Family in Transition

Family in Transition

**Rethinking Marriage,
Sexuality,
Child Rearing,
and Family Organization**

Sixth Edition

Arlene S. Skolnick
Jerome H. Skolnick
University of California, Berkeley

Scott, Foresman and Company
Glenview, Illinois   Boston   London

Library of Congress Cataloging-in-Publication Data

Family in transition.

   1. Family   I. Skolnick, Arlene S., 1933–
II. Skolnick, Jerome H.
HQ518.F336   1988   306.8'5   88-18615
ISBN 0-673-39879-X

1 2 3 4 5 6 7 8 9 10—MVN—94 93 92 91 90 89 88

Printed in the United States of America

Produced by R. David Newcomer Associates

Front cover photo credits, from the top:

  David Strickler/The Picture Cube
  Jeff Dunn/The Picture Cube
  Jeffry Myers/The Picture Cube
  Frank Siteman/The Picture Cube

For the sixth time, for Michael and Alexander

Preface to the Sixth Edition

Family life in America has been "in transition" since we began work on the first edition of this book in the Spring of 1970. Not only has family life changed, but the climate of opinion surrounding family issues has also shifted. New problems arise, and new approaches to earlier problems have emerged. Most strikingly perhaps, the state of the family has developed as a major public issue. At the same time, family scholarship continues to grow in quantity and quality.

In this edition, as in earlier ones, we have been torn between finding room for new material and keeping old favorites. As before, so much new and interesting quality writing on family and intimacy has appeared in just three years that more than half the articles are new. We have maintained the basic perspective of the book, but with somewhat altered themes to reflect current family research and controversies: among the new selections the reader will find discussions of surrogate motherhood and the new reproductive technologies, the increasing emotional value of children, the AIDS crisis, privacy rights and the Supreme Court's decision on homosexual behavior. We also include selections from two important new contributions to the continuing debate over the meaning of recent changes in family and personal life: *Habits of the Heart* by Robert Bellah and his colleagues, and *Love in America* by Francesca Cancian.

By now we have had so many useful conversations with colleagues that it is hard to single them out. Again, Nancy Chodorow's suggestions have been especially helpful. We also thank Karla Hackstaff for helping to search the literature and evaluate articles; and Celia Ronis for her organizational skills, intelligence, and unfailing good humor.

Arlene Skolnick
Jerome H. Skolnick
Berkeley, California
April 25, 1988

Contents

Introduction:
Family in Transition

Over the last three decades, family life in America has changed so dramatically that to many observers it has seemed as if "an earthquake had shuddered through the American family" (Preston, 1984). Divorce rates first skyrocketed, then they stabilized at historically high levels. Women have surged into the workplace. Birth rates have declined. The women's movement has changed the way men and women think and act towards one another, both inside the home and in the world at large. Furthermore, social and sexual rules that once seemed carved in stone have crumbled away: Unmarried couples can live together openly; unmarried mothers can keep their babies. Abortion has become legal. Remaining single and remaining childless, once unacceptable (though not illegal) options, have both become permissible.

A major result of these changes is that family life in America has become much more diverse than it was a generation ago. In the 1950s, the dominant family configuration was that of a male breadwinner and a full-time housewife living together with two or three, or sometimes even more children. The mass media celebrated "togetherness" and the rise of suburbia; social scientists viewed the middle-class suburban family as the most highly evolved version of a timeless social unit. Millions of people did not conform to the typical suburban model—the poor, blacks, city dwellers, ethnics, the working class—but the image did reflect both a cultural ideal and a set of trends affecting a majority of Americans.

Today most people live in ways that do not conform to the cultural ideal that prevailed in the '50s. In 1984 the traditional breadwinner/housewife family with minor children represented only 13 percent of all families. (Strober, in press). The "typical" American family in the last two decades of the twentieth century is likely to be one of four other kinds: the two-earner family, the single-parent family, the "bi-nuclear family" of remarriage (see Ahrons and Rodgers, Chapter 27 of this volume) or the "empty nest" couple whose children have grown up and moved out. Indeed, in 1984 fully half of American families had no children under age eighteen (Norton & Glick, 1986, p. 9). Apart from these variations, large numbers of people will spend part of their lives living apart from their families—as single young adults, as divorced singles, as older people who have lost a spouse.

The changes of recent decades have affected more than the forms of family life; they have been psychological as well. A major study of American attitudes over two decades revealed a profound shift in how people think about family life, work, and themselves (Veroff, Douvan, & Kulka, 1981). In 1957 four fifths of the respondents thought that a man or woman who did not want to marry was sick, immoral, and selfish. By 1976 only one fourth of the respondents thought that choice was bad. Two thirds were neutral, and one seventh viewed the choice as good. Summing up many complex findings, the authors conclude that America underwent a "psychological revolution" in the two decades between surveys. Twenty years earlier, people defined their satisfaction and problems—and indeed themselves—in terms of how well they lived up to traditional work and family roles. More recently, people have become more introspective, more attentive to inner experience. Fulfillment now means finding intimacy, meaning, and self-definition, rather than satisfactory performance of traditional roles.

A Dying Institution?

All of these changes, occurring as they did in a relatively short period of time, gave rise to fears about the decline of the family. By the early 1970s anyone watching television or reading *Time* or *Newsweek* magazines would hear again and again that the family is breaking down, falling apart, disintegrating, and even becoming "an endangered species." There also began a great nostalgia for the "good old days" when Mom was in the kitchen, families were strong and stable, and life was uncomplicated. This mood of nostalgia mixed with anxiety contributed to the rise of the conservative New Right and helped to propel Ronald Reagan into the White House.

In the early '80s, heady with victory, the conservative movement hoped that by dismantling the welfare state and overturning the Supreme Court's abortion decision, the clock could be turned back and the "traditional" family restored. As the Reagan presidency drew to a close, it became clear that such hopes had failed. Women had not returned to full-time homemaking; divorce rates had not returned to the levels of the 1950s. The "liberated" sexuality of the '60s and '70s had given way to greater restraint, largely due to fear of AIDS, although the norms of the '50s did not return.

Despite all the changes, however, the family in America is "here to stay" (Bane, 1976). The vast majority of Americans—at least 90 percent—marry and have children, and surveys repeatedly show that most people find family ties their deepest source of satisfaction and meaning. In sum, family life in America is a complex mixture of both continuity and change.

Meanwhile, during the same years in which the family was becoming the object of public anxiety and political debate, a torrent of new research on the family was pouring forth. Once something of a scholarly backwater in the field of sociology, the study of the family had come to excite the interest of scholars in a range of disciplines—history, demography, economics, law, psychology, and psychiatry.

As a result of this research, we now have much more information available about the family than ever before. Ironically, much of the new scholarship is at odds with the widespread assumption that family had a long stable history until hit by the social "earthquake" of the '60s and '70s. We have learned from historians that the "lost" golden age of family happiness and stability we yearn for never actually existed.

Because of the continuing stream of new family scholarship, as well as shifts in public attitudes toward the family, each edition of *Family in Transition* has been different from the one before it. In the first edition of this book we argued strenuously that the middle-class family patterns of the 1950s and early 1960s did not represent a model of the family in all times and places. Strange as it now seems, because the family was considered the basic building block of society, most family sociologists discounted the possibility that there could be serious changes in family roles, expectations, and behavior.

When we put together the first edition of this book in the early 1970s, the changes that are now commonplace were just beginning to be felt. The youth movements of the 1960s and the emerging women's movement were challenging many of the assumptions on which conventional marriage and family patterns had been based. The mass media were regularly presenting stories that also challenged in one way or another traditional views on sex, marriage, and family. People were becoming aware, for example, of "the population explosion" and of the desirability of "zero population growth." There was a growing realization that the ideal three-, four-, or five-child family of the '50s might not be very good for the country as a whole, or for every couple. Meanwhile, Hollywood movies were presenting a new and cynical view of marriage. It was almost taken for granted that marriages were unhappy, particularly if the spouses were middle class, middle aged, or affluent. Many people were openly defying conventional standards of behavior: College girls were beginning to live openly with young men, unwed movie actresses were publicizing rather than hiding their pregnancies, and homosexuals were beginning openly to protest persecution and discrimination.

It seemed as if something was happening to family life in America, even if there were no sharp changes in the major statistical indicators of family life, or in sexual behavior, or in the division of labor between husbands and wives. People seemed to be looking at sex, marriage, parenthood, and family life in new ways, even if behavior on a mass scale was not changing very noticeably. Thus, we argued that significant social and cultural change could happen even without massive changes in overt behavior patterns. John Gagnon and William Simon (1970) had observed that the moment of change may be when new forms of behavior seem "plausible." For example, even though there was no evidence that the homosexual population had grown, homosexuality had become a more plausible form of behavior. Knowing someone was a homosexual did not automatically mean that he or she was to be defined as a moral pariah. In the same way, whether or not there had been great changes in rates of premarital sex or unwed motherhood, the fact that people could now be open about such behavior and go on in normal ways with the rest of their lives seemed highly significant.

In putting together the readings for that first edition of *Family in Transition*, we found that the professional literature of the time seemed to deny that change was possible in family structure, the relations between the sexes, and parenthood. Most social scientists shared a particular set of assumptions about the nature of the family and its relation to society: human beings were equipped with a fixed set of psychological needs and tendencies, which were expressed in the family. An extreme version of this view was the statement by an anthropologist that the nuclear family (mother, father, and children) "is a biological phenomenon . . . as rooted in organs and physiological structures as insect societies" (LaBarre, 1954, p. 104). Any changes in the basic structure of the family roles or in childrearing were assumed to be unworkable, if not unthinkable.

The family in modern society was portrayed as a streamlined, more highly evolved version of a universal family. According to Talcott Parsons and his followers (1951, 1954), the modern family underwent structural differentiation or specialization. It transferred work and educational roles to other agencies and specialized in childrearing and emotional support. No less important for having relinquished certain tasks, the modern family was now the only part of society to carry out such functions.

These ideas about the family have lost their credibility. As Glenn Elder (1978) observed, the study of the family and its relations to social change during the postwar era was "shaped more by simplistic abstract theory and ideological preferences" than by the detailed study of the realities of family life in particular times, places, and circumstances.

The family theories of the postwar era were descriptively correct insofar as they portrayed the ideal middle-class family patterns of a particular society at a particular historical period. But they went astray in elevating the status quo to the level of a timeless necessity. In addition, the theories could not embrace variation in family life. For example, the working mother or the single-parent family could be seen only as deviant. Similarly, social change in family life on a large scale, as in the rise of women's employment or of divorce, could be interpreted only as social disorder and the disintegration of the social system.

Still another flaw in the dominant view was its neglect of major internal strains within the family, even when it was presumably functioning as it was supposed to. Paradoxically, these strains were vividly described by the very theorists who idealized the role of the family in modern society. Parsons, for example, observed that when home no longer functioned as an economic unit, women, children, and old people were placed in an ambiguous position. They became dependent on the male breadwinner and were cut off from society's major source of achievement and status.

Parsons saw women's roles as particularly difficult: Being a housewife was not a real occupation; it was vaguely defined, highly demanding, yet not considered real work in a society that measures achievement by the size of one's paycheck. The combination of existing strains and the demystifying effects of the challenges to the family status quo seems to have provided, as Judith Blake (1978, p. 11) points out, a classic set of conditions for social change.

A Time of Troubles

The recent changes in the family would have been unsettling even if other social conditions had remained stable. But everything else was also changing quickly. Despite assassinations and turmoil in the streets, the '60s were an optimistic period. Both dissidents and the establishment agreed that progress was possible, that problems could be solved, and that today's children would live in a better world. Both sides believed in limitless economic growth.

No one foresaw that the late 1970s would dramatically reverse this optimism and the social and economic conditions that had sustained it. Rather than hearing of limitless abundance and an end to scarcity and poverty, we began to hear of lowered expectations, survival, and lifeboat ethics. For the first time in history, Americans had to confront the possibility that their children and their children's children might not lead better lives. A popular country and western song expressed the national mood when it asked, "Are the good times really over for good?" (Haggard, 1982).

The "malaise" of the late 1970s, followed by the conservative renewal of the 1980s, once again changed the terms in which family issues were discussed and debated. There was a general withdrawal from political activity among all Americans, most surprisingly, perhaps, on the part of the young people who had been active in the 1960s and 1970s. (The movie *The Big Chill* was Hollywood's version of the transformation from activist to yuppie.) The return to a focus on private life was accelerated by the fact that the large baby boom generation, which had begun to enter college in the 1960s, was moving on to marriage and parenthood by the end of the 1970s.

Among family scholars and other social commentators, the terms of the debate about the family were also changed by shifts in feminist thinking. Some of the most vocal feminists of the 1960s had criticized the family as the major source of the oppression of women. By the 1970s, many feminists had articulated a new emphasis on nurturance, care, and intimacy. In fact, one of the surprising themes of recent years is the celebration of family in the name of social criticism. A new domesticity of the left has emerged on the intellectual scene. For example, one scholar argues that the family is the only institution that saves capitalistic societies from total domination by market values. Parental love and adult intimacy are an "affront" to an economic system that tries to put a price on everything.

Some radical attacks on the modern world and its ways seem consonant with traditional conservative arguments. Historian Christopher Lasch (1978) argues that while the family once provided a haven of love and decency in a heartless world, it no longer does so. The family has been "invaded" by outside forces—advertising, the media, experts, and family professionals—and stripped of its functions and authority. Corporate capitalism, with its need for limitless consumption, has created a "culture of narcissism," in which nobody cares about anybody else. Other scholars, as we noted earlier, insist that the family remains a vital and resilient institution.

The State of the Contemporary Family

What sense *can* be made of the current changes in family life? The various statistics we quoted earlier can and are being interpreted to show that the family is either thriving or falling apart. Falling birthrates can be taken to mean that people are too selfish to want to have any or many children. Or they can mean that people are no longer having children by accident, without thought, or because of social pressure, but because they truly want children. High divorce rates can signify that marriage either is an institution on the rocks or is considered so important that people will no longer put up with the kinds of dissatisfactions and empty-shell marriages previous generations tolerated. Is the rise in illegitimacy a sign of moral breakdown? Or does it simply reflect a different, more enlightened set of moral norms, a society no longer eager to punish unmarried mothers or to damage a child's life chances because of the circumstances of its birth?

Part of the confusion surrounding the current status of the family arises from the fact that the family is an inherently problematic area of study; there are few if any self-evident facts, even statistical ones.

Researchers have found, for example, that when the statistics of family life are plotted for the entire twentieth century, or back into the nineteenth century, a surprising finding emerges: today's young people—with their low marriage, high divorce, and low fertility rates—appear to be behaving in ways consistent with long-term historical trends (Cherlin, 1981; Masnick & Bane, 1980). The recent changes in family life only appear deviant when compared to what people were doing in the 1940s and 1950s. The now middle-aged adults who married young, moved to the suburbs, and had three, four, or more children comprised the generation that departed from twentieth-century trends. As one study put it, "Had the 1940s and 1950s not happened, today's young adults would appear to be behaving normally" (Masnick & Bane, 1980, p. 2).

Thus, the meaning of change in a particular indicator of family life depends on the time frame in which it is placed. If we look at trends over too short a period of time—say ten or twenty years—we may think we are seeing a marked change, when, in fact, an older pattern may be reemerging. For some issues, even discerning what the trends are can be a problem. Whether or not we conclude that there is an "epidemic" of teenage pregnancy depends on how we define adolescence and what measure of illegitimacy we use. Contrary to the popular notion of skyrocketing teenage pregnancy, teenaged childbearing has actually been on the decline during the past two decades (Furstenberg et al., 1981). It is possible for the *ratio* of illegitimate births to all births to go up at the same time as there are declines in the *absolute* number of such births and in the likelihood that an individual will bear an illegitimate child. This is not to say that concern about teenage pregnancy is unwarranted; but the reality is much more complex than the simple and scary notion of an "epidemic" implies.

Given the complexities of interpreting data on the family, it is little wonder that, as Joseph Featherstone observes (1979, p. 37), the family is a "great intellectual Rorschach blot." One's conclusions about the current state of the family often derive from deeper values and assumptions one holds in the first place about the definition and role of the family in society. We noted earlier that the family theories of the postwar era were largely discredited within sociology itself (Blake, 1978; Elder, 1978). Yet many of the assumptions of those theories continue to influence discussions of the family in both popular and scholarly writings. Let us look in more detail at these persistent assumptions.

1. The Assumption of the Universal Nuclear Family

To say that the family is the same everywhere is in some sense true. But the differences are more interesting, just as a portrait of an individual is interesting because of the person's uniqueness rather than because faces usually have eyes, ears, and a mouth. Families possess even more dissimilar traits than do faces. They vary in organization, membership, life cycles, emotional environments, ideologies, social and kin networks, and economic and other functions. Although anthropologists have tried to come up with a single definition of family that would hold across time and place, they generally have concluded that doing so is not useful (Geertz, 1965; Stephens, 1963).

The idea of the universal nuclear family is based on biology: A woman and a man must unite sexually to produce a child. But no social kinship ties or living arrangements flow inevitably from biological union. Indeed, the definition of marriage is not the same across cultures. Although some cultures have weddings and notions of monogamy and permanence, many cultures lack one or more of these attributes. In some cultures, the majority of people mate and have children without legal marriage and often without living together. In other societies, husbands, wives, and children do not live together under the same roof.

In our own society, the assumption of universality has usually defined what is normal and natural both for research and therapy and has subtly influenced our thinking to regard deviations from the nuclear family as sick or perverse or immoral. As Suzanne Keller (1971) points out:

> The fallacy of universality has done students of behavior a great disservice. By leading us to seek and hence to find a single pattern, it has blinded us to historical precedents for multiple legitimate family arrangements.

An example of this disservice is the treatment of illegitimacy. For decades the so-called principle of legitimacy, set forth by Malinowski (1930), was taken as evidence for the universality of the nuclear family. The principle stated that in every society a child must have a socially recognized father to give the child a status in the community. Malinowski's principle naturally leads to the assumption that illegitimacy is a sign of social breakdown.

Although the principle usually has been treated by social scientists as if it were a natural law, in fact it is based on certain prior assumptions about society (Goode, 1960; Blake, 1978). Chiefly, it assumes that children inherit their status from their father or from family origin rather than achieving it themselves. The traditional societies that anthropologists study are, of course, societies that do ascribe status in this way. Modern, democratic societies, such as the United States, are based, in theory at least, on achievement; a child's future is not supposed to be determined solely by who its father happens to be. The Malinowski principle, however compelling in understanding traditional societies, has decreasing relevance for modern ones. Current legal changes that blur the distinction between legitimate and illegitimate births may be seen as a way of bringing social practice in line with national ideal.

2.   The Assumption of Family Harmony

Every marriage, as Jessie Bernard (1973) points out, contains two marriages: the husband's and the wife's. Similarly, every family contains as many families as family members. Family members with differing perspectives may find themselves in conflict, occasionally in bitter conflict. Outside intervention is sometimes necessary to protect the weaker from the stronger.

To question the idea of the happy family is not to say that love and joy are not found in family life or that many people do not find their deepest satisfactions in their families. Rather, the happy family assumption omits important, if unpleasant, aspects of family life. Western society has not always assumed such a sentimental model of the family. From the Bible to the fairy tale, from Sophocles to Shakespeare, from Eugene O'Neill to the soap opera, there is a tragic tradition portraying the family as a high-voltage emotional setting, charged with love and hate, tenderness and spite, even incest and murder.

There is also a low-comedy tradition. George Orwell once pointed out that the world of henpecked husbands and tyrannical mothers-in-law is as much a part of the Western cultural heritage as is Greek drama. Although the comic tradition tends to portray men's discontents rather than women's, it scarcely views the family as a setting for ideal happiness.

Nor have social theorists always portrayed the family as harmoniously fulfilling the needs of its members and society. Around the turn of the century, the founders of sociology took for granted that conflict was a basic part of social life and that individuals, classes, and social institutions would struggle to promote their own interests and values. Freud and Simmel were among the leading conflict theorists of the family. They argued that intimate relations inevitably involve antagonism as well as love. This mixture of strong positive and negative feelings sets close relationships apart from less intimate ones.

In recent years, family scholars have been studying such family violence as child abuse and wife beating to understand better the realistic strains of family life. Long-known facts about family violence have recently been incorporated into a general analysis of the family. More police officers are killed and injured dealing with family fights than in dealing with any other kind of situation; of all the relationships between murderers and their victims, the family relationship is most common (Steinmetz & Straus, 1974). Recent studies of family violence reveal that it is much more widespread than had been assumed, cannot easily be attributed to mental illness, and is not confined to the lower classes. Family violence seems to be a product of psychological tensions and external stresses that can affect all families at all social levels.

The study of family interaction has also undermined the traditional image of the happy, harmonious family. About two decades ago, researchers and therapists began to bring mental patients and their families together to watch how they behaved with one another. Oddly, whole family groups had not been systematically studied before.

At first the family interactions were interpreted as pathogenic: a parent expressing affection in words but showing nonverbal hostility, alliances being made between different family members, families having secrets, one family member being singled out as a scapegoat to be blamed for the family's troubles, parents caring for children only as reflections of themselves, parents making belittling and sarcastic statements to children. As more and more families were studied, such patterns were found in many families, not just in those families with a schizophrenic child. Although family processes discovered by this line of research did not teach us much about the causes of mental illness, they made an important discovery about family life: so-called normal families can often be, in the words of one study, "difficult environments for interaction."

3. The Assumption of Parental Determinism

Throughout American history, the family has been seen as the basis of social order and stability. Through reproduction and socialization, the family presumably guarantees the continuation of society through time. Traditionally, theories of socialization have taken either of two perspectives. In the first—social molding— the child is likened to a blank slate or lump of clay, waiting to be written on or shaped by the environment. In the second—animal taming—the infant is a wild beast whose antisocial instincts need to be tamed by the parents.

Despite their differences, both views of socialization have much in common. Both consider children as passive objects and assign an all-powerful, Pygmalion-like role to parents. Both view the child's later life as a reenactment of early experience. Both view conformity to social norms as the outcome of successful socialization. Both tend to blame deviance of any kind (mental illness, crime, drug use) on the family. Finally, both share a view of socialization as a precarious enterprise, with failure and unhappiness the likely result of any parental mistake.

Although the belief that early family experience is the most powerful influence in a child's life is widely shared by social scientists and the public, there are serious flaws in two of its underlying assumptions: the assumption of the passive child and the assumption that parents independently exert influence in a virtual vacuum.

The model of the passive child is no longer tenable. Recent empirical work in human development shows that children come into the world with unique temperamental and other characteristics, so that children shape parents as much as parents shape children. Further, after two decades of intensive research in infancy and cognitive development, we know that the child's mind is not an empty vessel or a blank slate to be filled with parental instruction. Children are active agents in the construction of knowledge about the world.

Children also learn from the world around them. The parental-determinism model has encouraged the peculiar belief that children know nothing about the world except what parents teach. Poor black children therefore are said to do badly in school because their parents fail to use the right teaching techniques. It is easier to blame the parents than to change the neighborhood, the school, or the economy or to assume that ghetto children's correct perception of their life chances has something to do with school performance.

Finally, other kinds of research show that early experience is not the all-powerful, irreversible kind of influence it has been thought to be. An unfortunate childhood does not necessarily lead to a despairing adulthood. Nor does a happy childhood guarantee a similarly sunny adulthood. (Macfarlane, 1964; Emde & Harmon, 1984).

4.   The Assumption of a Stable, Harmonious Past

Laments about the current decay of the family imply some earlier era when the family was more stable and harmonious than it is now. But unless we can agree what earlier time should be chosen as a baseline and what characteristics of the family should be selected for, it makes little sense to speak of family decline. Historians have not, in fact, located a golden age of the family gleaming at us from the depths of history (Demos, 1975).

Recent historical studies of family life also cast doubt on the reality of family tranquility. Historians have found that premarital sexuality, illegitimacy, generational conflict, and even infanticide can best be studied as a part of family life itself rather than as separate categories of deviation. For example, William Kessen (1965), in his history of the field of child study, observes:

> Perhaps the most persistent single note in the history of the child is the reluctance of mothers to suckle their babies. The running war between the mother, who does not want to nurse, and the philosopher-psychologists, who insist she must, stretches over two thousand years (pp. 1–2).

The most shocking finding of the recent wave of historical studies is the prevalence of infanticide throughout European history. Infanticide has long been attributed to primitive peoples or assumed to be the desperate act of an unwed mother. It now appears that infanticide provided a major means of population control in all societies lacking reliable contraception, Europe included, and that it was practiced by families on legitimate children. Historians now believe that rises and falls in recorded birthrates may actually reflect variations in infanticide rates.

David Hunt's (1970) study of childrearing practices in early modern France found what would be considered by today's standards widespread mistreatment of children, although his study was limited to upper-class families. Rather than being an instinctive trait, having tender feelings toward infants—baby as a precious individual—seems to emerge only when infants have a decent chance of surviving and adults experience enough security to avoid feeling that children are competing with them in a struggle for survival. Throughout many centuries of European history, both of these conditions were lacking. In the allocation of scarce resources, European society, as one historian put it, preferred adults to children (Trexler, 1973, p. 110).

Even during more recent and prosperous historical times, the nostalgic image of a more stable and placid family turned out to be a myth. It is hard to comprehend how profoundly family life has been affected by the reduction in mortality and spread of contraception in the twentieth century. Although infant and child mortality rates had begun to decline a century earlier, the average family could not assume it would see all its infants survive to middle or old age. Death struck most often at children. But adults with an average life expectancy of about fifty years (Ridley, 1972) would often die in the prime of their productive years. The widow and widower with young children were more familiar figures on the social landscape than the divorced person is today.

To put it another way, it has been only during the twentieth century that a majority of people would expect to live out a normal family cycle: leaving home, marrying, having children, and surviving to age fifty with one's spouse still alive. Before 1900 only 40 percent of the female population experienced this life cycle. The majority either died before they got married, never married, died before childbirth, or were widowed while their children were still young (Uhlenberg, 1974).

Contrary to the myth of the three-generation family in past time, grandparents can almost be said to be a twentieth-century phenomenon (Hareven, 1978). In the past, when people lived shorter lives, they married later. The lives of parents and children thus had fewer years in which to overlap. As a result of these trends, there is for the first time in history a significant number of families with four generations alive at the same time.

A Heritage of Family Crisis

Our ancestors not only experienced chronic uncertainty in their personal family lives, but they also worried about the shakiness of the family as an institution. The idea that the family is falling apart is not really new. In fact, if we use a deep enough historical perspective, we see that the postwar era with its optimistic view of family life was the exception rather than the rule in American life. It was part of what one historian calls "the long amnesia" (Filene, 1975): the decades between the 1920s and the 1960s, during which concerns were muted about family crises, women's roles, childrearing, and declining morals, which had so agitated earlier generations. Anxiety about the family is an American tradition. Some historians trace it to the 1820s and the beginning of industrialism. Others would date the sense of crisis even earlier, from the time the first settlers set foot on American soil. Immigration, the frontier, geographic and social mobility—the basic ingredients of the American experience—were all disruptive of parental authority and familial bonds.

Although concern about the family may have begun earlier, anxiety increased during the second quarter of the nineteenth century, and discussions took on an entirely new tone. There began to be a widespread sense of alarm about the decline of the family and of parental authority. A new self-consciousness about family life emerged; writings about the family dealt anxiously with the proper methods of childrearing and with women's special roles.

In contrast to earlier periods, people began to experience a split between public and private life: The world outside the home came to be seen as cold, ugly, and threatening, while the home became a cozy retreat. The home was idealized as a place of perfect love and harmony, while at the same time it was blamed as the cause of juvenile delinquency, crime, and mental illness. These conflicting themes have a decidedly contemporary ring.

The Rise of the Modern Family

These anxieties about the family that began in the 1820s were in response to the changed circumstances brought about by "modernization." Although this is a much-debated term, it is useful as a shorthand way of referring to social changes that accompanied the massive growth of industrial capitalism in the nineteenth century. Although the changes and dilemmas to be discussed in the following paragraphs exist to some extent in all urbanized, advanced technological societies (i.e., in the Soviet Union and Eastern Europe as well as in the United States), they may be found in their purest and most acute form under advanced capitalism, particularly in America.

Modernization implies not merely economic or technological change but also profound social and psychological change. It affects all aspects of life: the physical environment, the types of communities people live in, the way they view the world, the way they organize their daily lives, the meaning of work, the emotional quality of family relationships, plus the most private aspects of individual experience.

It is, of course, a great oversimplification to talk about the effects of modernization on what is known as the family. Living in an industrial economy has had a different impact on people in different social classes and ethnic groups. Poor and working-class families were, and still are, confronted with survival issues: the need for steady incomes, decent housing, and health care, the tensions that result from not being sure basic needs will be met. In order to ensure survival and because their values tend to be familistic rather than individualistic, working-class, immigrant, and poor families have usually depended on strong networks of kin and kinlike friendships. Middle-class, affluent families, freed from worries about basic subsistence, confront in more acute ways the social and psychological dilemmas brought on by modernization. They more often fit the model of the inwardly turned, emotionally intense, relatively isolated nuclear family.

Since the nineteenth century, when the effects of industrialism and urbanization really began to be felt, scholars have debated the impact of industrialization on the family. Many scholars and laypeople were convinced that the family had outlived its usefulness. For the first time in history, men and women could find work and satisfy basic needs outside the bonds of blood or marriage. They felt, therefore, that the family would disintegrate.

The functional sociologists of the postwar era scoffed at predictions of family disintegration. As we saw earlier, they judged it to be more important than ever. The family nurtured and raised children and provided refuge for adults from the impersonality and competition of public and industrial life.

It now appears that both views were both right and wrong. Those who thought that life in a mass society would undermine family life were correct. But they were wrong in assuming that most people would want to spend their lives as isolated individuals. Those who argued that the conditions of urban-industrial society create exceptional needs for nurturant, intimate relationships were also correct. But they never understood that those same conditions would make it hard for the family to fulfill such needs. Family ties have become more intense than they were in the past, and yet at the same time they have become more fragile.

Although most western Europeans never lived in large extended-family households (Laslett & Wall, 1972), kinship ties extended much stronger constraints over the individual before the modern era. Work and marriage were not matters of individual choice. A person's economic and marital destinies were determined by hereditary status, tradition, and economic necessity. Continuity of marriages and conformity to prescribed behavior, both within the family and outside it, were enforced by severe economic, familial, and community sanctions.

Another extremely important aspect of family life in past times was its embeddedness in the community. The home was not set off as a private place, a refuge to make up for deprivations in the world of work. There was no world of work outside the home; family members were fellow workers. Nor did the world outside one's front door consist of strangers or half-strangers, as neighbors often are today. Rather, most people lived in a community of people known since childhood and with whom one would expect to have dealings for the rest of one's life. These outsiders could enter the household freely and were entitled, and even obligated, to intervene if relations between parents and children and husbands and wives were not as they should be. The most vivid example of community control over family life in preindustrial times was the practice known as *charivari:* community festivals in which people who violated family norms would be mocked and shamed (Shorter, 1975).

Modernization involves political as well as economic and social change. In English and American history, striking parallels exist between political ideals and the family, with the family being seen as a small version of the state—a little commonwealth. When the divine right of kings prevailed, the family ideal was likewise hierarchy and authority, with children and wives owing unquestioning obedience. When ideas about democracy and individual rights challenged the rule of kings, family ideologies also became more democratic (Stone, 1977). An ideology of liberation still accompanies replacement of the traditional pattern of work and family by the modern one. Modernization promises freedom of opportunity to find work that suits one's talents, freedom to marry for love and dissolve the marriage if it fails to provide happiness, and greater equality in the family between husband and wife and between parents and children (Goode, 1963).

In addition to promoting an ideology of individualism, modern technological societies change the inner experience of the self. The person living in an unchanging, traditional social world does not have to construct an identity to discover who he or she really is. "I am the son of this man, I came from that village, I work at that trade" would be enough to tell a man who he was.

There is still another source of the modern preoccupation with self. Much of daily life in modern society is spent in such roles as student, worker, customer, client. People begin to experience themselves as replaceable role players (Berger, Berger, & Kellner, 1973; Davis, 1973). As we become aware of a discrepancy between the role we are playing and our real and whole selves, we come to have a need for a private world, a set of relationships in which we can express those aspects of ourselves that must be repressed in role demands of work and public behavior. Individualization and intimacy are, as Howard Gadlin (1977) puts it, "the Siamese twins of modernization."

Although the need for intimacy increases, the very conditions creating that need make it more difficult to satisfy. For example, affluence may buy privacy, but, like King Midas' touch, family privacy is a drama that turns up unexpected costs when fulfilled. The family's "major burden," writes Napier (1972), "is its rootlessness, its aloneness with its tasks. Parents are somewhere else; the business you can't trust; the neighbors you never see; and friends are a help, when you see them, but never enough. Sometimes, late at night, the parent wakes up and on a sea of silence hears the ship creak, feels it drift, fragile and solitary, with its cargo of lives" (p. 540).

Family privacy needs illustrate only one example of how contradictory cultural instructions clash in the modern family. There is also the contradiction between a newer morality of enjoyment and self-fulfillment and an older morality of duty, responsibility, work, and self-denial. Fun morality is expressed by the advertising industry, credit cards, the buy-now-pay-later philosophy. The new morality can reunite families in activities that everyone can enjoy, but it also pulls family members apart in its emphasis on individual pursuit of enjoyment. Also, fun morality imposes a paradoxical demand: In the past, one could live up to demands of marriage and parenthood by doing one's duty. Today duty is not enough; we are also obliged to enjoy family life (Wolfenstein, 1954). As a result, pleasurable activities, including sex itself, become matters for evaluation and therefore of discontent.

Ironically, then, many of the difficulties besetting family life today are the consequences of some very positive changes: the decline of infant mortality and death rates in general, the fact that people are living longer, the use of birth control, the spread of mass education, and the increasing control of the individual over basic life decisions (whether to marry, when to marry, whom to marry, whether or not to have children, and how many children to have).

This very voluntariness can be disturbing. Freedom in modern family life is bought at the price of fragility and instability. Now the whole structure of family life comes to rest on a tenuous basis: the mutual feelings of two individuals. As George Simmel (1950, pp. 118–144) has shown, the couple or dyad is not only the most intimate of social relationships, it is also the most unstable. In traditional family systems, the inevitable tensions of marriage are contained by kin and community pressures, as well as by low expectations concerning the romance or happiness to be found in marriage.

Demographic and economic change has had a profound effect on women's roles. When death rates fall, as they do with modernization, women no longer have to have five or seven or nine children to make sure that two or three will survive to adulthood. Women today are living longer and having fewer children. After rearing children, the average woman can look forward to three or four decades without maternal responsibilities. Since traditional assumptions about women are based on the notion that women are constantly involved with pregnancy, childrearing, and related domestic concerns, the current ferment about women's roles may be seen as a way of bringing cultural attitudes in line with existing social realities.

As people live longer, they can stay married longer. Actually, the biggest change in twentieth-century marriage is not the proportion of marriages disrupted through divorce, but the potential length of marriage and the number of years spent without children in the home. Census data suggest that the statistically average couple marrying now will spend only 18 percent of their married lives raising young children, compared with 54 percent a century ago (Bane, 1976). As a result, marriage is becoming less of a union between parents raising a brood of children and more of a personal relationship between two people.

To sum it up then, a knowledge of family history reveals that the solution to contemporary problems will not be found in some lost golden age. Families have always struggled with outside circumstances and inner conflict. Our current troubles inside and outside the family are genuine, but we should never forget that many of the most vexing issues confronting us as men and women, parents and children, derive from the very benefits of modernization—benefits too easily taken for granted or forgotten in the lately fashionable denunciation of modern times. There was no problem of the aged in the past, because most people never aged; they died before they got old. Nor was adolescence a difficult stage of the life cycle when children worked, education was a privilege of the rich, and a person's place in society was determined by heredity rather than choice. And when most people were hungry illiterates, only aristocrats could worry about sexual satisfaction and self-fulfillment.

In short, there is no point in giving in to the lure of nostalgia. There is no golden age of the family to long for, nor even some past pattern of behavior and belief that would guarantee us harmony and stability if only we had the will to return to it. Family life is bound up with the social, economic, and ideological circumstances of particular times and places. We are no longer peasants, Puritans, pioneers, or even suburbanites circa 1955. We face conditions unknown to our ancestors, and we must find new ways to cope with them.

References

Ahrons, C. H. and Rodgers, R. H. 1987. *Divorced Families.* New York: W. W. Norton & Co.

Bane, M. J. 1976. *Here to Stay.* New York: Basic Books.

Berger, P., Berger, B., and Kellner, H. 1973. *The Homeless Mind: Modernization and Consciousness.* New York: Random House.

Bernard, J. 1973. *The Future of Marriage.* New York: Bantam.

Bernard, J. 1975. "Adolescence and Socialization for Motherhood." In Dragastin, S. E. and G. H. Elder. *Adolescence in the Life Cycle.* New York: Wiley, pp. 227–252.

Blake, J. 1978. "Structural Differentiation and the Family: A Quiet Revolution." Presentation at American Sociology Association, San Francisco.

Cherlin, A. J. 1981. *Marriage, Divorce, Remarriage.* Cambridge, Mass: Harvard University Press.

Davis, M. S. 1973. *Intimate Relations.* New York: The Free Press.

Demos, J. 1975. "Myths and Realities in the History of American Family Life," In H. Grunebaum and J. Christ (eds.). *Contemporary Marriage: Structure, Dynamics and Therapy.* Boston: Little, Brown and Company.

Elder, G. 1978. "Approaches to Social Change and the Family." In *Turning Points*, edited by J. Demos and S. S. Boocock, pp. 1–38. Supplement to *American Journal of Sociology,* vol. 84, p. S34.

Elstain, J. B. "Feminists Against the Family." *The Nation,* November 17, 1979, pp. 482ff.

Emde, R. N. and Harmon, R. J. (eds.). 1984. *Continuities and Discontinuities in Development.* New York: Plenum Press.

Featherstone, J. 1979. Family Matters, *Harvard Educational Review,* 49, No. 1, pp. 20–52.

Filene, P. 1975. *Him, Her, Self: Sex Roles in Modern America.* New York: Mentor.

Furstenberg, F. F., Jr., Lincoln, R., and Menken, J. 1981. *Teenage Sexuality, Pregnancy and Childbearing.* Philadelphia: University of Pennsylvania Press.

Gadlin, H. 1977. "Private Lives and Public Order." In *Close Relationships: Perspectives in the Meaning of Intimacy.* Amherst: University of Massachusetts Press, pp. 73–86.

Gagnon, J. H. and Simon, W. 1970. *The Sexual Scene.* Chicago: Transaction.

Geertz, G. 1965. "The Impact of the Concept of Culture on the Concept of Man." In *New Views of the Nature of Man,* edited by J. R. Platt, pp. 93–118. Chicago: University of Chicago Press.

Goode, W. J. 1960. "A Deviant Case: Illegitimacy in the Caribbean." *American Sociological Review,* vol. 25, pp. 21–30.

Goode, W. J. 1963. *World Revolution and Family Patterns.* New York: The Free Press.

Haggard, M. 1982. "Are the Good Times Really Over for Good?" Song copyright 1982.

Hareven, T. K. 1978. "Family Time and Historical Time." In *The Family,* edited by A. S. Rassi, J. Kagan, and T. K. Hareven. New York: W. W. Norton and Company, pp. 57–70. (Reprint of *Daedalus,* Spring 1977.)

Hunt, D. 1970. *Parents and Children in History: The Psychology of Family Life in Early Modern France.* New York: Basic Books.

ISR Newsletter. 1979. Institute for Social Research. The University of Michigan. Winter.

Keller, S. 1971. "Does the Family Have a Future?" *Journal of Comparative Studies,* Spring, 1971.

Keniston, K. 1977. *All Our Children: The American Family Under Pressure.* New York: Harcourt Brace Jovanovich.

Kessen, E. W. 1965. *The Child.* New York: John Wiley.

LaBarre, W. 1954. *The Human Animal.* Chicago: University of Chicago Press.

Lasch, C. 1978. *Haven in a Heartless World.* New York: Basic Books.

Laslett, P. and Wall, R. (eds.). 1972. *Household and Family in Past Time.* Cambridge, England: Cambridge University Press.

Macfarlane, J. W. 1964. "Perspectives on Personality Consistency and Change from the Guidance Study." *Vita Humana,* vol 7, pp. 115–126.

Malinowski, B. 1930. "Parenthood, the Basis of the Social Order." In *The New Generation,* Calverton and Schmalhousen, New York: Macauley Company, pp. 113–168.

Masnick, G. and Bane, M. J. 1980. *The Nation's Families: 1960–1990.* Boston: Auburn House.

Mason, K. O., Czajka, J., and Aiker, S. 1976. "Change in U.S. Women's Sex Role Attitudes, 1964–1974." *American Sociological Review,* 41, pp. 573–596.

Napier, A. 1972. Introduction to section four in *The Book of Family Therapy,* edited by A. Farber, M. Mendelsohn, and A. Napier. New York: Science House.

Norton, A. J. and Glick, P. C. 1986. "One-Parent Families: A Social and Economic Profile." *Family Relations,* 35, pp. 9–17.

Parsons, T. 1951. The Social System. Glencoe, Ill.: Free Press.

Parsons, T. 1954. The Kinship System of the Contemporary United States. In *Essays in Sociological Theory.* Glencoe, Ill.: Free Press.

Preston, S. H. 1984. Presidential address to the Population Association of America. Quoted in *Family and Nation* by D. P. Moynihan (1986). San Diego: Harcourt Brace Jovanovich.

Ridley, J. C. 1972. "The Effects of Population Change on the Roles and Status of Women." In *Toward a Sociology of Women,* edited by S. Safilios-Rothschild, Lexington, Mass.: Xerox College Publishing, pp. 372–386.

Rossi, A. S. 1978. "A Biosocial Perspective on Parenting." In *The Family,* edited by A. S. Rossi, J. Kagan, and T. K. Hareven. New York: W. W. Norton and Company. (Reprint of Daedalus, Spring 1977.)

Shorter, E. 1973. "Infanticide in the Past." *History of Childhood Quarterly,* Summer, pp. 178–180.

Shorter, E. 1975. *The Making of the Modern Family.* New York: Basic Books.

Simmel, G. 1950. *The Sociology of George Simmel,* edited by K. Wolff. New York: Free Press.

Steinmetz, D and Straus, M. A. (eds.) 1974. *Violence in the Family.* New York: Dodd, Mead Co.

Stephens, W. N. 1963. *The Family in Cross-Cultural Perspective.* New York: World.

Stone, L. 1977. *The Family, Sex and Marriage in England, 1500–1800.* New York: Harper and Row.

Strober, M. (in press). "Two-earner families." In *Feminism, Children, and the New Families,* edited by S. M. Dornbusch and M. H. Strober. New York: Guilford Press.

Trexler, R. C. 1973. "Infanticide in Florence: New Sources and First Results." *History of Childhood Quarterly,* Summer, pp. 98–116.

Trost, J. 1979. *Unmarried Cohabitation.* Vasteros, Sweden: International Library.

Uhlenberg, P. 1974. "Cohort Variations in Family Life Cycle Experiences of U.S. Females." *Journal of Marriage and the Family,* pp. 284–292.

Veroff, J., Douvan, E., and Kulka, R. A. 1981. *The Inner American: A Self-Portrait from 1957 to* New York: Basic Books.

Weed, J. A. 1981. *Status of Families.* Unpublished manuscript. Bureau of the Census, Population Division, September.

Wolfenstein, M. 1954. "Fun Morality: An Analysis of Recent American Child Training Literature." In *Childhood in Contemporary Cultures,* edited by M. Mead and M. Wolfenstein. Chicago: University of Chicago Press, pp. 168–178.

1

The Changing Family

Introduction

Chapter 1   Family Origins and History

Kathleen Gough
The Origin of the Family

Tamara K. Hareven
American Families in Transition: Historical Perspectives on Change

Ruth Schwartz Cowan
Twentieth-Century Changes in Household Technology

Linda Gordon
The Politics and History of Family Violence

Peter Uhlenberg
Death and the Family

Chapter 2   Demographic Trends

Andrew Cherlin
The Trends: Marriage, Divorce, Remarriage

Arthur J. Norton and Jeanne E. Moorman
Current Trends in Marriage and Divorce Among American Women

Martha Farnsworth Riche
Mysterious Young Adults

Thomas Exter
How to Figure Your Chances of Getting Married

Andrew J. Cherlin and Frank F. Furstenberg, Jr.
The Modernization of Grandparenthood

Introduction

The study of the family does not fit neatly within the boundaries of any single scholarly field; genetics, physiology, archeology, history, anthropology, sociology, psychology, and economics all touch upon it. Religious and ethical authorities claim a stake in the family. Also, troubled individuals and families generate therapeutic demands on family scholarship. In short, the study of the family is interdisciplinary, controversial, and necessary for the formulation of social policy and practices. Interdisciplinary subjects demand competence in more than one field. At a time when competent scholars find it difficult to master even one corner of a field—say the terminology of kinship, or the history of feminism, or the physiology of sexual arousal—intellectual demands on students of the family become vast. Although writers on the family confront many issues, their professional competence is usually limited. Thus a biologist may cite articles in psychology to support a position, without comprehending the tentativeness with which psychologists regard the researcher and his work. Similarly, a psychologist or sociologist may draw upon controversial biological studies. Professional competence means more than the ability to read technical journals; it includes informal knowledge—being "tuned in" to verbal understandings and evaluations of research validity. Usually a major theory or line of research is viewed more critically in its own field than outsiders realize.

Interdisciplinary subjects present other characteristic problems. Each discipline has its own assumptions and views of the world, which may not directly transfer into another field. Some biologists and physically oriented anthropologists, for example, analyze human affairs in terms of individual motives and instincts; for them, society is a shadowy presence, serving mainly as the setting for biologically motivated individual action. Many sociologists and cultural anthropologists, in contrast, perceive the individual as an actor playing a role written by culture and society; according to this view, the individual has no wholly autonomous thoughts and impulses. An important school of psychologists sees people neither as passive recipients of social pressures nor as creatures driven by powerful lusts, but as information processors trying to make sense of their environment. There is no easy way to reconcile such perspectives. Scientific paradigms—characteristic ways of looking at the world—determine not only what answers will be found, but what questions will be asked. This fact has perhaps created special confusion in the study of the family.

"We speak of families," R. D. Laing has observed, "as though we know what families are. We identify, as families, networks of people who live together over time, who have ties of marriage or kinship to one another" (Laing 1971, p. 3). Yet as Laing observes further, the more one studies the emotional dynamics of groups presently called "families," the less clear it becomes how these differ from groups not designated "families." Further, contemporary family patterns and emotional dynamics may not appear in other places and times.

As an object of study, the family is thus plagued with a unique set of problems. There is the assumption that family life, so familiar a part of everyday experience, is easily understood. But familiarity may breed a sense of destiny—what we experience is transformed into the "natural":

> One difficulty in the psychological sciences lies in the familiarity of the phenomena with which they deal. A certain intellectual effort is required to see how such phenomena can pose serious problems or call for intricate explanatory theories. One is inclined to take them for granted as necessary or somehow "natural." (Chomsky 1968, p. 21)

The selections in part 1 discuss both the concept of the family and the development of the family from prehistoric times through the contemporary United States. As one reads the selections, one observes the enormous variation that is possible in family structure and family organization through time and its accompanying economic and social conditions. Moreover, a careful examination of every family system reveals deeply embedded notions of propriety, health, legality, sex, and age role assignments. Only one thing seems constant through time and place with respect to relations among men, women, and children— everyone feels strongly about these. Moreover, prevailing family forms and norms tend to be idealized as the right and proper ones. Perhaps that is because, although the family is scarcely the building block of society claimed by early functional sociologists, it is without doubt the institution possessing the most emotional significance in society. If you believe in a woman's right to medical abortion, or if you don't, and if you have an egalitarian or subordinate vision of the roles of men, women, and children, you probably feel strongly about these. The family grabs us where we live. Not only do we become excited about it, but it seems more than any other institution to generate controversy and moral indignation.

References

Chomsky, N. 1968. *Language and Mind*. New York: Harcourt, Brace and World.
Laing, R. D. 1971. *The Politics of the Family*. New York: Random House.

Chapter 1

Family Origins and History

The Origin of the Family

Kathleen Gough

The trouble with the origin of the family is that no one really knows. Since Engels wrote *The Origin of the Family, Private Property and the State* in 1884, a great deal of new evidence has come in. Yet the gaps are still enormous. It is not known *when* the family originated, although it was probably between 2 million and 100,000 years ago. It is not known whether some kind of embryonic family came before, with, or after the origin of language. Since language is the accepted criterion of humanness, this means that we do not even know whether our ancestors acquired the basics of family life before or after they were human. The chances are that language and the family developed together over a long period, but the evidence is sketchy.

Although the origin of the family is speculative, it is better to speculate with than without evidence. The evidence comes from three sources. One is the social and physical lives of nonhuman primates—especially the New and Old World monkeys and, still more, the great apes, humanity's closest relatives. The second source is the tools and home lives of hunters and gatherers of wild provender who have been studied in modern times.

Each of these sources is imperfect: monkeys and apes, because they are *not* prehuman ancestors, although they are our cousins; fossil hominids, because they left so little vestige of social life; hunters and gatherers, because none of them has, in historic times, possessed a technology and society as primitive as those of early humans. All show the results of long endeavor in specialized marginal environments. But together, these sources give valuable clues.

From *Journal of Marriage and the Family*, November 1971, pp. 760–770. Copyrighted 1971 by the National Council on Family Relations, 1910 West County Road B, Suite 147, St. Paul, MN 55113. Reprinted by permission. Portions of the original have been deleted and several references have been added.

Defining the Family

To discuss the origin of something we must first decide what it is. I shall define the family as "a married couple or other group of adult kinsfolk who cooperate economically and in the upbringing of children, and all or most of whom share a common dwelling."

This includes all forms of kin-based household. Some are extended families containing three generations of married brothers and sisters. Some are "grand-families" descended from a single pair of grandparents. Some are matrilineage households, in which brothers and sisters share a house with the sisters' children, and men merely visit their wives in other homes. Some are compound families, in which one man has several wives, or one woman, several husbands. Others are nuclear families composed of a father, mother, and children.

Some kind of family exists in all known human societies, although it is not found in every segment or class of all stratified, state societies. Greek and American slaves, for example, were prevented from forming legal families, and their social families were often disrupted by sale, forced labor, or sexual exploitation. Even so, the family was an ideal which all classes and most people attained when they could.

The family implies several other universals. (1) Rules forbid sexual relations and marriage between close relatives. Which relatives are forbidden varies, but all societies forbid mother-son mating, and most, father-daughter and brother-sister. Some societies allow sex relations but forbid marriage between certain degrees of kin. (2) The men and women of a family cooperate through a division of labor based on gender. Again, the sexual division of labor varies in rigidity and in the tasks performed. But in no human society to date is it wholly absent. Child care, household tasks, and crafts closely connected with the household tend to be done by women; war, hunting, and government, by men. (3) Marriage exists as a socially recognized, durable, although not necessarily lifelong relationship between individual men and women. From it springs social fatherhood, some kind of special bond between a man and the child of his wife, whether or not they are his own children physiologically. Even in polyandrous societies, where women have several husbands, or in matrilineal societies, where group membership and property pass through women, each child has one or more designated "fathers" with whom he has a special social, and often religious, relationship. This bond of *social* fatherhood is recognized among people who do not know about the male role in procreation or where, for various reasons, it is not clear who the physiological father of a particular infant is. Social fatherhood seems to come from the division and interdependence of male and female tasks, especially in relation to children, rather than directly from physiological fatherhood, although in most societies, the social father of a child is usually presumed to be its physiological father as well. Contrary to the beliefs of some feminists, however, I think that in no human society do men, as a whole category, have *only* the role of insemination and *no* other social or economic role in relation to women and children. (4) Men in general have higher status and authority over the women of their families, although older women may have influence, even some authority, over junior men. The omnipresence of male authority, too, goes contrary to the belief of some feminists that in "matriarchal" societies, women were either completely equal to or had paramount authority over men, either in the home or in society at large.

It is true that in some matrilineal societies, such as the Hopi of Arizona or the Ashanti of Ghana, men exert little authority over their wives. In some, such as the Nayars of South India or the Minangkabau of Sumatra, men may even live separately from their wives and children, that is, in different families. In such societies, however, the fact is that women and children fall under greater or lesser authority from the women's kinsmen—their eldest brothers, mothers' brothers, or even their grown-up sons.

In matrilineal societies, where property, rank, office, and group membership are inherited through the female line, it is true that women tend to have greater independence than in patrilineal societies. This is especially so in matrilineal tribal societies where residence is matrilocal—that is, men come to live in the homes or villages of their wives. Even so, in all matrilineal societies for which adequate descriptions are available, the ultimate headship of households, lineages, and local groups is usually with men. (See Schneider and Gough, 1961, for common and variant features of matrilineal systems.)

There is in fact no true "matriarchal," as distinct from "matrilineal," society in existence or known for literature, and the chances are there never has been.* This does not mean that women and men have never had relations that were dignified and creative for both sexes, appropriate to the knowledge, skills, and technology of their times. Nor does it mean that the sexes cannot be equal in the future or that the sexual division of labor cannot be abolished. I believe that it can and must be. But it is not necessary to believe myths of a feminist Golden Age in order to plan for parity in the future.

Primate Societies

Within the primate order, humans are most closely related to the anthropoid apes (the African chimpanzee and gorilla and the Southeast Asian orang-utan and gibbon), and of these, to the chimpanzee and the gorilla. More distantly related are the Old, and then the New, World monkeys, and finally, the lemurs, tarsiers, and tree shrews.

All primates share characteristics without which the family could not have developed. The young are born relatively helpless. They suckle for several months

---

*The Iroquois are often quoted as a "matriarchal" society, but in fact Morgan himself refers to the "absence of equality between the sexes" and notes that women were subordinate to men, ate after men, and that women (not men) were publicly whipped as punishment for adultery. Warleaders, tribal chiefs, and *sachems* (heads of matrilineal lineages) were men. Women did, however, have a large say in the government of the long-house or home of the matrilocal extended family, and women figured as tribal counsellors and religious officials, as well as in arranging marriages. (Lewis H. Morgan: The League of the *Ho-de-ne Sau-nee or Iroquois,* Human Relations Area Files, 1954)

or years and need prolonged care afterwards. Childhood is longer, the closer the species is to humans. Most monkeys reach puberty at about four to five and mature socially between five and ten. Chimpanzees, by contrast, suckle for up to three years. Females reach puberty at seven to ten; males enter mature social and sexual relations as late as thirteen. The long childhood and maternal care produce close relations between children of the same mother who play together and help tend their juniors until they grow up.

Monkeys and apes, like humans, mate in all months of the year instead of in a rutting season. Unlike humans, however, female apes experience unusually strong sexual desire for a few days shortly before and during ovulation (the oestrus period) and have intensive sexual relations at that time. The males are attracted to the females by their scent or by brightly colored swellings in the sexual region. Oestrus mating appears to be especially pronounced in primate species more remote from humans. The apes and some monkeys carry on less intensive, month-round sexuality in addition to oestrus mating, approaching human patterns more closely. In humans, sexual desires and relations are regulated less by hormonal changes and more by mental images, emotions, cultural rules, and individual preferences.

Year-round (if not always month-round) sexuality means that males and females socialize more continuously among primates than among most other mammals. All primates form bands or troops composed of both sexes plus children. The numbers and proportions of the sexes vary, and in some species an individual, a mother with her young, or a subsidiary troop of male juveniles may travel temporarily alone. But in general, males and females socialize continually through mutual grooming* and playing as well as through frequent sex relations. Keeping close to the females, primate males play with their children and tend to protect both females and young predators. A "division of labor" based on gender is thus already found in primate society between a female role of prolonged child care and a male role of defense. Mates may also carry or take care of children briefly, and nonnursing females may fight. But a kind of generalized "fatherliness" appears in the protective role of adult males towards young, even in species where the sexes do not form long-term individual attachments.

Sexual Bonds Among Primates

Some nonhuman primates do have enduring sexual bonds and restrictions, superficially similar to those in some human societies. Among gibbons a single male and female live together with their young. The male drives off other males and the female, other females. When a juvenile reaches puberty it is thought to leave or be expelled by the parent of the same sex, and he eventually finds a mate elsewhere. Similar *de facto*, rudimentary "incest prohibitions" may have been passed on to humans from their prehuman ancestors and later codified and

---

*Combing the hair and removing parasites with hands or teeth.

elaborated through language, moral custom, and law. Whether this is so may become clearer when we know more about the mating patterns of the other great apes, especially of our closest relatives, the chimpanzees. Present evidence suggests that male chimpanzees do not mate with their mothers.

Orang-utans live in small, tree-dwelling groups like gibbons, but their forms are less regular. One or two mothers may wander alone with their young, mating at intervals with a male; or a male-female pair or several juvenile males may travel together.

Among mountain gorillas of Uganda, South Indian langurs, and hamadryas baboons of Ethiopia, a single, fully mature male mates with several females, especially in their oestrus periods. If younger adult males are present, the females may have occasional relations with them if the leader is tired or not looking.

Among East and South African baboons, rhesus macaques, and South American woolly monkeys, the troop is bigger, numbering up to two hundred. It contains a number of adult males and a much larger number of females. The males are strictly ranked in terms of dominance based on both physical strength and intelligence. The more dominant males copulate intensively with the females during the latter's oestrus periods. Toward the end of the oestrus a female may briefly attach herself to a single dominant male. At other times she may have relations with any male of higher or lower rank provided that those of higher rank permit it.

Among some baboons and macaques the young males travel on the outskirts of the group and have little access to females. Some macaques expel from the troop a proportion of the young males, who then form "bachelor troops." Bachelors may later form new troops with young females.

Other primates are more thoroughly promiscuous, or rather indiscriminate, in mating. Chimpanzees and also South American howler monkeys live in loosely structured groups, again (as in most monkey and ape societies) with a preponderance of females. The mother-child unit is the only stable group. The sexes copulate almost at random and most intensively and indiscriminately during oestrus.

A number of well-known anthropologists have argued that various attitudes and customs often found in human societies are instinctual rather than culturally learned and come from our primate heritage. They include hierarchies of ranking among men, male political power over women, and the greater tendency of men to form friendships with one another, as opposed to women's tendencies to cling to a man. (See, for example, Morris, 1967; Fox, 1967).

I cannot accept these conclusions and think that they stem from the male chauvinism of our own society. A "scientific" argument which states that all such features of female inferiority are instinctive is obviously a powerful weapon in maintaining the traditional family with male dominance. But in fact, these features are *not* universal among nonhuman primates, including some of those most closely related to humans. Chimpanzees have a low degree of male dominance and male hierarchy and are sexually virtually indiscriminate. Gibbons have a kind of fidelity for both sexes and almost no male dominance or hierarchy. Howler monkeys are sexually indiscriminate and lack male hierarchies or dominance.

The fact is that among nonhuman primates male dominance and male hierarchies seem to be adaptations to particular environments, some of which did become genetically established through natural selection. Among humans, however, these features are present in variable degrees and are almost certainly learned, not inherited at all. Among nonhuman primates there are fairly general differences between those that live mainly in trees and those that live largely on the ground. The tree dwellers (for example gibbons, orang-utans, South American howler, and woolly monkeys) tend to have to defend themselves less against predators than do the ground dwellers (such as baboons, macaques, or gorillas). Where defense is important, males are much larger and stronger than females, exert dominance over females, and are strictly hierarchized and organized in relation to one another. Where defense is less important there is much less sexual dimorphism (difference in size between male and female), less or no male dominance, a less pronounced male hierarchy, and greater sexual indiscriminacy.

Comparatively speaking, humans have a rather small degree of sexual dimorphism, similar to chimpanzees. Chimpanzees live much in trees but also partly on the ground, in forest or semiforest habitats. They build individual nests to sleep in, sometimes on the ground but usually in trees. They flee into trees from danger. Chimpanzees go mainly on all fours, but sometimes on two feet, and can use and make simple tools. Males are dominant, but not very dominant, over females. The rank hierarchy among males in unstable, and males often move between groups, which vary in size from two to fifty individuals. Food is vegetarian, supplemented with worms, grubs, or occasional small animals. A mother and her young form the only stable unit. Sexual relations are largely indiscriminate, but nearby males defend young animals from danger. The chances are that our prehuman ancestors had a similar social life. Morgan and Engels were probably right in concluding that we came from a state of "original promiscuity" before we were fully human.

Human Evolution

Judging from the fossil record, apes ancestral to humans, gorillas, and chimpanzees roamed widely in Asia, Europe and Africa some 12 to 28 million years ago. Toward the end of that period (the Miocene) one appears in North India and East Africa, Ramapithecus, who may be ancestral both to later hominids and to modern humans. His species were small like gibbons, walked upright on two feet, had human rather than ape cornerteeth, and therefore probably used hands rather than teeth to tear their food. From that time evolution toward humanness must have proceeded through various phases until the emergence of modern homo sapiens, about 70,000 years ago.

In the Miocene period before Ramapithecus appeared, there were several time spans in which, over large areas, the climate became dryer and subtropical forests dwindled or disappeared. A standard reconstruction of events, which I accept, is that groups of apes, probably in Africa, had to come down from the trees and adapt to terrestrial life. Through natural selection, probably over millions of years, they developed specialized feet for walking. Thus freed, the hands came to be used not only (as among apes) for grasping and tearing, but for regular carrying of objects such as weapons (which had hitherto been sporadic) or of infants (which had hitherto clung to their mothers' body hair).

The spread of indigestible grasses on the open savannahs may have encouraged, if it did not compel, the early ground dwellers to become active hunters rather than simply to forage for small, sick, or dead animals that came their way. Collective hunting and tool use involved group cooperation and helped foster the growth of language out of the call systems of apes. Language meant the use of symbols to refer to events not present. It allowed greatly increased foresight, memory, planning, and division of tasks—in short, the capacity for human thought.

With the change to hunting, group territories became much larger. Apes range only a few thousand feet daily; hunters, several miles. But because their infants were helpless, nursing women could hunt only small game close to home. This then produced the sexual division of labor on which the human family has since been founded. Women elaborated upon ape methods of child care and greatly expanded foraging, which in most areas remained the primary and most stable source of food. Men improved upon ape methods of fighting off other animals and of group protection in general. They adapted these methods to hunting, using weapons which for millennia remained the same for the chase as for human warfare.

Out of the sexual division of labor came, for the first time, home life as well as group cooperation. Female apes nest with and provide foraged food for their infants. But adult apes do not cooperate in food getting or nest building. They build new nests each night wherever they may happen to be. With the development of a hunting-gathering complex, it became necessary to have a G.H.Q., or home. Men could bring meat to this place for several days' supply. Women and children could meet men there after the day's hunting and could bring their vegetable produce for general consumption. Men, women, and children could build joint shelters, butcher meat, and treat skins for clothing.

Later, fire came into use for protection against wild animals, for lighting, and eventually for cooking. The hearth then provided the focus and symbol of home. With the development of cookery, some humans—chiefly women and perhaps some children and old men—came to spend more time preparing nutrition so that all people need spend less time in chewing and tearing their food. Meals—already less frequent because of the change to a carnivorous diet—now became brief, periodic events instead of the long feeding sessions of apes.

The change to humanness brought two bodily changes that affected birth and child care. These were head size and width of the pelvis. Walking upright produced a narrower pelvis to hold the guts in position. Yet as language developed, brains and hence heads grew much bigger relative to body size. To compensate, humans are born at an earlier stage of growth than apes. They are helpless longer and require longer and more total care. This in turn caused early women to concentrate more on child care and less on defense than do female apes.

Language made possible not only a division and cooperation in labor but also all forms of tradition, rules, morality, and cultural learning. Rules banning sex relations among close kinfolk must have come very early. Precisely how or why they developed is unknown, but they had at least two useful functions. They helped to preserve order in the family as a cooperative unit by outlawing competition for mates. They also created bonds *between* families, or even between separate bands, and so provided a basis for wider cooperation in the struggle for livelihood and the expansion of knowledge.

It is not clear when all these changes took place. Climatic change with increased drought began regionally up to 28 million years ago. The divergence between prehuman and gorilla-chimpanzee stems had occurred in both Africa and India at least 12 million years ago. The prehuman stem led to the Australopithecenes of East and South Africa, about 1,750,000 years ago. These were pygmylike, two-footed, upright hominids with larger than ape brains, who made tools and probably hunted in savannah regions. It is unlikely that they knew the use of fire.

The first known use of fire is that of cave-dwelling hominids (Sinanthropus, a branch of the Pithecanthropines) at Choukoutien near Peking, some half a million years ago during the second ice age. Fire was used regularly in hearths, suggesting cookery, by the time of the Acheulean and Mousterian cultures of Neanderthal man in Europe, Africa, and Asia before, during and after the third ice age, some 150,000 to 100,000 years ago. These people, too, were often cave dwellers and buried their dead ceremonially in caves. Cave dwelling by night as well as by day was probably, in fact, not safe for humans until fire came into use to drive away predators.

Most anthropologists conclude that home life, the family, and language had developed by the time of Neanderthal man, who was closely similar and may have been ancestral to modern homo sapiens. At least two anthropologists, however, believe that the Australopithecenes already had language nearly 2 million years ago, while another thinks that language and incest prohibitions did not evolve until the time of homo sapiens some 70,000 to 50,000 years ago. (For the former view, see Hockett and Ascher, 1968; for the latter, Livingstone, 1969.) I am myself inclined to think that family life built around tool use, the use of language, cookery, and a sexual division of labor must have been established sometime between about 500,000 and 200,000 years ago.

Hunters and Gatherers

Most of the hunting and gathering societies studied in the eighteenth to twentieth centuries had technologies similar to those that were widespread in the

Mesolithic period, which occurred about 15,000 to 10,000 years ago, after the ice ages ended but before cultivation was invented and animals domesticated.

Modern hunters live in marginal forest, mountain, arctic, or desert environments where cultivation is impracticable. Although by no means "primeval," the hunters of recent times do offer clues to the types of family found during that 99 percent of human history before the agricultural revolution. They include the Eskimo, many Canadian and South American Indian groups, the forest BaMbuti (Pygmies) and the desert Bushmen of Southern Africa, the Kadar of South India, the Veddah of Ceylon, and the Andaman Islanders of the Indian Ocean. About 175 hunting and gathering cultures in Oceania, Asia, Africa, and America have been described in fair detail.

In spite of their varied environments, hunters share certain features of social life. They live in bands of about 20 to 200 people, the majority of bands having fewer than 50. Bands are divided into families, which may forage alone in some seasons. Hunters have simple but ingenious technologies. Bows and arrows, spears, needles, skin clothing, and temporary leaf or wood shelters are common. Most hunters do some fishing. The band forages and hunts in a large territory and usually moves camp often.

Social life is egalitarian. There is of course no state or organized government. Apart from religious shamans or magicians, the division of labor is based only on sex and age. Resources are owned communally; tools and personal possessions are freely exchanged. Everyone works who can. Band leadership goes to whichever man has the intelligence, courage, and foresight to command the respect of his fellows. Intelligent older women are also looked up to.

The household is the main unit of economic cooperation, with the men, women, and children dividing the labor and pooling their produce. In 97 percent of the 175 societies classified by G. P. Murdock, hunting is confined to men; in the other 3 percent it is chiefly a male pursuit. Gathering of wild plants, fruits, and nuts is women's work. In 60 percent of societies, only women gather, while in another 32 percent gathering is mainly feminine. Fishing is solely or mainly men's work in 93 percent of the hunting societies where it occurs.

For the rest, men monopolize fighting, although interband warfare is rare. Women tend children and shelters and usually do most of the cooking, processing, and storage of food. Women tend, also, to be foremost in the early household crafts such as basketry, leather work, the making of skin or bark clothing, and, in the more advanced hunting societies, pottery. (Considering that women probably *invented* all of these crafts, in addition to cookery, food storage and preservation, agriculture, spinning, weaving, and perhaps even house construction, it is clear that women played quite as important roles as men in early cultural development.) Building dwellings and making tools and ornaments are variously divided between the sexes, while boat building is largely done by men. Girls help the women, and boys play in hunting or hunt small game until they reach puberty, when both take on the roles of adults. Where the environment makes it desirable, the men of a whole band or of some smaller cluster of households cooperate in hunting or fishing and divide their spoils. Women of nearby families often go gathering together.

Family composition varies among hunters as it does in other kinds of societies. About half or more of known hunting societies have nuclear families (father, mother, and children) with polygynous households (a man, two or more wives, and children) as occasional variants. Clearly, nuclear families are the most common among hunters, although hunters have a slightly higher proportion of polygynous families than do nonhunting societies.

About a third of hunting societies contain some stem-family households—that is, older parents live in together with one married child and grandchildren, while the other married children live in independent dwellings. A still smaller proportion live in large extended families containing several married brothers (or several married sisters), their spouses, and children. (For exact figures, see Murdock, 1957; Coult, 1965; and Murdock, 1967. In the last named survey, out of 175 hunting societies, 47 percent had nuclear family households, 38 percent had stem families, and 14 percent had extended families.) Hunters have fewer extended and stem families than do nonhunting societies. These larger households become common with the rise of agriculture. They are especially found in large, preindustrial agrarian states such as ancient Greece, Rome, India, the Islamic empires, and China.

Hunting societies also have few households composed of a widow or divorcee and her children. This is understandable, for neither men nor women can survive long without the work and produce of the other sex, and marriage is the way to obtain them. That is why so often young men must show proof of hunting prowess and girls of cooking before they are allowed to marry.

The family, together with territorial grouping, provides the framework of society among hunters. Indeed, as Morgan and Engels clearly saw, kinship and territory are the foundations of all societies before the rise of the state. Not only hunting and gathering bands, but the larger and more complex tribes and chiefdoms of primitive cultivators and herders organize people through descent from common ancestors or through marriage ties between groups. Among hunters, things are simple. There is only the family, and beyond it the band. With the domestication of plants and animals, the economy becomes more productive. More people can live together. Tribes form, containing several thousand people loosely organized into large kin groups such as clans and lineages, each composed of a number of related families. With still further development of the productive forces the society throws up a central political leadership, together with craft specialization and trade, and so the chiefdom emerges. But this, too, is structured through ranked allegiances and marriage ties between kin groups.

Only with the rise of the state does class, independently of kinship, provide the basis for relations of production, distribution, and power. Even then, kin groups remain large in the agrarian state and kinship persists as the prime organizing principle within each class until the rise of capitalism. The reduction in significance of the family that we see today is the outgrowth of a decline in the importance of "familism" relative to our institutions, that began with the rise of the state but became speeded up with the development of capitalism and machine industry. In most modern socialist societies, the family is even less significant as an organizing principle. It is reasonable to suppose that in the future it will become minimal or may disappear, at least as a legally constituted unit for exclusive forms of sexual and economic cooperation and of child care. [Some nineteenth century theorists, for example, Lloyd Morgan (1877) and Frederick Engels (1955)] thought that from a state of original promiscuity, early humans at first banned sex relations between . . . parents and children but continued to allow them . . . between brothers, sisters, and all kinds of cousins within the band. . . . They thought that later, all mating within the family or some larger kin group became forbidden, but that there was a stage . . . in which a group of sisters or other close kinsmen from one band were married jointly to a group of brothers or other close kinsmen from another. . . . Only later [according to this view] did the "pairing family" develop in which each man was married to one (or two) women individually.

These writers drew their conclusions not from evidence of actual group-marriage among primitive peoples but from the kinship terms found today in certain tribal and chiefly societies. Some of these equate all kin of the same sex in the parents' generation, suggesting brother-sister marriage. Others equate the father's brothers with the father and the mother's sisters with the mother, suggest-ing the marriage of a group of brothers with a group of sisters.

Modern evidence does not bear out these conclusions about early society. All known hunters and gatherers live in families, not in communal sexual arrange-ments. Most hunters even live in nuclear families rather than in large extended kin groups. Mating is individualized, although one man may occasionally have two wives, or (very rarely) a woman may have two husbands. Economic life is built primarily around the division of labor and partnership between individual men and women. The hearths, caves, and other remains of Upper Paleolithic hunters suggest that this was probably an early arrangement. We cannot say that Engel's sequences are completely ruled out for very early hominids—the evidence is simply not available. But it is hard to see what economic arrangements among hunters would give rise to group, rather than individual or pairing marriage arrangements, and this Engels does not explain.

Soviet anthropologists continued to believe in Morgan and Engel's early "stages" longer than did anthropologists in the West. Today, most Russian anthropologists admit the lack of evidence for "consanguineal" and "punaluan" arrangements, but some still believe that a different kind of group marriage intervened between indiscriminate mating and the pairing family. Semyonov, for example, argues that in the stage of group marriage, mating was forbidden within the hunting band, but that the men of two neighboring bands had multiple, visiting sex relations with women of the opposite band (Semyonov, 1967).

While such an arrangement cannot be ruled out, it seems unlikely because many of the customs which Semyonov regards as "survivals" of such group marriage (for example, visiting husbands, matrilineage dwelling groups, widespread clans, multiple sources for both sexes, men's and women's communal houses, and prohibitions of sexual intercourse inside the huts of the village) are actually found not so much among hunters as among horticultural tribes and even quite complex agricultural states. Whether or not such a stage of group marriage occurred in the earliest societies, there seems little doubt that pairing marriage (involving family households) came about with the development of elaborate methods of hunting, cooking, and the preparation of clothing and shelters—that is, with a fully fledged division of labor.

Even so, there *are* some senses in which mating among hunters has more of a group character than in archaic agrarian states or in capitalist society. Murdock's sample shows that sex relations before marriage are strictly prohibited in only 26 percent of hunting societies. In the rest, marriage is either arranged so early that premarital sex is unlikely, or (more usually) sex relations are permitted more or less freely before marriage.

With marriage, monogamy is the normal *practice* at any given time for most hunters, but it is not the normal *rule*. Only 19 percent in Murdock's survey prohibit plural unions. Where polygyny is found (79 percent) the most common type is for a man to marry two sisters or other closely related women of the same kin group—for example, the daughters of two sisters or of two brothers. When a woman dies it is common for a sister to replace her in the marriage, and when a man dies, for a brother to replace him.

Similarly, many hunting societies hold that the wives of brothers or other close kinsmen are in some sense wives of the group. They can be called on in emergencies or if one of them is ill. Again, many hunting societies have special times for sexual license between men and women of a local group who are not married to each other, such as the "lights out" games of Eskimo sharing a communal snow house. In other situations, an Eskimo wife will spend the night with a chance guest of her husband's. All parties expect this as normal hospitality. Finally, adultery, although often punished, tends to be common in hunting societies, and few if any of them forbid divorce or the remarriage of divorcees and widows.

The reason for all this seems to be that marriage and sexual restrictions are practical arrangements among hunters designed mainly to serve economic and survival needs. In these societies, some kind of rather stable pairing best accomplishes the division of labor and cooperation of men and women and the care of children. Beyond the immediate family, either a larger family group or the whole band has other, less intensive but important kinds of cooperative activities. Therefore, the husbands and wives of individuals within that group can be summoned to stand in for each other if need arises. In the case of Eskimo wife lending, the extreme climate and the need for lone wandering in search for game dictate high standards of hospitality. This evidently becomes extended to sexual sharing.

In the case of sororal polygny or marriage to the dead wife's sister, it is natural that when two women fill the same role—either together or in sequence—they should be sisters, for sisters are more alike than other women. They are likely to care more for each other's children. The replacement of a dead spouse by a sister or a brother also preserves existing intergroup relations. For the rest, where the economic and survival bonds of marriage are not at stake, people can afford to be freely companionate and tolerant. Hence, premarital sexual freedom, seasonal group license, and a pragmatic approach to adultery.

Marriages among hunters are usually arranged by elders when a young couple are ready for adult responsibilities. But the couple know each other and usually have some choice. If the first marriage does not work, the second mate will almost certainly be self-selected. Both sexual and companionate love between individual men and women are known and are deeply experienced. With comparative freedom of mating, love is less often separated from or opposed to marriage than in archaic states or even than in some modern nations.

The Position of Women

Even in hunting societies it seems that women are always in some sense the "second sex," with greater or less subordination to men. This varies. Eskimo and Australian aboriginal women are far more subordinate than women among the Kadar, the Andamanese, or the Congo Pygmies—all forest people.

I suggest that women have greater power and independence among hunters when they are important food obtainers than when they are mainly processors of meat or other supplies provided by men. The former situation is likelier to exist in societies where hunting is small-scale and intensive than where it is extensive over a large terrain, and in societies where gathering is important by comparison with hunting.

In general in hunting societies, women are less subordinated in certain crucial respects than they are in most, if not all, of the archaic states, or even in some capitalist nations. These respects include men's ability to deny women sexuality or to force it upon them, to command or exploit their labor or to control their produce, to control or rob them of their children, to confine them physically and prevent their movement, to use them as objects in male transactions, to cramp their creativeness, or to withhold from them large areas of the society's knowledge and cultural attainments.

Especially lacking in hunting societies is the kind of male possessiveness and exclusiveness regarding women that leads to such situations as savage punishments or death for female adultery, the jealous guarding of female chastity and virginity, the denial of divorce to women, or the ban on a woman's remarriage after her husband's death.

For these reasons, I do not think we can speak, as some writers do, of a class division between men and women in hunting societies. True, men are more mobile than women and they lead in public affairs. But class society requires that one class control the means of production, dictate its use by the other classes, and expropriate the surplus. These conditions do not exist among hunters. Land and other resources are held communally, although women may monopolize certain gathering areas, and men, their hunting grounds. There is rank difference, role difference, and some difference respecting degrees of authority between the sexes, but there is reciprocity rather than domination or exploitation.

As Engels saw, the power of men to exploit women systematically springs from the existence of surplus wealth and, more directly, from the state, social stratification, and the control of property by men. With the rise of the state, because of their monopoly over weapons, and because freedom from child care allows them to enter specialized economic and political roles, some men—especially ruling-class men—acquire power over other men and over women. Almost all men acquire it over women of their own or lower classes, especially within their own kinship groups. These kinds of male power are shadowy among hunters.

To the extent that men *have* power over women in hunting societies, this seems to spring from the male monopoly of heavy weapons, from the particular division of labor between the sexes, or from both. Although men seldom use weapons against women, they *possess* them (or possess superior weapons) in addition to their physical strength. This does give men an ultimate control of force. When old people or babies must be killed to ensure band or family survival, it is usually men who kill them. Infanticide—rather common among hunters, who must limit the mouths to feed—is more often female infanticide than male.

The hunting of men seems more often to require them to organize in groups than does the work of women. Perhaps because of this, 60 percent of hunting societies have predominantly virilocal residence. That is, men choose which band to live in (often, their fathers'), and women move with their husbands. This gives a man advantages over his wife in terms of familiarity and loyalties, for the wife is often a stranger. Sixteen to 17 percent of hunting societies are, however, uxorilocal, with men moving to the households of their wives, while 15 to 17 percent are bilocal—that is, either sex may move in with the other on marriage.

Probably because of male cooperation in defense and hunting, men are more prominent in band councils and leadership, in medicine and magic, and in public rituals designed to increase game, to ward off sickness, or to initiate boys into manhood. Women do, however, often take part in band councils; they are not excluded from law and government as in many agrarian states. Some women are respected as wise leaders, story tellers, doctors, or magicians or are feared as witches. Women have their own ceremonies of fertility, birth, and healing, from which men are often excluded.

In some societies, although men control the most sacred objects, women are believed to have discovered them. Among the Congo Pygmies, religion centers about a beneficent spirit, the Animal of the Forest. It is represented by wooden trumpets that are owned and played by men. Their possession and use are hidden from the women and they are played at night when hunting is bad, someone falls ill, or death occurs. During the playing men dance in the public campfire, which is sacred and is associated with the forest. Yet the men believe that women originally owned the trumpet and that it was a woman who stole fire from the chimpanzees or from the forest spirit. When a woman has failed to bear children for several years, a special ceremony is held. Women lead in the songs that usually accompany the trumpets, and an old woman kicks apart the campfire. Temporary female dominance seems to be thought necessary to restore fertility.

In some hunting societies women are exchanged between local groups, which are thus knit together through marriages. Sometimes, men of different bands directly exchange their sisters. More often there is a generalized exchange of women between two or more groups or a one-way movement of women within a circle of groups. Sometimes the husband's family pays weapons, tools, or ornaments to the wife's in return for the wife's services and, later, her children.

In such societies, although they may be well treated and their consent sought, women are clearly the moveable partners in an arrangement controlled by men. Male anthropologists have seized on this as evidence of original male dominance and patrilocal residence. Fox and others, for example, have argued that until recently, *all* hunting societies formed outmarrying patrilocal bands, linked together politically by the exchange of women. The fact that fewer than two-thirds of hunting societies are patrilocal today and only 41 percent have band-exogamy is explained in terms of modern conquest, economic change, and depopulation.

I cannot accept this formula. It is true that modern hunting societies have been severely changed, deculturated, and often depopulated by capitalist imperialism. I can see little evidence, however, that the ones that are patrilocal today have undergone less change than those that are not. It is hard to believe that in spite of enormous environmental diversity and the passage of thousands, perhaps millions, of years, hunting societies all had band exogamy with patrilocal residence until they were disturbed by western imperialism. It is more likely that early band societies, like later agricultural tribes, developed variety in family life and the status of women as they spread over the earth.

There is also some likelihood that the earliest hunters had matrilocal rather than patrilocal families. Among apes and monkey, it is almost always males who leave the troop or are driven out. Females stay closer to their mothers and their original site; males move about, attaching themselves to females where availability and competition permit. Removal of the wife to the husband's home or band may have been a relatively late development in societies where male cooperation in hunting assumed overwhelming importance.* Conversely, after the development of horticulture (which was probably invented and is mainly carried out by women), those tribes in which horticulture predominated over stock raising were most

*Upper Palaeolithic hunters produced female figurines that were obvious emblems of fertility. The cult continued through the Mesolithic and into the Neolithic period. Goddesses and spirits of fertility are found in some patrilineal as well as matrilineal societies, but they tend to be more prominent in the latter. It is thus possible that in many areas even late Stone Age hunters had matrilocal residence and perhaps matrilineal descent, and that in some regions this pattern continued through the age of horticulture and even—as in the case of the Nayars of Kerala and the Minangkabau of Sumatra—into the age of plow agriculture, or writing, and of the small-scale state.

likely to be or to remain matrilocal and to develop matrilineal descent groups with a relatively high status of women. But where extensive hunting of large animals or, later, the herding of large domesticates, predominated, patrilocal residence flourished and women were used to form alliances between male-centered groups. With the invention of metallurgy and of agriculture as distinct from horticulture after 4000 B.C., men came to control agriculture and many crafts, and most of the great agrarian states had patrilocal residence with patriarchal, male-dominant families.

Conclusions

The family is a human institution, not found in its totality in any prehuman species. It required language, planning, cooperation, self-control, foresight, and cultural learning and probably developed along with these.

The family was made desirable by the early human combination of prolonged child care with the need for hunting with weapons over large terrains. The sexual division of labor on which it was based grew out of a rudimentary prehuman division between male defense and female child care. But among humans this sexual division of functions for the first time became crucial for food production and so laid the basis for future economic specialization and cooperation.

Morgan and Engels were probably right in thinking that the human family was preceded by sexual indiscriminacy. They were also right in seeing an egalitarian group quality about early economic and marriage arrangements. They were without evidence, however, in believing that the earliest mating and economic patterns were entirely group relations.

Together with tool use and language, the family was no doubt the most significant invention of the human revolution. All three required reflective thought, which above all accounts for the vast superiority in consciousness that separates humans from apes.

The family provided the framework for all prestate society and the fount of its creativeness. In groping for survival and for knowledge, human beings learned to control their sexual desires and to suppress their individual selfishness, aggression, and competition. The other side of this self-control was increased capacity for love—not only love of a mother for her child, which is seen among apes, but of male for female in enduring relationships and of each sex for ever-widening groups of humans. Civilization would have been impossible without this initial self-control, seen in incest prohibitions and in the generosity and moral orderliness of primitive family life.

From the start, women have been subordinate to men in certain key areas of status, mobility, and public leadership. But before the agricultural revolution, and even for several thousands of years thereafter, the inequality was based chiefly on the unalterable fact of long child care combined with the exigencies of primitive technology. The extent of inequality varied according to the ecology and the resulting sexual division of tasks. But in any case it was largely a matter of survival rather than of man-made cultural impositions. Hence the impressions we receive of dignity, freedom, and mutual respect between men and women in primitive hunting and horticultural societies. This is true whether these societies are patrilocal, bilocal, or matrilocal, although matrilocal societies, with matrilineal inheritance, offer greater freedom to women than do patrilocal and patrilineal societies of the same level of productivity and political development.

A distinct change occurred with the growth of individual and family property in herds, in durable craft objects and trade objects, and in stable, irrigated farmsites or other forms of heritable wealth. This crystallized in the rise of the state, about 4000 B.C. With the growth of class society and of male dominance in the ruling class of the state, women's subordination increased and eventually reached its depths in the patriarchal families of the great agrarian states. Knowledge of how the family arose is interesting to women because it tells us how we differ from prehumans, what our past has been, and what have been the biological and cultural limitations from which we are emerging. It shows us how generations of male scholars have distorted or overinterpreted the evidence to bolster beliefs in the inferiority of women's mental processes—for which there is no foundation in fact. Knowing about early families is also important to correct a reverse bias among some feminist writers, who hold that in "matriarchal" societies women were completely equal with or were even dominant over men. For this, too, there seems to be no basis in evidence.

The past of the family does not limit its future. Although the family probably emerged with humanity, neither the family itself nor particular family forms are genetically determined. The sexual division of labor—until recently, universal—need not, and in my opinion should not, survive in industrial society. Prolonged child care ceases to be a basis for female subordination when artificial birth control, spaced births, small families, patent feeding, and communal nurseries allow it to be shared by men. Automation and cybernation remove most of the heavy work for which women are less equipped than men. The exploitation of women that came with the rise of the state and of class society will presumably disappear in poststate classless society—for which the technological and scientific basis already exists.

The family was essential to the dawn of civilization, allowing a vast qualitative leap forward in cooperation, purposive knowledge, love, and creativeness. But today, rather than enhancing them, the confinement of women in homes and small families—like their subordination in work—artificially limits these human capacities. It may be that the human gift for personal love will make some form of voluntary, long-term mating and of individual devotion between parents and children continue indefinitely, side by side with public responsibility for domestic tasks and for the care and upbringing of children. There is no need to legislate personal relations out of existence. But neither need we fear a social life in which the family is no more.

References

Coult, Allen D. *Cross Tabulations of Murdock's World Ethnographic Sample.* Columbia: University of Missouri Press, 1965.

Engels, F. *The Origin of the Family, Private Property and the State.* Moscow: Foreign Language Publishing House, 1955.

Fox, Robin. *Kinship and Marriage.* London: Pelican Books, 1967.

Hockett, Charles F., and Robert Ascher. "The Human Revolution." In *Man in Adaptation: The Biosocial Background,* edited by Yehudi A. Cohen. Chicago: Aldine, 1968.

Livingstone, Frank, B. "Genetics, Ecology and the Origin of Incest and Exogamy." *Current Anthropology,* February 1969.

Morgan, L. F. *Ancient Society* (1877). New York: Holt, reprinted 1963.

Morris, Desmond. *The Naked Ape.* Jonathan Cape, 1967.

Murdock, G. P. "World Ethnographic Sample." *American Anthropologist,* 1957.

Murdock, G. P., *Ethnographic Atlas.* Pittsburgh: University of Pittsburgh, 1967.

Schneider, David M., and Kathleen Gough. *Matrilineal Kinship.* Berkeley and Los Angeles: University of California Press, 1961.

Semyonov, Y. I. "Group Marriage, Its Nature and Role in the Evolution of Marriage and Family Relations." In *Seventh International Congress of Anthropological and Ethnological Sciences.* Vol. IV. Moscow, 1967.

American Families in Transition: Historical Perspectives on Change

Tamara K. Hareven

Introduction: Myths About the Past

The American family has recently been the subject of much concern. Anxiety over its future has escalated over the past decade; the youth movement of the 1960s, and subsequently the women's movement, have brought it under scrutiny and attack. Policy debates over governmental family welfare programs have also directed attention to it. More recently, the emergence of the elderly in American society as a significant group with its own problems has led to a further examination of inadequacies of the family that contribute to the isolation of older people in modern America.

The consequences of all these developments, combined with the impact of increasing divorce rates and declining birth rates and the increase in the proportion

From Froma Walsh, ed., *Normal Family Processes,* pp. 446–466 © 1982 The Guilford Press, New York. Reprinted by permission.

of single-parent families, have given rise to the fear that the family might be breaking down or going out of existence. Anxiety over family breakdown is not unique to our times. It appears that since the time of the Founding Fathers every generation has expressed its doubts about the stability and continuity of the family. This very intense concern over the fate of the family both in the past and today points to the crucial place that the family holds in American culture. Yet the question still needs to be asked: Is the family in crisis, or is it simply undergoing some important changes? What can we learn from the past about the transitions the family life is undergoing and the directions in which it is heading?

Through much of American history, the family has been seen as the linchpin of the social order and the basis for stable governance. Even though changes appear more gradually in the family than they do in other institutions, educators, moralists, and social planners frequently express fear of family breakdown under the pressures of social changes. Every generation has thought itself to be witnessing the breakdown of the "traditional" family. In the era of the American Revolution, much anxiety was expressed about the possible disappearance of the American family, and during the Civil War the nation's crisis was projected onto the fate of the family itself. More than any other developments, however, industrialization and urbanization have been viewed as the major threats to traditional family life over the past decade and a half.

Family disorganization has been identified as a major characteristic of industrial society and has been associated with the loss of a Utopian preindustrial past. Even the adaptation of functions of and within the family that developed in response to social change were frequently interpreted as manifestations of breakdown.

Perceptions of American family life today are governed by commonly held myths about American family life in the past. Such myths maintain that there once was a golden age of family relations, when three generations lived together happily in the same household. This belief in a lost golden age has led people to depict the present as a period of decline and family breakdown. Nostalgia for a mythical past has resulted in the idealization of such families as the Waltons of TV and the world that supposedly produced them.

In order to come to grips with the problems of the present, it is essential to examine changes in family life over the past two centuries. A historical consideration of the family places some of the changes in their proper context. Looking at developments over time enables us better to assess the uniqueness of present conditions, and it also helps us to distinguish between long-term trends and temporary developments. To what extent are some of these changes part of a continuing historical process, and to what extent are they new departures? Most importantly, a historical consideration enables us to distinguish between passing fads and critical changes, and it can even offer some precedents from the past that could be revived and applied to present conditions.

In the ensuing discussion, I first examine major historical changes in the American family in relation to the current, seemingly "dramatic" transitions. I discuss changes in the following areas: organization of the family and kin; family functions and values; and changes in the life course.

Change and Continuity in Family Structure

Recent research on the family in preindustrial American society has dispelled the myths about the existence of ideal three-generational families in the American past (Demos, 1970; Goode, 1963; Greven, 1970; Laslett, 1965; Laslett & Wall, 1972).[1] There has never been in American society an era when three generations were coresiding in the same household. The "great extended families" that have become part of the folklore of modern industrial society were rarely actually in existence. Households and families were simple in their structure and not drastically different in their organization from contemporary families. Nuclear households, consisting of parents and their children, were characteristic residential units (although, as will be suggested later, they often contained strangers in addition to nuclear family members). Three generations rarely lived together in the same household. Given the high mortality rate in preindustrial societies, most parents could not have expected to live with their grandchildren (Davis, 1972; Glick, 1947, 1957). (On the changing life cycles of American women in particular, see Uhlenberg, 1969.) It would thus be futile to argue that industrialization destroyed the great extended family of the past, since such a family type rarely existed. And, as will be shown below, the process of industrialization had actually contributed in many ways to strengthening family ties and to increasing the chances of family members to stay together in the same place for longer time periods.

Contrary to popular assumption, preindustrial households were thus not filled by large numbers of extended kin. These households did contain strangers, however, who lived in the home as boarders, lodgers, apprentices, or servants. In this respect, the composition of the household in the preindustrial and early industrial period was significantly different from that in contemporary society. The tendency of families to include strangers in the household was connected with an entirely different concept of family life. In contrast to the current emphasis on the family as a private retreat, the household of the past was the site of a broad array of functions and activities that transcended the more restricted circle of the nuclear family. This fact had especially important implications for the role of women: it meant that women were involved in a variety of domestic management tasks beyond the care of their immediate family members. They took care of apprentices, boarders, and possibly other strangers who were placed with the

---

[1]Historians have frequently confused "family" with "household." This distinction must be made clear, however, if changes in the family are to be put in proper perspective. The "household" is the residential unit, which has also been recorded in the population censuses. The "family" can contain kin living inside the household, as well as relatives outside the household. It is now clear that preindustrial households were not extended. But this does not mean that the family was nuclear and isolated. Although several relatives did not reside in the same household, they were still interactive (see Hareven, 1971, 1974).

family because they were delinquent youth, orphaned children, or abandoned old men or women.

The household then, was not the exclusive abode of the nuclear family. It did not include relatives other than nuclear family members, but it did include strangers. The presence of strangers in the household continued in different forms throughout the 19th and into the early 20th century. Although apprentices virtually disappeared from households by the middle of the 19th century, and dependent, delinquent, and sick people were being placed in institutions, the practice of taking strangers into the household persisted—primarily through boarding and lodging. Throughout the 19th and early 20th centuries, about one-fourth to one-third of the population either had lived in someone's household as a boarder or had taken in boarders or lodgers at some point in their lives (Modell & Hareven, 1973). Boarding and lodging fulfilled the function of what Taeuber has referred to as "the social equalization of the family" (1969, p. 5). Young men and women in their late teens and 20s who had left their own parents' households, or who had migrated from other communities, lived as boarders in the households of older people whose own children had left home. This practice thus enabled young people to stay in surrogate family arrangements, while at the same time it provided old people with the opportunity to continue heading their own households without being isolated.

The practice of taking in boarders and lodgers was extremely valuable in providing continuity in urban life and in allowing new migrants and immigrants to adapt to urban living. Its existence suggests the great flexibility in families and households, flexibility that has been lost over the past half century. Increasing availability in housing and the spread of the values of privacy in family life have led to the phasing out of this practice. The practice has survived to some extent among black families, but it has almost virtually disappeared from the larger society. With its disappearance, the family has lost some of its major sources of resilience and adaptability to urban living. Thus, the most important change in American family life has not been the breakdown of a three-generational family pattern, but, rather, the loss of flexibility in regard to taking strangers into the household.

The practice of boarding and lodging has been replaced since the 1920s by solitary living. The increase in the rates of "primary individual" households, as the Census Bureau refers to the households of individuals residing alone, is a spreading phenomenon. While in the 19th century solitary residence was almost unheard of, now a major portion of the population resides alone. The disquieting aspect of this pattern is in the high percentage of aging widows living alone. Thus, solitary residence for a major portion of the population is not a matter of free choice, but rather an unavoidable and often unbearable arrangement. Again, what has been lost is not a great extended family of the past, but the flexibility of the family that enabled households to expand when necessary and to take people in to live in surrogate family settings rather than in isolation (Kobrin, 1976).

Another pervasive myth about family life in the past has been the assumption that industrialization broke up traditional kinship ties and destroyed organic interdependence between the family and the community. Once again, historical research has shown that industrialization led to the redefinition of the family's roles and functions, but by no means broke up traditional family patterns. In industrial communities, the family continued to function as a work unit. Relatives acted as recruitment, migration, and housing agents for industrial laborers, helping each other to shift from rural to industrial work. Preindustrial family patterns and values were carried over into the industrial system, providing important continuities between rural and urban industrial life (Anderson, 1971; Hareven, 1978, 1982 forthcoming). Rather than being a passive victim, the family was an active agent in the process of industrialization. Families migrated into groups to industrial centers, recruiting workers into the factory system, and often several family members continued to work in the same place. Migration to industrial communities did not break up traditional kinship ties. Rather, families used these ties to facilitate their own transitions into industrial life.

Despite changes wrought under the impact of industrialization, reliance on kin as the most basic resource for assistance persisted. Throughout the 19th and 20th centuries, kin in rural and urban areas continued to engage in mutual assistance and in reciprocal services. Kin performed a crucial role in initiating and organizing migration from rural areas to factory towns locally and from rural communities abroad to American factories. While rural/urban or overseas migration temporarily depleted kinship groups, networks were gradually reconstructed in the new location through chain migration. Thus, although people did not share the same household with relatives outside the nuclear family, they were still enmeshed in close ties with their kin outside the household.

The 19th-century American cities, chain migration facilitated transition and settlement, assured a continuity in kin contacts, and made mutual assistance in personal and family crises an important factor in the adjustment of immigrants to the urban environment. Even in the later part of the last century and in the early parts of this one, workers who migrated from rural areas to cities in most industrializing communities carried major parts of their kinship ties and family traditions into new settings. Young unmarried sons and daughters of working age, or young married couples without their children, tended to migrate first. After they found jobs and housing, they would send for their relations. Chain migration thus helped maintain ties and continuities between family members in their new communities of settlement. In factories or other places of employment, newly arrived workers utilized the good offices of their relatives who were already working in the establishment to facilitate the hiring of their newly arrived kin.

Hiring and placement through kin often continued even in large-scale modern factories. Kinship networks were able to permeate and infiltrate formal, bureaucratized industrial cooperatives and the cluster within them. Even where they worked in different locales, kin made collective decisions about the work careers of their members. Workers migrated in kin groups and carried with them traditional patterns of kin assistance, but adapted these to the requirements of modern industrial organizations. Immigrants successfully adapted their traditional kinship patterns to modern modes of production and the organization of work, which required familiarity with bureaucratic structures and organizations, adherence to modern work schedules, responsiveness to the rhythms of industrial employment, and specialization in technological skill (Anderson, 1971; Hareven, 1978, 1982 forthcoming).

Changing Family Functions and Values

Industrialization, however, did affect major changes in family functions. Through a process of differentiation, the family gradually surrendered functions previously concentrated within it to other social institutions. During the preindustrial period, the family not only reared children, but also served as a workshop, a school, a church, and an asylum. Preindustrial families meshed closely with the community and carried a variety of public responsibilities within the larger society. "Family and community," writes Demos, "private and public life, formed part of the same moral equation. The one supported the other and they became in a sense indistinguishable" (1970, p. 186).

In preindustrial society, most of the work took place in the household. Reproductive roles were therefore congruent with social and economic roles. Children were considered members of the work force and were seen as economic assets. Childhood was a brief preparatory period terminated by apprenticeship and the commencement of work, generally before puberty. Adolescence was virtually unknown as a distinct stage of life. Such a social system encouraged the integration of family members into common economic activities. The segregation along sex and age lines that characterizes middle-class family life in modern society had not yet appeared.

As long as the household functioned as a workshop as well as a family home, there was no clear separation between family life and work life. Even though preindustrial families contained large numbers of children, women invested relatively less time in motherhood than their successors in the 19th century and in our time did and still do. The integration of family and work allowed for an intensive sharing of labor between husbands and wives and between parents and children that would not exist in industrial society.

Even though households were nuclear, family members were not totally isolated from kin who were residing in the neighborhood. Consequently, the tasks of child rearing did not fall exclusively on mothers; other relatives living nearby also participated in this function. As long as the family was a production unit, housework was inseparable from domestic industries or agricultural work, and it was valued, therefore, for its economic contribution. Since children constituted a viable part of the labor force, motherhood, too, was valued for its economic contributions, and not only for its nurturing qualities.

Under the impact of industrialization, many of these functions were transferred to agencies and institutions outside the family. The work place was separated from the home, and functions of social welfare were transferred from the family to asylums and reformatories. "The family has become a *more specialized agency* than before," note Parsons and Bales, "probably more specialized than in any previous known society . . . but not in any general sense less important, because the society is dependent *more* exclusively on it for the performance of *certain* of its vital functions" (1955, pp. 9–10). These vital functions included (and include) childbearing, child rearing, and socialization. The family ceased to be a work unit and limited its economic activities primarily to consumption and child care.

The transformation of the household from a busy work place and social center to a private family abode involved the withdrawal of strangers, such as business associates, partners, journeymen, apprentices, and boarders and lodgers, from the household; it also involved a more rigorous segregation in the tasks and the work responsibilities of different family members. New systemized work schedules led to the segregation of husbands from wives and fathers from children in the course of the work day. In middle-class families, housework lost its economic and productive value. Since it was not paid for, and since it no longer led to the production of visible goods, it had no place in the occupational hierarchy.

Differentiation and specialization in work schedules significantly altered the daily lives of men and women who worked outside the home. Housework, on the other hand, continued to be governed by traditional time schedules, remaining throughout the 19th century a nonindustrial occupation. This is another reason (in addition to economic ones) why housework has been devalued in modern society, where achievement is measured not only by products but also by systematic time and production schedules. This may also explain why, since the 19th century, the home economics movement has been so intent on introducing efficient management and industrial time schedules into the home. For several decades, reformers maintained the illusion that if housework were more systematically engineered, it would become more respectable.

In trying to assess the significance of the changes in family life brought about by industrialization, we must recognize the fact that these changes were gradual, and that they varied significantly from class to class as well as among different ethnic groups. While historians have sometimes generalized for an entire society on the basis of middle-class experience, it is now becoming clear that preindustrial family patterns persisted over longer time periods in rural and in urban working-class families. Since the process of industrialization was gradual, domestic industries and a variety of small family enterprises carried over into the industrial system. In New England, for example, during the first half of the 19th century, rural families were sending their daughters to work in factories while the farm continued to be the family's economic base (Dublin, 1979). In most working-class families, work continued to be considered a family enterprise, even if it did not take place in the home. In such families, the work of wives, sons, and daughters was carefully regulated by the collective strategies of the family unit. Many of what we perceive today as individual work careers were actually part of a collective family effort.

Even though the process of industrialization offered women opportunities for independent work outside their homes, women continued to function as an integral part of the productive effort of the family unit, even when they worked in factories. Working women were bound by family obligations and contributed most of their earnings to their parents—a woman's work was considered part of the family's work, not an independent career. Even during periods of large-scale industrial development, families continued to function as collective economic units, in which the husbands, wives, and children were all responsible for the well-being of the family unit. This continuity in the function of the family economy as a corporate enterprise is significant for understanding the limited changes in working-class gender roles under the impact of the industrial revolution. Industrialization changed the nature and the pace of the work, but these families survived as collective economic units for a long time to come (Hareven, 1982 forthcoming).

Industrialization, however, had a more dramatic effect on the experience of the middle class. The separation between the home and the work place that followed in the wake of industrialization led to the glorification of the home as a domestic retreat from the outside world. The new ideology of domesticity that developed in the first half of the 19th century relegated women to the home and glorified their domestic role. (On the cult of domesticity, see Jeffrey, 1972; Sennett; 1971; Welter, 1966; Young & Wilmott, 1973.)

These changes were closely connected with the decline in the number of children a woman had and with the new attitudes toward childhood. The discovery of childhood as a distinct stage of life was intimately tied to the emergence of the middle-class family in Europe and in the United States in the early 19th century. Stripped of the multiplicity of functions that had been previously concentrated in the household, these families developed into private, domestic, and child-centered retreats. Children were no longer expected to join the work force until their late teens, a major indication of the growing recognition of childhood as a distinct stage of development. Instead of considering children as potential working members of the family group, parents perceived them as dependent subjects of tender nurture and protection. This was the emergence of the domestic middle-class family as we know it today (Aries, 1962; Bremner, Barnard, Hareven, & Mennel, 1970–1974; Demos, 1970; Greven, 1970; Kett, 1971).

The glorification of motherhood as a full-time career served both to enshrine the family as a domestic retreat from the world of work and to make families child-centered. The gradual separation of the home from the work place that had started with industrialization reached its peak in the designation of the home as a therapeutic refuge from the outside world. As custodians of this retreat, women were expected to have attributes distinctly different from those of the working wife who had been an economic partner in the family. Tenderness, gentleness, affection, sweetness, and a comforting demeanor were all considered ideal char-

acteristics for the domestic wife. Sentiment began to replace instrumental relationship. (On family sentiment, see Aries, 1962, 1981.)

The ideology of domesticity and the new view of childhood combined to revise
expectations of parenthood. The roles of husbands and wives became gradually
segregated; a clear division of labor replaced the old economic partnership, with
the husband now responsible for economic support and the wife's efforts directed
toward homemaking and child rearing. With men leaving the home to work
elsewhere, time invested in fatherhood occurred primarily during leisure hours.
Thus, the separation of husbands from wives and parents from children for major
parts of the day came about. The cult of domesticity emerged as a major part of the
ideology of family life in American society. One of its central assumptions was
the role of women as custodians of the domestic retreat and as full-time mothers.
The very notion has dominated perceptions of women's roles in American society
until very recently and has shaped the prevailing assumptions governing family life. One of its major consequences was the insistence that women confine
their main activities to the domestic sphere, and that women's work in the labor
market would be harmful to the family and to society (Lerner, 1969; Scott, 1970;
Welter, 1966).

Ironically, the ideology was adopted by middle-class families just at the point in
time when rural and immigrant women were recruited into the newly established
giant textile centers. Even though the ideology of domesticity originated in urban
middle-class families, it emerged as part of the ideology of American family life
in the larger society. Second- and third-generation immigrant families embraced
this outlook as part of their "Americanization" process. The ideals of urban
middle-class life emerged as the ideology of the larger society and subsequently
handicapped the role of women as workers outside the home as well.

The impact of the ideology of domesticity became apparent in patterns of
women's labor force participation. In the late 19th century, despite the convergence of many factors that could actually have facilitated women's work outside
the home, very few women actually took advantage of the opportunity. Demographic changes, combined with technological advances, offered advantageous
conditions for the entry of married women into the labor force. By the late 19th
century the birth rate had declined, particularly among native-born families.
Women had fewer children and at the same time benefited from the new laborsaving appliances, which should have freed up their time considerably. Expanded
industrial and commercial facilities, made easily accessible by new transportation
systems, provided increased employment opportunities for women. But despite
all this, 97% of all married women did not assume gainful employment, because
ideological barriers placed women's domestic and work roles in conflict (Kenniston & Kenniston, 1964; Smuts, 1959; Sweet, 1973; Tilly & Scott, 1978).

The ideology of domesticity also began to influence working-class and immigrant families during the early part of the 20th century. As immigrants became
"Americanized," particularly in the second generation, they internalized the

values of domesticity and began to view women's work outside the home as demeaning, as having low status, or as compromising for the husband and dangerous for the children. Consequently, married women entered the labor force only when driven by economic necessity.

It is important to realize, however, that despite its threat in the larger society, and despite its adoption as the dominant ideology in "American culture," a majority of working-class and ethnic families continued to adhere to the earlier way of life; most importantly, they maintained a collective view of the family and its economy. In contrast to the values of individualism that govern much of family life today, the traditional values of family collectivity persisted at this level of American society.

With the growth of industrial child labor in the 19th century, working-class families continued to recognize the economic value of motherhood, as they had in rural society. Segregation along age groups within working-class families was almost nonexistent. Children were socialized for industrial work from an early age and began to contribute to the family's work effort at a lower age than specified by law. They were considered an asset, both for their contribution to the family's economy during their youth and for the prospect of their support during their parents' old age. Parents viewed their efforts in child rearing as investments in future social security.

The relationships between husbands and wives, parents and children, and other kin were based upon reciprocal services, support, and assistance. Such exchange relationships, often defined as "instrumental," were based on the assumption that family members were all engaged in mutual obligations and in reciprocal relationships. Although such obligations were not specifically defined by contract, they rested on the accepted social norms of what family members owed to each other. In the period preceding the welfare state and public assistance, instrumental relationships provided important supports to individuals and families, particularly during the critical life situations (Anderson, 1971; Hareven, 1978).

A collective view of familial obligations was the very basis of survival. From such a perspective, marriage and parenthood were not merely love relationships, but partnerships governed by family economic and social needs. In this respect, the experience of 19th-century working-class families and of ethnic families in the more recent past was drastically different from that of middle-class ones, in which sentimentality emerged as the dominant base of family relationships. This is not to argue that husbands and wives in the past did not love each other or that parents harbored no sentiment for their children. It suggests, rather, that sentiment was secondary to family needs and survival strategies. Under such conditions, child-bearing and work were not governed by individual decisions. Mate selection and the timing of marriage were regulated in accordance with collective family considerations, rather than directed by strictly individual whim. The transfer of property and work partnerships were important considerations in the selection of partners. At times, such collective family "plans" took priority over individual preferences. Parents tried to delay the marriage of the last child in the household—commonly that of a daughter—in order to secure continued economic support, especially in later life when they were withdrawing from the labor force.

The major historical change in family values has been a change from a collective view of the family to one of individualism and sentiment. These have led to an increasing emphasis on individual priorities and preferences over collective family needs. They have also led to an exaggerated emphasis on emotional nurture, intimacy, and privacy as the major justification for family relations. This shift in values has contributed considerably to the "liberation of individuals," but it has also eroded the resilience of the family and its ability to handle crises. Moreover, it has contributed to a greater separation among family members and especially to the isolation of older people.

Changes in the Life Course

The full impact of changes in family values and functions on the condition of the family today can be best understood in the context of demographic changes affecting the time of life transitions, such as marriage, parenthood, the "empty nest," and widowhood. Since the end of the 19th century, important changes have occurred in the family cycle that have affected age configurations within the family and generational relations (Hareven, 1977).

Beginning in the early 19th century, the American population has experienced a steady decline in the birth rate. Over the 19th and 20th centuries, the birth rate of the American population went down steadily; it declined from an average of 7.04 children per family in 1800 to 3.56 children per family in 1900. This decline and the subsequent decline since 1900 have had a profound impact on the cycle of family life, especially on the timing of marriage, the birth of the first child and of subsequent children, and the spacing of children. They have also considerably affected the meaning of marriage and of parenthood. In traditional society, little time elapsed between marriages and parenthood, since procreation was the major goal of marriage. In modern society, contraception has permitted a gap between these two stages of the family cycle. Marriage has become recognized as important in its own right, rather than merely as a transition to parenthood (Smith, 1974; Wells, 1971; Yasuba, 1961).

One widely held myth about the past is that the timing of family transitions was once more orderly and stable than it is today. The complexity that governs family life today and the variations in family roles and in transitions into them are frequently contrasted to this more placid past. The historical record, however, frequently reveals precisely the opposite condition: patterns of family timing in the past were often more complex, more diverse, and less orderly than they are today. Voluntary and involuntary demographic changes that have come about since the late 19th century have in fact paradoxically resulted in greater uniformity in the timing of transitions along the life course, despite greater social complexity. The growing uniformity in timing has been accompanied by a shift from involuntary to voluntary factors affecting the timing of family events. The increase in life expectancy, the decline in fertility, and the earlier marriage age have, for example, greatly increased the chances for temporal overlap in the lives of family members. Families are now able to go through a life course much less subject to sudden change than that experienced by the majority of the population in the 19th century.

The "typical" family cycle of modern American families includes early marriage and early commencement of childbearing, but a small number of children. Families following this type of family cycle experience a compact period of parenthood in the middle years of life; then an extended period encompassing one-third of their adult life, without children; and finally, often, a period of solitary living following the death of a spouse, most frequently that of the husband (Glick, 1955, 1977; Glick & Parke, 1965).

This type of cycle has important implications for the composition of the family and for relationships within it in current society: husbands and wives are spending a relatively longer lifetime together; they invest a shorter segment of their lives in child rearing; and they more commonly survive to grandparenthood. This sequence has been uniform for the majority of the population since the beginning of the 20th century. In contrast to past times, most families see their children through to adulthood with both parents still alive. As Uhlenberg (1974) points out, the normal family cycle for women—a sequence of leaving home, marriage, family formation, child rearing, launching, and survival at age 50 with the first marriage still intact—unless broken by divorce—has not been the dominant pattern of family timing before the early 20th century. Prior to 1900, only about 40% of the female population in the United States experienced this ideal family cycle. The remainder either never married, never reached marriageable age, died before childbirth, or were widowed while their offspring were still young children.

In the 19th century, the combination of a later age at marriage and higher fertility provided little opportunity for a family to experience an "empty nest" stage. Prior to the decline in mortality among the young at the beginning of the 20th century, marriage was frequently broken by the death of a spouse before the end of the child-rearing period. Even when fathers survived the child-rearing years, they rarely lived beyond the marriage of their second child. As a result of higher fertility, children were spread over a wider age range; frequently, the youngest child was just entering school as the oldest was preparing for marriage. The combination of later marriage, higher fertility, and widely spread childbearing resulted in a different timing of family transitions. Individuals became parents later, but carried child-rearing responsibilities almost until the end of their lives. Consequently, the lives of parents overlapped with those of their children for shorter periods than they do currently.

Under demographic conditions of the 19th century—higher mortality and higher fertility—functions within the family were less specifically tied to age, and members of different age groups were consequently not so completely segregated by the tasks they were required to fulfill. The spread of children over a larger age spectrum within the family had important implications for family relationships, as well as for their preparations for adult roles. Children were accustomed to growing up with larger numbers of siblings and were exposed to a greater variety of models from which to choose than they would have been in a small nuclear family. Older children often took charge of their younger siblings. Sisters, in particular, carried a major share of the responsibility for raising the youngest siblings, and they frequently acted as surrogate mothers if the mother worked outside the home or had died. The smaller age overlap between children and their parents was also significant: the oldest child was the one most likely to overlap with its father in adulthood, and the youngest child was the least likely to do so.

The oldest child would have been most likely to embark on an independent career before the parents reached old-age dependency; the youngest children were most like to carry responsibilities for parental support and to overlap in adulthood with a widowed mother. The oldest child had the greatest chance to overlap with grandparents, the youngest child the least. Late-marrying children were most likely to be responsible for the support of a widowed mother, while early-marrying children depended on their parents' household space after marriage. One can better grasp the implications of these differences in age at marriage, number of children, assigned tasks, and generational overlap when one takes into consideration the uncertainties and the economic precariousness that characterized the period. These made the orderly sequence of progression along stages of the family cycle, which sociologists have observed in the contemporary American population, impossible for the 19th-century family.

Another comparison between what is considered the "normal" family cycle today and its many variants in the 19th century reverses one more stereotype about the past—namely, that American society has been experiencing breakdown and diversification in family organization. In reality, the major transitions in family roles have been characterized by greater stability and conformity because of the greater opportunity for generational continuities. The opportunity for a meaningful period of overlap in the lives of grandparents and grandchildren is a 20th-century phenomenon, a surprising fact that runs counter to the popular myth of a family solidarity in the past that was based on three-generational ties.

The relative significance of transition into family roles also differed in the 19th century. In the 19th century, when conception was likely to take place very shortly after marriage, the major transition in a woman's life was represented by marriage itself. But, as the interval between marriage and first pregnancy has increased in modern society, the transition to parenthood has become more significant than the transition to marriage. Family limitation has also had an impact on the timing of marriage. Since marriage no longer inevitably leads to parenthood, postponing marriage is no longer needed to delay it. On the other end of the life course, transitions into the "empty nest" roles are much more critical today than they were in the past, when parental or surrogate-parental roles encompassed practically the entire life span. Completion of parental roles today involves changes in residence, changes in work, and, perhaps eventual removal into institutions or retirement communities (Chudacoff & Hareven, 1978).

The overall historical pattern of family behavior has thus been marked by a shift from involuntary to voluntary forces controlling the timing of family events. It has also been characterized by greater rigidity and uniformity in the timing of the passage from one family role to another. In their comparison of such transitions in 19th-century Philadelphia with those of the present, Modell, Furstenberg, and Hershberg (1976) conclude that transition into adult roles (departure from the family of origin, marriage, and the establishment of a household) follow a more ordered sequence and are accomplished over a shorter time period in a young person's life today than they were in the 19th century. Such transitions to familial roles also coincide today with transitions into occupational roles: "Transitions are today more contingent, more integrated because they are constrained by a set of formal institutions. 'Timely' action to nineteenth-century families consisted of helpful response in times of trouble; in the twentieth century, timeliness connotes adherence to a schedule" (Modell, Furstenberg, & Hershberg, 1976, p. 30).

The demographic changes that have led to this isolation, continued with the decline in "instrumental" relations in the family discussed earlier, have caused isolation of older people in American society—a problem that is much more severe and immediate than the issue of "family breakdown." While the major historical changes in family functions occurred in the 19th and early 20th centuries, changes in the timing of family transitions are much more strictly 20th-century phenomena and particularly affect the family in our times. Changes in the family cycle, such as the emergence of the "empty nest," extensions of the period of widowhood, and increasing age segregation in the family and the larger society, reflect major discontinuities that have resulted in increasing problems in the middle and later years of life. It is precisely in this area that one needs to be concerned with future changes in the family.

Implications of Change

One of the major causes of the anxiety about the future of the family is rooted not so much in reality as in the tension between the idealized expectation in the culture and the reality itself. Nostalgia for a lost family tradition that in fact never existed has prejudiced our understanding of the conditions of families in contemporary society. Thus, the current anxiety over the fate of the family reflects not merely problems in the family, but a variety of fears about other social problems that are eventually projected onto the family.

The real problems that the American family is facing today are not symptoms of breakdown, as is often suggested. Rather, they reflect the difficulties that the family faces in its adaptation to recent social changes, particularly in the loss of diversity in household membership it had in the past, the reduction of the variety of its functions, and, to some extent, the weakening of its adaptability. The idealization of the family as a refuge from the world and the myth that the work of mothers is harmful have added considerable strain. The continuous emphasis on the family as a universal private retreat and as an emotional haven is misguided in light of the historical experience. In the past, the family fulfilled a broad array of functions, not merely emotional ones. Most of its functions in the past were intertwined with the larger community. Rather than being the custodian of privacy, the family prepared its members for interaction with the larger society. Family relationships were valued not merely for their emotional contents, but for a wide array of services and contributions to the collective family unit. By contrast, one of the major sources of the crisis of nuclear families today is its difficulty in adapting to the emotional functions thrust upon it and to the expectations of romantic love that accompany marriage, precisely because these functions and expectations represent an artificial boundary between individuals and the larger society.

Concentration on the emotional functions of the family has grown at the expense of another of its much-needed roles in industrial society; namely, the preparation of its members for their interaction with bureaucratic institutions. In American society, the education and welfare systems have made dramatic inroads into areas that had previously been the private preserve of the family. At the same time, however, the tendency of the family to shelter its members from the social institutions has weakened its ability to affect the structure of or to influence the programs and legislation that public agencies have directed at the family.

Attitudes towards family life in American society have been governed by the stereotype of the "ideal family," which is based on the middle-class nuclear family. In reality, American society has contained within it great diversities in family types and family behavior that were associated with the recurring entrance of new immigrant groups into American society. Ethnic, racial, cultural, and class differences have also resulted in diversity in family behavior. The tensions between family behavior in the dominant culture and the traditional patterns of the black family and of immigrant families have been a continuing pattern in American life (Hareven & Modell, 1980).

There has been a tendency toward homogenization of American culture, through the absorption of ethnic traditions on the one hand, and immigrant acceptance of the dominant cultural models on the other. Immigrants, primarily in the second generation, adopted "American" family behavior, and this adoption has been reflected in several areas: a decline in fertility, earlier marriage, growing privatization of the family, withdrawal of women and children from the labor force, and changing patterns of consumption and tastes. However, this ongoing process did not result in total assimilation of family ways and traditional customs, because the influx of new immigrants kept introducing new cultural variety. The result has been continuing diversity in family patterns. Contrary to the official creed of the "melting pot," a great many varieties of ethnic family behavior have survived in American society, and new patterns are still being introduced through recent migration. It is therefore unrealistic to talk simply about *the* American family.

For over a century, until very recently, the stereotype of the private nuclear family as the ideal family in American society has been dominant. Alternative forms of family organization, such as those of the black family or of other ethnic families, were misinterpreted as "family disorganization" simply because they did not conform to the official stereotype. But actually, over the past decade, the strength and resilience of ethnic and black family ways has been recognized. These traditional resources of family and kinship among black and ethnic families have been rediscovered as the middle-class nuclear family, besieged by its own isolation, has proven its limitations in coping with stress.

One of the most unique features of American families today is their cultural and ethnic diversity; this diversity, which is in itself a continuation of a historical pattern, is now being valued as a source of strength and continuity, rather than, as in the past, being decried as a manifestation of deviance. One of the challenges today faced by individuals and policy makers is the creative use of these family patterns in coping with contemporary problems.

An understanding of the historical changes over the past century provides a different perspective of family life today. There is no question that American families have been undergoing important transitions over the past century. But the main question is that of whether these changes represent family breakdown and whether they threaten the disappearance of the family. Some of these traditions represent the continuation of a long historical process: the decline in the birth rate, the earlier marriage rate, and changes in the timing of life transitions are all the result of a continuing process of change over the past century and a half. Similarly, the moratorium from adult responsibilities that teenagers now experience and the increasing isolation of older people on the other end of the cycle, are both the results of long-term historical changes.

On the other hand, the increase in divorce rates and the concomitant increase in single-parent households represent a much more dramatic transition in our times. But the rise in divorce as such, which has been often cited as a symptom of family breakdown, should not be necessarily misconstrued. In the 19th century people did not resort to divorce as frequently as they do now, because divorce was considered socially unacceptable. This does not mean, however, that families were living happily and in harmony. A high rate of desertion and separation of couples replaced legal divorce. And incompatible couples who did not resort to divorce or separation lived together as strangers or in deep conflict. Thus, the increase in divorce statistics as such is no proof of family breakdown. In some respects, it is proof that people care enough about the contents and quality of family life and marriage to be willing to dissolve an unsatisfactory marriage (and commonly to replace it with a more successful one).

Much anxiety has also been expressed over the increase in the proportion of couples living together unmarried, over homosexual partners or parents, and over a whole variety of alternative family forms and life styles. What we are witnessing in all these varieties of life styles are not necessarily new inventions. Many different forms have been in existence all along, but they have been less visible. The more recent forms of alternative life styles have now become part of the official fiber of society, because they are now being tolerated much more than in the past. In short, what we are witnessing is not a fragmentation of traditional family patterns, but, rather, the emergence of a pluralism in family ways.

Thus, from a long-range perspective, the greatest concerns over family life in America need not be divorce, the declining birth rate, or alternative life styles. Of much greater concern for the future, and especially for policy, should be the problem of the isolation of the elderly and the inability of families in all ages to cope with inflation and with diminishing resources.

The historical lesson is valuable in demonstrating the extent to which a variety of traditional family ways and continuities with the past are still surviving in American society today. It is particularly helpful in revealing the salient role of surrogate families (taking in boarders and lodgers), as well as in emphasizing the effectiveness of kinship ties in coping with migration, economic insecurity, and personal family crises. The persistence of kinship ties as a major source of support has been a source of resilience and strength in urban neighborhoods. This rediscovery of the strength of kin should not lead us, however, to a new myth of self-reliance. It would be a mistake to assume that the fact that family members are helping each other in times of crisis means that families should be left to take care of their own. The historical experience also suggests the high price that family members had to pay in order to support their kin and help aging parents. The pressures on the nuclear family today, combined with economic and technological stresses, would make it difficult if not impossible for families to sustain continued assistance and support for their kin, especially for aging relatives.

A creative and constructive family policy will have to take into consideration, therefore, both the survival of support networks among kin and the escalating pressures on individuals and families. Such a policy, by necessity, will have to provide public programs and assistance where informal support networks fall short. It will also need to strengthen kinship and neighborhood support networks without bureaucratizing them.

Acknowledgments

An earlier version of this chapter was prepared for the Research Forum on Family Issues, White House Conference on Families, April 1980.

I am grateful to Kathleen Adams for her editorial help.

References

Anderson, M. *Family structure in nineteenth-century Lancashire.* Cambridge, England: Cambridge University Press, 1971.

Aries, P. [*Centuries of childhood*] (R. Baldick, trans.). New York: Knopf, 1962.

Aries, P. [*The hour of our death*] (H. Weaver, trans.). New York: Knopf, 1981.

Bremmer, R. H., Barnard, J., Hareven, T. K., & Mennel, R. M. (Eds.). *Children and youth in America* (3 vols.). Cambridge: Harvard University Press, 1970–1974.

Chudacoff, H. P., & Hareven, T. K. The later years of life and the family cycle. In T. K. Hareven (Ed.), *Transitions: The family and the life course in historical perspective.* New York: Academic Press, 1978.

Davis, K. The American family in relation to demographic change. In C. F. Westoff & R. Parke, Jr. (Eds.), *Demographic and social aspects of population growth.* Washington, D.C.: U.S. Government Printing Office, 1972.

Demos, J. *A little commonwealth: Family life in Plymouth Colony.* New York: Oxford University Press, 1970.

Dublin, T. *Women at work: The transformation of work and community in Lowell, Massachusetts, 1826–1860.* New York: Columbia University Press, 1979.

Glick, P. C. The family cycle. *American Sociological Review,* 1947, *12,* 164–174.

Glick, P. C. The life cycle of the family. *Marriage and Family Living,* 1955, *18,* 3–9.

Glick, P. C. *American families.* New York: Wiley, 1957.

Glick, P. C. Updating the life cycle of the family. *Journal of Marriage and the Family,* 1977, *39,* 5–13.

Glick, P. C., & Parke, R., Jr. New approaches in studying the life cycle of the family. *Demography,* 1965, *2,* 187–212.

Goode, W. J. *World revolution and family patterns.* New York: Macmillan, Free Press, 1969.

Greven, P. *Four generations: Population, land and family in colonial Andover, Massachusetts.* Ithica, N.Y.: Cornell University Press, 1970.

Hareven, T. K. The history of the family as an interdisciplinary field. *Journal of Interdisciplinary History,* 1971, *2,* 399–414.

Hareven, T. K. The family as process: The historical study of the family cycle. *Journal of Social History,* 1974, *7,* 322–329.

Hareven, T. K. Family time and historical time. *Daedalus,* Spring 1977, pp. 57–70.

Hareven, T. K. The dynamics of kin in an industrial community. In J. Demos & S. Boocock (Eds.), *Turning points.* Supplement to *American Journal of Sociology,* 1978, *84.*

Hareven, T. K. *Family time and industrial time.* New York: Cambridge University Press, 1982 forthcoming.

Hareven, T. K. & Modell, J. Ethnic families. In S. Thernstrom (Ed.), *Harvard encyclopedia of American ethnic groups.* Cambridge: Harvard University Press, 1980.

Jeffrey, K. The family as Utopian retreat from the city: The nineteenth-century contribution. In S. TeSelle (Ed.), *The family, communes, and Utopian societies.* New York: Harper & Row, 1972.

Kenniston, E., & Kenniston, K. An American anachronism: The image of women and work. *American Scholar,* 1964, *33,* 353–375.

Kett, J. H. Growing up in rural New England, 1800–1840. In T. K. Hareven (Ed.), *Anonymous Americans: Exploration in nineteenth century social history.* Englewood Cliffs, N.J.: Prentice-Hall, 1971.

Kobrin, F. The fall in household size and the rise in the primary individual in the United States. *Demography,* 1976, *13,* 127–138.

Laslett, P. *The world we have lost.* London: Methuen, 1965.

Laslett, P., & Wall, R. (Eds.). *Household and family in past time.* Cambridge, England: Cambridge University Press, 1972.

Lerner, G. The lady and the mill girl. *Mid-Continent American Studies Journal,* 1969, *10,* 5–14.

Modell, J., Furstenberg, F., & Hershberg, T. Social change and transitions to adulthood in historical perspective. *Journal of Family History,* 1976, *1,* 7–32.

Modell, J., & Hareven, T. K. Urbanization and the malleable household. An examination of boarding and lodging in American families. *Journal of Marriage and Family,* 1973, *35,* 467–478.

Parsons, T., & Bales, R. F. *Family socialization and interaction process.* Glencoe, Ill.: Free Press, 1955.

Scott, A. F. *The Southern lady: From pedestal to politics, 1830–1930.* Chicago: University of Chicago Press, 1970.

Sennett, R. *Families against the city: Middle-class homes of industrial Chicago, 1872–1890.* Cambridge: Harvard University Press, 1971.

Smith, D. S. Family limitation, sexual control, and domestic feminism in Victorian America. In M. S. Hartman & L. Banner (Eds.), *Clio's consciousness raised: New perspectives on the history of women.* New York: Harper & Row, 1974.

Smuts, R. W. *Women and work in America.* New York: Columbia University Press, 1959.

Sweet, J. *Women in the labor force.* New York: Academic Press, 1973.

Tauber, I. B. Change and transition in family structures. In *The family in transition* (Fogarty International Center Proceedings). Washington, D.C.: U.S. Government Printing Office, 1969.

Tilly, L., & Scott, J. *Women, work, and families.* New York: Holt, Rinehart & Winston, 1978.

Uhlenberg, P. R. A study of cohort life cycles: Cohorts of native-born Massachusetts women. 1830–1920. *Population Studies,* 1969, *23,* 407–420.

Uhlenberg, P. R. Cohort variations in family life cycle experiences in United States females. *Journal of Marriage and the Family,* 1974, *36,* 284–292.

Wells, R. V. Demographic change and the life cycle of American families. *Journal of Interdisciplinary History,* 1971, *2,* 273–282.

Welter, B. The cult of true womanhood, 1820–1860. *American Quarterly,* 1966, *18,* 151–174.

Yasuba, Y. *Birth rates of the white population in the United States, 1800–1860.* Baltimore: Johns Hopkins University Press, 1961.

Young, M. D., & Wilmott, P. *The symmetrical family: A study of work and leisure in the London region.* London: Routledge & Kegan Paul, 1973.

Twentieth-Century Changes in Household Technology

Ruth Schwartz Cowan

Conventional wisdom has been telling us—for many decades now—that twentieth-century technology has radically transformed the American household, by turning it from a unit of production to a unit of consumption. Put into plain English, this means that the food and clothing that people once made in their homes is now produced in factories, and what we do in our homes (eat the food, get dressed in the clothes, occasionally launder them) actually has little economic significance.

Now this particular piece of conventional wisdom (which, ironically enough, seems to be subscribed to by people as diverse as sociology professors and newspaper editors, political conservatives and Marxists) is a cultural artifact of vast importance, because it has two corollaries that guide people in the conduct of their daily lives: first, that as American families passed from being units of production to being units of consumption, the economic ties that once bound family members so tightly to each other came undone; and, second, that as factory production replaced home production, nothing was left for adult women to do at home. Many Americans believe that these corollaries are true, and they act on this belief in various ways: some hope to reestablish family solidarity by relearning lost productive crafts such as baking bread or tending a vegetable garden; others dismiss the women's liberation movement as "simply a bunch of affluent housewives who have nothing better to do with their time"; husbands complain that their wives spend too much time doing inconsequential work ("What *do* you do all day, dear?"); and housewives can find no reasonable explanation for why they are perpetually exhausted.

The conventional wisdom was once not so conventional; it has its roots in the painstaking sociological observations and patient economic research undertaken by pioneer social scientists who did their most important empirical and theoretical work in the years from 1890 to 1930. All of them were, in one way or another, keen and disciplined observers of the world in which they lived. They witnessed monumental technological changes in their own lifetimes (from the steam engine to the electric motor, from the horse to the automobile, from handmade to factory-made clothing, from gas lamps to electric lights), and they were not unreasonably impressed with the impact that those changes were having on the daily life—and on the communal life—of their contemporaries. Unfortunately the conclusions that these social scientists reached may not be as fine a guide to our past (and to our present) as we have let ourselves believe.

Twentieth-century household technology consists of not one, but of eight, interlocking technological systems: the systems that supply us with food, clothing, health care, transportation, water, gas, electricity, and petroleum products. Some of these systems have followed the conventional model—moving production out of the home and into the factories; but (and this is the crucial point) some of them have not. Indeed, some of the systems cannot even be made to fit this model at all. A brief historical sketch of the development of these eight systems, tracing them back, in some cases, to their nineteenth-century origins, should reveal, rather quickly, why the conventional model is, at best, incomplete and, at worst, grossly misleading.

 . . . [I]n all three of these technological systems (for food, clothing, and health care) the shift from production to consumption occurred slowly, over a long period—but with increasing momentum as the twentieth century approached. Butchering, milling, textile making, and leatherwork had departed from many homes by 1860. Sewing of men's clothing was gone, roughly speaking, by 1880, of women's and children's outerwear by 1900, and finally of almost all items of clothing for all members of the family by 1920. Preservation of some foodstuffs— most notably peas, corn, tomatoes, and peaches—had been industrialized by 1900; the preparation of dairy products such as butter and cheese had become a lost art, even in rural districts, by about the same date. Factory-made biscuits and quick cereals were appearing on many American kitchen tables by 1910, and factory-made bread had become commonplace by 1930. The preparation of drugs and medications had been turned over to factories or to professional pharmacists by 1900, and a good many other aspects of long-term medical care had been institutionalized in hospitals and sanitariums thirty years later. Individual families no doubt differed in the particular times and particular patterns by which they made (or underwent) this transition. Those who lived in urban areas probably had shifted from the production to the consumption of most goods earlier than those who lived in rural districts, and those who were economically comfortable before those who were economically deprived—but there were significant variations in these overall patterns. The urban poor received hospital care long before the urban rich, and some of the rural poor were probably wearing ready-made clothes decades before the urban rich (or even the urban middle classes) had made the same transition. Personal idiosyncracies also make generalizations difficult because there were surely people who—for reasons of pride in skills well learned, or reverence for traditions, or religious scruple, or aesthetic judgment, or pure intransigence—refused to give up brewing their own beer when everyone else was buying theirs in bottles, or continued to make strawberry jam when everyone else was settling for store-bought, or continued to construct hand-made clothes when everyone else was getting theirs from the catalogues or the department stores.

A Shift in the Other Direction: Transportation

Yet whatever variations of social station or personal inclination there may have been, the general pattern that most American families would adhere to in most of the arrangements for providing food, clothing, and health care had been settled, at the very latest, by 1930. This, of course, is the social trend that the earliest social scientists so correctly observed. What they did not observe—perhaps because the Depression and the Second World War gave them other problems to worry about, or perhaps because the postwar years found them either in retirement or in pursuit of other realms of investigation—was the impact that developments in the fourth of the household technological systems—the transportation system—would have on the work processes of housework and on the time allocations for housewives. As most modern housewives know far too well, you cannot consume frozen T.V. dinners or acrylic knit sweaters or aspirin or a pediatrician's services unless you can get to them, or unless someone is willing to deliver them to your door. In either case you, or someone else, is dependent upon whatever means of transportation is most convenient. Consequently, in order to understand why housework did not magically disappear when twentieth-century factories, pharmacies, and hospitals took over the work that nineteenth-century women once had done, the history of urban and rural transportation must also be considered.

The household transportation system has developed in a pattern that is precisely the opposite of the food, clothing, and health-care systems: households have moved from the net consumption to the net production of transportation services—and housewives have moved from being the receivers of purchased goods to being the transporters of them. During the nineteenth century, many household goods and services were delivered virtually to the doorsteps of the people who had purchased them—and many others were offered for sale in retail establishments located a short walk from the houses in which people lived. Peddlers carried pots and pans, linens, and medicines to farmhouses and to the halls and stairways of urban tenements. Seamstresses almost always came to the homes of the women and children for whom they were fashioning clothing; and tailors occasionally provided the same service for men. Milk, ice, and coal were regularly delivered directly to kitchens and basements of middle-class urban dwellers and not infrequently also into the homes (or at least to the curbsides) of those who were poor. Butchers, greengrocers, coffee merchants, and bakers employed delivery boys to take orders from and then carry purchases back to the homes of their more prosperous customers. Smoked, dried, and pickled fish, fruits and vegetables, secondhand clothing, and linens were routinely sold from pushcarts that lined the curbs and traveled the back alleys of poor neighborhoods. Knife sharpeners traveled the streets with flintstones and grindstones on their backs or in their carts, and frequently so did the man who repaired shoes and other leathergoods. Bakeries and grocery stores were located in every city neighborhood, so that housewives, children, and servants could "run out" for extra supplies whenever they were needed. Even doctors made house calls. Under ordinary circumstances the individual urban householder, whether rich or poor, rarely had to travel far from his or her own doorstep in order to have access to the goods and services required for sustenance. For rural households such convenience was not feasible: what shopping there was to be done in rural areas usually waited for the weekly, monthly, or even, in some cases, the annual trip into town or arrival of the peddler.

In the latter decades of the nineteenth century, this pattern of shopping began to change. In urban areas department stores flourished: Marshall Field went into business in Chicago in 1852; Stewart's opened in New York in 1861; and Wanamaker's, in Philadelphia one year later. At first these stores (which, by definition, sold more than one category of goods) were patronized only by the "carriage trade"—people who could afford to keep a horse and carriage and hence could travel to such a store to do their shopping; but later in the century, the range of their business expanded somewhat as horse-drawn omnibuses and trolley and subway cars made it possible for people of lesser means to travel. Even after the turn of the century, however, the department stores still did not appeal to the poor, and their total sales represented only a fraction of the retail sales in most urban areas. Most people living in cities, especially those who were in less comfortable economic circumstances, still acquired most of the goods that they needed, day in and day out, without having to spend much time either getting to the places where goods were offered for sale, or in getting their purchases home.

In rural areas, toward the end of the century, the total time spent in shopping for and transporting goods was additionally decreased by the widespread popularity of mail-order catalogues. A good part of the business done by urban department stores had always been either by mail (or, later, by telephone) ordering; in the last decades of the nineteenth century, this service became available to rural Americans as well. Montgomery Ward and Sears Roebuck (as well as hundreds of smaller enterprises) had entered the mail-order business during the 1870s; and by the time twenty years had passed, there was virtually nothing—from soup to nuts, from underwear to outerwear, from nails to screws to plows and buggies—that rural residents could not order from a catalogue. And clearly they did: the mail-order companies were among the country's leading business enterprises by the turn of the century—and continued to flourish for decades afterward. The creation of rural free-delivery services, which were begun on an experimental basis in the 1890s and extended to most parts of the country before the First World War, further increased the accessibility of this service. Rural women, like their urban counterparts, simply did not have to spend much time either in shopping or in transporting the goods they were buying—even though, as the decades passed, they were buying more than their mothers and grandmothers ever had.

Prior to the advent of the motorcar, many transportation services were provided—when they were provided by the household at all—by men or by servants. Stereotypically, it was the man of the family who hitched the horse to the buggy and went into town to get the mail and buy the flour and the cloth or whatever else it was that his family required. Similarly, in urban middle-class families it was the servant who fetched the doctor, or went to market in search of fresh meat or vegetables, or drove the family carriage through the streets. Among some immigrant groups men were responsible for handling the family's money and hence for making the family's purchases in the marketplace—carrying over into the New World traditions of the Old; and in these families, at least in the first generation of immigrants, women were not regular participants in shopping expeditions or decisions. Needless to say, in actual practice stereotype conditions did not always prevail. There must have been many occasions when, for one reason or another, mother rather than father made the trip into town, or a middle-class urban housewife chose to do her marketing herself; and there were certainly immigrant groups (for example, the Jews) among whom the standard of sex-role behavior dictated that purchases of food and clothing were made by women rather than by men. Yet even when these exceptions are included, it seems a fair generalization to say that in the years before (roughly) 1920 what shopping and transporting there was took little time, and that a large part of that time was spent by men and servants.

In the years just before and after the First World War, all this began to change—and the agent of change was, of course, the motor car. "Why on earth do you need to study what's changing this country," one person asked Helen and Robert Lynd during 1925, when they were studying social conditions in Muncie, Indiana. "I can tell you what's happening in just four letters: A–U–T–O." The speed with which the automobile became an integral part of daily life in America was, in historical terms, astounding. In 1890, for all intents and purposes, the automobile simply did not exist, except in the dreams of a few willful inventors. A decade later, there were already several dozen American entrepreneurs in the business of manufacturing automobiles, but their products were extremely expensive and intended for the delight of only the wealthiest segment of the population. By 1910, Henry Ford was already manufacturing the Model T, in a determined effort to lower the cost and thus increase the diffusion rate of the motor car to all classes of the population—and twenty years afterward, just at the onset of the Depression, he had virtually succeeded. In 1921, President Harding told the Congress that "the motorcar has become an indispensable instrument in our political, social and industrial life." By 1930, just as bad times were beginning, there were roughly thirty million households in the United States—and twenty-six million registered automobiles. Allowing for some households that had two automobiles (not yet a common practice, even in the upper middle classes) and for some automobiles that were used only for business purposes, it still seems reasonable to conclude that the daily lives of at least half the people then living in the United States had been touched by this newfangled mode of transportation before the advent of the Depression. When horse transport had been the rule, a private carriage was beyond the means of all but the very rich; everyone else depended upon his or her feet, on public transport, and—in rural areas—on saddled horses or open carts. The automobile brought the advantage not just of speed in transport but also of privacy to more Americans than had ever before had this privilege. The Lynds estimated that, in Muncie in the 1890s, only 125 families owned a horse and buggy—and they were all members of the élite; by 1923, there were 6,222 passenger cars in the city, "roughly one for every 6.1 persons, or, two for every three families." And what was happening in Muncie was apparently happening nationwide (with the possible exception of the older Eastern cities which were well supplied with public transportation systems): people of many social classes were finding that it was possible for them to get where they wanted to go faster, over longer distances, according to their own schedules—and with carrying capacity attached.

Interestingly enough, when the automobile began to replace feet and horses as the prime mode of transportation, women began to replace men as household suppliers of the service. For reasons that may be clear only to anthropologists and psychologists, automobile driving was not stereotypically limited to men. This situation may have arisen because advertisers of automobiles made a special effort to attract the interest of women, or because the advent of the automobile coincided with the advent of what was then called the "new girl"—more athletic, better educated, less circumscribed by traditional behavior patterns—or for a host of other reasons presently beyond our ken, but it unquestionably happened. The woman who could drive even became something of an ideal for a time:

> Like the breeze in its flight, or the passage of light,
> Or swift as the fall of a star.
> She comes and she goes in a nimbus of dust
> A goddess enthroned on a car.
> The maid of the motor, behold her erect
> With muscles as steady as steel.
> Her hand on the lever and always in front
> The girl in the automobile.

The girl who drove an automobile in 1907 (when this jingle was published) was a middle-aged matron by 1930—and then what she was driving to was not the moon but the grocery store. As the nation shifted from an economy dominated by the horse to an economy dominated by the automobile—and as the Depression created stiff competition among retailers for shares of a declining market—

delivery services of all kinds began to disappear. The owners of grocery shops and butcher's markets began to fire their delivery boys in an effort to lower prices and thus more effectively to compete with the chain stores and supermarkets which were cropping up throughout the land. Some of the chain stores began to eliminate these services as the Depression deepened. The supermarkets (self-service markets with many departments) almost by definition had never had them. After the Second World War, mail-order companies such as Sears Roebuck and Montgomery Ward discovered that they could compete effectively with department stores by opening retail outlets of their own, thus converting their mail-order customers into shoppers. Department stores discovered that many of their customers had moved out of the central city neighborhoods and so opened suburban branches—which were accessible only by car. Physicians discovered that they could stop making house calls and require that all ambulatory patients (in itself an ironic euphemism) be brought to their offices—without losing a significant number of patients. Indeed, a survey of private practitioners in Philadelphia in 1929 revealed that physicians were spending roughly six hours a week making house calls during an average working week of fifty hours; the rest of the time they were in offices, hospitals, or clinics. Medical care, in general, became more dependent upon the availability of complex and expensive equipment (X-ray machines, iron lungs, intravenous feedings, anesthetics), so that visiting nurses were less able to cope, and hospital visits (which required transporting the patient back and forth, rather than waiting at home for the nurse to arrive) became more frequent.

These various individual and corporate decisions were spread out over two decades, but they all conspired in the same direction—to shift the burden of providing transportation services from the seller to the buyer. By the end of the 1930s, the general notion that businesses could offer lower prices by cutting back on services to customers was ingrained in the pattern of business relations. The growth of suburban communities in the postwar years did little to alter that pattern: as more and more businesses converted to the "self-service" concept, more and more households became dependent upon "herself" to provide the service.

By midcentury the time that housewives had once spent in preserving strawberries and stitching petticoats was being spent in driving to stores, shopping, and waiting in lines; and the energy that had once gone into bedside care of the sick was now diverted into driving a feverish child to the doctor, or racing to the railroad station to pick up a relative, or taking the baseball team to the next town for a game. The automobile had become, to the American housewife of the middle class, what the cast-iron stove in the kitchen would have been to her counterpart of 1850—the vehicle through which she did much of her most significant work, and the work locale where she could most often be found.

The Household Utility Systems: Water

The historical development of four household utility systems—those that supply us with water, gas, electricity, and petroleum products—reveals other deficiencies in the "production to consumption" model; and thus their history is appropriately considered separately. The ways in which water and energy are supplied to households are important determinants of the work processes of housework, yet the details of these systems have rarely been considered by those who are convinced that women's work had been markedly lightened in the last one hundred years. . .

In terms of the processes of housework, the introduction of modern water systems had multiple effects, some of which have been ignored by the conventional model. People of all ages and sexes no longer had to carry water long distances (which was back-breaking work), and women no longer had to heat water on stoves and carry it to the place where their laundry was to be done. In this sense, obviously, burdensome tasks were eliminated for all members of the household, and grateful they must have been for the change. In addition, the installation of indoor plumbing made it possible to improve personal cleanliness, family health, and, ultimately, public health as well—improvements that all of us who now take them for granted would be wise not to ignore.

Women shared in the general lightening of labor that occurred when taps replaced pumps and hot water heaters replaced kettles, but the advent of indoor plumbing created a new task, one that had never existed before; because of the way households were organized at that time, that task naturally fell to women. By the 1920s and 1930s, most men were employed (when employment was available) outside their homes, and most children spent most of their youth in school. Adult women remained at home, and thus it was to them that the burden of cleaning the bathroom fell: in any event, women had traditionally been responsible for household cleaning, whether they were employed outside their home or not. Cleaning a bathroom was not light work; and, given the frequency with which the room was used, and the seriousness of the diseases that might result from unsanitary conditions, it was not casual work either. The bathroom was not then just one more room to be cleaned, but a room that had to be thoroughly and frequently cleaned if the health of the family was to be maintained.

Thus, if it makes sense to say that, in the absence of modern water-supply systems, women (and other members of the family) had to "produce" water for cooking and hot water for bathing and laundering, then it also makes sense to say that, *with* such systems, women have to "produce" clean toilets, bathtubs, and sinks. The item produced has changed, but the fact of production has not. Indeed, as we all know, standards of personal and household cleanliness have increased markedly during the twentieth century (sheets, underclothes, table linens are changed more frequently; floors, carpets, fixtures are kept freer of dust and grime); or—to put it somewhat more accurately—more people are becoming accustomed to living at standards of cleanliness that were once possible only for the very rich. "Increased standards of cleanliness," when translated into the language of production and consumption, essentially means "increased productivity." Women have always been responsible for keeping their families and their homes clean; with modern water (and other utility) systems, they became responsible for keeping them even cleaner. Given the stereotypical sex-role division of labor in the early twentieth century, it was inevitable that this work would fall to women. Hot and cold running water in the kitchen and the bath eliminated some of the hard labor that women had done, but it also eliminated some of the work that men and children had once done (and thus left them increasingly free to labor in other places) and created new chores and new standards (which women would have to undertake and to meet). The conventional model accounts for the first of these changes, but not for the second and the third.

The Household Utility Systems: Gas, Electricity, and Oil

Considered together, the other household utility systems had a similar impact on the work processes of housework, in part because they reached a stage of fairly complete development—at least in the United States—at about the same time as the water-supply system.

Thus, with the exception of central heating and some advanced electrical appliances, many Americans made the transition to modern fuels in many aspects of their daily life before the outbreak of the Second World War. The symbolic nineteenth-century kitchen—dominated by the great coal- or wood-burning stove—was transformed into the symbolic twentieth-century kitchen—dominated by the gas, oil, or electric range. Hand tools were replaced by power tools; human energy, by chemical and mechanical energy. Scrubbing boards were discarded, and power washing machines took their place; carpet beaters and sweepers were thrown away, and vacuum cleaners acquired. Gas lights and kerosene lamps were wired and fitted with electric bulbs. Coal and wood no longer had to be hauled into the kitchen, and ashes no longer had to be hauled out of it. Cast-iron stoves no longer had to be rubbed with stoveblack; kitchens and parlors were no longer plagued by a constant residue of greasy ash. Light and heat could now be obtained, at almost any hour of the day or night, without much attention to the maintenance of the appliance or to the supply of fuel (aside from paying the bills). Some terribly burdensome chores were either eased or totally eliminated when the new kitchen came into being, which is no doubt why most people seem to have acquired conveniences and appliances as soon as they were in a position to pay for them and, given the prevalence of installment-credit plans after 1918, sometimes even sooner than that.

The multitudinous chores that constitute housework were totally reorganized by these technological changes; and yet—as with the impact of the water-supply system—the impact of these changes on the nature and the amount of work that housewives had to do was ambiguous. Consider for a moment the three parts of the work process of cooking which are directly connected to the appliance that we call a stove: fuel must be supplied, pots must be tended, and, subsequently, the appliance must be cleaned. Modernization of the fuel-supply system for stoves eliminated only one of those steps, the first; and *that* was the step which, in the coal and wood economy, was most likely to be assigned to the men and boys in the family. Or, consider the process of doing laundry: washing sheets with an automatic washing machine is considerably easier than washing them with one that has a wringer, itself considerably easier than washing them with a scrubboard and tub. Yet the easiest solution of all (at least from the point of view of the housewife) is to have someone else do it altogether—common practice in many households in the nineteenth century and even in the first few decades of the twentieth. Laundresses were the most numerous of all specialized houseservants; many women who did their own cooking, sewing, and housecleaning would have a laundress "in" to do the wash or, failing that, would send some of it "out" to be done. "Out" might have been the home of the laundress herself, or it might—especially in the early decades of the century—have been a commercial laundry, business establishments that were especially numerous in urban and suburban communities. The advent of the electrically powered washing machines (as well as of synthetic washable fabrics) coincided with the advent of "do-it-yourself" laundry, so that the women endowed with a Bendix would have found it *easier* to do her laundry but, simultaneously, would have done *more* laundry, and more of it herself, than either her mother or grandmother had.

I could multiply examples endlessly, but these two should suffice to reveal the reasons that modern fuel-supply systems did not necessarily lighten the work of individual housewives, although they certainly did reorganize it. Some of the work that was eliminated by modernization was work that men and children—not women—had previously done: carrying coal, carrying water, chopping wood, removing ashes, stoking furnaces, cleaning lamps, beating rugs. Some of the work was made easier, but its volume increased: sheets and underwear were changed more frequently, so there was more laundry to be done; diets became more varied, so cooking was more complex; houses grew larger, so there were more surfaces to be cleaned. Additionally, some of the work that, when done by hand had been done by servants, came to be done by the housewife herself when done by machine; indeed, many people purchased appliances precisely so that they could dispense with servants. It is not, consequently, accidental that the proportion of servants to households in the nation dropped (1 servant to every 15 households in 1900; 1 to 42 in 1950) just when washing machines, dishwashers, vacuum cleaners, and refrigerators were increasing just as markedly. Finally, some of the work that had previously been allocated to commercial agencies actually returned to the domain of the housewife—laundry, rug cleaning, drapery cleaning, floor polishing—as new appliances were invented to make the work feasible for the average housewife, and the costs of labor (all labor, that is, except the labor of the housewife) continued to escalate in the postwar years.

Conclusion

Thus, the changes that occurred in household technology during the twentieth century had two principal effects. The first was to separate the work of men and children from the work of women, continuing a process that had begun in the previous century; and the second was markedly to increase the productivity of the average housewife. This conclusion can be put more succinctly by saying that, in the second phase of industrialization, American households and American housewives shifted not from production to consumption but from the production of one type of commodity to the production of another in even greater quantities. Prior to industrialization (which means, in the United States, prior to 1860), American households (and the adult women who lived in them) produced goods intended for sale in the market place, but they also produced goods and services that were intended for use at home: foodstuffs, clothing, medicines, meals, laundry, health care—and much more. During the first phase of industrialization (say, between 1860 and 1910), households stopped producing goods for sale. They did not, however (and this is the crucial point), cease to be productive locales: they continued to produce goods and services intended for use at home or, as the Marxists would say, for the production and the reproduction of labor power. During the second phase of industrialization (after 1910), those latter productive functions did not leave the home. The industrialization of the household did not entail, as that of the market had, the centralization of all productive processes; the household continued to be the locale in which meals, clean laundry, healthy children, and well-fed adults were "produced"—and housewives continued to be the workers who were principally responsible. What changed most markedly was the productivity of these workers: modern technology enabled the American housewife of 1950 to produce singlehandedly what her counterpart of 1850 needed a staff of three or four to produce: a middle-class standard of health and cleanliness for herself, her spouse, and her children.

Moreover, from the perspective of the household, the transportation system had developed in a direction that was precisely the opposite of the one taken by the food, the clothing, and the health systems. The shift from production to consumption of such goods as strawberry jam, petticoats, and medicine meant that less time needed to be spent in housework in order to provide the same standard of living; but the shift from the horse and buggy to the automobile canceled many of the potential benefits of this extra time.

Our commonly received notions about the impact of twentieth-century household technology have thus deceived us on two crucial grounds. They have led us to believe that households no longer produce anything particularly important, and that, consequently, housewives no longer have anything particularly time consuming to do. Both notions are false, deriving from an incomplete understanding of the nature of these particular technological changes. Modern laborsaving devices eliminated drudgery, not labor. Households are the locales in which our society produces healthy people, and housewives are the workers who are responsible for almost all of the stages in that production process. Before industrialization, women fed, clothed, and nursed their families by preparing (with the help of their husbands and children) food, clothing, and medication. In the post-industrial age, women feed, clothe, and nurse their families (without much direct assistance from anyone else) by cooking, cleaning, driving, shopping, and waiting. The nature of the work has changed, but the goal is still there and so is the necessity for time-consuming labor. Technological systems that might have truly eliminated the labor of housewives could have been built; but such systems would have eliminated the home as well—a result that most Americans were consistently and insistently unwilling to accept.

The Politics and History of Family Violence

Linda Gordon

In the past twenty-five years, family violence has appeared as a substantial social problem in the United States. Starting with a wave of concern about child abuse in the 1960s, the concern widened to include wife-beating, incest (the sexual abuse of children in the family), and marital rape, as the women's liberation movement of the 1970s drew those crimes to public attention. The actual extent of family violence is controversial; estimates of child abuse vary, for example, from 50,000 to 1.5 million cases a year in the United States. Whatever the real figure, the general awareness of the problem has increased substantially.

For most of these two and half decades, I was not a family-violence scholar. My responses were probably typical: First, I wondered how anyone could be so bestial as to beat or mutilate their children (beating and mutilation were at first the dominant media representations of child abuse); then, as I gathered how widespread the problem was, I wondered that so many could have so little self-control; then, as I began to meet former victims and perpetrators, I began to suspect that the boundary separating me from those experiences was by no means invulnerable. Finally, the issue provoked my historian's curiosity. I noticed that family violence had had virtually no history; that most who discussed it—experts, journalists, friends—assumed they were discussing a *new* problem. As my preliminary forays into libraries revealed that it was an old problem, I began to notice the distortions created in the public discussion by the lack of a history.

One example is the tendency of the media to cover only the most cruel cases, creating the impression that these were typical. I learned that, a century ago, the problem had also gained public attention through sensational cases, while the majority of cases were ambiguous, not life-threatening, more often crimes of neglect than of assault. Another example is that many diagnoses of the *causes* of family violence—e.g., the increasing permissiveness of recent family and sexual

No. G 160222

DATE 11/08/88

ITEM NO.   QTY

039879   2

life—assume that the problem is unprecedented, which is not the case. By contrast, the ebb-and-flow pattern of concern about family violence over the last century suggests that its incidence has not changed as much as its visibility.

The changing visibility of family violence is, in my opinion, the leading indicator of the necessity of an historical approach to understanding it. Concern with family violence has been a weathervane identifying the prevailing winds of anxiety about family life in general. The periods of silence about family violence are as significant as periods of concern. Both reveal the longing for peaceful family life, the strength of the cultural image of home life as a harmonious, loving, and supportive environment. One response to this longing has been a tendency to deny, even suppress, the evidence that families are not always like that. Denying the problem serves to punish the victims of family violence doubly by forcing them to hide their problems and to blame themselves. Even the aggressors in family violence suffer from denial, since isolation and the feeling that they are unique make it difficult to ask for the help they want.

About 110 years ago there arose for the first time a different response—an attempt to confront the facts of family violence and to stop or at least control it. The first social agencies devoted to family-violence problems arose in the 1870s, called Societies for the Prevention of Cruelty to Children. They originally focused only on child abuse, but were soon drawn into other forms of family violence as well. It is important to learn and evaluate this history for its contemporary value as well as its historical interest.

The central argument of this [selection] is that family violence has been historically and politically constructed. I make this claim in a double sense. First, the very definition of what constitutes unacceptable domestic violence, and appropriate responses to it, developed and then varied according to political moods and the force of certain political movements. Second, violence among family members arises from family conflicts which are not only historically influenced but political in themselves, in the sense of that word as having to do with power relations. Family violence usually arises out of power struggles in which individuals are contesting real resources and benefits. These contests arise not only from personal aspirations but also from changing social norms and conditions.

The historical developments that influenced family violence—through the behavior of family members and the responses of social-control agencies— include, prominently, changes in the situation of women and children. Another major argument of this [work], therefore, is that family violence cannot be understood outside the context of the overall politics of the family. Today's anxiety about family issues—divorce, sexual permissiveness, abortion, teenage pregnancy, single mothers, runaway or allegedly stolen children, gay rights—is not unprecedented. For at least 150 years there have been periods of fear that "the family"—meaning a popular image of what families were supposed to be like, by no means a correct recollection of any actual "traditional family"—was in decline; and these fears have tended to escalate in periods of social stress.

Anxieties about family life, furthermore, have usually expressed socially conservative fears about the increasing power and autonomy of women and children, and the corresponding decline in male, sometimes rendered as fatherly, control of family members. For much of the history of the family-violence concern, moreover, these anxieties have been particularly projected onto lower-class families. Thus an historical analysis of family violence must include a view of the changing power relations among classes, sexes, and generations.

Yet family-violence policy is mainly discussed today without an historical dimension, and with its political implications hidden. The result has been a depoliticization of family-violence scholarship, as if this were a social problem above politics, upon which "objective" scientific expertise could be brought to bear. The questions raised by proposed remedies cannot be answered by "neutral" experts, but only by public decisions about the extent and limits of public responsibility.

A few examples may offer an introductory sense of what it means to call family violence a political problem. For over a century there has been a consensus that there must be some limits placed on the treatment family "heads" can mete out to their dependents. But setting and enforcing those limits encounters a fundamental tension between civil liberties and social control. In policing private behavior, one person's right may be established only by invading another person's privacy. Moreover, social control of family violence is made difficult by our dominant social norm that families ought to be economically independent. There is a consensus that children ought to have some minimal guarantees of health and welfare, no matter how poor their parents. Yet there is a consistent tendency to insist that social welfare be a temporary expedient, made uncomfortable, and its recipients stigmatized. These dilemmas must be confronted by political choices; they cannot be ironed out by expert rationalization.

The political nature of family violence is also revealed in the source of the campaign against it. For most of the 110 years of this history, it was the women's-rights movement that was most influential in confronting, publicizing, and demanding action against family violence. Concern with family violence usually grew when feminism was strong and ebbed when feminism was weak. Women's movements have consistently been concerned with violence not only against women but also against children. But this does not mean that anti-family-violence agencies, once established, represented feminist views about the problem. On the contrary, anti-feminism often dominated not only among those who would deny or ignore the problem but also among those who defined and treated it. In some periods the experts confronted wife-beating and sexual assault, male crimes, while in others they avoided or soft-pedaled these crimes and emphasized child neglect, which they made by definition a female crime. In some periods they identified class and in others gender inequalities as relevant, and in still others ignored connections between family violence and the larger social structure.

Political attitudes have also affected research "findings" about family violence.

For example, in the last two decades, experts on the problem have tended to divide into two camps. A psychological interpretation explains the problem in terms of personality disorders and childhood experience. A sociological explanatory model attributes the problem primarily to social stress factors such as poverty, unemployment, drinking, and isolation. In fact, these alternatives have been debated for a century, and the weight of opinion has shifted according to the dominant political mood. More conservative times bring psychological explanations to the foreground, while social explanations dominate when progressive attitudes and social reform movements are stronger. The debate is intense because it is not mainly about diagnoses but about their implications for policy. Social diagnoses imply social action and demand resources; psychological diagnoses may point to the need for psychotherapy but also justify criminal penalties and remove family violence from the range of problems called upon to justify welfare spending. When caseworkers lack the resources to help clients materially, they may focus on psychological problems—which are usually present—because at least something can be done about them. Those opposed to the commitment of resources on social spending are more likely to focus on individual psychological deviance as the problem. But both sides have often ignored the gender politics of family-violence issues, and the gender implications of policy recommendations, not only when women or girls were the victims of men, but also when women were the abusers.

Political attitudes have determined the very *meanings* of family violence. Family violence is not a fixed social illness which, like tuberculosis, can have its causal microorganism identified and then killed. Rather, its definitions have changed substantially since it first appeared as a social problem. Most of the discussion of family violence today assumes that what makes it problematic and requires social action is self-evident. Yet what was considered spanking a century ago might be considered abusive today, and the standards for what constitutes child neglect have changed greatly.

To insist that family violence is a political issue is not to deny its material reality as a problem for individuals—a painful, often terrifying reality. If there were any doubt, the victims', and often aggressors', pleas for help would erase it. But to discuss the violence itself without attention to the conflicts that give rise to it is to avoid the roots of the problem.

It is equally important to look at the history of attempts to control family violence. These efforts illustrate many of the general problems of "social control," a phrase often used to describe processes by which deviant and, presumably, dangerous behavior is disciplined by the larger society. Agencies devoted to the problem of family violence are in many ways typical of the entire welfare state. They have faced great difficulties in maintaining a balance between social order and privacy, between protecting the rights of some individuals and preserving the autonomy of others, and they have often been the means of imposing dominant values on subordinate groups. As with other activities of the state, social control of family violence could hardly be expected to be administered fairly in a society of such great inequalities of power. Yet it is precisely those inequalities that create such desperate need for the intervention of a welfare state.

Thus the example of family violence also produces a more complex view of social control than has been customary among social theorists. One of the most striking findings of this study is how often the objects of social control themselves asked for intervention from child-protection agencies. Clients were troubled by their inability to raise children according to their own standards, or to escape domestic violence themselves, and were eager for outside help. Moreover, once becoming clients, they attempted aggressively to influence agency policy and the definitions of the problems themselves, sometimes successfully.

Types of Family Violence

Four major types of family violence predominated in the eighty years covered by this study. The original one was cruelty to children, a notion which evolved into the modern category: child abuse. In 1880, as today, child-saving propaganda emphasized violent assault as the archetypical problem. In fact, child abuse is (and was) less common than child neglect, but it is more dramatic, less ambiguous, and—above all—it stimulates more outrage and financial generosity. Social workers in the nineteenth century, as those today, were aware that for effective fund-raising, they had to offer a distorted image of the nature of their work.

Child neglect soon became the most common form of family "violence" met by agencies. Its definition is of course extremely variable and relative to economic class, cultural standards, and family structure. What child-neglect cases have in common is that they must by definition project an inverse standard, a norm of proper child-raising.

Sexual abuse of children in the family—incest—figured prominently in family-violence case records. The "discovery" of child sexual abuse in the last decade has been only a rediscovery of a problem well known to social workers in the nineteenth century and the Progressive era.

Finally, wife-beating was also common in the case records. Logically, this should not have been the case, since the agencies studied here were exclusively devoted to child welfare. But women frequently and energetically attempted to force child-welfare agencies to defend their own interests as well as their children's. Included in their complaints were accusations of what we would today call marital rape, usually seen along with beatings as part of a generic male violence.

These themes are addressed through a case study: how Boston-area social-work agencies approached family-violence problems, from 1880 to 1960. These dates cover the period since the "discovery" of family violence in the late 1870s, stopping just before the latest wave of alarm about child abuse. Although the data in this [work] come exclusively from the Boston metropolitan area, which had certain demographic and social peculiarities, there is reason to consider the findings of this study typical of the urban United States. The largest environmental factors affecting family violence (e.g., poverty, unemployment, illness, alcoholism) were common to many areas. Moreover, the "discovery" of this social problem occurred simultaneously throughout the United States and in much of Europe, in the course of a single decade, suggesting similar patterns. The agencies whose records formed the source material for this study were local, but they were part of a national social-work profession—indeed, for most of this period the Boston groups were a leading influence in national family-violence policy.

The Clients

The protagonists of this story are the victims and assailants in family-violence cases: unusual heroes and heroines, to be sure, for they were almost always quite wretched, innocent and guilty alike. Nevertheless they were people with aspirations and complex emotions as well as ill luck and, often, self-destructive impulses.

These clients of children's protective agencies were mainly poor immigrants of non-elite ethnic and racial backgrounds. These groups were the most numerous, not because they are the only ones involved in family violence, but because they were more likely to be "caught."

Because I mean to describe these people as individuals rather than statistical generalizations, it will be useful here to offer a general profile of these clients. This profile cannot be construed to tell us anything about the characteristics that promote family violence, however, because this was not a controlled study. For example, the clients I studied were mostly poor and uneducated; but I have no way of knowing how many other poor and uneducated people did not have family-violence problems, or how many prosperous and educated people did. My guesses about the characteristics that contribute to family violence will rely on qualitative, not quantitative, evidence. But the reader will be able to know these people better, to understand their problems more readily, with a general description of the social and economic outlines of their lives.

The clients' most pronounced characteristic was their poverty. Twenty-one percent were lacking basic necessities, such as food and fuel, and an additional 48 percent lived in constant insecurity as to whether they could maintain bare subsistence. Relatively more clients were extremely poor in the last century, confirming what is known about the disastrous living conditions in poor urban neighborhoods in the nineteenth century. While there was a decline in the poorest categories after 1910, the number of prosperous or even middle-class clients did not increase greatly.

The clients' poverty was reflected in how they supported themselves. Once federal welfare aid developed in the 1930s, 42 percent relied on it chronically and only one-quarter had never received welfare. The proportion of fathers who were main supporters of their families went down over time, not because women were increasingly employed, but because welfare contributed more. Very few of the client families contained regularly employed women. Employed women were probably less likely to need the help of, or to come to the attention of, child-protection agencies, because their families were better off and because they themselves had more independence and self-esteem. The extreme poverty of the clients was also indicated by the fact that for 40 percent of families, children were vital contributors to the family budget. After World War II, when child labor had become virtually negligible in the urban population, 31 percent of these clients still needed their children's wages to survive.

The clients were extremely transient. Forty-one percent had lived at their present address less than two years, and only 18 percent more than five years. The clients also appeared rather isolated, judging from the few social contacts they seemed to have. These characteristics do not necessarily distinguish family-violence clients, since poor people are often more isolated than the prosperous, but they illustrate one of the indirect ways in which poverty, through the lack of community rootedness it creates, reduced their social resources of coping with family conflict.

There is a common view that large households promote family violence, either directly or through the correlation of large families with poverty and overcrowding. On the contrary, neither the families nor the households of the clients were consistently larger than average, and in the first four decades of this study, they were a little smaller than Boston's average. This was probably because of the tendency to family disorganization associated with poverty and family violence: children tended to leave home earlier, marital separation and illegitimacy were frequent, and living arrangements with boarders were unstable.

The clients were mainly immigrants or children of immigrants. Until World War II, the foreign-born were overrepresented in proportion to their numbers in Boston's population, but not in proportion to their numbers among the poor. The leading foreign ethnic groups among the family-violence clients were the Irish, the Italians, and the Canadians. In later years, Afro-Americans and West Indian blacks became another large ethnic group in this study. No ethnic group was significantly overrepresented in any of the four major types of family violence (child abuse, child neglect, wife-beating, and sexual abuse). The proportion of foreign-born clients shifted from 70 percent in the first decades of this study to just under 20 percent at the end, a decline consistent with the slowing of immigration.

However, there were behavioral differences among ethnic groups which affected family-violence problems. Perhaps the most notorious of them was the heavy drinking of the Irish. Although there is no reason to share the caseworkers' (many of whom were abstainers) moralistic condemnations, the case records provide evidence that the Irish were heavier drinkers than any other nationality. The Irish stood out even more in the amount of women's drinking. With respect to family violence, Irish alcoholism contributed to unusually high rates of desertion, poverty, dependency, infant mortality, and fighting. In the case records of this study, while the Irish were not disproportionately represented in cases of wife-beating, they did more often engage in mutual marital combat. But there is no reason to focus on liquor as the cause of this: the combativeness of Irish women may result from other factors in Irish and Irish-American history which accustomed Irish women to unusual independence.

The Italians were the poorest of Boston's ethnic groups at the turn of the century. Yet unlike the Irish, they were underrepresented in the city's almshouses. This contradiction may be explained by the strong family cohesion among Italian-Americans, as evidenced, for example, in their low desertion rates. Moreover, heavy drinking was rare among Italians. There was less street brawling and marital fighting than among the Irish, yet plenty of wife-beating. The Italian-American families in these case records included many of the most patriarchal, in terms of fathers' control over wives, authority over sons, and sequestering of daughters. (These patterns were shared by other southern-European and Mediterranean immigrants, such as the Lebanese, Syrians, and Greeks, of whom there were many fewer in Boston.)

The Canadian immigrants were of French, Scotch, and English origin, and had no single ethnic identity. Many had lived long in Canada, particularly Nova Scotia, before coming to the United States; others, particularly French Canadians, had lived in northern New England before migrating to Boston. Thus many Boston clients of Canadian origin had relatives with farms in New England or Canada to whom they turned for help, a substantial advantage in coping with family stress which European immigrants did not have. According to studies of Massachusetts as a whole, the French Canadians resembled the Irish in their extreme poverty and concentration in unskilled jobs, but resembled more the Italians in their low rates of female employment; like all the rural immigrants, they had high rates of child labor.

There were few Afro-Americans in the first decades of this study, and even by 1960 Boston had a much smaller black population than most other large eastern cities. Like all the other "ethnic" groups, they were overrepresented in family-violence case records in proportion to their numbers in the population, but not in proportion to their numbers among the poor. As with other ethnic groups, the increase of the black population came mainly from migration, and in many ways they shared with other immigrants the stresses of being alien. Contrary to what contemporary expectations might suggest, blacks were not overrepresented in any characteristic relevant to family violence: not poverty, or single-mother families, or drinking.

Overall these ethnic cultural differences were of minimal importance in constructing family-violence problems in comparison to the general influence of being poor, migratory, or alien. The single ethnic patterns that can be identified as influential were Irish drinking-and-fighting behavior and Italian fathers' patriarchal control over family members. Even these fade in comparison to experiences that were common to all ethnic groups in this study. Yet that commonness was not perceived by the clients themselves. Ethnic stereotyping was practiced, of course, not only by agency workers but also among clients. They experienced themselves as ethnically unique and frequently attempted to interpret their behavior to caseworkers in terms of ethnic traditions. Among the clients themselves a

kind of "pluralistic ignorance" is visible: Irish women, for example, were convinced that desertion was unique to their men; Italian women that wife-beating
was an Italian problem. They were wrong in these analyses. Yet their frequent
references to their cultural origins and traditions were attempts to assert to social
workers something important about their identities, vital for caseworkers to
understand if they were to help.

The "clients" in this study were as varied as any collection of several thousand
people, perhaps more so, since many of them had recently come from separate
foreign cultures. Yet they also had a great deal in common: their poverty, above
all, and their experience of helplessness in the context of radical social and
economic change, the more acute for those who had recently immigrated from
agrarian societies into the metropolis of Boston. Most of them were inadequately
housed; many of their children had serious medical problems; many of the men
were frequently and sometimes chronically unemployed or underemployed. For
the purposes of this study, what united them most was their common experience as
"clients" of an agency of social control, devoted to protecting their children—
from themselves. The very definition of their problems arose through their
interactions with individual caseworkers and the developing child-welfare
establishment.

The Child Protectors and Their Records

In tracking the history of family violence, I turned to a source relatively new to
historians: case records of social work agencies devoted to child protection. Case
records are rich in detail about daily life and personal relations. They are not,
however, universally reliable, understandable, or easy to use. Since the nature of
these records affects so much how I know what I assert in this [work], it is
important to discuss briefly here the nature of the records and their limitations.

This study is based on the work of three Boston agencies, each exemplary of a
certain type of child welfare agency, and each involved in family violence in a
different way. The major source, and the dominant type of agency in this field,
was the Massachusetts Society of the Prevention of Cruelty to Children (MSPCC,
or the Society). Societies for the Prevention of Cruelty to Children (SPCCs), or
child-protection agencies, as they were later called, arose throughout the United
States and Europe in the 1870s; nearly every state in the United States had such an
agency, and the Massachusetts SPCC was one of the most influential. The
MSPCC investigated and prosecuted parents for child abuse and neglect and, in
cooperation with other governmental and private agencies, arranged the placements of children ordered removed from their parents.

A second agency active in child-saving, the Boston Children's Service Association (BCSA), developed from alms-giving and asylum-providing groups. While
the BCSA always conceded to the MSPCC primary jurisdiction over protective
work, the MSPCC in turn referred to the BCSA much of the arrangement and
supervision of placements.

A third major type of child-saving agency, which came into existence toward the end of the Progressive era, were clinics offering psychological diagnosis and treatment for disturbed or delinquent children. The example used in this study, one of the leading such clinics in the United States, is the Judge Baker Guidance Center (JBGC), established in Boston in 1917. This clinic was the major place of referral by the courts and by other social work agencies, including the MSPCC and BCSA, when children were thought to need professional mental health services. A substantial proportion of JBGC clients had backgrounds of family violence, making its records a rich source of data for the second half of this period of study.

The keeping of case records was a basis for the professionalization of social work. In the nineteenth century, when the agencies studied here where charities, using volunteer and/or untrained labor, their record-keeping was skimpy and inconsistent. They used ledger books in which handwritten notes were entered about cases as they came in. If a "case" continued for more than one day, the worker might or might not remember to write on the bottom of the first entry, say, "cont'd volume IX p. 396." After five or six further entries, it was very easy to lose the trail. Since a worker had to pull down many heavy volumes to trace the history of a case, it seems reasonable to surmise that many did not bother to do this. The Progressive-era transformation of social work in the early twentieth century brought modern record-keeping: card files and a "loose-leaf" system, generally a folder and a case number for each case, so that new material could be added continually. Thus, from the point of view of the historian, the quality of records took a great advance around 1910, and that is reflected [here] in the disproportion of quotations from case histories after 1910.

Despite improvements, case records continued uneven in the information they contained. There were many reasons for this: sometimes the clients were so reluctant to cooperate at all that the workers did not want to struggle to get information beyond the absolutely necessary; sometimes the workers simply deemed some information irrelevant; sometimes the client interviewed did not know what the worker wanted; sometimes the workers were hurried. Case records varied also in length: from one paragraph to several hundred pages. All, however, consisted primarily of notes written by the caseworker(s), summarizing contacts with and information from or about clients. There were many interagency memoranda and, infrequently, notes from the clients themselves. With few exceptions, the case records represent the caseworkers' opinions, even when they were trying to represent the clients' point of view.

Thus agency workers, "child protectors," are also protagonists in this story, but only collectively. I have not attempted to individualize them here (indeed, I would have had no basis on which to do so, for *their* foibles and problems were not laid out in agency records). In that neglect, I am simplifying an already extremely complicated tale; I do not wish to distract attention too far from the central position of the clients. In avoiding distinctions among social workers, I am doing some of them an injustice; the limitations of the agencies as a whole did not pertain to each of the workers. But some might benefit from my generalizations, too, since some were even more limited in what they offered than the norm.

The bias, not to mention outright prejudice, of these caseworkers was often substantial. For the first twenty-five years of this study the workers were almost always male, while the clients were virtually all female. For the first fifty years of this study, the workers were almost always white, native-born Protestants, dealing with clients who were in the majority Catholic immigrants. Lack of adequate translators was a chronic problem. The most common result was the conclusion that clients were stupid or ignorant because of their inadequacy in answering questions or following instructions. Sometimes the caseworkers could not gather basic family information accurately because of their lack of language skills. Often case records were duplicated because, due to mistakes in spelling foreign names, workers did not find a previously existing record.

Social workers often disdained many aspects of the ethnic and religious cultures of their clients; for most of the period of this study, the child protectors were overwhelmingly native-born white Protestents, while the clients were immigrant or second-generation Catholics. Most caseworkers, reflecting the cultures in which they had been raised, assumed subnormal intelligence among their poorer clients. The agents' comments and expectations about immigrants in this early period were similar to views of black clients in the mid-twentieth century. The records abound with derogatory references, even when made with kind intent. One girl making an incest allegation against her father in 1910, and being accused of lying, was called "a romancer but not more so than the average foreign born child." Black women were described as "primitive," "limited," "not nearly as talkative as many of her race, but apparently truthful," "fairly good for a colored woman." White immigrants came in for similar abuse: e.g., "a typical low-grade Italian woman." The characterizations of clients were also saturated with class arrogance. "A young girlish appearing woman with dark bobbed curly hair, ignorant, brassy, indifferent . . . coarse, had very poor standards. . . . Seemed to lack feeling, sympathy and understanding, decidedly hard." Some social workers disdained their clients partly because they *were* clients: "typical Puerto Ricans who loved fun, little work and were dependent people," a caseworker wrote in 1960.

After about 1920 these informal judgments were supposed to be replaced by scientific intelligence tests. It has been well documented that these tests were biased against immigrant, non-English-speaking, and poor people, and the case records provide direct evidence for that conclusion. In the Judge Baker records, the children's actual tests, in their own handwriting, are included, and one can imagine the experience of immigrant children in trying to answer them. Some 1930 examples: Make as many words as you can from the letters AEIRLP; Fill in the blanks: "The poor baby _____ as if it were _____ sick"; Answer: "Why did the Pilgrims come to this country?" Moreover, the testing merely supplemented, but did not replace, arbitrary race and class labeling of clients. I compared the epithets used by MSPCC caseworkers, the least professionalized of the agencies in this study, to those used by Judge Baker professionally trained psychiatric social workers, for the same years (1910–17). The MSPCC records called clients shiftless, coarse, low type, uncouth, immoral, feebleminded, lazy, and worthless (or occasionally, positively, good or sober); Judge Baker workers characterized their clients as low-grade, of weak character, ignorant type, degenerate, of low mentality (or once, positively, as refined)—hardly a more scientific set of categories. Yet the caseworkers were often so in thrall to the objectivity of such testing that they credited it above the evidence of their own observation: "The psychological testing brought forth the fact very plainly that the child [Italian-born, fifteen years old] has a very distinct language handicap that is not evident when one is talking with her."

Equally questionable was the use of testing to evaluate parents, almost always mothers. Test results might decide whether girls were placed in institutions; they might decide whether mothers could keep their children. For example:

> . . . she graded at a median mental age of $7\frac{3}{12}$ years, which is $6\frac{9}{12}$ years below the average. As she could speak no English, test had to be given through an interpreter. . . . Although initial performance on Healy A was total failure, she showed good learning ability after demonstration. She did surprisingly well on problems of simple change from Stanford scale though she failed to count backwards from 20 to 1. . . . Her method on tests was a combination of chance, trial and error, and some elements of planning. . . . Although this woman . . . can neither read nor write Italian, speaks only a few words of English, is unable to spell her own name, does not know the year or the month, she does, however, know the date . . . that every child was born, is able to make change and manifests fairly good practical ability. She will probably be capable of caring for two or more of her children. Her responsibilities, however, should be carefully guarded and it should be kept constantly before her that the return of the children is to be the reward for the effort she makes to care for them. [This woman, deserted by her husband and left with four children, had come herself to a family service agency seeking help. . . .]

In the face of such discriminatory attitudes and procedures, and of such power to disrupt clients' lives, it is to be expected that clients would not be frank with caseworkers. Even caseworkers trying to avoid arrogance and to help clients achieve their own goals met uncooperativeness and lack of understanding. From the clients' point of view, even well-meaning caseworkers could do a good deal of damage through misunderstandings and the structural inflexibilities of the system. What caseworkers saw as professional standards and procedures had entirely different meanings to clients. When the former asked personal questions, clients did not understand their relevance, considered them nosy, and did not trust the confidentiality of their responses. Most child-protection workers had no material aid to offer clients, but had to rely primarily on moral exhortation, counseling, or threats of punitive measures, even with clients who had themselves asked for help with violence problems. Clients interpreted this emphasis on talk instead of action as meaning that the caseworkers did not really want to help. Clients so often had something to hide—who among us would agree to allow caseworkers free entry to their homes at any time? Boyfriends, liquor, boarders and guests, children not at school, luxuries that might provide evidence against needed relief, baby and child care that did not conform to expert recommendations, food that did not conform to American tastes—all these and many other infractions that clients might not even notice could convince a caseworker that the client was an unfit parent.

These mutually distrustful relationships were by no means the fault of individual caseworkers. Many caseworkers managed despite these limitations to offer sympathy and help to clients. These useful services were of many types: sometimes what clients wanted was exactly what agencies could provide, as in cases of prosecution of child abusers or wife-beaters; sometimes caseworkers provided referrals to other agencies that did have material aid to offer; sometimes the child protectors themselves provided encouragement, advice, confirmation of a client's own good judgment, or a brake on bad judgment; sometimes they offered informal support quite beyond the bounds of the professional minimum, ranging from small gifts to trips to the country to an ongoing, steady relationship.

The caseworker in her turn faced pressures that militated against scrupulously honest case records. These records were often the basis of the worker's evaluation by her superior and she needed, therefore, to note what she ought to have done, not what she did do. Furthermore, she needed to justify her actions by showing that they were appropriate to her clients—evidence that would mainly be taken from the record she prepared. She sometimes had to disguise both her inadequacies and her excellence; the case record could be allowed to show neither too little nor too much action for clients. I tried, where possible, to check caseworkers' characterizations against more reliable, objective data. Where caseworkers said that clients were mainly drunkards, I tried to look myself for clear evidence of alcohol abuse, for example. But since the evidence was usually presented or suppressed by the caseworker, these efforts were limited.

The interpretation of such records involves the historian's creativity, even imagination—although not necessarily more so than with other sorts of historical sources. Their status as historical documents does not make them infallible; their truth must be gathered from among the varied and often conflicting stories they contain, and from the complex relationships that they expressed—between agency representatives, clients, and family members. In trying to grasp the will of the clients, I weighed what they did more heavily than what they said (i.e., what caseworkers said clients said). I tried to identify the actions taken by agency workers, not their promises and waverings.

I argued above that individual outcomes were not determined, that the collectively greater power of the social workers and the social order they represented could not predict any individual case. The interactions between client and worker which are central to my argument, central to the whole historical construction of family violence, can only be revealed in actual case histories. Throughout . . . I have chosen to tell, as much as possible, whole stories rather than excerpts from stories, so that the peculiarities of every situation are inescapable, and so that my generalizations are seen for what they are: abstractions, not "typical cases." I also tell whole stories in order to maximize the readers' opportunity to "see" my interpretation and to argue with it, conscious that readers do not immediately have access to these confidential case records as they might to other forms of historical documents.

As we turn now to examine the historical construction and reconstruction of definitions of family violence, one such case history will serve an an example of the interaction of client and social worker. The "Amatos" were clients of MSPCC from 1910 to 1916. They had five young children from the current marriage and Mrs. Amato had three from a previous marriage, two of them still in Italy and one daughter in Boston. Mrs. Amato kept that daughter at home to do housework and look after the younger children while she earned money doing home piece-rate sewing. This got the family in trouble with a truant officer, and they were also accused, in court, of lying, saying that the father had deserted when he was in fact at home. Furthermore, once while left alone, probably in charge of a sibling, one of the younger children fell out of a window and had to be hospitalized, making the mother suspect of negligence.

Despite her awareness of these suspicions against her, Mrs. Amato went to many different agencies, starting with those of the Italian immigrant community and then reaching out to elite (Protestant) social work agencies, seeking help, reporting that her husband was a drunkard, a gambler, a non-supporter, and a wife-beater. The Massachusetts Society for the Prevention of Cruelty to Children agents at first doubted her claims because Mr. Amato impressed them as a "good and sober man," and blamed the neglect of the children on his wife's incompetence in managing the wages he gave her. The Society ultimately became convinced of her story because of her repeated appearance with severe bruises and the corroboration by the husband's father. Mr. Amato, Sr., was intimately involved in the family troubles, and took responsibility for attempting to control his son. Once, he came to the house and gave the son "a warning and a couple of slaps," after which the son improved for a while. Another time he extracted from his son a pledge not to beat his wife for two years.

Mrs. Amato did not trust this method of controlling her husband. She begged the MSPCC agent to help her get a divorce; then she withdrew this request; later she claimed that she had not dared take this step because his relatives threatened to beat her if she tried it. Finally Mrs. Amato's daughter (from her previous marriage) took action, coming independently to the MSPCC to bring an agent to the house to help her mother. As a result of this complaint Mr. Amato was convicted of assault once and sentenced to six months. During that time Mrs. Amato survived by "a little work" and help from "Italian friends," according to her caseworker. Her husband returned more violent than before: he went at her with an ax, beat the children so much on the head that their "eyes wabbled" [*sic*], and supported his family so poorly that the children went out begging. This case closed, like so many, without a resolution.

The Amatos, it must be remembered, exist only as they were interpreted for us by social workers in a particular historical period—the Progressive era. I want to press the Amatos into service to help illustrate the historicity and political construction of family violence, by imagining how social workers might have responded to the Amatos differently in different periods. A summary of these changes produces a rough periodization of the history of family violence:

1. The late nineteenth century, approximately 1875–1910, when family violence agencies were part of the general charity organization and moral reform movement, influenced by feminism.
2. The Progressive era and its aftermath, approximately 1910–1930, when family violence work was incorporated into professional social work and a reform program relying heavily on state regulation.
3. The Depression, when intrafamily violence was radically deemphasized in favor of amelioration of economic hardship.
4. The 1940s and 1950s, when psychiatric categories and intensely "pro-family" values dominated the social work approach to family problems.
5. The 1960s and 1970s, when feminist and youth movements began a critique of the family which forced open the doors of closets that hid family problems.

Nineteenth-Century Child-Saving, 1875–1910

The nineteenth-century definition of the problem was cruelty to children, a concept subtly but importantly different from child abuse, which it later became. The former was a moralistic notion, directing attention to the cruel culprit, usually presumed to be an ignorant, "depraved, immigrant man," more than to the victim. This consciousness reflected the values of the social movements from which it grew. It shared the feminist emphasis on illegitimate male power, the moralism characteristic of the social purity (anti-drinking, anti-prostitution) campaigns, and the socially elite assumptions of both.

The anti-cruelty-to-children movement was particularly influenced by the temperance movement, and blamed drinking for virtually all family irregularities. The temperance orientation, too, contained a feminist interpretation: male cruelty was the constant subtext of anti-drinking propaganda. The image of maternal cruelty, less prevalent, also focused on alcoholism: a negligent mother, lying abed in a drunken stupor while her children cried for food.

The emphasis on drink, and the envisioning of cruelty to children as something that "they"—the immigrant poor—did, never "us"—the respectable classes— allowed even anti-feminist moral reformers to include wife-beating within their jurisdiction. They did not have to take the feminist message personally, so to speak. Similarly, child-protection agencies were able to prosecute many incest cases without offending anti-feminists. It was even recognized as an exclusively male crime, but was attributed to a male depravity that occurred only in the lower classes.

Had the Amato case appeared in 1890, the child-savers might have been quicker to see Mr. Amato as a brutal man, depraved, of inferior stock. The sympathy thus engendered for Mrs. Amato, however, would have been condescending and would have associated her problems primarily with alcohol rather than with her structural position in the family and city. They would not have helped her seek economic independence as a route to safety but would more likely have offered two choices: either reforming her husband through a combination of moralizing and punishment or institutionalizing her children to protect them from the husband.

The Progressive Era and Its Aftermath, 1910–1930

Social work as a whole was becoming professionalized and "scientific" during the Progressive era, and a new group of middle-class "experts" replaced upper-class charity workers as those who set standards for family life. Environmentalist analyses led to an emphasis on child neglect (as opposed to abuse) as the major category of improper parenting. Neglect was, of course, the fundamental concern in the Amato case, which dated from this period. A decreased emphasis on alcohol opened the way for caseworkers to identify other sorts of stress—poverty, unemployment, illness—as contributors to child neglect. But understanding environmental stresses did not lessen the racism and class bias in family-violence diagnoses. The broader causal analysis revealed a deep dilemma in anti-family-violence work, vividly reflected in the Amato case: difficulty in distinguishing culpable parental negligence from the results of poverty.

The Progressive reformers, more than their nineteenth-century predecessors, believed that they were seeing an overall weakening of the family. One of their greatest fears was the apparent increase in single-mother families, a problem noticed in part because of the overrepresentation of single mothers in child-neglect cases. The agency workers' hostility to Mrs. Amato's desire for independence reflected a fear of establishing female-headed households.

Moreover, the Progressive era produced a cover-up of wife-beating as a form of family violence, which was evident in the reluctance to recognize Mrs. Amato's victimization. The old feminist diatribes against drunken, brutal men came to seem moralistic and unscientific. Instead, marital violence was portrayed as mutual, resulting from environmental stress, lack of education, or lack of mental hygiene. This was the diagnosis of Mrs. Amato's difficulties (and in response the agency undertook regular supervision of the family, attempting to "Americanize" them, to instruct Mrs. Amato in proper child care and housekeeping methods).

The cover-up also extended to that other highly gendered form of family violence, incest. In a pattern familiar to those who have followed the public alarm about sexual assault of children in the 1980s, in the decades 1910–1930 sexual assault by strangers was emphasized and incest—that is, sexual assault within the family—deemphasized. Sexual abuse of children was increasingly blamed on "dirty old men," who were considered sick or "perverted." Incest and sexual abuse were fit into a new category, sexual delinquency. In this new understanding, the victims, almost always girls, were labeled as sexually deviant and criminal, even when they had been raped or mistreated at young ages, and were often incarcerated in industrial schools. These developments were conditioned by the decline of feminism.

The Depression

One of the major characteristics of Depression-era social work was a policy of defending the "conventional" nuclear family. This meant working against all centrifugal forces in the family, at the expense of asking women and children to suppress their own aspirations. The great advances in provision of general welfare necessitated by the massive unemployment of the 1930s have tended to obscure more conservative implications of social policy at that time. In treatment of conflict between the sexes, Depression-era family-violence agencies strengthened still further the Progressive-era tendency to deemphasize male violence as a significant family problem. A sympathy arose for the unemployed husband, the stress and role conflict that frequently engendered his violence; remarkably less sympathy was mustered for the situation of mothers doing double shifts—at work and at home—in attempts to hold their families together. Indeed, women were consistently held responsible for the treatment of children and the general mood of the family, as men were not. The treatments of preference for family violence were reconciliation and economic aid. The very meaning of family violence had shifted: it was seen as an epiphenomenon of extrafamilial events.

Indeed, violence altogether was deemphasized, and the SPCCs devoted themselves almost exclusively to child neglect, now conceived primarily in terms of economic neglect, such as malnutrition or inadequate medical care. But relief alone was no answer to family violence, since poverty alone does not cause family violence. After all, most poor children are neither abused nor neglected. A Depression-era agency might have offered Mrs. Amato relief, perhaps even in return for her agreement to work at reconciliation with her husband, and ignored her other aspirations, problems, and complaints.

World War II and The 1950s

The defend-the-conventional-family policy in social work continued straight through the 1940s and 1950s. These decades represented the low point in public awareness of family-violence problems and in the status of child-protection work within the social-work profession. Family casework was, however, no longer reluctant to inquire into the roots of intrafamily conflict, but did so now in psychiatric categories. The goal of the new psychiatric therapy was individual maturity, and this was often measured by the patient's ability to adjust to a nuclear family life. The roots of most interpersonal problems were sought in individual "complexes," not in cultural or structural arrangements. The most notorious example of the psychiatric influence in family-violence work was in the blaming of wives for their abuse by husbands—again, a double standard in requirements of individual responsibility for their actions. The "nagging wife" of traditional patriarchal folklore was now transformed into a woman of complex mental ailments: failure to accept her own femininity and attempting to compete with her husband; frustration as a result of her own frigidity; a need to control resulting from her own sexual repression; masochism. These neuroses required diagnosis and treatment by professionals—friends were unlikely to be of help. Moreover, these neuroses indicated treatment not of the assailant but of the victim. Mrs. Amato, a battered wife, might have been urged to question how and why she provoked her husband, what were the angers she felt toward her second set of children, what was her part in her husband's failure to support.

Psychiatry in family-violence work also affected problems with children, and it is here that we see the most marked change from Depression-era social-work thought. Child-neglect cases were increasingly seen as products not of poverty but of neurotic rejection or negligence. Indeed, an entirely new category of cruelty to children was now developed: emotional neglect. Emotional neglect was a gendered form of child abuse—only mothers could be guilty of it. Emotional neglect as a category allowed the mystification of incest in a new way, the "discovery" of emotional incest, seductiveness between mother and child. I do not mean to deny the possibility that such seductiveness exists and might be bad for children. I am merely pointing to the irony of child-protection policies which avoided acknowledging the occurrence of actual sexual molestation of children but evinced interest rather in symbolic sexual behavior in the form of certain inappropriately intimate emotional relations indulged in by women.

The 1960s and 1970s

In order to avoid violating clients' privacy any more than necessary, I chose not to read any currently ongoing case records, which required ending the research in 1960. It will be helpful, nonetheless, to contrast this historical material with the contemporary context of family-violence discussion. Professional and public responses to family violence have undergone significant changes since 1960. One such change has been the increased medicalization of the issue. The first wave of anti-cruelty-to-children work had been a campaign of upper-class charity volunteers. In the Progressive-era child-protection work became a branch of the new profession of social work—indeed, it helped to build that profession—and remained primarily a social-work concern to the end of this study. In the 1960s, by contrast, child abuse was seized upon by doctors, particularly pediatricians, its diagnosis and treatment medicalized, also as a means of building the prestige of the group. If I were attempting similar research for the last two decades, I would turn not only to casework but also to medical records.

More importantly, the context of the rediscovery and redefinition of family violence in the last two decades was the civil-rights, anti-war, student, and women's movements, all of them challenging family norms in different ways. Combined, these movements raised critical questions about the sanctity of family privacy, the privileged position of the male head of family, and the importance of family togetherness at all costs. The movements created an atmosphere in which child abuse, wife-beating, and incest could again be pulled out of the closet. Moreover, the critique of family violence was situated in an atmosphere of criticism of more accepted forms of violence as well—military, political, and cultural. In challenging the ideology of separate public and private spheres, the new social movements also challenged the power of professionals to define and then cure social problems. Their anti-authoritarian interpretive framework stimulated collective citizen's action on family violence. Self-help organizations of family-violence victims and assailants started competing with professionals for hegemony. Mrs. Amato might have gone to a battered women's shelter and discovered her commonality with many other women. She might have been encouraged by the shelter atmosphere, or that of other self-help projects such as Parents Anonymous, to identify her own goals and strategies for change. These projects render evident what was previously disguised—the role of victims, "clients," in defining the problems and remedies.

This chronology is schematic, not only because the transitions between different periods were gradual and the boundaries blurred, but also because the histories of the four types of family violence with which this [work] is concerned were different. . . .

[M]y premise is that family violence is a problem inseparable from the family norms of a whole society or from the overall political conflicts in that society. It is a changing historical and cultural issue, not a biological or sociobiological universal. As a public issue, family violence has been a virtual lightning rod for different social and political perspectives. Born as a social problem in an era of a powerful women's rights movement, the 1870s, campaigns against child abuse and wife-beating have tended to lose momentum and support, even to disappear altogether, when feminist influence is in decline. In such periods family togetherness is often sought at the expense of individual rights and by ignoring intrafamily problems, rather than by exposing and attacking them. Alternatively, in periods without much feminist influence family-violence problems are redefined in ways less threatening to myths of the harmony of the normative family.

Death and the Family

Peter Uhlenberg

The impact of mortality change upon family structure, although sometimes mentioned, has been seriously neglected in studies of family history. Many of the most significant changes in the American family—the changing status of children, the increasing independence of the nuclear family, the virtual disappearance of orphanages and foundling homes, the rise in societal support of the elderly, the decline in fertility, the rise in divorce—cannot be adequately understood without a clear recognition of the profound changes that have occurred in death rates. And the decline in mortality in this century has been dramatic. At the beginning of this century about 140 infants out of every 1,000 born died in the first year of life; now only 14 out of 1,000 die. In this same period the average life span has increased from less than 50 to 73. The mortality decline in this century is greater than the total mortality decline that occurred during the 250 years preceding 1900.

In searching for the meaning of aggregate statistics on death for individuals and families, we must consider the effects of a death upon the survivors. Habenstein suggests that,

> Each death initiates significant responses from those survivors who in some way have personally or vicariously related to the deceased. Inevitably, the collectivities in which the dead person held membership also react (1968:26).

The family is often the most important group in which an individual has membership and in which close relationships exist, so it is here that we should expect death to have its greatest impact. The loss of a parent, a child, a sibling, or a spouse disrupts established family patterns and requires readjustment. As the experience of losing intimate family members moves from a pervasive aspect of life to a rare event, adjustments in family structure become imperative.

If the mortality decline since 1900 has been so large and if this decline has major repercussions for the family, why has it been neglected in studies of family change?[1] One important reason is the difficulty involved in trying to measure accurately the effects of a mortality change. Suppose, for example, that we want to describe the effect of mortality upon the family position of children at various historical times. If we attempt to specify the situation in its full complexity, we must deal with the age of mothers and fathers at the birth of their children, the birth position of children, and the age-sex configuration of siblings. Furthermore,

From *Journal of Family History,* Fall 1980. Copyrighted 1980 by the National Council on Family Relations, 1910 West County Road B, Suite 147, St. Paul, MN 55113. Reprinted by permission.

[1]Several studies have discussed the significance of mortality level for the social structure (Blauner, 1966; Aries, 1962; Habenstein, 1968), but they do not present quantitative information regarding its effect upon the family.

we must recognize that cohorts of individuals live out their lives in a dynamic environment in which the force of mortality is constantly changing. Even if we could construct a conceptually complex model to elaborate the detailed mortality experiences of individuals, we would not have the necessary statistics to make use of it. Nor can a retrospective survey provide the data we would need, since only survivors to the present could be interviewed.

The purpose of this article is to suggest an alternative approach by constructing relatively simple measures of how different mortality levels affect important aspects of the family. Rather than attempting to summarize the total impact of mortality upon a cohort, the present study develops hypothetical situations to provide insights into the dynamic role of death in family life. The emphasis is upon ways in which mortality impinges upon family structure, and how observed changes in mortality over this century have encouraged change in the American family.

For perspective on historical change in mortality, I will focus upon three dates in the twentieth century: approximately 1900, 1940, and 1980 (actually, 1976). At each date, the role of mortality will be considered from the perspective of individuals at four different locations in the life course. The stages of life are: childhood, young adulthood, middle age, and old age. The calculations use period life tables[2] for each date, which means that the measures do not reflect the actual experience of any cohort. Rather, the picture presented reveals the implications of mortality conditions at specific points in time. In other words, the question asked is how would mortality at the 1900 (or 1940 or 1980) level impinge upon the family experience of individuals?

Childhood

Mortality change has affected the family experience of children in three ways. First, an increasing likelihood that a newborn will survive through childhood may influence the nature of parent-child relations. Second, declining mortality in the middle years of life affects the chances of orphanhood for children. Third, changing adult mortality also alters the prospects for having grandparents alive during childhood.

Parent-Child Relations

There is widespread agreement that mortality levels in a society constrain attitudes and feelings that parents have toward their infant children. As Ariès writes, under conditions of very high infant and childhood mortality "people

---

[2]The life tables are the U.S. white population.

could not allow themselves to become too attached to something that was regarded as a probable loss" (1962:38; also see Blauner, 1966). As infant mortality has declined, childhood has become a more clearly differentiated stage of life, and families have increasingly focused upon children and emphasized the nurturance of children. Comparing the modern and historical American family, Skolnick concludes,

> What seems to have changed is the psychological quality of the intimate environment of family life. . . . Within the home the family has become more intense emotionally (1978:115).

Surely other factors in addition to changed mortality encouraged the deepening of emotional bonds between family members. But a look at the extent of changing survival prospects for infants since 1900 points clearly to the critical role that this change played in the increased intimacy of the parent-child relationship.

Several calculations to demonstrate the magnitude of the drop in child deaths since 1900 are presented in Table 1. First, the probability that an individual baby would survive his or her childhood increased from .79 in 1900, to .98 in 1976. The second calculation answers the question, what is the probability that a couple bearing three children would have at least one child die before reaching age 15? The answer is that under 1900 mortality conditions half of the parents would experience the loss of a child; under 1976 conditions only 6 percent would. But the rate of birth as well as death fell over this century. As a result, the probability of an average parent experiencing the death of a child changed even more. Women bearing children around 1900 had, on average, 4.2 children, while projections suggest that women currently bearing children will average about 2.1. Thus the third calculation in Table 1 shows that the probability of a child dying for parents with an average number of children for that period dropped from .62 in 1900 to only .04 in 1976. As the parental experience of having a child die changed from routine to exceptional, the stimulus to invest greater emotion and resources has grown.

Orphanhood

The dependency of children upon adults for care and socialization necessitates fully developed social arrangements to deal with orphans in societies with high rates of mortality. Adoption within an extended kinship system and placement of children in orphanages were two mechanisms used to deal with the social problem of orphans in nineteenth-century America. But during the twentieth century orphanhood changes from a common occurrence to a rare event. Consequently, social institutions designed to deal with this problem have virtually disappeared. From the perspective of successive cohorts of children, the change has profoundly altered their experiences in families.

Table 1.   Measures of Death to Children in Families: 1900; 1940; 1976.

Year	Probability of surviving from 0 to 15	Probability of 1 or more dying out of 3	Average number of children per mother[a]	Probability of 1 or more dying out of average number of births
1900	.79	.50	4.2	.62
1940	.94	.17	2.8	.16
1976	.98	.06	2.1	.04

[a]For 1900 and 1940 this is the average completed family size for women who were aged 25–29 at these dates. For 1976 the figure is the expected completed family size for women aged 25–29 in 1976.
   Sources: U.S. Public Health Service, 1969; NCHS, 1978; Grabill *et al.*, 1958; U.S. Bureau of the Census, 1978a.

Table 2 contains data which show the effect of varying mortality levels upon the probability of orphanhood. Since probability of death is related to age, some assumption about the age of men and women at occurrence of parenthood is required. Over this century the median age of women at the birth of their children has ranged from 27.2 to 25.4, and fathers have, on average, been about 3 years older than mothers. Therefore, the choice of a mother aged 27 and a father aged 30 for the calculations in Table 2 is a reasonable approximation to the typical experience over this time interval.[3] From the table we can read the probability of orphanhood for those born under these circumstances.

If mortality levels characteristic of 1900 persisted over time and the probability of death for the father and mother was independent, about 24 percent of the children born would loose at least one parent before reaching age 15; one out of 62 would have both parents die. Under mortality conditions existing in 1976, only 5 percent of children would see a parent die, while one in 1,800 would lose both parents. So declining mortality has operated to increase greatly the family stability of children.

Of course, increasing divorce has had the counter influence of increasing family disruption for children. At current levels of divorce, about 36 percent of all children will experience a disrupted family (Bumpass, 1978). But the social significance of disruption due to death differs from disruption due to divorce. Current discussions of the effects of family disruption upon children should consider the very high rate of family instability that has been the historical experience of children prior to the modern era of low mortality. Further, those interested in designing social policy for the family would benefit from studying the historical ways of dealing with orphans.

In addition to the reduced probability of losing a parent during childhood, there has also been a great reduction in the probability of a sibling dying. One good

[3]Varying the ages of parents at the birth of the child a few years in either direction has negligible effects upon the probability of orphanhood. For example, if the mother was 25 and the father 28, the probability in 1900 would be .23 instead of .24, and the probability in 1976 would be unchanged.

Table 2. Probabilities of Parents and Siblings Dying Before a Child Reaches Age 15: 1900; 1940; 1976.[a]

Year	Probability of 1 or more parent dying	Probability of 1 or more of 2 siblings dying	Probability of death to member of nuclear family
1900	.24	.36	.51
1940	.10	.12	.21
1976	.05	.04	.09

[a]See text for specific family context of the child.
Sources: U.S. Public Health Service, 1969; NCHS, 1978.

example indicates the magnitude of this change. Consider the situation of a first-born child to a mother aged 27 and a father aged 30, where the parents have two additional children at two-year intervals. That is, the first-born child has siblings born when he or she is two and four. What is the probability that this child will experience the death of a sibling before reaching age 15? Under 1900 mortality conditions the probability is .36, while under the 1976 conditions, it is only .04. Combined with the possibility of a parent or sibling dying during childhood, the chances of a child losing someone in the nuclear family before he or she reaches age 15 drops from .51 to .09. Since the average number of siblings for a child born later in this century is much lower than for someone born earlier, the actual experience of encountering the death of an intimate family member has declined even more dramatically than these calculations suggest. Compared to the past, children now are almost entirely shielded from the death of close relatives, except that of elderly grandparents.

Grandparents' Survival

Not only did the mortality decline improve the likelihood that all members of the nuclear family would survive one's childhood, but also it increased the average number of living grandparents. Consider the probability of a child having grandparents alive if he or she is born to a father aged 30 and mother aged 27 and if both parents were similarly born when their fathers and mothers were 30 and 27 respectively. Under 1900 mortality conditions, one-fourth of the children would have all grandparents alive at birth; by 1976 it increased to almost two-thirds (Table 3). The probability of three or more grandparents being alive when the child was age 15 increased from .17 to .55. Thus, mortality change has greatly increased the potential for family interaction across more than two generations. The actual role of grandparents in the lives of children cannot be determined from these simple demographic data. But the increased presence of grandparents suggests that statements about their declining importance in the lives of children are probably exaggerated or wrong.

Table 3.   Distribution of Children by Number of Living Grandparents When Child Is Aged 0 and 15 Under Conditions of 1900, 1940, 1976.[a]

Year	Number of grandparents alive at age 0				Number of grandparents alive at age 15			
	0–1	2	3	4	0–1	2	3	4
1900	.08	.26	.42	.25	.48	.35	.15	.02
1940	.02	.13	.40	.46	.29	.39	.26	.06
1976	.00	.05	.31	.63	.12	.33	.39	.16

[a]See text for details.
Sources: Same as Table 2.

Young Adults

The mortality decline since 1900 has greatly altered the prospects that a marriage between young adults will be broken by death before old age. If a man and woman marry when they are aged 25 and 22, the probability that either of them will die within 40 years after their marriage dropped from .67 in 1900 to .36 in 1976. This decline in early widowhood more than offsets the rise in divorce (Table 4), so that the stability of marriages during the childrearing years has actually increased over this century. When the declining age at completion of childbearing (Glick, 1977) is also considered, the higher probability of both husband and wife surviving to the empty nest stage of life is even more marked.

With current low mortality the prospective view of married life is quite different from what it was in the past. A man and a woman marrying at the average marriage age can anticipate jointly surviving a median of 45 years, i.e., until the husband is 70 years old. The prospect of living with one person over such a long period, especially when one anticipates significant but unknown social change, may influence one's view of marriage. In particular, it may cause higher uncertainty about whether or not the marriage can survive until broken by death. If a couple enters in marriage accepting the option of divorce as a possibility, the chances of actually ending the marriage with a divorce are probably increased. Further, the period of time in which a divorce can occur has been lengthened. Thus it seems likely that the decreasing likelihood of marital disruption due to death has contributed to the increased rate of divorce in recent years.

Another, and more frequently noted, effect of lowered death rates upon the family behavior of young adults concerns fertility decisions. As shown in Table 1, the experience of having an infant or child die has moved from a common to a very uncommon event for American parents. The great variability that existed in 1900 between the number of children ever born and the number who eventually reached adulthood has disappeared. It is now possible for parents to anticipate the survival of all their children through childhood. Thus, the planning of family size has

Table 4. Probability of Marital Disruption Due to Death or Divorce Within the First 40 Years: 1900; 1940; 1976.

Year	Broken by death[a]	Broken by death or divorce[a]
1900	.67	.71
1940	.50	.63
1976	.36	.60

[a]Assuming husband is 25 and wife is 22 at time of marriage.
Sources: Same as Table 2; plus Preston and McDonald, 1979; Glick, 1977.

become feasible, and the need to have additional children to protect against possible loss no longer exists. A couple bearing two children can now be almost 95 percent confident that both will reach age 20. Consequently, an interesting effect of lowered mortality is the downward pressure it exerts upon fertility.

Middle Aged

Discussions of the family role of the middle-aged have generally emphasized the changes involved as children leave home and as relationships with adult children are developed. Two ways of viewing the changes that occur when parents no longer have dependent children are noted by Winch (1971). On the positive side:

> With the fulfillment of the parental role and the consequent reduction of responsibilities comes the promise of a more relaxed mode of life and the ultimate leisure of retirement.

While on the negative side:

> The "empty nest" psychology implies that since the parents' job is completed, they are no longer needed. They may look forward to declining strength, declining productivity, declining health, and, usually, in retirement to diminished income.

Both of these views picture the post-parental phase as a period of greatly reduced family responsibility. Clearly the average length of this segment of life has grown as the probability of surviving into old age has increased. But interestingly, the fall in mortality is also altering the nature of the empty nest stage of life. Brody (1978) has nicely captured this change when she writes, "The 'empty nests' of some of the grandparents generation are being refilled with members of the great-grandparent generation."

An increasing number of persons entering the "young-old" stage of life have parents who are still living and who are in need of substantial assistance. Older people are not generally abandoned by their children. Rather, adult children are

Table 5.   Distribution of Middle-Aged Couples by Number of Their Parents Still
Alive Under Conditions in 1900, 1940, and 1976.

	Number of parents alive:			
Year	*0*	*1*	*2+*	*Total*
1900	.52	.38	.10	1.00
1940	.37	.43	.20	1.00
1976	.14	.39	.47	1.00

Sources: Same as Table 2.

now, as in the past, the primary care givers to the elderly in American society
(Brody, 1978; Sussman, 1976). The big change has not been in norms regarding
the responsibility of children to their elderly parents, but in the likelihood of a
middle-aged person faced with the actual situation of having parents still alive. A
quantitative assessment of the increased presence of parents for the middle-aged is
given in Table 5.

The number of parents and parents-in-law still alive for a husband aged 55 and
wife aged 52 under mortality conditions prevailing at selected historical periods is
shown. The calculations assumed that both husband and wife were born when
their fathers were aged 30 and their mothers were aged 27 (which is close to the
average age at parenthood over this century). As in the previous calculations,
period life tables are used to capture mortality conditions at specific time periods,
so the data do not reflect the experiences of actual cohorts. A shift from 1900
mortality conditions to those of 1976 implies an increase in the proportion of
middle-aged couples who have living parents from 48 to 86 percent. With 1976
mortality conditions, half of all middle-aged couples would have two or more
elderly parents alive.

Old Age

As discussed earlier, marital instability prior to old age has declined over this
century. At the same time, the remarriage rate for those with disrupted marriages
has increased. Consequently, a much larger proportion of men and women are
married and living with a spouse when they arrive at old age, and a slightly higher
proportion of the total older population is now married (51 percent in 1900 vs. 52
percent in 1970). But while these data indicate an increased involvement of older
persons in nuclear families, it is also true that the average number of years that
women spend in widowhood has greatly increased. The increased period of
widowhood is a result of the much greater improvement in life expectancy for
women than for men. The lengthening old-age period of life is increasingly
divided into two parts for women: an earlier phase in which they are married and a
later phase in which they are widows.

Table 6. Average Years of Life Remaining at Selected Ages for Men and Women in the U.S.: 1900; 1940; 1976.

	Life table values					
Year	$_a(1)$ $e22(F)$	$_a(2)$ $e25(M)$	(3) $(1)-(2)$	$_a(41)$ $e62(F)$	$_a(5)$ $e65(M)$	(6) $(4)-(5)$
1900	42.3	38.5	3.8	14.0	11.5	2.5
1940	49.5	43.3	6.2	15.6	12.1	3.5
1976	56.8	47.1	9.7	20.4	13.7	6.7

Sources: Same as Table 2.

Selected values of life expectancy from life tables for men and women are presented in Table 6. From these values it can be seen that under the given mortality conditions, the average number of years that a typical wife can expect to outlive her husband has increased from 3.8 in 1900 to 9.7 currently. Primarily as a consequence of the increasing survival advantage of females over males, the ratio of widows to widowers over age 65 has grown from 2.2:1 in 1900 to 5.6:1 in 1976. With such a large imbalance, remarriage is clearly an option for very few of the older widows. Therefore, mortality change has created a major increase in the significance of the final stage of life for women, a period of widowhood in which very few men are around. What the family experience of the rapidly growing number of older women, whose children themselves are approaching old age, will be is not entirely clear. In 1976, however, about 70 percent of the widows over age 65 were living either alone or in institutions (Metropolitan Life, 1977). Thus, a large majority of older women are now living their last years of life outside of a family context. Of course, this does not mean that they necessarily lack significant kinship links, but it does indicate that their daily life is not enmeshed in a family.

Conclusion

Declining mortality during the twentieth century has had a major impact upon the American family. The role of mortality as an independent variable producing change has been noted in the following areas:

1. Increasing survival prospects for infants has encouraged stronger emotional bonds between parents and children.
2. Decreasing deaths to adults aged 20 to 50 has reduced the proportion of children who experience orphanhood.
3. Decreasing mortality has eliminated the experience of a member of the nuclear family dying for most children.
4. Increasing survival rates has increased the number of living grandparents for children.

5. Decreasing mortality has increased the number of years that marriages survive without being disrupted by death. This change has probably contributed to the increase in divorce.
6. Decreasing infant and child deaths has allowed more careful planning of family size and has encouraged a reduction in fertility.
7. Increasing survival rates has lengthened the "empty nest" stage of the family.
8. Decreasing mortality has increased the number of elderly persons dependent upon middle-aged children.
9. Increasing survival advantages for women relative to men has lengthened the period of widowhood at the end of the life course.

Bibliography

Ariès, Phillippe
  1962   Centuries of Childhood: A Social History of Family Life. Robert Baldick, trans. New York: Random House.
Blauner, Robert
  1966   "Death and Social Structure," Psychiatry 29:378–394.
Brody, Elaine M.
  1978   "The Aging of the Family." The Annals 438:13–27.
Bumpass, Larry and Ronald Rindfuss
  1978   "Children's Experience of Marital Disruption." Paper presented at the Annual Meeting of the Population Association of America.
Glick, Paul
  1977   "Marrying, Divorcing, and Living Together in the U.S. Today." Population Bulletin 32.
Grabill, Wilson H., Clyde V. Kiser and Pascal K. Whelpton
  1958   The Fertility of American Women. New York: Wiley.
Habenstein, Robert W.
  1968   "The Social Organization of Death." In David L. Sills, ed. International Encyclopedia of the Social Sciences 4:26–28.
Metropolitan Life
  1977   "Widows in the United States." Statistical Bulletin 58:8–10.
NCHS
  1978   Vital Statistics of the United States, 1976, vol. 2-Section 5. Life Tables. Hyattsville: U.S. Department of HEW.
Preston, Samuel H. and John McDonald
  1979   "The Incidence of Divorce with Cohorts of American Marriages Contracted Since the Civil War." Demography 16:1–25.
Skolnick, Arlene
  1978   The Intimate Environment: Exploring Marriage and the Family. 2nd ed. Boston: Little, Brown and Co.
Sussman, Marvin B.
  1976   "The Family Life of Old People." In Robert H. Binstock and Ethel Shanas, eds., Handbook of Aging and the Social Sciences. New York: Van Nostrand Reinhold.
U.S. Bureau of the Census
  1978a   Current Population Reports, Series P-23, No. 70.
  1978b   Current Population Reports, Series P-23, No. 77.
U.S. Public Health Service
  1969   Vital Statistics of the United States: 1967, Vol. 2, Part A.
Winch, Robert F.
  1971   The Modern Family, 3rd ed. New York: Holt, Rinehart & Winston.

Chapter 2

Demographic Trends

The Trends: Marriage, Divorce, Remarriage

Andrew Cherlin

We often think of social change in terms of the differences between one generation and the next—between our parents' lives and our own lives or between our own lives and our children's lives. When we look at the trends in marriage, divorce, and remarriage in the United States since World War II, the experiences of two successive generations stand in sharp contrast: the men and women who married and had children in the late 1940s and 1950s, and their sons and daughters, who entered adulthood in the late 1960s and 1970s. Most of the members of the older generation were born in the 1920s and the 1930s, and they grew up during the Great Depression and the war years. This group is relatively small because fewer babies were born during the late 1920s and the hard times of the 1930s. But when they reached adulthood, this generation had a large number of children. About five out of six of the women whose peak childbearing years occurred in the 1950s gave birth to at least two children, and those births were bunched at an earlier time in their lives. The result was a great increase in births between the end of World War II and 1960, an increase which we now call the postwar baby boom. In 1957, at the peak of the boom, 4.3 million babies were born in the United States, compared to 2.4 million in 1937. (By comparison, there were 3.5 million births in 1979.) Thus the relatively small generation of parents in the 1950s gave birth to a much larger generation—the children of the baby boom.

In the 1950s, when the members of the older generation were in their twenties and thirties, the country's marriage rate was high and rising, and its divorce rate was relatively low and stable. But as the younger generation matured, all that changed. The divorce rate began to rise in the early 1960s and doubled between

1966 and 1976. As more and more young people put off marrying, the marriage rate fell, though the number of couples living together without marrying more than doubled in the 1970s. The birth rate fell to an all-time low.

In this chapter I compare the experiences of these two generations as they have married, divorced, and remarried. But we must be careful not to assume that just because the older generation came first, their family patterns were more typical of twentieth-century American family life. Put another way, we shouldn't assume that all the changes since the 1950s were deviations from the usual way of family life in the United States. In fact, I argue that the 1950s were the more unusual time, that the timing of marriage in the 1970s was closer to the typical twentieth-century pattern than was the case in the 1950s. The divorce experiences of both generations differed from the long-term trend in divorce. In addition, the rate of childbearing in the 1950s was unusually high by twentieth-century standards. A close look at the historical record, then, suggests that in some ways the 1970s were more consistent with long-term trends in family life than were the 1950s. . . .

Entering Marriage

One hardly needs to have the latest national statistics to know that young adults are not marrying as quickly as they were just ten or twenty years ago. Anyone who knows recent college graduates, for example, realizes that more and more of them are postponing marriage until their mid- or late twenties. Getting married within weeks of graduation—seemingly a symbol of success for many college women in the 1950s and early 1960s—is now much less common. In the past decade there also has been a great increase in the number of young adults who have moved in with someone of the opposite sex without marrying first. Some observers have expressed concern that the later age at marriage and the increase in "cohabitation" or "living together" might indicate a weakening of our system of marriage and family life. Others are more sanguine but believe that these changing patterns of coupling will alter American family life.

Almost every adult in the United States eventually marries, although is some eras people tend to marry earlier than in others. In the postwar period there have been sharp fluctuations in the timing of marriage, with an especially noticeable difference between the 1950s and the 1970s, as can be seen by comparing the lifetime experiences of several cohorts. Figure 1 shows the actual and projected marriage experiences of women born in the periods 1910 to 1914, 1920 to 1924, 1930 to 1934, 1940 to 1944, and 1950 to 1954. The graph displays for each cohort the estimated age at which 25, 50, and 75 percent of those who will ever marry [will] have already done so.

Figure 1 shows that there has been little change in the age by which one-quarter of all those women who will ever marry have done so. The age at which 50 percent have married—the median age of marrying for each cohort—shows more change. It was highest for the oldest cohort, then it declined by about one and one-half years for women born in the 1930s and 1940s, and more recently it has risen again.

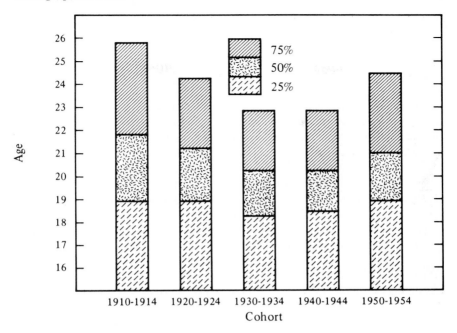

Figure 1.   Cumulative Percentage of All Marriages Occurring by a Given Age, for Five Birth Cohorts of Women from 1910 to 1954.

The figure that shows the most change is the age at which three-fourths have married: it was above twenty-five years for the 1910–1914 cohort, fell below twenty-three for the middle cohorts, and now has risen above twenty-four for the youngest cohort.

This pattern of change suggests that so far in this century a fixed proportion of women in any cohort marry early, regardless of the historical circumstances. Conversely, the variation in the timing of marriage mainly reflects the changing behavior of those women who tend to wait until their early twenties to marry. Among women born in the 1930s and 1940s, those who remained single through their teenage years married relatively quickly when they reached their early twenties. But in the preceding and succeeding cohorts, single women in their twenties took longer to marry. As a result, the spread between the 25 and 75 percent marks decreased from nearly seven years for the 1910 to 1914 cohort to about four years in the middle cohorts, and more recently it has increased to about five and a half years for the 1950 to 1954 cohort.

These changes do not necessarily imply that large numbers of the young women of the early 1980s will remain unmarried throughout their lives. Currently, as Figure 1 suggests, the timing of marriage for young women is becoming increasingly similar to that of cohorts born early in the century, and more than nine out of ten women in these older cohorts married eventually. In fact, more than 90 percent of the members of every birth cohort on record (records extend back to the mid-1800s) have eventually married. . . .

Childbearing

A brief look at trends in childbearing may tell us something about the differences between the parental generation of the 1950s and their children's generation. Most people are familiar with the broad outlines of the postwar trend in childbearing, or fertility, to use the demographer's term for childbearing: the annual birth rate spurted upward just after the war and then, after a brief respite, increased sharply during the 1950s. It then fell just as sharply in the 1960s and 1970s. We now know that during the 1950s women were having their first child earlier in their lives, and subsequent children were born closer together; after 1960 women had their first child at a later age and spaced subsequent children further apart. These trends in the timing of fertility—the accelerated pace of the 1950s and the postponement of the 1960s and 1970s—amplified the peaks and valleys of the baby boom and bust as measured by annual birth rates. We can obtain a more meaningful picture of the trends by examining the lifetime levels of fertility for different cohorts. The lifetime levels measure changes in the volume of childbearing over time, independent of changes in the timing of births during women's reproductive years.

Figure 2 displays the cohort total fertility rate for single-year birth cohorts of women born between 1891 and 1950, based on data assembled by Norman B. Ryder. The cohort total fertility rate is the mean number of children born per woman in a particular cohort. For cohorts of women past their reproductive years, this rate can be calculated from survey or birth registration data; for the more recent cohorts, future levels of fertility must be estimated. As can be seen in Figure 2, the mean number of births per woman born in 1891 was 3.0. This figure, as best we can tell, declined throughout the nineteenth century: it was 4.1 for the 1867 cohort and perhaps 7 or 8 for those born in the early 1800s. The total fertility rate declined to a low of 2.3 for the 1908 cohort—who came of age early in the depression—and then rose precipitously to a high of 3.2 for the 1933 cohort—who came of age in the 1950s—before beginning a steep slide to the estimated level of 1.9 for the 1950 cohort.

The graph demonstrates that trends in lifetime levels of childbearing in this century have followed a single, massive wave pattern that peaked with the cohorts of women who married and began to bear children in the decade following World War II. This great rise in fertility is at variance with the long-term historical decline in childbearing over the past 150 years. To be sure, Figure 2 and our sketchy knowledge of nineteenth-century fertility patterns also suggest that the fertility of the cohorts who reached adulthood during the depression was unusually low. And the fertility of the most recent cohorts appears to be at an all-time low, although that seems to be in line with the longer historical decline. The more

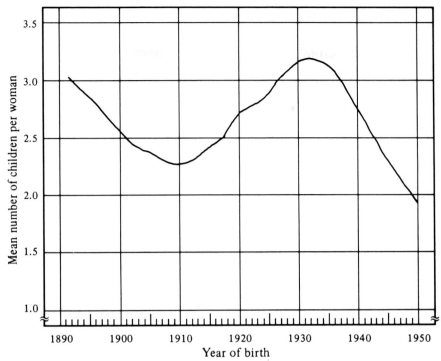

Source: Norman B. Ryder, "Components of Temporal Variations in American Fertility," in Robert W. Hiorns, ed., *Demographic Patterns in Developed Societies* (London: Taylor and Francis, 1980). pp. 15–54.

Figure 2   Cohort Total Fertility Rate for Single-Year Birth Cohorts, 1891 to 1950.

unusual phenomenon, in a long-term perspective, is the great increase in child-bearing among those born during the 1920s and 1930s. Cohort trends in childbearing, like trends in age at marriage, suggest that the cohorts who grew up during the depression and the war years—not the cohorts who grew up during the postwar years—stand out as more historically distinctive.

Marital Dissolution

No trend in American family life since World War II has received more attention or caused more concern than the rising rate of divorce. The divorce rate, however, has been rising since at least the middle of the nineteenth century. Figure 3 shows the number of divorces per 1,000 existing marriages (after 1920, per 1,000 married women) in every year between 1860 (the earliest year for which data are available) and 1978. These are annual measures, reflecting the particular social and economic conditions of each year. We can see, for example, that the annual

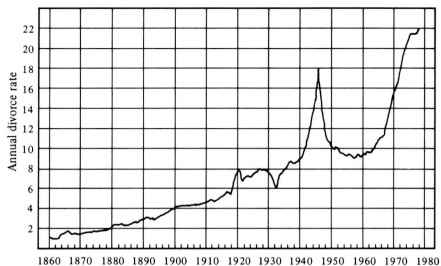

Sources: 1860–1920, Paul H. Jacobson, *American Marriage and Divorce* (New York: Rinehart, 1959), Table 42; 1920–1967, U.S. National Center for Health Statistics, Vital and Health Statistics, series 21, no. 24, *100 Years of Marriage and Divorce Statistics* (1973), Table 4; 1968–1978, U.S. National Center for Health Statistics, Vital Statistics Report, Advance Report, vol. 29, no. 4, supplement, *Final Divorce Statistics 1978,* Table 2.

Figure 3   Annual Divorce Rates, United States. For 1920–1978: Divorces Per 1,000 Married Women Aged 51 and over; for 1860–1920: Divorces Per 1,000 Existing Marriages.

rate of divorce increased temporarily after every major war: there is a slight bulge in the graph following the Civil War, a rise in 1919 and 1920 following World War I, and a large spike in the years immediately after World War II. We can also see how the depression temporarily lowered the divorce rate in the early 1930s: with jobs and housing scarce, many couples had to postpone divorcing until they could afford to do so.

Ignoring for the moment the temporary movements induced by war and depression, there is a slow, steady increase in the annual rate of divorce through the end of World War II. Since the war, however, the graph looks somewhat different. In the period from 1950 to about 1962 the annual rates are lower than what we would expect on the basis of the long-term rise. Then starting about 1962, the annual rates rise sharply, so that by the end of the 1970s the rate of divorce is well above what would be predicted from the long-term trend. Thus if we compare the annual rates from the 1950s with those from the 1970s, as many observers have tended to do, we are comparing a period of relatively low rates with a time of very high rates. The result is to make the recent rise loom larger than it would if we took the long-term view.

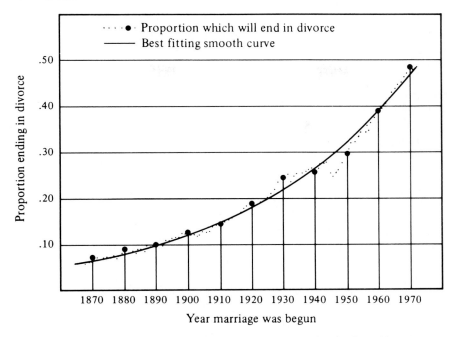

Figure 4   Proportion of Marriages Begun in Each Year that Will End in Divorce, 1867 to 1973.

It is true that the rise in annual divorce rates in the 1960s and 1970s is much steeper and more sustained than any increase in the past century, but to gauge the significance of this recent rise, it is necessary to consider the lifetime divorce experiences of adults, rather than just the annual rates of divorce. In Figure 4 the dotted line is an estimate of the proportion of all marriages begun in every year between 1867 and 1973 which have ended, or will end, in divorce before one of the spouses dies. Following conventional usage among demographers, I refer to all people marrying in a given year as a "marriage cohort." For marriage cohorts after 1910, the lifetime record is incomplete, and I have relied on projections prepared by Samuel H. Preston, John McDonald, and James Weed. Any projection, of course, can be undermined by future events, so the importance of Figure 4 lies more in the general trend it shows than in its precise estimates for recent marriage cohorts. We can see from the dotted line that the proportion of all marriages in a given year that eventually end in divorce has increased at a faster and faster rate since the mid-nineteenth century. Moreover, the increase has been relatively steady, without the large fluctuations which the annual rates show in times of war or depression.

In order to make the underlying long-term trend clearer, the graph also shows the smooth curve that most clearly fits the pattern of change in the proportions.

People who married in the years when the dotted line is above the smooth curve were more likely to become divorced than the long-term historical trend would lead us to expect; people who married in years when the dotted line is below the smooth curve were less likely to become divorced than would be expected. We can see, for instance, that although the annual divorce rates were temporarily low in the early 1930s, more of the people who married just before or during the depression eventually became divorced than we would expect from the long-term trend. The hardship and distress families suffered when husbands lost their jobs irrevocably damaged some marriages, and many unhappy couples later divorced after economic conditions improved enough to allow them to do so. Conversely, Figure 4 indicates that the lifetime proportions ever divorced for those marrying between the end of the war and the late 1950s probably will not reach the expected levels based on the long-term trend. To be sure, a greater proportion of them will divorce than was the case for previous marriage cohorts, but the increase will be modest by historical standards.

On the other hand, for those who married in the 1960s and early 1970s, the increase may exceed what would be predicted by the long-term trend. Couples who married in 1970, for instance, lived the early years of their marriage during a period of very high annual divorce rates. By 1977, only seven years after they had married, one-quarter of these couples had already divorced. In contrast, it was twenty-five years before one-quarter of those who married in 1950 had divorced. If the annual divorce rates stay the same in the 1980s and 1990s as they were in 1977, 48 percent of those who married in 1970 will eventually divorce, according to a recent estimate. . . . Scholars disagree on how fast the divorce rate will increase in the near future, but almost no one expects a drop in the annual rates. Barring an unforeseen downturn in divorce in the near future, then, for those marrying in the late 1960s and early 1970s the lifetime proportions ever divorced are likely to be exceptionally high, even compared to the long-term rise in divorce.

In sum, although annual measures of divorce often show large fluctuations from year to year or decade to decade, the lifetime proportions ever divorced for people marrying in a given year have risen in a regular fashion for the past century, with some variations. Those who married during the depression and those who married in the 1960s and early 1970s experienced even higher levels of divorce over their lifetimes than the historical trend would predict. And those who married in the decade or so following the war were the only cohorts in the last hundred years to show a substantial, sustained shortfall in their lifetime levels of divorce. This latter group, of course, includes most of the parents of the baby boom children. Figure 4 suggests that the lifetime level of divorce for the baby boom parents was unusually low: for their children it will be unusually high. . . .

Remarriages have been common in the United States since its beginnings, but until this century almost all remarriages followed widowhood. In the Plymouth Colony about one-third of all men and one-quarter of all women who lived full lifetimes remarried after the death of a spouse, but there was little divorce. Even as late as the 1920s, brides and grooms who were remarrying were more likely to have been widowed than divorced. Since then, however, the increase in divorce and the decline in mortality have altered the balance: by 1978, 87 percent of all brides who were remarrying were previously divorced, and 13 percent were widowed. For grooms who were remarrying in 1978, 89 percent were divorced. Thus it is only in recent decades that remarriage after divorce has become the predominant form of remarriage. And since the turn of the century, such remarriages have increased as a proportion of all marriages. In 1900 only 3 percent of all brides—including both the single and previously married—were divorced. In 1930 9 percent of all brides were divorced, and in 1978, 28 percent of all brides were divorced.

Part of this increase is caused simply by the greater proportion of divorced people in the general population. In addition, a greater proportion of divorced people remarry each year today than earlier in the century. In 1920 and again in 1940, about 100 out of every 1,000 divorced and widowed women aged fourteen to fifty-four remarried each year, but by the late 1960s the remarriage rate had jumped to more than 150 per 1,000. Although the rate has since dropped to 134 per 1,000 in the period 1975 to 1977, it is still considerably above earlier levels. The recent decline in the annual remarriage rates may mean that fewer divorced people will remarry in the future, but it also may reflect only a postponement of remarriage.

The upshot of all this is that most people who get divorced remarry. About five out of six men and about three out of four women remarry after a divorce, according to the experiences of the older generations alive today. And those who are going to remarry do so soon after their divorce: about half of all remarriages take place within three years after divorce. In addition, the average age at which people remarry appears to have declined somewhat during the century. Women born in 1910 to 1914 who remarried following divorce had a median age of about thirty-five when they remarried; for young adults in the 1970s and early 1980s, that median will probably be about thirty. . . .

An Overview

The indicators I have reviewed show that in attempting to summarize the changes in marriage, divorce, and remarriage since World War II, it is important to choose our frame of reference with care. We often contrast the situation of the 1950s with that of the 1970s, implicitly assuming that the 1950s were representative of family life throughout the first half of the century. Thus we sometimes conclude that the family patterns of the 1970s differ sharply overall from what was experienced in the past. But as I have shown in this chapter, this sweeping conclusion is unwarranted; in many respects it is the 1950s that stand out as more unusual.

Current Trends in Marriage and Divorce Among American Women

Arthur J. Norton and Jeanne E. Moorman

This study examines recent trends and future prospects regarding marriage and divorce patterns among women in the United States. Results indicate that first marriages are taking place later, more adult women will never marry at all, divorce has likely peaked, remarriage after divorce is becoming less frequent, and among current adult cohorts of women, those representing the first ten years of the baby boom are expected to have the highest incidence of divorce.

In the United States the period spanning the last two decades has been a time of remarkable change in attitudes and behavior regarding marriage. Change has been manifest in the frequency and timing of marriage as well as in the frequency and timing of marriage disruptions through separation and divorce.

The rise in the rate of divorce, particularly between 1965 and 1980, has been well documented (Cherlin, 1981; Glick, 1984). The relative stability in the rate of divorce since 1980 has been noted (Kemper, 1983), but largely because of the recency of this development, it has been subject to little research. Trends in age at marriage and in marriage rates, on the other hand, have continued into the 1980s to move in a pattern first established in the early 1970s. Age at first marriage has been increasing and marriage rates have been declining (Rogers and Thornton, 1985).

This article examines recent trends and future prospects regarding marriage and divorce among women in the United States. It focuses on first marriage, separation, divorce, and remarriage among adult women, with the emphasis on women in various age groups within the general range of 20 to 54 years old. This age span extends from the age representing the beginning of marriage and divorce experiences to the age by which most of the marrying and divorcing of women is completed.

The principal data in this article are from the June 1985 marriage and fertility history supplement to the Current Population Survey. This set of data is from the latest in a series of quinquennial surveys conducted by the Bureau of the Census and sponsored by the National Institute of Child Health and Human Development. These data provide the most recent comprehensive national information on marriage and divorce in the United States. The present study is one of the first of what will likely be many explorations of the 1985 data. In this survey, detailed marriage history questions were asked only of women. Earlier surveys in this series asked similar questions of men, but because of the high rate of proxy responses and the

This article is a revised version of a paper presented at the annual meeting of the Population Association of America, San Francisco, California, April 1986. From *Journal of Marriage and the Family*, February 1987, 49:1, pp. 3–14. Copyrighted 1987 by the National Council on Family Relations, 1910 West County Road B, Suite 147, St. Paul, MN 55113. Reprinted by permission.

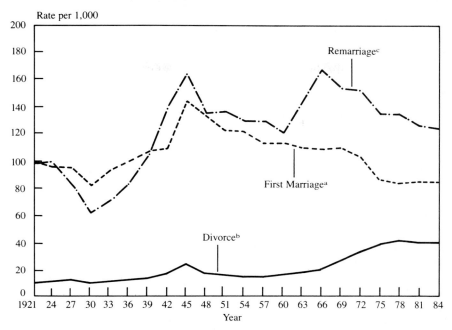

Rate per 1,000

Year

Source: U.S. National Center for Health Statistics, 1985a.
[a]First marriages per 1,000 single women 14 to 44 years old.
[b]Divorces per 1,000 married women 14 to 44 years old.
[c]Remarriages per 1,000 widowed and divorced women 14 to 54 years old.

Figure 1   Rates of First Marriage, Divorce, and Remarriage for U.S. Women: 1921–1984 (3-year averages).

resulting uncertainty regarding the quality of the survey results for men, they were dropped from the universe of the detailed section of the 1985 survey.

Basic Rates

Marriage, divorce, and remarriage rates have fluctuated considerably over the last half century, often in response to specific historical events (Norton and Glick, 1979). Figure 1 shows the change that has occurred in these rates during the last several years. The first marriage rate declined during the 1970s and has remained at low levels into the 1980s; the divorce rate increased sharply during the 1970s but has shown little movement thus far in the 1980s; the remarriage rate has continued a decline begun most recently during the late 1960s. The recent stabilizing of many of these rates may indicate a period-based hiatus, a reflection of differential cohort behavior, or the acceptance of and adjustment to a new set of societal norms or standards. It seems that a combination of these possibilities has resulted in the present situation and will dictate trends in the near future.

Table 1 shows the general nature of recent trends in marriage behavior by offering both a cohort and a period perspective covering the years from 1975 to 1985. The proportion ever married for 5-year age groups of young women 20 through 39 years old has declined. At ages 40 to 54, there is little difference in the proportions ever married for each 5-year age group at each date shown. Although about 95% of all women 40 to 54 were reported as ever having been married according to surveys in 1975, 1980, and 1985, there is a strong possibility that this overall proportion may fall somewhat for several of the younger cohorts. It seems unlikely, given the extent of nonmarriage (as of 1985) among women under 35, that these women will marry at sufficiently higher rates in their later years to attain an ultimate proportion ever marrying of 95%. A 90% proportion ever marrying seems more plausible.

There were significant increases in divorce after first marriage for 5-year cohorts of women over age 30 during the 1975–1985 period. However, for women in their 20s, the proportion divorced after first marriage rose between 1975 and 1980 but did not change significantly between 1980 and 1985. Insofar as divorce is and will continue to be disproportionately an activity of young adults, these figures may suggest the beginning of an overall stabilization, if not diminution, of the rate of divorce after first marriage for women currently in their 20s. Possible stabilization notwithstanding, the figures for divorce after first marriage indicate that divorce overall is more prevalent than ever before and that women currently in their 30s will probably establish record high proportions ever divorced, as nearly one-third of ever-married women 35 to 39 in 1985 had already ended a first marriage by divorce.

As the frequency of divorce has increased, so has the proportion of ever-married women who have been married more than once. Among women 35 to 39 and 40 to 44, the proportion married more than once has risen from 17% in 1975 to 22% in 1985. Largely, this increase reflects patterns of remarriage after divorce. Given the overall increase in divorce, one might have expected the increase in the percentage married more than once (among ever-married women who were old enough to have had a reasonable risk of marital dissolution and subsequent remarriage) to be greater than it has been. This would have been the case if the remarriage proportions for 1975 had remained constant for 1980 and 1985. However, the overall remarriage proportion for women 20 to 54 had dropped since 1975, and although remarriage remains widespread, it seems reasonable to expect that the eventual proportion of divorced women who remarry will fall from the 75% usually cited (Norton and Glick, 1979; Glick, 1984). The data in Table 1 do not reflect duration in status and therefore the period comparisons are offered as general indicators only.

As divorce and remarriage have become more common, the incidence of redivorce has also risen and now numerically offers a more reasonable possibility than before for statistical presentation and analysis. An estimated 1.3 million women 20 to 54 years old in 1985 had redivorced. They represent 16% of the 7.9 million women of that age who had remarried after divorce and about 10% of the 12.6 million women who ended a first marriage in divorce.

Table 1. Marriage Experience for Women 20 to 54 Years Old, by Age, Race, and Spanish Origin: 1975, 1980, and 1985

Category	All races			White			Black			Spanish origin	
	1975[a]	1980	1985	1975	1980	1985	1975	1980	1985	1980	1985
Percentage ever married											
20–54	87.5	82.5	79.9	88.6	84.2	82.1	79.8	70.6	64.7	81.4	81.1
20–24	62.5	49.5	43.3	64.9	52.2	46.6	47.5	33.3	23.9	55.4	56.7
25–29	87.2	78.6	74.0	88.8	81.0	77.4	76.5	62.3	53.4	80.2	78.4
30–34	93.1	89.9	85.8	93.9	91.6	88.1	87.1	77.9	70.9	88.3	88.0
35–39	95.5	94.3	91.6	96.2	95.3	93.1	90.1	87.4	80.7	91.2	91.6
40–44	95.8	95.1	94.6	95.9	95.8	95.6	95.1	89.7	86.1	94.2	90.3
45–49	95.9	95.9	94.4	95.9	96.4	95.1	95.4	92.5	88.4	94.4	91.1
50–54	95.8	95.3	95.2	96.0	95.8	95.4	94.6	92.1	93.4	95.0	92.5
Percentage divorced after first marriage											
20–54	18.4	23.1	26.8	18.1	22.8	26.7	21.7	27.4	30.6	18.3	19.5
20–24	11.2	14.2	13.9	11.3	14.7	14.4	10.6	10.5	11.0	9.4	11.0
25–29	17.1	20.7	21.0	17.7	21.0	21.5	15.3	20.2	18.2	13.9	14.8
30–34	19.8	26.2	29.3	20.0	25.8	29.0	20.5	31.4	34.4	21.1	19.2
35–39	21.5	27.2	32.0	21.2	26.7	32.0	22.7	32.9	34.6	21.9	26.3
40–44	20.5	26.1	32.1	19.7	25.5	32.0	27.4	33.7	36.9	19.7	22.8
45–49	21.0	23.1	29.0	20.3	22.7	28.4	26.9	29.0	36.0	23.9	24.3
50–54	18.0	21.8	25.7	16.8	21.0	24.6	29.7	29.0	33.7	22.5	21.8
Percentage remarried after divorce											
20–54	66.0	62.7	62.2	67.5	64.4	64.3	55.9	51.2	45.7	54.1	55.1
20–24	47.9	45.5	44.3	50.1	47.0	46.0	(B)	(B)	(B)	(B)	(B)
25–29	60.2	53.4	55.3	62.0	56.4	58.3	43.1	27.9	25.4	(B)	50.5
30–34	64.4	60.9	61.4	67.5	63.3	64.3	41.8	42.0	41.1	58.3	44.9
35–39	69.5	64.9	63.0	70.9	66.9	64.9	62.6	50.6	44.8	45.2	57.1
40–44	69.7	67.4	64.7	71.9	68.6	67.5	57.1	58.4	45.4	(B)	50.6
45–49	69.6	69.2	67.9	70.7	70.4	69.6	61.7	62.7	54.6	(B)	78.9
50–54	73.5	72.0	68.2	73.4	72.6	68.4	73.7	72.7	64.3	(B)	(B)
Percentage redivorced after remarriage											
20–54	NA	22.9	26.0	NA	23.0	25.6	NA	22.0	30.7	17.7	25.7
20–24	NA	8.5	8.7	NA	9.0	8.3	NA	—	—	—	(B)
25–29	NA	15.6	18.2	NA	15.6	18.1	NA	(B)	(B)	(B)	(B)
30–34	NA	19.1	20.0	NA	19.4	18.8	NA	19.6	33.1	(B)	(B)
35–39	NA	24.7	26.9	NA	25.4	27.4	NA	16.9	20.6	(B)	22.6
40–44	NA	28.4	33.0	NA	29.2	31.8	NA	23.8	45.8	(B)	(B)
45–49	NA	25.1	33.8	NA	26.4	34.8	NA	17.0	28.0	(B)	(B)
50–54	NA	29.0	27.3	NA	27.5	26.9	NA	35.9	28.9	(B)	(B)

Note: (B) = base is less than 75,000.
— = value rounds to zero.
[a]U.S. Bureau of the Census, 1976 and 1977.

White and black women and women of Spanish origin (who may be of any race) have followed the same overall patterns of change in marriage behavior as the general population, although intergroup differences do exist. Compared to white women, black women have had lower proportions ever married at young ages over the last several decades, but generally the proportions ultimately marrying have been similar (around 95%). However, the data for 1975 through 1985 indicate a widening of the differential between blacks and whites in the overall likelihood of ever marrying (blacks less likely). Black women experienced much more dramatic drops during the past 10 years in the proportion ever married at ages 30 to 34 and 35 to 39 than white women (whose experiences mirror those of the total population)—a development that could result in a differential of at least 10% between white and black women in proportion eventually marrying. Women of Spanish origin, for whom survey marriage history data are available only for 1980 and 1985, have patterns of entry into first marriage that are similar to those of white women.

Black women have maintained higher divorce proportions than white women. In recent years the difference between young black and white women in the incidence of divorce after first marriage appears to have diminished. Women of Spanish origin have shown a slight upward trend in divorce after first marriage during the period from 1980 to 1985 but overall maintained a lower rate of divorce than either white or black women.

Remarriage after divorce, without being controlled for length of exposure, appears to be more likely for white women than for black women. The number of cases in the survey is too small for meaningful analytic comparisons of remarriage and redivorce proportions by race and Spanish origin.

Timing of Marital Events

Age at first marriage has risen in recent years, as shown through depressed marriage rates and the estimates of the median age at first marriage that are routinely published in annual Census Bureau reports. The latter show an increase of more than two years in the estimated median age at first marriage for women, from 21.1 in 1975 to 23.3 in 1985 (U.S. Bureau of the Census, 1985b). The well-established trend of increasing age at first marriage has been accompanied by fluctuations in the lengths of intervals between other marital events. Figure 2 shows the median duration of first marriage before first divorce, of first divorce before remarriage, and of remarriage before redivorce for 1975, 1980, and 1985. In each case, the interval declined between 1975 and 1980 and increased between 1980 and 1985. These figures indicate that the period of the late 1970s was not only a time of climbing divorce rates but also that divorce, remarriage, and redivorce were taking place within a relatively shorter span of years than has been the case since 1980. Other data indicate that a shortening of these intervals began in the late 1960s (Glick and Norton, 1973) and continued through the 1970s. Thus, the years spanning 1980 to 1985 differ considerably from those of the 1970s with

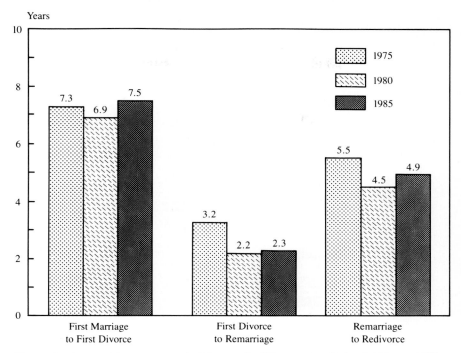

Figure 2   Interval between Marital Events for Women Aged 15 to 74 Years: 1975, 1980, and 1985.

respect to marital events beyond first marriage in that the last five years may be characterized as a time of relatively stable rates and relatively longer (or at least unchanging) durations in status. These aggregate medians for all women could change appreciably once women in the currently younger age groups complete their marrying and divorcing experience.

Figures 3 shows median intervals between marital events for women by race and Spanish origin. Between 1980 and 1985, the durations between events generally increased and did so in a way that reduced the differences between the groups. The median duration of first marriage before divorce was virtually the same for white, black, and Spanish-origin women according to the 1985 data, whereas the 1980 data show some evidence that blacks had a shorter interval than whites. Even though timing patterns for remarriage after divorce and for redivorce are becoming more alike, the differentials between white and black women in the probability of remarriage and redivorce are increasing. Whites are more likely than blacks to remarry after divorce, but among those who do remarry, blacks are more likely than whites to redivorce. Data for women of Spanish origin indicate little change during the 1980–85 period in the occurrence of divorce, remarriage, and redivorce—they have the lowest probability of divorce and in 1985 were intermediate between whites and blacks in remarriage.

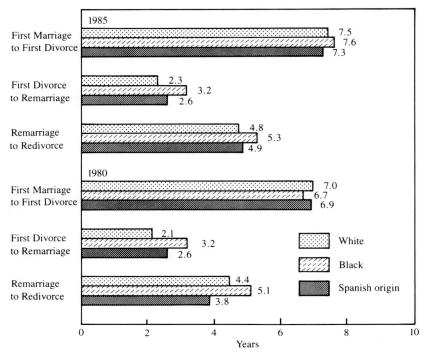

Figure 3   Interval Between Marital Events for Women Aged 15 to 74 Years, by Race and Spanish Origin: 1985 and 1980.

Questions regarding the date of physical separation from spouses were asked for the first time in a Census Bureau survey in June 1980 and repeated in the June 1985 survey. Thus, data on the time from marital separation to divorce is available from the 1980 and 1985 surveys. Perhaps the most important information about separation to be gained from the recent surveys pertains to the length of time spent in a separated status prior to ending a marriage in divorce, because this interval is often a period of the most intense need for those involved in a marital disruption. There has been an increase in the estimated median interval of separation before first divorce, from .8 years in 1980 to 1.2 years in 1985. The intervals for white women and women of Spanish origin in 1985 were identical at 1.1 years, while black women had an interval of 1.4 years between separation and divorce. The facts that the median interval between separation and divorce is still relatively brief and that the interval between divorce and remarriage is increasing (and that the frequency of remarriage is declining) appear to contradict the notion that the prospect of imminent remarriage is the primary motivation for ending a separation in divorce. On the other hand, one might argue that the increase between 1980 and

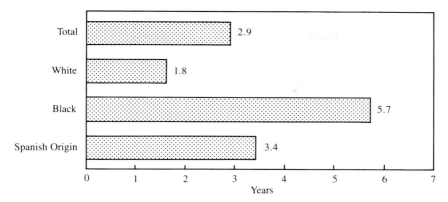

Figure 4   Median Years Separated After First Marriage for Currently Separated Women Aged 15 Years and Over, by Race and Spanish Origin: 1985.

1985 in the interval between separation and divorce implies more uncertainty regarding remarriage prospects. Still, the decision to divorce eventually may be less tied to remarriage prospects than was once supposed.

Being separated and not yet divorced or reconciled is a much more likely status for black women than for women of Spanish origin or white women, although the differential seems to be decreasing. In 1980, 17% of black women who had been married once were reported as separated at the survey date, compared with 8% of the women of Spanish origin and 3% of white women. By 1985, the percentage of once-married black women who were separated dropped to 13%, while the proportions separated for women of Spanish origin and white women remained at their 1980 levels. In both years, black women were disproportionately represented among separated women. Forty percent of the separated women in 1980 were black, while black women comprised only about 10% of all women. This over-representation existed in 1985, but to a slightly lesser extent, with black women representing 36% of all separated women and 10% of all women. This pattern is the same for twice-married women, but the differentials are smaller. It has been said that black separated women are more likely to be involved in long-term separations than other groups of women (Cherlin, 1981). In recent years, divorce has become much more readily available to all economic and demographic groups, and as was shown earlier, the frequency and times of divorce is becoming more homogeneous across traditionally disparate groups. Nevertheless, there remains a significant difference in the level and character of separation between black and other women. Figure 4 shows that the median duration of separation for all women who were still separated from their first husband at the survey date, June 1985, was 2.9 years. For white women, the median time separated was 1.8 years, for women of Spanish origin it was 3.4 years, and for black women it was 5.7 years. Although differences are becoming less distinct over time between

Table 2.   Percentage of Women Divorced from Their First Spouse, by Age at First Marriage

Age at first marriage	1985	1980[a]	1970[b]
Total	23.2	20.2	14.2
Under 20 years	32.4	27.5	19.6
20 to 24 years	18.2	16.2	10.9
25 to 29 years	13.6	12.9	9.2
30 years and over	11.8	13.8	9.1

[a]U.S. Bureau of the Census, 1985a.
[b]U.S. Bureau of the Census, 1973.

black women and other women with respect to first marriage disruption, blacks apparently still rely more heavily than other groups on separation as a way of functionally ending a marriage.

Additional Stratifiers

The probability of divorce and the probability of remarriage have been found to vary considerably by sociodemographic status (Glenn and Supancic, 1984. Glick, 1984). This section explores the relationship between marriage behavior and certain sociodemographic characteristics.

Table 2 shows that the long-standing increased risk of teenage marriages ending in divorce has continued into the mid-1980s. The percentage of ever-married women who had ended their first marriage in divorce increased from 14.2 in 1970 to 23.2 in 1985. For women who first married before age 20, however, the figures were 19.6% in 1970 and 32.4% in 1985—roughly twice the comparable percentages for women who first married in their 20s. It has been reported that women who first marry after age 30 are also more likely to divorce than those who marry in their 20s (Glick and Norton, 1979). While there was surface evidence to support this finding in 1980, closer inspection of available data indicates that when timing patterns of divorce are considered, women who marry after age 30 may actually have more stable marriages than women who marry in their 20s. For the 1970 and 1980 census data shown in Table 3, the proportion divorced for marriages of 5 or fewer years duration was higher for women first married after age 30 than for women first married in their 20s.

This higher proportion divorced for women first married at age 30 years or older is not evident in the 1985 CPS data nor when the marriage occurred more than 10 years prior to the census. The reason for this apparent increased incidence of divorce within 5 years of marriage in the census data for women first married after age 30 can be explained as a timing difference. Table 4 shows that 47% of those first married at age 30 years or older who had divorced had done so within 5 years of marriage, while only 41% of those married at younger ages who subsequently

Table 3.   Percentage of Women Divorced After First Marriage

Age at First Marriage	Years married prior to census or survey		
	0 to 5	6 to 10	11 to 20
	Year of first marriage		
CPS: 1985	1980–1985[a]	1975–1979	1965–1974
Total	8.0	24.6	33.8
Under 20 years	12.3	33.5	44.3
20 to 24 years	6.8	20.0	26.1
25 to 29 years	5.8	18.0	22.0
30 years and over	6.4	16.8	19.6
	Year of first marriage		
Census: 1980[b]	1975–1980[c]	1970–1974	1960–1969
Total	9.1	23.6	28.0
Under 20 years	11.6	30.1	36.3
20 to 24 years	7.2	19.2	22.3
25 to 29 years	7.2	17.0	19.3
30 years and over	12.4	19.1	19.0
	Year of first marriage		
Census: 1970[d]	1965–1970[e]	1960–1964	1950–1959
Total	5.4	13.3	16.4
Under 20 years	7.4	18.0	22.6
20 to 24 years	3.6	9.1	11.9
25 to 29 years	3.9	8.3	10.5
30 years and over	6.2	9.8	10.5

[a]January 1980 to June 1985.
[b]U.S. Bureau of the Census, 1985a.
[c]January 1975 to April 1980.
[d]U.S. Bureau of the Census, 1973.
[e]January 1965 to April 1970.

divorced had done so within the 5-year period. The median duration of marriage for women who divorce is 7.4 years, while the median for women first marrying at age 30 years or older is 6.1 years. These results suggest that women married at age 30 or older are less likely to divorce, but that if a divorce is going to occur, it will occur relatively earlier in the marriage. Further evidence that this is a timing difference can be seen when one compares the 1975–1980 marriage cohort from the 1980 census data with the 1975–1979 cohort from the 1985 CPS data. There is some evidence that by 1985 the percentage divorced for those married after age 30 was less than for those married in their 20s, rather than greater.

Table 4.   Percentage of Women Divorced, by Age at First Marriage and Duration of Marriage: 1985

| | | Duration of first marriage | | | | | |
Age at first marriage	Total divorced (in thousands)	0–5 Years	6–10 Years	11–15 Years	16–20 Years	21 or more years	Median
Total	17,141	40.6	25.1	15.0	9.2	10.2	7.4
Under 20 years	9,884	41.1	25.1	15.2	9.2	9.3	7.3
20 to 24 years	5,636	39.2	25.1	15.1	8.8	11.8	7.6
25 to 29 years	1,145	40.0	25.6	12.9	10.8	10.8	7.5
30 years and over	474	47.3	23.5	13.5	8.3	7.5	6.1

The change over time in the percentage divorced for recent marriages (0 to 5 years prior to the census or survey) by age at first marriage is quite remarkable. Between the 1970 census and the 1985 CPS, the percentage of recent marriages of teenagers that had ended in divorce within 5 years increased from 7.4% to 12.3%. For all other age-at-first-marriage cohorts, the percentage increased between the censuses but declined between the 1980 census and the 1985 CPS. It seems clear that a general inverse relationship between age at first marriage and prospects for divorce can be asserted and that the difference in the likelihood of divorce between women who marry in their teens and women who marry at older ages is growing.

The marital and fertility history surveys allow the analyst to consider the effects of premarital childbearing on eventual marital stability. About 9% of ever-married women in 1985 had at least one premarital birth and 10% had a premarital conception (birth within 7 months of marriage). Twenty-seven percent of women with a premarital birth or conception had ended their first marriage in divorce by the survey date, while 22% of women with no premarital births or conceptions were divorced from their first husband. This higher proportion divorced for women with premarital births or conceptions holds for all age groups (Table 5), ranging from a difference of 3 to 4 percentage points for those aged 20 to 29 years to a difference of 5 to 6 percentage points for those aged 50 to 59 years. Thus, having borne or conceived a child before marriage increases the likelihood of eventual divorce.

In the context of the overall relationship between childbearing and divorce, one might expect that one of the consequences of divorce would be reduced childbearing as a result of reduced exposure time for legitimate childbearing. This does in fact hold true, but only for divorced women over age 60 at the time of the 1985 survey and for those divorced women who have not remarried. Those who have remarried after divorce from their first spouse actually have a higher average number of children ever born (2.40) than those in an intact first marriage (2.22), while those in an intact first marriage have a higher average than those who are

Table 5.   Percentage of First Marriages Ending in Divorce, by Age and Whether the Woman had a Premarital Birth or Conception: 1985

| | | | | Percentage divorced | |
| | | | | *Premarital birth or conception* | | |
Age	*Total ever-married (in thousands)*	*Total*	*None*	*Conception*	*Birth*
15 years or older	73,971	23.2	22.2	27.4	27.3
Under 20 years	575	4.4	6.1	0	(B)[a]
20 to 29 years	12,473	18.4	17.6	21.3	20.5
30 to 39 years	16,770	30.6	29.4	35.2	34.4
40 to 49 years	12,443	30.7	29.4	35.5	35.4
50 to 59 yeras	11,100	23.5	22.7	27.5	28.6
60 years or older	20,646	15.8	15.6	16.2	18.2

[a](B) = base is less than 75,000.

divorced from their first spouse and have not remarried (1.99). The average number of children born before divorce from a first spouse, on the other hand, is only 1.41 for women who have remarried, which suggests that a considerable amount of childbearing occurs after divorce from their first husband (1.41 children born before divorce and 2.40 children ever born).

The presence (or absence) of children is a topic often included in the discussion of divorce. The U.S. National Center for Health Statistics (1985b) reports that over 1 million children were involved in divorces each year since 1972. They indicate that there is no evidence that divorcing couples have either more or fewer children than the general population of married couples. In 1982 the average number of children per divorce decree was 0.94, while the average number of children in married-couple families was 0.93.

Data from the June 1985 CPS for women aged 15 to 75 with 0 to 5 children show that 29% of women were childless at the time of divorce, 51% had 1 or 2 children, 17% had 3 children, and 3% had 4 or 5 children. This represents very little, if any, change since June 1975 (28%, 51%, 12%, and 9%, respectively). There was, similarly, little change in the distribution of women by age at divorce and number of children at the time of divorce. The only notable change is the increase in the percentage of divorced women aged 30 to 39 at divorce with 3 children (19% in 1975, 27% in 1985) and the corresponding decrease in the percentage with 4 or 5 children (16% in 1975, 5% in 1985). A similar trend is seen for women over age 40 at divorce. This is probably a reflection of the lower parity of younger women. Other than this one shift, there is little difference in these data between the 1975 and 1985 surveys.

Not unexpectedly, a majority of women (age 15–75 with 0 to 5 children) who had divorced from their first marriage had remarried by the time of the survey

(64%). Again, consistent with earlier survey figures, the younger the woman was at the time of divorce, the more likely she was to have remarried (74% for women under age 30 at divorce). At first glance, childless women also appear to be more likely to have remarried (70%) than women with one child or two or more children (67% and 58%, respectively). However, when both age at divorce and number of children are considered, the apparent effect of number of children is diminished and, in some cases, reversed. Among women in their 30s at the time of the divorce, there was no statistically significant difference between the remarriage percentages for women with one or more children and childless women. Childless women divorced before age 30 were the most likely to have remarried (77%); however, only slightly fewer women under age 30 who had children had also remarried (73%). Clearly, age at divorce has the greater effect on remarriage, while the number of children at the time of divorce has little, if any, effect within age-at-divorce cohorts. Koo and Suchindran (1980) found similar results using the June 1975 survey.

Table 6 shows the percentage of ever-married women who divorced after first marriage and the percentage of divorced women who remarried by education for women in the age groups 35 to 39 and 45 to 49 years. These ages were chosen because they represent women who are old enough to have completed their education and to have had meaningful exposure to the risk of marriage, divorce, and remarriage. The data on divorce and education appear to support the so-called Glick effect (Glenn and Supancic, 1984), which suggests that people with an incomplete education (e.g., those who apparently stopped short of earning a diploma or degree) are more likely to divorce than people who attain exact diploma or degree levels. However, the comparison by education category from the 1985 data do not in themselves show statistically significant differences at the 95% confidence level. Table 6 also indicates a generally inverse relationship between educational attainment and percentage remarried.

Summary and Conclusions

This article has described recent trends in marriage behavior among American women. Survey results reflecting the marriage histories of women have been used to show that first marriages are taking place later, and more currently young adult women (particularly blacks) than ever before will never marry during their lifetimes—although a large majority will still marry; that remarriage after divorce is becoming less frequent; that the first five years of the 1980s have been quite different from the last 5 years of the 1970s (the late 1970s represent a time when marital dissolution in the United States very likely reached its highest point, while the early 1980s appear to represent the beginning of a period of relative stability); and that data for the 1980s indicate that divorce rates are leveling, after increasing for nearly two decades. Certain variables commonly thought of as being associated with divorce and remarriage have been investigated, with the following results: women who first marry in their teens are more likely to have ended that

Table 6.   Divorce and Remarriage by Education for Women, by Age: 1985

Years of school completed and marriage experience	*Age (years)*	
	35 to 39	*45 to 49*
Percentage divorced after first marriage		
0–11 years	38.5	31.3
12 years	31.8	27.9
13 to 15 years	35.2	31.6
16 years	24.1	22.6
17 or more years	26.4	32.1
Percentage remarried after divorce		
0–11 years	66.7	79.0
12 years	64.0	70.2
13 to 15 years	61.0	59.3
16 years	62.3	53.9
17 or more years	56.2	45.1

marriage in divorce, as are women who marry after a premarital birth or give birth within 7 months after marriage; first marriages of older women (over age 30) are the most stable, although those who do divorce tend to do so sooner than women who marry at younger ages; the presence or absence of children does not affect either divorce or remarriage figures to an appreciable degree; a considerable amount of childbearing occurs among women who remarry after divorce from their first spouse; women with incomplete units of education are most likely to divorce; and educational attainment is inversely related to remarriage.

Recent surveys and other data sources have provided the basis for reporting trends through 1985 and the basis for analytic judgments about the meaning of the trends. We now take judgmental speculation one step further and offer some projections of the eventual levels of divorce, remarriage, and redivorce for selected cohorts of women. For these estimates we used basic double decrement life table methodology with a slight variation. Rather than assuming that current age-specific divorce rates would remain constant, we allowed the divorce rates to vary. For the life table for women currently 35 to 39 years old, the age-specific rates for each successively older age group were increased by 50%. For the life table for women currently 25 to 29 years old, the age-specific rates were decreased by 5%. These figures were chosen to reflect the changes in the percentage divorced by age as shown in Table 1 and the generally slower pace of entry into first marriage for the youngest women. The age-specific divorce rates used as a baseline were 1983 vital statistic rates; and it was assumed that no divorce occurred after age 74.

Figure 5 shows projected levels of divorce for women 25 to 29, 35 to 39, and 45 to 49 in 1985. The age groups were selected to represent a cohort that has

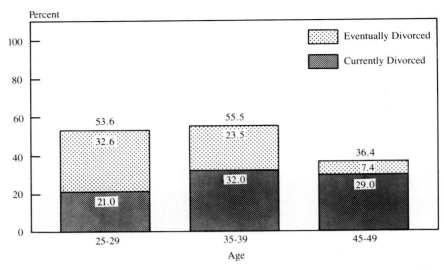

Figure 5   Percentage Currently (1985) and Eventually Divorced After First Marriage for Ever-Married Women, by Age.

completed most of its relevant marriage experience (45 to 49 years old), a cohort that represents, in the extreme, the uniqueness of the baby boom (35 to 39 years old), and a cohort that has had some marriage experience but is still young enough to be considered at the initial stages of the marital life course (25 to 29 years old).

Figure 5 shows that nearly one-third of ever-married women aged 35 to 39 had ended a first marriage in divorce by the 1985 survey date and that a projected figure of about 56% may eventually end a first marriage in divorce. The projection for this age group is greater than that for women 10 years older and 10 years younger. About 36% of the women 45 to 49 years old may eventually end a first marriage through divorce and about 54% of the women aged 25 to 29 may be expected to do so. Each of these projections indicates a very high divorce experience, but especially for the cohort 35 to 39 years old. This group is unique for a number of reasons, one of which is that they represent the vanguard of the post-World War II baby boom. A decade ago it was apparent that the first members of the baby boom to reach adulthood were deviating from past patterns of marriage and divorce. Figure 5 shows not only how extreme their deviation has been and is expected to be but also how their actions have possibly influenced other cohorts. It can be argued that the oldest baby boomers were at once deviant and trend setters whose extraordinarily high divorce experience, although somewhat anomalous, also helped to establish new normative societal standards that permit a generally high rate of divorce. To illustrate how dramatically things have changed within the span of a generation (defined here as 20 years), one need only consider the projected proportion to divorce eventually among women aged 55 to 59 in 1985—24%. Divorce rates are also sensitive to nondemographic events, and it is certain that the rates presented in this article are the result of a number of interacting factors. For example, the war in Vietnam, technical advances in fertility control, and the rising employment of women also may have been associated with the divorce behavior of the early baby boomers (Cherlin, 1981). Thus, economic cycles, political events, technological developments, and social, cultural, and psychological changes as well as demographic characteristics collectively and sometimes individually influence behavior.

Economic cycles or rapid technological development generally exercise a "period" influence on divorce (e.g., the rates rise or fall according to some momentary stimuli). Characteristics of a particular birth cohort (as in the special case of the baby boom cohorts) can exercise an overriding "cohort" influence on divorce rates. The rising divorce rates of the 1970s and the stable rates of the first half of the 1980s reflect a combination of period and cohort influences. The oldest members of the baby boom were of peak divorcing age in the 1970s, which was also a time of rapid institutional change in many other spheres. In the 1980s, the early baby boomers have aged just beyond the highest divorcing years, while society at large may have entered a period of adjusting to several new behavioral standards created during the previous decade. These are the most plausible theoretical explanations for recent divorce trends. Other factors, such as uncertainty associated with a recession economy (in the early 1980s), may also have made an important contribution to stabilizing the divorce rate.

The majority of women who divorce eventually remarry. However, the proportion remarrying appears to be declining. Recent analyses of this topic have indicated that about three-quarters of the women who divorce ultimately remarry (Glick, 1984). The results of the 1985 survey imply that remarriage following divorce will be somewhat less common in the future than in the recent past. An informed guess about the percentage of divorced women who eventually remarry would be that the overall proportion will fall to at least 70%. This speculation is based upon inspection of results of the 1975, 1980, and 1985 surveys. The data show an impressive pattern of decline for adult age groups in the proportion of divorced women who had remarried by the survey date.

Redivorce for women married twice has also shown signs of decline. Overall, the data suggest that in the future the incidence of redivorce may be quite similar to the incidence of first divorce.

These exercises to predict future marriage patterns are intended only to illustrate in the broadest possible way what the general direction of the future may be. It appears that both first marriages and remarriages after divorce will be relatively more stable than in the past and that first marriages and remarriages will be relatively less frequent than in the past. Divorce, remarriage, and redivorce may have peaked in the late 1970s and will probably recede to some new normative level. If this happens, it will be an important but not dramatic change. Most adults will marry, and the incidence of divorce in the United States is likely to remain among the highest in the world.

This article is intended to chronicle recent change and suggest some plausible future trends. Marriage, separation, divorce, remarriage, and redivorce are all a prominent and permanent part of our social system. Each status has important consequences for social and economic institutions and for individuals touched by these events. We now accept and are trying to adjust to a more complex human life course and to develop meaningful relational networks as well as programs and policies that will assist people (children, adults, and the elderly) as they pass into and out of various statuses in life.

References

Cherlin, Andrew J. 1981. *Marriage, Divorce, Remarriage*. Cambridge, MA: Harvard University Press.

Glenn, Norval, and Michael Supancic. 1984. "The social and demographic correlates of divorce and separation in the United States: An update and reconsideration." *Journal of Marriage and the Family* 46: 563–576.

Glick, Paul C. 1984. "Marriage, divorce, and living arrangements: Prospective changes." *Journal of Family Issues* 5: 7–26.

Glick, Paul C., and Arthur J. Norton. 1973. "Perspectives on the recent upturn in divorce and remarriage." *Demography* 10: 301–314.

Glick, Paul C., and Arthur J. Norton. 1979. "Marrying, divorcing, and living together in the U.S. today." *Population Bulletin* 32 (February): 1–40.

Kemper, Theodore D. (1983). "Predicting the divorce rate: Down?" *Journal of Family Issues* 4: 507–524.

Koo, Helen P., and C. M. Suchindran. 1980. "Effects of children on women's remarriage prospects." *Journal of Family Issues* 1: 497–516.

Norton, Arthur J., and Paul C. Glick. 1979. "Marital instability in America: Past, present, and future." Pp. 6–19 in George Levinger and Oliver Moles (eds.), *Divorce and Separation*. New York: Basic Books.

Rodgers, Willard L., and Arland Thornton. 1985. "Changing patterns of first marriage in the United States." *Demography* 22: 265–279.

U.S. Bureau of the Census. 1973. *1970 Census of Population, Subject Reports, Age at First Marriage*. Washington, DC: Government Printing Office.

U.S. Bureau of the Census. 1976. *Number, Timing, and Duration of Marriages: June 1975*. Current Population Reports, Series P-20, No. 297. Washington, DC: Government Printing Office.

U.S. Bureau of the Census. 1977. *Marriage, Divorce, Widowhood, and Remarriage by Family Characteristics: June 1975*. Current Population Reports, Series P-20, No. 312. Washington, DC: Government Printing Office.

U.S. Bureau of the Census. 1985a. *1980 Census of Population, Subject Reports, Marital Characteristics*. Washington, DC: Government Printing Office.

U.S. Bureau of the Census. 1985b. *Households, Families, Marital Status, and Living Arrangements: March 1985*. Current Population Reports, Series P-20, No. 402. Washington, DC: Government Printing Office.

U.S. National Center for Health Statistics. 1985a. *Monthly Vital Statistics: December 1984*. Washington, DC: Government Printing Office.

U.S. National Center for Health Statistics. 1985b. *Monthly Vital Statistics Report, Advance Report of Final Divorce Statistics, 1982*. Washington, DC: Government Printing Office.

Mysterious Young Adults

Martha Farnsworth Riche

When young people do things differently, it makes society nervous. Older generations do not know whether their youthful counterparts are just trying to be different, or whether they are responding to real changes in the world around them. The older baby boomers turned the country upside-down as they rejected their parents' values in the 1960s and 1970s. Now younger people are setting a new course.

First cocktail-party conversations, then newspaper and magazine articles pointed to a new trend—grown children who won't leave home. The phenomenon cuts across the income distribution—even millionaires are troubled by it. According to Thomas Stanley, director of the Atlanta-based Affluent Market Institute, one millionaire turned his college-student son's bedroom into a billiard room only to find the new graduate back home, sleeping on an air mattress atop the billiard table.

Are the young adults who won't leave home spoiled, suffering from downward mobility, or responding to a temporarily weak economy? Or are the stories about children who won't leave home just anecdotes, without any statistics to back them up? Are today's young adults more likely than those in the past to live with Mom and Dad?

In 1985, 35 percent of Americans aged 22 to 24 and 14 percent of those aged 25 to 29 were living in their parents' homes, according to the Current Population Survey.* Men were more likely to live with their parents than women. Living with a parent was, in fact, the most common living arrangement for men younger than age 25. Forty-two percent of 22-to-24-year-old men, compared to only 29 percent of women in that age group, lived with their parents. Among 25-to-29-year-olds, 17 percent of men versus 11 percent of women lived with their parents.

The proportion of young people who live at home is greater than it used to be. Among 18-to-24-year-olds, the proportion of men living at home in 1985 was up from what it was in the last three censuses: 60 percent in 1985 versus 54 percent in 1980 and 1970, and 52 percent in 1960. For women aged 18 to 24, the proportion rose even more: 48 percent lived at home in 1985 versus 43 percent in 1980, 41 percent in 1970, and 35 percent in 1960. Among men and women aged 25 to 34, the proportion who live at home rose only slightly over the last 25 years, from 11 to 13 percent for men and from 7 to 8 percent for women.

Living with Mom and Dad does not fit the image people have of young adults, nor does it match with how young adults think they will live. Among high school

From *American Demographics*, February 1987. © American Demographics 1987. Reprinted with permission.

*Unmarried college students in dormitories are included in the Current Population Survey's estimate of people living in their parents' household.

seniors in 1980, for example, 75 percent of the men and 65 percent of the women expected to live independently before marriage.

But a minority of young adults live alone or with nonrelatives, though over the past 25 years the nonfamily household has become an increasingly common living arrangement. Only 3 percent of men and 2 percent of women aged 18 to 24 lived alone or with friends in 1960. By 1985, the proportions were 10 and 7 percent, respectively. Among men aged 25 to 34, only 4 percent lived in a nonfamily household in 1960, while 16 percent did in 1985. For women in this age group, the proportion increased from 2 percent to 10 percent.

Why Leave Home?

Eventually, young adults do leave the nest. Among women aged 30 to 34, only 5 percent lived in a parent's household in 1985; among men in that age group, only 9 percent lived with their parents. For those aged 35 to 39, the proportions were 3 and 4 percent, respectively. But as in the past, marriage remains the major event the pulls young adults from their parents' homes. One reason that a larger proportion of young adults live with Mom and Dad today is that they are waiting longer to marry.

In 1985, only 16 percent of men and 32 percent of women aged 18 to 24 were married and living in their own household. In 1960, the proportions were 32 percent for men and 51 percent for women. Among men aged 25 to 34, only 60 percent were married and living in their own households in 1985, down from 79 percent in 1960. Among women aged 25 to 34, 76 percent were married and in their own households in 1985, down from 86 percent in 1960. Almost all of the decline in the proportion of young adults who are married and in their own households has occurred since 1970.

Marriage makes a dramatic difference in the living arrangements of young adults. For example, 60 percent of all young adults aged 20 and 21 were living with their parents in 1985. But among married young adults in this age group, only 4 percent were living with their parents. Overwhelmingly, young married people leave home.

But divorce often drives them back: Some people make up for the loss of a spouse by returning home. Among people aged 25 to 29 who were living with their parents in 1985, 13 percent were divorced or separated compared to 10 percent of those who were not living with their parents. Among people aged 30 to 34, nearly 25 percent of those who were living with their parents were divorced or separated, compared to 14 percent of those who were living on their own. The pattern was the same for men and women.

The majority of the young adults who were living with their parents continued to be the never-married, however: 80 percent of 25-to-29-year-olds and 66 percent of 30-to-34-year-olds who were living with their parents in 1985 were still single.

The proportion of married sons and daughters who stay on in the old homestead is even smaller than it was a few years ago. The proportion of young married men aged 18 to 24 who live in their parents' household dropped from 4 percent in 1970 to 1 percent in 1985. At the same time the proportion of single men who live at home grew from 60 to 72 percent.* For married men aged 25 to 34, the proportion who live with a parent has remained a negligible 1 percent. The proportion of single men that age who live at home has fallen from 45 percent to 36 percent.

For single women aged 18 to 24, the proportion who live with a parent rose from 62 percent in 1970 to 69 percent in 1985, while the proportion of the marrieds who live at home declined slightly, from 5 percent to 4 percent. For women aged 25 to 34, the proportion of singles who live in their parents' household dropped substantially, from 43 percent to 28 percent, while the proportion of marrieds remained at 1 percent. Among people in their late 20s, single women were much less likely than single men to be living with their parents.

One reason that more single, young adults are living at home may be that a large proportion of them are in school. The Current Population Survey asks respondents what their primary activity was during the survey week. In 1985, 29 percent of all young men aged 18 to 19 said school was their primary activity, but this proportion was 32 percent for those who lived with a parent and only 13 percent for those who lived on their own. Men in their early 20s who were attending school were eight times as likely to be living with their parents than men not attending school. Of men aged 20 to 24 who were attending school, 74 percent lived with their parents.** In contrast, of those whose primary activity was a job, 45 percent lived with their parents.

Thirty-two percent of young women aged 18 to 19 who were living with a parent were going to school, compared to only 14 percent of those who were living on their own. As with men, women attending school were much more likely to be living at home than were those who work; 75 percent of those aged 20 to 24 in school lived with parents compared to only 39 percent of those who were working. Working women aged 20 to 24 were less likely to live with their parents than working men in that age group.

Addicted to Money

Parents once breathed a sigh of relief when their children turned 18 and they could send them off to work, to school, or to marry. The expectation that the kids now were on their own may have been realistic in the past, but it is taking longer today for parents to empty their nest. Children can't leave home until they are self-supporting, and it is not until age 20 that most young adults report work as their primary activity.

Sixty-four percent of men and 68 percent of women aged 22 to 24 said work was their primary activity, and working women were more likely to leave home than working men. Forty-six percent of working women aged 20 and 21 had left home,

*Some of this increase may be due to differences in measures. The 1985 Current Population Survey figure includes college students living in dormitories, while the 1970 census figure does not.

**Some of them were in college dormitories, but most were not.

Table 1. Nesting Patterns: Percent of Men and Women Living With and Apart from Their Parents, by Age and Selected Characteristics (Note: Most Young

				Living with Mom and/or Dad				
	Total (1,000's)	Number (1,000's)	Percent of total	Percent in school	Percent working	Percent never married	Percent married	Percent divorced/ separated	Percent in households with incomes of $50,000 +
Aged 18–19									
Men	3,640	3,058	84%	32%	50%	99%	—*	—*	25%
Women	3,738	2,765	74	32	49	98	2%	1%	27
Aged 20–21									
Men	3,907	2,549	65	23	56	98	1	1	33
Women	4,066	2,176	54	25	57	95	2	3	32
Aged 22–24									
Men	6,148	2,565	42	14	64	95	2	3	36
Women	6,345	1,818	29	13	68	89	4	7	35
Aged 25–29									
Men	10,420	1,821	17	9	69	84	5	11	34
Women	10,686	1,168	11	5	70	75	6	18	31
Aged 30–34									
Men	9,764	864	9	1	66	73	6	21	22
Women	9,987	493	5	4	65	58	10	30	22
Aged 35–39									
Men	8,460	366	4	2	60	63	10	27	12
Women	8,762	255	3	2	65	57	11	29	14

*Note: — means less than 1 percent.
Source: U.S. Bureau of the Census, March 1985. Current Population Survey.

versus only 40 percent of working men. Among working women aged 22 to 24, 70 percent had left home, compared to 63 percent of working men. [See Table 1.]

For each succeeding age group of men, a growing proportion of those who have left home are working. But among those still living in their parents' home, an increasingly smaller proportion report work as their primary activity. In 1985, while 69 percent of men aged 25 to 29 who were living in their parents' household were working, that figure drops to 66 percent for men aged 30 to 34, and to 60 percent for those aged 35 to 39.

The role of adult women in their parents' home is different. In 1985, around 60 percent of women aged 22 to 39 were working, but unlike men, women living with their parents were more likely to work than women who had left home. One-third of women aged 22 to 39 who were on their own reported that their primary action was keeping house, versus 11 percent of women who were living with their parents.

The role of income in determining a young adult's decision to leave the parental nest is crucial. Of the men aged 22 to 24 in 1985, over 70 percent of those living in their parents' home had a personal income below $10,000, compared to just over 40 percent of those who had left home. This disparity widens with age: for those

Adults Aged 18 to 21 Live With Their Parents, but Even Among Those Aged 22 and Older, a Sizable Proportion Continue to Live at Home.)

				Living apart from Mom and Dad				
	Total (1,000's)	Number (1,000's)	Percent of total	Percent in school	Percent working	Percent never married	Percent married	Percent divorced/ separated	Percent in households with incomes of $50,000 +
Aged 18–19									
Men	3,640	582	16%	13%	65%	85%	15%	—*	6%
Women	3,738	973	26	14	46	55	41	4%	4
Aged 20–21									
Men	3,907	1,358	35	9	69	65	34	1	5
Women	4,066	1,890	46	6	55	44	52	5	4
Aged 22–24									
Men	6,148	3,583	58	6	77	50	47	4	5
Women	6,345	4,527	71	3	63	35	57	8	5
Aged 25–29									
Men	10,420	8,599	83	2	84	29	63	8	10
Women	10,686	9,518	89	2	62	20	68	11	9
Aged 30–34									
Men	9,764	8,900	91	1	86	16	73	11	13
Women	9,987	9,494	95	1	63	11	72	16	13
Aged 35–39									
Men	8,460	8,093	96	—*	86	8	81	27	19
Women	8,762	8,508	97	1	65	7	75	17	19

Note: — means less than 1 percent.
Source: U.S. Bureau of the Census, March 1985. *Current Population Survey.*

aged 30 to 34, for example, 55 percent of those who were living with a parent had a personal income below $10,000, compared with only 18 percent of those who had left home.

Moreover, these data support the suggestion that young adults from affluent families take longer to leave their parents' home because it will take them longer to replicate their parents' living standards. In 1985, over one-third of men aged 25 to 29 who were living with their parents were in households with an annual income of $50,000 or more. The reasoning behind this fact is not mysterious.

As with men up to age 30, the higher the parents' household income, the higher the proportion of young women who live at home. But a sizable group—15 percent of women and 20 percent of men in their 30s who were living at home— had personal incomes above $20,000, suggesting that they supported their parents' household.

No Mystery

All in all, the story behind the rising proportion of young adults who live with their parents is not such a mystery, nor is it really a cause for worry. Delayed marriage is the major explanation, and with divorce rates for early marriages as high as they are, this is probably a good thing. Economic doomsayers might argue that young adults are postponing marriage precisely because they can't afford to feather their own nest, but the trend toward delayed marriage is longstanding and began with the older baby boomers who matured into a more favorable economic climate.

If anyone deserves pity, it's the affluent parent who has feathered such a nice nest that the fledglings won't leave. But whether this is a sorry or happy state will vary from family to family. What the numbers show is that the process of leaving home is longer and more flexible than it used to be. So, it seems, is parenthood.

How to Figure Your Chances of Getting Married

Thomas Exter

More couples marry in June than in any other month. If you're going to marry this year, chances are you'll do it in June. But what are your chances of marrying this year—or ever? Marriage rates are down to historic lows. Fewer than 100 marriages will occur this year per 1,000 unmarried women aged 15 to 44, down from the peak of 199 per 1,000 in 1946 (the first year of the baby boom).

The probability of marrying in a given year increases from near zero at age 15 to over one in ten between ages 20 and 24. That is, one in ten people aged 20 will marry before he or she turns 25. After age 24 your chances of marrying drop each year.

The recent brouhaha over the results of the Harvard-Yale and Census Bureau studies on marriage rates is largely a debate over the steepness of the decline in marriage probabilities from age 25 to age 50.* The Harvard-Yale authors assume that your chances of marrying drop precipitously after age 25 so that, by age 45, a never-married, college-educated woman has a negligible (0.003 percent) chance of ever marrying. The Census Bureau, on the other hand, assumes a more gradual decline in the chances of marrying for college-educated women. The Census Bureau study reports that 45-year-old, never-married, college-educated women have a 10 percent chance of marrying by age 65.

Both studies recognize that college-educated women marry later, on average,

---

*Neil G. Bennett, David E. Bloom, and Patricia H. Craig, "Black and White Marriage Patterns: Why So Different?" unpublished paper, February 1986. Jeane E. Moorman, "The History and Future of the Relationship Between Education and Marriage," a paper prepared by the Marriage and Family Statistics Branch of the U.S. Bureau of the Census, 1987.

From *American Demographics*, June 1987. © American Demographics 1987. Reprinted with permission.

than those with no college education. The studies differ, however, on whether college-educated women marry as quickly or more slowly after leaving college as earlier generations of women married after leaving high school.

The Harvard-Yale study concludes that women are marrying as quickly and those who have postponed marriage may have foregone it altogether, either by design or by default.

The Census Bureau study concludes that most college-educated women who postponed marriage will eventually marry, but they are creating a new pattern of age at first marriage. The Census Bureau believes that most women who postponed marriage have no intention of foregoing it.

The truth may lie somewhere between the results of the two studies. The Census Bureau points out, however, that among never-married, white, college-educated women aged 25 to 29 in 1980, 35 percent had married by 1985 when they were aged 30 to 34. The proportion of this cohort who had ever married increased from 68 percent in 1980 to 79 percent in 1985. Since the Harvard-Yale study concluded that only 78 percent of this group would ever marry, any more marriages among them will cast doubt on the Harvard-Yale results.

Among never-married, white, college-educated women aged 30 to 34 in 1980, 29 percent had married by 1985 when they were aged 35 to 39. The proportion of all women in that cohort who had married at least once increased from 84 percent in 1980 to 89 percent in 1985. Again, since the Harvard-Yale study predicted that only 84 percent of these women would ever marry, the fact that the proportion ever-married surpassed the prediction by 1985 suggests that the Harvard-Yale study underestimates marriage probabilities.

The Probabilities

Researchers base their calculations of the probability of ever marrying on assumptions about the future. They combine historical data with current trends to judge the reasonableness of their assumptions.

The Harvard-Yale study assumes that college-educated women will have about the same chances of marrying as women with only a high school education, though their average age at first marriage will be older. The Census Bureau study assumes that today's college-educated women have established a new pattern of postponed marriage.

Each study uses a method of analysis appropriate to each set of assumptions. The results yield starkly different probabilities of ever marrying, especially when comparing women with and without a college education.

For example, the Census Bureau's study concluded that among never-married high school graduates aged 25, only 65 percent will marry before they turn 65. Among college-educated women aged 25, fully 85 percent will marry by age 65. The Harvard-Yale study concludes that 56 percent of never-married women aged 25 with a high school education or less will ever marry. And among the college-educated, only 52 percent will ever marry.

Table 1.   The Probabilities: probabilities of never-married women marrying by age 65*

| | Census Bureau Study | | Harvard-Yale Study** | |
Age	With four years high school	With four years college	With high school or less	With four years college or more
25	65%	85%	56%	52%
30	47	58	22	20
35	32	32	6	5
40	21	17	1	1
45	12	9	0	0

*Numbers [in the two studies] not strictly comparable due to different measures of education.
**Results refer to white women aged 25–29; 1982.

The Harvard-Yale study gives similar probabilities of ever marrying to women regardless of their educational level. Among never-married women aged 30, only about 1 in 5 will ever marry; among those aged 35, about 1 in 20 will marry; and among those aged 40, only about 1 in 100 will marry.

According to Census Bureau calculations, however, among women still unmarried by age 35 about one in three will marry.

To figure your probability of ever marrying, find the numbers in Table 1 that correspond to your age and educational level. If you are unmarried but still want to marry, your chances are probably closer to the Census Bureau figures. If you are not sure you want to marry, then your chances are probably closer to those of the Harvard-Yale study. Your intentions may make all the difference in the world.

The Availabilities

Other factors can improve your chances of marrying, such as the number of people of the opposite sex available for marriage. Stories about the marriage squeeze suggest that women on the leading edge of the baby boom—those born between 1946 and 1958—face a man shortage because women usually marry men who are older than they are. But men have postponed marriage at least as much as women. Fully 22 percent of men aged 30 to 34 versus just 14 percent of women were unmarried in 1986. Among men aged 35 to 39, 11 percent were unmarried in 1986, versus just 8 percent of women.

Table 2 shows the number of men and women in each age group who had never married by 1986, and the number who had married at least once. As a result of postponing marriage, the number of unmarried men outnumbers the number of unmarried women in every age group to age 65.

In 1986, fully 41 percent of men aged 25 to 29 had never married, compared with only 19 percent of men that age in 1970. Among women aged 25 to 29 in 1986, 28 percent had never married, up from 11 percent in 1970. As a result, there

Table 2:   The Availabilities

Age	Number of never-married women (1,000's)	Number of never-married men (1,000's)	Number of never-married men to 100 women (1,000's)	Percent of age group who have ever married (all women)	Percent of age group who have ever married (w/ college)	Percent of age cohorts who will marry by age 65*
15–19	8,563	9,027	105	0%	0%	88%
20–24	5,883	7,390	126	24	3	88
25–29	3,054	4,451	146	65	46	90
30–34	1,453	2,266	156	83	75	92
35–39	781	1,021	131	91	87	94
40–44	398	588	148	94	93	96
45–49	550	647	118	94	92	95

*According to the Census Bureau study.

were 146 never-married men for every 100 never-married women between the ages of 25 and 29 in 1986. These are good odds for single women who want to marry, and the odds remain good even for women in their 40s. For women, then, the marriage market is a buyer's market.

A meterologist will tell you the chances of rain on a given day. But either it rains or it doesn't. A 30 percent probability of rain means that out of 100 similar days, it will rain on 30 of them. But on a single day, the chances of rain are either one or zero. Because each person, like each day, is unique, those are the real marriage probabilities as well.

The Modernization of Grandparenthood

Andrew J. Cherlin and Frank F. Furstenberg, Jr.

Writing a book about grandparents may seem an exercise in nostalgia, like writing about the family farm. We tend to associate grandparents with old-fashioned families—the rural, extended, multigenerational kind much celebrated in American mythology. Many think that grandparents have become less important as the nation has become more modern. According to this view, the shift to factory and office work meant that grandparents no longer could teach their children and grandchildren the skills needed to make a living; the fall in fertility and the rise in divorce weakened family ties; and the growth of social welfare programs meant that older people and their families were less dependent on each other for support. There is some truth to this perspective, but it ignores a powerful set of historical facts that suggest that grandparenthood—as a distinct and nearly universal stage of family life—is a post–World War II phenomenon.

Consider first the effect of falling rates of death. Much of the decline in mortality from the high preindustrial levels has occurred in this century. According to calculations by demographer Peter Uhlenberg, only about 37 percent of all males and 42 percent of all females born in 1870 survived to age sixty-five; but for those born in 1930 the comparable projections were 63 percent for males and 77 percent for females. The greatest declines in adult mortality have occurred in the last few decades, especially for women. The average number of years that a forty-year-old white woman could expect to live increased by four between 1900 and 1940; but between 1940 and 1980 it increased by seven. For men the increases have been smaller, though still substantial: a two-year increase for forty-year-old whites between 1900 and 1940 and a four-year increase between 1940 and 1980. (The trends for nonwhites are similar.) Consequently, both men and women can expect to live much longer lives than was the case a few decades ago, and more and more women are outliving men. In 1980, the average forty-year-old white woman could expect to live to age eighty, whereas the average forty-year-old white man could expect to live only to age seventy-four. As a result, 60 percent of all the people sixty-five and over in the United States in 1980 were women. Thus, there are many more grandparents around today than just a few decades ago simply because people are living longer—and a majority of them are grandmothers.

This decline in mortality has caused a profound change in the relationship between grandparents and grandchildren. For the first time in history, most adults live long enough to get to know most of their grandchildren, and most children have the opportunity to know most of their grandparents. A child born in 1900, according to Uhlenberg, had a better than nine-out-of-ten chance that two or more of his grandparents would be alive. But by the time that child reached age fifteen, the chances were only about one out of two that two or more of his grandparents would still be alive. Thus, some children were fortunate enough to establish relationships with grandparents, but in many other families the remaining grandparents must have died while the grandchild was quite young. Moreover, it was unusual for grandchildren at the turn of the century to know all their grandparents: only one in four children born in 1900 had four grandparents alive, and a mere one in fifty still had four grandparents alive by the time they were fifteen. In contrast, the typical fifteen-year-old in 1976 had a nearly nine-out-of-ten chance of having two or more grandparents still alive, a better than one-out-of-two chance of having three still alive, and a one-out-of-six chance of having all four still alive. Currently, then, nearly all grandchildren have an extended relationship with two or more grandparents, and substantial minorities have the opportunity for extended relationships with three or even all four.

Indeed, Americans take survival to the grandparental years pretty much for granted. The grandparents we spoke to rarely mentioned longer life when discussing the changes since they were children. *Of course* they were still alive and reasonably healthy; that went without saying. But this taken-for-grantedness is a new phenomenon; before World War II early death was a much greater threat, and far fewer people lived long enough to watch their grandchildren grow up.

Most people are in their forties or fifties when they first become grandparents. Some observers have mistakenly taken this as an indication that grandparents are younger today than in the past. According to one respected textbook:

> Grandparenting has become a phenomenon of middle age rather than old age. Earlier marriage, earlier childbirth, and longer life expectancy are producing grandparents in their forties.

But since the end of the nineteenth century (the earliest period for which we have reliable statistics) there has been little change in the average age at marriage. The only exception was in the 1950s, when ages at marriage and first birth did decline markedly but only temporarily. With the exception of the unusual 1950s, then, it is likely that the age when people become grandparents has stayed relatively constant over the past century. What has changed is the amount of time a person spends as a grandparent: increases in adult life expectancy mean that grandparenthood extends into old age much more often. In our national sample of the grandparents of teenagers, six out of ten had become grandparents while in their forties. When we interviewed them, however, their average age was sixty-six. Grandparenting has been a phenomenon of middle age for at least the past one hundred years. The difference today is that it is now a phenomenon of middle age *and* old age for a greater proportion of the population. To be sure, our notions of what constitutes old age also may have changed, as one woman in our study implied when discussing her grandmother:

> She stayed home more, you know. And I get out into everything I can. That's the difference. That is, I think I'm younger than she was at my age.

Moreover, earlier in the century some middle-aged women may have been too busy raising the last of their own children to think of themselves as grandmothers. Nevertheless, in biological terms, the average grandparent alive today is older, not younger, than the average grandparent at the turn of the century.

Consider also the effects of falling birth rates on grandparenthood. As recently as the late 1800s, American women gave birth to more than four children, on average. Many parents still were raising their younger children after their older children had left home and married. Under these conditions, being a grandparent often overlapped with being a parent. One would imagine that grandparenthood took a back seat to the day-to-day tasks of raising the children who were still at home. Today, in contrast, the birth rate is much lower; and parents are much more likely to be finished raising their children before any of their grandchildren are born. In 1900, about half of all fifty-year-old women still had children under eighteen; but by 1980 the proportion had dropped to one-fourth. When a person becomes a grandparent now, there are fewer family roles competing for his or her time and attention. Grandparenthood is more of a separate stage of family life, unfettered by child care obligations—one that carries its own distinct identification. It was not always so.

The fall of fertility and the rise of life expectancy have thus greatly increased the supply of older persons for whom grandparenthood is a primary intergenerational role. To be sure, there always have been enough grandparents alive so that everyone in American society (and nearly all other societies, for that matter) was familiar with the role. But until quite recently, an individual faced a considerable risk of dying before, or soon after, becoming a grandparent. And even if one was fortunate enough to become a grandparent, lingering parental obligations often took precedence. In past times, when birth and death rates were high, grandparents were in relatively short supply. Today, as any number of impatient older parents will attest, grandchildren are in short supply. Census data bear this out: in 1900 there were only twenty-seven persons aged fifty-five and over for every one hundred children fourteen and under; but by 1984 the ratio had risen to nearly one-to-one. In fact, the Bureau of the Census projects that by the year 2000, for the first time in our nation's history, there will be more persons aged fifty-five and over than children fourteen and under.

Moreover, technological advances in travel and long-distance communication have made it easier for grandparents and grandchildren to see or talk to each other. . . . [T]he grandparents at one senior citizen center had to remind us that there was a time within their memories when telephone service was not universal. We tend to forget that only fifty years ago the *Literary Digest* predicted a Landon victory over Roosevelt on the basis of responses from people listed in telephone directories—ignoring the crucial fact that telephones were to be found disproportionately in wealthier, and therefore more often Republican, homes. As late as the end of World War II, only half the homes in the United States had a telephone. The proportion rose quickly to two-thirds by the early 1950s and three-fourths by the late 1950s. Today, more than 97 percent of all homes have telephones. About one-third of the grandparents in our survey reported that they had spoken to the study child on the telephone once a week or more during the previous year.

Nor did most families own automobiles until after World War II, as several grandparents reminded us:

> I could be wrong, but I don't feel grandparents felt as close to grandchildren during that time as they do now. . . . Really back there, let's say during the twenties, transportation was not as good, so many people did not have cars. Fortunately, I can say that as far back as I remember my father always had a car, but there were many other people who did not. They traveled by horse and buggy and some even by wagons. And going a distance, it did take quite some time. . . .

Only about half of all families owned automobiles at the end of the war. Even if a family owned an automobile, long trips still could take quite some time:

> Well, I didn't see my grandmother that often. They just lived one hundred miles from us, but back then one hundred miles was like four hundred now, it's the truth. It just seemed like clear across the country. It'd take us five hours to get there, it's the truth. It was an all-day trip.

But in the 1950s, the Federal government began to construct the interstate highway system, which cut distances and increased the speed of travel. The total number of miles driven by passenger vehicles increased from about 200 million miles in the mid-1930s to about 500 million miles in the mid-1950s to over a billion miles in the 1980s. Not all of this increase represents trips to Grandma's house, of course; but with more cars and better highways, it became much easier to visit relatives in the next county or state.

But weren't grandparents and grandchildren more likely to be living in the same household at the turn of the century? After all, we do have a nostalgic image of the three-generation family of the past, sharing a household and solving their problems together. Surprisingly, the difference between then and now is much less than this image would lead us to believe. To be sure, there has been a drastic decline since 1900 in the proportion of older persons who live with their adult children. In 1900 the proportion was more than three out of five, according to historian Daniel Scott Smith; in 1962 it was one out of four; and by 1975 it had dropped to one in seven. What has occurred is a great increase in the proportion of older people who live alone or only with their spouses. Yet the high rates of co-residence in 1900 do not imply that most grandparents were living with their grandchildren—much less that most grandchildren were living with their grandparents. As Smith's data show, older persons who were married tended to live with unmarried children only; children usually moved out when they married. It was mainly widows unable to maintain their own households who moved in with married children. Consequently, according to Smith's estimates, only about three in ten persons sixty-five and over in 1900 lived with a grandchild, despite the great amount of co-residence between older parents and their adult children. What is more, because of the relative shortage of grandparents, an even lower percentage of grandchildren lived with their grandparents. Smith estimates that about one in six children under age ten in 1900 lived in the same household with someone aged fifty-five or over. Even this figure overestimates the number of children living with their grandparents, because some of these elderly residents were more distant kin, boarders, or servants.

There were just too many grandchildren and too few grandparents for co-residence to be more common. In the absence of more detailed analyses of historical censuses, however, the exact amount of change since 1900 cannot be assessed. Nor was our study designed to provide precise estimates of changes in co-residence. But it is still worth noting that just 30 percent of the grandparents in our sample reported that at least one of their grandparents ever lived with them while they were growing up. And 19 percent reported that the teenaged grandchild in the study had lived with them for at least three months. Undoubtedly, some of the grandparents in our study had shared a household with some of their own grandchildren, although we unfortunately did not obtain this information. Thus, although our study provides only imperfect and incomplete data on this topic, the responses are consistent with our claim that the change in the proportion of grandparents and grandchildren who share a household has been more modest than the change in the proportion of elderly persons who share a household with an adult child.

Grandparents also have more leisure time today, although the trend is more pronounced for men than for women. The average male can now expect to spend fifteen years of his adult life out of the labor force, most of it during retirement. (The labor force comprises all persons who are working for pay or looking for work.) The comparable expected time was ten years in 1970, seven years in 1940, and only four years in 1900. Clearly, a long retirement was rare early in this century and still relatively rare just before World War II. But since the 1960s, workers have begun to leave the labor force at younger ages. In 1961, Congress lowered the age of eligibility for Social Security benefits from sixty-five to sixty-two. Now more than half of all persons applying for Social Security benefits are under sixty-five. Granted, some of the early retirees are suffering from poor health, and other retirees may have difficulty adjusting to their new status. Still, when earlier retirement is combined with a longer life span, the result is a greatly extended period during which one can, among other things, get to know and enjoy one's grandchildren.

The changes in leisure time for women are not as clear because women have always had lower levels of labor force participation than men. To be sure, women workers also are retiring earlier and, as has been noted, living much longer. And most women in their fifties and sixties are neither employed nor raising children. But young grandmothers are much more likely to be employed today than was the case a generation ago; they are also more likely to have aged parents to care for. Young working grandmothers, a growing minority, may have less time to devote to their grandchildren.

Most employed grandparents, however, work no more than forty hours per week. This, too, is a recent development. The forty-hour work week did not become the norm in the United States until after World War II. At the turn of the century, production workers in manufacturing jobs worked an average of fifty hours per week. Average hours dropped below forty during the depression, rose above forty during the war, and then settled at forty after the war. Moreover, at the turn of the century, 38 percent of the civilian labor force worked on farms, where long hours were commonplace. Even in 1940, about 17 percent of the civilian labor force worked on farms; but currently only about 3 percent work on farms. So even if they are employed, grandparents have more leisure time during the work week than was the case a few decades ago.

They also have more money. Living standards have risen in general since World War II, and the rise has been sharpest for the elderly. As recently as 1960, older Americans were an economically deprived group; now they are on the verge of becoming an economically advantaged group. The reason is the Social Security system. Since the 1950s and 1960s, Congress has expanded Social Security coverage, so that by 1970 nearly all nongovernment workers, except those in nonprofit organizations, were covered. And since the 1960s, Congress has increased Social Security benefits far faster than the increase in the cost of living. As a result, the average monthly benefit (in constant 1980 dollars, adjusted for changes in consumer prices) rose from $167 in 1960, to $214 in 1970, to $297 in 1980. Because of the broader coverage and higher benefits, the proportion of the elderly who are poor has plummeted. In 1959, 35 percent of persons sixty-five and over had incomes below the official poverty line, compared to 22 percent of the total population. By 1982 the disparity had disappeared: 15 percent of those sixty-five and over were poor, as were 15 percent of the total population. The elderly no longer were disproportionately poor, although many of them have incomes not too far above the poverty line. Grandparents, then, have benefitted from the general rise in economic welfare and, as they reach retirement, from the improvement in the economic welfare of the elderly.

Because of the postwar prosperity and the rise of social welfare institutions, older parents and their adult children are less dependent on each other economically. Family life in the early decades of the century was precarious; lower wages, the absence of social welfare programs, and crises of unemployment, illness, and death forced people to rely on their kin for support to a much greater extent than is true today. There were no welfare checks, unemployment compensation, food stamps, Medicare payments, Social Security benefits, or government loans to students. Often there was only one's family. Some older people provided assistance to their kin, such as finding a job for a relative, caring for the sick, or tending to the grandchildren while the parents worked. Sometimes grandparents, their children, and their grandchildren pooled their resources into a single family fund so that all could subsist. Exactly how common these three-generational economic units were we do not know; it would be a mistake to assume that all older adults were cooperating with their children and grandchildren at all times. In fact, studies of turn-of-the century working-class families suggest that widowed older men—past their peak earning capacity and unfamiliar with domestic tasks as they were—could be a burden to the households of their children, while older women—who could help out domestically—were a potential source of household assistance. Nevertheless, these historical accounts suggest that intensive intergenerational cooperation and assistance was more common than it is today. Tamara Hareven, for example, studied the families of workers at the Amoskeag Mills in Manchester, New Hampshire, at the turn of the century. She found that the day-to-day cooperation of kin was necessary to secure a job at the mill, find housing, and accumulate enough money to get by. Cooperation has declined because it is not needed as often: social welfare programs now provide services that only the family formerly provided; declining rates of illness, death, and unemployment have reduced the frequency of family crises; and the rising standard of living—particularly of the elderly—has reduced the need for financial assistance.

The structure of the Social Security system also has lessened the feelings of obligation older parents and their adult children have toward each other. Social Security is an income transfer system in which some of the earnings of workers are transferred to the elderly. But we have constructed a fiction about Social Security, a myth that the recipients are only drawing out money that they put into the fund earlier in their lives. This myth allows both the younger contributors and the older recipients to ignore the economic dependency of the latter. The elderly are free to believe that they are just receiving that to which they are entitled by virtue of their own hard work. The tenacity of this myth—it is only now breaking down under the tremendous payment burden of our older age structure—demonstrates its importance. It allows the elderly to accept financial assistance without compromising their independence, and it allows children to support their parents without either generation openly acknowledging as much.

All of these trends taken together—changes in mortality, fertility, transportation, communications, the work day, retirement, Social Security, and standards of living—have transformed grandparenthood from its pre–World War II state. More people are living long enough to become grandparents and to enjoy a lengthy period of life as grandparents. They can keep in touch more easily with their grandchildren; they have more time to devote to them; they have more money to spend on them; and they are less likely still to be raising their own children.

2

Gender and Sex

Introduction

Introduction

American society has experienced both a sexual revolution and a sex-role revolution. The first has liberalized attitudes toward erotic behavior and expression; the second has changed the roles and status of women and men in the direction of greater equality. Both revolutions have been brought about by the rapid social changes in recent years, and both revolutions also represent a belated recognition that traditional beliefs and norms did not reflect how people actually behaved and felt.

The conventional idea of sexuality defines sex as a powerful biological drive continually struggling for gratification against restraints imposed by civilization. The notion of sexual instincts also implies a kind of innate knowledge: A person intuitively knows his or her own identity as male or female, he or she knows how to act accordingly, and he or she is attracted to the "proper" sex object—a person of the opposite gender. In other words, the view of sex as biological drive pure and simple implies "that sexuality has a magical ability, possessed by no other capacity, that allows biological drives to be expressed directly in psychological and social behaviors" (Gagnon & Simon, 1970, p. 24).

The whole issue of the relative importance of biological versus psychological and social factors in sexuality and sex differences has been obscured by polemics. On the one hand, there are the strict biological determinists who declare that anatomy is destiny. On the other hand, there are those who argue that all aspects of sexuality and sex-role differences are matters of learning and social conditioning.

There are two essential points to be made about the nature-versus-nurture argument. The first is that extreme positions overlook the connection between biology and experience:

> In the theory of psychosexual differentiation, it is now outmoded to oppose or juxtapose nature vs. nurture, the genetic vs. psychological, or the instinctive vs. the environmental, the innate vs. the acquired, the biological vs. the psychological, or the instinctive vs. the learned. Modern genetic theory avoids these antiquated dichotomies. (Money & Ehrhardt, 1972, p. 1)

The second and related point concerns a misconception about how biological forces work. Both biological determinists and their opponents assume that if a biological force exists, it must be overwhelmingly strong. But the most sophisticated evidence concerning both gender development *and* erotic arousal suggests that physiological forces are gentle rather than powerful. Acknowledging the possible effects of prenatal sex hormones on the brains of human infants, Robert Stoller (1972) thus warns against "biologizing":

> While the newborn presents a most malleable central nervous system upon which the environment writes, we cannot say that the central nervous system is neutral or neuter. Rather, we can say that the effects of these biological systems, organized prenatally in a masculine or feminine direction, are almost always . . . too gentle in humans to withstand the more powerful forces in human development, the first and most powerful of which is mothering. (p. 211)

Research into the development of sex differences thus suggests not an opposition between genetics and environment but an interaction. Gender identity as a child and occupation as an adult are primarily the product of social learning rather than anatomy and physiology.

In terms of scholarship, the main effect thus far of the sex-role and sexual revolutions has been on awareness and consciousness. For example, much social science writing was suddenly revealed to have been based on sexist assumptions. Many sociologists and psychologists took it for granted that women's roles and functions in society reflect universal physiological and temperamental traits. Since in practically every society women were subordinate to men, inequality was interpreted as an inescapable necessity of organized social life. Such analysis suffers from the same intellectual flaw as the idea that discrimination against nonwhites implies their innate inferiority. All such explanations fail to analyze the social institutions and forces producing and supporting the observed differences. In approaching the study of either the physical or the social relations between the sexes, it is therefore important to understand how traditional stereotypes have influenced both popular and professional conceptions of sexuality and sex differences.

Jessie Bernard's and William J. Goode's articles on male and female sex roles develop this theme in different ways, but generally examine how stereotyping influences and sets limits on male and female socialization. These limits rob both men and women of a broader potential—for example, gentleness for men, achievement for women. Stereotyping thus diminishes the capacity of both women and men to fulfill a broader potential than conventional sex roles dictate.

The study by Dana V. Hiller and William W. Philliber of the division of labor in contemporary marriage shows how persistent are traditional gender-role scripts for the actual division of labor in contemporary marriage. Even when women worked outside the home, as they did in some 70 percent of the cases studied, the husband's expectations about the division of labor proved powerful predictors of performance, indicating that male prerogatives in marital-role bargaining are still quite strong.

As Karen Rosenblum's article suggests, it is not news that American society's formulation of gender roles breeds conflict and male dominance. Rosenblum maintains, however, that the reason for this conflict is broader and deeper than students of gender roles have heretofore considered. She argues that there are conflicts both between and within gender roles, and that the unintended consequences of within-gender conflicts are more significant than conflicts between the genders. Thus, masculinity, which affirms the values of equality and autonomy, actually produces hierarchy and dependence.

Such values as equality and autonomy are implicit in the idea of the sexual revolution. Both men and women were presumably freer to follow their desires. In practice, however, the sexual revolution has also produced new problems and anxieties. Lillian Breslow Rubin's selection deals with the difficulties experienced by blue-collar couples trying to cope with the new sexuality. For wives caught between the new standards for sexual performance and their own and their husband's earlier training, having an orgasm can often seem to be just another chore in a life already full of chores. Middle-class women, more comfortable with the idea of sexual experimentation, feel guilty about the hang-ups that may prevent them from acting on their liberated beliefs. For their part, men who encourage their wives to be more erotically active may be turned off if the women become so.

Gender differences in intimate relations are explored further in Francesca M. Cancian's article examining the relationship between love and power in private and public spheres. Cancian argues that the traditional social organization of love—that women seem to have and enjoy a greater capacity for tender intimacy while men appear to prefer outright sexuality—is related to the dependencies associated with the traditional female role and the relative economic independence of men. Thus, she argues, male and female conceptions of love will likely move toward one another as power positions in the public sphere are more equitably shared by women and men.

References

Gagnon, J. H. and Simon, W. 1970. *The Sexual Scene.* Chicago: Aldene.
Money, J. and Ehrhardt, A. A. 1972. *Man and Woman, Boy and Girl.* Baltimore: Johns Hopkins Press.
Stoller, R. J. 1972. "The Bedrock of Masculinity and Femininity: Bisexuality." *Archives of General Psychiatry,* 26, pp. 207–212.

Chapter 3

Gender and Equality

The Good-Provider Role: Its Rise and Fall

Jessie Bernard

Abstract

The general structure of the "traditional" American family, in which the husband-father is the provider and the wife-mother is the housewife, began to take shape early in the 19th century. This structure lasted about 150 years, from the 1830s to 1980, when the U.S. Census no longer automatically denominated the male as head of the household. As "providing" became increasingly mediated by cash derived from participation in the labor force or from commercial enterprises, the powers and prerogatives of the provider role augmented, and those of the housewife, who lacked a cash income, declined. Gender identity became associated with the work site as well as with work. As affluence spread, the provider role became more and more competitive and escalated into the good-provider role. There were always defectors from the good-provider role, and in recent years expressed dissatisfaction with it increased. As more and more married women entered the labor force and thus assumed a share of the provider role, the powers and prerogatives of the good-provider role became diluted. At the present time a process that Ralph Smith calls "the subtle revolution" is realigning family roles. A host of social-psychological obstacles related to gender identity have to be overcome before a new social-psychological structure can be achieved.

The Lord is my shepherd, I shall not want. He sets a table for me in the very sight of my enemies; my cup runs over (23rd Psalm). And when the Israelites were complaining about how hungry they were on their way from Egypt to Canaan, God told Moses to rest assured: There would be meat for dinner and bread for breakfast the next morning. And, indeed, there were quails that very night,

From *American Psychologist*, Vol 36, No. 1, January 1981, pp. 1–12. Copyright 1981 by the American Psychological Association. Reprinted by permission of the publisher.

143

enough to cover the camp, and in the morning the ground was covered with dew that proved to be bread (Exodus 16:12–13). In fact, in this role of good provider, God is sometimes almost synonymous with Providence. Many people, like Micawber, still wait for him, or Providence, to provide.

Granted, then, that the first great provider for the human species was God the Father, surely the second great provider for the human species was Mother, the gatherer, planter, and general factotum. Boulding (1976), citing Lee and deVore, tells us that in hunting and gathering societies, males contribute about one fifth of the food of the clan, females the other four fifths (p. 96). She also concludes that by 12,000 B.C. in the early agricultural villages, females provided four fifths of human subsistence (p. 97). Not until large trading towns arose did the female contribution to human subsistence decline to equality with that of the male. And with the beginning of true cities, the provisioning work of women tended to become invisible. Still, in today's world it remains substantial.

Whatever the date of the virtuous woman described in the Old Testament (Proverbs 31:10–27), she was the very model of a good provider. She was, in fact, a highly productive conglomerate. She woke up in the middle of the night to tend to her business; she oversaw a multiple-industry household; *her* candles did not go out at night; there was a ready market for the high-quality linen girdles she made and sold to the merchants in town; and she kept track of the real estate market and bought good land when it became available, cultivating vineyards quite profitably. All this time her husband sat at the gate talking with his cronies.

A recent counterpart to the virtuous woman was the busy and industrious shtetl woman:

> The earnings of a livelihood is sexless, and the large majority of women . . . participate in some gainful occupation if they do not carry the chief burden of support. The wife of a "perennial student" is very apt to be the sole support of the family. The problem of managing both a business and a home is so common that no one recognizes it as special. . . . To bustle about in search of a livelihood is merely another form of bustling about managing a home; both are aspects of . . . health and livelihood. (Zborowski & Herzog, 1952, p. 131)

In a subsistence economy in which husbands and wives ran farms, shops, or businesses together, a man might be a good, steady worker, but the idea that he was *the* provider would hardly ring true. Even the youth in the folk song who listed all the gifts he would bestow on his love if she would marry him—a golden comb, a paper of pins, and all the rest—was not necessarily promising to be a good provider.

I have not searched the literature to determine when the concept of the good provider entered our thinking. The term *provider* entered the English language in 1532, but was not yet male sex typed, as the older term *purveyor* already was in 1442. Webster's second edition defines the good provider as "one who provides, especially, colloq., one who provides food, clothing, etc. for his family; as, he is a good or an adequate provider." More simply, he could be defined as a man whose wife did not have to enter the labor force. The counterpart to the good provider was the housewife. However the term is defined, the role itself delineated relationships within a marriage and family in a way that added to the legal, religious, and other advantages men had over women.

Thus, under the common law, although the husband was legally head of the household and as such had the responsibility of providing for his wife and children, this provision was often made with help from the wife's personal property and earnings, to which he was entitled:

> He owned his wife's and children's services, and had the sole right to collect wages for their work outside the home. He owned his wife's personal property outright, and had the right to manage and control all of his wife's real property during marriage, which included the right to use or lease property, and to keep any rents and profits from it. (Babcock, Freedman, Norton, & Ross, 1975, p. 561)

So even when she was the actual provider, the legal recognition was granted the husband. Therefore, whatever the husband's legal responsibilities for support may have been, he was not necessarily a good provider in the way the term came to be understood. The wife may have been performing that role.

In our country in Colonial times women were still viewed as performing a providing role, and they pursued a variety of occupations. Abigail Adams managed the family estate, which provided the wherewithal for John to spend so much time in Philadelphia. In the 18th century "many women were active in business and professional pursuits. They ran inns and taverns; they managed a wide variety of stores and shops; and, at least occasionally, they worked in careers like publishing, journalism and medicine" (Demos, 1974, p. 430). Women sometimes even "joined the menfolk for work in the fields" (p. 430). Like the household of the proverbial virtuous woman, the Colonial household was a little factory that produced clothing, furniture, bedding, candles, and other accessories, and again, as in the case of the virtuous woman, the female role was central. It was taken for granted that women provided for the family along with men.

The good provider as a specialized male role seems to have arisen in the transition from subsistence to market—especially money—economies that accelerated with the industrial revolution. The good-provider role for males emerged in this country roughly, say, from the 1830s, when de Tocqueville was observing it, to the late 1970s, when the 1980 census declared that a male was not automatically to be assumed to be head of household. This gives the role a life span of about a century and a half. Although relatively short-lived, while it lasted the role was a seemingly rock-like feature of the national landscape.

As a psychological and sociological phenomenon, the good-provider role had wide ramifications for all of our thinking about families. It marked a new kind of marriage. It did not have good effects on women: The role deprived them of many chips by placing them in a peculiarly vulnerable position. Because she was not reimbursed for her contribution to the family in either products or services, a wife was stripped to a considerable extent of her access to cash-mediated markets. By discouraging labor force participation, it deprived many women, especially affluent ones, of opportunities to achieve strength and competence. It deterred young women from acquiring productive skills. They dedicated themselves instead to winning a good provider who would "take care of" them. The wife of a more successful provider became for all intents and purposes a parasite, with little to do except indulge or pamper herself. The psychology of such dependence could become all but crippling. There were other concomitants of the good-provider role.

Expressivity and the Good-Provider Role

The new industrial order that produced the good provider changed not so much the division of labor between the sexes as it did the site of the work they engaged in. Only two of the concomitants of this change in work site are selected for comment here, namely, (a) the identification of gender with work site as well as with work itself and (b) the reduction of time for personal interaction and intimacy within the family.

It is not so much the specific kinds of work men and women do—they have always varied from time to time and place to place—but the simple fact that the sexes do different kinds of work, whatever it is, which is in and of itself important. The division of labor by sex means that the work group becomes also a sex group. The very nature of maleness and femaleness becomes embedded in the sexual division of labor. One's sex and one's work are part of one another. One's work defines one's gender.

Any division of labor implies that people doing different kinds of work will occupy different work sites. When the division is based on sex, men and women will necessarily have different work sites. Even within the home itself, men and women had different work spaces. The woman's spinning wheel occupied a different area from the man's anvil. When the factory took over much of the work formerly done in the house, the separation of work space became especially marked. Not only did the separation of the sexes become spatially extended, but it came to relate work and gender in a special way. The work site as well as the work itself became associated with gender; each sex had its own turf. This sexual "territoriality" has had complicating effects on efforts to change any sexual division of labor. The good provider worked primarily in the outside male world of business and industry. The homemaker worked primarily in the home.

Spatial separation of the sexes not only identifies gender with work site and work but also reduces the amount of time available for spontaneous emotional give-and-take between husbands and wives. When men and women work in an economy based in the home, there are frequent occasions for interaction. (Consider, for example, the suggestive allusions made today to the rise in the birth rate nine months after a blackout.) When men and women are in close proximity, there is always the possibility of reassuring glances, the comfort of simple physical presence. But when the division of labor removes the man from the family dwelling for most of the day, intimate relationships become less feasible. De Tocqueville was one of the first to call our attention to this. In 1840 he noted that

> almost all men in democracies are engaged in public or professional life; and . . . the limited extent of common income obliges a wife to confine herself to the house, in order to watch in person and very closely over the details of domestic economy. All these distinct and compulsory occupations are so many natural barriers, which, by keeping the two sexes asunder, render the solicitations of the one less frequent and less ardent—the resistance of the other more easy. (de Tocqueville, 1840, p. 212)

Not directly related to the spatial constraints on emotional expression by men, but nevertheless a concomitant of the new industrial order with the same effect, was the enormous drive for achievement, for success, for "making it" that escalated the provider role into the good-provider role. De Tocqueville (1840) is again our source:

> The tumultuous and constantly harassed life which equality makes men lead [becoming good providers] not only distracts from the passions of love, by denying them time to indulge in it, but it diverts them from it by another more secret but more certain road. All men who live in democratic ages more or less contract ways of thinking of the manufacturing and trading classes. (p. 221)

As a result of this male concentration on jobs and careers, much abnegation and "a constant sacrifice of her pleasures to her duties" (de Tocqueville, 1840, p. 212) were demanded by the American woman. The good-provider role, as it came to be shaped by this ambience, was thus restricted in what it was called upon to provide. Emotional expressivity was not included in that role. One of the things a parent might say about a man to persuade a daughter to marry him, or a daughter might say to explain to her parents why she wanted to, was not that he was a gentle, loving, or tender man but that he was a good provider. He might have many other qualities, good or bad, but if a man was a good provider, everything else was either gravy or the price one had to pay for a good provider.

Lack of expressivity did not imply neglect of the family. The good provider was a "family man." He set a good table, provided a decent home, paid the mortgage, bought the shoes, and kept his children warmly clothed. He might, with the help of the children's part-time jobs, have been able to finance their educations through high school, and, sometimes, even college. There might even have been a little left over for an occasional celebration in most families. The good provider made a decent contribution to the church. His work might have been demanding, but he expected it to be. If in addition to being a good provider, a man was kind, gentle, generous, and not a heavy drinker or gambler, that was all frosting on the cake. Loving attention and emotional involvement in the family were not part of a woman's implicit bargain with the good provider.

By the time de Tocqueville published his observations in 1840, the general outlines of the good-provider role had taken shape. It called for a hard-working man who spent most of his time at his work. In the traditional conception of the role, a man's chief responsibility is his job, so that "by definition any family behaviors must be subordinate to it in terms of significance and [the job] has priority in the event of a clash" (Scanzoni, 1975, p. 38). This was the classic form of the good-provider role, which remained a powerful component of our societal structure until well into the present century.

Costs and Rewards of the Good-Provider Role for Men

There were both costs and rewards for those men attached to the good-provider role. The most serious cost was perhaps the identification of maleness not only with the work site but especially with success in the role. "The American male looks to his breadwinning role to confirm his manliness" (Brenton, 1966, p. 194).[1] To be a man one had to be not only a provider but a *good* provider. Success in the good-provider role came in time to define masculinity itself. The good provider had to achieve, to win, to succeed, to dominate. He was a bread*winner*. He had to show "strength, cunning, inventiveness, endurance—a whole range of traits henceforth defined as exclusively 'masculine' " (Demos, 1974, p. 436). Men were judged as men by the level of living they provided. They were judged by the myth "that endows a money-making man with sexiness and virility, and is based on man's dominance, strength, and ability to provide for and care for 'his' woman" (Gould, 1974, p. 97). The good provider became a player in the male competitive macho game. What one man provided for his family in the way of luxury and display had to be equaled or topped by what another could provide. Families became display cases for the success of the good provider.

The psychic costs could be high:

> By depending so heavily on his breadwinning role to validate his sense of himself as a man, instead of also letting his roles as husband, father, and citizen of the community count as validating sources, the American male treads on psychically dangerous ground. It's always dangerous to put all one's psychic eggs into one basket. (Brenton, 1966, p. 194)

The good-provider role not only put all of a man's gender-identifying eggs into one psychic basket, but it also put all the family-providing eggs into one basket. One individual became responsible for the support of the whole family. Countless stories portrayed the humiliation families underwent to keep wives and especially mothers out of the labor force, a circumstance that would admit to the world the

[1]Rainwater and Yancy (1967), critiquing current welfare policies, note that they "have robbed men of their manhood, women of their husbands, and children of their fathers. To create a stable monogamous family we need to provide men with the opportunity to be men, and that involves enabling them to perform occupationally" (p. 235).

male head's failure in the good-provider role. If a married woman had to enter the labor force at all, that was bad enough. If she made a good salary, however, she was "co-opting the man's passport to masculinity" (Gould, 1974, p. 89) and he was effectively castrated. A wife's earning capacity diminished a man's position as head of the household (Gould, 1974, p. 99).

Failure in the role of good provider, which employment of wives evidenced, could produce deep frustration. As Komarovsky (1940, p. 20) explains, this is "because in his own estimation he is failing to fulfill what is the central duty of his life, the very touchstone of his manhood—the role of family provider."

But just as there was punishment for failure in the good-provider role, so also were there rewards for successful performance. A man "derived strength from his role as provider" (Komarovsky, 1940, p. 205). He achieved a good deal of satisfaction from his ability to support his family. It won kudos. Being a good provider led to status in both the family and the community. Within the family it gave him the power of the purse and the right to decide about expenditures, standards of living, and what constituted good providing. "Every purchase of the family—the radio, his wife's new hat, the children's skates, the meals set before him—all were symbols of their dependence upon him" (Komarovsky, 1940, pp. 74–75). Such dependence gave him a "profound sense of stability" (p. 74). It was a strong counterpoise vis-à-vis a wife with a stronger personality. "Whether he had considerable authority within the family and was recognized as its head, or whether the wife's stronger personality . . . dominated the family, he nevertheless derived strength from his role as a provider" (Komarovsky, 1940, p. 75). As recently as 1975, in a sample of 3,100 husbands and wives in 10 cities, Scanzoni found that despite increasing egalitarian norms, the good provider still had "considerable power in ultimate decision-making" and as "unique provider" had the right "to organize his life and the lives of other family members around his occupation" (p. 38).

A man who was successful in the good-provider role might be freed from other obligations to the family. But the flip side of this dispensation was that he could not make up for poor performances by excellence in other family roles. Since everything depended on his success as provider, everything was at stake. The good provider played an all-or-nothing game.

Different Ways of Performing the Good-Provider Role

Although the legal specifications for the role were laid out in the common law, in legislation, in legal precedents, in court decisions, and, most importantly, in custom and convention, in real-life situations the social and social-psychological specifications were set by the husband or, perhaps more accurately, by the community, alias the Joneses, and there were many ways to perform it.

Some men resented the burdens the role forced them to bear. A man could easily vent such resentment toward his family by keeping complete control over all expenditures, dispensing the money for household maintenance, and complaining about bills as though it were his wife's fault that shoes cost so much. He could, in effect, punish his family for his having to perform the role. Since the money he earned belonged to him—was "his"—he could do with it what he pleased. Through extreme parsimony he could dole out his money in a mean, humiliating way, forcing his wife to come begging for pennies. By his reluctance and resentment he could make his family pay emotionally for the provisioning he supplied.

At the other extreme were the highly competitive men who were so involved in outdoing the Joneses that the fur coat became more important than the affectionate hug. They "bought off" their families. They sometimes succeeded so well in their extravagance that they sacrificed the family they were presumably providing for to the achievements that made it possible (Keniston, 1965).[2]

The Depression of the 1930s revealed in harsh detail what the loss of the role could mean both to the good provider and to his family, not only in the loss of income itself—which could be supplied by welfare agencies or even by other family members, including wives—but also and especially in the loss of face.

The Great Depression did not mark the demise of the good-provider role. But it did teach us what a slender thread the family hung on. It stimulated a whole array of programs designed to strengthen that thread, to ensure that it would never again be similarly threatened. Unemployment insurance was incorporated into the Social Security Act of 1935, for example, and a Full Employment Act was passed in 1946. But there proved to be many other ways in which the good-provider role could be subverted.

Role Rejectors and Role Overperformers

Recent research in psychology, anthropology, and sociology has familiarized us with the tremendous power of roles. But we also know that one of the fundamentel principles of role behavior is that conformity to role norms is not universal. Not everyone lives up to the specifications of roles, either in the psychological or in the sociological definition of the concept. Two extremes have attracted research attention: (a) the men who could not live up to the norms of the good-provider role or did not want to, at one extreme, and (b) the men who overperformed the role, at the other. For the wide range in between, from blue-collar workers to professionals, there was fairly consistent acceptance of the role, however well or poorly, however grumblingly or willingly, performed.

---

[2]Several years ago I presented a critique of what I called "extreme sex role specialization," including "work-intoxicated fathers." I noted that making success in the provider role the only test for real manliness was putting a lot of eggs into one basket. At both the blue-collar and the managerial levels, it was dysfunctional for families. I referred to the several attempts being made even then to correct the excesses of extreme sex role specialization: rural and urban communes, leaving jobs to take up small-scale enterprises that allowed more contact with families, and a rebellion against overtime in industry (Bernard, 1975, pp. 217–239).

First the nonconformists. Even in Colonial times, desertion and divorce occurred:

> Women may have deserted because, say, their husbands beat them; husbands, on the other hand, may have deserted because they were unable or unwilling to provide for their usually large families in the face of the wives' demands to do so. These demands were, of course, backed by community norms making the husband's financial support a sacred duty (Scanzoni, 1979, pp. 24–25)

Fiedler (1962) has traced the theme of male escape from domestic responsibilities in the American novel from the time of Rip Van Winkle to the present:

> The figure of Rip Van Winkle presides over the birth of the American imagination; and it is fitting that our first successful home-grown legend should memorialize, however playfully, the flight of the dreamer from the shrew—into the mountains and out of time, away from the drab duties of home . . . anywhere to avoid . . . marriage and responsibility. One of the factors that determine theme and form in our great books is this strategy of evasion, this retreat to nature and childhood which makes our literature (and life) so charmingly and infuriatingly "boyish." (pp. xx–xxi)

Among the men who pulled up stakes and departed for the West or went down to the sea in ships, there must have been a certain proportion who, like their mythic prototype, were fleeing the good-provider role.

The work of Demos (1974), a historian, offers considerable support for Fiedler's thesis. He tells us that the burdens thrust on men in the 19th century by the new patterns of work began to show their effects in the family. When "the [spatial] separation of the work lives of husbands and wives made communication so problematic," he asks, "what was the likelihood of meaningful communication?" (Demos, 1974, p. 438). The answer is, relatively little. Divorce and separation increased, either formally or by tacit consent—or simply by default, as in the case of a variety of defaulters—tramps, bums, hoboes—among them.

In this connection, "the development of the notorious 'tramp' phenomenon is worth noticing," Demos (1974, p. 438) tells us. The tramp was a man who just gave up, who dropped out of the role entirely. He preferred not to work, but he would do small chores or other small-scale work for a handout if he had to. He was not above begging the housewife for a meal, hoping she would not find work for him to do in repayment. Demos (1974) describes the type:

> Demoralized and destitute wanderers, their numbers mounting into the hundreds of thousands, tramps can be fairly characterized as men who had run away from their wives. . . . Their presence was mute testimony to the strains that tugged at the very core of American family life. . . . Many observers noted that the tramps had created a virtual society of their own [a kind of counterculture] based on a principle of single-sex companionship. (p. 438)

A considerable number of them came to be described as "homeless men" and, as the country became more urbanized, landed ultimately on skid row. A large part of the task of social workers for almost a century was the care of the "evaded" women they left behind.[3] When the tramp became wholly demoralized, a chronic alcoholic, almost unreachable, he fell into a category of his own—he was a bum.

Quite a different kettle of fish was the hobo, the migratory worker who spent several months harvesting wheat and other large crops and the rest of the year in cities. Many were the so-called Wobblies, or Industrial Workers of the World, who repudiated the good-provider role on principle. They had contempt for the men who accepted it and could be called conscientious objectors to the role. "In some IWW circles, wives were regarded as the 'ball and chain.' In the West, IWW literature proclaimed that the migratory worker, usually a young, unmarried male, was 'the first specimen of American manhood . . . the leaven of the revolutionary labor movement' " (Foner, 1979, p. 400). Exemplars of the Wobblies were the nomadic workers of the West. They were free men. The migratory worker, "unlike the factory slave of the Atlantic seaboard and the central states, . . . was most emphatically 'not afraid of losing his job.' No wife and family cumbered him. The worker of the East, oppressed by the fear of want for wife and babies, dared not venture much" (Foner, 1979, p. 400). The reference to fear of loss of job was tell taken; employers preferred married men, disciplined into the good-provider role, who had given hostages to fortune and were therefore more tractable.

Just on the verge between the area of conformity to the good-provider role—at whatever level—and the area of complete nonconformity to it was the non-good provider, the marginal group of workers usually made up of "the under-educated, the under-trained, the under-employed, or part-time employed, as well as the under paid, and of course the unemployed" (Snyder, 1979, p. 597). These included men who wanted—sometimes desperately—to perform the good-provider role but who for one reason or another were unable to do so. Liebow (1966) has discussed the ramifications of failure among the black men of Tally's corner: The black man is

> under legal and social constraints to provide for them [their families], to be a husband to his wife and a father to his children. The chances are, however, that he is failing to provide for them, and failure in this primary function contaminates his performance as father in other aspects as well. (p. 86)

[3]In one department of a South Carolina cotton mill early in the century, "every worker was a grass widow" (Smuts, 1959, p. 54). Many women worked "because their husbands refused to provide for their families. There is no reason to think that husbands abandoned their duties more often than today, but the woman who was burdened by an irresponsible husband in 1890 usually had no recourse save taking on his responsibilities herself. If he deserted, the law-enforcement agencies of the time afforded little chance of finding and compelling him to provide support" (Smuts, 1959, p. 54). The situation is not greatly improved today. In divorce child support is allotted in only a small number of cases and enforced in even fewer. "Roughly half of all families with an absent parent don't have awards at all. . . . Where awards do exist they are usually for small amounts, typically ranging from $7 to $18 per child" (Jones, 1976, abstract). A summary of all the studies available concludes that "approximately 20 percent of all divorced and separated mothers receive child support regularly, with an additional 7 percent receiving it 'sometimes': 8 percent of all divorced and separated women receive alimony regularly or sometimes" (Jones, 1976, p. 23).

In some cases, leaving the family entirely was the best substitute a man could supply. The community was left to take over.[4]

At the other extreme was the overperformer. De Tocqueville, quoted earlier, was already describing him as he manifested in the 1830s. And as late as 1955 Warner and Ablegglen were adding to the considerable literature on industrial leaders and tycoons, referring to their "driving concentration" on their careers and their "intense focusing" on interests, energies, and skills on these careers, "even limiting their sexual activity" (pp. 48–49). They came to be known as workaholics or work-intoxicated men. Their preoccupation with their work even at the expense of their families was, as I have already noted, quite acceptable in our society.

Poorly or well performed, the good-provider role lingered on. World War II initiated a challenge, this time in the form of attracting more and more married women into the labor force, but the challenge was papered over in the 1950s with an "age of togetherness" that all but apotheosized the good provider, his house in the suburbs, his homebody wife, and his third, fourth, even fifth, child. As late as the 1960s most housewives (87%) still saw breadwinning as their husband's primary role (Lopata, 1971, p. 91).[5]

Intrinsic Conflict in the Good-Provider Role

Since the good-provider role involved both family and work roles, most people believed that there was no incompatibility between them or at least that there should not be. But in the 1960s and 1970s evidence began to mount that maybe something was amiss.

De Tocqueville had documented the implicit conflict in the American business-man's devotion to his work at the expense of his family in the early years of the 19th century; the Industrial Workers of the World had proclaimed that the good-provider role which tied a man to his family was an impediment to the great revolution at the beginning of the 20th century; Fiedler (1962) had noted that throughout our history, in the male fantasy world, there was freedom from the responsibilities of this role; about 50 years ago Freud (1930/1958) had analyzed the intrinsic conflict between the demands of women and the family on one side and the demands of men's work on the other:

> Women represented the interests of the family and sexual life, the work of civilization has become more and more men's business; it confronts them with ever harder tasks, compels them to sublimations of instinct which women are not easily able to achieve. Since man has not an unlimited amount of mental

[4]Even though the annals of social work agencies are filled with cases of runaway husbands, in 1976 only 12.6% of all women were in the status of divorce and separation, and at least some of them were still being "provided for." Most men were at least trying to fulfill the good-provider role.

[5]Although all the women in Lopata's (1971) sample saw breadwinning as important, fewer employed women (54%) than either nonemployed urban (63%) or suburban (64%) women assigned it first place (p. 91).

energy at his disposal, he must accomplish his tasks by distributing his libido to the best advantage. What he employs for cultural [occupational] purposes he withdraws to a great extent from women, and his sexual life; his constant association with men and his dependence on his relations with them even estrange him from his duties as husband and father. Woman finds herself thus forced into the background by the claims of culture [work] and she adapts an inimical attitude towards it. (pp. 50–51)

In the last two decades, researchers have been raising questions relevant to Freud's statement of the problem. They have been asking people about the relative satisfactions they derive from these conflicting values—family and work. Among the earliest studies comparing family–work values was a Gallup poll in 1940 in which both men and women chose a happy home over an interesting job or wealth as a major life value. Since then there have been a number of such polls, and considerable body of results has now accumulated. Pleck and Lang (1979) and Hesselbart (Note 1) have summarized the findings of these surveys. All agree that there is a clear bias in the direction of the family. Pleck and Lang conclude that "men's family role is far more psychologically significant to them than is their work role" (p. 29), and Hesselbart—however critical she is of the studies she summarizes—believes they should not be dismissed lightly and concludes that they certainly "challenge the idea that family is a 'secondary' valued role" (p. 14).[6] Douvan (Note 2) also found in a 1976 replication of a 1957 survey that family values retained priority over work: "Family roles almost uniformly rate higher in value production than the job role does" (p. 16)[7]

The very fact that researchers have asked such questions is itself interesting. Somehow or other both the researchers and the informants seem to be saying that all this complaining about the male neglect of the family, about the lack of family involvement by men, just is not warranted. Neither de Tocqueville nor Freud was right. Men do value family life more than they value their work. They do derive their major life satisfactions from their families rather than from their work.

It may well be true that men derive the greatest satisfaction from their family

---

[6]Pleck and Lang (1979) found only one serious study contradicting their own conclusions: "Using data from the 1973 NORC (National Opinion Research Center) General Social Survey, Harry analyzed the bivariate relationship of job and family satisfaction to life happiness in men classified by family life cycle stage. In three of the five groups of husbands . . . job satisfaction had a stronger association than family satisfaction to life happiness" (pp. 5–6).

[7]In 1978, a Yankelovich survey on "The New Work Psychology" suggested that leisure is now becoming a strict competitor for both family and work as a source of life satisfactions: "Family and work have grown less important than leisure; a majority of 60 percent say that although they enjoy their work, it is not their major source of satisfaction" (p. 46). A 1977 survey of Swedish men aged 18 to 35 found that the proportion saying that the family was the main source of meaning in their lives declined from 45% in 1955 to 41% in 1977; the proportion indicating work as the main source of satisfaction dropped from 33% to 17%. The earlier tendency for men to identify themselves through their work is less marked these days. In the new value system, the individual says, in effect, "I am more than my role. I am myself" (Yankelovich, 1978). Is the increasing concern with leisure a way to escape the dissatisfaction with both the alienating relations found on the work site and the demands for increased involvement with the family?

roles, but this does not necessarily mean they are willing to pay for the benefit. In any event, great attitudinal changes took place in the 1960s and 1970s.

Douvan (Note 2), on the basis of surveys in 1957 and 1976, found, for example, a considerable increase in the proportion of both men and women who found marriage and parenthood burdensome and restrictive. Almost three fifths (57%) of both married men and married women in 1976 saw marriages as "all burdens and restrictions," as compared with only 42% and 47%, respectively, in 1957. And almost half (45%) also viewed children as "all burdens and restrictions" in 1976, as compared with only 28% and 33% for married men and married women, respectively, in 1957. The proportion of working men with a positive attitude toward marriage dropped drastically over this period, from 68% to 39%. Working women, who made up a fairly small number of all married women in 1957, hardly changed attitudes at all, dropping only from 43% to 42%. The proportion of working men who found marriage and children burdensome and restrictive more than doubled, from 25% to 56% and from 25% to 58%, respectively. Although some of these changes reflected greater willingness in 1976 than in 1957 to admit negative attitudes toward marriage and parenthood—itself significant—profound changes were clearly in process. More and more men and women were experiencing disaffection with family life.[8]

"All Burdens and Restrictions"

Apparently, the benefits of the good-provider role were greater than the costs for most men. Despite the legend of the flight of the American male (Fiedler, 1962), despite the defectors and dropouts, despite the tavern habitués "ball and chain" cliché, men seemed to know that the good-provider role, if they could succeed in it, was good for them. But Douvan's (Note 2) findings suggest that recently their complaints have become serious, bone-deep. The family they have been providing for is not the same family it was in the past.

Smith (1979) calls the great trek of married women into the labor force a subtle revolution—revolutionary not in the sense of one class overthrowing a status quo and substituting its own regime, but revolutionary in its impact on both the family and the work roles of men and women. It diluted the prerogatives of the good-provider role. It increased the demands made on the good provider, especially in the form of more emotional investment in the family, more sharing of household responsibilities. The role became even more burdensome.

However men may now feel about the burdens and restrictions imposed on them by the good-provider role, most have, at least ostensibly, accepted them. The

---

[8]Men seem to be having problems with both work and family roles. Veroff (Note 3), for example, reports an increased "sense of dissatisfaction with the social relations in the work setting" and a "dissatisfaction with the affiliative nature of work" (p. 47). This dissatisfaction may be one of the factors that leads men to seek affiliative-need satisfaction in marriage, just as in the 19th century they looked to the home as shelter from the jungle of the outside world.

tramp and the bum had "voted with their feet" against the role; the hobo or Wobbly had rejected it on the basis of a revolutionary ideology that saw it as enslaving men to the corporation; tavern humor had glossed the resentment habitués felt against its demands. Now the "burdens-and-restrictions" motif has surfaced both in research reports and, more blatantly, in the male liberation movement. From time to time it has also appeared in the clinicians' notes.

Sometimes the resentment of the good provider takes the form of simply wanting more appreciation for the life-style he provides. All he does for his family seems to be taken for granted. Thus, for example, Goldberg (1976), a psychiatrist, recounts the case of a successful businessman:

> He's feeling a deepening sense of bitterness and frustration about his wife and family. He doesn't feel appreciated. It angers him the way they seem to take the things his earnings purchase for granted. They've come to expect it as their due. It particularly enrages him when his children put him down for his "materialistic middle-class trip." He'd like to tell them to get someone else to support them but he holds himself back. (p. 124)

Brenton (1966) quotes a social worker who describes an upper-middle-class woman: She has "gotten hold of a man who'll drive himself mad to get money, and [is] denigrating him for being too interested in money, and not interested in music, or the arts, or in spending time with the children. But at the same time she's subtly driving him—and doesn't know it" (p. 226). What seems significant about such cases is not that men feel resentful about the lack of appreciation but that they are willing to justify their resentment. They are no longer willing to grin and bear it.

Sometimes there is even more than expressed resentment; there is an actual repudiation of the role. In the past, only a few men like the hobo or Wobbly were likely to give up. Today, Goldberg (1976) believes, more are ready to renounce the role, not on theoretical revolutionary grounds, however, but on purely selfish ones:

> Male growth will stem from openly avowed, unashamed, self-oriented motivation. . . . Guilt-oriented "should" behavior will be rejected because it is always at the price of a hidden build-up of resentment and frustration and alienation from others and is, therefore, counterproductive. (p. 184)

The disaffection of the good provider is directed to both sides of his role. With respect to work, Lefkowitz (1979) has described men among whom the good-provider role is neither being completely rejected nor repudiated, but diluted. These men began their working lives in the conventional style, hopeful and ambitious. The found a job, married, raised a family, and "achieved a measure of economic security and earned the respect of . . . colleagues and neighbors" (Lefkowitz, 1979, p. 31). In brief, they successfully performed the good-provider role. But unlike their historical predecessors, they in time became disillusioned with their jobs—not jobs on assembly lines, not jobs usually characterized as alienating, but fairly prestigious jobs such as aeronautics engineer and government economist. They daydreamed about other interests. "The common theme which surfaced again and again in their histories, was the need to find a new social connection—to reassert control over their lives, to gain some sense of freedom" (Lefkowitz, 1979, p. 31). These men felt "entitled to freedom and independence." Middle-class, educated, self-assured, articulate, and for the most part white, they knew they could talk themselves into a job if they had to. Most of them did not want to desert their families. Indeed, most of them "wanted to rejoin the intimate circle they felt they had neglected in their years of work" (p. 31).

Though some of the men Lefkowitz studied sought closer ties with their families, in the case of those studied by Sarason (1977), a psychologist, career changes involved lower income and had a negative impact on families. Sarason's subjects were also men in high-level professions, the very men least likely to find marriage and parenthood burdensome and restrictive. Still, since career change often involved a reduction in pay, some wives were unwilling to accept it, with the result that the marriage deteriorated (p. 178). Sometimes it looked like a no-win game. The husband's earlier career brought him feelings of emptiness and alienation, but it also brought financial rewards for the family. Greater work satisfaction for him in lower paying work meant reduced satisfaction with life-style. These findings lead Sarason to raise a number of points with respect to the good-provider role. "How much," he asks, "does an individual or a family need in order to maintain a satisfactory existence? Is an individual being responsible to himself or to his family if he provides them with little more than the bare essentials of living?" (p. 178). These [are] questions about the good-provider role that few men raised in the past.

Lefkowitz (1979) wonders how his downwardly mobile men lived when they left their jobs. "They put together a basic economic package which consisted of government assistance, contributions from family members who had not worked before and some bartering of goods and services" (p. 31). Especially interesting in this list of income sources are the "contributions from family members who had not worked before" (p. 31). Surely not mothers and sisters. Who, of course, but wives?

Women and the Provider Role

The present discussion began with the woman's part in the provider role. We saw how as more and more of the provisioning of the family came to be by way of monetary exchange, the woman's part shrank. A woman could still provide services, but could furnish little in the way of food, clothing, and shelter. But now that she is entering the labor force in large numbers, she can once more resume her ancient role, this time, like her male counterpart the provider, by way of a monetary contribution. More and more women are doing just this.

The assault of the good-provider role in the Depression was traumatic. But a modified version began to appear in the 1970s as a single income became inadequate for more and more families. Husbands have remained the major providers, but in an increasing number of cases the wife has begun to share this role. Thus, the proportion of married women aged 15 to 54 (living with their husbands) in the labor force more than doubled between 1950 and 1978, from 25.2% to 55.4%. The proportion for 1990 is estimated to reach 66.7% (Smith, 1979, p. 14). Fewer women are now full-time housewives.

For some men the relief from the strain of sole responsibility for the provider role has been welcome. But for others the feeling of degradation resembles the feeling reported 40 years earlier in the Great Depression. It is not that they are no longer providing for the family but that the role-sharing wife now feels justified in making demands on them. The good-provider role with all its prerogatives and perquisites has undergone profound changes. It will never be the same again.[9] Its death knell was sounded when, as noted above, the 1980 census no longer automatically assumed that the male member of the household was its head.

The Current Scene

Among the new demands being made on the good-provider role, two deserve special consideration, namely, (1) more intimacy, expressivity, and nurturance—specifications never included in it as it originally took shape—and (b) more sharing of household responsibilities and child care.

As the pampered wife in an affluent household came often to be an economic parasite, so also the good provider was often, in a way, a kind of emotional parasite. Implicit in the definition of the role was that he provided goods and material things. Tender loving care was not one of the requirements. Emotional ministrations from the family were his right; providing them was not a corresponding obligation. Therefore, as de Tocqueville had already noted by 1840, women suffered a kind of emotional deprivation labeled by Robert Weiss "relational deficit" (cited in Bernard, 1976). Only recently has this male rejection of emotional expression come to be challenged. Today, even blue-collar women are imposing "a host of new role expectations upon their husbands or lovers. . . . A new role set asks the blue-collar male to strive for . . . deep-coursing intimacy" (Shostak, Note 4, p. 75). It was not only vis-à-vis his family that the good provider was lacking in expressivity. This lack was built into the whole male role script. Today not only women but also men are beginning to protest the repudiation of expressivity prescribed in male roles (David & Brannon, 1976; Farrell, 1974; Fasteau, 1974; Pleck & Sawyer, 1974).

Is there any relationship between the "imposing" on men of "deep-coursing intimacy" by women on one side and the increasing proportion of men who find marriage burdensome and restrictive on the other? Are men seeing the new

---

[9]Among the indices of the waning of the good-provider role are the increasing number of married women in the labor force; the growth in the number of female-headed families; the growing trend toward egalitarian norms in marriage; the need for two earners in so many middle-class families; and the recognition of these trends in the abandonment of the identification of head of household as a male.

emotional involvement being asked of them as "all burdens and restrictions"? Are they responding to the new involvements under duress? Are they feeling oppressed by them? Fearful of them?

From the standpoint of high-level pure-science research there may be something bizarre, if not even slightly absurd, in the growing corpus of serious research on how much or how little husbands of employed wives contribute to household chores and child care. Yet is is serious enough that all over the industrialized world such research is going on. Time studies in a dozen countries—communist as well as capitalist—trace the slow and bungling process by which marriage accommodates to changing conditions and by which women struggle to mold the changing conditions in their behalf. For everywhere the same picture shows up in research: an image of women sharing the provider role and at the same time retaining responsibility for the household. Until recently such a topic would have been judged unworthy of serious attention. It was a subject that might be worth a good laugh, for instance, as when an all-thumbs man in a cartoon burns the potatoes or finds himself bumbling awkwardly over a diaper, demonstrating his—proud—male ineptness at such female work. But it is no longer funny.

The "politics of housework" (Mainardi, 1970) proves to be more profound than originally believed. It has to do not only with tasks but also with gender—and perhaps more with the site of the tasks than with their intrinsic nature. A man can cook magnificently if he does it on a hunting or fishing trip; he can wield a skillful needle if he does it mending a tent or a fishing net; he can even feed and clean a toddler on a camping trip. Few of the skills of the homemaker are beyond his reach so long as they are practiced in a suitably male environment. It is not only women's work in and of itself that is degrading but any work on female turf. It may be true, as Brenton (1966) says, that "the secure man can wash a dish, diaper a baby, and throw the dirty clothes into the washing machine—or do anything else women used to do exclusively—without thinking twice about it" (p. 211), but not all men are that secure. To a great many men such chores are demasculinizing. The apron is shameful in a man in the kitchen; it is all right at the carpenter's bench.

The male world may look upon the man who shares household responsibilities as, in effect, a scab. One informant tells the interviewer about a conversation on the job: "What, are you crazy?" his hard-hat fellow workers ask him when he speaks of helping his wife. "The guys want to kill me. 'You son of a bitch! You are getting us in trouble.' . . . The men get really mad" (Lein, 1979, p. 492). Something more than persiflage is involved here. We are fairly familiar with the trauma associated with the invasion by women of the male work turf, the hazing women can be subjected to, and the male resentment of admitting them except into their own segregated areas. The corresponding entrance of men into the traditional turf of women—the kitchen or the nursery—has analogous but not identical concomitants.

Pleck and Lang (1979) tell us that men are now beginning to change in the direction of greater involvement in family life. "Men's family behavior is beginning to change, becoming increasingly congruent with the long-standing psychological significance of the family in their lives" (p. 1). They measure this greater involvement by way of the help they offer with homemaking chores. Scanzoni (1975), on the basis of a survey of over 3,000 husbands and wives, concludes that at least in households in which wives are in the labor force, there is the "possibility of a different pattern in which responsibility for households would unequivocally fall equally on husbands as well as wives" (p. 38). A brave new world indeed. Still, when we look at the reality around us, the pace seems intolerably slow. The responsibilities of the old good-provider role have attenuated far faster than have its prerogatives and privileges.

A considerable amount of thought has been devoted to studying the effects of the large influx of women into the work force. An equally interesting question is what the effect will be if a large number of men actually do increase their participation in the family and the household. Will men find the apron shameful? What if we were to ask fathers to alternate with mothers in being in the home when youngsters come home from school? Would fighting adolescent drug abuse be more successful if fathers and mothers were equally engaged in it? If the school could confer with fathers as often as with mothers? If the father accompanied children when they went shopping for clothes? If fathers spent as much time with children as do mothers?

Even as husbands, let alone as fathers, the new pattern is not without trauma. Hall and Hall (1979), in their study of two-career couples, report that the most serious fights among such couples occur not in the bedroom, but in the kitchen, between couples who profess a commitment to equality but who find actually implementing it difficult. A young professional reports that he is philosophically committed to egalitarianism in marriage and tries hard to practice it, but it does not work. He even feels guilty about this. The stresses involved in reworking roles may have an impact on health. A study of engineers and accountants finds poorer health among those with employed wives than among those with nonemployed wives (Burke & Wier, 1976). The processes involved in role change have been compared with those involved in deprogramming a cult member. Are they part of the increasing sense of marriage and parenthood as "all burdens and restrictions"?

The demise of the good-provider role also calls for consideration of other questions: What does the demotion of the good provider to the status of senior provider or even mere coprovider do to him? To marriage? To gender identity? What does expanding the role of housewife to that of junior provider or even coprovider do to her? To marriage? To gender identity? Much will of course depend on the social and psychological ambience in which changes take place.

A Parable

I began this essay with a proverbial woman. I close it with a modern parable by William H. Chafe (Note 5), a historian who also keeps his eye on the current scene. Jack and Jill, both planning professional careers, he as doctor, she as lawyer, marry at age 24. She works to put him through medical school in the expectation that he will then finance her through law school. A child is born during the husband's internship, as planned. But in order for him to support her through professional training as planned, he will have to take time out from his career. After two years, they decide that both will continue their training on a part-time basis, sharing household responsibilities and using day-care services. Both find part-time positions and work out flexible work schedules that leave both of them time for child care and companionship with one another. They live happily ever after.

That's the end? you ask incredulously. Well, not exactly. For, as Chafe (Note 5) points out, as usual the personal is also political:

> Obviously such a scenario presumes a radical transformation of the personal values that today's young people bring to their relationships as well as a readiness on the part of social and economic institutions to encourage, or at least make possible, the development of equality between men and women. (p. 28)

The good-provider role may be on its way out, but its legitimate successor has not yet appeared on the scene.

Reference Notes

1. Hasselbart, S. *Some underemphasized issues about men, women, and work.* Unpublished manuscript, 1978.
2. Douvan, E. *Family roles in a twenty-year perspective.* Paper presented at the Radcliffe Pre-Centennial Conference. Cambridge, Massachusetts, April 2–4, 1978.
3. Veroff, J. *Psychological orientations to the work role: 1957–1976.* Unpublished manuscript. 1978.
4. Shostak, A. *Working class Americans at home: Changing expectations of manhood.* Unpublished manuscript, 1973.
5. Chafe, W. *The challenge of sex equality: A new culture or old values revisited?* Paper presented at the Radcliffe Pre-Centennial Conference. Cambridge, Massachusetts, April 2–4, 1978.

References

Babcock, B., Freedman, A. E., Norton, E. H., & Ross, S. C. *Sex discrimination and the law: Causes and remedies.* Boston: Little, Brown, 1975.

Bernard, J. *Women, wives, mothers.* Chicago: Aldine, 1975.

Bernard, J. Homosociality and female depression. *Journal of Social Issues,* 1976, *32,* 207–224.

Boulding, E. Familial constraints on women's work roles. *SIGNS: Journal of Women in Culture and Society,* 1976, *1,* 95–118.

Brenton, M. *The American male.* New York: Coward-McCann, 1966.

Burke, R., & Weir, T. Relationships of wives' employment status to husband, wife and pair satisfaction and performance. *Journal of Marriage and the Family,* 1976, *38,* 279–287.

David, D. S., & Brannon, R. (Eds.). *The forty-nine percent majority: The male sex role.* Reading, Mass.: Addison-Wesley, 1976.

Demos, J. The American family in past time. *American Scholar,* 1974, *43,* 422–446.

Farrell, W. *The liberated man.* New York: Random House, 1974.

Fasteau, M. F. *The male machine.* New York: McGraw-Hill, 1974.

Fiedler, L. *Love and death in the American novel.* New York: Meredith, 1962.

Foner, P. S. *Women and the American labor movement.* New York: Free Press, 1979.

Freud, S. *Civilization and its discontents.* New York: Doubleday-Anchor, 1958. (Originally published, 1930.)

Goldberg, H. *The hazards of being male.* New York: New American Library, 1976.

Gould, R. E. Measuring masculinity by the size of a paycheck. In J. E. Pleck & J. Sawyer (Eds.), *Men and masculinity.* Englewood Cliffs, N.J.: Prentice-Hall, 1974. (Also published in *Ms.,* June 1973, pp. 18ff.)

Hall, D., & Hall, F. *The two-career couple.* Reading, Mass.: Addison-Wesley, 1979.

Jones, C. A. *A review of child support payment performance.* Washington, D.C.:Urban Institute, 1976.

Keniston, K. *The uncommitted: Alienated youth in American society.* New York: Harcourt, Brace & World, 1965.

Komarovsky, M. *The unemployed man and his family.* New York: Dryden Press, 1940.

Lefkowitz, B. Life without work. *Newsweek,* May 14, 1979, p. 31.

Lein, L. Responsibility in the allocation of tasks. *Family Coordinator,* 1979, *28,* 489–496.

Liebow, E. *Tally's corner.* Boston: Little, Brown, 1966.

Lopata, H. *Occupational housewife.* New York: Oxford University Press, 1971.

Mainardi, P. The politics of housework. In R. Morgan (Ed.), *Sisterhood is powerful.* New York: Vintage Books, 1970.

Pleck, J. H., & Lang, L. Men's family work: Three perspectives and some new data. *Family Coordinator,* 1979, *28,* 481–488.

Pleck, J. H., & Sawyer, J. (Eds.), *Men and masculinity.* Englewood Cliffs, N.J.: Prentice-Hall, 1974.

Rainwater, L., & Yancy, W. L. *The Moynihan report and the politics of controversy.* Cambridge, Mass.: M.I.T. Press, 1967.

Sarason, S. B. *Work, aging, and social change.* New York: Free Press, 1977.

Scanzoni, J. H. *Sex roles, life styles, and childbearing: Changing patterns in marriage and the family.* New York: Free Press, 1975.

Scanzoni, J. H. An historical perspective on husband-wife bargaining power and marital dissolution. In G. Levinger & O. Moles (Eds.), *Divorce and separation in America.* New York: Basic Books, 1979.

Smith, R. E. (Ed.), *The subtle revolution.* Washington, D.C.: Urban Institute, 1979.

Smuts, R. W. *Women and work in America.* New York: Columbia University Press, 1959.

Snyder, L. The deserting, non-supporting father: Scapegoat of family non-policy. *Family Coordinator,* 1979, *38,* 594–598.

Tocqueville, A. de. *Democracy in America.* New York: J. & H. G. Hangley, 1840.

Warner, W. L., & Ablegglen, J. O. *Big business leaders in America.* New York: Harper, 1955.

Yankelovich, D. The new psychological contracts at work. *Psychology Today,* May, 1978, pp. 46–47; 49–50.

Zborowski, M., & Herzog, E. *Life is with people.* New York: Schocken Books, 1952.

Why Men Resist

William J. Goode

Although few if any men in the United States remain entirely untouched by the women's movement, to most men what is happening seems to be "out there" and has little direct effect on their own roles. To them, the movement is a dialogue mainly among women, conferences of women about women, a mixture of just or exaggerated complaints and shrill and foolish demands to which men need not even respond, except now and then. When men see that a woman resents a common male act of condescension, such as making fun of women in sports or management, most males are still as surprised as corporation heads are when told to stop polluting a river.

For the time being, men are correct in this perception if one focuses on the short run only. It is not often that social behavior deeply rooted in tradition alters rapidly. Over the long run, they are not likely to be correct, and indeed I believe they are vaguely uneasy when they consider their present situation. As against numerous popular commentators, I do not think we are now witnessing a return to the old ways, a politically reactionary trend, and I do not think the contemporary attack on male privilege will ultimately fail.

The worldwide demand for equality is voiced not only by women; many groups have pressed for it, with more persistence, strength, and success over the past generation than in any prior epoch of world history. It has also been pressed by more kinds of people than ever before; ethnic and racial groups, castes, subnational groups such as the Scots or Basques, classes, colonies, and political regimes. An ideal so profoundly moving will ultimately prevail, in some measure, where the structural bases for traditional dominance are weakened. The ancient bases for male dominance are no longer as secure as they once were, and male resistance to these pressures will weaken.

Males will stubbornly resist, but reluctantly adjust, because women will continue to want more equality than they now enjoy and will be unhappy if they do not get it; because men on average will prefer that their women be happy; because a majority of either sex will not find an adequate substitute for the other sex; and because neither will be able to build an alternative social system alone. When dominant classes or groups cannot rig the system as much in their favor as they once did, they will work within it just the same; to revise an old adage, if that is the only roulette wheel in town, they will play it even if it is honest and fair.

To many women, the very title of my essay is an exercise in banality, for there is no puzzle. To analyze the peculiar thoughtways of men seems unnecessary, since ultimately their resistance is that of dominant groups throughout history: They enjoy an exploitive position that yields them an unearned profit in money, power, and prestige. Why should they give it up?

The answer contains of course some part of the truth, but we shall move more effectively toward equality only if we grasp much more of the truth [than] that bitter view reveals. If it were completely true, then the greater power of men would have made all societies male-vanity cultures, in which women are kept behind blank walls and forced to work at productive tasks only with their sisters, while men laze away their hours in parasitic pleasure. In fact, one can observe that the position of women varies a good deal by class, by society, and over time, and no one has succeeded in proving that those variations are the simple result of men's exploitation.

Indeed there are inherent socioeconomic contradictions in any attempt by males to create a fully exploitative set of material advantages for all males. Moreover, there are inherent *emotional* contradictions in any effort to achieve full domination in that intimate sphere.

As to the first contradiction, women—and men in the same situation—who are powerless, slavish, and ignorant are most easily exploitable, and thus there are always some male pressures to place them in that position. Unfortunately, such women do not yield much surplus product. In fact, they do not produce much at all. Women who are freer and more in command of productive skills, as in hunting and gathering societies and increasingly in modern industrial ones, produce far more, but they are also more resistant to exploitation or domination. Without understanding that powerful relationship, men have moved throughout history toward one or the other of these great choices, with their built-in disadvantages and advantages.

As to emotional ties, men would like to be lords of their castle and to be loved absolutely—if successful, this is the cheapest exploitative system—but in real life this is less likely to happen unless one loves in return. In that case what happens is what happens in real life: Men care about the joys and sorrows of their women. Mutual caring reduces the degree to which men are willing to exploit their wives, mothers, and sisters. More interesting, their caring also takes the form of wanting to prevent *other* men from exploiting these women when they are in the outside world. That is, men as individuals know that *they* are to be trusted, and so should have great power, but other men cannot be trusted, and so the laws should restrain such fellows.

These large sets of contrary tensions have some effect on even those contemporary men who do not believe that the present relations between men and women are unjust. Both sets, moreover, support the present trend toward greater equality. In short, men do resist, but these and other tensions prevent them from resisting as fully as they might otherwise, while not so much as a cynical interpretation of their private attitudes would expect. On the other hand, they do resist somewhat more strenuously than we should predict from their public assertion in favor of, for example, equal pay, or slogans like "liberty and justice for all."

This exposition is necessarily limited. Even to present the latest data on the supposed psychological traits of males would require more space than is available here. I shall try to avoid the temptation of simply describing men's reactions to the women's movement, although I do plan to inform you of men's attitudes toward some aspects of equality. I shall try to avoid defending men, except to the extent that explaining them may be a defense. And, as is already obvious, I shall not assert that we are on the brink of a profound, sudden change in sex-role allocations, in the direction of equality, for we must never underestimate the cunning or the staying power of those in charge. Finally, because all of you are also observers of men, it is unlikely that I can bring forward many findings that are entirely unknown to you. At best, I can suggest some fruitful, perhaps new, ways of looking at male roles. Within these limitations, I shall focus on the following themes:

1. As against the rather narrow definition of men's roles to be found in the current literature on the topic, I want to remind you of a much wider range of traditionally approved roles in this and other cultures.
2. As against the conspiracy theory of the oppression of women, I shall suggest a modest "sociology of the dominant group" to interpret men's behavior and thinking about male roles and thus some modest hypotheses about why they resist.
3. I shall point to two central areas of role behavior, occupations and domestic tasks, where change seems glacial at present and men's resistance strong.
4. As against those who feel that if utopia does not arrive with the next full moon, we should all despair, I shall point to some processes now occurring that are different from any in recorded history and that will continue to press toward more fundamental changes in men's social positions in this as well as other countries of the world.

The Range of Sex Roles

Let me begin by reminding you of the standard sociological view about the allocation of sex roles. Although it is agreed that we can, with only small error, divide the population into males and females, the biological differences between the two that might affect the distribution of sex roles—which sex is supposed to do which social tasks, which should have which rights—are much too small to determine the large differences in sex-role allocation within any given society or to explain the curious doctrines that serve to uphold it. Second, even if some differences would give an advantage to men (or women) in some tasks or achievements, the overlap in talent is so great that a large minority of men (or women) could do any tasks as well as could members of the other sex. Third, the biological differences are too fixed in anatomy and physiology to account for the wide diversity of sex-role allocation we observe when we compare different societies over time and cultures.

Consequently, most sex-role allocation must be explained by how we rear children, by the sexual division of labor, by the cultural definitions of what is appropriate to the sexes, and by the social pressures we put on the two sexes. Since human beings created these role assignments, they can also change them. On the other hand, these roles afford large advantages to men (e.g., opportunity, range of choices, mobility, payoffs for what is accomplished, cultivation of skills, authority, and prestige) in this and every other society we know. Consequently, men are likely to resist large alterations in roles. They will do so even though they understand that in exchange for their privileges, they have to pay high costs in morbidity, mortality, and failure.[1] As a consequence of this fact about men's position, it can be supposed that they will resist unless their ability to rig the system in their favor is somehow reduced. It is my belief that this capacity is in fact being undermined somewhat, though not at a rapid rate.

A first glance at descriptions of the male role, especially as described in the literature about mass media, social stereotypes, family roles, and personality attributes, suggests that the male role is definite, narrow, and agreed upon. Males, we are told, are pressed into a specific mold. For example, ". . . the male role prescribes that men be active, aggressive, competitive, . . . while the female role prescribes that women should be nurturant, warm, altruistic . . . and the like."[2] The male role requires the suppression of emotion, or "the male role, as personally and socially defined, requires men to appear tough, objective, striving, achieving, unsentimental. . . . If he weeps, if he shows weakness, he will likely be viewed as unmanly. . . ." Or: "Men are programmed to be strong and 'aggressive.' "[3]

We are so accustomed to reading such descriptions that we almost believe them, unless we stop to ask, first, how many men do we actually know who carry out these social prescriptions (i.e., how many are emotionally anesthetized, aggressive, physically tough and daring, unwilling or unable to give nurturance to a child)? Second, and this is the test of a social role, do they lose their membership cards in the male fraternity if they fail in these respects? If socialization and social pressures are so all-powerful, where are all the John Wayne types in our society? Or, to ask a more searching question, how seriously should we take such sex-role prescriptions if so few men live up to them?

The key fact is not that many men do not live up to such prescriptions; rather, it is that many other qualities and performances are also viewed as acceptable or admirable, and this is true even among boys, who are often thought to be strong supporters of sex stereotypes. The *macho* boy is admired, but so is the one who edits the school newspaper, who draws cartoons, or who is simply a warm friend. There are at least a handful of ways of being an admired professor. Indeed a common feminist complaint against the present system is that women are much more narrowly confined in the ways they are permitted to be professors, or members of any occupation.

But we can go further. A much more profound observation is that oppressed groups are *typically* given narrow ranges of social roles, while dominant groups afford their members a far wider set of behavior patterns, each qualitatively different but each still accepted or esteemed in varying degrees. One of the privileges granted, or simply assumed, by ruling groups, is that they can indulge in a variety of eccentricities while still demanding and getting a fair measure of authority or prestige. Consider in this connection, to cite only one spectacular example, the crotchets and quirks cultivated by the English upper classes over the centuries.

Moreover, if we enlarge our vision to encompass other times and places, the range becomes even greater. We are not surprised to observe Latin American men embrace one another, Arab or Indian boys walk together hand in hand, or seminary students being gentle. The male role prescriptions that commonly appear in the literature do not describe correctly the male ideal in Jewish culture, which embodied a love of music, learning, and literature; an avoidance of physical violence; an acceptance of tears and sentiments, nurturance, and a sensitivity to others' feelings. In the South that I knew a half a century ago, young rural boys were expected to nurture their younger siblings, and male-male relations were ideally expected to be tender, supporting, and expressed occasionally by embraces. Among my own kin, some fathers then kissed their school-age sons; among Greek-Americans in New York City, that practice continues many decades later. Or, to consider England once more, let us remember the admired men of Elizabethan England. True enough, one ideal was the violent, daring Francis Drake and the brawling poet Ben Jonson. But men also expressed themselves in kissing and embracing, writing love poems to one another, donning decorative (not to say gaudy and efflorescent) clothing, and studying flowers as well as the fiery heavens.

We assert, then, that men manage to be in charge of things in all societies but that their very control permits them to create a wide range of ideal male roles, with the consequence that large numbers of men, not just a few, can locate rewarding positions in the social structure. Thereby, too, they considerably narrow the options left for feminine sex roles. Feminists especially resent the narrowness of the feminine role in informal interaction, where they feel they are dealt with only as women, however this may be softened by personal warmth or affection.

We can recognize that general relationship in a widespread male view, echoed over the centuries, that males are people, individuals, while women are lumped together as an aggregate. Or, in more modern language: Women have roles, a delimited number of parts to play, but men cannot be described so simply.

Nor is that peculiar male view contradicted by the complaint, again found in all major civilizations, that women are mysterious, unpredictable, moved by forces outside men's understanding, and not controllable. Even that master of psychodynamics Sigmund Freud expressed his bewilderment by asking, "What do women want?" Men have found their women difficult to understand for a simple reason: They have continued to try to think of them as a set of roles (above all else, mothers and wives), but in fact women do not fit these roles, not only not now, but not in the past either. Some women were great fighting machines, not compliant; some were competitive and aggressive, not nurturant; many were incompetent or reluctant mothers. They have been queens and astronomers, moralists and nurturers, leaders of religious orders as well as corporations, and so on. At any point, men could observe that women were ignoring or breaking out of their social molds, and men experienced that discrepancy as puzzling. However, it is only recently that many have faced the blunt fact that there is no feminine riddle at all: Women are as complex as men are, and always will escape the confinements of any narrow set of roles.

The Sociology of Superordinates

That set of relationships is only part of the complex male view, and I want to continue with my sketch of the main elements in what may be called the "sociology of superordinates." That is, I believe that there are some general principles or regularities to be found in the view held by superordinates—here, the sex-class called males—about relations with subordinates, in this instance women. These regularities do not justify, but they do explain in some degree, the modern resistance of men to their new social situation.[4] Here are some of them:

1. The observations made by either men or women about members of the other sex are limited and somewhat biased by what they are most interested in and by their lack of opportunity to observe behind the scenes of each others' lives.[5] However, far less of what men do is determined by women; what men do affects women much more. As a consequence, men are often simply less motivated to observe carefully many aspects of women's behavior and activity because women's behavior does not usually affect what men propose to do. By contrast, almost everything men do will affect what women *have* to do, and thus women are motivated to observe men's behavior as keenly as they can.
2. Since any given cohort of men know they did not create the system that gives them their advantages, they reject any charges that they conspired to dominate women.
3. Since men, like other dominants or superordinates, take for granted the system that gives them their status, they are not aware of how much the social structure, from attitude patterns to laws, pervasively yields small, cumulative, and eventually large advantages in most competitions. As a consequence, they assume that their greater accomplishments are actually the result of inborn superiority.
4. As a corollary to this male view, when men weigh their situation, they are more aware of the burdens and responsibilities they bear than of their unearned advantages.
5. Superiors, and thus men, do not easily notice the talents or accomplishments of subordinates, and men have not in the past seen much wisdom in giving

women more opportunities for growth, for women are not capable of much anyway, especially in the areas of men's special skills. Thus, in the past, few women have embarrassed men by becoming superior in those areas. When they did, their superiority was seen, and is often still seen, as an odd exception. As a consequence, men see their superior position as a just one.

6. Men view even small losses of deference, advantages, or opportunities as large threats. Their own gains, or their maintenance of old advantages, are not noticed as much.[6]

Although the male view is similar to that of superordinates generally, as the foregoing principles suggest, one cannot simply equate the two. The structural position of males is different from that of superordinate groups, classes, ethnic populations, or castes. Males are, first, not a group, but a social segment or a statistical aggregate within the society. They share much of a common destiny, but they share few if any *group* or *collective* goals (within small groups they may be buddies, but not with all males). Second, males share with certain women whatever gain or loss they experience as members of high or low castes, ethnic groups, or classes. For example, women in a ruling stratum share with their men a high social rank, deference from the lower orders, and so on; men in a lowly Indian caste share that rank with their women, too. In modern societies, men and women in the same family are on a more or less equal basis with respect to "inheritance, educational opportunity (at least undergraduate), personal consumption of goods, most rights before the law, and the love and responsibility of their children."[7] They are not fully equal, to be sure, but much more equal than are members of very different castes or social classes.

Moreover, from the male view, women also enjoy certain exemptions: "freedom from military conscription, whole or partial exemption from certain kinds of heavy work, preferential courtesies of various kinds." Indeed, men believe, on the whole, that their own lot is the more difficult one.[8]

Most important as a structural fact that prevents the male view from being simply that of a superordinate is that these superordinates, like their women, do not live in set-apart communities, neighborhoods, or families. Of course, other such categories are not sequestered either, such as alcoholics, ex-mental patients, or the physically handicapped, but these are, as Goffman points out, "scattered somewhat haphazardly through the social structure." That is not so for men; like their women, they are allocated to households in a nonrandom way, for "law and custom allow only one to a household, but strongly encourage the presence of that one."[9]

A consequence of this important structural arrangement is that men and women are separated from their own sex by having a stake in the organization that gives each a set of different roles, or a different emphasis to similar roles: women especially come to have a vested interest in the social unit that at the same time imposes inequalities on them. This coalition between the two individuals makes it difficult for members of the same sex to join with large numbers of persons of their own sex for purposes of defense or exploitation. This applies equally to men and women.

One neat consequence may be seen in the hundreds of family law provisions created over the centuries that seem to run at cross-purposes. Some gave more freedom to women in order to protect them from predatory or exploitative males (i.e., in the male view, *other* men), and some took freedom away from women and put it in the hands of supposedly good and kindly men (i.e., heads of families, *themselves*). Or, in more recent times, the growing efforts of some fathers to press their daughters toward career competence so that they will not be helpless when abandoned by their future husbands, against those same fathers' efforts to keep their daughters docile and dutiful toward their protecting fathers.

You will note that male *views* are not contradictory in such instances, even though their *actions* may be. In coalition with their women, they oppose the exploitative efforts of outside men; within the family unit, however, they see little need for such protections against themselves, for they are sure of their own goodheartedness and wisdom.

That men see themselves as bound in a coalition with their families and thus with their daughters and wives is the cause of much common male resistance to the women's movement, while some have instead become angered at the unfair treatment their wives and daughters have experienced. The failure of many women to understand that complex male view has led to much misunderstanding.

Responses of Superordinates to Rebellion[10]

First, men are surprised at the outbreak. They simply had not known the depth of resentment that many women harbored, though of course many women had not known it either. Second, men are also hurt, for they feel betrayed. They discover, or begin to suspect, that the previously contented or pleasant facade their women presented to them was false, that they have been manipulated to believe in that presentation of self. Because males view themselves as giving protection against anyone exploiting or hurting their women, they respond with anger to the hostility they encounter, to the discovery that they were deceived, and to the charge that they have selfishly used the dominant position they feel they have rightfully earned.

A deeper, more complex source of male anger requires a few additional comments, for it relates to a central male role, that of jobholder and breadwinner. Most men, but especially most men outside the privileged stratum of professionals and managers, see their job as not yielding much intrinsic satisfaction, not being fun in itself, but they pride themselves on the hard work and personal sacrifice they make as breadwinners. In the male view, men make a gift of all this to their wives and children.[11]

Now they are told that it was not a gift, and they have not earned any special deference for it. In fact, their wives earned what they received, and indeed nothing is owing. If work is a sacrifice, they are told, so were all the services, comforts, and self-deprivations women provided. Whatever the justice of either claim, clearly if you think you are giving or sacrificing much to make gifts to someone over a period of time, and then you learn he or she feels the gifts were completely deserved, for the countergifts are asserted to have been as great and no gratitude or special debt was incurred, you are likely to be hurt or angry.[12]

I am reasonably certain about the processes I have just described. Let me go a step further and speculate that the male resentment is the greater because many fathers had already come to suspect that their children, especially in adolescence, were indifferent to those sacrifices, as well as to the values that justified them.[13] Thus, when women too begin to assert that men's gifts are not worth as much as men thought, the worth of the male is further denied.

Some Areas of Change and Nonchange

Although I have not heard specific complaints about it, I believe that the most important change in men's position, as they experience it, is a loss of centrality, a decline in the extent to which they are the center of attention. In our time, other superordinates have also suffered this loss: colonial rulers, monarchs and nobles, and U.S. whites both northern and southern, to name a few.

Boys and grown men have always taken for granted that what they were doing was more important than what the other sex was doing, that where they were was where the action was. Their women accepted that definition. Men occupied the center of the stage, and women's attention was focused on them. Although that position is at times perilous, open to failure, it is also desirable.

Men are still there of course, and will be there throughout our lifetime. Nevertheless, some changes are perceptible. The center of attention shifts to women more now than in the past. I believe that this shift troubles men far more, and creates more of their resistance, than the women's demand for equal opportunity and pay in employment.

The change is especially observable in informal relations, and men who are involved with women in the liberation movement experience it most often. Women find each other more interesting than in the past, and focus more on what each other is doing, for they are in fact doing more interesting things. Even when they are not, their work occupies more of their attention, whether they are professionals or factory workers. Being without a man for a while does not seem to be so bereft a state as it once was. I also believe that this change affects men more now than at the time of the suffragist movement half a century ago, not only because more women now participate in it but also because men were then more solidary and could rely on more all-male organizations and clubs; now, they are more dependent on women for solace and intimacy.

As a side issue, let me note that the loss of centrality has its counterpart among feminist women too, and its subtlety should be noted. Such women now reject a certain type of traditional centrality they used to experience, because its costs are too great. Most women know the experience of being the center of attention:

When they enter a male group, conversation changes in tone and subject. They are likely to be the focus of comments, many of them pleasurable; affectionate teasing, compliments, warmth. However, these comments put women into a special mold, the stereotyped female. Their serious comments are not welcomed or applauded, or their ideas are treated as merely amusing. Their sexuality is emphasized. Now, feminist women find that kind of centrality less pleasant—in fact, condescending—and they avoid it when they can. In turn, many men feel awkward in this new situation, for their repertory of social graces is now called boorish.

Although I have noted men's feelings of hurt and anger, I want to emphasize that I believe no backlash of any consequence has been occurring, and no trend toward more reactionary male attitudes exists. Briefly, there is a continuing attitude change on the part of both men and women, in favor of more equality. The frequent expressions of male objection, sometimes labeled "backlash" in the popular press, can be attributed to two main sources: (1) The discovery, by some men who formerly did pay lip service to the principle of equality, that they do not approve of its concrete application; and (2) active resistance by men and women who simply never approved of equality anyway and who have now begun to oppose it openly because it can no longer be seen as a trivial threat. Most of this is incorrectly labeled "backlash," which ought instead to refer only to the case in which people begin to feel negative toward a policy they once thought desirable, because now it has led to undesirable results. Those who oppose women's rights like to label any support they get a backlash because thereby they can claim that "women have gone too far."

It may surprise you to learn that it is not possible to summarize here all the various changes in public opinion about sex roles, as attitudes have shifted over the past generation, simply because pollsters did not bother to record the data. They often did not try to find out about social trends and thus only rarely asked the same questions in successive decades. One unfortunate result is that one of the most fiercely debated events of this period, the women's liberation movement, almost does not appear in the polls.[14]

The single finding that seems solid is that no data show any backward or regressive trend in men's attitudes about women's progress toward equality. The most often repeated question is not a profound one: whether a respondent would vote for a qualified woman for President. Favorable answers rose from about one-fourth of the men in 1937 to two-thirds in 1971, and to four-fifths among men and women combined in 1975. Another repeated question is whether a married woman should work if she has a husband able to support her, and here the answers of men and women combined rose from 18 percent in 1936 to 62 percent in 1975. In contrast to these large changes, a large majority favored equal pay, in principle at least, as early as 1942, and later data report no decrease.

In 1953, 21 percent of men said it made no difference whether they worked for a man or woman, and that figure rose slightly to 32 percent in 1975.[15] Polls in 1978 show that a large majority of the nation, both men and women, was in favor of the enforcement of laws forbidding job discrimination against women or discrimination in education; and most agreed that more women should be elected to public office.[16]

A plurality of only about 40 percent held such favorable opinions in 1970. On such issues, men and women did not differ by much, although, until recently, men's attitudes were somewhat more favorable. Divisions of opinion are sharper along other lines: The young are in favor more than the old, the more educated more favorable than the less educated, city dwellers more than rural people, blacks more than whites. Whatever the difference, clearly no substantial amount of male backlash has appeared. Through men's eyes, at least the *principle* of equality seems more acceptable than in the past. Their resistance is not set against that abstract idea. Modest progress, to be sure, but progress nonetheless.

I cannot forego making references to a subvariety of the backlash, which has been reported in hundreds of articles, that is, that more men are impotent because of women's increased sexual assertiveness. This impotence, we are told, appears when women discover the delights of their own sexuality, make it clear to their men that they will play coy no more, and indeed look at their men as sexual objects, at least sometimes.

The widespread appearance of male impotence as an answer to, or an escape from, increased female willingness would certainly be news,[17] but it violates the sexual view of most men, and much worse, it runs counter to the only large-scale data we have on the topic.[18] The male view may be deduced, if you will permit the literary reference, from traditional pornography, which was written by men and expressed male fantasies. Briefly, in such stories, but entirely contrary to real life, everything went smoothly: At every phase of the interaction, where women in real male experience are usually indifferent if not hostile, the hero encounters enthusiasm, and in response he himself performs miracles of sexual athleticism and ecstasy.

Nothing so embroidered is found in social science data, but it seems reasonably certain that in the five-year period ending in 1970, the married men of the United States increased the frequency of their lovemaking with their wives. Doubtless, there were pockets of increased impotence, but with equal security we can assert that most husbands did not have that experience.

The reason is clear, I think: The message of permission had finally been received by women, and they put it into action. In millions of how-to-do-it books and articles, they were not only told to enjoy themselves but were urged to do so by seducing their men. Since the most important sex organ is the human mind, these changes in the heads of both men and women caused changes in the body. Without question, the simplest and most effective antidote to male impotence, or even lassitude and nonperformance, is female encouragement and welcome. Even if a few cases of the backlash of impotence have occurred, that has not, I think, been a widespread trend among males in our time, as a psychological response to women's move toward some equality in sexuality itself. To this particular change among women, men have offered little resistance.

Domestic Duties and Jobs

So far, the opinion data give some small cause for optimism. Nevertheless, all announcements of the imminent arrival of utopias are premature. Men's approval of more equality for women has risen, but the record in two major areas of men's roles—the spheres of home and occupation—gives but little reason for optimism. Here we can be brief, for though the voluminous data are very complex, the main conclusion can easily be summarized.[19] The striking fact is that very little has changed, if we consider the society as a whole and focus on changes in behavior.

Let us consider the domestic role of men. They have contributed only slightly more time to their duties in the home than in the past—although "the past" is very short for time budgets of men's child-care and homemaking activities. By contrast, the best record now indicates that homemakers without jobs spend somewhat less time at their domestic tasks than they did ten years ago. Working wives allocate much less time (26–35 hours a week) to the home than do stay-at-home wives (35–55 hours), but *husbands* of working wives do almost as little as husbands of stay-at-home wives (about 10–13 hours weekly). We hear much these days about Russian husbands who expect their wives to hold jobs and also take care of housework and child care, but so do American husbands. Moreover, that is as true of the supposedly egalitarian Swedish or Finnish husbands as it is of German and French ones.[20]

Of course, there are some differences. If a child two years or younger is in the house, the father does more. Better-educated husbands do a bit more, and so do younger husbands. But the massive fact is that men's domestic contribution does not change much whether or not they work, and whether or not their wives work.[21] Still more striking is the fact that the past decade has shown little change in the percentage of women who want their husbands to take a larger share of domestic work, though once again it is the vanguard of the young, the educated, and the black who exhibit the largest increase. Studies have reported that only about 20 to 25 percent of wives express the wish for more domestic participation by their husbands, and that did not change greatly until the late 1970s.[22]

With reference to the second large area of men's roles, job holding, we observe two further general principles of the relations between superordinates and those of lesser ranks. One is that men do not, in general, feel threatened by competition from women if they believe the competition is fair and women do not have an inside track. Men still feel that they are superior and will do better if given the chance. Without actually trying the radical notion of genuinely fair competition, they have little reason to fear as yet: Compared with women, they were better off in wages and occupational position in the 1970s than in the 1950s.

The second principle is that those who hold advantaged positions in the social structure (men, in this case) can perceive or observe that they are being flooded by people they consider their inferiors—by women, blacks, or the lower classes— while the massive statistical fact is that only a few people are rising by much. There are several causes of this seeming paradox.

First, the new arrivals are so visible, so different from those who have held the jobs up to this time. The second cause is our perception of relative numbers. Since there are far fewer positions at higher levels, only a few new arrivals constitute a fair-sized minority of the total at that level. Third, the mass media emphasize the hiring of women in jobs that seem not to be traditional for them, for that is considered news. Men's structural position, then, causes them to perceive radical change here, and they resist it.

Nevertheless, the general conclusion does not change much. The amount of sex segregation in jobs is not much different from the past.[23] More important, there is no decrease in the gap between the earnings of men and women; at every job level, it is not very different from the past, and in the period from 1955 to 1971 the gap actually became somewhat larger. That is, a higher percentage of women entered the labor force, and at better wages than in the past, but men rose somewhat faster than they.

Although the mass figures are correct, we need not discount all our daily observation. We see women entering formerly masculine jobs from garbage collecting to corporate management. That helps undermine sex stereotypes and thereby becomes a force against inequality. For example, women bus drivers were hardly to be found in 1940, but they now make up 37 percent of that occupation; women bartenders now form 32 percent of that occupation, but a generation ago made up only 2.5 percent.[24] Although occupational segregation continued strong in the 1970s, it did decline in most professions (e.g., engineering, dentistry, science, law, medicine) between 1960 and 1970. That is, the percentage of women in these professions did rise.[25] Women now constitute over one-fourth of the law school classes in the higher-ranking law schools of the country. In occupations where almost everyone was once male, it is not possible to recruit, train, and hire enough women to achieve equality in a few years, but the trend seems clear.

A secondary effect of these increasing numbers should be noted. Percentages are important, but so are absolute numbers. If women lawyers increase from about seven thousand to forty thousand, they become a much larger social force, even though they may be only about 10 percent of the total occupation. When women medical students, while remaining a small percentage of their classes, increase in number so that they can form committees, petition administrators, or give solidarity to one another against the traditional masculine badgering and disesteem, they greatly increase their impact on discriminatory attitudes and behavior. That is, as their rise in numbers permits the formation of real groups, their power mounts faster than the numbers or even (except at the start) the percentages. Thus, changes occur even when the percentage of the occupation made up of women is not large.

Bases of Present Changes

Most large-scale, objective measures of men's roles show little change over the past decade, but men do feel now and then that their position is in question, their security is somewhat fragile. I believe they are right, for they sense a set of forces that lie deeper and are more powerful than day-to-day negotiation and renegotiation of advantage among husbands and wives, fathers and children, or bosses and those who work for them. Men are troubled by this new situation.

The conditions we live in are different from those of any prior civilization, and they give less support to men's claims of superiority than perhaps any other historical era. When these conditions weaken that support, men can rely only on previous tradition, or their attempts to socialize their children, to shore up their faltering advantages. Such rhetoric is not likely to be successful against the new objective conditions and the claims of aggrieved women. Thus, men are correct when they feel they are losing some of their privileges, even if many continue to laugh at the women's liberation movement.

The new conditions can be listed concretely, but I shall also give you a theoretical formulation of the process. Concretely, because of the increased use of various mechanical gadgets and devices, fewer tasks require much strength. As to those that still require strength, most men cannot do them either. Women can now do more household tasks that men once felt only they could do, and still more tasks are done by repair specialists called in to do them. With the development of modern warfare, there are few if any important combat activities that only men can do. Women are much better educated than before.

With each passing year, psychological and sociological research reduces the areas in which men are reported to excel over women and disclose far more overlap in talents, so that even when males still seem to have an advantage, it is but a slight one. It is also becoming more widely understood that the top posts in government and business are not best filled by the stereotypical aggressive male but by people, male or female, who are sensitive to others' needs, adept at obtaining cooperation, and skilled in social relations. Finally, in one sphere after another, the number of women who try to achieve rises, and so does the number who succeed.

Although the pressure of new laws has its direct effect on these conditions, the laws themselves arise from an awareness of the foregoing forces. Phrased in more theoretical terms, the underlying shift is toward the decreasing marginal utility of males, and this I suspect is the main source of men's resistance to women's liberation. That is, fewer people believe that what the male does is indispensable, nonsubstitutable, or adds such a special value to any endeavor that it justifies his extra "price" or reward. In past wars, for example, males enjoyed a very high value not only because it was felt that they could do the job better than women but also because they might well make the difference between being conquered and remaining free. In many societies, their marginal utility came from their contribution of animal protein through hunting. As revolutionary heroes, explorers, hunters, warriors, and daring capitalist entrepreneurs, men felt, and doubtless their women did too, that their contribution was beyond anything women could do. This earned men extra privileges of rank, authority, and creature services.

It is not then as individuals, as persons, that males will be deemed less worthy in the future or their contributions less needed. Rather, they will be seen as having no claim to *extra* rewards solely because they are members of the male sex-class. This is part of a still broader trend of our generation, which will also increasingly deny that being white, or an upper-caste or upper-class person, produces a marginally superior result and thus justifies extra privileges.

The relations of individuals are subject to continuous renegotiation as people try to gain or keep advantages or cast off burdens. They fail or succeed in part because one or the other person has special resources or lacks that are unique to those individuals. Over the long run, however, the outcome of these negotiations depends on the deeper social forces we have been describing, which ultimately determine which qualities or performances are more or less valued.

Now, men perceive that they may be losing some of their advantages and that more aspects of their social roles are subject to public challenge and renegotiation than in the past. They resist these changes, and we can suppose they will continue to do so. In all such changes, there are gains and losses. Commonly, when people at lower social ranks gain freedom, those at higher ranks lose some power or centrality. When those at the lower ranks also lose some protection, some support, those at the higher ranks lose some of the burden of responsibility. It is also true that the care or help given by any dominant group in the past was never as much as members believed, and their loss in political power or economic rule was never as great as they feared.

On the other hand, I know of no instance when a group or social stratum gained its freedom or moved toward more respect and then had its members decide that they did not want it. Therefore, although men will not joyfully give up their rank, in spite of its burdens, neither will women decide that they would like to get back the older feminine privileges, accompanied with the lack of respect and material rewards that went with those courtesies.

I believe that men perceive their roles as being under threat in a world that is different from any in the past. No society has yet come even close to equality between the sexes, but the modern social forces described here did not exist before either. At the most cautious, we must concede that the conditions favoring a trend toward more equality are more favorable than at any prior time in history. If we have little reason to conclude that equality is at hand, let us at least rejoice that we are marching in the right direction.

Notes

1. Herbert Goldberg, *The Hazards of Being Male* (New York: Nash, 1976); and Patricia C. Sexton, *The Feminized Male: Classrooms, White Collars, and the Decline of Manliness* (New York: Random House, 1969). On the recognition of disadvantages, see J. S. Chafetz, *Masculine/ Feminine or Human?* (Itasca, Ill.: Peacock, 1974), pp. 56 ff.
2. Joseph H. Pleck, "The Psychology of Sex Roles: Traditional and New Views," in *Women and Men: Changing Roles, Relationship and Perceptions*, ed. Libby A. Carter and Anne F. Scott

(New York: Aspen Institute for Humanistic Studies, 1976), p. 182. Pleck has carried out the most extensive research on male roles, and I am indebted to him for special help in this inquiry.

3. For these two quotations, see Sidney M. Jourard, "Some Lethal Aspects of the Male Role," p. 22, and Irving London, "Frigidity, Sensitivity and Sexual Roles," p. 42, in *Men and Masculinity*, ed. Joseph H. Pleck and Jack Sawyer (Englewood Cliffs, N.J.: Prentice-Hall, 1974). See also the summary of such traits in I. K. Braverman et. al., "Sex-Role Stereotypes: A Current Appraisal," in *Women and Achievement*, ed. Martha T. S. Mednick, S. S. Tangri, and Lois W. Hoffman (New York: Wiley, 1975), pp. 32–47.

4. Robert Bierstedt's "The Sociology of the Majority," in his *Power and Progress* (New York: McGraw-Hill, 1974), pp. 199–220, does not state these principles, but I was led to them by thinking about his analysis.

5. Robert K. Merton, in "The Perspectives of Insiders and Outsiders," in his *The Sociology of Science* (Chicago: University of Chicago Press, 1973), pp. 99–136, has analyzed this view in some detail.

6. This general pattern is noted at various points in my monograph *The Celebration of Heroes: Prestige as a Social Control System* (Berkeley: University of California Press, 1979).

7. Erving Goffman, "The Arrangement Between the Sexes," *Theory and Society* 4 (1977): 307.

8. Hazel Erskine, "The Polls: Women's Roles," *Public Opinion Quarter* 35 (Summer 1971).

9. Goffman, "Arrangement Between the Sexes," p. 308.

10. A simple analysis of these responses presented in William J. Goode, *Principles of Sociology* (New York: McGraw-Hill, 1977), pp. 359 ff.

11. See Joseph H. Pleck, "The Power of Men," in *Women and Men: The Consequences of Power*, ed. Dana V. Hiller and R. Sheets (Cincinnati: Office of Women's Studies, University of Cincinnati, 1977), p. 20. See also Colin Bell and Howard Newby, "Husbands and Wives: The Dynamic of the Deferential Dialectic," in *Dependent and Exploitation in Work and Marriage*, ed. Diana L. Barker and Sheila Allen (London: Longman, 1976), pp. 162–63; as well as Richard Sennett and Jonathan Cobb, *The Hidden Injuries of Class* (New York: Vintage, 1973), p. 125. On the satisfactions of work, see Daniel Yankelovich, "The Meaning of Work," in *The Worker and the Job*, ed. Jerome Rosow (Englewood Cliffs, N.J.: Prentice-Hall, 1974), pp. 19–49.

12. Whatever other sacrifices women want from men, until recently a large majority did *not* believe men should do more housework. On this matter, see Joseph H. Pleck, "Men's New Roles in the Family: Housework and Child Care," to appear in *Family and Sex Roles*, ed. Constantina Safilios-Rothschild, forthcoming. In the mid-1970s, only about one-fourth to one-fifth of wives agreed to such a proposal.

13. Sennett and Cobb, *The Hidden Injuries of Class*, p. 125.

14. To date, the most complete published summary is that by Erskine, "The Polls: Women's Roles," pp. 275–91.

15. Stephanie Greene, "Attitudes Toward Working Women Have 'A Long Way to Go,' " *Gallup Opinion Poll*, March 1976 p. 33.

16. *Harris Survey*, 16 February 1978; see also *Harris Survey*, 11 December 1975.

17. It is, however, in harmony with one view expressed by many women (as well as men), that men in the past were a bit necrophiliac (i.e., they preferred to hop on unresponsive women, take their quick crude pleasure, and hop off). It does not accord much with what we know of people generally (they gain more pleasure when their partner does) or even of bawds and lechers (they brag about the delirium they arouse in the women they seduce).

18. See Charles F. Westoff, "Coital Frequency and Contraception," *Family Planning Perspectives* 6 (Summer 1974): 136–41.

19. The most extensive time budget data on a cross-national basis are found in A. Szalai, ed. *The Use of Time* (The Hague: Mouton, 1972). The most useful summary of the data on the above points is in Joseph H. Pleck, "The Work-Family Role System," *Social Problems* 24 (1977): 417–27. See also his "Developmental Stages in Men's Lives: How Do They Differ From Women's?" (National Guidance Association, Hartland, Michigan, 1977), mimeo.

20. Elina Haavio-Mannila, "Convergences Between East and West: Tradition and Modernity in Sex Roles in Sweden, Finland, and the Soviet Union," in Midnick et al., *Women and Achievement*, pp. 71–84. Further data will appear in J. Robinson, *How Americans Use Time*, forthcoming.

21. Pleck, "Men's New Roles in the Family." For details on men's contribution to child care, see Philip J. Stone, "Child Care in Twelve Countries," in Szalai, *The Use of Time*.

22. These data are to be found in Pleck, "Men's New Roles in the Family." However, 1977 data show that in Detroit this figure has risen to over 60 percent: Arland Thornton and Deborah S. Freedman, "Changes in the Sex Role Attitudes of Women 1962–1977," *American Sociological Review* 44 (October 1979): 833.

23. The expansion of women's jobs has occurred primarily in "female" jobs or through new occupations defined as female or (less frequently) by women taking over formerly male jobs. See Council of Economic Advisers, *Economic Report of the President,* 1973, p. 155; and Barbara R. Bergman and Irma Adelman, "The 1973 Report of the President's Council of Economic Advisors: The Economic Role of Women," *American Economic Review,* September 1973, pp. 510–11. In 1960, about 24 percent of the labor force was made up of women in occupations where women are predominant; in 1970, the figure was 27 percent according to Myra H. Strober, "Women and Men in the World of Work: Present and Future," in Cater et al., *Women and Men: Changing Roles, Relationships, and Perceptions,* pp. 128–33.

24. Jean Lipman-Blumen, "Implications for Family Structure of Changing Sex Roles," *Social Casework* 57 (February 1976): pp. 67-79.

25. Victor R. Fuchs, "A Note on Sex Segregation in Professional Occupations," *Explorations in Economic Research* 2, no. 1 (Winter 1975): 105–111.

The Division of Labor in Contemporary Marriage: Expectations, Perceptions, and Performance

Dana V. Hiller and William W. Philliber

Married women have moved into the labor market at a dramatic pace during the second half of the twentieth century. In 1950, 12 percent of wives with pre-schoolers were employed while in 1980 50 percent of this group were employed (Biachi and Spain, 1983). However, the institutions of North American society are still geared to meet the needs of two-parent families with only one employed partner.

Partners in a two-job marriage may be overloaded with demands on their time and energy, and that pressure in turn may generate rigid role performances as well as emotional exhaustion. Such conditions create an environment ripe for marital dissent. Two outside jobs demand that couples take time to negotiate a household division of labor that once was a given, while at the same time employment absorbs more time and requires greater efficiency in the performance of household tasks.

The underlying issue for individual spouses is equity and fairness in the distribution of costs and rewards within the relationship. With a majority of wives employed in the United States, a new definition of an equitable marital role bargain is emerging which suggests men should take a more active role in housekeeping and childcare. Yet, sharing the responsibilities for housework, parenting, and nurturing others is difficult when tradition has delegated those tasks solely to women. Not surprisingly, Huber and Spitze (1983) have found that "thought of divorce" is strongly related to division of labor in the family. We believe that the extent to which the role expectations of a husband and wife differ will be critical to their ability to negotiate a mutually acceptable role bargain and, ultimately, to their marital stability.

We interviewed 489 midwestern married couples (two-thirds of them were dual-earner couples) to discern what each partner's expectations were and how they actually behaved, and to determine what factors were likely to influence those expectations and behaviors. Assuming that a couple's situational definitions are also important, we studied the perceptions spouses have of their partners' expectations. The specific purpose of this study was to answer the following questions: (1) Do husbands and wives hold different role expectations?; (2) How accurately does each partner perceive the other's expectations?; (3) How do expectations and behavior differ?; and (4) How is the division of labor between a couple affected by the expectations of husbands or wives? In general, we find that tradition endures even in modern, dual-earner families, and that the husband's view of marital roles strongly influences actual behavior.

Previous Research

The literature on gender role attitudes and marital role expectations suggests more attention should be paid to the perceptions partners have of their spouses' attitudes. Research indicates that men and women hold differing marital role expectations, with men tending to have somewhat more traditional expectations (Komarovsky, 1973; Mason and Bumpass, 1975; Osmond and Martin, 1975). Both men and women—but especially women—have come to prefer less rigid gender roles in the labor markets and in family relationships (Mason et al., 1976; Parelius, 1975a).

It is unclear whether men really lag behind women in their preference for more egalitarian roles or whether women simply perceive that they do. Very early, McKee and Sheriffs (1959) found that women perceive men as wanting them to show more feminine qualities than men actually do. Parelius (1975b) concluded that women's expectations for themselves have changed, but that women perceive the expectations of men to have changed little. Osmond and Martin (1975) found more men saying their own self-esteem would not be hurt if their wives earned more money, while most women thought that their husband's self-esteem would be hurt.

Others have found that expectations and perceptions of expectations influence married women's decisions to work. Scanzoni (1979) found that a wife's attitude toward her gender role affects the probability that she will participate in the labor force. Spitze and Waite (1981) demonstrated that whether the wife perceived her husband's attitude to be positive or negative was important for her employment.

Husbands and wives also have different perceptions about behavior. Condran and Bode (1982) point out what they call the Rashomon effect—a significant disjuncture between wives' and husbands' perceptions about how much the husbands participate in household duties. Husbands see themselves as participating more than wives believe they do. Regardless of the perceptions, actual behavior with respect to housework and childcare has been slow to change (Meissner et al., 1975; Vanek, 1974). Typically only one partner is interviewed in these studies. Thus, there has been no way to determine whether partners actually differ in their expectations, or whether they just believe that they have different expectations than their partners. By using couples in our sample, we hope to clarify this issue.

Sample

In 1983, personal interviews were conducted with a stratified sample of 489 married couples in Hamilton County (Cincinnati), Ohio. Participants were selected by randomly dialing households in the target area and securing appointments for interviews to be conducted separately but simultaneously with husbands and wives in their home. Men interviewed husbands, and women interviewed wives. The overall acceptance rate was 47 percent.[1] Because we were particularly interested in professional and managerial women, the sample was stratified to over-sample dual-earner couples, and especially dual-earner couples in which wives held professional and managerial positions. This stratified sample was drawn as callers dialed random numbers and screened subjects. In the final sample, husbands only were employed in 153 couples, wives only were employed in 39 couples, both spouses were employed with the wife in a non-professional or non-managerial occupation in 240 couples, and both spouses were employed and the wife held a professional or managerial position in 57 couples.

Comparing this sample with the 1980 census and with a sample of the non-respondents suggests that the socio-economic status of these subjects is somewhat higher than in the general population and among those who refused to participate. The average family income for the comparable population in Hamilton County is $28,711; in the sample it is $38,260. The census indicates this population to be 12.5 percent black; the sample is 7 percent black. Equal percentages in the census data and the sample were in their first marriages. Demographic variables appear sensitive to response rates, but we believe marital variables to be less so (see Hiller and Philliber, 1985). In all analyses the sample has been weighted to match the actual proportions of Hamilton County households which are dual-earner households, husband-only-earner households, and wife-only-earner households.

Measures

Role Expectations. The four family roles for which expectations were analyzed were childcare, housework, money management, and income earning. The first two are traditionally considered to be in the wife's domain, and the second two in the husband's. Participants were asked to indicate on a five-point scale whether they thought each of these four family roles should be carried out entirely or mostly by themselves, by both partners equally, or mostly or entirely by their spouses.

Perceptions of Spouse's Role Expectations. Using the same five-point scale, we asked participants who they thought their spouses thought should take respon-

[1]Callers contacted 1,037 households in which a married couple lived and at least one spouse was employed. Of these, 489 couples agreed to be interviewed, producing an acceptance rate of 47 percent. Both men and women callers screened households between 6 and 9 P.M. weeknights and on Saturdays, and interviews were scheduled at the convenience of the subjects. Addresses were sought from eligible couples who hesitated to make interview appointments, and information about the study was mailed. This letter was followed by a call back, and, if necessary, a second letter and call back. Those who refused to give addresses or who initially refused to answer the screening question were also called a second time. Subjects were not paid but gave their time voluntarily. More details about the sampling and data collection processes for this study appear in Hiller and Philliber (1985) and are presented in a working paper available from the authors upon request.

sibility for these family roles. In addition, husbands were asked how they felt about their wives being employed, and wives were asked how they thought their husbands felt about their being employed.

Accuracy of Perception. We computed a three-fold difference score for the relationship between an individual's expectation and his or her spouse's perception of that expectation. Individuals were classified either as having a *more traditional* expectation than perceived by their partners, having an expectation *congruent* with their partner's perception, or having a *less traditional* expectation than perceived by their partners.

Attachment to Roles. Marriage partners were asked how important it was to them to be better than their spouses at each of the four family roles: raising children; keeping house; managing finances; and earning income. Responses were scored on a four-point scale from very important to not important at all.

Perception of Division of Household Labor. Both husbands and wives were presented with a list of 20 household and childcare tasks, and were asked whether these tasks were done mostly by themselves, mostly by their spouses, equally by both, mostly by children, or mostly by someone hired. In these analyses, the children and hired help responses are eliminated.

Findings

Differences in Expectations

Within each couple, we compared the spouses' views of who should do what.[2] Table 1 indicates that, irrespective of the family role in question, over two-thirds of the couples had similar expectations. However, for roles traditionally thought to be the wife's, 84 percent agree that childcare should be shared, but only 38 percent agree housework should be. Almost as many couples, 30 percent, agree that housework should be the wife's responsibility. For the roles traditionally assigned to husbands, 69 percent agree that the management of money should be shared, but only 24 percent agree that earning it should be. Almost twice as many— 43 percent—agree that earning money is the husband's responsibility.

When couples disagree, the spouses who traditionally perform a given role believe they should continue to do so, while their partners believe those tasks should be shared. A greater number of husbands wish to maintain traditional roles

---

[2]For roles traditionally fulfilled by wives, responses were dichotomized by grouping perceptions that the role should be carried out entirely or mostly by the wife as ''wife's job,'' while perceptions that the role should be shared or done entirely or mostly by the husband were classified as ''shared job.'' The same procedure was followed for roles traditionally carried out by husbands with the categories reversed accordingly.

Table 1.   Comparison of Spouses' Expectations About Who Should Perform Marital Roles

Expectations for wife's traditional roles	Childcare	Housework
Agree job should be shared	84%	38%
Agree it is wife's job	2	30
Husband: wife's job/Wife: should share	7	13
Husband: should share/Wife: wife's job	8	20
Total	101%	101%
(N)	(483)	(488)

Expectations for husband's traditional roles	Money Management	Income earning
Agree job should be shared	69%	24%
Agree it is husband's job	9	43
Wife: husband's job/Husband: should share	5	9
Wife: should share/Husband: husband's job	17	25
Total	100%	101%
(N)	(487)	(484)

in money matters, and more women than men thought they, the women, should be responsible for domestic matters. This suggests that few husbands or wives want to give up the prerogatives belonging to their traditional marital roles, yet some are interested in expanding their activities into non-traditional roles.

Differences Between Expectations and Partner's Perceptions

Table 2 compares one partner's expectations about the division of family roles with his or her spouse's perceptions of those expectations. First, spouses misperceive their partners' expectations fairly often. In five of the nine comparisons, over 40 percent inaccurately perceive their partner's expectations. In two of those comparisons—wife's perceptions of husband's attitude about her working and about who should manage money—the majority were incorrect. Second, husbands perceive their spouses' expectations more accurately than their wives perceive theirs. On each of the four items which were available for both husbands and wives, husbands were accurate more often than wives.

Third, inaccurate perceptions about housekeeping and childcare roles occur most often because husbands are less traditional and wives more traditional than their partners expect. On the one hand, sizable percentages of wives believe their husbands expect them to do housework and childcare when, in fact, their husbands believe these should be shared roles. On the other hand, husbands are especially likely to believe their wives expect them to share housework when, in fact, wives do not expect this.

Table 2. Accuracy of Spouse's Perception of Partner's Expectations for Marital Roles

	Accuracy of wife's perception				Accuracy of husband's perception			
	Husband more traditional	Perception accurate	Husband less traditional	Total (N)	Wife more traditional	Perception accurate	Wife less traditional	Total (N)
Having a working wife	26%	38	36	100% (482)	a	a	a	a
Doing childcare	6%	73	21	100% (483)	11%	82	7	100% (485)
Doing housework	9%	55	36	100% (487)	27%	65	8	100% (487)
Managing money	37%	44	19	100% (488)	18%	51	31	100% (485)
Earning income	22%	55	23	100% (484)	13%	61	26	100% (484)

Note: a. Variable not measured.

Finally, inaccuracies in perceptions of expectations for roles traditionally assigned to men occur most often because husbands are more traditional and wives less traditional than their partners expect. Wives tend to perceive husband's expectations about managing money to be less traditional than they actually are. Husbands more often perceive wive's expectations about both managing and earning money to be more traditional than they actually are.

Differences Between Expectations and Behavior

How do the expectations spouses have of themselves and each other match the actual behavior in their marriages? The discrepancies between expectations and actual behavior become apparent when Table 1 is compared to data on task performance in Table 3. Fifty-eight percent of husbands say housework should be shared; yet, except for two tasks listed in Table 3, not more than a third of the husbands either share or do regular household tasks, even by their own estimate. Thirty-three percent of the husbands report they shop for food, and 43 percent wash dishes. Note that the percentages of wives who see their husbands doing or sharing these tasks is lower than the percentages of husbands who see themselves doing them (although the percentages tend to vary in the same direction across all tasks). Both husbands and wives report that money management is the only regular household task either done by or shared by a majority of husbands.

Although wives perform the more regular household tasks, a number of husbands do household tasks which are less regular or are needed on an occasional

Table 3.   Husband's and Wife's Perceptions of Division of Labor

	Wife's perception				Husband's perception				Percent agreement between spouses
	Wife does %	Both do %	Husband does %	(N)	Wife does %	Both do %	Husband does %	(N)	
Regular Household Tasks									
Food shopping	70%	20%	10%	(489)	67%	23%	10%	(489)	86%
Meal preparation	85	10	5	(481)	82	13	5	(487)	81
House cleaning	80	17	3	(453)	73	23	4	(456)	78
Washing dishes	66	29	5	(451)	57	36	7	(453)	87
Washing clothes	84	10	6	(475)	81	14	5	(473)	76
Ironing	90	7	3	(489)	90	7	3	(450)	90
Managing money	42	31	27	(489)	30	38	32	(488)	65
Less Regular Household Tasks									
Household repairs	7	13	80	(440)	2	7	91	(458)	82
Yard work	11	29	60	(382)	6	24	70	(405)	71
Supervision of help	72	24	4	(174)	51	34	15	(226)	56
Entertaining preparation	52	46	2	(487)	44	53	3	(489)	61
Major purchases	14	82	4	(489)	9	85	6	(488)	79
Planning recreation	16	80	4	(476)	11	83	7	(476)	72
Planning vacations	8	85	7	(472)	8	82	10	(482)	79
Childcare Tasks									
Arranging activities	61	36	3	(280)	58	40	2	(325)	63
Take kids to doctor	74	23	3	(309)	62	34	4	(333)	73
Stays home when kids are sick	62	36	2	(332)	48	48	4	(340)	52
Get kids ready for bed	60	34	6	(253)	48	47	5	(300)	71
Get kids ready for school	82	11	7	(218)	80	16	4	(267)	81
Help kids with homework	45	41	14	(235)	35	54	11	(266)	65

basis. Almost all husbands take primary responsibility for household repairs and yard work, and most share in making major purchases, planning recreation, and planning vacations. Many also share in the supervision of help and in preparations for entertainment.

Analyses of perceptions of childcare task performance were limited to those couples who still have children at home (which accounts for the reduced sample size for these items in Table 3). While 84 percent of all these couples agree that childcare should be shared, a majority of fathers say they participate equally or more in only three of the six childcare tasks—staying with ill children, getting children ready for bed, and helping kids with homework. Moreover, according to wives' reports, only about a third of their husbands participate equally or more in any childcare tasks, except for helping with homework.

As shown in the far right-hand column of Table 3, couples generally agree about

Table 4.   Importance of Superior Role Performance for Husband and Wife

Importance of role	Childcare		Housework		Money Management		Income Earning	
	Husband	Wife	Husband	Wife	Husband	Wife	Husband	Wife
Very important	4%	15%	2%	14%	9%	7%	26%	2%
Somewhat important	22	28	7	26	30	25	32	10
Not very important	43	30	43	33	36	41	24	44
Not at all important	31	27	48	27	25	27	18	44
Total	100%	100%	100%	100%	100%	100%	100%	100%
(N)	(481)	(481)	(488)	(486)	(487)	(486)	(488)	(485)

who does what around the house. With the exception of money management, at least three-quarters agree about whether regular household tasks are done primarily by the wife, the husband, or are shared. There is somewhat lower agreement about who does non-regular household tasks and even less about who does childcare; but for every task the majority of couples agree. Across the board, both husbands and wives see themselves participating more than their spouses see them participating. Husbands are especially more likely to see tasks as shared, while wives see themselves with major responsibility.

Personal Attachment to Roles

Table 4 shows that 58 percent of husbands consider it important to be better than their wives at earning income—suggesting that the men are still very attached to their traditional breadwinning role. Neither husbands nor wives are overwhelmingly attached to the role of managing finances. However, 43 percent of wives consider it important to be better than their husbands at childcare, and 38 percent feel that way about housekeeping. The majority of wives do not consider it important to exceed their husbands in performance of the traditional female roles.

Table 5 indicates husbands' feelings about their wives' employment. While the majority of men in this sample consider it important to earn more income than their

Table 5.   Husband's Attitude Toward Wife's Employment

	Husbands with employed wife	Husbands with non-employed wife	All husbands
Likes wife working	74%	37%	63%
Does not care	11	26	15
Dislikes wife working	15	37	22
Total	100%	100%	100%
(N)	(341)	(141)	(482)

wives, three-fourths of those with employed wives like the fact that their spouses are working, and over a third with unemployed wives would like their wives to be working. Less than a fourth of the total sample of husbands prefer that their wife be unemployed.

Effects of Expectations and Perceptions on Performance

To discern how expectations and perceptions of expectations affect performance, measures of the division of labor in four major areas were subjected to multiple regression analysis. We constructed a summary measure of who does childcare by adding responses to the six childcare items. Similarly, we obtained a measure of who does housework by adding the six regular household tasks, excluding money management. Money management was kept as a separate item. We calculated income earning as the percent of family income earned by the wife. On all four measures, a high score indicates the wife takes greater responsibility for the role.[3]

The four regression equations included as predictors each spouse's expectations for the specific marital role, perceptions of partner's expectations, and husband's and wife's attachments to the role.[4] In addition, we included family income, wife's employment, presence of children in the home, and length of marriage to examine and control their possible effects on performance of each role.

Table 6 indicates that the only variable with a significant effect on childcare is the wife's employment. Specifically, the husband is more likely to share in childcare if the wife is employed than if the wife stays at home.

Several variables significantly affect performance of housework. The wife does more of the housework if she is not employed, has a husband who believes she should do the housework, perceives that to be his expectation, and has a husband who perceives it to be her expectation. She does less housework if her husband feels it is important for him to be able to do it well, or if the family has a relatively high income. The strongest effect is that of wife's perception of husband's expectation. In general, the husband's attitudes about housework appear to be more important than the wife's.

Money management is affected by expectations, perceptions, and role attachment in much the same way as housework, except that the wife's attitudes are somewhat more important. The wife is more likely to manage the money if she is employed, if both she and her husband feel she should to it and perceive the other

[3]Because of the reasonably high agreement between husbands and wives, only husband's perception of who does childcare, housework, and money management were analyzed.

[4]Zero-order correlations, means, and standard deviations for the variables in the four regression equations are available from the first author. As might be expected, several of the independent variables in these analyses are significantly correlated, but none so highly that multicollinearity would be of great concern. The total N varies across the four analyses because of different levels of missing data (deleted listwise) and sub-sample selection on the dependent variable (i.e., analysis only of couples with children or a working wife).

Table 6.   Standardized Effects of Independent Variables on Household Division of Labor as Reported by Husband

Predictor	Marital role			
	Childcare (N = 209)	Housework (N = 336)	Money management (N = 395)	Income earning (N = 185)
Family Income	−.01	−.13**	.01	−.19**
Wife's Employment	−.25***	−.14**	.09**	b
Children in the Home	a	.06	−.05	−.11
Length of Marriage	−.10	.07	−.05	−.13
Husband's Role Expectations	.12	.17**	.31***	.02
Wife's Role Expectations	.01	−.09	−.08	−.04
Husband's Perception of Wife's Expectation	−.05	−.23***	−.22***	.21*
Wife's Perception of Husband's Expectation	.11	.27***	.28***	−.18*
Importance of Role to Husband	.09	−.11*	−.09**	−.01
Importance of Role to Wife	.08	.07	.08*	.01
R^2 =	.16	.42	.56	.15

Notes: a. Analysis limited to couples with children in the home.
b. Analysis limited to couples with an employed wife.
   *$p < .05$
 **$p < .01$
***$p < .001$

to feel that way, and if performance of that role is important to her and unimportant to him. Again, the most influential variables are husband's expectation and wife's perception of that expectation.

Three predictors are significantly related to income earning. First, the lower the total income of a family, the higher the percentage earned by the wife. Also, the percentage of income earned by the wife is greater if (a) the husband perceives that his wife expects to earn money, and (b) the wife perceives that her husband expects her to share in income earning.

Discussion and Conclusions

What do partners in contemporary marriages expect of one another? How do they see their spouse's expectations? And, how do these definitions of the marital relationship relate to the traditional division of labor in the household? We have attempted to move beyond previous efforts to answer these questions by basing our inquiry on the perspectives of both husbands and wives. The picture of their marriages portrayed in our results is complex, but it is still heavily colored by traditional expectations about spouses' respective role responsibilities.

We did find widespread agreement among couples that childcare and money management should be shared responsibilities. Most couples expected to share childrearing equally, and two-thirds expected to take equal responsibility for managing money. However, differences between and within couples were more apparent for two other areas of responsibility—housework and income earning. Although many spouses agreed that these tasks should be shared equally, nearly a third of the couples agreed that housework is the wife's job, and 43 percent agreed that income earning is the husband's job. In another third of these couples, partners held different expectations about housework and income earning. In these cases, the wife tended to be more traditional with respect to responsibility for housework, and the husband was more likely to hold traditional expectations toward income earning. These results suggest that many spouses were willing to share in the traditional roles of the opposite sex but did not expect to relinquish primary responsibility for their own traditional roles in marriage.

Focusing specifically on the key issue of income earning in these households, we found that nearly two-thirds of the husbands liked (or would have liked) their wives being employed. Yet, a majority of the men in our sample (58 percent) felt that it is important to earn more than their wives earn, and nearly three-fourths of them held to the traditional view that income earning is the husband's job. Apparently, most husbands were comfortable with having their wives work—as long as the man is still the main breadwinner. While over half of the wives similarly expected the husband to be the primary earner of household income, our results seemingly contradict Osmond and Martin's (1975) finding that women were more likely than men to believe that a husband would be hurt if his wife earned more money.

Turning to the question of how partners perceive their spouses' expectations about household responsibilities, we found that husband's perceptions were consistently more accurate than were wives' perceptions. Perhaps wives are more likely to express their feelings about who should perform household tasks, giving their husbands a better reading of these expectations. When partners misperceived their spouses' expectations, this often occurred because the spouse actually expected to take more responsibility for the traditional role of the opposite sex than the partner perceived. For instance, many wives underestimated their husbands' willingness to share childcare and housework. Likewise, substantial proportions of the husbands seemed unaware that their wives expected to share in managing and earning household income. On the other hand, spouses tended to be more traditional about their own sex-specific responsibilities—i.e., husbands expecting to manage the money and wives expecting to do the housework—than their partners thought they would be.

Spouses' respective perceptions of the actual division of labor in their household were generally consistent with one another. In those instances where spouses disagreed about who performed a given task, both husbands and wives tended to see themselves as doing more than their spouses said they did. These discrepancies reflect the Rashomon effect noted previously by Condran and Bode (1982). However, the dominant pattern in spouses' ratings of task performance, especially for routine tasks, was one of agreement. Consequently, we focused on husband's reports in our subsequent analyses of the household division of labor.

Even when measured by husband's reports of behavior, the performance of key household tasks departed markedly from spouses' expectations about shared responsibilities. For instance, over four-fifths of these couples expected to share childcare, but less than half actually did so. Over half of these spouses expected to share housekeeping chores, but only a third of the husbands reported sharing even two tasks equally (dishwashing and shopping). For most couples, then, these activities continued to follow traditional patterns in spite of spouses' expectations for greater equality in their relationship.

This brings us to our final question: What factors do affect the household division of labor? Perhaps the most important and far-reaching finding of our multivariate analysis is that perceptions of partners' expectations strongly influence spouses' behavior. Spouses' views of what their partners expected significantly affected performance of housework, money management, and income earning. Clearly, these definitions of the marital situation have real consequences for the behavior of married men and women, even when they define their partner's expectations incorrectly. This important link between perceptions and behavior in the marital relationship deserves attention in future research.

Our analysis also indicated that the husband's prerogatives continue to have a more pronounced impact on marital role bargains than do the wife's employment or other family characteristics. We found that money management was more strongly affected by the husband's expectations—and by the wife's perception of those expectations—than by whether the wife worked. Similarly the husband's expectations and wife's perceptions of his preferences were the most important factors in the allocation of the housework. The only area where the wife's employment had a leading influence was in childcare.

Therefore, despite the fact that 69 percent of the wives in our sample were working outside the home, the traditional division of labor and dominant role of the male "head-of-household" were still very much in evidence in these marriages. Although some signs of change were apparent in spouses' expectations about sharing certain household tasks, we did not find indications of dramatic change in the husband's position as the "primary" wage earner or in the wife's day-to-day responsibilities for housework and childcare. As Pleck (1977) has argued, the traditional priorities of work and marital roles reflected in our results form an interdependent system that will be difficult to alter. Until women's earnings are more comparable to men's, it seems unlikely that role bargaining in the intimate marital relationship will change drastically. Conversely, the ability of women to compete equally with men in the public worlds of work and politics will suffer until they are equally free of—or equally burdened by—the constraints of housework and childcare.

References

Bianchi, Susanne M. and Daphne Spain
    1983   American Women: Three Decades of Change (DCS-80-8). Washington, DC: U.S. Bureau of
        the Census.
Condran, John G. and Jerry G. Bode
    1982   "Rashomon, working wives, and family division of labor: Middletown, 1980." Journal of
        Marriage and the Family 44:421–26.
Hiller, Dana V. and William W. Philliber
    1985   "Maximizing confidence in married couple sample." Journal of Marriage and the Family
        47:729–32.
Huber, Joan and Glenna Spitze
    1983   Sex Stratification: Children, Housework, and Jobs. New York: Academic Press.
Komarovsky, Mirra
    1973   "Cultural contradictions and sex roles: the masculine case." American Journal of Sociology
        78:873–84.
Mason, Karen Oppenheimer and Larry L. Bumpass
    1975   "U.S. women's sex-role ideology, 1970." American Journal of Sociology 80:1212–19.
Mason, Karen Oppenheimer, John L. Czajka and Sara Arber
    1976   "Change in U.S. women's sex-role attitudes, 1964–1974." American Sociological Review
        41:573–96.
McKee, John P. and Alex C. Sheriffs
    1959   "Men's and women's beliefs, ideals, and self-concepts." American Journal of Sociology
        64:356-63.
Meissner, Martin, Elizabeth Humphreys, Scott Meis and William Scheu
    1975   "No exit for wives: sexual division of labor and the cumulation of household demands."
        Canadian Review of Sociology and Anthropology 12:424–39.
Osmond, Marie Withers and Patricia Yancy Martin
    1975   "Sex and sexism: a comparison of male and female sex-role attitudes." Journal of Marriage
        and the Family 37:744–53.
Parelius, Ann P.
    1975a "Change and stability in college women's orientations toward education, family and work."
        Social Problems 22:420–32.
    1975b "Emerging sex-roll attitudes, expectations, and strains among college women." Journal of
        Marriage and the Family 37:146–53.
Pleck, Joseph H.
    1977   "The work-family role system." Social Problems 24:417–27.
Scanzoni, John
    1977   "Sex-role influences on married women's status attainments." Journal of Marriage and the
        Family 41:793–800.
Spitze, Glenna D. and Linda J. Waite
    1981   "Wife's employment: the role of husband's perceived attitudes." Journal of Marriage and the
        Family 42:117–24.
Vanek, Joann
    1974   "Time spent in housework." Scientific American 231:116–20.

Chapter 4

Gender and Intimacy

The Conflict Between and Within Genders: An Appraisal of Contemporary American Femininity and Masculinity

Karen E. Rosenblum

When we look at popular attitudes about gender, two assumptions appear to be pervasive: first, that there are significant differences in the "nature," i.e., personal attributes, of men and women (Ruble, 1983; Ruble and Ruble, 1982; Huston-Stein and Higgins-Trenk, 1978);[1] and second, that these differences produce conflict between the sexes. The presumption of difference has been pursued—both implicitly and explicitly—by a wide range of sociological and psychological research, and there is some support for it although to a lesser extent than what popular opinion would hold (e.g., Maccoby and Jacklin, 1974). In this article, the second of these assumptions—that difference implies conflict and opposition—will be examined. My argument, however, is that the conflict which attends gender has been understated rather than overstated, and that it does not exist so much between gender formulations as within each of them.

What follows does not survey all the manifestations of conflict which attend gender. Rather, the aim is to assess the nature and scope of the conflict inherent in gender as it is formulated in contemporary American culture. The discussion begins with identification of what appear to be the core features of femininity and masculinity and then examines the conflicts which are implicit to these constructions. In all, this discussion seeks the empirical basis of the popular assumption that in the realm of sex and gender, difference implies conflict.

Reprinted from *Sociological Inquiry*, Vol. 56, No. 1, Winter 1986. Copyright © 1986 by the University of Texas Press. By permission of the author and the publisher.

The Core Features of Gender in Contemporary American Society

In a much-acclaimed addition to the social-psychological literature on moral development, Carol Gilligan (1982) argued that women and men operate from different understandings of morality, i.e., that it is possible to distinguish between a "feminine" and "masculine" ethic.[2] Her analysis provides a useful starting point for the appraisal of key features of gender in American society.

Gilligan's work can be sketched by focusing first on the processes of attachment and separation. Following recent psychoanalytic approaches (e.g., Chodorow, 1978; Dinnerstein, 1976), Gilligan attributes sex-differentiated moralities to women's preeminence in child-rearing. Since women are the primary parents, the achievement of masculinity requires from boys a separation from and opposition to that parent. For girls, sharing a gender identity with their primary parent means that separation is not so pressing and attachment may thus be extended. Girls, then, "emerge . . . with a basis for empathy built into their primary definition of self in a way that boys do not. Girls emerge with a stronger basis for experiencing another's needs or feelings as one's own" (Chodorow, 1978:167).

The encouragement of attachment or separation implicit to child-rearing practices have implications for an individual's perception and resolution of moral dilemmas. From interviews with college students, women seeking abortion, and individuals across the life cycle, Gilligan concluded that among boys and men the resolution of moral dilemmas entailed separation, both in terms of the method by which moral dilemmas were resolved and in terms of the specific content of morality.

The method of a masculine morality appeared to be categorical and rule-bound. Gilligan's male respondents approached ethical dilemmas by abstracting the conflict from its interpersonal specifics and applying impersonal rules. One example was the "Heinz dilemma": Heinz's wife is dying, the drug which could save her will cost more money than Heinz has, and the druggist will not reduce the price. What should Heinz do? In this situation, masculine morality saw a conflict of rights, specifically between life and property, which could be resolved by reference to a particular canon. Thus, a masculine morality endorsed separation through the application of abstract principles and the decontextualization of the conflict as a method by which to resolve ethical dilemmas.

Similarly, the content of a masculine morality stressed achievement, autonomy, individuation (Kohlberg, 1981; Levinson, 1978; Valliant, 1977)—all manifestations of separation. Acting morally meant not only respecting others' rights and allowing others to be autonomous, but also keeping others from delimiting one's own autonomy. As Gilligan noted, even Kohlberg's developmental stages reflect that value, his highest stage of development being the recognition of "the rights of others as these are defined naturally or intrinsically; the human being's right to do as he pleases without interfering with somebody else's rights" (1973:29–30).

Among girls and women, however, situational and interpersonal contexts emerged as more important. For them, the responsibility to care for the network of others, i.e., attachment, was both the method which guided decision making and the value by which a decision was judged to be "good." "[W]hile Kohlberg's [male] subject worries about people interfering with each other's rights, . . . [women worry] about the possibility of omission, of not helping others when you could help them" (Gilligan, 1982:21). In "conventional" feminine morality, being bad was being selfish, placing one's own needs above others'; being good was doing what others wanted or needed, pursuing submission and self-sacrifice in the service of attachment.[3] In its method, a feminine morality was context-bound rather than categorical; thus Gilligan's female respondents were often taken aback when presented with *hypothetical* ethical dilemmas. In its content a "good" decision was one which took the specifics of others' needs into account.

These, then, are sex-differentiated moralities. In a feminine ethic, the goal is to decide one's action in light of others' specific needs. In a masculine ethic, the goal is precisely the opposite: to respect other's rights, but not to let others affect one's decisions. In one case, morality means caring, being responsible for others, seeking particularized resolutions which maintain networks of relations. In the other, acting morally means presuming autonomy, being fair, resolving dilemmas by application of abstract principles. Each reveals a distinct *Weltanschauung*. As Gilligan concluded, an ethic of fairness and rights presupposes equality among individuals, while an ethic of caring presumes differences in needs and abilities. In all, one ethic stands as an elaboration of assumptions about autonomy, the other as an elaboration of assumptions about care.

The Significance and Limitations of the Care/Autonomy Distinction

Clearly, these two ethics embody very different understandings of the term "moral." Yet what Gilligan has tapped is not simply a difference in conceptions of morality or even in social-psychological development, but a constituent element of gender in contemporary American society. The operation of a care/autonomy distinction as a marker of gender can be seen in a variety of social processes, but perhaps becomes most clear when violated. For example, if women's commitment to non-domestic achievement takes precedence over a commitment to family, their orientation is characterized, often pejoratively, as "masculine." Similarly, men who choose family over career are "feminine." Such characterizations may be a consequence of sex-stereotypes, or role reversal, or the actual qualities of autonomy and care embodied in particular roles. In each case, however, the autonomy/care distinction is a central—perhaps even critical—means by which gender is assessed and/or displayed. Thus, the distinction offers a particularly useful framework from which to assess the nature and scope of gender-related conflict.

Still, caution must be exercised in the application of such a framework. For example, Gilligan's appraisal of the origin of the care/autonomy distinction is problematic. We do not so far have a body of evidence supporting the key hypotheses—that attachment specifically results from the shared gender-identity of primary parent and child, or that separation results when that identity is not shared. Confirming such a connection not only demands a focus on a somewhat infrequent family constellation (single-parent fathers raising sons), but also requires attention to a number of complicating factors, such as the effects of divorce, death, or absence of a parent or the impact of sex differences in parenting. Socialization is an exceedingly complex process (e.g., see Safilios-Rothschild, 1979); finding a correlation between sex of parent/child and attachment or separation is quite different from demonstrating that the two are causally related. Thus, insofar as Gilligan draws on the work of Chodorow and Dinnerstein, she is potentially liable to much of the same criticism they have met (e.g., see Lorber, 1981; Bart, 1977, 1983).

Most importantly, one need not involve the single-sex nature of child-rearing or posit stages of psycho-social development to explain the care/autonomy distinction. After all, the normative injunctions which prescribe self-sacrifice as evidence of femininity are longstanding and highly developed. From the early nineteenth century "cult of true womanhood," in which women were enjoined to guard the morality of their husbands and children, to the turn-of-the-century "social housekeepers," devoted to the purification of an entire society, to contemporary working women concerned to show that their employment benefits their family rather than themselves (Levitin, Quinn, and Staines, 1971), and even to the concentration of women workers in the service sector of the labor force, femininity has both been equated with and displayed by care for others rather than self. A similar point can be made regarding masculinity; self-reliance, achievement (Stearns, 1979; Brannon, 1976), and "putting the self over and against other people" (Cicone and Ruble, 1978:11) characterize both the contemporary and historic American expectations about masculinity. American men have been expected and socialized to display autonomy just as women have been urged toward care. Thus, while Gilligan offers an important key toward conceptualizing the nature of gender in American society, the features which are illuminated by her work are just as likely to be rooted in culture as in the psycho-dynamics of parent-child interactions.

Care, Autonomy, and Conflict

If we accept the care/autonomy distinction as a key feature of American gender, what conflict is suggested by that distinction? To pursue the question systematically, we will look for conflict in two general domains: (1) in the interaction of femininity and masculinity, i.e., "inter-gender" conflict, and (2) within each construction of gender, i.e., "intra-gender" conflict.

Inter-Gender Conflict

Conflict in the interaction of femininity and masculinity is usually the reference of popular conceptions about gender conflict. The expectation that sex difference yields conflict is most often understood as conflict between the sexes. A focus on the conflict between gender constructions has also characterized much scholarly work. As a consequence, there is considerable evidence that men and women bring different needs and expectations to their interactions with one another—and even that they have substantially divergent understandings of those interactions (e.g., Bernard, 1971; LeMasters, 1975; Rubin, 1976, 1983).

As the care/autonomy distinction plays itself out in the interpersonal realm, it produces an interesting juxtaposition: while femininity is displayed by care for the network of others, masculinity is affirmed by independence from that network. Contrary to the general view, however, that femininity and masculinity are affirmed via the display of care or autonomy does not necessarily argue for any structural conflict between them. As functionalists might contend, there is no inherent conflict involved in one party "caring" and the other party demonstrating "independence." Rather, conflict is likely to be engendered by expectations of reciprocity, i.e., that one should receive the same treatment one dispenses. Only because the care/autonomy distinction is set against a cultural and personal value of heterosexual, companionate relations and romantic love, which embody expectations of reciprocity and mutual understanding (Shorter, 1975), do they collide. Thus, despite the prevalence of the assumption that gender itself is responsible for conflict between the sexes, conflict is more reasonably attributed to culturally specific expectations about the nature of heterosexual interactions.

Intra-Gender Conflict

The notion of intra-gender conflict, on the other hand, encompasses those conflicts which are embedded within gender prescriptions and proscriptions, those which devolve from the "fit" between the dictates of gender and the nature of social life, as well as those which emerge when the dictates of gender are compared to its latent functions.

In regard to the latter, Gilligan argued that conventional feminine morality, because it endorsed making decisions in terms of others' needs, functioned to reduce women's power. Neither her conclusion nor the underlying assumption that the dictates of gender are directly reproduced in behavior is unusual. They emerge regularly in scholarly, political, and popular treatments of gender. Still, such an analysis stops at the level of manifest function.

A look at the latent consequences of femininity provides a somewhat different picture. While a feminine morality appears to concede power, it is also the case that a strategy of sacrifice is a reasonable tactic for those who lack other means by which to exercise control (Janeway, 1971, 1981). In the absence of control over external resources or expertise, sacrifice utilizes that resource which *is* available—the ostensive giving up of one's own interests. As Sennett and Cobb (1973) argued in regard to social class, self-sacrifice can function as a "gift" which obligates, and thereby exercises some control over, a recipient. Indeed, women's acts of sacrifice for the sake of the network of relations are likely to have a special strength since the dictates of gender impel men to ignore those same relations. While sacrifice provides only a weak resource, both because it depends on others needing what one has to offer and because it is unlikely to result in one's being *seen* as powerful (Johnson, 1976), it is a resource nonetheless. Through its commitment to care even at the expense of one's own apparent interests, conventional American femininity simultaneously accrues some degree of power and endorses the giving up of power. Thus, femininity requires that one ignore or at least deny the power which derives from sacrifice, since such power is "selfish" and thereby "unfeminine" (e.g., see Bart, 1972).

While the tenets of American femininity conflict with its function, they are also at odds with the nature of social life. Within an ethic of self-sacrifice, one is of course *choosing* to sacrifice, but the operation of choice is masked by the injunction to please others. However, when the needs of others are in conflict or run counter to one's own desires, the presence of volition both becomes more apparent and is likely to entail inflicting injury. As Gilligan concluded, the goal of pleasing others inevitably collides with situations in which no matter what one does, someone will be hurt. Thus, the nature of social life requires action which may violate the value of attachment: one must sometimes make decisions which sever rather than maintain networks of relations. When conventional femininity meets the exigencies of the social world, the desire to be good runs headlong into the unavoidability of inflicting injury. Even the desire to be selfless may be countered by the fact that pleasing others sometimes fulfills one's own "selfish" needs. Since it is impossible never to inflict injury (always to please others and never to put one's own interests first), the social world inevitably frustrates the realization of conventional feminine "goodness."

Occasionally one hears the argument that women's conflicts would be resolved if they abandoned their commitment to care and adopted a more masculine ethic. But masculinity also entails conflicts, the most encompassing of which are revealed in an examination of its latent functions.

First, a masculine affirmation or presumption of "equality" may be problematic in its realization. An ethic of autonomy—of a generalized commitment to "protect from interference the rights to life and self-fulfillment" (Gilligan, 1982:100)—presumes equality and would appear to militate against the creation of hierarchy and the exercise of dominance. Yet that outcome certainly has not been realized in the vast array of male-created and -dominated institutions. More importantly, it does not emerge in informal male interaction, an arena somewhat less affected by historic pressures toward stratification. For example, as those observing conversation in sex-segregated groups have observed, members of all-male groups move quickly to establish and maintain a hierarchy of speakers; all-female groups tend to a system of shared turn-taking, with the more dominant members often taking steps to ensure that everyone has an opportunity to talk (Aries, 1976).[4] Thus, the manifest function of an ethic of autonomy, i.e., the cultivation of relations of equality, fails to materialize. Instead, one finds hierarchy.

From a different arena, research on love and marriage indicates that men fall in love more quickly and suffer more at the end of an intimate relation (Rubin, 1973). Further, on physical and psychological measures, marriage appears to be "better" for men than for women (Bernard, 1971). Such findings stand in contrast to the values of separation and autonomy—they would imply that at least in the domestic sphere, an ethic of autonomy yields dependence rather than independence.

Thus, for both masculinity and femininity in contemporary America, a clear contrast exists between the dictates of gender and the social effects of following those dictates. With femininity, gender denies power but produces it nonetheless. With masculinity, gender affirms autonomy but produces dominance in the public arena and dependence in the private.

That masculinity urges autonomy but functions to produce hierarchy can be attributed, in part, to a conflict embedded within it. On the one hand, masculinity endorses a blanket protection of individuals' rights and autonomy. On the other, it requires putting others aside, "standing over and against them," in order to pursue a self-determined vision. Thus, within contemporary masculinity, we find reproduced the classic antagonism between the needs and rights of the collectivity and those of the individual.

How is this conflict within masculinity resolved? Consider the interplay of masculinity and the nature of social life. Because masculinity values differentiation and separation—the right to do as one pleases—it both presupposes and requires opposition to the social world. Because achievement and individuation are critical for masculinity, the social world becomes the background from which one must differentiate oneself. Thus, one's own needs come to supersede the generalized endorsement of autonomy. Although masculinity values autonomy and the protection of rights, the injunction to differentiate oneself from others promotes stratification. While the nature of the social world frustrates the realization of conventional femininity, conventional masculinity conflicts with social life because its tenets require asocial, even antisocial, behavior.

Indeed, it is the opposition of the individual to the *social* aspect of social life which sociologists have identified as an underlying conflict of American culture. When, for example, Sennett and Cobb (1973) or Slater (1970) depict American culture as valuing the loner—the one who stands out as both special and independent, who is needed but not needy—they are actually talking about masculinity, not simply culture.

If conventional femininity is evinced by a commitment to a network of relations even at the cost of individual achievement, then it stands in sharp contrast to prevailing American values. While the culture stresses individuation and self-promotion, femininity encourages one to self-sacrifice and subordination. Indeed, it is the American—and masculine—goal of autonomous choice which femininity foregoes in order to be responsive to others' needs. Because American culture values achievement, individuality, and future-orientation, a feminine morality with its emphasis on responsibility to others and self-sacrifice becomes virtually "un-American" (Walum, 1977:9–12).

This contrast has been tapped by research eliciting Americans' stereotypes about the personality traits of males, females, and the "normal, healthy, American adult, sex unspecified" (e.g., Ruble, 1983; Broverman, 1970, 1972; Rosenkrantz, 1968). Such research regularly finds that the traits attributed to the healthy American adult are substantially the same as those attributed to males. The traits which are associated with masculinity are the traits which are culturally valued; hence, the prevailing cultural values are by themselves masculine. The conflict between gender and culture exists, then, only in the realm of femininity. The conflict between femininity and culture could as effectively account for individuals' movement to a "post-conventional" morality as Gilligan's contention that feminine development results from the crisis engendered by an over-commitment to care. After all, while the tenets of femininity might encourage women to sacrifice for others, the cultural values provide little external validation or reward for that sacrifice.

Conclusions

That conflict attends contemporary American formulations of masculinity and femininity is a virtual truism. What this discussion has suggested is that the conflict is broader and deeper than might have been expected, and that it operates more fully *within* the formulations of gender than between them.

One implication of this conclusion is that explorations of gender may have overlooked a fruitful direction of investigation. While inter-gender conflict cannot be discounted, it is intra-gender conflict which seems more significant. The intra-gender conflicts revealed even in this preliminary discussion are extensive. We have seen that masculinity, which presumes equality and autonomy, actually functions to produce hierarchy and dependence; that it involves an internal contradiction between the principle of blanket autonomy and the pursuit of one's own interests; and that it requires an asocial, even anti-social, stance. By the same token, femininity embodies an ethic of powerlessness which produces power, a commitment to care which cannot be realized, a masking of the fact that sacrifice is a matter of choice, and a contravention of cultural values.

Thus, within these gender constructions one finds not simply internal contradictions, but consequences which are antithetical to the dictates which produced them and behaviors which run counter to the basic features of social life and American culture. None of this is inherent to gender *per se,* rather it is specific to the formulation of gender as a care/autonomy distinction within the context of American society. In all, the implications of inter-gender conflict are certainly rivaled by those in intra-gender conflict, i.e., the contradictions American women and men both face as they grapple with their socially constructed genders.

Endnotes

1. Beliefs about the personal attributes of each sex, i.e., *sex* stereotypes, must be distinguished from beliefs about the appropriate behavior for each sex, i.e., *sex role* stereotypes (Ruble and Ruble, 1982:194). Sex stereotypes and sex role stereotypes must also be distinguished from actual behavioral differences, as well as from the actualities of sex differentiation and segregation (e.g., Bernard, 1981).
2. The terms "masculine" and "feminine" are empirically derived but not exclusive. Thus, a feminine ethic is more likely to be produced by women and a masculine ethic more likely to be produced by men, but some women may display a "masculine" ethic, some men a "feminine" one, and some persons both.
3. Gilligan treats each ethic as having its own developmental "trajectory," the stages of which are labeled pre-conventional, conventional, and post-conventional. The discussion in this article focuses exclusively on what is called the "conventional" stage.

   In the pre-conventional feminine morality, caring is explicitly rejected so as to be "selfish." In pre-conventional masculine morality, the social world is seen as lacking shared values or norms and thus requiring dogged self-interest and a battle of needs. Conventional feminine morality seeks "goodness," i.e., attempts to respond to others and to avoid inflicting injury even if it means hurting oneself. The shift to a post-conventional morality entails the extension of caring to one's self, and the factoring in of one's own needs and desires. Thus, post-conventional femininity militates against self-sacrifice and submission. For men, post-conventional morality involves the attenuation of separation, recognizing the need for caretaking to correct "the potential indifference of a morality of non-interference and turn attention from the logic to the consequences of choice" (Gilligan, 1982:100).
4. These patterns do not hold in mixed-sex conversations, however (Aries, 1976).

References

Aries, Elizabeth
    1976   "Interaction patterns and themes of male, female, and mixed groups." Small Group Behavior 7:7–18.

Bart, Pauline
    1972   "Depression in middle-aged women." Pp. 163–186 in V. Gornick and B. K. Moran (eds.), Women in Sexist Society. New York: New American Library.
    1977   "The Mermaid and the Minotaur: A fishy story that's part bull." Contemporary Psychology.
    1983   "Review of Chodorow's Reproduction of Mothering." Pp. 147–152 in J. Trebilcot (ed.), Mothering: Essays in Feminist Theory. Totowa, N.J.: Rowman and Allanheld. Originally published in 1981.

Bernard, Jessie
    1971   "The paradox of the happy marriage." Pp. 145–163 in V. Gornick and B. K. Moran (eds.), Woman in Sexist Society. New York: New American Library.
    1981   The Female World. New York: Free Press.

Brannon, Robert
    1976   "The male sex role." Pp. 1–45 in D. David and R. Brannon (eds.), The 49% Majority: The Male Sex Role. Reading, Mass.: Addison-Wesley.

Broverman, Inge, D. Broverman, F. Clarkson, P. Rosenkrantz, and S. Vogel
    1970   "Sex-role stereotypes and clinical judgments of mental health." Journal of Consulting and Clinical Psychology 34:1–7.
    1972   "Sex-role stereotypes: A current appraisal." Journal of Social Issues 28:59–70.

Chodorow, Nancy
    1978   The Reproduction of Mothering. Berkeley: University of California Press.

Cicone, Michael, and D. Ruble
    1978   "Beliefs about males." Journal of Social Issues 34:5–16.

Dinnerstein, Dorothy
    1976   The Mermaid and the Minotaur: Sexual Arrangements and Human Malaise. New York: Harper and Row.

Gilligan, Carol
   1982   In a Different Voice: Psychological Theory and Women's Development. Cambridge, Mass.:
          Harvard University Press.
Huston-Stein, A., and A. Higgins-Trenk
   1978   "The development of females: Career and feminine role aspirations." In P. B. Baltes (ed.),
          Life-Span Development and Behavior. Vol I. New York: Academic Press.
Janeway, Elizabeth
   1971   Man's World, Woman's Place. New York: Dell.
   1981   Powers of the Weak. New York: Morrow.
Johnson, Paula
   1976   "Women and power: Toward a theory of effectiveness." Journal of Social Issues 32:99–110.
Kohlberg, Lawrence
   1973   "Continuities and discontinuities in childhood and adult moral development revisited." In
          Collected Papers on Moral Development and Moral Education. Moral Education Research
          Foundation. Cambridge, Mass.: Harvard University Press.
   1981   The Philosophy of Moral Development. San Francisco: Harper and Row.
LeMasters, E. E.
   1975   Blue Collar Aristocrats. Madison, Wis: University of Wisconsin Press.
Levinson, Daniel
   1978   The Seasons of a Man's Life. New York: Vintage.
Levitin, T., R. P. Quinn, and G. L. Staines
   1971   "Sex discrimination against the American working woman." American Behavioral Scientist
          15:237–254.
Lorber, Judith
   1981   "Is there (and should there be) a woman's culture?" SWS Network 11:4–5.
Maccoby, Eleanor, and C. Nagy Jacklin
   1974   The Psychology of Sex Differences. Stanford, Calif: Stanford University Press.
Rosenkrantz, Paul, S. Vogel, H. Bee, I. Broverman, and D. Broverman
   1968   "Sex-role stereotypes and self-concepts in college students." Journal of Consulting and
          Clinical Psychology 32:287–295.
Rubin, Lillian
   1976   Worlds of Pain: Life in the Working Class Family. New York: Basic Books.
   1983   Intimate Strangers: Men and Women Together. New York: Harper and Row.
Rubin, Zick
   1973   Liking and Loving: An invitation to Social Psychology. New York: Holt, Rinehart and
          Winston.
Ruble, Diane, and T. Ruble
   1982   "Sex stereotypes." Pp. 188–252 in A. G. Miller (ed.), In the eye of the Beholder:
          Contemporary Issues in Stereotyping. New York: Praeger.
Ruble, Thomas
   1983   "Sex stereotypes: Issues of change in the 1970s." Sex Roles 9:397–402.
Safilios-Rothschild, Constantina
   1979   Sex Role Socialization and Sex Discrimination: A Synthesis and Critique of the Literature.
          Washington, D.C.: U.S. Dept. of Health, Education, and Welfare.
Sennett, Richard and J. Cobb
   1973   The Hidden Injuries of Class. New York: Vintage.
Shorter, Edward
   1975   The Making of the Modern Family. New York: Basic Books.
Slater, Philip
   1970   The Pursuit of Loneliness: American Culture at the Breaking Point. Boston: Beacon Press.
Stearns, Peter
   1979   Be a Man: Males in Modern Society. New York: Holmes and Meier.
Valliant, George
   1977   Adaptation to Life. Boston: Little, Brown.
Walum, Laurel
   1977   The Dynamics of Sex and Gender: A Sociological Perspective. Chicago: Rand McNally.

Blue-Collar Marriage and the Sexual Revolution

Lillian Breslow Rubin

> Experimental? Oh, he's much more experimental than I am. Once in awhile, I'll say, "Okay, you get a treat; we'll do it with the lights on." And I put the pillow over my head. [Thirty-year-old woman, married twelve years]

> Experimental? Not Ann. I keep trying to get her to loosen up; you know, to be more—What would you call it?—adventurous. I mean, there's lots of different things we could be doing. She just can't see it. Sometimes I mind; but then sometimes I think, "After all, she was brought up in a good family, and she always was a nice, sweet girl." And that's the kind of girl I wanted, so I guess I ain't got no real right to complain. [Twenty-seven-year-old man, married seven years]

These comments, typical of a significant number of the fifty white working-class couples* with whom I spoke, made me wonder: Is *this* the revolution in sexual behavior I had been reading about? And if so, were these the issues of the working class alone? To answer the second question, I also talked with twenty-five professional middle-class couples whose characteristics matched the working-class group in all but education and occupation.

Not one couple is without stories about adjustment problems in this difficult and delicate area of marital life—problems not just in the past, but in the present as well. Some of the problem areas—such as differences in frequency of sexual desire between men and women—are old ones. Some—such as the men's complaints about their wives' reluctance to engage in variant and esoteric sexual behaviors—are newer. All suggest that there is, in fact, a revolution in sexual behavior in the American society that runs wide and deep—a revolution in which sexual behaviors that formerly were the province of the college-educated upper classes now are practiced widely at all class and education[al] levels.

The evidence is strong that more people are engaging in more varieties of sexual behavior than ever before—more premarital, post-marital, extra-marital sex of all kinds. In 1948, for example, Kinsey found that only 15 percent of high-school–educated married men ever engaged in cunnilingus, compared to 45 percent of college-educated men. But the world changes quickly. Just twenty-five years later, a national survey shows that the proportion of high-school–educated men engaging in cunnilingus jumped to 56 percent.[1] And among the people I met, the figure stands at 70 percent.

*For the purpose of this study, class was defined by both education and occupation. All the families were intact, neither husband nor wife had more than a high-school education, and the husband was employed in what is traditionally defined as a blue-collar occupation. In addition, because I was interested in studying relatively young families, the wife was under 40 and at least one child under 12 was still in the home. Median age of the women was 28; of the men, 31.

But to dwell on these impressive statistics which tell us what people *do* without attention to how they *feel* about what they do is to miss a profoundly important dimension of human experience—that is, the *meaning* that people attribute to their behavior. Nowhere is the disjunction between behavior and attitude seen more sharply than in the area of sexual behavior. For when, in the course of a single lifetime, the forbidden becomes commonplace, when the border between the conceivable and the inconceivable suddenly disappears, people may *do* new things, but they don't necessarily *like* them.

For decades, novelists, filmmakers, and social scientists all have portrayed working-class men as little more than boorish, insensitive studs—men whose sexual performance was, at best, hasty and perfunctory; at worst, brutal— concerned only with meeting their own urgent needs. Consideration for a woman's needs, variety in sexual behavior, experimentation—these, it is generally said, are to be found largely among men of the upper classes; working-class men allegedly know nothing of such amenities.[2]

If such men ever lived in large numbers, they surely do no longer. Morton Hunt's study, *Sexual Behavior in the 1970s,* which does not control for class but does give data that are controlled for education, provides evidence that men at all educational levels have become more concerned with and more sensitive to women's sexual needs—with the greatest increase reported among high-school–educated men. Comparing his sample with the 1948 Kinsey data on the subject of foreplay, for example, he notes that Kinsey reported that foreplay was "very brief or even perfunctory" among high-school–educated husbands, while college-educated husbands reported [foreplay took] about ten minutes. Twenty-five years later, Hunt found that the median for non-college and college-educated husbands was the same—fifteen minutes. Similar changes were found in the variety of sexual behaviors, the variety of positions used, and the duration of coitus—with especially sharp increases reported among high-school–educated men.

Not surprisingly, it is the men more often than the women who find these changing sexual norms easier to integrate—generally responding more positively to a cultural context that offers the potential for loosening sexual constraints. For historically, it is men, not women, whose sexuality has been thought to be unruly and ungovernable—destined to be restrained by a good (read: asexual) woman. Thus, it is the men who now more often speak of their wish for sex to be freer and with more mutual enjoyment:

> I think sex should be that you enjoy each other's bodies. Judy doesn't care for touching and feeling each other though.

. . . who push their wives to be sexually experimental, to try new things and different ways:

> She thinks there's just one right position and one right way—in the dark with her eyes closed tight. Anything that varies from that makes her upset.

. . . who sometimes are more concerned than their wives for her orgasm:

> It's just not enjoyable if she doesn't have a climax, too. She says she doesn't mind, but I do.

For the women, these attitudes of their men—their newly expressed wish for sexual innovation, their concern for their wives' gratification—are not an unmixed blessing. For in any situation, there is a gap between the ideal statements of a culture and the reality in which people live out their lives—a time lag between the emergence of new cultural forms and their internalization by the individuals who must act upon them. In sexual matters, that gap is felt most keenly by women. Socialized from infancy to experience their sexuality as a negative force to be inhibited and repressed, women can't just switch "on" as the changing culture or their husbands dictate. Nice girls don't! Men *use* bad girls but *marry* good girls! Submit, but don't enjoy—at least obviously so! These are the injunctions that have dominated their lives—injunctions that are laid aside with difficulty, if at all.

The media tells us that the double standard of sexual morality is dead. But with good reason, women don't believe it. They know from experience that it is alive and well, that it exists side-by-side with the new ideology that heralds their sexual liberation. They know all about who are the "bad girls" in school, in the neighborhood; who are the "good girls." Everybody knows! Nor is this knowledge given only among the working class. The definition of "good girl" and "bad girl" may vary somewhat according to class, but the fundamental ideas those words encompass are not yet gone either from our culture or our consciousness at any class level.

We need only to look at our own responses to two questions to understand how vital the double standard remains. When we are asked, "What kind of woman is she?" we are likely to think about her sexual behavior; is she "easy" or not. But the question, "What kind of man is he?" evokes thoughts about what kind of work he does; is he strong, weak, kind, cruel? His sexual behavior is his private business, no concern of ours.

Whether these issues are especially real for working-class women, or whether women of that class are simply more open in talking about them than their middle-class counterparts, is difficult to say. Most of the middle-class women I spoke with came to their first sexual experiences at college where, during the early-to-middle 1960s, they suddenly entered a world where sexual freedom was the by-word. These were the years when it was said, "Sex is no different than a handshake"; when it was insisted that if women would only "do what comes naturally," they'd have no problems with sexual enjoyment; when the young women who did have such problems experienced themselves as personally inadequate; when it was "uncool" for a girl to ask questions about these issues—even, God forbid, to say no. Thus for well over a decade, these college-educated women have lived in an atmosphere that was at once sexually permissive and coercive—permissive in that it encouraged them to unfetter and experience their sexuality; coercive, in that it gave them little room to experience also the constraints upon that sexuality that their culture and personal history until then had imposed upon them. That combination, then, would make them at once less guilty about their sexuality *and* less ready to speak of the inhibitions that remain.

All that notwithstanding, one thing is clear. Among the people I met, working-class and middle-class couples engage in essentially the same kinds of sexual behaviors in roughly the same proportions. But working-class wives express considerably more discomfort about what they do in the marriage bed than their middle-class sisters.

Take, for example, the conflict that engages many couples around the issue of oral-genital stimulation. Seventy percent of the working-class and 76 percent of the middle-class couples engage in such sexual activity. A word of caution is necessary here, however, because these gross figures can be misleading. For about one-third of each group, engaging in oral-genital stimulation means that they tried it once, or that it happens a few times a year at most. Another 30 percent of the middle-class couples and 40 percent of the working-class couples said they have oral sex only occasionally, meaning something over three times but less than ten times a year. Thus, only about one-fourth of the working-class couples and one-third of the middle-class couples who engage in oral sex use this sexual model routinely as a standard part of their repertoire of sexual techniques. Still, fewer of the working-class women say they enjoy it unreservedly or without guilt. Listen to this couple, married twelve years. The husband:

> I've always been of the opinion that what two people do in the bedroom is fine; whatever they want to do is okay. But Jane, she doesn't agree. I personally like a lot of foreplay, caressing each other and whatever. For her, no. I think oral sex is the ultimate in making love; but she says it's revolting. [With a deep sigh of yearning] I wish I could make her understand.

The wife . . .

> I sure wish I could make him stop pushing me into that (Ugh, I even hate to talk about it), into that oral stuff. I let him do it, but I hate it. He says I'm old-fashioned about sex and maybe I am. But I was brought up that there's just one way you're supposed to do it. I still believe that way, even though he keeps trying to convince me of his way. How can I change when I wasn't brought up that way? [With a pained sigh] I wish I could make him understand.

Notice her plaintive plea for understanding—"I wasn't brought up that way." In reality, when it comes to sex, she, like most of us, wasn't brought up *any* way. Girls generally learn only that it's "wrong" before marriage. But what that "it" is often is hazy and unclear until after the first sexual experience. As for the varieties of sexual behavior, these are rarely, if ever, mentioned to growing children, let alone discussed in terms of which are right or wrong, good or bad, permissible or impermissible.

Still, the cry for understanding from both men and women is real. Each wishes to make the other "understand," to transform the other into oneself for a brief moment so that the inner experience can be apprehended by the other. Yet, given the widely divergent socialization practices around male and female sexuality, the wish is but another impossible fantasy. The result; he asks; she gives. And neither is satisfied with the resolution. Despairing of finding a solution with which both are comfortable, one husband comments . . .

> Either I'm forcing my way on her or she's forcing her way on me. Either way, you can't win. If she gives in, it isn't because she's enjoying it, but because I pushed her. I suppose you could say I get what I want, but it doesn't feel that way.

It's true, on the question of oral sex, most of the time she "gives in"— hesitantly, shyly, uncomfortably, even with revulsion. Sometimes women act from a sense of caring and consideration . . .

> We don't do it much because it really makes me uncomfortable, you know [making a face], a little sick. But sometimes, I say okay because I know it means a lot to him and I really want to do it for him.

Sometimes from a sense of duty . . .

> Even though I hate it, if he needs it, then I feel I ought to do it. After all, I'm his wife.

Sometimes out of fear of losing their men . . .

> He can find someone to give it to him, so I figure I better do it.

Sometimes out of resignation and a sense of powerlessness . . .

> I tell him I don't want to do it, but it doesn't do any good. If it's what he wants, that's what we do.

And sometimes it is offered as a bribe or payment for good behavior—not surprisingly in a culture that teaches a woman that her body is a negotiable instrument:

> He gets different treats at different times, depending on what he deserves. Sometimes I let him do that oral stuff you're talking about to me. Sometimes when he's *very* good, I do it to him.

While most of the working-class women greet both cunnilingus and fellatio with little enthusiasm or pleasure, cunnilingus is practiced with slightly greater frequency and with slightly less resistance than fellatio. Partly, that's because many women are talked into cunnilingus by their husbands' "If-I'm-willing-why-do-you-care?" argument . . .

> I don't like him to do it, but I can't figure out what to say when he says that I shouldn't care if *he* doesn't.

. . . and partly, and perhaps more important, because cunnilingus is something that is done *to* a woman—an act not requiring her active engagement as fellatio does; and one, therefore, not quite so incongruent with her socialization to passivity. In all areas of life, she has been raised to wait upon the initiative of another, to monitor both behavior and response carefully so as not to appear too forward or aggressive. Nowhere are these lessons more thoroughly ingrained than in her sexual behavior; nowhere has she learned better to be a reflector rather than a generator of action. Thus, fellatio, perhaps more than any other sex act, is a difficult one for women.

Even those women who do not express distinctly negative feelings about oral sex are often in conflict about it—unsure whether it is really all right for them to engage in, let alone enjoy, such esoteric sexual behavior, worrying about whether these are things "nice girls" do. One twenty-eight-year-old mother of three, married ten years, explained . . .

> I always feel like it's not quite right, no matter what Pete says. I guess it's not the way I was brought up, and it's hard to get over that. He keeps telling me it's okay if it's between us, that anything we do is okay. But I'm not sure about that. How do I know in the end he won't think I'm cheap.
>
> Sometimes I enjoy it, I guess. But most of the time I'm too worried thinking about whether I ought to be doing it, and worrying what he's *really* thinking to get much pleasure.

"How do I know he won't think I'm cheap"—a question asked over and over again, an issue that dominates these women and their attitudes toward their own sexuality. Some husbands reassure them . . .

> She says she worries I'll think she's a cheap tramp, and she doesn't really believe me when I keep telling her it's not true.

Such reassurances remain suspect, however, partly because it's so hard for women to move past the fear of their own sexuality with which they have been stamped; and partly because at least some men are not without their own ambivalence about it, as is evident in this comment from one young husband . . .

> No, Alice isn't that kind of girl. Jesus, you shouldn't ask questions like that. [A long, difficult silence] She wasn't brought up to go for all that [pause] fancy stuff. You know, all those different ways and [shifting uncomfortably in his chair, lighting a cigarette, and looking down at the floor] that oral stuff. But that's okay with me. There's plenty of women out there to do that kind of stuff with. You can meet them in any bar any time you want to. You don't have to marry those kind.

As long as that distinction remains, as long as men distinguish between the girl they marry and the girl they use, many women will remain unconvinced by their reassurances and wary about engaging in sexual behaviors that seem to threaten their "good girl" status.

Those assurances are doubly hard to hear and to believe when women also know that their husbands are proud of their naivete in sexual matters—a pride which many men take little trouble to hide.

> It took a long time for me to convince her that it didn't have to be by the books. She was like an innocent babe. I taught her everything she knows.

Even men whose wives were married before will say with pleasure . . .

> It's funny how naive she was when we got married. She was married before, you know, but still she was kind of innocent. I taught her just about everything she knows.

For the women, the message seems clear: he wants to believe in her innocence, to believe in the special quality of their sexual relationship, to believe that these things she does only for him. She is to be pupil to his teacher. So she echoes his words—"He taught me everything I know." Repeatedly that phrase or a close equivalent is used as women discuss their sexual behavior and their feelings about it. And always it is said with a sure sense that it's what her husband wants and needs to believe, as these incongruent comments from a woman now in her second marriage show.

> One thing I know he likes is that he taught me mostly all I know about sex, so that makes him feel good. It also means that I haven't any habits that have to be readjusted to his way or anything like that.
> *That seems a strange thing to say when you were married for some years before.*

Startled, she looked at me, then down at her hands uncomfortably.

> Yeah, I guess you'd think so. Well, you know, he likes to feel that way so why shouldn't he, and why shouldn't I let him?

Given that knowledge, even if it were possible to do so on command, most women would not dare risk unleashing their sexual inhibitions. From where a woman stands, the implicit injunction in her husband's pride in her innocence is that her sexuality be restrained. And restrain it she does—a feat for which she is all too well trained. The price for that training in restraint is high for both of them, however. He often complains because she doesn't take the initiative . . .

> She never initiates anything. She'll make no advances at all, not even subtleties.

She often replies . . .

> I just can't. I guess I'm inhibited, I don't know. All I know is it's very hard for me to start things up or to tell him something I want.

On the other hand, not infrequently when women put aside that restraint and take the initiative, they may find themselves accused of not being feminine enough.

> It isn't that I mind her letting me know when she wants it, but she isn't very subtle about it. I mean, she could let me know in a nice, feminine way. Being feminine and, you know, kind of subtle, that's not her strong point.

Sensitive to the possibility of being thought of as "unfeminine" or "aggressive," most women shy away from any behavior that might bring those words down upon their heads. For it is painful for any woman of any class to hear herself described in these ways.

> I don't like to think he might think I was being aggressive, so I don't usually make any suggestions. Most of the time it's okay because he can usually tell when I'm in the mood. But if he can't, I just wait.

These, then, are some of the dilemmas and conflicts people face around the newly required and desired sexual behaviors. Among working-class women, isolation and insulation compound their problems. It is one thing to read about all these strange and exotic behaviors in books and magazines, another to know others like yourself who actually do these things.

> He keeps trying to get me to read those books, but what difference would it make? I don't know who those people are. There's a lot of people do lots of things; it doesn't mean I have to do them.

If the books aren't convincing, and it's not culturally acceptable to discuss the intimate details of one's sex life with neighbors, friends, co-workers, or even family, most women are stuck with their childhood and adolescent fears, fantasies, and prohibitions. Small wonder that over and over again during my visit the atmosphere in the room changed from anxiety to relief when subjects such as oral sex were treated casually, with either the implicit or explicit understanding that it is both common and acceptable sexual practice.

> Jim keeps telling me and telling me it's okay, that it's not dirty. But I always worry about it, not really knowing if that's true or not. I read a couple of books once, but it's different. I never talked to anyone but Jim about it before. [Smiling, as if a weight had been lifted from her shoulders] You're so cool about it; talking to you makes it seem not so bad.

In contrast, discussion of these issues with the middle-class women was considerably more relaxed. Regardless of their own feelings about engaging in oral sex, it was clear that most middle-class women recognize that it is widely practiced and acceptable behavior. In fact, more often than not, they tended to feel guilty and uncomfortable about their own inhibitions, not because they weren't able to please their husbands but because they believed their constraint reflected some inadequacy in their personal sexual adjustment. It was also from middle-class women that I more often heard complaints when their husbands were unwilling to experience with oral-genital sex. Of the working-class couples who never engage in oral sex, only one woman complained about her husband's unwillingness to do so. Of the middle-class couples in a similar situation, four women offered that complaint.

But it is also true that, generally, the husbands of these middle-class women send fewer ambiguous and ambivalent messages about their wives' sexuality, tend less to think in good-bad girl terms, [and] more often expect and accept that their wives had other sexual experiences before they met. Further, these middle-class women were more often in contact with others like themselves in an environment where discussion of sexual issues is encouraged—a course in human sexuality, a women's group, for example.

Still, the recitation of these differences in experience ought not to be read to suggest that middle-class women are now sexually free and uninhibited. The most that can be said on that score is that more of them live in an atmosphere that more seriously encourages that goal, hence more—especially those under thirty—may be closer to its attainment. Meanwhile, at all class levels, most women probably feel comfortable enough with their own sexual responses to be willing participants in sexual intercourse. But when it comes to oral sex—especially among the working-class—generally they submit just as their mothers before them submitted to more traditional sexual behaviors.

Sexual conflicts in marriage are not always constellated around such erotic issues, however; nor, as I have said, are any of them the exclusive problem of a particular class. Thus, although what follows rests on material taken from my discussion with working-class couples, much of it applies to the professional middle class as well. True, the middle-class couples more often are able to discuss some of their issues more openly with each other. But despite the current, almost mystical, belief in communication-as-problem-solving, talk doesn't always help. True, middle-class couples much more often seek professional help with these problems. But sexual conflicts in a marriage are among the most intractable—the recent development and proliferation of sex therapies notwithstanding. Those therapies can be useful in dealing with some specific sexual dysfunction—prematurely ejaculating men or nonorgasmic women. But the kinds of sexual conflicts to be discussed here are so deeply rooted in the socio-cultural mandates of our world that they remain extraordinarily resistant regardless of how able the psychotherapeutic help we can buy. Thus, while there are subtle differences between the two classes in the language and tone with which the problems are dealt, in the amount of discussion about them, and in their ability and willingness to seek professional help, in this instance, those differences are not as important as the similarities that remain.

In fact, the earliest sexual problems rear their heads with the couple's first fight. Regardless of what has gone before, at bedtime, he's ready for sex; she remains cold and aloof. Listen to this couple in their mid-to-late-twenties, married nine years. The wife . . .

> I don't understand him. He's ready to go any time. It's always been a big problem with us right from the beginning. If we've hardly seen each other for two or three days and hardly talked to each other, I can't just jump into bed. If we have a fight, I can't just turn it off. He has a hard time understanding that. I feel like that's all he wants sometimes. I have to know I'm needed and wanted for more than just jumping into bed.

The husband . . .

> She complains that all I want from her is sex, and I try to make her understand
> that it's an expression of love. I'll want to make up with her by making love, but
> she's cold as the inside of the refrig. Sure I get mad when that happens. Why
> shouldn't I? Here I'm trying to make up and make love, and she's holding out for
> something—I don't know what.

The wife . . .

> He keeps saying he wants to make love, but it just doesn't feel like love to me.
> Sometimes I feel bad that I feel that way, but I just can't help it.

The husband . . .

> I don't understand. She says it doesn't feel like love. What does that mean,
> anyway? What does she think love is?

The wife . . .

> I want him to talk to me, to tell me what he's thinking about. If we have a fight, I
> want to talk about it so we could maybe understand it. I don't want to jump in bed
> and just pretend it didn't happen.

The husband . . .

> Talk! Talk! What's there to talk about. I want to make love to her and she says she
> wants to talk. How's talking going to convince her I'm loving her.

In sex, as in other matters, the barriers to communication are high; and the
language people use serves to further confuse and mystify. He says, "I want to
make love." She says, "It doesn't feel like love." Neither quite knows what the
other is talking about; both feel vaguely guilty and uncomfortable—aware only
that somehow they're passing each other, not connecting. He believes he already
has given her the most profound declaration of love of which a man is capable. He
married her; he gives her a home; he works hard each day to support her and the
children.

> What does she want? Proof? She's got it, hasn't she? Would I be knocking myself
> out to get things for her—like to keep up this house—if I didn't love her. Why
> does a man do things like that if not because he loves his wife and kids? I swear, I
> can't figure what she wants.

This is one time when *she* knows what she wants.

> I want him to let me know in other ways, too, not just sex. It's not enough that he
> supports us and takes care of us. I appreciate that, but I want him to share things
> with me. I need for him to tell me his feelings. He keeps saying no, but to me,
> there's a difference between making love and sex. Just once, I'd like him to love
> me without ending up in sex. But when I tell him that, he thinks I'm crazy.

For him, perhaps, it *does* seem crazy. Split off, as he is, from the rest of the
expressive-emotional side of himself, sex may be the only place where he can

allow himself the expression of deep feelings, the one place where he can experience the depth of that affective side. His wife, on the other hand, closely connected with her feeling side in all areas *but* the sexual, finds it difficult to be comfortable with her feelings in the very area in which he has the greatest— sometimes the only—ease. She keeps asking for something she can understand and is comfortable with—a demonstration of his feelings in non-sexual ways. He keeps giving her the one thing he can understand and is comfortable with—his feelings wrapped in a blanket of sex. Thus do husbands and wives find themselves in an impossibly difficult bind—another bind not of their own making, but one that stems from the cultural context in which girls and boys grow to adulthood.

I am suggesting, then, that a man's ever-present sexual readiness is not simply an expression of urgent sexual need but also a complex compensatory response to a socialization process that *constricts the development of the emotional side of his personality in all but sexual expression.* Conversely, a woman's insistent plea for an emotional statement of a nonsexual nature is a response to a process that *encourages the development of the affective side of her personality in all but sexual expression.*[3]

Such differences between women and men about the *meaning* of sex make for differences between wives and husbands in frequency of desire as well—differ- ences which lead to a wide discrepancy in their perceptions about the frequency of the sexual encounter.[4] Except for a few cases where the women are inclined to be more sexually active than the men, he wants sex more often than she. To him, therefore, it seems as if they have sex less often than they actually do; to her, it seems more often. But the classical caricature of a wife fending off her husband's advances with a sick headache seems not to apply among working-class women. Once in a while, a woman says . . .

> I tell him straight. I'm not in the mood, and he understands.

Mostly, however, women say . . .

> I don't use excuses like headaches and things like that. If my husband wants me, I'm his wife, and I do what he wants. It's my responsibility to give it to him when he needs it.

Whether she refuses outright or acquiesces out of a sense of duty or respon- sibility, the solution is less than satisfactory for both partners. In either case, he feels frustrated and deprived. He wants more than release from his own sexual tension; he wants her active involvement as well. Confronted with his ever-present readiness, she feels guilty . . .

> I feel guilty and uncomfortable when he's always ready and I'm not, like I'm not taking care of him.

. . . coerced . . .

> I feel like it hangs over my head all the time. He always wants it; twice a day

> wouldn't be too much for him. He says he doesn't want me just to give in to him,
> but if I didn't he'd be walking around horny all the time. If we waited for me to
> want it, it would never be enough for him.

. . . and also deprived . . .

> Before I ever get a chance to feel really sexy, he's there and waiting. I'd like to
> know what it feels like sometimes to really want it that bad. Oh, sometimes I do.
> But mostly I don't get the chance.

Thus, she rarely has the opportunity to experience the full force of her own sexual
rhythm, and with it, the full impact of her sexuality. It is preempted by the urgency
and frequency of his desires.

Finally, there is plenty of evidence that the battle between the sexes is still being
waged in the marriage bed, and in very traditional ways. Several couples spoke of
their early sexual adjustment problems in ways that suggest that the struggle was
not over sex but over power and control. Often in the early years, when she wants
sex, he's tired; when he wants sex, she's uninterested. For many couples, the
pattern still repeats itself once in awhile. For about one-fifth of them, the scenario
continues to be played out with great regularity and sometimes with great drama,
as this story of one early-thirties couple illustrates.

In six months of premarital and ten years of marital coitus, the woman had
never had an orgasm.

> We had sex four or five times a week like clockwork all those years, and I just laid
> there like a lump. I couldn't figure out what all the noise was about.

Asked how he felt about her passivity during that period, her husband—a taci-
turn, brooding man, whose silence seemed to cover a wellspring of hostility—
replied . . .

> If she couldn't, she couldn't. I didn't like it, but I took what I needed. [After a
> moment's hesitation] She's always been hard to handle.

A year ago, attracted by ideas about women's sexuality that seemed to her to be
"in the air," she began to read some of the women's literature on the subject. From
there, she moved on to pornography and one night, as she tells it . . .

> The earth shook. I couldn't believe anything could be so great. I kept wondering
> how I lived so long without knowing about it. I kept asking Fred why he'd never
> made me understand before. [Then, angrily] But you'll never believe what
> happened after that. My husband just lost interest in sex. Now, I can hardly ever
> get him to do it any more, no matter how much I try or beg him. He says he's too
> tired, or he doesn't feel well, or else he just falls asleep and I can't wake him up. I
> can hardly believe it's happening sometimes. Can you imagine such a thing? I
> even wonder whether maybe I shouldn't have made such a big fuss about it.
> Maybe it scared him off or something.

Her husband refused my attempts to explore the issue with him, insisting that all is
well in their sex, but adding . . .

> She's always asking for something, of hollering about something. I don't have any control around this house any more. Nobody listens to me.

It would seem, then, that as long as he could "take what I needed," he could feel he was asserting some control over his wife and could remain sexually active and potent. When she unexpectedly became an assertive and active participant in the sex act, the only possibility for retaining control was to move from the active to the passive mode. Thus, he felt impotent. His wife, now acutely aware of her sexual deprivation, is left torn between anger, frustration, and the terrible fear that somehow she is responsible for it.

A dramatic story? Certainly, but one whose outlines are clear in 20 percent of these marriages where three women complained about their husbands' impotence and seven about sexual withholding—not surprisingly, a problem most of the men were unwilling to talk about. In the three cases where the husband did address the issue at all, either he denied its existence, "It's no problem; I'm just tired"; or blamed his wife, "She doesn't appeal to me," or "She's too pushy." The last has been a subject of recent concern expressed publicly by psychologists and widely publicized in the mass media. The performance demands being laid on men are extraordinary, we are told, and women are cautioned that their emergent assertiveness—sexual and otherwise—threatens the sexual performance of their men. The time has come, these experts warn, to take the pressure off.

Nowhere, however, do we hear concern about the effects of the performance demand on women. Yet, never in history have heavier demands for sexual performance been laid on them. Until recently, women were expected to submit passively to sex; now they are told their passivity diminishes their husbands' enjoyment. Until recently, especially among the less educated working class, orgasm was an unexpected gift; now it is a requirement of adequate sexual performance.[5] These new definitions of adequacy leave many women feeling "under the gun"—fearful and anxious if they do not achieve orgasm; if it does not happen at the "right" moment—that is, at the instant of their husbands' ejaculation; or if they are uncomfortable about engaging in behaviors that feel alien or aberrant to them.[6] If anxiety about one's ability to perform adequately has an untoward effect on the male orgasm, is there any reason to believe it would not inhibit the female's as well?

In fact, the newfound concern with their orgasm is a mixed and costly blessing for many women. For some, it has indeed opened the possibility for pleasures long denied. For others, however, it is experienced as another demand in a life already too full of demands. Listen to this thirty-five-year-old woman who works part time, takes care of a house, a husband, six children, and an aging, sick father . . .

> If feels like somebody's always wanting something from me. Either one of the kids is hanging on to me or pulling at me, or my father needs something. And if it's not them, then Tom's always coming after me with that gleam in his eye. Then, it's not enough if I just let him have it, because if I don't have a climax, he's

not happy. I get so tired of everybody wanting something from me all the time. I sometimes think I hate sex.

While it is undoubtedly true that more women have more orgasms more often than ever before—and that most of them enjoy sex more than women in earlier generations—it is also true that there are times when a husband's wish for his wife's orgasm is experienced as oppressive and alienating—when it seems to a woman that her orgasm is more a requirement of his pleasure than her own. We may ask: How rational are these thoughts? And we may wonder: Why should it be a matter of question or criticism if, in the course of pleasuring their wives, men also pleasure themselves? When phrased that way, it should not be questioned! But if we look at the discussion around female orgasm or lack of it a little more closely, we notice that it is almost invariably tied to male pleasure. If a woman doesn't have an orgasm, it is a problem, if not for her, then because both her man's pleasure and his sense of manhood are diminished. Can anyone imagine a discussion of male impotence centering around concern for women? In fact, when we talk about the failure of men to achieve erection or orgasm, the discourse takes place in hushed, serious, regretful tones—always in the context of concern about how those men experience that failure. How many of us have ever thought, "What a shame for his woman that he can't have an erection." Any woman who has shared that experience with a man knows that her concern was largely for him, her own frustration becoming irrelevant in that moment. Any man who has experienced impotence knows that his dominant concern was for the failure of his manhood.

It is not surprising, therefore, that several of the women I talked to were preoccupied with their orgasm, not because it was so important to them, but because their husband's sense of manhood rested on it. Holding her head, one woman said painfully . . .

> I rarely have climaxes. But if it didn't bother my husband, it wouldn't bother me. I keep trying to tell him that I know it's not his fault, that he's really a good lover. I keep telling him it's something the matter with me, not with him. But it scares me because he doesn't believe it, and I worry he might leave me for a woman who will have climaxes for him.

With these final words, she epitomizes the feelings of many women, whether orgasmic or not, at least some of the time: *her orgasm is for him, not for her.* It is his need to validate his manhood that is the primary concern—his need, not hers. For women of the working class, who already have so little autonomy and control over their lives, this may well be experienced as the ultimate violation.

To compound the anxiety, now one orgasm is not enough. One woman, having read that some women have multiple orgasms, worried that her husband would soon find out.

> It's really important for him that I reach a climax, and I try to every time. He says it just doesn't make him feel good if I don't. But it's hard enough to do it once! What'll happen if he finds out about those women who have lots of climaxes?

These, then, are some dimensions of sexual experience in the 1970s that are buried under the sensational reports of changing sexual mores. Undoubtedly, there is a loosening of sexual constraints for both women and men; undoubtedly, more people are enjoying fuller sexual experiences than ever before. Certainly, it is important that these changes are discussed publicly, that the subject of sex has come out of the closet. But that is not enough. For we must also understand that such changes are not without cost to the individuals who try to live them out, who must somehow struggle past powerful early training to a new consciousness. For women especially—women of any class—that training in repressing and inhibiting their sexuality makes this a particularly difficult struggle.

It is both sad and ironic now to hear men complain that their wives are too cautious, too inhibited, or not responsive enough in bed. Sad, because the deprivation men experience is real; ironic, because these are the costs of the sexual limitations that generations of their forebears have imposed on women. Changing such historic patterns of thought and behavior will not be easy for either men or women. For certainly, many men are still not without ambivalence about these sexual issues with reference to their women—a subtlety that is not lost on their wives. But even where men unambivalently mean what they say about wanting their wives to be freer in the marriage bed, it will take time for women to work through centuries of socially mandated denial and repression . . .

> All I know is, I can't just turn on so easy. Maybe we're all paying the price now because men didn't used to want women to enjoy sex.

. . . and probably will require their first being freer in other beds as well.

> I was eighteen when we got married, and I was a very young eighteen. I'd never had any relations with anybody, not even my husband, before we were married. So, we had a lot of problems. I guess I was kind of frigid at first. But you know, after all those years when you're holding back, it's hard to all of a sudden get turned on just because you got married.

Yes, it is "hard to all of a sudden get turned on just because you got married." And as long as women's sexuality continues to be subjected to capricious demands and treated as if regulated by an on-off switch—expected to surge forth fully and vigorously at the flick of the "on" switch and to subside quietly at the flick of the "off"—most women will continue to seek the safest path, in this case, to remain quietly someplace between "on" and "off."

Notes

1. Morton Hunt, *Sexual Behavior in the 1970s* (Chicago: Playboy Press, 1974). This study, conducted for *Playboy* magazine, included a representative sample of urban and suburban adults, of whom 982 were men and 1,044 were women. Seventy-one percent of the sample were married (not to each other), 25 percent were never married, and 4 percent had been married.
2. For a good description of this stereotype, see Arthur B. Shostak, "Ethnic Revivalism, Blue-Collarites, and Bunker's Last Stand." In *The Rediscovery of Ethnicity,* edited by Sallie TeSelle (New York: Harper Colophon, 1973). See also Mirra Komarovsky, *Blue Collar Marriage* (New

York: Vintage Books, 1962) who, while noting that the stereotype applied to "only a small minority" of the families she studied, found that only 30 percent of the women said they were very satisfied with their sexual relations. And some of the data she presents do indeed validate the stereotype more forcefully and very much more often than among my sample where it is practically nonexistent.

3. Cf. William Simon and John Gagnon, "On Psychosexual Development." In *Handbook of Sociali- zation Theory and Research,* edited by David A. Goslin (Chicago: Rand McNally, 1969) and John Gagnon and William Simon, *Sexual Conduct: The Social Sources of Human Sexuality* (Chicago: Aldine Publishing, 1973) whose work is a major contribution toward understanding the differences in male-female sexuality as an expression of the different socialization patterns for women and men. These authors also point to the masculine tendency to separate love and sex and the feminine tendency to fuse them. They suggest, in fact, that the male "capacity for detached sexual activity, activity where the only sustaining motive is sexual . . . may actually be the hallmark of male sexuality in our culture." For an exploration of the ways in which social structure and personality intersect from the psychoanalytic perspective, see Nancy Chodorow, *The Reproduction of Mother- ing: Family Structure and Feminine Personality* (Berkeley: University of California Press, 1977, forthcoming), who argues that the root of the differences in male-female personality and the concomitant differences in the development of psychosexual needs and responses lie in the social structure of the family.

   See also Ben Barker-Benfield, "The Spermatic Economy: A Nineteenth Century View of Sexuality." In *The American Family in Social-Historical Perspective,* edited by Michael Gordon (New York: St. Martin's Press, 1973) for a portrait of nineteenth century definitions of male and female sexuality and the fear and abhorrence with which men viewed female sexuality in that era.

4. It is for this reason that studies relying on the recollection of only one spouse for their data—as most do—risk considerable distortion. Thus, for example, when Morton Hunt reports that almost 26 percent of the married women ages twenty-five to thirty-four report having sexual intercourse between 105 and 156 times a year, we know only that this is the wife's perception, and we can assume that the recollection is filtered through her *feelings* about the frequency of the sexual encounter.

5. Again, Hunt's data, while not controlled for class, are suggestive. Using the 1948 Kinsey data as a comparative base, he reports that marital coitus has increased in frequency at every age and educational level. Comparing the Kinsey sample with his own at the fifteenth year of marriage, Hunt reports "a distinct increase in the number of wives who always or nearly always have orgasm (Kinsey: 45 percent; *Playboy:* 53 percent) and a sharp decrease in the number of wives who seldom or never do (Kinsey: 28 percent; *Playboy:* 15 percent)."

6. For a rebuke of the self-styled male "experts" on women's sexuality that is both wonderfully angry and funny as it highlights the absurdity of their advice to women, see Ellen Frankort, *Vaginal Politics* (New York: Bantam Books, 1973): 172–180. She opens this section of her book, entitled "Carnal Ignorance," by saying:

   > For the longest time a woman wasn't supposed to enjoy sex. Then suddenly a woman was neurotic if she didn't achieve orgasm simultaneously with her husband. Proof of a woman's health was her ability to come at the very moment the man ejaculated, in the very place he ejaculated, and at the very rate ordained for him by his physiology. If she couldn't, she went to a male psychiatrist to find out why.

Gender Politics: Love and Power in the Private and Public Spheres*

Francesca M. Cancian

Introduction

Love has been a feminine specialty and preoccupation since the nineteenth century, a central part of women's sphere. Women's dependency on men's love has been attacked by feminists as a mystification that gives men power over women (Flax, 1982). And their argument makes sense in terms of an exchange theory of power—if women need men more than men need women, then men will have the power advantage in marriage and couple relationships.

This chapter presents a perspective on the social organization of love that clarifies the links between love, dependency, and power. My perspective is based, first of all, on the empirical generalization that women and men prefer different styles of love that are consistent with their gender role. Women prefer emotional closeness and verbal expression; men prefer giving instrumental help and sex, forms of love that permit men to deny their dependency on women. Second, I argue that love is feminized in our society; that is, only women's style of love is recognized, and women are assumed to be more skilled at love and more in need of it.

My perspective clarifies how the social organization of love bolsters the power of men over women in close relationships, but it also suggests that men's power advantage in the private sphere is quite limited. It is primarily in the public sphere that feminized love promotes inequality in power. The feminization of love implies that men are independent individuals and by so doing obscures relations of dependency and exploitation of the work place and the community.

Definitions

Let me begin by defining love and power. I will then describe the feminization of love, summarize the evidence on men's and women's styles of love, and consider the effects of love on power.

My definition of love includes instrumental assistance and emotional expression and deemphasizes verbal self-disclosure. I define love between adults as a relatively enduring bond where a small number of people are affectionate and emotionally committed to each other, define their collective well-being as a major

*I am indebted to Frank Cancian, Henry Fagin, Steven Gordon and Ann Swidler for helpful comments and discussions.

219

goal, and feel obliged to provide care and practical assistance for each other. People who love each other also usually share physical contact; they talk to each other frequently and cooperate in some routine tasks of daily life. This definition is similar to definitions of companionate love as opposed to passionate love (Walster & Walster, 1978). It resembles Tönnies' concept of *Gemeinschaft* and is very different from the Parsonian conception of love as expressive but not instrumental.[1]

I define power as the ability to impose one's will on others despite resistance or the ability to prevail when decisions are made (Blau, 1964).

The Feminization of Love

In contrast to the broad definition of love that I have just given, our culture has been dominated by a much narrower conception of love for over a century, which I label "feminized love" (see Douglas, 1977).

The feminization of love in contemporary culture is evident in the way love is defined. Researchers who study love, intimacy, and close friendship often use operational definitions of love that consider only emotional expression, verbal self-disclosure, and affection. They typically ignore providing instrumental help or sharing physical activities.

For example, the study of marriage by Stinnett, Carter, and Montgomery (1972) among older people emphasized emotional expression and cognitive understanding in defining the basic needs in marriage. Six basic marital needs were identified: Love, personality fulfillment, respect, communication, finding meaning, and integrating past experiences. Love was measured by four questions about feelings, for example, whether one's spouse expressed "a feeling of being emotionally close to me." Providing money, practical help, or sex were not considered to be among the basic needs satisfied by marriage (Stinnett et al., 1972).

Research on friendship usually distinguishes close friends from acquaintances on the basis of how much personal information is disclosed (Booth & Hess, 1974; Lowenthal & Haven, 1968), and many recent studies of married couples and lovers emphasize communication and self-disclosure. Thus, a recent book on marital love by Lillian Rubin (1983) focuses on intimacy, which she defines as "reciprocal expression of feeling and thought, not out of fear or dependent need, but out of a wish to know another's inner life and be able to share one's own" (p. 90). She argues that intimacy is distinct from nurturance or caretaking, and that men are usually unable to be intimate.

The general public also defines love primarily as expressing feelings and verbal

---

[1]Alternative definitions of love are reviewed in Walster and Walster (1978), Hendrick and Hendrick (1983), and Reedy (1977). Frederich Tönnies' concept of *Gemeinschaft* includes economic exchange, physical proximity, routine cooperation, and affection; later generations of sociologists, like myself, incorrectly believed that Talcott Parsons' pattern variables restated Tönnies' *Gemeinschaft-Gessellschaft* distinction. In fact, Tönnies' *Gemeinschaft* tends to integrate the instrumental and expressive aspects of action.

disclosure, not as instrumental help; this is especially true for middle-class as opposed to working-class people.[2] In a study I conducted in 1980, 130 adults from a wide range of social backgrounds were interviewed about the qualities that make a good love relationship. The most frequent response referred to honest and open communication. Similar findings have been reported by others (Quinn, 1982; Swidler, 1982). Finally, *Webster's New Collegiate Dictionary* (1977) defines love as "strong affection for another rising out of kinship or personal ties" and as attraction based on sexual desire, affection, and tenderness.

These contemporary definitions of love obviously focus on qualities that are seen as feminine in our culture. A study of gender roles by Rosenkrantz, Vogel, Bee, Broverman and Broverman (1968) found that warmth, expressiveness, and talkativeness were usually seen as appropriate for females but not males. When this study was repeated in 1978, the core features of gender stereotypes were unchanged although fewer qualities were seen as appropriate for only one sex. Expressing tender feelings, being gentle, and being aware of the feelings of others were still ideal qualities for women and not men. The desirable qualities for men but not women included being independent, competent, unemotional, and interested in sex (Rosenkrantz, 1982). Thus, sexuality is the only masculine component in our culture's conception of love.

Evidence on Women's and Men's Style of Love

There is a fairly extensive body of research on women's and men's styles of love—on the kind of behavior that each sex prefers in close relationships with their lovers, spouse, or close friends. The results show that women prefer to talk about their personal experiences, especially their fears and troubles, and want to feel emotionally close and secure. Men prefer to show their love by instrumental help, doing activities together, and sex (see reviews of this research in Cancian, n.d.[b]; Peplau & Gordon, in press).

For example, the two styles of love emerged clearly in a study of seven couples by Wills, Weiss and Patterson (1974). The couples recorded their own interactions for several days. They noted how pleasant their relations were and also counted how often their spouse did a helpful chore, like cooking a good meal or repairing a faucet, and how often the spouse expressed acceptance or affection. The social scientists followed traditional usage and labeled practical help as "instrumental behavior" and expressing acceptance as "affectionate behavior," thereby denying the affectionate aspect of practical help. The wives seemed to be using the same scheme; they thought their marital relations were pleasant that day if their husband

---

[2]The greater emphasis on mutual aid and instrumental love among poor people is described in Miller and Riessman (1964), Rapp (1982), and Rubin (1976). The masculine role also seems less focused on independence and individualism in the working class. In the middle class, love is more feminized and women are more dependent on love with a man, probably because middle-class men can provide a high income and enviable lifestyle. Working-class women are more likely to look to their kin and children for intimacy, not their husbands (see Schneider & Smith, 1973).

had directed a lot of affectionate behavior to them, regardless of his positive instrumental behavior. But the husbands' enjoyment of their marital relations depended on their wife's instrumental actions, not her affection (Wills et al., 1974). One husband, when told by the researchers to increase his affectionate behavior toward his wife, decided to wash her car, and was surprised when neither his wife nor the researchers accepted that as an "affectionate" act.

Other studies of married couples and friends report similar findings. Margaret Reedy (1977) surveyed 102 married couples and asked them how well a series of statements described their marriage. The men emphasized practical help and spending time together and gave higher ratings to statements like: "When she needs help I help her," and "She would rather spend her time with me than with anyone else." Men also described themselves as more sexually attracted. The women emphasized emotional security and were more likely to describe the relationship as secure, safe, and comforting. Another study of the ideal and actual relationship of several hundred young couples found that the husbands gave greater emphasis to feeling responsible for the partner's well-being and putting the spouse's needs first, as well as to spending time together. The wives gave greater importance to emotional involvement and the verbal self-disclosure (Parelman, 1980). In friendships also, men value sharing activities, while women emphasize confiding their troubles and establishing a supportive emotional attachment (Dickens & Perlman, 1981).

There is also a large body of research showing that women are more skilled and more interested in love than men. Women are closer to their relatives and are more likely to have intimate friends (Adams, 1968; Dickens & Perlman, 1981). Women are more skilled in verbal self-disclosure and emotional expression (Henley, 1977; Komarovsky, 1962). When asked about what is most important in their lives, women usually put family relations first, while men are more likely to put work first.

However, this evidence of women's superiority in love is not so strong as it first seems. Many of the studies show very small differences between the sexes, and the measures of love are usually biased against men and focus on verbal self-disclosure or willingness to say one "feels close" to someone. For example, in a careful study of kinship relations among young adults in a Southern city, Bert Adams found that women were much more likely than men to say that their parents and relatives were very important to their lives (58% of women and 37% of men). However, when he looked at actual contact with relatives, he found much smaller differences (88% of women and 81% of men whose parents lived in the city saw their parents weekly). He concludes that "differences between males and females in relations with parents are discernible primarily in the subjective sphere; contact frequencies are quite similar" (Adams, 1968, p. 169).

In sum, women and men have different styles of love, but love is feminized. It is identified with qualities that are stereotypically feminine and with styles of love that women prefer.

Social historians help us identify the causes of this social organization of love.

They describe how love became feminized in the nineteenth century as economic production became separated from the home and from personal relationships (see Degler, 1980; Ryan, 1979, 1981; Welter, 1966). They have shown how the increasing divergence of men's and women's daily activities produced a polarization of gender roles. Wives became economically dependent on their husbands, and an ideology of separate spheres developed that exaggerated the differences between women and men and between the loving home and the ruthless work place.

Building on this historical research, I interpret the feminization of love and gender differences in styles of love as caused primarily by: (1) the sexual division of labor that makes wives economically dependent on their husbands and makes women responsible for childrearing; (2) the separation of the public and private spheres; and (3) beliefs about gender roles. Thus, there are both socioeconomic and cultural causes of our social organization of love.

Love and the Power of Men over Women

In the private sphere of marriage and close relationships, the social organization of love bolsters men's power over women in two ways. First it exaggerates women's dependency on men. If most people believe that women need heterosexual love more than men, then women will be at a power disadvantage, as many feminists have pointed out (Flax, 1982).

In fact, there is strong medical and sociological evidence that men depend on marriage as much as, or more than, women. For example, the mortality rate of unmarried men is much higher than married men, while marriage has a weaker effect on the mortality of women (Gove, 1973). The fact that men's health benefits from marriage more than women's health suggests that men depend more on marriage, whether or not they acknowledge this need. Men's dependency on marriage is also suggested by the tendency for women to have closer ties with friends and relatives than men; thus, men are more dependent on their spouses for social support (Cancian, n.d.[a], chap. 3). Men also remarry at higher rates than women (Stein, 1981, p. 358) and when they are asked about their major goals in life, a happy marriage is usually first or second on their list (Campbell, Converse, & Rodgers, 1976). But the centrality of independence to the masculine role seems to make us forget these facts. A dominant picture of gender politics in our culture is still a woman trying to entrap a man into an enduring love relationship, while all he wants is temporary sex.

Because of the social organization of love, men's dependency on close relationships remain covert and repressed, whereas women's dependency is overt and exaggerated. And it is overt dependency that affects power, according to social exchange theory. Thus, a woman gains power over her husband if he clearly places a high value on her company or if he expresses a high demand or need for what she supplies (Blau, 1964; Homans, 1967). If his need for her and high evaluation of her remain covert and unexpressed, her power will be low.

The denial of dependency is also evident in the styles of love that men prefer. Insofar as men admit that they are loving, their styles of love involve fulfilling women's needs and not on being dependent and needy themselves. Providing practical help, protection, and money implies superiority over the one who receives these things. Sex also expresses male dominance insofar as the man takes the initiative and intercourse is defined either as him "taking" his pleasure or being skilled at "giving" her pleasure, in either case defining her as passive. The man's power advantage will also be strengthened if the couple assumes that his need for sex can be filled by any attractive woman, while her sexual needs can only be filled by the man she loves.

In contrast, women's preferred ways of loving involve admitting dependency and sharing or losing power. The intimate talk about personal troubles that appeals to women requires a mutual vulnerability, an ability to see oneself as weak and in need of support. Women's love is also associated with being responsive to the needs of others; this leads to giving up control, in the sense of being "on call" to provide care whenever it is required.[3]

In addition to affecting the balance of dependency between women and men, the feminization of love bolsters men's power by devaluing women's sphere of activities. Defining love as expressive devalues love, since our society tends to glorify instrumental achievement and to disparage emotional expression as sentimental and foolish (Fiedler, 1966; Inkeles, 1979). In fact, much of women's love consists of instrumental acts like preparing meals, washing clothes, or providing care during illness, but this is obscured by focusing on the expressive side of love. In our culture, a woman washing her husband's shirt tends to be seen as expressing loving feelings, while a man washing his wife's car tends to be seen as doing a job.

The well-known study of gender stereotypes among mental health workers by Broverman, Broverman, Clarkson, Rosenkrantz and Vogel (1970) vividly demonstrates how defining love as expressive is connected to decreasing women's status and power. In the study, therapists were asked to describe mentally healthy adults, femininity, and masculinity. They associated both mental health and masculinity with being independent, unemotional, dominant, and businesslike, qualities that the researchers labeled as "competence." In contrast, "expressive" qualities like being tactful, gentle, or aware of the feelings of others were associated with femininity and not with mental health. These results document a devaluation of femininity and show how the dominant concept of mental health is biased against women and against love and attachment (see Gilligan, 1982).

In sum, the power of men over women in close relationships is strengthened by the feminization of love and by men's and women's different styles of love.

---

[3] A nurturant woman can be a formidable power, and taking care of someone easily slides over into controlling them; but the tendency to deny the active and powerful aspect of women's nurturance often obscures this aspect of women's power.

But Men Are Not That Powerful

Men clearly dominate women in close relationships. Husbands tend to have more power in making decisions, a situation that has not changed in recent decades (Blood & Wolfe, 1960; Duncan, Schuman, & Duncan, 1973). The evidence on the superior mental and physical health of married men vs. women has led some researchers, like Jessie Bernard (1972), to conclude that the institution of marriage is controlled by men for men's benefit.

However, given that power means the ability to get what one wants from another, men's power over women in intimate relationships is severely limited by the social organization of love. First, the legitimacy of men's style of love is denied. He will probably fail to persuade her that his practical help is a sign of love and that his sexual advances are a request for intimacy. As one of the working-class husbands interviewed by Lillian Rubin said, "She complains that all I want from her is sex, and I try to make her understand that it's an expression of love"; and a wife commented, "he keeps saying he wants to make love, but it just doesn't feel like love to me" (1976, p. 146). In contrast, the legitimacy of her desire for intimate communications is supported by the mass media and by therapists. Thus, there is probably more social pressure for him to express his feelings than for her to enjoy sex.

Moreover, because of the avoidance of dependency associated with the male role, he may not even know what he wants or needs from her and, therefore, may be unable to try to get it. Thus, the covert nature of a man's dependency may increase his power by hiding his neediness from women. But it may also decrease his power by hiding his needs from himself.

Women's responsibility for love and their overt dependence can also leave both partners feeling controlled by the other.[4] Insofar as love is defined as the woman's "turf," an area where she sets the rules and expectations, a man is likely to feel threatened and controlled when she seeks more intimacy. Talking about the relationship, like she wants, feels like taking a test that she made up and he will fail. The husband is likely to react with withdrawal and passive aggression. He is blocked from straightforward counterattack insofar as he believes that intimacy is good.

From a woman's perspective, since love is in her sphere and she is responsible for success, she is very highly motivated to have a successful relationship. When there are problems in the relationship, she typically wants to take steps to make things better. She is likely to propose solutions such as discussing their problem or taking a vacation; and he is likely to respond with passive resistance and act as if

---

[4]Other negative consequences of women's dependency on love are described in Cancian (1984); for example, her dependency may lead her to seek frequent reassurance from him that he loves her, and she may be so needy that he will inevitably fail to meet her needs.

she were pushy, demanding, and unfeminine. His withdrawal and veiled accusations will probably make her feel helpless and controlled.

Thus, a woman's control of the sphere of love ends up making her feel less powerful, not more, because she can succeed in her sphere only by getting the right response from him. Women's separate sphere of love and the family probably produced much more power for women in Victorian times, when a woman could succeed in love through her relations with her children and women friends and through sacrificing herself for her husband; in those times, being a loving woman was less dependent on the behavior of men (Ryan, 1979).

In these times, one of the most frequent marital conflicts reported by therapists is the conflict between a woman who wants more intimacy, more love, something more from from her husband, and the man who withdraws and feels pressured (Raush, Barry, Hertel, & Swain, 1974; Rubin, 1983). The same pattern showed up in a survey of middle-class couples that asked how people wanted their spouse to change. The major sex difference was that husbands wanted their spouse to be less emotional and create less stress, while wives wanted their spouse to be more responsive and receptive (Burke, Weir, & Harrison, 1976).

Similar conflicts emerge from interview studies, although men's sexual frustrations come out more clearly in interviews (Cancian, 1984; Rubin, 1976). One young wife who had been married 3 years exploded: "Words! If only my husband could talk to me more. Sometimes he listens, but he hardly ever talks back. It's hard to talk to a drunk, and yet it's the only time he shows me any real feelings." Her husband acknowledges: "She always says that I don't talk to her. I don't understand. I'm sure she knows what I'm thinking, but that isn't good enough for her." For him, "I feel we have really communicated after we have made love."[5]

In sum, feminized love seems to give men some power advantage, but neither sex wins in the conflict it creates.

Power in the Public Sphere

Love may have a more important effect on power relations in the public sphere than in the private sphere. Feminized love covers up the material dependency of women on men and the interdependence of all people. It is part of a world view that explains people's life situation by their inherent nature and not by the relations of exchange, sharing, or exploitation between them.

The way feminized love mystifies social relations of dependency and exploitation was especially clear in the nineteenth century, when wives were totally dependent economically on their husbands and the ideology of woman's special sphere of love was emerging. A central argument in this ideology was that women

---

[5]This quote is from an interview by Cynthia Garlich, a student in an undergraduate seminar I taught, in which students did intensive, open-ended interviews about close relationships.

were powerless and dependent because they were naturally submissive and affectionate. An article by an antislavery writer in the mid-nineteenth century illustrates this perspective:

> The comparison between women and the colored race is striking. Both are characterized by affection more than by intellect; both have a strong development of the religious sentiment; both are exceedingly adhesive in their attachments; both, comparatively speaking, have a tendency to submission, and hence, both have been kept in subjection by physical force, and considered rather in the light of property, than as individuals. (Rose, 1982, p. 45)

This perspective denies the material basis of women's dependency. It also defines religious morality and the need for affection as qualities peculiar to women.

The other side of defining women as naturally dependent, moral, and affectionate is defining men as naturally independent, amoral, and isolated. As Marxist scholars have pointed out, the ideology of the isolated individual accompanied and justified the rise of capitalism (Zaretsky, 1976). Men were encouraged to see themselves as independent, competitive, and self-made. If they were rich or poor, it was the result of their own individual merit, not relationships of dependency with other people. And if they were real men, they would thrive on the impersonal, competitive relationships that prevailed at work.

Contemporary views of human nature often perpetuated the ideology of separate spheres and the self-made man. They assume that independence is the central human virtue, and dependency and attachments are feminine qualities associated with weakness. As Carol Gilligan has documented (1982), current psychological theories of human development assert that a healthy person develops from a dependent child to an independent, autonomous adult. For example, Daniel Levinson's conception of development for men centers on the "Dream" of glorious achievement in his occupation. Attachments are subservient to the goals of becoming an autonomous person and attaining the "Dream"; a man who has not progressed towards his "Dream" by mid-life should break out of his established way of life by "leaving his wife, quitting his job, or moving to another region" (1978, p. 206). This concept of a healthy man condemns men without challenging careers, which includes most middle- and working-class men. It also ignores the fact that "successful" men depend on others: on wives and mothers who raised them and their children, on men and women who worked with them and for them. In many ways, Levinson's position is a restatement of the ideology of the self-made man, an excellent justification of meritocracy and inequality.

Thus, defining affection and dependency as feminine supports inequality in the public sphere in addition to maintaining men's power over women at home. It also motivates men to work hard at impersonal jobs and to blame themselves for their poverty or failure.

More generally, the ideology of separate spheres leads people to tolerate immoral, exploitative relationships in the work place or the community.[6] For example, this ideology suggests that it is acceptable for a manager to underpay his workers or for the faculty at a university to ignore an assistant professor who has been fired. Their behavior is not unloving or immoral; they are being businesslike or are respecting individual privacy. From this perspective, it is natural to treat people like objects at work; personal relationships, morality, and love are reserved for the private sphere and the feminine role.

These are other ways that the social organization of love contributes to economic and political inequality (see Sokoloff, 1980). In particular, it strengthens the power of men over women at the work place not only by encouraging women to devote themselves to love and the family but also by supporting the belief that money and dreams of achievement are not very important to women.

The consequences of love would be more positive if love were the responsibility of men as well as women and if love were defined more broadly to include instrumental help as well as emotional expression. Our current social organization of love maintains a situation where at home, women and men are in conflict, and where at work, men oppress women and managers oppress workers.

Conclusion

I have focused on how love effects power relations. In conclusion, I want to return to the causes of our current social organization of love. The foregoing analysis suggests that one reason for the persistence of the feminization of love and the accompanying emphasis on the independence of men is that these patterns serve the interests of the ruling classes. This functional explanation is weak until we can specify the mechanisms by which ruling groups manage to establish beliefs and social practices that benefit them. The historical research on the origins of the feminization of love in the nineteenth century suggests that the major causes were the differentiation of the harsh public sphere and the loving private sphere also the sexual division of labor, especially the economic dependency of women on men.

This explanation suggests that our conceptions of love will change now that women are economically dependent. It also suggests that in societies where the public sphere is seen as cooperative and helpful, love will be identified with men as well as women and with instrumental as well as expressive activity; a small socialist society might be an example. These issues should be explored in future research. We also need to focus on the masculine gender role and clarify how men's identification with the marketplace effects gender roles and love relationships. By clarifying the causes of our patterns of love, hopefully we can also clarify the social conditions that would encourage a more androgynous kind of love that combined expression and practical help and acknowledged the interdependence of men and women.

---

[6]The concept of *love* has been closely tied to moral values in American culture, as Ann Swidler (1980) has pointed out.

References

Adams, B. *Kinship in an urban setting*. Chicago, Ill.: Markham, 1968.

Bernard, J. *The future of marriage*. New York: Bantam Books, 1972.

Blau, P. M. *Exchange and power in social life*. New York: John Wiley, 1964.

Blood, R. O., & Wolfe, D. *Husbands and wives*. New York: The Free Press, 1960.

Booth, A. & Hess, E. Cross-sex friendship. *Journal of Marriage and the Family*, 1974, *36*, 38–47.

Broverman, I. K., Broverman, D. M., Clarkson, F., Rosenkrantz, P., & Vogel, S. Sex-role stereo-types and clinical judgments of mental health. *Journal of Consulting Psychology*, 1970, *34*, 1–7.

Burke, R., Weir, T., & Harrison, D. Disclosure of problems and tensions experienced by marital partners. *Psychological Reports*, 1976, *38*, 531–542.

Campbell, A., Converse, P. E., & Rodgers, W. *The quality of American life*. New York: Russell Sage Foundation, 1976.

Cancian, F. M. Marital conflict over intimacy. In G. Handel (Ed.), *The psychosocial interior of the family* (3rd ed.). New York: Aldine, 1984.

Cancian, F. M. *Attachment and freedom*. Unpublished manuscript, University of California, Irvine, n.d.(a)

Cancian, F. M. *The feminization of love*. Unpublished manuscript, University of California, Irvine, n.d.(b)

Degler, C. N. *At odds: Women and the family in America from the Revolution to the present*. New York: Oxford University Press, 1980.

Dickens, W., & Perlman, C. Friendship over the life cycle. In S. Duck & R. Gilmour (Eds.), *Personal relationships* (Vol. 2). London: Academic Press, 1981.

Douglas, A. *The feminization of American culture*. New York: Knopf, 1977.

Duncan, O. D., Schuman, H., & Duncan, B. *Social change in a metropolitan community*. New York: Russell Sage Foundation, 1973.

Fiedler, L. *Love and death in the American novel*. New York: Stein and Day, 1966.

Flax, J. The family in contemporary feminist thought: A critical review. In J. Elshtain (Ed.), *The family in political thought*. Amherst, Mass.: University of Massachusetts Press, 1982.

Gilligan, C. *In a different voice*. Cambridge, Mass.: Harvard University Press, 1982.

Gove, W. Sex, marital status and mortality. *American Journal of Sociology*, 1973 *79*, 45–67.

Hendrick, C., & Hendrick, S. *Liking, loving and relating*. Belmont, Calif.: Wadsworth, 1983.

Henley, N. *Body politics*. Englewood Cliffs, N.J.: Prentice-Hall, 1977.

Homans, G. Fundamental social processes. In N. Smelser (Ed.), *Sociology*. New York: John Wiley, 1967.

Inkeles, A. Continuity and change in the American national character. In S. Lipset (Ed.), *The third century*. Stanford, Calif.: Hoover Institution Press, 1979.

Komarovsky, M. *Blue-collar marriage*. New York: Random House, 1962.

Levinson, D. J. *The seasons of a man's life*. New York: Knopf, 1978.

Lowenthal, M. F., & Haven, C. Interaction and adaption: Intimacy as a critical variable. *American Sociological Review*, 1968, *33*, 20–40.

Miller, S. M., Riessman, F. The working-class subculture. In A. Shostak & W. Greenberg (Eds.), *Blue-collar world*. Englewood Cliffs, N.J.: Prentice-Hall, 1964.

Parelman, S. A. *Dimensions of emotional intimacy in marriage*. Unpublished doctoral dissertation, University of California, Los Angeles, 1980.

Peplau, L., & Gordon, S. Women and men in love: Sex differences in close relationships. In V. O'Leary, R. Unger, & B. Wallston (Eds.), *Women, gender and social psychology*. Hillsdale, N.J.: Erlbaum, in press.

Quinn, N. Commitment in American marriage. *American Ethnologist*, 1982, *9*, 775–798.

Rapp, R. Family and class in contemporary America. In B. Thorne (Ed.), *Rethinking the family*. New York: Longman, 1982.

Raush, H. L., Barry, W. A., Hertel, R. K., & Swain, M. A. *Communication, conflict and marriage*. San Francisco: Jossey-Bass, 1974.

Reedy, M. *Age and sex differences in personal needs and the nature of love*. Unpublished doctoral dissertation, University of Southern California, 1977.

Rose, W. L. Reforming women. *New York Review of Books, 29*, October 7, 1982.

Rosenkrantz, P. Changes in stereotypes about men and women. *Second Century Radcliffe News*, June 1982.

Rosenkrantz, P., Vogel, S. R., Bee, H., Broverman, I. K., & Broverman, D. M. Sex role stereotypes and self-concepts in college students. *Journal of Consulting and Clinical Psychology.* 1968, *32,* 287–295.

Rubin, L. B. *Worlds of pain.* New York: Basic Books, 1976.

Rubin, L. B. *Intimate strangers.* New York: Harper and Row, 1983.

Ryan, M. *Womanhood in America* (2nd ed.). New York: New Viewpoints, 1979.

Ryan, M. *The cradle of the middle class: The family in Oneida County, New York, 1790–1865.* New York: Cambridge University Press, 1981.

Schneider, D. M., & Smith, R. *Class difference and sex roles in American kinship and family structure.* Englewood Cliffs, N.J.: Prentice-Hall, 1973.

Sokoloff, N. *Between money and love: The dialectics of women's home and market work.* New York: Praeger, 1980.

Stein, P. *Single life.* New York: St. Martin's Press, 1981.

Stinnett, N., Carter, L., & Montgomery, J. Older persons' perception of their marriages. *Journal of Marriage and the Family,* 1972, *34,* 665–670.

Swidler, A. Love and adulthood in American culture. In N. Smelser & E. Erikson (Eds.), *Themes of work and love in adulthood.* Cambridge, Mass.: Harvard University Press, 1980, pp. 120–147.

Swidler, A. *Ideologies of love in middle class America.* Paper presented to the Annual Meeting of Pacific Sociological Association, San Diego, 1982.

Walster, E., & Walster, W. G. *A new look at love.* Reading, Mass.: Addison-Wesley, 1978.

Welter, B. The cult of true womanhood: 1820–1860. *American Quarterly,* 1966, *18,* 151–174.

Wills, T., Weiss, R., & Patterson, G. A behavioral analysis of the determinants of marital satisfaction. *Journal of Consulting and Clinical Psychology,* 1974, *42,* 802–811.

Zaretsky, E. *Capitalism, the family and personal life.* New York: Harper & Row, 1976.

3

Coupling

Introduction

Chapter 5   Sex and Love

Carol A. Darling, David, J. Kallen, and Joyce E. VanDusen
Sex in Transition, 1900–1980

Peter Davis
Exploring the Kingdom of AIDS

Graham B. Spanier
Cohabitation in the 1980s: Recent Changes in the United States

Philip Blumstein and Pepper Schwartz
American Couples

Chapter 6   Marriage

John F. Cuber and Peggy B. Harroff
Five Types of Marriage

Rosanna Hertz
More Equal Than Others: Women and Men in Dual-Career Marriages

Murray A. Straus, Richard Gelles, and Suzanne Steinmetz
The Marriage License and a Hitting License

Chapter 7   Divorce and Remarriage

Lenore J. Weitzman and Ruth B. Dixon
The Transformation of Legal Marriage Through No-Fault Divorce

Terry Arendell
Mothers and Divorce: Downward Mobility

Susan E. Krantz
The Impact of Divorce on Children

Constance R. Ahrons and Roy H. Rodgers
The Remarriage Transition

Introduction

To many people, the current state of marriage seems to provide the clearest evidence that the family is falling apart. In the past two decades, marriage rates have declined, divorce rates have gone up, and increasing numbers of couples have come to live together without being married. Yet these changes do not necessarily mean that people no longer want long-term commitments or that they are psychologically incapable of forming deep attachments. Rather, they reflect the fact that in the modern world marriage is increasingly a personal relationship between two people. Over time there have come to be fewer and fewer reasons for couples to remain in unsatisfactory relationships. And as the standards for emotional fulfillment in marriage have risen, the level of discontent may have increased also.

In the preindustrial past, the emotional relationship between husband and wife was the least important aspect of marriage. A marriage was an exchange between kin groups, a unit of economic production, and a means of replenishing populations with high death rates. In traditional societies, parents often selected their children's mates. Parents were more interested in the practical consequences of choice than in romantic considerations.

By contrast, in our modern society, people are supposed to marry for "love." They may marry for practical reasons or for money; nevertheless they often follow their culture's rules and decide they are "in love." People may also decide they are in love and want to live together but do not care to have their union licensed by the state or blessed by the clergy.

Couple relationships are thus influenced by a new fluidity and openness with regard to social norms in general and sexual behavior in particular. At one time, a relationship between a man and a woman could be easily categorized: it was either "honorable" or "dishonorable." An "honorable" relationship went through several distinct stages of commitment: dating, keeping company, going steady, agreeing to be married, announcing the engagement, and finally getting married, presumably for life. Divorce was regarded as a personal tragedy and social disgrace. Sexual relations at any point before marriage were also shameful, especially for the woman, although the shamefulness decreased as the marriage drew nearer.

Today the system of courtship has given way to a new pattern of couple relationships—less permanent, more flexible, more experimental. Utilizing the most recent demographic findings, two of the selections make this point very clearly. The first, by Darling, Kallen, and VanDusen, finds that premarital sexual intercourse has become widely acceptable, and indeed has become the norm for both men and women, based upon similar motives and meanings. But sexual freedom isn't what it used to be, even only a few years ago. As of the 1986 edition of this book, we had not heard much about AIDS. Now, just three years later, AIDS has become a major public health policy issue. The Surgeon General has urged that nonmonogamous sexually active persons use condoms to protect themselves against the fatal disease. When that sort of warning and threat is widely disseminated, it must affect nonmarital sex. Peter Davis's article suggests that even though heterosexuals are not considered a major risk group, the threat of AIDS, however remote, has generated significant changes in the sexual conduct and attitudes of heterosexuals.

The choice, of course, is not simply between multiple sexual partners and marriage. In a closely related set of findings, the selection by Spanier concludes that cohabitation without marriage is no longer shameful and appears to be a growing phenomenon. It has now become an acceptable pattern of coupling, even in mainstream America.

Philip Blumstein and Pepper Schwartz have recently completed a major re-search study of American couples—based on thousands of questionnaires and more than 300 intensive interviews. In the excerpt we reprint here, they address two general questions: First, what does the "institution" of marriage mean to couples today? An institution is a way of life with clear rules and expectations. Thus, it is not clear what marriage means in a time when the rules are in flux and couples can simply live together without getting married. The second question involves gender: How do couple relationships work when there are no male/female differences with which to contend? For example, how do couples consisting of two females differ from couples in which both partners are male?

As it happens, our cultural ideals of marital happiness and emotional fulfillment are often at odds with the realities of everyday married life. The article by John F. Cuber and Peggy Harroff reveals that enduring and satisfying marriages can vary a great deal from one another as well as from the ideals of happy marriage.

The dual-career marriage has begun to be considered the vanguard of gender equality and family integration. In the selection reprinted here, Rosanna Hertz attempts to cut into the mythology of the dual-career pattern as representing the quintessential "modern couple." It is true, she finds, that dual-career marriage and family can benefit positively those involved. Because two jobs bring in more income than one, dual-career couples enjoy a more affluent lifestyle—and one that is also more secure financially, because they are less dependent on the success of one career. At the same time, this autonomy is contingent upon a number of other factors, such as the availability of two jobs, outside help, and the often competing demands made by separate employers. These observations are interesting in that they draw our attention to the difficulties as well as the benefits of marriage, even when the couples enjoy each other and a widely sought-after lifestyle.

Whether dual career or not, family life can show considerable, even severe strains. Nowhere is this more evident than in the increasing recognition that violence within the family, while not quite as American as apple pie, is not so unusual either. In the article we reprint here, Murray A. Straus, Richard Gelles, and Suzanne Steinmetz explore the prevalence of and reasons for contemporary wife-beating. As might be expected, violence is reported more frequently in marriages ending in divorce.

Traditional societies do not necessarily have happier marriages or even lower divorce rates—some have higher rates than ours. Still, strong kin groups in traditional societies either keep couples together regardless of how they feel or make it easier for couples to break up without severe disruption. Nevertheless, traditional societies were quite conservative in their view of marriage, which was regarded as a permanent moral commitment that the church, and later the state, was to protect and preserve. Traditional marriage was also based on a division of labor between the sexes. The husband was to be head of the family and its chief provider; the wife was to provide services in the form of child care and housework. Divorce could be granted only through either the failure of one of the spouses to live up to his or her role or the betrayal of a spouse through adultery or cruelty.

The new divorce laws, as the article by Lenore J. Weitzman and Ruth B. Dixon points out, abolish this notion of fault or blame; instead, "irreconcilable differences" are grounds for the dissolution of marriage. Further, the new laws attempt to establish more equal rights and obligations between husband and wife, both during the marriage and at the time of divorce. While it is still too early to judge the ultimate effects of the new laws on marriage as an institution, it is clear that they codify a very different conception of marriage and divorce than previously existed in the law.

Moreover, as the piece by Terry Arendell suggests, despite the positive intentions of those who wrote the new laws, divorce often has a negative economic impact on middle-class women, a finding confirmed by Weitzman's research as well.

Divorce, however, touches 2 million children every year, and by 1990, it is expected to be experienced by over half of American children under age 18. Researchers are coming to view divorce not as a single event, but as a complex process that unfolds across the course of the child's life. Susan E. Krantz's article reviews the current state of research about the effects of divorce on children's functioning. What is it about divorce that influences children? The absence of a parent? The conflict between the parents? Economic hardship? Looking at the relevant research, Krantz concludes that children's adjustment is a product of many interacting factors, including characteristics of the child, the family, and the economic and social resources, as well as the child's interpretation of the situation. This complexity makes research difficult, and there is a shortage of well-controlled studies. Nevertheless, it seems clear that divorce is stressful for children and may lead, in some children, to emotional difficulties that persist for long periods. The paper concludes that easing the financial hardships of custodial parents and their children, along with improved social services, can help prevent or shorten the period of emotional trauma experienced by children of divorce.

Another impact of divorce is the possibility of remarriage by one or both spouses. Such remarriages generate interesting and problematic kinship structures and relationships that have scarcely been studied and for which we may not even have names. We know something about stepparents and stepchildren. But is there a difference between the way a father acts to his own children of his first marriage who live part of the time with his first wife, and the children of his second marriage who live full-time with him and his second wife? What of half-brothers, and -sisters? What of the relationship between a father's first-marriage children, second wife's first-marriage children, and children of both of the second marriage? The selection by Constance R. Ahorns and Roy H. Rodgers discusses the family complexities generated by divorce and modern remarriage that challenge the traditional assumptions underlying the conception of the so-called "nuclear family."

Despite all its difficulties, marriage is not likely to go out of style in the near future. Ultimately we agree with Jessie Bernard (1972), who, after a devastating critique of marriage from the point of view of a sociologist who is also a feminist, has this to say:

> The future of marriage is as assured as any social form can be . . . For men and women will continue to want intimacy, they will continue to want to celebrate their mutuality, to experience the mystic unity which once led the church to consider marriage a sacrament. . . . There is hardly any probability such commitments will disappear or that all relationships between them will become merely casual or transient. (p. 301)

References

Bernard, Jessie. 1972. *The Future of Marriage*. New York: World.
Cherlin, Andrew. 1978. "Remarriage as an Incomplete Institution." *American Journal of Sociology*, 84, pp. 634–650.
Weitzman, Lenore J. *The Divorce Revolution*. New York: Free Press. 1985.

Chapter 5

Sex and Love

Sex in Transition, 1900–1980

Carol A Darling, David J. Kallen, and Joyce E. VanDusen[1]

Introduction

The influence of sexuality on our lives has changed through time. This change has affected the meanings and attitudes attached to sexuality and sexual behaviors. The past decade and a half, in particular, has seen a major increase in the extent to which adolescents and young adults have been involved in heterosexual intercourse. Furthermore, there has been a major shift in the rates of coital involvement among young females so that their age-adjusted rates now approximate those of young males.

This paper examines trends in sexual behavior in the United States from the early 1900s to the present. It does not present a historical review of the sexual literature; rather, it provides a meta-analysis of scientific studies of sexual behavior of youth, with an emphasis on the changing rates of coital involvement among males and females. Implications about the meaning of these changing rates are also presented. Although over the years "premarital intercourse" has been the terminology utilized by researchers when discussing the sexual behavior of never-married persons, the authors have chosen not to employ this term due to the implication that intercourse is necessarily followed by marriage, an implication which is not correct today.

The transition from virgin to nonvirgin represents a move into a new status (Jessor and Jessor, 1975). Since this status change can be made only once in the lifetime of an individual, it has considerable meaning for the individual as well as for society. The symbolic meaning of this transition evolves from a societal need to control reproduction and entry into adulthood. Beliefs about the range of sexual

From *Journal of Youth and Adolescence*, Vol. 13, No. 5, 1984. Reprinted by permission of Plenum Publishing Corporation. Portions of the original have been omitted.

behaviors that are acceptable are embedded in normatic systems and vary according to individual factors, group membership, and social changes. Thus, sexual behavior is social behavior which is regulated by society and learned through the socialization process (Kallen, 1980).

Major changes have occurred in the sexual standards and behaviors of adolescents and young adults in recent years. While this transformation has been more rapid during the last two decades than during the earlier part of the century, an analysis of published data from the last 80 years helps to depict social trends in the reorganization of sexual relations among unmarried youth. Hence, the focus of this paper is on a broad examination of the transition of sexual behavior within the societal context of this century.

Methodology

Data for this trend analysis were obtained from 35 published studies which examined some phase of sexual behavior among never-married youth and young adults. These studies were selected through the use of literature and computer searches and employed a number of criteria to ensure that the studies were methodologically acceptable and represented behavioral patterns of the time. These included the following.

- The study must be of a cross-sectional sample, not of a specially selected group. Thus, studies which utilized participants in birth-control clinics, retrospective samples of married persons reporting on their premarital behavior, patients in psychiatric treatment, etc., were not included.
- The research method used must be within a generally acceptable range of social and behavioral science research.
- The data must have been published either in book form or, more probably, in a reasonably accessible journal.

Due to the wide variety of samples and methods employed in the studies, this review is focused primarily upon two elements: coital rates and year of data collection. The year of data collection was utilized rather than the date of publication since the time lapse between these two dates could result in some confusion and allow for a misrepresentation of trends in sexual behavior. While several aspects of sexual behavior could have been utilized as a basis of comparison over the years, using proportions of nonvirgins reported by each study was selected because of the significance of this status change for society and the individual who makes this transition. . . .

Findings

. . . The data show three major trends in sexual behavior during the twentieth century in the United States.

1. Through time there has been an increase in the proportion of both males and females reporting coital involvement prior to marriage.
2. There has been a converging of the coital rates reported by males and females, with two subtrends: (a) in 1958 the highest reported rate for females and the lowest reported rate for males overlapped; and (b) prior to 1970 the reported rate for males was approximately twice that for females, while after 1970 the reported rates for males and females were within about 10 percentage points of each other.
3. There was a dramatic upswing in the reported coital rates after 1970, particularly among women, so that coital involvement now appears to be statistically normative among the age group reported upon.

While the overall summary of the trends is impressive, there are a number of methodological cautions which must be taken into consideration. These include the following.

* The sample sizes varied greatly, from 22 to 2453 (Freedman, 1965; Lewis and Burr, 1975).
* The number of years to collect data ranged up to 12 (Kinsey, 1953) or was obtained from combining two samples taken from 2 different years (Zuckerman, 1973).
* The age of respondents differed from college-age students in lower- or upper-division studies to samples representing all four class levels.
* The randomness of sample selection varied depending on the use of classes or adherence to various randomization procedures.
* The research design included such methods as mail surveys, questionnaires, interviews, and longitudinal studies.
* The geographical locations of the sample either represented various sections of the country or were part of a sample from the total United States.
* The background of college institutions varied from state-supported institutions to private religious schools and from liberal to conservative schools.

As a result of these discrepancies, it is realized that a comparison of these studies may carry some risk but, nevertheless, will provide valuable insights into both research variations and social-sexual trends. This is particularly so since the trends are clear and consistent through time. . . .

The data . . . indicate an increasing incidence of coitus among never-married youth. This increase holds for both males and females; however, the increase for females has been much more [dramatic. The data] clearly [show] the wide variation of male and female coital rates from the 1900s to the mid-1960s. While an early scientific study of female sexuality in 1903 (Dickerson and Beam, 1915) found a coital rate of 12%, an early study of males (Exner, 1915) reported a coital rate of 36%. However, in the 1970s coital rates increased to a range of 70 to 80% for each sex (Jessor and Jessor, 1975; Murstein and Holden, 1979).

From the mid-1960s to 1980, the coital rates for males and females not only increased but also converged. In the early part of the century, there was a large difference between the proportion of males and that of females reporting coitus; this spread began to diminish during the mid-1960s, when in some studies the coital rate for females (43%) (Luckey and Nass, 1969) was higher than the coital rate for males (37%) (Christensen and Gregg, 1970). This convergence continued into the 1970s, when according to Jessor and Jessor (1975) coital rates for females and males showed little difference (senior males, 82%; senior females 85%).

. . . [T]he sudden change . . . occurred during the late 1960s, when major increases occurred in the coital rates of both males and females. At the same time there was also a marked increase in the number of studies of sexuality. It seems probable that these two increases are related; while more adolescents and young adults were changing status from virgin to nonvirgin, social concern with the extent and meaning of the change led to an increase in the number of studies of sexual behavior. At the same time, it also seems possible that the liberalization of sexual norms and standards increased subjects' willingness to report their sexual behavior in a study.

The period of sudden change from 1968 to 1980 illustrates the importance of paying attention to the year of data collection when examining research findings. For example, Carns (1973) utilized data from 1967, while Lewis and Burr (1975) collected their data in 1967–1968. . . . [T]his time lapse occurred at a critical period of transition in sexual behavior and, hence, researchers must be mindful of the resultant confusion that could result from inattentiveness to the data year.

Discussion

It was suggested at the beginning of this paper that changes in the influence of sexuality on our lives affect sexual meanings and attitudes as well as sexual behaviors. Furthermore, it was suggested that the increase in studies of sexual behavior in recent years may reflect general social concern with sexual behavior. Kallen (1980) and Kallen and Stephenson (1982) have interpreted recent trends in sexual behavior and the reports that youth give about their sexual behavior as indicating a major shift in the norms and standards affecting decisions about coital involvement. Three general eras, characterized by different sexual standards, have been identified. The first, which lasted until the late 1940s or early 1950s, was the era of the double standard, in which sexual behavior was permitted for males and prohibited for females. In the second, the era of "permissiveness with affection" (Reiss, 1967), premarital intercourse was allowable as long as it was in a love relationship and the relationship was expected to lead to marriage. This era lasted until approximately 1970. In the recent era, which began about 1970, intercourse is a natural and expected part of a love relationship for both males and females, without an expectation that the relationship will lead to marriage. Under this standard, while intercourse is also acceptable for both males and females in a nonaffectual relationship, physical or emotional exploitation of the sexual partner is not.

These changes in sexual behavior and in the standards which govern it are correlated with a variety of other changes. Between 1900 and 1980 the proportion of males and females of college age actually attending college increased a number of times, with a corresponding shift in the social background of the students. While the increase in the proportions of students reporting intercourse is not regarded as an artifact of the change in student characteristics, the differing nature of the population is one of the factors producing a complicated change in standards and in behavior.

Another change is the revival in sex education. The concept of sex education was "alive and well" in the United States as early as 1900. Educative pioneers had a goal of trying to protect the young from "distorted" knowledge or ideas (Keyes, 1906). The distortions, they feared, related to a revolutionary idea that pleasure might be an acceptable motivation for sex. Therefore, youth must be taught the "right" information about sex, in that self-control and restraint were imperative (Penland, 1981). The only acceptable purpose for sex was procreation, and if sex was so practiced, restraint was assured. Sex instruction was predominantly for prophylactic purposes. Furthermore, according to a statement from the American Society of Sanitary and Moral Prophylaxis in 1905, sexual physiology and hygiene need not be formally taught to girls but should be taught to every boy when mental and sexual puberty makes him capable of beneficially utilizing the knowledge (Valentine, 1906). This divergence of sexual communications to males and females was part of the double standard which resulted in a wide variation of sexual behavior between the sexes at the beginning of the century.

The 1940s and early 1950s brought a resurgence of a moralistic view on sexuality as a part of family life. Sex education was now expected to help contribute toward the long-term sexual adjustment of individuals (Youth Education Today, 1938). Sex information was taught under the broader concept of "social hygiene," which was generally presented in sex-segregated classes so as not to draw too much inappropriate attention to sexual discussions in mixed groups (Kirkendall, 1940; Penland, 1981). Thus, during this period different sexual messages were being given to males and females which were consistent with the double standard and resulted in quite different coital frequencies for males and females.

As prosperity increased during the 1960s and 1970s an expansion occurred in the exploration of new life-styles which was reflected in a new openness about sex. Two sequential changes in sexual standards took place. The first was the development of the standard of "permissiveness with affection," in which intercourse was permitted before marriage in a relationship of affection with the assumption that the relationship would lead to marriage (Reiss, 1967). The second, reflected in the sharp increase in proportions of females reporting coitus during the late 1960s, is the current standard in which intercourse is an expected part of love relationships and is permitted in nonlove relationships provided there is no exploitation of the partner. These shifts . . . paralleled many social changes of the time. Technological advances led to an expansion of travel and job opportunities for both men and women, with the resulting decreased emphasis on the role of the nuclear family. Increasing numbers of women entered the labor force, with the consequent development of greater economic independence for them. In addition, a highly technological society needed more highly educated people. As college enrollments swelled, young adults were involved in an intellectual milieu which encouraged questioning and thinking about both societal regulations on sexual behavior and individual rights to self-enhancement and fulfillment (Juhasz, 1976). The mass media also played an important role in changing attitudes and advocating personal gratification by publicizing and legitimizing a variety of role models for differing interpersonal relationships. During this period the contraceptive pill, the Supreme Court decision legalizing abortion, and innovative life-styles such as coed college dormitories, cohabitation, open marriages, and gay liberation helped to undercut old patriarchal values and contribute to the convergence of male and female sexual behaviors (Francoer, 1980).

The major shift in behavior among females, which occurred after 1970, may be regarded as a true revolution. While the genesis of this revolution is in the same forces which led to the development of the standard of permissiveness with affection, the size and suddenness of this shift to the expectation of intercourse within a love relationship are not fully explained by the earlier trends. [Recent studies of high school–aged populations indicate that the sexual behavior characteristic of college students is also characteristic of high-school students (Zelnik and Kantner, 1980; Chilman, 1978). That is, more and more adolescents are having intercourse at younger and younger ages, but primarily in affectional relationships.]

If the interpretation is correct that there has, indeed, been a revolutionary shift in standards governing the sexual behavior of young people, then the trend toward increased affectional and recreational sexuality should persist, and young men and young women will continue to be equally involved in relationships which include the overt expression of sexuality. While medical problems associated with the perceived epidemic of herpes of the 1980s (Leo, 1982) may limit the risk taking of recreational sex in casual, nonexploitative relationships, neither it nor the risk of pregnancy (Koenig and Zelnik, 1982) will limit the function of sexual intercourse as confirmatory of an emotional attachment. Thus, the concern with herpes may reinforce the present standard of sex and love going together.

This alliance of sexual and emotional expression without the expectation of the relationship leading to marriage may be one of the major sources of value conflict between parents and children today. Parents provide contradictory sexual messages in relation to current sexual behavioral trends (Darling and Hicks, 1982). These messages, which are predominantly negative in nature, evolve from an age cohort who began their sexual involvements prior to the sudden sexual shift in the late 1960s. As these adults and parents attempt to pass down the sexual socialization messages they received to today's youth, confusion, guilt, and conflict can result. Alternatively, it may lead to an ignoring of parental messages on the assumption that parental experience is not valid for guidance. This is particularly apt to occur if the experience of the individual indicates that the parental message is not credible. Hence, the heirs of the hypothesized "sexual revolution" have to learn how to adjust to the varying rates of transition between intergenerational communications and current behavioral norms.

In an analysis of the forces affecting dissemination of information about the transition from virgin to nonvirgin from a study of college students in 1967, Carns (1973) hoped that as a result of the then predicted sexual revolution, "the genders do not pass each other in the night, women on their part seeking the genital expression so long denied them by a sexually repressive culture, men looking for situations of affection and tenderness unallowed by the performance principle forced upon them by the restrictions of hypermasculinity" (p. 687). In an analysis of the same forces from a study of college students conducted in 1976, Kallen and Stephenson (1982) note that new patterns of revelation of the status change "are perhaps as much signs of differential definition and movement through a common social space as they are of significant differences in the social space through which the genders now move" (p. 22). The data presented in this paper seem to support the latter view. While examining coital rates for males and females through time does not provide information about meanings of sexual behavior for the participants, the extent to which the behavioral trends have become identical for both genders is supportive of the belief that sexual behavior is currently based on similar motives and similar meanings. Furthermore, it provides the bases for defining premarital intercourse as normal rather than deviant (Durkheim, 1938), since if most young people are sexually involved, it is not possible to regard sexual involvement as socially deviant. Furthermore, it seems likely that this normality will persist, at least in situations of affection, as new norms and new standards become institutionalized.

References

Bauman, I. E., and Wilson, R. R. (1971). Sexual behavior of unmarried university students in 1968 and 1972. *J. Sex Res.* 10(4): 327–333.

Bell, R. R., and Chaskes, J. B. (1970). Premarital sexual experience among coeds, 1958 and 1968. *J. Marriage Family* 32: 81–84.

Bromley, D., and Britton, F. (1938). *Youth and Sex: A Study of 1300 College Students*, Harper and Brothers, New York.

Carns, D. (1973). Talking about sex: Notes on first coitus and the double sexual standard. *J. Marriage Family* 35(4): 677–688.

Chilman, C. S. (1974). Some psychological aspects of female sexuality. *Family Coord.* 23: 123–131.

Chilman, C. S. (1978). Adolescent sexuality in a changing American society: Societal and psychological perspectives. DHEW Publication No. (NIH) 79–1426, U.S. Department of Health, Education, and Welfare, Public Health Service, National Institutes of Health.

Christenson, H. T., and Gregg, C. F. (1970). Changing sex norms in America and Scandinavia. *J. Marriage Family* 32: 616–627.

Croak, J. W., and James, B. E. (1973). A four year comparison of premarital sexual attitudes. *J. Sex Res.* 9(2): 91–96.

Darling, C. A. (1976). Research critique: Sexual behavior among never-married adults. Unpublished paper, Department of Family and Child Sciences, Michigan State University, East Lansing.

Darling, C. A. (1979). *Parental Influence on Love, Sexual Behavior, and Sexual Satisfaction*, Unpublished dissertation, Department of Family Ecology, Michigan State University, East Lansing.

Darling, C. A., and Hicks, M. (1983). Parental influence on adolescent sexuality: Implications for educators. *J. Youth Adoles.* 11(3): 231–245.

DeLameter, J., and MacCorquodale, P. (1979). *Premarital Sexuality: Attitudes, Relationships, Behavior*, University of Wisconsin Press, Madison.

Dickerson, R. L., and Beam, L. (1915). *The Single Woman*, Williams and Wilkins, Baltimore.

Durkheim, E. (1938). In Catlin, G. E. G. (ed.), *The Rules of Sociological Method*, The Free Press, Glencoe, Ill.

Ehrmann, W. (1954). *Premarital Dating Behavior*, Henry Holt, New York.

Exner, M. J. (1915). *Problems and Principles of Sex Education: A Study of 948 College Men*, Association Press, New York.

Finger, F. W. (1947). Sex beliefs and practices among male college students. *J. Abnorm. Soc. Psychol.* 42: 57–67.

Francoer, R. T. (1980). The sexual revolution: Will hard times turn back the clock? *Futurist* 14(2): 3–12.

Freedman, M. B. (1965). The sexual behavior of American college women: An empirical study and historical survey. *Merrill-Palmer Q.* 11: 33–48.

Fujita, B. N., Wagner, N. N., and Pion, R. J. (1971). Contraceptive use among single college students. *Am. J. Obstet. Gynecol.* 109: 787–793.

Guralnik, D. B. (ed.) (1976). *Webster's New World Dictionary,* 2nd ed., Williams Collins and World, New York.

Haeck, P. (1974). Rates of premarital intercourse among college students through the years. Unpublished paper, Department of Human Development, Michigan State University, East Lansing.

Hopkins, J. R. (1977). Sexual behavior in adolescence. *J. Soc. Issues* 33(2) 67–85.

Jessor, S. L., and Jessor, R. (1975). Transition from virginity to nonvirginity among youth: A social-psychological study over time. *Dev. Psychol.* 11(4): 473–484.

Juhasz, A. M. (1976). Changing patterns of premarital sexual behavior. *Intellect Mag.* 103: 511–514.

Kaats, G. R., and Davis, K. E. (1970). The dynamics of sexual behavior of college students. *J. Marriage Family* 32: 390–399.

Kallen, D. J. (1974). The sexual and contraceptive behavior of college students. Research grant proposal to the National Institutes of Health.

Kallen, D. J. (1980). Les adolescents decident de leur sexuality. In *Medicine et Adolescents; Les Cahiers de Bioetheique, Vol. 3*, Le Presses de L'Universite laval, Quebec, Canada.

Kallen, D. J., and Stephenson, J. (1982). Talking about sex revisited. *J. Youth Adoles.* 11(1): 11–23.

Keyes, E. (1906). If education upon sexual matters is to be offered to youth, what should be its nature and scope, and at what age should it commence? *N.Y. Med. J.* 83: 274–275.

King, K., Balswick, J. O., and Robinson, I. F. (1977). The continuing premarital sexual revolution among college females. *J. Marriage Family* 39(3): 455–459.

King, M., and Sobel, D. (1975). Sex on the college campus: Current attitudes and behavior. *J. Coll. Stud. Person.* (May): 205–209.

Kinsey, A. C., Pomeroy, W. B., and Martin, C. E. (1948). *Sexual Behavior in the Human Male*, W. B. Saunders, Philadelphia.

Kinsey, A. C., Pomeroy, W. B., Martin, C. E., and Gebhard, P. H. (1953). *Sexual Behavior in the Human Female*, W. B.Saunders, Philadelphia.

Kirkendall, L. (1940). Building a program of sex education for the secondary school, *J. Soc. Hygiene* 26: 305–311.

Koenig, M. A., and Zelnik, M. (1982). The risk of premarital first pregnancy among metropolitan area teenagers: 1976 and 1979. *Family Plan. Perspect.* 14(5): 239–247.

Leo, J. (1982). The new scarlet letter. *Time* 120(5): 62–66.

Lewis, R. A., and Burr, W. R. (1975). Premarital coitus and commitment among college students. *Arch. Sex. Behav.* 4(1): 73–79.

Luckey, E., and Nass, G. (1969). A comparison of sexual attitudes and behavior of an international sample. *J. Marriage Family* 31: 346–379.

McCary, J. L. (1978). *Human Sexuality,* Van Nostrand Reinhold, New York.

Murstein, B. I., and Holden, C. C. (1979). Sexual behavior and correlates among college students. *Adolescence* 4(56): 625–639.

Needle, R. H. (1975). The relationship between first sexual intercourse and ways of handling contraception among college students. *J. Am. Health Assoc.* 244: 106–111.

Otto, H. A. (1971). The new sexuality: An introduction. In Otto, H. A. (ed.), *The New Sexuality*, Science and Behavior Books, Palo Alto, Calif.

Peck, M. W., and Wells, F. L. (1925). Further studies in the psychosexuality of college graduate men. *Ment. Hygiene* 9: 502–520.

Penland, L. R. (1981). Sex education in 1900, 1940, and 1980: An historical sketch. *J. School Health* 51(4): 305–309.

Peterson, R. (1938). *Early Sex Information and Its Influence on Later Sex Concepts,* Unpublished master's thesis, University of Colorado, Boulder.

Porterfield, A. E., and Salley, H. E. (1945). Current folkways of sexual behavior. *Am. J. Sociol.* 52: 209–216.

Prince, A. J., and Shipman, G. (1957). Attitudes of college students towards premarital sex experience. *Family Life Coord.* 6: 60–67.

Reevy, W. R. (1959). Premarital petting behavior and marital happiness prediction. *Marriage Family Liv.* 23: 349–355.

Reiss, I. F. (1967). *The Social Context of Premarital Sexual Permissiveness,* Rinehart and Winston, New York.

Robinson, I., and Jedlicka, D. (1982). Change in sexual attitudes and behavior of college students from 1965 to 1980: A research note. *J. Marriage Family* 44(1): 237–240.

Robinson, I., King, K., Dudley, C., and Clune, F. (1968). Changes in sexual behavior and attitudes of college students. *Family. Coord.* 16:119–124.

Ross, R. T. (1950). Measures of the sex behavior of college males compared with Kinsey's results. *J. Abnorm. Soc. Psychol.* 45: 753–755.

Simon, W., Berger, A., and Gagnon, J. (1972). Beyond anxiety and fantasy: The coital experiences of college youth. *J. Youth Adoles.* 1(3): 203–222.

Valentine, F. (1906). Education in sexual subjects. *N.Y. Med. J.* 82: 276–278.

Vincent, M. L., and Stelling, F. H. (1973). A survey of contraceptive practices and attitudes of unwed college students. *J. Am. Coll. Health Assoc.* 21: 357–363.

Weichman, G. H., and Ellis, A. (1969). A study of the effects of sex education on premarital petting and coital behavior. *Family Coord.* 18: 231–234.

Youth Education Today (1938). *16th Yearbook,* American Association of School Administrators, Washington, D.C.

Zelnik, M., and Kantner, J. F. (1980). Sexual activity, contraceptive use and pregnancy among Metropolitan area teenagers: 1971–1979. *Family Plan. Perspect.* 12(5): 230–237.

Zuckerman, M. (1973). Scales for sex experience for males and females. *J. Consult. Clin. Psychol.* 41(1): 27–29.

Exploring the Kindgom of AIDS

Peter Davis

I spent a month recently in the imaginary kingdom of AIDS, tracking what experts say is the designated future of the disease: its coming assault upon the heterosexual community.[*] What I was looking at was the behavior of heterosexuals surrounded by the same storm warnings yet acting in a wide variety of ways.

Since it is primarily contracted through sex and the use of drugs, two activities associated with both desire and free will, acquired immune deficiency syndrome tests us as no disease ever has. It is the first plague in the history of mankind whose regulation is entirely dependent upon our *knowing* behavior.

Threatened or unthreatened by the disease, we find ourselves displayed with embarrassing clarity in the searchlight AIDS throws on our attitudes and feelings. As a married man with three sons and a daughter, I thought I was open-minded, accepting of diversity, hopeful the near future would bring a cure for something I didn't understand. I discovered that where AIDS is concerned, I was insatiably curious sexually, morally ambivalent, and politically angry.

Meanwhile, in the imaginary AIDS kingdom, I found moods ranging from panic to defiance to a kind of jubilant apathy. And over everything hung a blanket of confusion, the heavy fog in the AIDS kingdom that will not blow away. Why would people given the same facts and information and theories respond so differently?

Two glamorous women spoke heatedly, intimately. They are very close to each other and remarkably alike, both bicoastal, both fashionably dressed. At first glance, the principal difference between them is age; a quarter-century ago the older one had given birth to the younger.

"How long have you known him?" the mother asked.

"Not long," the daughter answered. "Maybe two months."

"Astonishing. What possesses you to get married so soon?"

"Mother, he'll make a perfect first husband."

"What? Aren't you planning for the rest of your life here?"

"Maybe he'll outgrow me, maybe I'll outgrow him, but at the moment this seems a very constructive move, Mother."

" 'A very constructive move,' " the mother mimicked. "The sheer pragmatism stuns me. Come on, now, why are you doing this?"

"Frankly, Mother, I don't want to stay in the singles stream. I'm afraid I might get AIDS."

[*For a more complete and recent discussion of the future spread of AIDS, see the Report of the Presidential Commission on the Human Immunodeficiency Virus Epidemic, submitted to the President on June 24, 1988. U.S. Government Printing Office.]

As the daughter sizes up her future, she is better off throwing part of her life away on someone she does not love rather than throwing her entire life away on someone else she may sleep with but also not love. If a chance rendezvous can be fatal, the relationship between sex and death, anciently understood in art and ritual, is restored.

In the kingdom of AIDS, a penis itself, often likened to a sword in folk tales, again becomes a deadly weapon. This young woman tries to protect herself by a hasty marriage. Another, an elegant divorced woman of 41, celebrated for her beauty and passion, swore herself to celibacy when her relationship with a financier broke up six months ago. "It is agony," she said, "but I may never share my bed again with anyone."

Watching the fear rise among many whose behavior is not generally considered to be risky—that is, among heterosexual men who do not use drugs, and among women who are neither drug users nor involved with bisexual men—I have been struck by a fear of my own: that the panic may so far outstrip the disease as to be ludicrous. The danger is that when the panic is finally recognized as silly, sensible precaution will disappear along with unreasonable fear.

Is the panic justified? In interviews with more than 100 New Yorkers, many of whom had friends with AIDS, I have not heard of a single case where the disease was passed sexually by one non-drug-using, untransfused heterosexual to another. Most Americans who will have AIDS in 1991 are among the estimated 1.5 million already infected with the virus, carrying around a live epidemiological bullet in their sexual organs and bloodstreams. More than 90 percent of the 35,000 AIDS victims in the United States thus far have been men.

On the other hand—AIDS has more hands than an orgy—the HIV virus does take all that time to incubate, up to five years, perhaps longer. As in Schnitzler's play, "La Ronde," a man sleeps with a woman who sleeps with another man who sleeps with another woman. . . . Somewhere in that circle may be a bisexual or an intravenous drug user.

Ratios can shift. In central Africa, the disease has spread primarily among heterosexuals, and slightly more women than men have it. Who can say conclusively the panic is not justified? And with AIDS, expectation is all: since our perception of the threat presumably determines our behavior, perhaps only an exaggerated depiction of the danger AIDS now poses for heterosexuals will prevent that worst-case scenario from ultimately becoming the reality. It seems paradoxical; but the result is we are being warned that we are all bombs, and some of our fuses have been lighted.

A 38-year-old woman in publishing broke off a lengthy relationship last summer. For months she didn't allow herself to have a date. Finally, her old boyfriend from college, freshly divorced in Darien, Conn., asked to take her to dinner.

"He's still a drip," she told me, "but it was safe psychologically for me so I went. Well, I brought him back to the apartment and we made love. Then we're lying there, you know, right afterward, and he says to me, 'You're friends with a lot of people in show business, aren't you?' *Darien!* It was my own fault.

"So I say, 'I guess I know a few.' Whereupon he props himself up rather starchily on one elbow and says, 'I suppose I'd better start to worry about AIDS now, hadn't I?' Right after making love! There I'd been, flattered he wanted me after all these years, and suddenly he sees me as his executioner. Sex is always so fraught with possibilities for humiliation anyway. Now we're being taught that it's also Russian roulette."

Fear, guilt, hostility, violent fantasies, rage, the life impulse or a death wish— the dynamics of people's responses to AIDS often mirror their feelings about sex. For those scared by sex, AIDS is the penalty for feeling sexual in the first place. Sex is associated with aggression, and aggression must be punished. What more effective punishment than AIDS itself, the ultimate castration?

A divorced 40-year-old man told me he would "never again sleep with a woman I haven't checked out thoroughly." He might have been talking about a new car. Men and women are acting more afraid of one another than ever before in this century. The ease with which people began to treat each other during the 1960's is vanishing. Men and women talk of one another almost as if two separate races are involved.

"I'm your total yuppie profile, from the Ivy League education to the job to the expectations," said a young woman I'll call Amy Flagg, a show business executive not yet out of her 20's. The spate of articles about AIDS had literally iced the passions of Amy and her friends.

"Yesterday I was at lunch with another woman executive and two young TV writers we'd like to do business with," she continued. "Everybody had read at least two AIDS cover stories and was petrified. What would a few months ago have been a slightly flirtatious occasion combined with business instead became this sober deadly consideration of something no one wanted to talk about yet couldn't stop thinking about."

"You find out someone had a drug problem three years ago, forget it. A bisexual, forget it, forget it, forget it. Even if a guy you know is straight but is kind of promiscuous, forget it. The people I know aren't yet taking the, uh, precautions when they do have sex. I guess we're all going to start soon. God, I wish I could have just one lunch in the Russian Tea Room where we talk about something else besides AIDS. Herpes, maybe."

Samantha Ellis, as I'll call a 31-year-old investment banker noted among her friends for both her independence and abandon, was furious, and herpes was part of the reason. "The medical profession cried wolf on herpes, and the journalists tagged right along," she said. "It turned out to be a hoax. Why should we believe any of you now? Frankly, I'm someone who adores lovemaking. I think the enjoyment of one's sexuality is such a precious gift and attribute—like a flower blooming—that I bitterly resent anyone attempting to crush it."

I asked whether Samantha has changed the way she lives.

"The stories had no effect on me until recently," she said. "I just can't handle the idea of prophylactics. I'd have no hesitancy about buying them myself but I'd find it difficult to ask someone to actually use them."

The injunction not to "exchange bodily fluids" not only denies a fundamental aspect of intercourse—since sex by definition involves the sharing of selves—but it also means that a newly formed couple must pause to negotiate a delicate pathway around infection: "Do you mind using a condom?" "Oh, ah, do you happen to have any with you?" "Have you ever been with an IV drug user?"

"I'm a lot more careful now about sleeping with someone I think is bisexual," says Samantha. "This is, in a way, a tyranny, part of the inexorable return to conservatism. It's so antithetical to intermingling, so antidemocratic, it destroys the integrity and openness achieved by the sexual revolution. People are saying you should sleep only with your own kind."

Last year, on a business trip to the Midwest, Samantha met a stagehand she liked. She brought him back to New York for a while. "We had a lot of fun and although this wasn't the point, we broadened each other's horizons. He didn't have a habit, but occasionally he shot drugs into his arm. If I met him today I wouldn't sleep with him. We never would have had the relationship. I resent so much what's happening."

For the larger community, as for Samantha Ellis, the holiday is over. Doctor's orders. Whether the heterosexual citizenry is following the helpful hints to safer sex and longer life, hints packaged like scouting handbooks on how to tie different kinds of knots, few are unaware of a change in circumstance. People who felt guilty about sex or about not enjoying it as much as they had been told in the previous two decades that they should, have just quit. They have the perfect excuse. It used to be good for you, like aerobics and Brussels sprouts; goodbye to all that because now it is dangerous to your health, like smoking and hang gliding.

The baby boom's babies are supposed to turn back the clock, never easy when the hands are racing forward as they tend to do at 21. The urges of youthful rebellion—young people pushing out against the limits set by their parents—are now directed to the "sensible" instead of the experimental. The 45-year-old former radicals are now expected to teach their children how to be reactionary.

"What a frightful time to be young!" said a society lady, known for her cosmopolitan views but celibate since she stopped living with someone last summer. "The new caring man and independent woman we heard so much about, the lovers keeping their own apartments just in case, uh, something interesting turns up while you're away, dear, a little tentative shall we say, exploration, all that is out, out, out.

"Two years ago, when our gay friends were dying, we thought real men not only didn't eat quiche, they didn't get AIDS. Now the campaign is on among us, and we have all these grand New York matrons showing up at benefits puckering their lips to lecture gravely that it won't be possible to have anal intercourse anymore, it's *passé,* my dear, *ça ne se fait plus,* as though mankind is being robbed of one of the wonders of the world, the Pyramids are collapsing perhaps.

"As for our friends the gays, they are not so very gay anymore, my dear, nor so wild with abandon, nor leading the charge anymore against established sexual practices. They opened the door and rushed through. And they felt the earliest warning signal."

I decided to look deeper, into the trenches of the imaginary AIDS kingdom, the bars where young people go to make new acquaintances. Dorrian's Red Hand on Second Avenue has had a reputation as an easy place to find a pick-up. (It became notorious one night last summer when Jennifer Dawn Levin met Robert E. Chambers Jr. there, and the two left for a sexual encounter in Central Park that ended in Miss Levin's death.) Preppies and junior yuppies still swagger around in Dorrian's as if they owned the sexual turf, but according to at least a dozen customers there is far less action than there was a year ago.

"I won't sleep with anyone unless I really, really know him," said a slender young woman wearing huge gold earrings and a long black sweaterdress. A young man in a crew-neck sweater leaned against the bar, watching her. "AIDS has me scared to death," she added. "I always thought I could do anything; now I know I can't."

I asked how she knew.

"The media hype got me. I guess I changed about a year and a half ago."

"You didn't change that long ago," said the man in the crew-necked sweater.

"O.K.," said the woman with the gold earrings, "but on my last experience I used a condom."

"I remember."

"Next time bring your own, moron."

Three 24-year-old men—call them Tom, Dick and Harry—all described themselves as extremely worried about AIDS. Two years out of college, Tom is a building-supply salesman hoping to become a veterinarian, Dick is a real-estate salesman, and Harry a medical student.

Of the three, only Tom wore a condom the last time he had sex, which was with a prostitute who made him use one. Harry the medical student carries condoms with him all the time; he just doesn't always use them. Dick had bought some for the first time a few weeks earlier. He had met a girl he knew he was going to sleep with on the second date, so he made the purchase. But his last previous experience before I met him was with an old girlfriend.

"I figured I was safe so I didn't use a rubber," Dick said. "What bothers me is this incubation period, because two, three and four years ago I was having sex with girls I didn't know at all."

"As worried as I am," he went on, "I'm a young single male, and I'm going to be meeting people and picking them up. I'll just have to be more careful."

"The trouble with condoms," Tom said, "they take the pleasure out."

"They take some of the pleasure out, but they beat dying," Dick said. "You use a condom at first, then later you can forget about them."

"Right," said Harry, "you get serious, you throw away your rubbers."

At a table nearby three 23-year-old women in advertising—let them be Alice, Betty and Carol—worried about stopping AIDS without stopping sex. They said Dorrian's had changed and they had changed. When 3 A.M. rolled around they no longer saw people leaving with somebody different every night.

"One good thing about AIDS is it kind of wakes everybody up," Alice said. "It's like, 'Knock, knock in there, anybody home? Time to take care of your life, you know.' "

"Really," Betty said. "I can't believe condoms are the final answer though. I haven't used a rubber in eight years, not since my first experience when I was 15. Believe me, I don't want to go through that again."

"I used one once," Alice said, "but I didn't like it."

"It's like there's something between you and him, some kind of barrier," Carol said. "We all believe in precautions, but we don't necessarily take them," Carol said. "Like I know cigarettes are harmful and have killed a lot more people than AIDS, but I haven't stopped smoking them."

What will make people really "take precautions?" And what is the degree of danger for heterosexuals anyway?

I asked Dr. Mervyn F. Silverman, the former public health director for San Francisco and now president of the American Foundation for AIDS Research, what level of concern he thought was appropriate among heterosexuals.

"Today the amount of virus floating around available to heterosexuals is small," he said, "but the paradox is we can't let ourselves think that way, because if we operate on that premise we'll wake up one day with an overwhelming problem. We walk a tightrope between Chicken-Little-the-sky-is-falling and apathy. Neither one is helpful."

But aren't the specialists inevitably spreading not merely precaution but panic when they project a huge AIDS population in the near future?

"Probably," Dr. Silverman said, "but just because there's no reason to panic doesn't mean there's no reason to be careful. What I want most is for someone to say to me five years from now, 'You were all wet. AIDS never made a dent in the heterosexual community.' It'll mean we did our job."

I thought of Dr. Silverman's paradox as I watched the scene in P.J. Clarke's. Though not a singles bar, Clarke's appeals to many up-scale New Yorkers with a variety of tastes.

"Hey, I'm not going with anyone right now, but condoms are not for me," said Chuck, a 25-year-old stockbroker, to his friend, Steve. "If I do meet someone, I'll probably end up just winging it."

"Me too," said Steve, who is 24. "I wing it."

"I've thought about condoms," said Mariel, a 20-year-old college student, "but I always end up winging it myself."

Kevin, a 24-year-old insurance salesman who was the only black person in the group, let his friends finish before saying anything. "The war stories have got to me," he said. "I know a woman who was once married to an addict. She left him six years ago, but she's dying now. A gay man I used to work with is already dead. I've been celibate for six months because of AIDS. I'm waiting until I meet someone I'm really interested in. Then I'll have to date for a while. Then I'll use a condom."

What had really gotten to Kevin, what had really made him change his behavior, as he made clear, was not press coverage but personal experience. With AIDS killing two of his friends, he was taking no chances.

"Hey, listen," Chuck said, motioning for another round of beers, "sex is the lifeblood of the nation. I say go for it, ha ha."

Frequently, in suburban bars even more than in New York City, I heard the remark that "we only go out with people we know." As Samantha Ellis said, AIDS has done away with the democratic element that the 60's introduced to sex. "Safe sex" did not mean only condoms and spermicides; it also meant staying within one's prescribed circle. The old taboos against outsiders are coming back again now.

The problem is that "safe sex" is a contradiction in terms. The familiar, as happily married couples know, can be filled with variation and the unexpected, but if something is entirely and predictably safe, with no elements of adventure or the unknown, it's not very sexy. If, as a number of men and women on Long Island told me, they now come to public places in prearranged groups and have resolved to meet new friends only in their churches and synagogues, the choice of romantic partners is further restricted to members of one's own religion. The political conservatism that swept the land in the early 1980's is being joined by its social (and therefore sexual) counterpart.

I saw the politics of AIDS become increasingly polarized as I toured its kingdom. Essentially, the battle was between those who saw the disease as a medical problem and those who used it as a moral opportunity. Within the Reagan Administration, Surgeon General C. Everett Koop was virtually alone in hoping to treat AIDS as a medical issue. A conservative who strongly opposes abortion, Dr. Koop has emerged as a champion of instruction for schoolchildren in the prevention of AIDS, which inevitably involves sex education.

Rejecting Dr. Koop's plea, President Reagan has urged schoolchildren to abstain from sex as the best method of avoiding AIDS. "After all," he asked, "when it comes to preventing AIDS, don't medicine and morality teach the same lesson?"

Well, no. Medicine does not teach abstinence any more than philosophy teaches happiness. The medical profession looks for ways a disease may spread, can be prevented, and finally cured; it hardly advises mankind not to engage in reproductive activity. As for morality, of course, it all depends on whose morals are being promoted. George Bernard Shaw's would be considerably different from Billy Graham's, and it is not entirely clear that even President Reagan's friends would all choose the latter.

The President's Domestic Policy Council has urged educators to "place sexuality within the context of marriage" and pretty much let it go at that. In addition to being a message that could have been promulgated by the McKinley Administration, it totally ignores the presence—almost the omnipresence—of sex among adolescents. The message also implies that sex itself is the cause of AIDS, and that AIDS may therefore be considered a proper punishment for those who enjoy sex in an unsanctioned context.

But sex is no more the cause of AIDS than swimming was the cause of polio. Indiscriminate sex with partners whose behavior is risky constitutes risky behavior, just as swimming in crowded public pools exposed one to the polio virus. We were never lectured that swimming needed to be considered in the context of joining an exclusive pool club; we were told only that the polio virus could swim around, like us, in pools.

It is not that I have no stronger moral feelings about sexuality than about swimming, because I do. Sex can be an unstoppable force, a force that can destroy relationships, if ungoverned, as well as confirm love and create life. But none of that has anything to do with the prevention of AIDS. To confuse the prevention of AIDS with the promotion of a specific morality is to defeat both resoundingly.

To raise young people's awareness of the AIDS problem, to stop them from "winging it," many schools have begun special programs for their students, programs that vary widely depending on the school. At the elite Dalton School in Manhattan, for example, a frequent question from students is: Can you catch AIDS from French kissing? The standard answer is: It hasn't been proved but why take the chance.

French kissing is not what they are worried about in the New York City public schools, an obviously crucial battleground of the AIDS kingdom. What they are worried about, in addition to AIDS, is needles in veins and babies in teen-agers. A poster at the back of Maggi Zadek's classroom at John Bowne High School in Queens shows two crossed arms with sleeves rolled up ready to receive an injection of heroin. Underneath, it reads: "AIDS IS DEADLY—Don't Pass the Spike!"

In her elective course on adolescent sexuality, the peppy Ms. Zadek, a 42-year-old divorced woman who could qualify as any team's head cheerleader in the big game against AIDS, drilled her 11th- and 12th-grade students on the disease and how to fight it. She bounced from her desk to the blackboard, wheeling to face her charges, marching to their desks to insure wakefulness, joking, always in motion to engage the 27 young minds that had been entrusted to her. Since Ms. Zadek's principal subject was, after all, sex, there was a live possibility that she might succeed.

"All right, why are we suddenly so conscious of AIDS—Sabrina?"

"Because it's in the straight community now."

"Right. Why is AIDS so scary—Shawn?"

"It's fatal."

"I see. Does AIDS kill—Curtis?"

"No. It breaks down the cells in your immune system to let other diseases kill you."

"That's it. You die of opportunistic diseases."

"Now if we are going to have intercourse, what should we do to stop AIDS—Jenny?"

"Use condoms."

"Why not the pill? I'll tell you—because condoms can stop AIDS passing through them. If I'm the man with AIDS, it's in my semen, and I could pass it to you."

"Now we've mentioned rough sex," Ms. Zadek went on, "during which capillaries can be broken, allowing blood and semen to mix. We're not talking about an annoying herpes rash. We're talking death here. Jason?"

"We live in our glands, not our brains."

"But we can at least use our brains to save our glands. Jason, you don't want to risk your whole life on a girl at 16."

"Seventeen."

"All right. Hey, Jason, be in control of your life."

The problem for Jason, for Maggie Zadek, and for the rest of us is that AIDS is a problem with no solution. Education will always help, but it will only help—not save us. With our multiplicity of orientations, we will continue to take the same warnings, information and confusions and act differently in response to them. We are faced with a disease for which there is no preventive vaccine, no cure, and no sure end but death. Can it be so surprising if our responses to this disease range from paranoia to denial?

In this respect, the threat of AIDS is not unlike that of nuclear annihilation. In both cases, the will to act, either personally or collectively, must be preceded by a perceived and immediate danger. With AIDS, that perception is rising among us. A generation ago, a President, speaking of the cold war, warned Americans they were in for a long twilight struggle. He might as well have been predicting AIDS.

Cohabitation in the 1980s: Recent Changes in the United States

Graham B. Spanier

Social scientists can point to few trends in contemporary American society that have manifested such a dramatic pace of change and that have exhibited such consistent upward growth as the trend in unmarried cohabitation. The objective of this chapter is to document and explain this development and to test the explanation against some characteristics of cohabiting couples.

About four million American adults are living with a partner of the opposite sex whom they have not married (U.S. Bureau of the Census, 1983a, 1984). Some observers may regard the number as small in a population of 238 million. Yet

From Kingsley Davis and Amyra Grossbard-Shechtman, eds., *Contemporary Marriage: Comparative Perspectives on a Changing Institution* (New York: Russell Sage Foundation, 1986). Reprinted by permission.

Table 1.   Households with Two Unrelated Adults of Opposite Sex Sharing Living Quarters, by Presence of Children: 1970, 1980, 1984

	1984		1980		1970	
	Number (in thousands)	Percent	Number (in thousands)	Percent	Number (in thousands)	Percent
Total	1,988	100.0%	1,589	100.0%	523	100.0%
No children present	1,373	69.1	1,159	72.9	327	62.5
Children present[a]	614	30.9	431	27.1	196	37.5

[a]For the year 1970, children in unmarried-couple households are under 14. For the years 1980 and 1984, children are under 15.

Source: U.S. Bureau of the Census, *Current Population Reports,* Series P-20, No. 391, 1984.

cohabitation usually involves persons who are eligble for an important life transition—marriage—or who have recently experienced another critical transition—divorce. Thus the study of the features of marriage entails at least some study of cohabitation.

By definition, an unmarried cohabiting individual is an adult sharing living quarters with one unrelated adult of the opposite sex. No other adult may be present in the household although children may or may not be present. The data are drawn primarily from the March 1980 *Current Population Survey* conducted by the U.S. Bureau of the Census and secondarily from more recent *Current Population Surveys*. It is reasonable to assume that most heterosexual unmarried couples with no other adults in the household live together because they are romantically involved. This assumption is important to note because the data featured here are demographic and do not provide the respondents' reports of their attitudes, motivations, and plans. The demographic data, however, do allow us to address many of the questions raised in this chapter. For example, although our definition of unmarried cohabitation encompasses such arrangements as an elderly woman who rents a room to a male college student or an elderly man who employs a live-in nurse or housekeeper, fewer than 1 percent of unmarried cohabiting couples fit this profile. Most unmarried couples differ in age by no more than a few years.

Trends in Unmarried Cohabitation

A profound increase in unmarried cohabitation occurred during the 1960s and 1970s and has continued into the 1980s; only recently are there signs that the rate of increase may be leveling off.

Table 1 compares figures for 1970, 1980, and 1984. In 1980 three times as many unmarried couples lived together as in 1970, the number nearly doubling between 1975 and 1980. In 1980 the trend continued to grow, showing a 14 percent increase by 1981. In 1984, there were two million unmarried-couple households (U.S.

Table 2. Partners in Unmarried-Couple Households, By Sex, Age, and Marital History: 1981 (Numbers in Thousands)

	Men		Women	
	Number	*Percent*	*Number*	*Percent*
Total	1,808	100.0%	1,808	100.0%
Age				
Under 25	435	24.1	687	38.0
25–34	780	43.1	686	37.9
35–44	252	13.9	151	8.4
45–64	232	12.8	181	10.0
65 years or more	111	6.1	99	5.5
Marital history				
Never married	958	53.0	991	54.8
Ever married	850	47.0	817	45.2

Source: U.S. Bureau of the Census, *Current Population Reports,* Series P-20, No. 372, 1982.

Bureau of the Census, 1984), a 25 percent increase since 1980. About 4 percent of all couples living together in the United States are unmarried.

Table 1 also reveals that about 27 percent of all unmarried-couple households have at least one child in the household. When children as well as adults are included, more than 4.6 million persons live in the households of unmarried couples.

Table 2 verifies a finding noted in earlier data, namely that primarily young adults find unmarried cohabitation attractive as a living arrangement. One-fourth of the men and nearly two-fifths of the women are under 25 years old; two-thirds of the men and three-fourths of the women are under 35. Although unmarried couples consist of persons of all ages, the phenomenon continues to involve younger persons disproportionately.

Between 1970 and 1981 one particularly noteworthy trend was a significant decline in the proportion of unmarried couples involving persons 65 and over. The absolute number of elderly persons remained relatively constant. For example, in 1970 approximately 115,000 persons 65 or older were unmarried and cohabiting, constituting 22 percent of all households with no children present. In 1981 there were approximately 120,000 such couples, only 7 percent of those with no children present. Given a possibly greater reluctance to report such a living arrangement in 1970 than in 1981, the negligible change in the number of unmarried cohabiting older persons during a period when the elderly population increased significantly is noteworthy. Changes in Social Security regulations, which make remarriage more practical for the elderly, may account for some of the inertia in cohabitation.

Another interesting subgroup are persons legally married to someone other than the person they live with. In 1981 there were an estimated 282,000 such individuals—about 8 percent of the total number of persons cohabiting. The partners of individuals in this category most frequently either have never married or have been divorced. To a lesser extent, the partners share the same status, namely, still married to someone else.

Contrary to previous speculation suggesting that unmarried couples typically involve never-married persons, Glick and Spanier (1980) found that about half of the individuals living together had been married previously. More recent data confirm this finding. Although never-married cohabiting individuals tend to be young (81 percent of the men and 88 percent of the women are under 35), those who have been married are more evenly distributed across the adult years— 40 percent of the men and 31 percent of the women are 35–54 years old, and 24 percent and 22 percent, respectively, are 65 or older. One of the more notable changes between 1975 and 1980 is the increase in the proportion of cohabitants under 35 who have been married. In other words, among the ever-married, a larger share of the increase can be attributed to those under 35. This change undoubtedly stems somewhat from the continuing high divorce rate, which rose from 4.9 to 5.2 per 1,000 population during the period (National Center for Health Statistics 1981, 1982). The change may also reflect a possibly longer period between divorce and remarriage, although such a trend has not yet been established. Since divorce disproportionately affects younger adults, a growing pool of previously married individuals now has the option of remarrying or of living with someone as an unmarried couple.

Glick and Spanier (1980) reported that between 1960 and 1975 the number of unmarried couples in households with children present had not varied much. The increase in nonmarital cohabitation was accounted for primarily by young couples without children. This pattern changed between 1975 and 1980 when both the number and the proportion of households with children increased. Thus, the recent growth in nonmarital cohabitation comes both from couples with children and from couples without children.

As with married couples, most young unmarried cohabiting adults live with someone of the same race. In 1980 nearly 98 percent of married couples and 95 percent of unmarried couples were of the same race. In 1980 about 2.2 percent of all marriages with the woman under 35 involved persons of different races, compared to 1.2 percent in 1975. The largest share of this increase occurred among couples with a white man or woman married to a person who designated a race other than black or white. Black men are far more likely to be living with white women than are black women to be living with white men. Individuals neither black nor white are as likely to have a partner of a different race as of the same race.

Unmarried partners generally are in the same or an adjacent age group. The ages of the partners tend to be widest apart when the man was previously married and least widely apart when he was never married. Whereas 45 percent of the previously married cohabiting men are in an older five-year age cohort than their wives, 71 percent of the previously married cohabiting men are in an older category than their unmarried partners. These findings reflect a tendency for men either to live with and then marry younger women or simply to live with a younger woman following a disrupted marriage.

It is interesting to point out that whereas only 4 percent of married women are in an older five-year cohort than their husbands, about 12 percent of the couples with a never-married man, and about 6 percent with one previously married, have such a profile. In general, therefore, young unmarried women, regardless of their marital history, are more likely than married women to be older than their partners.

The increase in cohabitation in recent years has encompassed persons of all educational backgrounds, but particularly has involved those with less than a college degree. In 1975, for example, 25 percent of the men and 21 percent of the women of cohabiting couples involving a never-married man were college graduates; in 1980 the percentages had dropped to 18 and 16.

Unemployment in 1980 was about twice as high for unmarried cohabiting women as it was for married men. An unmarried working man or woman exhibits a much higher tendency to live with an unemployed partner than does his or her married counterpart. However, unemployment does not seem to afflict both members of a cohabiting relationship simultaneously. Only 2 percent of unmarried-couple households possessed both an unemployed man and an unemployed woman.

The statistics are similar for both partners' participation in the labor force. In 1980, in only 3 percent of unmarried-couple households both the man and the woman were not in the labor force. However, unmarried women are much more likely than married women to be supporting a man who is not in the labor force. On the other side of the coin, married men are more likely than their cohabiting counterparts to support a woman not in the labor force.

Of all unmarried couples in which the woman is under 35 years old, nearly half are ones in which neither partner has ever been married. This represents an increase (48 percent compared to 43 percent) between 1975 and 1980. In another 15 percent of the cases, both the man and the woman have been divorced and in another 23 percent one partner has never been married while the other has been divorced.

Among these relatively young couples, widowhood is rare, as are relationships involving individuals still married to another partner. Cohabiting men and women who are still married to another person are much more frequent among couples in which the woman is over 35.

In 1980 in unmarried households, the proportion of separated persons was only half of what it had been in 1975, while the proportion of divorced persons was larger. This shift suggests that individuals are now more likely than before to terminate a failing marriage by divorce rather than to allow it to continue legally. Divorce may be sought sooner by persons who wish to live with someone else; moreover, divorce laws now more readily permit a speedy dissolution of a marriage.

Explaining the Trend

Increased unmarried cohabitation suggests that attitudes have changed. Cohabitation is viewed as a more acceptable form of living, and individuals are now more willing to live together. If so, if both attitude and behavior have changed, what are the causes of the change?

One factor has been the increase in the average age at first marriage, which has accompanied the rising incidence of cohabitation. After the 1950s, when the median age at first marriage reached a low for both men and women in the United States, the marital age rose steadily. In the most recent twenty-five-year period the median age climbed by more than two full years for both men and women (U.S. Bureau of the Census 1983a). It can be argued that among never-married persons cohabitation provides a contemporary extension of the courtship process, perhaps contributing to the postponement of marriage. Of course, if individuals first decide to postpone marriage, then cohabitation has more time to flower. Thus additional explanations are in order as to why these trends have covaried.

Several trends pertaining to sexual behavior and fertility have been well-documented during the last twenty-five years. In particular, the incidence of premarital coitus has increased, effective contraception is more readily available, fertility rates among young women have declined, and young married women are waiting longer after the wedding to commence childbearing (U.S. Bureau of the Census 1983b; Zelnik and Kantner 1980).

The prospect of sexual intimacy probably offered young adults of a generation ago a powerful incentive to consider marriage and to schedule it with some dispatch. Since the significant upward trend in cohabitation appears to have begun in the early 1960s, let us consider the 1950s as a period of comparison with today. In the 1950s, as Andrew Cherlin points out (Cherlin 1981), home and family life were highly regarded. It was a period of prosperity, high birth rates, and geographical dispersion to family-centered suburbs. In these and other ways, society provided a climate conducive to early marriage, early childbearing, and relatively high birth rates. Cohabitation had no prominent place given the norms of the time. Since the public consciousness largely disapproved of sexual intercourse outside of marriage—although it was fairly common—marriage provided young people with the only pragmatic route to sexual intimacy on a continuing basis. Since the 1950s, however, premarital sexual activity has become more prevalent, has involved less risk, and has tended to begin earlier. Society accepts such behavior more readily. Contraception more readily available to young people reduces or even eliminates the fear of pregnancy. The availability of abortion and the increased awareness of abortion as a method of controlling fertility undoubtedly also play some role.

Society's changing views of sex and marriage have made it possible to de-emphasize or even to eliminate access to a sexual partner as a primary motivation for marriage. With this motivation removed, it is logical on the average that marriage would tend to occur later. Simultaneously, the period during which cohabitation can occur has extended and there now exists a diminished need for a cohabitational relationship to be formalized. Since a woman can almost completely eliminate the risk of pregnancy, the couple also can avoid what in the 1950s would have been a very compelling reason for early marriage—a birth out of wedlock or premarital pregnancy.

Society has changed in another way that may contribute to increased unmarried cohabitation. In the 1950s people assumed that women would marry relatively early, in part to begin childbearing, and that most mothers would remain at home to raise the children. The impressive movement of women into the labor force during the intervening years has changed this picture. Women now possess a much greater propensity to have attended college in order to pursue a career or to have an interest in working during their early adult years. Consequently, they have a diminished desire to marry during their early twenties or to have children at a time when their careers are being launched. With the internal and external pressures to marry and have children lessened, it is likely that young women would want to consider other options, such as cohabitation without marriage, during the years when their counterparts a generation ago were already married and beginning families.

Higher education, in its own right, may also influence cohabitation in two ways. First, since more young women leave home for college today than did so in the 1950s, they are more likely to become socially independent of their parents. The contemporary woman has increased opportunities to interact with eligible men, usually in an environment that tends to be less restrictive than that at home. Second, women attending college today expect to integrate both family and career, whereas women a generation ago viewed college as a transition to marriage. The college climate today directs women toward careers, not toward mate selection and marriage.

Urbanization, similarly, may be conducive to nonmarital cohabitation. The urban environment and its characteristic anonymity allow for cohabitation with fewer sanctions than a small town or rural environment might provide. Men and women may live together out of wedlock with little concern about what others will think. With urbanization, the level of surveillance of personal behavior has declined, thus making cohabitation easier to consider.

Finally, we may cite the increased prospect of divorce as a contributor to the upward trend in cohabitation. Although few brides and grooms expect to get divorced, there is now a very real awareness of the increased propensity to divorce. Many young men and women have experienced a divorce in their own families of orientation. The delay in marriage and the increased likelihood of cohabitation as a temporary alternative to marriage reflect to some degree a reluctance to rush into a relationship that runs some risk of divorce. In other words, young couples today may be weighing the prospects for marriage more carefully, deciding to marry only after reaching a degree of commitment higher than that required two or three decades earlier.

Although the discussion above focuses on young adults never yet married, parallel arguments can be presented for the phenomenon of divorced persons cohabiting after their marriages have been dissolved. One common trend in all of these explanations is that couples do not necessarily equate living together with a permanent and lasting alternative to marriage, but rather associate it with a postponement of marriage or regard it as a temporary matter of convenience without an explicit understanding of what lies ahead. Indeed for many couples, the link between cohabitation and marriage is unclear from the outset because of other overriding concerns such as educational or job mobility. Couples may wish to delay marriage because one individual is preparing to go to graduate school and views marriage as a distant possibility. They may delay marriage because of job offers in differing locations. Economic concerns also suggest why a couple may prefer temporary cohabitation. They may be reluctant to marry before they are financially secure or when one or both partners are unemployed. Cohabitation can thus be viewed as an extension of the traditional courtship process, having many of the same conceptual features as engagement.

This discussion suggests that nonmarital cohabitation increased over the course of a generation when other fundamental changes also took place in society. Cohabitation, I believe, is best viewed not as a cause or effect of such changes, but rather as a phenomenon that occurred simultaneously and logically with other changes. We may generalize that cohabitation allows for intimacy without the commitment of marriage, providing for some couples the opportunity to satisfy the needs traditionally met in a family context. Cohabitation also affords the opportunity to terminate a relationship without the messy legal tangles (although they are not always avoided) and without the stigma that can accompany divorce. Cohabitation may serve an important economic function, since two individuals living together can usually live more cheaply than two individuals living apart. It may also be more economical than living together as a married couple due to the structure of our income tax system. Unmarried cohabitation may be like engagement in that it signifies to others that a formal, committed relationship short of marriage exists. It can be a period where the advisability of marriage is determined. Unlike engagement, however, which implies an imminent wedding, cohabitation may function in a contrary manner, allowing the indefinite postponement of a wedding date.

Some aspects of the demography of cohabitation must be viewed in a broader historical context. For example, the racial differences in social and economic characteristics of unmarried cohabitants are so substantial that they cannot be explained solely in terms of contemporary history. It is likely that nonmarital unions have different meanings for blacks and whites. The history of black family life in Africa and during the period of slavery in the United States suggests that black women and men possessed a greater degree of independence than did men and women in traditional European society. Of course, other fundamental differences exist between blacks and whites that may be responsible for the cohabitational variation. Differing employment patterns for blacks than for whites, the higher rate of economic instability for blacks than for whites, the higher rate of illegitimate births among blacks, and the sex ratio resulting in fewer black men available for marriage to black women as compared to whites may all play some role in explaining the differences presented.

The following sections highlight the social and economic characteristics of unmarried cohabitating men and women compared with married men and women of similar age categories. We can look to these data to verify some of the tentative ideas presented above.

Profile of Social Characteristics

Table 3 presents a broad view of individual social characteristics in three types of living arrangements. Individuals are classified by sex and age, and are cross-classified by education, metropolitan-nonmetropolitan residence (sizes of the Standard Metropolitan Statistical Area), and race. The estimates for unmarried cohabiting individuals include persons married to someone other than their current partner. The Current Population Survey assigns weights, determined by sampling variability, to individual and household records to allow for population estimates. Estimates for unmarried men and women are based on weights associated with their own individual records, whereas estimates for unmarried couples are based on weights for the male cohabitor. This procedure results in totals for unmarried men and women that are not precisely comparable.

One of the several generalizations that can be offered is that the numbers of never-married and ever-married cohabiting women are approximately equal, whereas the number of men shows a somewhat more heavy representation in the ever-married category. Thus, a previously married man has a greater tendency to cohabit with a never-married woman than vice versa. This trend may imply an increase in the proportion of never-married women in this living arrangement. This change may stem from the recent rise in the median age at first marriage (U.S. Bureau of the Census 1981a) and the greater acceptance of unmarried cohabitation for young women.

In 1975 Glick and Spanier (1980) found significant educational differences between married and unmarried persons. By 1980 many of the differences still existed, although they had tended to diminish. For example, in 1975 only three in ten of the married women in the youngest age group had attended college, compared to one-half of the never-married cohabiting women. By 1980 the gap had narrowed from both directions to the corresponding figures of 35 and 41 percent. In all age categories married men are more likely than unmarried cohabitating men to have graduated from college and less likely to have dropped out of high school. These differences also characterize married women in relation to previously married cohabiting women. However, never-married cohabiting women fail to fit into any of these generalizations. Such women are more likely than women in any other living arrangement to have a college degree. The differences are particularly large among the never-married women over age 55, of whom 62 percent are college graduates.

Table 3.   Selected Social Characteristics of Adults According to Living Arrangements, by Sex and Age: 1980

| | Living with unrelated person of opposite sex | | | | | | Married, living with spouse | | |
| | Never married | | | Ever married | | | | | |
Characteristic[a]	Under 35 years	35–54 years	55 + years	Under 35 years	35–54 years	55 + years	Under 35 years	35–54 years	55 + years
Men									
Education									
0–11 years	18.3	39.9	77.3	21.6	33.0	59.6	14.9	25.0	47.2
12 years	36.6	21.2	9.9	37.7	38.4	27.6	40.5	36.2	28.8
13–15 years	27.2	12.4	b	22.9	14.5	4.4	21.3	14.9	10.6
16 years or more	18.0	26.6	12.8	18.0	14.2	8.4	23.2	24.0	13.4
SMSA size									
3 million or more	18.1	31.2	17.4	20.1	21.6	27.7	14.0	16.0	15.5
1–3 million	29.3	31.6	37.9	24.1	25.4	23.1	20.6	21.8	19.7
Less than 1 million	25.7	21.4	15.0	30.3	30.5	19.7	28.4	26.0	26.1
Not in SMSA	26.9	15.8	29.7	25.5	22.5	29.5	37.1	36.1	38.9
Race									
White	83.7	53.6	67.8	87.8	69.5	70.8	90.7	91.2	92.6
Black	14.8	44.1	32.2	10.9	28.9	28.5	7.2	7.0	6.4
Other	1.5	2.3	b	1.3	1.6	0.7	2.1	1.8	1.0
N (in thousands)	808	121	71	376	420	250	13,898	18,550	15,139
Total (in thousands)		999			1,046			47,587	
Women									
Education									
0–11 years	17.6	44.8	21.9	25.3	39.3	61.9	16.2	23.1	42.2
12 years	41.3	29.6	15.0	45.2	34.1	29.3	48.6	48.6	39.0
13–15 years	21.9	6.9	1.3	19.9	17.3	5.0	19.0	14.3	10.5
16 years or more	19.2	18.8	61.9	9.4	9.4	3.9	16.2	14.1	8.4
SMSA size									
3 million or more	19.6	44.6	58.3	20.0	16.7	21.5	14.3	16.1	15.4
1–3 million	30.3	24.5	12.8	21.4	26.5	22.9	10.8	21.6	19.6
Less than 1 million	26.0	14.6	15.5	30.1	31.5	19.0	27.6	26.3	26.2
Not in SMSA	24.2	16.3	13.3	28.5	25.3	36.0	37.3	36.1	38.9
Race									
White	82.2	74.9	90.7	88.5	78.3	72.9	90.6	91.1	93.3
Black	15.6	21.6	9.3	9.3	18.8	26.6	7.1	7.1	5.7
Other	2.3	3.5	b	2.2	2.9	0.5	2.3	1.9	1.0
N (in thousands)	805	64	47	424	285	204	16,899	18,262	12,425
Total (in thousands)		916			914			47,587	

[a]Total for each characteristic is 100 percent.
[b]Zero or rounds to zero.
Source: March 1980 *Current Population Survey*.

Where do unmarried couples live? The figures for 1980 maintain the 1975 finding that unmarried couples have a greater tendency than their married counterparts to reside in metropolitan areas. For example, for people under 35 years old, about half of all never-married cohabitants lived in communities with at least one million residents, compared to only 35 percent of married persons.

In 1975 blacks, relative to whites, showed a disproportionate representation among unmarried couples. The cohabitation rate among blacks was three times that of whites. Although such differences continue to persist, they have moderated somewhat to a cohabitation rate about twice as high for blacks as for whites. In 1980 only 15 percent of never-married cohabitants and 10 percent of ever-married cohabitants under 35 were black. These figures represent significant declines over the five-year period. Among persons in the 35–54 and 55-and-above age groups, however, blacks continue to be quite heavily represented relative to whites and contrast sharply with the relative proportion of whites and blacks among married couples.

Profile of Economic Characteristics

Table 4 presents information on three economic correlates of living arrangements. Comparisons with 1975 data reveal that, although the proportion of married men in the labor force under age 35 remained virtually unchanged in 1980, the proportion employed increased in all other categories. Employment of married women in this age group increased from 44 to 55 percent; unmarried couples with a never-married man showed increases from 71 to 78 percent for men and from 68 to 72 percent for women; and unmarried couples with the man ever-married jumped from 77 to 85 percent for men and from 59 to 73 percent for women.

These developments reflect two changes. The first change is the rather familiar pattern of young women continuing to move into the labor force. The second change stems from an incipient convergence of the social and economic characteristics of married and unmarried couples. As suggested earlier, unmarried couples apparently are being drawn more fully into the mainstream of society, and people are more willing to ignore marital status, or at least are more willing to consider unmarried cohabitation as a regular living arrangement, if only on a temporary basis.

Despite the changes, unmarried cohabiting men are still less likely to be employed than married men, and unmarried cohabiting women are still more likely to be employed than married women. In the more recent data, differences also persist in the occupational categories of employed persons. Married men continue to be more likely than unmarried cohabiting men to have white-collar jobs. The reverse is true of service-worker jobs.

For women, differences in occupational group by living arrangement are harder to find. Fewer unmarried women have never worked or are not in the labor force. This difference may reflect the more tenuous nature of unmarried cohabitation,

Table 4. Selected Economic Characteristics of Adults According to Living Arrangements, by Sex and Age: 1980

| | Living with unrelated person of opposite sex | | | | | | Married, living with spouse | | |
| | Never married | | | Ever married | | | | | |
Characteristic[a]	Under 35 years	35–54 years	55+ years	Under 35 years	35–54 years	55+ years	Under 35 years	35–54 years	55+ years
Men									
Employment status									
Employed	78.0	80.4	31.6	84.7	84.0	45.2	92.1	92.4	48.1
Unemployed or not in labor force	22.0	19.6	68.4	15.3	16.0	54.8	7.6	7.6	32.0
Occupational group									
White collar	30.7	30.3	10.0	33.4	32.3	17.4	39.0	46.3	25.6
Blue collar	54.0	45.0	15.9	56.8	49.5	23.1	50.8	41.8	21.9
Service workers	10.4	7.9	9.5	7.1	10.4	9.5	6.0	5.4	4.9
Farm workers	1.4	1.5	0.4	0.6	1.1	1.5	2.5	3.0	3.6
Never worked or not in labor force	3.5	15.4	64.3	2.0	6.8	48.5	1.8	3.6	44.0
Family income									
Less than 10,000	53.3	46.4	97.8	34.4	34.7	68.6	12.5	7.8	27.6
10,000–14,999	25.8	30.3	1.6	30.3	25.6	10.4	16.8	8.9	19.2
15,000–19,999	12.4	12.0	0.7	16.7	18.4	4.2	20.7	13.7	12.8
20,000 and over	8.5	11.3	b	18.5	21.3	16.8	50.0	69.7	40.4
N (in thousands)	808	121	71	376	420	250	13,398	18,550	15,139
Total (in thousands)	999			1,046			47,587		
Women									
Employment status									
Employed	72.1	57.3	37.9	73.3	72.3	28.2	55.2	57.2	23.7
Unemployed or not in labor force	27.9	42.7	62.1	26.7	27.7	71.8	44.8	42.8	76.3
Occupational group									
White collar	53.4	28.5	12.0	52.6	43.4	11.3	47.4	43.0	18.0
Blue collar	14.1	17.8	3.7	12.5	11.3	5.3	9.9	9.8	4.2
Service Workers	20.0	17.6	22.2	19.1	20.9	17.4	12.4	11.0	6.1
Farm Workers	0.8	b	b	1.1	1.2	0.2	0.9	1.2	0.7
Never worked or not in labor force	11.8	36.1	62.1	14.8	22.8	65.8	29.5	35.0	70.7
Family income									
Less than 10,000	77.5	71.9	96.0	68.3	57.7	84.9	12.3	8.2	30.7
10,000–14,999	14.7	8.9	4.0	22.8	26.5	9.9	15.9	9.0	20.6
15,000–19,999	5.2	12.2	b	6.8	9.9	3.5	20.0	13.0	12.8
20,000 and over	2.6	7.0	b	1.5	6.0	1.7	51.8	69.9	36.0
N (in thousands)	805	64	47	424	285	204	16,899	18,262	12,425
Total (in thousands)	916			914			47,587		

[a]Total for each characteristic is 100 percent.
[b]Zero or rounds to zero.
Source: March 1980 *Current Population Survey.*

which requires more independence and more financial self-reliance. Of course, it is also likely that some women who are a priori more independent and financially self-reliant experience less pressure or less motivation to marry. They are therefore more willing to consider unmarried cohabitation. Apart from this difference, however, the distribution of job types is roughly similar for all women. In all three living arrangements most women have white-collar jobs; service work is the next most prevalent form of employment, followed by blue-collar work.

Table 4 includes information on income, a variable that reveals perhaps the most profound difference between married couples and unmarried couples. Table 4 combines the incomes of the man and the woman into "family income" for married couples but not for unmarried couples. Yet this procedure does not negate the differences between the two groups, partially because the differences are so profound. In 1975 and again in 1980 low income was found to be especially characteristic of unmarried couples. The recent data reveal, for example, that approximately half of cohabiting men receive less than $10,000 per year, compared to fewer than one in eight families of married men.

In addition, whereas more than half of married men have family incomes surpassing $20,000, about one in twelve never-married cohabiting men and about one in five ever-married cohabiting men fall in this income category.

Conclusion

Our data on the social and economic characteristics of couples provide some confirmation of our explanation for the upward trend in cohabitation. The data presented here, when compared with similar data prepared five years earlier, suggest an overall picture of consistency in the demographic characteristics of unmarried couples. However, differences between unmarried couples and married couples are diminishing. Unmarried couples are evidently being drawn more fully into the mainstream of society. Society is more willing to ignore marital status in its evaluation and treatment of individuals, and those already in the mainstream of society are more willing to consider unmarried cohabitation as an acceptable living arrangement.

Much of our earlier discussion about the trend in nonmarital cohabitation probably makes the most sense from the perspective of middle and upper-middle class Americans—people who have benefited from clear norms governing mate selection and from a college education and job mobility. But our profile of social and economic characteristics, while not contradicting any of these explanations, suggests that most unmarried cohabitants are not in the middle or upper-middle class at all. A disproportionate share of such persons have a high school diploma at best, are blue-collar or service workers—or are unemployed—and earn less than $10,000 per year. Blacks are overrepresented. Thus, we must examine the possibility that two simultaneous phenomena have provided the force for changes in nonmarital cohabitation. The first relies on the dynamics cited already in this chapter and applies mostly to middle class young adult men and women who have never been married or who were previously married. The other explanation of the trend must focus on the large working class and lower class population, particularly blacks, for whom cohabitation may be principally a response to economic hardship, family disruption, and elusive mate selection and marriage norms.

When applied to the second group, the upward trend in unmarried cohabitation correlates with the high level of illegitimacy, single parenthood, and divorce among individuals in the lowest socioeconomic statuses. Among blacks, for example, only 42 percent of children live with two parents. Among black children with one parent, the largest share live with a never-married mother. The incidence of such arrangements has increased substantially over the past decade, paralleling the increase in nonmarital cohabitation (U.S. Bureau of the Census 1983b).

What lies in the future? An overall increase in cohabitation is likely to occur, although more slowly than in recent years, since the conditions that have been conducive to nonmarital cohabitation or that perhaps have contributed to its increase will continue to be present. Since the age at first marriage probably will continue its increase, cohabitation will remain prominent in our society. If the divorce rate continues at its current level, or even declines slightly, a large population of previously married individuals will be free to cohabit, many in a transition to remarriage. The beginnings of a trend toward postponement of remarriage, undoubtedly corresponding with the trend in postponement of first marriage, is likely to continue, thus increasing unmarried cohabitation arrangements.

Although the pace of the increase shows signs of deceleration, the large numbers of individuals who now cohabit and who have caused significant changes in our society have bequeathed to us a demographic history that will not go unnoticed by the next generation. Future cohorts will find the freedoms and flexibility of cohabitation attractive, and, almost certainly, behavior across social class lines will converge. To the extent that social and economic conditions improve, cohabitation for lower-status individuals should level off or decline. Yet a continuing increase in cohabitation due to other factors mentioned certainly will compensate for this leveling effect. The collective outcome is likely to be one of convergence among social classes within the larger framework of a continuing increase nationally in cohabitation. A comparison of 1975, 1980, and later data indicates that this prediction may have some merit.

References

Cherlin, A. J. *Marriage, Divorce, Remarriage.* Cambridge, Mass.: Harvard University Press, 1981.

Glick, P. C., and Spanier, G. B. "Married and Unmarried Cohabitation in the United States." *Journal of Marriage and the Family* 42(1980):19–30.

National Center for Health Statistics. "Annual Summary of Births, Deaths, Marriages, and Divorces: United States, 1980." *Monthly Vital Statistics Report,* Vol. 29, No. 13, September 17. Washington, D.C.: Department of Health and Human Services, 1981.

National Center for Health Statistics. "Births, Marriages, Divorces, and Deaths for 1981." *Monthly Vital Statistics Report,* Vol. 30, No. 12, March 18. Washington, D.C.: Department of Health and Human Services, 1982.

U.S. Bureau of the Census. "Marital Status and Living Arrangements: March 1980." *Current Population Reports,* Series P-20, No. 365. Washington, D.C.: U.S. Government Printing Office, 1981a.

U.S. Bureau of the Census. "Household and Family Characteristics: March 1980." *Current Population Reports,* Series P-20, No. 366. Washington, D.C.: U.S. Government Printing Office, 1981b.

U.S. Bureau of the Census. "Marital Status and Living Arrangements: March 1981." *Current Population Reports,* Series P-20, No. 372. Washington, D.C.: U.S. Government Printing Office, 1982.

U.S. Bureau of the Census. "Marital Status and Living Arrangements: March 1982." *Current Population Reports,* Series P-20, No. 380. Washington, D.C.: U.S. Government Printing Office, 1983a.

U.S. Bureau of the Census. "Fertility of American Women: June 1981." *Current Population Reports,* Series P-20, No. 378. Washington, D.C.: U.S. Government Printing Office, 1983b.

U.S. Bureau of the Census. "Households, Families, Marital Status, and Living Arrangements: March 1984 (Advanced Report)." *Current Population Reports,* Series P-20, No. 391. Washington, D.C.: U.S. Government Printing Office, 1984.

Zelnik, M., and Kantner, J. F. "Sexual Activity, Contraceptive Use and Pregnancy Among Metropolitan-Area Teenagers: 1971–1979." *Family Planning Perspectives* 12(1980):230–237.

American Couples

Philip Blumstein and Pepper Schwartz

We did this study because we, like many others in this country, were becoming increasingly aware that relationships in general and marriage in particular were in flux, that they seemed to be getting more fragile, and that we were witnessing social change that needed to be understood. We wanted to know if the institution of our past—marriage—would be the institution of the future. We wanted to know whether any intimate relationship could meet modern challenges, be satisfying, and last for a lifetime.

What do we mean by *institution*? An institution is a way of life that is very resistant to change. People know about it; they can describe it; and they have spent a lifetime learning how to react to it. The *idea* of marriage is larger than any individual marriage. The *role* of husband or wife is greater than any individual who takes on that role.

Institutions set up standards and practices that let people fall neatly into niches, giving them roles and rules of conduct that help interaction proceed smoothly. Each relationship does not have to deal with the same problem as if it has never occurred before. Trust can be assumed because of the nature of the rules. This is illustrated by one of the major differences between marriage and cohabitation: Marriage has no need for the kind of financial bookkeeping so common among cohabitors because the rules help keep people together and help make for an orderly exit if the relationship ends. Bookkeeping is alienating. It implies the possibility of a breakup or suggests that partners will not do their share unless watched, or that the relationship has to be fifty-fifty and that anything else is a bad bargain.

At the present time, marriage is an institution that seems to be in danger of collapse. We understand it in its pure form. Indeed, every schoolchild understands what marriage is supposed to be like. Ask a young child to explain marriage and he or she can tell its essential parts: that there are a husband and wife, and eventually a mommy and a daddy, that it entails a ceremony, and that the two people live together for the rest of their lives. The child knows just as well as the adult that there are marriages that do not look like this. He may have seen his own parents divorce. But he will not describe real life when he describes marriage—he will describe the "ideal type." The question is, Is that ideal disappearing because of the exceptions to it? Is marriage becoming less an institution because of the prevalence of divorce, because of new roles for husbands and wives, and because society is debating what relationships are and should be? Are there now different types of marriage, and if so, does that strengthen the institution or weaken it? Moreover, if institutionalization is intrinsically good—if it gives shape to a relationship so that partners know what to expect of one another and can predict what their future together will be like—is this something that our other three kinds of couples should aim for? Indeed, do any of these three already have institutional aspects to their relationships?

Types of Relationship

In looking at marriage in the last part of the twentieth century, we see that there are different marital forms. At one end of the continuum there is traditional marriage, with the man working outside the home and having unquestioned authority, the woman a homemaker, and no possibility of divorce. At the other end of the continuum are the most experimental forms of marriage.

It may be that this continuum will start to break off into little clusters, each a different kind of marriage. We may see, for example, that "voluntary marriage" will take on a recognizable profile. These are the marriages that last only while the couple is in love. Based as they are on "happiness" and "compatibility," they may be expected to be less stable than relationships grounded in a presumption of permanence. Such marriages might be seen as requiring special contracts, renewable every year or every five years. Partners would anticipate the fact that their high expectations made permanence improbable. If voluntary marriage became an institution people would say, "I'm entering into a voluntary marriage," to their friends and their friends would immediately know this was different from any other form of marriage. For example, economic arrangements might be quite specific and separate.

The question is, however, Does voluntary marriage simply create a new form of marriage, or does it have deeper implications? Does the mere concept of voluntary marriage undermine the institution so thoroughly that even the most traditional of vows lose their effect, thereby bringing the permanence of the marital institution, its most critical aspect, into question?

Another modern variation may be cohabitation as a "trial marriage." Trial marriages, as we have seen, are quite conservative and it might be said that they are exactly like marriage except that the couple has not yet made the final decision. But trial marriage is really quite different from the *institution* of marriage. It is not the mere anticipation of marriage but the actual experience of it that shapes people's lives. A woman who intends to quit her job will not do so until the marriage has occurred. No children will be born until their future can be assured by the safeguards of marriage. While trial marriage may be the nonmarital form closest to marriage (because it presumes an eventual lifetime commitment), it is still not marriage.

Traditionalists see voluntary marriage and trial marriage as truly threatening alternatives because they *seem* to be supportive of the institution while in fact they are not. Allowing such variation erodes the historic nature of marriage. And society does not sit by complaisantly and allow its institutions to change radically. Those who champion voluntary marriage and argue that what modern society needs is many different forms of intimate life-style are ignoring the fact that such a development would be a revolutionary one.

There have already been revisions in the concept of marriage that may prove shattering. Society now questions whether husbands should have absolute authority. Soon it may be taken for granted that the working wife will be a financial partner, sharing even the man's provider role. This gives a woman more power because many of the justifications for the couple's division of labor were predicated on one person, the male, directing the relationship because his work made survival possible. If he is no longer the provider, he may lose his legitimacy as ultimate decision-maker. Other decisions, such as who chooses where they will live become problematic. (We are already, for example, seeing one outcome of such a situation, wherein couples commute rather than live together because each partner values his or her job and neither will compromise success by moving to the other person's location.) Changes such as these do not simply modify the institution; they alter the very meaning of marriage so drastically that it may cease to be an institution in the way we have always known it. We are not arguing that these changes should not occur. We are merely saying that if and when they do, the institution may fail and need to be reconstructed according to a different model.

What about other kinds of couples? It could be argued that cohabitors who plan never to marry are attempting to create a new institution. The whole idea behind lifetime cohabitation is that people who love each other can create a bond that does not need the state's participation and can be durable and satisfying. But relationships are both public and private. It is difficult to create an institution without support from society and this society still recognizes only marriages as an institution.

Furthermore, to be an institution, cohabitation would have to have a predictable shape, and at present cohabitation takes too many forms. The fact that two partners often have very different concepts of what cohabitation means is evidence that it is not yet institutionalized. It is not recognized as a stable *form* by law or society; it is seen as a *situation* which may change at any moment. Its lack of predictability and the absence of clear understandings about what the relationship means to the participants themselves make establishing the institution of cohabitation very difficult.

Before cohabitation can become an institution, its properties must be clear to any schoolchild. It must be seen as legitimate. Both partners must have the same level of commitment (or lack thereof) to the future. At the present time, we think that because there are so many possible permutations of cohabitation, partners may have trouble being sure they both want the same thing out of the relationship. There is often no basis for trust, no mutual cooperation, and no ability to plan.

Currently, cohabitation as a way of life is unstable. Cohabitors may be dismayed by this because they feel their love is enough and that all it takes to create a way of life is two people who see eye to eye. But they do not take into account the importance of society's reactions and how poorly society is equipped to accommodate them. For example, parents may not want to acknowledge a cohabitor's partner as a family member. Even if they want to be welcoming, they may be unsure of what to expect of such a person; they may not know how to act toward him or her. One symptom of this confused state of affairs is that cohabitation has been widely discussed and openly practiced for the past fifteen years, and yet we still do not have a term the two people can use for one another. Couples who want to create an institution should be aware of what an awesome task they have taken on. It is very hard to anticipate the results when one tries to create a new tradition and it is very hard to maintain one's resolve in the face of an unsupportive society. After all, it has taken a long time for Western marriage to evolve the features that it has. Institutions are not made or redesigned overnight.

Moreover, we think it will be hard for cohabitation to become an institution while the traditional model of marriage still exists. As long as marriage retains its image as the highest form of commitment, it acts as a lure to cohabiting couples who want to prove their love for each other. So they are likely either to get married or to break up once their commitment falters. If cohabition is to be a unique institution, it must be perceived as different from marriage, and marriage cannot be allowed to be seen as a better or next step in the relationship. But, the establishment of cohabitation as a lifetime alternative to marriage is an implied criticism of the latter, and hence is likely to be resisted by government and society in an attempt to defend the concept of matrimony. Society accepts cohabitation now only because it is thought of as a phase in a person's life. It is not understood as challenging the legitimacy of marriage.

Do same-sex couples exist as an institution? Certainly not in the general community. Neither schoolchildren nor heterosexual adults can explain accurately how such couples function. Furthermore, because of the general antipathy toward homosexuality in American society, gay men and lesbians are not encouraged to be open about their sexual preference or about their relationships. Hence they are seldom extended such commonplace courtesies as having a partner invited to an office party or to a retirement banquet. Even heterosexuals who might like to welcome a gay friend's partner may [not] know how to go about doing so.

Are same-sex couples an institution within the gay and lesbian community? At present, we think not. There is a general fear in both gay and lesbian circles that relationships are unlikely to last. Long-lasting relationships are seen as quite special. They are unexpected, and therefore newly formed couples are not treated as though they will remain together for fifty years. People are less likely to ask, "How's Jerry?" and more likely to say, "Are you still with your lover?" This is particularly true for gay men. But it happens with both men and women, and when a couple is not treated as inviolate, the less likely it is that the partners will see themselves that way.

We might expect that the existence of a gay culture would help the development of "couple" status. A community could offer the support of public opinion, the reinforcement of a relationship by friends, and censure of a person who treats his or her partner badly or dissolves a well-thought-of partnership. Conventions could be established and a couple who violated them would have an awareness that they might be headed for trouble. Role models would be present to show that relationships can last, and more important, to show how.

The problem with gay male culture is that much of it is organized around singlehood or maintaining one's sexual marketability. Meeting places like bars and baths promote casual sex rather than couple activities. The problem with the lesbian world is quite different. Women are often in tight-knit friendship groups where friends and acquaintances spend so much intimate time together that, it seems to us, opportunities arise for respect and companionship to turn into love and a meaningful affair. Thus, gay men imperil their relationship because of the availability of a singles market that draws men out of their relationships; lesbians are in jeopardy because of opportunities to fall in love. We have found that when gay women are involved in the gay world, they break up more [often], not less. If couplehood were an institution, participation in the gay world would not be detrimental; it would be supportive.

What would give institutional status to gay relationships? They would not need to look like marriage or to have the same rules as marriage. But they would have to have some predictable elements so that couples could agree on their obligations. Ideally there might be a public witness to the couple's vows to one another, perhaps even a ceremony. The couple might want to be legally joined by the state and have reciprocal legal responsibilities that would make it emotionally and financially harder to break up. Sometimes gay men and lesbians have put each other in their wills; sometimes one has adopted the other. These are attempts to give the relationship stronger ties than the couple's private promises to one another.

The chance to marry legally, however, is denied to gay people. We think the courts, as agents of the broader society, have resisted same-sex petitions to wed, partly because of anti-homosexual precedents and prejudices and partly because it would be the most fundamental change ever made to the institution of marriage. The judiciary understands that if gay people are allowed to marry, it would help institutionalize their relationships; the courts do not want to do this. Nor do they want to create parallel institutions to marriage. Just as the courts once enforced laws that forbade blacks and whites to marry because white America feared an interracial society, so they also prohibit gay marriage, fearing it would in some way encourage homosexuality. Courts are by nature conservative; they enforce the status quo and resist change. They do not want to redefine marriage.

This is very upsetting to many gay people, but they should also remember that there are some minuses to balance the pluses institutions provide. For one thing, when relationships become institutions, this reduces pluralism. There becomes only one model of how to live as a couple. In addition, the more the couple is extolled, the more the single person is excluded. At present, the fluidity of couple status in the gay community makes it easier to be a single gay man or lesbian than it is to be a single heterosexual person. Institutional standing for same-sex couples may reduce some of the freedom the gay community offers.

A more important drawback is that the institution of marriage, at least until now, has been organized around inequality, and attempts to change this framework have not yet been very successful. The traditional married couples in our study often laid their solid foundation on roles that stabilized the relationship but gave the woman some of the less pleasant responsibilities, such as housework, and assigned her duties, such as the buyer role. If tasks were allotted on the basis of efficiency or affinity, we would expect that married couples could reassign household chores and have the institution remain as durable as ever. We have found, however, that when roles are reversed, with men doing housework and women taking over as provider, couples become dreadfully unhappy. Even couples who willingly try to change traditional male and female behavior have difficulty doing so. They must not only go against everything they have learned and develop new skills, but they have to resist the negative reaction of society. Thus we have learned that while the institution is bigger than the individuals within it, it may not be bigger than the assignment of roles by gender.

Gender

Gender has been a second theme running through this study. We have described many differences among the four types of couples, but we have also observed that heterosexual men have traits in common with homosexual men, and this is also true of heterosexual and homosexual women. It has been clear that a person's gender affects what he or she desires in a relationship and how he or she behaves in one. It is equally clear that the way people expect their partners to behave depends on whether the partner is male or female; thus gender requirements set the stage for how individuals will interact as a couple.

An extremely important effect of having one male and one female in heterosexual couples is that each gender is automatically assigned certain duties and privileges. A couple does not have to think about how the house is going to be cleaned or money is going to be earned, if they depend on tradition to guide the male's efforts in one direction and the female's in another. All this is taken for granted except when people are trying to reject tradition or when they have no gender differences to guide them. Then the true complexity of running a household and running a relationship become evident. Each element of the couple's life—from cooking a meal to initiating sex to writing Christmas cards—becomes a potential point of debate. Both may want to take on a responsibility or neither may be so inclined. Both may have been trained to do certain things, or neither may know anything about them. For heterosexual couples, gender provides a shortcut and avoids the decision-making process.

With this enormous advantage comes two enormous disadvantages. First, while the heterosexual model offers more stability and certainty, it inhibits change, innovation, and *choice* regarding roles and tasks. Second, the heterosexual model, which provides so much efficiency, is predicated on the man's being the dominant partner. Giving one person the final say guarantees less argument about the organization of the relationship—as long as neither partner sees this as unfair. Historically the man's authority was questioned by neither the man nor the woman. But today, the right of men to have authority over women is widely debated and it is not as clear what the internal organization of the relationship will be. Same-sex couples cannot, obviously, rely on gender to guide their decisions about who will do what in the relationship. But they do not have the inequality that gender builds into heterosexual relationships. Some individual gay male or lesbian couples may not have equality, but that is either the happenstance of that individual relationship or perhaps the result of modeling their relationship on marriage. It is not thrust upon them as part of the nature of their relationship. Same-sex couples who wish to build a relationship based on equality are a step ahead of heterosexual couples, but the price they pay is the lack of traditions or guidelines.

When asked how they came to organize their relationship the way they do, same-sex couples usually refer to trial and error, both partners minimizing the number of tasks they hate doing, or say they had to discover which partner was more talented in one area or another. If heterosexual couples today wish to avoid the hierarchy that gender places on them and to escape from adherence to notions of "men's work" and "women's work," they often arrange their lives so that each performs the jobs he or she prefers or to which he or she is better suited. They do not fully realize, however, that growing up male or female shapes one's prefer-ences and one's skills, so choosing tasks on the basis of personal preference still brings them within the traditional framework.

What is there about men's and women's roles that enhances relationships, and what is there that undermines them? What are the properties of gender that men and women prize in their relationships, and which do they wish to discard? Among the heterosexuals we find that men are still invested in their work and treat it as a major focus of their lives. The provider role, however, is in jeopardy. Husbands are still in the work force supporting their families, but many are now joined by their wives who help carry financial responsibility. Many husbands told us in the interviews that they no longer wish to be totally responsible for a partner's economic well-being. Looking at the cohabitors, we can see that when relationships between men and women are less scripted, men can, and indeed do, cast off that responsibility. Their ambition to achieve, however, is not diminished even though they are no longer the sole support of their partners. The world of work has not lost its allure for men, even though a major reason for conquering it is disappearing. It is too important a source of respect for them. What may be lessening, however, is their ability to use their responsibilities to family or [the] relationship as a rationale for devoting themselves to work. In the future a man's excessive attachment to his work may be viewed as selfish rather than selfless.

There is another reason why work is an important part of a man's self-image. For most married couples, it is still the man's work that remains sacrosanct. His superior earning power means it is in the couple's best interest to make choices that will support his presence in the work world. It is interesting that even when the couple shares the provider responsibility, the husband's career will probably continue to be put first. This is extremely important for gender hierarchy. This assures that he will remain a dominant force in the relationship.

His work gives him a great deal of influence. Historically, a husband's influence came from the fact of his being male and therefore the head of the household. While there is a residue of this kind of authority left, it seems to us that it is fast disappearing and that it is being shored up by a man's achievements. Thus men may be even more attached to their work because they now derive their influence from how well they do as well as from who they are.

When the husband was making the only money the couple had, it was tradi-tional for the wife to make his life at home as comfortable as possible. Since his labor was synonymous with the couple's welfare, doing things for him was doing something for the whole family. Men learned to be indulged without feeling particularly selfish. They learned to make decisions without consulting the rest of the family because of their authority and the importance of their comforts. They felt it was their due to be taken care of in return for the burdens they carried. They became accustomed to doing no housework unless they wished to be magnani-mous, and it was unquestionably their right to have their sexual needs and desires shape the couple's sex life. Although times are changing, it is still difficult for men to give up these privileges. The assumption that they should be indulged shapes the lives of heterosexual men, both married and cohabitors. Men are starting to give up the costs of being male, but they are moving much more slowly in giving up benefits that were their due in an earlier age.

Women in relationships with men increasingly see employment as part of their self-image, although this does not yet include taking on the provider role. We believe that this role is still foreign to most of them. They wish to work, but not as the primary support of the family. Further, while some women in our study are "work-centered," it remains a minority. We think that most employed women continue to value their role as companion and caretaker. Women in the study seem to want respect for both roles and are seeking a way to perform them both successfully. They also want to preserve part of men's traditional commitment to the world of work: They still want their partners to achieve. When they enter the world of work, they do not want him to leave. Women want to look up to, or at least directly across at, their male partner if they are to respect them.

Women, like men, want to be admired for their success at their jobs. Men, however, are more likely to see their own work as more important and the woman's work as auxiliary. This is partly because she generally earns less money, but it may also reflect the belief that her work is more voluntary or done more for her self-fulfillment than for the couple's welfare. In established married couples, if the woman wanted to quit working, if it were financially feasible, her husband would probably acquiese. If the man wanted to quit working, it would be considered a central change in the relationship. There is still some residue of the provider role, and in a man any reluctance to work would be seen as abandoning his responsibilities.

Cohabiting men and women feel that neither should be responsible for the other's economic welfare and so they are more likely to see the woman's work as a duty rather than as a choice. Cohabiting men and women do not give the woman or the man a provider role. They are likely to invoke the rule of doing one's fair share. Cohabiting women seem pleased to be as self-sufficient as possible and to contribute to the financial needs of the relationship, but their desire for equality is often stymied by the fact that women still do not earn as much as men. The woman with a high income may easily do her fair share and more, but in general, cohabiting women are struggling to keep up with their partners. Until women earn as much as men, even cohabiting women would like to base their financial participation on what they can afford. These women have rejected most aspects of traditional female subordination and they do not like to be in a less than equal position in the relationship. But while some cohabiting men subscribe to an equitable arrangement of splitting expenses, many prefer absolutely equal contribution. This is frustrating to a woman because it puts her at a disadvantage and gives her less influence. The fact that the woman brings in less income keeps the couple from operating along egalitarian lines, and it is a reminder to her that she is in a second-class position. There are of course more traditional cohabitors, those intending to marry, who are not as taken up with the idea of equality, but most cohabiting women want respect for their ability to pay their own way. It seems to us that this may be evidence that dependency, financial or otherwise, will eventually cease to be such a large part of the female role.

Furthermore, it seems likely that women will press for some changes in men's roles. Women, in exchange for sharing financial responsibilities, want more help with burdensome chores, and in most of the areas we have studied, would like to move closer to equality. They do not want to dominate their men any more than men want to be dominated. But they want enough power so that they can have their desires considered and so the relationship does not always operate on their partner's terms. This may be accomplished as work plays a more important role in their lives and, by making them less dependent, moves the relationship more toward equal decision-making.

The gay men, like the heterosexual men, derive much of their self-esteem from the world of work and the ability to make a good income. As men, they expect to work. Because they have a male partner, they expect him to work as well. The provider role lapses because it is really suitable only in a heterosexual context. Men do not expect to provide for other men. They ask of their partners the same things they ask of themselves: ambition, earning power, and initiative. This can create a problem for the internal dynamics of couples where one man clearly does better in the world of work than the other or where one man is clearly more powerful than the other. Men do not do well in such relationships. The more dominant man finds it difficult to respect his partner and not punish him for being less successful or for not being forceful and aggressive. The man who is less powerful may have trouble staying in a relationship where he is unable to see himself as an equal. A man might like to cook or keep house, or be less invested in his work, but if these things bring him less respect or power from his partner—as they may well do—this is likely to be disturbing to all but a small proportion of gay men. Relaxing some of the demands of the male role seems to be less of a problem than assuming roles that have traditionally been held by women.

It seemed to us that, at least in some ways, lesbians also find the female role demeaning and wish to change it. Like the other women, they still value being companions and they still want their relationships to be at the center of their lives. These are parts of the traditional female role that they continue to prize. But while we spoke to lesbians who had relationships where one woman supported the other or where one was content to be clearly subordinate, our overwhelming impression is that most lesbians, young or old, affluent or poor, wish to avoid being dependent or having a dependent partner. There is a strong emphasis on being able to take care of oneself. If, for example, one woman seemed to need a lot of help making decisions or was clearly glad to be supported, the more dominant partner was usually unhappy about it. Lesbians are vigilant for signs of weakness or lack of initiative in themselves or in their partners. They want their partners to be ambitious and to enter the world of work, and they are careful to divide evenly the tasks like housework that remind them of women's subordinate status in heterosexual relationships. They do not want a partner to dominate them, and just like heterosexual women, they have no desire to dominate. As we saw when we looked at the data on who broke up, the woman who was in a more dominant role was the woman more likely to leave the relationship. Lesbians are in a double bind: On the one hand, they want a great deal of attention and communication from a partner. On the other hand, they do not want a partner who is so relationship-centered that she has no ambition or attachment to work. Lesbians want an intense home life, but they also want a strong, ambitious, and independent partner. They want to give a great deal, but only if their partner gives as much. They demand a lot, but not more than they can return in kind. They do not want to be provider, but neither do they wish to be provided for.

This gives us a clue to why lesbians have such a high breakup rate. They are the vanguard in changing women's roles in the 1980s. They have many conflicting desires in their relationships, none of which can be solved by reverting to the traditional female role. Both partners are rejecting the comfortable support position that women have been trained for in favor of being a full and equal partner in a relationship. This endangers their desire to place their relationship at the center of their lives and their need for emotional intensity because it means that both women need to be equally ambitious outside the relationship. Moreover, they are at the same time moving away from male traits that they feel provide inequality. They do not wish to dominate in their relationship or take too much initiative. They know that if they do, their partner may actually relax into what they see as a traditional female dependency, and this they refuse to allow. Thus lesbians are rejecting almost all available gender directives at once.

The lesbians are trying to carve out a new female role. This is an exceptionally difficult challenge and it is a testimony to their persistence that so many of their relationships do thrive. We think that one reason some are successful is because lesbians still retain women's desire for closeness and nurturance. Most are still relationship-centered and are willing to put time and effort into working out their problems and being attentive to their partner's emotional needs.

We have tried to describe some of the major issues that will be confronting couples in this decade and perhaps for far longer. Institutions evolve slowly and change slowly. Gender roles are entrenched, and they are difficult to change even when they are no longer satisfying. We hope that after seeing where the conflicts and successes lie, couples will be more aware of where the directives imposed by gender serve them well and where they serve them badly.

We have focused a great deal of attention on the problems couples face, their sources of conflict, and the factors that stand in the way of their contentment. These are the issues that challenged us as sociologists and these are the issues we felt that couples would most want to understand. What we have not shown is why so many couples can face up to extremely difficult problems and yet endure and be happy. We have been impressed with the energy that human beings are willing to put out to conquer problems against great odds, to make compromises, and to achieve enough satisfaction to stay and work things out. We have tried to stress the reasons why some kinds of couples face greater hurdles than others. We hope that while drawing attention to the conflicts that can erode a couple's relationship, we have also offered insights into what can make them stronger. Many of the problems we have discussed have no easy solution, and this is particularly true because a couple does not live in a vacuum. The modern world in which they are trying to create a life together is full of complexities. There are demands made of men and women by virtue of their gender that they may resist because they see them as an affront to their individual values—only to find it difficult to invoke new, better, and fairer guidelines. People may avoid marriage because of the inequalities built into its traditional design only to find that there are pitfalls in not having rules and regulations and social recognition.

Looking at marriage and its alternatives, we see advantages both in the institution and in nonmarital forms. As we look at the impact of being male or female, we see no evidence that historic gender-role traditions and restrictions help solve *all* issues for couples. We believe that the time for orthodoxy is past. Neither, however, do we reject the idea that gender differences may be valuable for a couple in certain areas of their life together. Gay couples face problems that arise from "sameness" of gender; these give us an indication of where it might be wise for partners to be different. Heterosexuals face problems that arise from their "differences"; these give us guidance about where it might be better for two partners to be more alike.

There is, of course, no perfect composite picture that will fit every couple's needs. But we hope that the findings of this study will help a couple identify roles and develop understandings that will help make their relationship satisfactory and long-lasting. As the institution of marriage loses its predictability for heterosexuals, and while homosexual couples have no institution to enter, each couple will have to establish guidelines for making gender work for, not against, the possibility of a lifetime relationship.

Chapter 6

Marriage

Five Types of Marriage

John F. Cuber and Peggy B. Harroff

The qualitative aspects of enduring marital relationships vary enormously. The variations described to us were by no means random or clearly individualized, however. Five distinct life styles showed up repeatedly and the pairs within each of them were remarkably similar [in the ways in] which they lived together, found sexual expression, reared children, and made their way in the outside world.

The following classification is based on the interview materials of those people whose marriages had already lasted ten years or more and who said that they had never seriously considered divorce or separation. While 360 of the men and women had been married ten or more years to the same spouse, exclusion of those who reported that they had considered divorce reduced the number to 211. The discussion in this chapter is, then, based on 211 interviews: 107 men and 104 women.

The descriptions which our interviewees gave us took into account how they had behaved and also how they felt about their actions past and present. Examination of the important features of their lives revealed five recurring configurations of male-female life, each with a central theme—some prominent distinguishing psychological feature which gave each type its singularity. It is these preeminent characteristics which suggested the names for the relationship; the *Conflict-Habituated*, the *Devitalized*, the *Passive-Congenial*, the *Vital*, and the *Total*.

The Conflict-Habituated

We begin with the conflict-habituated not because it is the most prevalent, but because the overt behavior patterns in it are so readily observed and because it

Reprinted by permission of Hawthorn Books, Inc., from John Cuber and Peggy B. Harroff, *The Significant American*. Copyright, © 1965, pp. 43–65. All rights reserved.

presents some arresting contradictions. In this association there is much tension and conflict—although it is largely controlled. At worst, there is some private quarreling, nagging, and "throwing up the past" of which members of the immediate family, and more rarely close friends and relatives, have some aware-ness. At best, the couple is discreet and polite, genteel about it in the company of others—but after a few drinks at the cocktail party the verbal barbs begin to fly. The intermittent conflict is rarely concealed from the children, though we were often assured otherwise. "Oh, they're at it again—but they always are," says the high-school son. There is private acknowledgment by both husband and wife as a rule that incompatibility is pervasive, that conflict is ever-potential, and that an atmosphere of tension permeates the togetherness.

An illustrative case concerns a physician of fifty, married for twenty-five years to the same woman, with two college-graduate children promisingly established in their own professions.

> You know, it's funny; we have fought from the time we were in high school together. As I look back at it, I can't remember specific quarrels; it's more like a running guerrilla fight with intermediate periods, sometimes quite long, of pretty good fun and some damn good sex. In fact, if it hadn't been for the sex, we wouldn't have been married so quickly. Well, anyway, this has been going on ever since. . . . It's hard to know what it is we fight about most of the time. You name it and we'll fight about it. It's sometimes something I've said that she remembers differently, sometimes a decision—like what kind of car to buy or what to give the kids for Christmas. With regard to politics, and religion, and morals—oh, boy! You know, outside of the welfare of the kids—too much and that's just abstract—we don't really agree about anything. . . . At different times we take opposite sides—not deliberately; it just comes out that way.
>
> Now these fights get pretty damned colorful. You called them arguments a little while ago—I have to correct you—they're brawls. There's never a bit of physical violence—at least not directed to each other—but the verbal gunfire gets pretty thick. Why, we've said things to each other that neither of us would think of saying in the hearing of anybody else. . . .
>
> Of course we don't settle any of the issues. It's sort of a matter of principle *not* to. Because somebody would have to give in then and lose face for the next encounter. . . .
>
> When I tell you this in this way, I feel a little foolish about it. I wouldn't tolerate such a condition in any other relationship in my life—and yet here I do and always have. . . .
>
> No—we never have considered a divorce or separation or anything so clear-cut. I realize that other people do, and I can't say that it has never occurred to either of us, but we've never considered it seriously.
>
> A number of times, there has been a crisis, like the time I was in the automobile accident, and the time she almost died in childbirth, and then I guess we really showed that we do care about each other. But as soon as the crisis is over, it's business as usual.

There is a subtle valence in these conflict-habituated relationships. It is easily missed in casual observation. So central is the necessity for channeling conflict and bridling hostility that these considerations come to preoccupy much of the interaction. Some psychiatrists have gone so far as to suggest that it is precisely the deep need to do psychological battle with one another which constitutes the cohesive factor insuring continuity of the marriage. Possibly so. But even from a surface point of view, the overt and manifest fact of habituated attention to handling tension, keeping it chained, and concealing it, is clearly seen as a dominant life force. And it can, and does for some, last for a whole lifetime.

The Devitalized

The key to the devitalized mode is the clear discrepancy between middle-aged reality and earlier years. These people usually characterized themselves as having been "deeply in love" during the early years, as having spent a great deal of time together, having enjoyed sex, and, most importantly of all, having had a close identification with one another. The present picture, with some variation from case to case, is in clear contrast—little time is spent together, sexual relationships are far less satisfying qualitatively or quantitatively, and interests and activities are not shared, at least not in the deeper and meaningful way they once were. Most of their time together now is "duty time"—entertaining together, planning and sharing activities with children, and participating in various kinds of required community responsibilities. They do as a rule retain, in addition to a genuine and mutual interest in the welfare of their children, a shared attention to their joint property and the husband's career. But even in the latter case the interest is contrasting. Despite a common dependency on his success and the benefits which flow therefrom, there is typically very little sharing of the intrinsic aspects of career—simply an acknowledgment of their mutual dependency on the fruits.

Two rather distinct subtypes of the devitalized take shape by the middle years. The following reflections of two housewives in their late forties illustrate both the common and the distinguishing features:

> Judging by the way it was when we were first married—say the first five years or so—things are pretty matter-of-fact now—even dull. They're dull between us, I mean. The children are a lot of fun, keep us pretty busy, and there are lots of outside things—you know, like Little League and the P.T.A. and the Swim Club, and even the company parties aren't always so bad. But I mean where Bob and I are concerned—if you followed us around, you'd wonder why we ever got *married*. We take each other for granted. We laugh at the same things sometimes, but we don't really laugh together—the way we used to. But, as he said to me the other night—with one or two under the belt, I think—"You know, you're still a little fun now and then." . . .
>
> Now, I don't say this to complain, not in the least. There's a cycle to life. There are things you do in high school. And different things you do in college. Then you're a young adult. And then you're middle-aged. That's where we are now. . . . I'll admit that I do yearn for the old days when sex was a big thing and going out was fun and I hung on to everything he said about his work and his ideas as if they were coming from a genius or something. But then you get the children and other responsibilities. I have the home and Bob has a tremendous burden of responsibility at the office. . . . He's completely responsible for

> setting up the new branch now. . . . You have to adjust to these things and we both try to gracefully. . . . Anniversaries though do remind you kind of hard. . . .

The other kind of hindsight from a woman in a devitalized relationship is much less accepting and quiescent:

> I know I'm fighting it. I ought to accept that it has to be like this, but I don't like it, and I'd do almost anything to bring back the exciting way of living we had at first. Most of my friends think I'm some sort of a sentimental romantic or something—they tell me to act my age—but I do know some people—not very darn many—who are our age and even older, who still have the same kind of excitement about them and each other that we had when we were all in college. I've seen some of them at parties and other places—the way they look at each other, the little touches as they go by. One couple has grandchildren and you'd think they were honeymooners. I don't think it's just sex either—I think they are just part of each other's lives—and then when I think of us and the numb way we sort of stagger through the weekly routine, I could scream. And I've even thought of doing some pretty desperate things to try to build some joy and excitement into my life. I've given up on Phil. He's too content with his balance sheets and the kids' report cards and the new house we're going to build next year. He keeps saying he has everything in life that any man could want. What do you *do?*

Regardless of the gracefulness of the acceptance, or the lack thereof, the common plight prevails: on the subjective, emotional dimension, the relationship has become a void. The original zest is gone. There is typically little overt tension or conflict, but the interplay between the pair has become apathetic, lifeless. No serious threat to the continuity of the marriage is generally acknowledged, however. It is intended, usually by both, that it continue indefinitely despite its numbness. Continuity and relative freedom from open conflict are fostered in part because of the comforts of the "habit cage." Continuity is further insured by the absence of any engaging alternative, "all things considered." It is also reinforced, sometimes rather decisively, by legal and ecclesiastical requirements and expectations. These people quickly explain that "there are other things in life" which are worthy of sustained human effort.

This kind of relationship is exceedingly common. Persons in this circumstance frequently make comparisons with other pairs they know, many of whom are similar to themselves. This fosters the comforting judgment that "marriage is like this—except for a few oddballs or pretenders who claim otherwise."

While these relationships lack visible vitality, the participants assure us that there is "something there." There are occasional periods of sharing at least somethng—if only memory. Even formalities can have meanings. Anniversaries can be celebrated, if a little grimly, for what they once commemorated. As one man said, "Tomorrow we are celebrating the anniversary of our anniversary." Even clearly substandard sexual expression is said by some to be better than nothing, or better than a clandestine substitute. "A good man" or a "good mother for the kids" may "with a little affection and occasional attention now and then, get you by." Many believe that the devitalized mode is the appropriate mode in which a man and woman should be content to live in the middle years and later.

The Passive-Congenial

The passive-congenial mode has a great deal in common with the devitalized, the essential difference being that the passivity which pervades the association has been there from the start. The devitalized have a more exciting set of memories; the passive-congenials give little evidence that they had ever hoped for anything much different from what they are currently experiencing.

There is therefore little suggestion of disillusionment or compulsion to make believe to anyone. Existing modes of association are comfortably adequate—no stronger words fit the facts as they related them to us. There is little conflict, although some admit that they tiptoe rather gingerly over and around a residue of subtle resentments and frustrations. In their better moods they remind themselves (and each other) that "there are many common interests" which they both enjoy. "We both like classical music." "We agree completely on religious and political matters." "We both love the country and our quaint exurban neighbors." "We are both lawyers."

The wife of a prominent attorney, who has been living in the passive-congenial mode for thirty years, put her description this way:

> We have both always tried to be calm and sensible about major life decisions, to think things out thoroughly and in perspective. Len and I knew each other since high school but didn't start to date until college. When he asked me to marry him, I took a long time to decide whether he was the right man for me and I went into his family background, because I wasn't just marrying him; I was choosing a father for my children. We decided together not to get married until he was established, so that we would not have to live in dingy little apartments like some of our friends who got married right out of college. This prudence has stood us in good stead too. Life has moved ahead for us with remarkable orderliness and we are deeply grateful for the foresight we had. . . .
>
> When the children were little, we scheduled time together with them, although since they're grown, the demands of the office are getting pretty heavy. Len brings home a bulging briefcase almost every night and more often than not the light is still on in his study after I retire. But we've got a lot to show for his devoted effort. . . .
>
> I don't like all this discussion about sex—even in the better magazines. I hope your study will help to put it in its proper perspective. I expected to perform sex in marriage, but both before and since, I'm willing to admit that it's a much overrated activity. Now and then, perhaps it's better. I am fortunate, I guess, because my husband has never been demanding about it, before marriage or since. It's just not that important to either of us. . . .
>
> My time is very full these days, with the chairmanship of the Cancer Drive, and the Executive Board of the (state) P.T.A. I feel a little funny about that with my children already grown, but there are the grandchildren coming along. And besides so many of my friends are in the organizations, and it's so much like a home-coming.

People make their way into the passive-congenial mode by two quite different routes—by default and by intention. Perhaps in most instances they arrive at this way of living and feeling by drift. There is so little which they have cared about deeply in each other that a passive-congenial mode is a deliberately intended arrangement for two people whose interests and creative energies are directed elsewhere than toward the pairing—into careers, or in the case of women, into children or community activities. They say they know this and want it this way. These people simply do not wish to invest their total emotional involvement and creative effort in the male-female relationship.

The passive-congenial life style fits societal needs quite well also, and this is an important consideration. The man of practical affairs, in business, government service, or the professions—quite obviously needs "to have things peaceful at home" and to have a minimum of distraction as he pursues his important work. He may feel both love and gratitude toward the wife who fits this mode.

A strong case was made for the passive-congenial by a dedicated physician:

> I don't know why everyone seems to make so much about men and women and marriage. Of course, I'm married and if anything happened to my wife, I'd get married again. I think it's the proper way to live. It's convenient, orderly, and solves a lot of problems. But there are other things in life. I spent nearly ten years preparing for the practice of my profession. The biggest thing to me is the practice of that profession, to be of assistance to my patients and their families. I spend twelve hours a day at it. And I'll bet if you talked with my wife, you wouldn't get any of that "trapped housewife" stuff from her either. Now that the children are grown, she finds a lot of useful and necessary work to do in this community. She works as hard as I do.

The passive-congenial mode facilitates the achievement of other goals too. It enables people who desire a considerable amount of personal independence and freedom to realize it with a minimum of inconvenience from or to the spouse. And it certainly spares the participants in it from the need to give a great deal of personal attention to "adjusting to the spouse's needs." The passive-congenial menage is thus a mood as well as a mode.

Our descriptions of the devitalized and the passive-congenials have been similar because these two modes are much alike in their overt characteristics. The participants' evaluations of their *present situations* are likewise largely the same—the accent on "other things," the emphasis on civic and professional responsibilities; the importance of property, children, and reputation. The essential difference lies in their diverse histories and often in their feelings of contentment with their current lives. The passive-congenials had from the start a life pattern and a set of expectations essentially consistent with what they are now experiencing. When the devitalized reflect, however, when they juxtapose history against present reality, they often see the barren gullies in their lives left by the erosions of earlier satisfactions. Some of the devitalized are resentful and disillusioned; others, calling themselves "mature about it," have emerged with reasonable acceptance of their existing devitalized modes. Still others are clearly ambivalent, "I wish life would be more exciting, but I should have known it couldn't last. In a way, it's calm and quiet and reassuring this way, but there are times when I get very ill at ease—sometimes downright mad. Does it *have* to be like this?"

The passive-congenials do not find it necessary to speculate in this fashion. Their anticipations were realistic and perhaps even causative of their current marital situation. In any event, their passivity is not jarred when teased by memory.

The Vital

In extreme contrast to the three foregoing is the vital relationship. The vital pair can easily be overlooked as they move through their worlds of work, recreation, and family activities. They do the same things, publicly at least; and when talking for public consumption say the same things—they are proud of their homes, love their children, gripe about their jobs, while being quite proud of their career accomplishments. But when the close, intimate, confidential, empathic look is taken, the essence of the vital relationship becomes clear: the mates are intensely bound together psychologically in important life matters. Their sharing and their togetherness is genuine. It provides the life essence for both man and woman.

> The things we do together aren't fun intrinsically—the ecstasy comes from being *together in the doing*. Take her out of the picture and I wouldn't give a damn for the boat, the lake, or any of the fun that goes on out there.

The presence of the mate is indispensable to the feelings of satisfaction which the activity provides. The activities shared by the vital pairs may involve almost anything: hobbies, careers, community service. Anything—so long as it is closely shared.

It is hard to escape the word *vitality*—exciting mutuality of feelings and participation together in important life segments. The clue that the relationship is vital (rather than merely expressing the joint activity) derives from the feeling that it is important. An activity is flat and uninteresting if the spouse is not a part of it.

Other valued things are readily sacrificed in order to enhance life within the vital relationship.

> I cheerfully, and that's putting it mildly, passed up two good promotions, because one of them would have required some traveling and the other would have taken evening and weekend time—and that's when Pat and I *live*. The hours with her (after twenty-two years of marriage) are what I live for. You should meet her. . . .

People in the vital relationship for the most part know that they are a minority and that their life styles are incomprehensible to most of their associates.

> Most of our friends think we moved out to the country for the kids; well—the kids *are* crazy about it, but the fact of the matter is, we moved out for ourselves—

just to get away from all the annoyances and interferences of other people—our friends actually. We like this kind of life—where we can have almost all of our time together. . . . We've been married for over twenty years and the most enjoyable thing either of us does—well, outside of the intimate things—is to sit and talk by the hour. That's why we built that imposing fireplace—and the hi-fi here in the corner. . . . Now that Ed is getting older, that twenty-seven-mile drive morning and night from the office is a real burden, but he does it cheerfully so we can have our long uninterrupted hours together. . . . The children respect this too. They don't invade our privacy any more than they can help—the same as we vacate the living room when Ellen brings in a date, she tries not to intrude on us. . . . Being the specialized kind of lawyer he is, I can't share much in his work, but that doesn't bother either of us. The *big* part of our lives is completely mutual. . . .

Her husband's testimony validated hers. And we talked to dozens of other couples like them, too. They find their central satisfaction in the life they live with and through each other. It consumes their interest and dominates their thoughts and actions. All else is subordinate and secondary.

This does not mean that people in vital relationships lose their separate identities, that they may not upon occasion be rivalrous or competitive with one another or that conflict may not occur. They differ fundamentally from the conflict-habituated, however, in that when conflict does occur, it results from matters that are important to them, such as which college a daughter or son is to attend; it is devoid of the trivial "who said what first and when" and "I can't forget when you. . . ." A further difference is that people to whom the relationship is vital tend to settle disagreements quickly and seek to avoid conflict, whereas the conflict-habituated look forward to conflict and appear to operate by a tacit rule that no conflict is ever to be truly terminated and that the spouse must never be considered right. The two kinds of conflict are thus radically different. To confuse them is to miss an important differentiation.

The Total

The total relationship is like the vital relationship with the important addition that it is more multifaceted. The points of vital meshing are more numerous—in some cases all of the important life foci are vitally shared. In one such marriage the husband is an internationally known scientist. For thirty years his wife has been "his friend, mistress, and partner." He still goes home at noon whenever possible, at considerable inconvenience, to have a quiet lunch and spend a conversational hour or so with his wife. They refer to these conversations as "our little seminars." They feel comfortable with each other and with their four grown children. The children (now in their late twenties) say that they enjoy visits with their parents as much as they do with friends of their own age.

There is practically no pretense between persons in the total relationship or between them and the world outside. There are few areas of tension, because the items of difference which have arisen over the years have been settled as they arose. There often *were* serious differences of opinion but they were handled, sometimes by compromise, sometimes by one or the other yielding; but these outcomes were of secondary importance because the primary consideration was not who was right or who was wrong, only how the problem could be resolved without tarnishing the relationship. When faced with differences, they can and do dispose of the difficulties without losing their feeling of unity or their sense of vitality and centrality of their relationship. This is the mainspring.

The various parts of the total relationship are reinforcing, as we learned from this consulting engineer who is frequently sent abroad by his corporation.

> She keeps my files and scrapbooks up to date. . . . I invariably take her with me to conferences around the world. Her femininity, easy charm and wit are invaluable assets to me. I know it's conventional to say that a man's wife is responsible for his success and I also know that it's often not true. But in my case I gladly acknowledge that it's not only true, but she's indispensable to me. But she'd go along with me even if there was nothing for her to do because we just enjoy each other's company—deeply. You know, the best part of a vacation is not *what* we do, but that we do it together. We plan it and reminisce about it and weave it into our work and other play all the time.

The wife's account is substantially the same except that her testimony demonstrates more clearly the genuineness of her "help."

> It seems to me that Bert exaggerates my help. It's not so much that I only want to help him; it's more that I want to do those things anyway. We do them together, even though we may not be in each other's presence at the time. I don't really know what I do for him and what I do for me.

This kind of relationship is rare, in marriage or out, but it does exist and can endure. We occasionally found relationships so total that all aspects of life were mutually shared and enthusiastically participated in. It is as if neither spouse has, or has had, a truly private existence.

The customary purpose of a classification such as this one is to facilitate understanding of similarities and differences among the cases classified. In this instance enduring marriage is the common condition. The differentiating features are the dissimilar forces which make for the integration of the pair within each of the types. It is not necessarily the purpose of a classification to make possible a clear-cut sorting of all cases into one or another of the designated categories. All cannot be so precisely pigeon-holed; there often are borderline cases. Furthermore, two observers with equal access to the facts may sometimes disagree on which side of the line an unclear case should be placed. If the classification is a useful one, however, placement should *as a rule* be clear and relatively easy. The case is only relative because making an accurate classification of a given relationship requires the possession of amounts and kinds of information which one rarely has about persons other than himself. Superficial knowledge of public or professional behavior is not enough. And even in his own case, one may, for reasons of ego, find it difficult to be totally forthright.

A further caution. The typology concerns relationships, not personalities. A clearly vital person may be living in a passive-congenial or devitalized relationship and expressing his vitality in some other aspect of life—career being an important preoccupation for many. Or, possibly either or both of the spouses may have a vital relationship—sometimes extending over many years—with someone of the opposite sex outside of the marriage.

Nor are the five types to be interpreted as *degrees* of marital happiness or adjustment. Persons in all five are currently adjusted and most say that they are content, if not happy. Rather, the five types represent *different kinds of adjustment* and *different conceptions of marriage*. This is an important concept which must be emphasized if one is to understand the personal meanings which these people attach to the conditions of their marital experience.

Neither are the five types necessarily stages in a cycle of initial bliss and later disillusionment. Many pairings started in the passive-congenial stage; in fact, quite often people intentionally enter into a marriage for the acknowledged purpose of living this kind of relationship. To many the simple amenities of the "habit cage" are not disillusionments or even disappointments, but rather are sensible life expectations which provide an altogether comfortable and rational way of having a "home base" for their lives. And many of the conflict-habituated told of courtship histories essentially like their marriages.

While each of these types tends to persist, there *may* be movement from one type to another as circumstances and life perspectives change. This movement may go in any direction from any point, and a given couple may change categories more than once. Such changes are relatively *in*frequent however, and the important point is that relationship types tend to persist over relatively long periods.

The fundamental nature of these contexts may be illustrated by examining the impact of some common conditions on persons of each type.

Infidelity, for example, occurs in most of the five types, the total relationship being the exception. But it occurs for quite different reasons. In the conflict-habituated it seems frequently to be only another outlet for hostility. The call girl and the woman picked up in a bar are more than just available women; they are symbols of resentment of the wife. This is not always so, but reported to us often enough to be worth noting. Infidelity among the passive-congenial, on the other hand, is typically in line with the stereotype of the middle-aged man who "strays out of sheer boredom with the uneventful, deadly prose" of his private life. And the devitalized man or woman frequently is trying for an hour or a year to recapture the lost mood. But the vital are sometimes adulterous too; some are simply emancipated—almost bohemian. To some of them sexual aggrandizement is an accepted fact of life. Frequently, the infidelity is condoned by the partner and in some instances even provides an indirect (through empathy) kind of gratification. The act of infidelity in such cases is not construed as disloyalty or as a threat to continuity, but rather as a kind of basic human right which the loved one ought to be permitted to have—and which the other perhaps wants also for himself.

Divorce and separation are found in all five of the types, but the reasons, when viewed realistically and outside of the simplitudes of legalistic and ecclesiastical fiction, are highly individual and highly variable. For example, a couple may move from a vital relationship to divorce because for them the alternative of a devitalized relationship is unendurable. They can conceive of marriage only as a vital, meaningful, fulfilling, and preoccupying interaction. The "disvitality" of any other marriage form is abhorrent to them and takes on "the hypocrisy of living a public lie." We have accounts of marriages which were unquestionably vital or total for a period of years but which were dissolved. In some respects relationships of this type are more readily disrupted, because these people have become adjusted to such a rich and deep sharing that evidences of breach, which a person in another type of marriage might consider quite normal, become unbearable.

> I know a lot of close friendships occur between men and women married to someone else, and that they're not always adulterous. But I know Betty—and anyhow, I personally believe they eventually do become so, but I can't be sure about that. Anyway, when Betty found her self-expression was furthered by longer and longer meetings and conversations with Joe, and I detected little insincerities, not serious at first, you understand, creeping into the things we did together, it was like the little leak in the great dike. It didn't take very long. We weren't melodramatic about it, but it was soon clear to both of us that we were no longer the kind of pair we once were, so why pretend. The whole thing can go to hell fast—and after almost twenty years!

Husbands in other types of relationships would probably not even have detected any disloyalty on the part of the wife. And even if they had, they would tend to conclude that "you don't break up a home just because she has a passing interest in some glamourous writer."

The divorce which occurs in the passive-congenial marriage follows a different sequence. One of the couple, typically a person capable of more vitality in his or her married life than the existing relationship provides, comes into contact with a person with whom he gradually (or suddenly) unfolds a new dimension to adult living. What he had considered to be a rational and sensible and "adult" relationship can suddenly appear in contrast to be stultifying, shallow, and an altogether disheartening way to live out the remaining years. He is left with "no conceivable alternative but to move out." Typically, he does not do so impulsively or without a more or less stubborn attempt to stifle his "romanticism" and listen to well-documented advice to the effect that he should act maturely and "leave the romantic yearning to the kids for whom it is intended." Very often he is convinced and turns his back on his "new hope"—but not always.

Whether examining marriages for the satisfactions and fulfillments they have brought or for the frustrations and pain, the overriding influence of life style—or as we have here called it, relationship type—is of the essence. Such a viewpoint helps the observer, and probably the participant, to understand some of the apparent enigmas about men and women in marriage—why infidelities destroy some marriages and not others; why conflict plays so large a role for some couples and is so negligible for others; why some seemingly well-suited and harmoniously adjusted spouses seek divorce while others with provocations galore remain solidly together; why affections, sexual expression, recreation, almost everything observable about men and women is so radically different from pair to pair. All of these are not merely different objectively; they are perceived differently by the pairs, are differently reacted to, and differently attended to.

If nothing else, this chapter has demonstrated that realistic understanding of marital relationships requires use of concepts which are carefully based on perceptive factual knowledge. Unfortunately, the language by which relationships between men and women are conventionally expressed tends to lead toward serious and pervasive deceptions which in turn encourage erroneous inferences. Thus, we tend to assume that enduring marriage is somehow synonymous with happy marriage or at least with something comfortably called adjustment. The deception springs from lumping together such dissimilar modes of thought and action as the conflict-habituated, the passive-congenial, and the vital. To know that a marriage has endured, or for that matter has been dissolved, tells one close to nothing about the kinds of experiences, fulfillments, and frustrations which have made up the lives of the people involved. Even to know, for example, that infidelity has occurred, without knowledge of circumstances, feelings, and other essences, results in an illusion of knowledge which masks far more than it describes.

To understand a given marriage, let alone what is called "marriage in general," is realistically possible only in terms of particular sets of experiences, meanings, hopes, and intentions. This chapter has described in broad outline five manifest and recurring configurations among the Significant Americans.

More Equal Than Others:
Women and Men in Dual-Career Marriages

Rosanna Hertz

In contrast to the myth and hyperbole surrounding the "modern couple," this study has attempted to analyze the opportunities and constraints faced by the dual-career marriage and family, stressing the relationship between work, family, and gender as a way to emphasize the reciprocity between *autonomy* and *contingency* for individuals, couples, and social classes. The marriage of two careers and incomes has bought a measure of autonomy for these couples and for the individuals involved. As a couple, they can pursue a lifestyle unprecedented for anyone but the rich; as individuals, they are less subject to the vagaries of a single source of income, less dependent on the success of one career. Yet the existence of the dual-career marriage and family is contingent on the availability of career positions, outside labor to perform household and childcare chores, and, perhaps most important, the capacity of couples to adapt themselves to competing employer demands. These couples experience the interplay between autonomy and contingency as a series of difficult choices.

This study also offers an important insight about how ideologies are shaped by changes in social structures and institutions. The dual-career couples in this study have not consciously chosen a new relationship or family form because of some revolutionary shift in their beliefs or attitudes toward the family or male-female relationships. Rather, their pursuit of career success, financial well-being, and self-sufficiency is an attempt to play out their (and their parents') version of the American dream. Having graduated from college into the era of women's liberation, the women in this study are more aware of the available possibilities. Likewise, the men were not unaffected by the women's movement. But such possibilities had to materialize in the form of careers for women—careers that were an intersection of feminism and the American dream. It was the possibility of achievement and independence rather than the desire to make a political statement that pushed these women to have careers.

Once married, two-career couples must come to grips with both the externally imposed demands of the organizations that employ them and the lack of an appropriate ideology to guide them in creating marital relationships. The ideology of the traditional family simply does not work—the wife cannot stay home and do the housework. But it is not political (feminist) ideology that leads these couples to construct new marriages or new approaches to marital roles; instead, their employers' demands and their own desires for individual and combined career success lead them toward these changes. The ideology of equality, particularly in marital roles, emerges out of common opportunities and constraints, not out of a prior commitment to a feminist philosophy.

This point is crucial. It is a common misunderstanding that all one needs to do is wish or want another way of life and that somehow marriages, family, work, or even politics will be altered by our dreams and desires. This study demonstrates that these lifestyle "pioneers" did nothing of the sort; they reconstructed family forms not because they desired to blaze new social trails but because the constraints of work and the value placed on success altered the practices of their daily lives. Once established, these practices give rise to new ideologies of marriage and the family.

This article begins with a clarification of the class and family context in which the dual-career couple must be understood, draws together major findings about dual-career couples, offers suggestions for future research, and concludes by focusing on the implications that merging two careers has for the future of the marital bond.

Class and Family Structure

To most outside observers, the couples in this study would probably appear "successful." They all have careers and seem destined to occupy increasingly privileged positions. As individuals and as families, they rank near the top of the income pyramid. Each couple has, to this point at least, navigated the choppy waters of a two-career marriage and maintained a viable relationship. Some have even managed to integrate careers, marriage, and children.

Yet, the term *successful* is misleading because it implies the existence of an ideal situation or ideal type against which marriages can and should be measured. If high incomes, high-status jobs, and durable marriages are the ideal, then these couples would probably be judged as successful. However, if other criteria—such as a strong commitment to home life and traditional marital relations—are valued, then it is not clear that the dual-career couples of this study would be judged so favorably. Success is a subjective valuation, and this subjectivity affects both the criteria used and the applicability of the term to different situations. If, as many sociologists have argued, objective factors (such as one's income, gender, race, or family background) affect the evaluative frame one adopts (what one values or devalues), then it is conceivable that for some readers these couples are far from successful. These cautionary statements are intended to suggest that for people in categorically different situations (for example, different social classes), what is considered successful might often be tempered by what is possible. These couples are successful in integrating careers and marriage and in questioning traditional gender roles largely because it has been possible for them to do so; such opportunities may be unattainable for others.

These distinctions are more than just semantic points. Work, family, and gender roles, far from being independent of one another, are interactive and mutually determining. Because these dual-career couples occupy social and organizational positions that carry with them high earnings and continued upward mobility, they are set apart from other categories of families. These social and monetary advantages allow, although they do not require, differences in family organization and gender roles, in comparison to other families. Money may make a difference in the way families are organized and in the social relations between husbands and wives, but the structure of work and occupations and the economy in general are responsible for the differential distribution of money and wealth.

Compare, for instance, the experiences of these upper-middle-class dual-career couples with those of the working-class couples interviewed by Rubin (1976).[1] The "worlds of pain" that working-class couples experience contrast dramatically with the world experienced by dual-career couples. Desiring release from conflict and tension in their parents' home, young working-class men and women attempt to gain independence by rebelling, having early sexual experiences, and establishing their own individual lifestyles. Yet, as Rubin shows, the flight from parental restriction and economic dependence often leads to other and more oppressive bonds: a lack of sexual experience (particularly for women) and early pregnancy channel many young couples into marriage and parenthood. Early family responsibilities, combined with inadequate formal education, yoke working-class husbands into lower-status, dead-end jobs; working-class wives are saddled with children, and, because of their lack of skills, have extremely limited opportunities for continued education or subsequent investment in work-related skills. Men can struggle to improve their family's economic lot; but cyclical unemployment, tiring work, and organizational barriers to white-collar work create an iron curtain that prevents escape from the working class.

The result, as Rubin argues and the couples themselves describe, is a situation in which the family becomes a social and psychological pressure cooker. Husbands, seemingly blocked at every turn in their struggle to fulfill the American dream, become angry and frustrated and blame themselves; in some cases, they turn to alcohol and abuse their wives and children. Wives, living with financial insecurity and their husbands' anger and frustration, respond with anger and

---

[1]Rubin's study, intended to document and explain the struggles of working-class families, was built on an explicit comparison with the life experiences and values of middle-class managerial and professional families, arguing that a family's class position largely determined its economic resources and opportunities and, by extension, the relations between husbands and wives. However, two factors impeded the class-based comparison. First, data on the two classes of families were uneven. Although neither group was randomly selected, far more detail was presented on working-class families, whereas middle-class families tended to be depicted in broader terms. Thus, a systematic comparison could not be constructed, and class-based explanations of differences were less convincing than they might have been. Second, a conceptual framework for understanding social stratification by class was lacking. Conceptualizing the connection between class and family structure is by no means an easy undertaking, largely because the connection is indirect. . . . Rarely are the relations among classes of families direct—even when one employs or purchases the labor of another—in the same sense that there is no immediate, tangible connection between rich and poor neighborhoods. Thus, in Rubin's analysis, the "worlds of pain" in which working-class couples live are not produced by middle-class couples; yet these couples are connected by their relation to an underlying economic system that creates them both.

frustration of their own, often venting their feelings on husbands and children. Children simply experience a repeat of their parents' early years and adolescence.

Although some came from working-class families, the dual-career couples in this study were able to avoid early entrapment in marriage, children, and jobs. The time they spent at college provided sufficient opportunity to experiment (both sexually and intellectually) without the threat that such experiments would turn into inescapable obligations. Their diplomas, social networks, and college work experience opened doors to a broader set of possibilities than existed for their working-class counterparts. Their work demanded commitment and responsibility, but then rewarded these efforts with higher income, security, and opportunities for real advancement. The American dream . . . came quickly and in some instances unexpectedly.

It might be argued that dual-career couples have something working-class couples lack: motivation, ambition, or desire. But it would be a mistake to overlook the ways in which such "traits" are acquired: from parents whose resources made college possible; from instructors and peers who encouraged these individuals in college; from employers who offer enticements and incentives; and from their pleasurable lifestyle itself, which requires continued effort to sustain it. The women in this study offer the best evidence against using inherent motivation as an explanation for why some people get ahead and others do not. In describing their career beginnings, . . . many women claimed that they had no plans for careers while in college or, in some instances, after college. Careers "emerged" in various ways, primarily through labor market shifts but also through husbands' encouragement and, significantly, through the recognition by these women that they could do the work they saw others (men) doing.

These points are not intended to devalue motivation or the accomplishments of dual-career couples. Rather, they are intended to focus attention on the systematic differences in objective circumstances and possibilities that face people from different social classes. The advantages dual-career couples enjoy and build on do not result from their direct exploitation of working-class couples or the working-class wives who perform household and childcare chores. Instead, the class structure that results from the organization of the economy into owners and managers on the one hand and workers on the other creates two distinct groups in relation to household and childcare services: those who need the work done but do not have the time do it, and those who have little alternative but to do it for pay. Hiring labor is only one possibility that enables dual-career couples to save time. Yet, hiring the labor of working-class women tangibly creates a relationship that already exists at an underlying social structural level.

If family structure is understood within the context of class-stratified society, then a similar argument must be made concerning gender. Without recapitulating the extensive debates among feminists and leftist theoreticians on the relationship between gender and class inequalities, it is undeniable that the opportunity for women in this study to pursue careers is partially dependent on the availability of other women to work in the home. . . . As women often pointedly argued, . . . daycare workers are essential to maintaining the household; moreover, they make it possible for career women to organizationally and economically compete with men and at the same time strive for the personally and socially valued status of mother. Career women are making a rational set of choices in the face of organizational demands; they do not consider hiring labor to be exploitative. The issue is not that some women hire other women and thereby exploit them. (Indeed, the increasing number of career women and dual-career households have created a small boom in the employment market for unskilled labor.) Rather, the ability of dual-career couples to enjoy the privileges of careers is predicated on the availability of lower-paid household and childcare workers; that is, on a systematic and unequal distribution of advantages and disadvantages.

It is not inconceivable that other categories of families could achieve a measure of the equity between husbands and wives that I found among these dual-career couples. However, the structure of work and the opportunities available to those other families reduce the possibility that society-wide equality would result. For example, in a family situation where only the husband works outside the home, earns a modest income, and has little likelihood of significant increases in his earning power over time, the wife may be trapped in a situation in which her labor in the home is necessary simply to sustain the family as a viable unit. Such a division of labor would be experienced not as a conscious choice but instead as the product of an economic system that values a man's activity less than that of many others (such as managers) but more than the wife's. The subjective valuation of that division of labor reinforces the inequality between husband and wife and replicates the general system of economic inequality that has created a hierarchy of families.

The Marriage of Careers

The focused examination of a particular type of family—the dual-career family—has made it possible to consider the relationship of work, family, and gender roles against the backdrop of the broader system of class and economic inequality. Particular attention has been devoted to family organization and gender roles in situations where class is held constant; that is, whether more equal relations between husbands and wives, and between men and women in general, develop when partners in a marriage have relatively equal status and income. What follows here is a summary of the findings and implications of this study as they pertain to family gender roles.

Family

Middle-class notions of family self-sufficiency and autonomy are myths. Even with their financial resources, dual-career couples must purchase individual and institutional services in order to fulfill traditional family functions. The image of self-sufficiency masks the wide range of private exchanges between dual-career couples and other actors in the socioeconomic system on whom these couples depend. Because arrangements for these services are made privately, the myth of self-sufficiency is maintained. Conversely, the desire for such self-sufficiency directs the effort to fulfill these functions into the private sphere. The solutions these couples have implemented run counter to the feminist and Marxist visions of the consequences of women's entry into the labor force, namely, that women's participation would lead to demands for the communal satisfaction of domestic needs. Instead of demanding that private domestic needs be made public, these women have insisted on keeping domestic services private—partly because there are few collective services available and partly to perpetuate the image of self-sufficiency promised by sizeable income. In effect, they have brought the market into the home instead of taking the housework into the market.

Money does not buy self-sufficiency. On the contrary, money ties these people into the economic system in a different way than it does for those who have fewer resources. Dual-career couples trade time for money, and, instead of bartering their own labor with friends and relatives as lower-class families do, . . . they buy domestic services from strangers. Moreover, they are trapped into a system in which they require two incomes to make the purchases they desire. This system may be seen as a "treadmill of reproduction," analogous to Schnaiberg's . . . "treadmill of production." Their lifestyle has been inflated to the point where both incomes are necessary to maintain their way of life and to ensure the persistence of their high-level jobs.

Couples fully recognize the necessity of two incomes when they contemplate having children. The decisions to have children, when to have them, and how to care for them are the most difficult family issues these couples face. Rarely do other personal or family problems infringe on work demands to the extent that child-related issues do. Yet, corporate (and professional) career trajectories are still based on the assumption that there is one type of family—the traditional nuclear family. Even though the gender composition of the corporate work force has changed, the demands and structure of careers within these firms have remained relatively static. Thus, career women postpone childbearing until they have been promoted to higher ranks in their firms. There is little evidence that women who want to have children make it in the corporate world; those who have children prior to critical career promotions are often later denied these promotions. The heavy career investment these women must make early in their work lives leads to the postponement of children, and thus they do not combine working with childbearing in the early stages of their careers. Therefore, employers share responsibility for, yet are unresponsive to, the timing of the birth of children to the women they employ. Further, the corporate environment prevents women from voicing collective concerns and demands by making individual deals and special arrangements with the few women who are seen as indispensable to the organization.

Pushed into a corner by their career demands and desire to succeed, these couples (and women in particular) face anxieties for which few social scientists have ready responses. Two concerns are paramount for these couples. First, the timing of children causes couples to worry about how to synchronize biological and career clocks. There are no convenient pauses in either timeframe, and as couples seek to establish their careers, time threatens to run out.[2] The second concern is for the potential long-term consequences for children of the dual-career family environment. . . . [C]ouples hinted at their fear that their children will lack nurturance—social and psychological—when both parents are away from home all day, and sometimes into the night. These fears have caused many couples to use what is popularly called "quality time" with their children as a way to salve their consciences and as a response to a society that tends to be unfavorably predisposed against surrogate childcare. Without definitive clinical or scientific evidence about the effects of parental absence from the home, anxieties grow, and couples seek individual solutions rather than making demands on employers for more time with their families.

When these couples bring other individuals into the nuclear family for childcare and housekeeping, there are important though unintended consequences. Fictive kin ties are created, even if the relationships are expected to exist only for short periods of time. For example, many couples found themselves involved in the personal and family lives of people they hired and sometimes helped solve problems for these people—lending money, finding housing, helping with bureaucratic intricacies, and socializing with employees' relatives—largely out of a vested interest in keeping their hired help. Regardless of motive, however, this effort involved these couples in new and unanticipated networks.

A final point concerning family focuses on the issue of stability. Middle-class and upper-middle-class one-career families employed by corporations in past decades have achieved economic stability at the expense of geographic stability. This is not the case for these dual-career couples, who have remained geographically rooted in the Chicago area. Chicago is a major corporate city in which two careers can thrive without repeated geographic disruption. But more important than Chicago's career opportunities is the dual-earner character of these marriages. Spouses are not forced to relocate at the whim of their employing firm; instead, they have more freedom to switch careers and to be more selective about career moves because the other spouse's career acts as a backstop. The conjoining

---

[2]A related issue involves the potential burden faced by children whose parents are approaching retirement. Couples who have their first child in their mid- to late thirties could eventually prove a financial or emotional burden later in life, just as their children are embarking on their own careers. This issue clearly deserves further research.

of two careers in one marriage enhances the likelihood of geographic stability for this group.

Gender Roles

Interviews conducted for this study strongly suggest that concerns about equity between husbands and wives rarely precede the construction of the dual-career marriage. The practice of combining two careers rather than the adherence to a nonsexist ideology informs change. In this respect work is the leading factor shaping the domestic sector. Two careers shape the career marriage, but at some point the career marriage may begin to impinge on the two individual careers and in turn shape them. In the process, gender roles can be altered.

Although work creates external pressure for equality between spouses, there is no guarantee that equity within the home will result from career equity. I have highlighted two aspects of this problem: the type of budgets that couples implement, and the differing values attached to fathering versus mothering roles. A large income does make a difference in husband-wife relations. How that money is conceptualized and used by the couple, however, continues to play a crucial role in power relations between husbands and wives. Equity and equal salaries alone cannot change relations between spouses.

The division of labor in the home is transformed simply because equal work demands are made on husbands and wives. However, until the status of housework is elevated or, more important, until fathering acquires an equivalent normative meaning for men, women will continue to be responsible for childrearing (and to feel the corresponding guilt over working, something husbands do not share). Rarely did fathers in these couples talk about fathering as important to them; however, the women placed great importance on mothering as something they *should* provide. Therefore, an asymmetry still exists between husbands and wives in terms of parenting, further reinforced by a cultural ideology and social norms that applaud women for having careers, yet react with horror when mothers continue to work while their children are young. . . .

Because the existence of more high-powered careers for women is relatively recent, women are more likely to be glad they have a career than to push for compensation equal to their male co-workers'. Some women even believe that they must work harder to prove their commitment to their employers, and how they handle maternity leaves can become a "test of manhood." For the immediate future, these women look for equity in a more immediate environment—at home, with their husbands. The problems of equity between men and women in general are more distant and much more amorphous. Thus, the problems of sexual politics are still being staged behind closed doors. It is ironic that in order for gender differences to *significantly* decline, there must be relative equity in incomes and in work between husbands and wives.

Corporate Employers: The Silent Partners

This study has emphasized how the partners in dual-career couples negotiate, bargain, trade, and occasionally battle with each other in an effort to shape work, marriage, and children into a complex but livable arrangement. Couples are required to make these adjustments because, with few exceptions, employers have not felt compelled to respond to the new phenomenon of dual-career marriage. At this point most positive responses by employers have been exceptions to the rule (such as special dispensations for pregnant female executives). Negative corporate responses, which are often continuations of out-of-date restrictive policies, are such that they "prevent" the corporation from having to respond to changed circumstances (such as the decision to have no maternity leave policy). Corporations define these matters as nonissues or nonproblematic. . . . Even less direct challenges to corporate policy—such as refusals to relocate as part of a dual-career strategy—have not been dealt with systematically by most employers. In the experiences of the respondents in this study, such refusals are commonly treated either as momentary indiscretions (which can be overlooked by a compassionate boss) or as signals that the employee in question is not as "serious" as his or her co-workers. And, as many people in this study stated, they will go to great lengths to keep their jobs, even if there is a price for having children or a spouse with a career. In short, corporations treat these matters as private troubles rather than as social issues. . . .

Corporate employers have been and still remain the silent (and relatively intransigent) partners in the dual-career marriage. But the deals they strike with their employees are not intended to promote dual-career marriage, only to condone it if it is necessary to satisfy a given valued employee. Thus, it is left to the couple to accommodate the contradictions, pressures, and dissatisfactions of the corporate world and to build a wall around themselves in order to survive the double demands made on them by their employers. The result, ironically, is these couples' increased emphasis on the marriage as a third career. But this career must buffer the couple from outside pressures *and* act as a selective membrane that allows only part of the world to permeate into the home environnment.

The Future of Dual-Career Marriage

In view of the complex struggles in which these couples engage—with each other as well as with employers, children, relatives, and employees—it is remarkable that dual-career marriages even exist. But do they have a future? This study in itself cannot adequately answer this question; only intact couples were interviewed, and only past and current experiences could be analyzed. However, several findings can be put together to generate some hypotheses for future research.

In contrast to the normative model of the traditional marriage, the majority of couples in this study did not base a family division of labor on separate spheres of activity and experience. The traditional role of bread-winner and, by extension, husband is shared by both men and women. Neither can claim that status solely, by virtue of equivalent career demands, and neither can be relegated to the position of nonproductive spouse. Thus, the traditional implicit exchange between husbands and wives—he supports the family economically and in exchange she maintains the home—is abrogated. The couples in this study demonstrate that an independent income brings to the surface questions of equity and symmetry that are largely unheard of and often actively discouraged in the traditional family. The keeping of separate financial accounts makes the equity issue more visible. Husbands can no longer legitimate their authority over financial and political matters on the basis of their greater experience with or knowledge of the outside world. In dual-career marriages, both partners have intimate knowledge of that world.

Following the logic of the traditional model, the dual-career marriage has no future. Aside from the stresses of two careers, the disruption of the traditional exchange between husbands and wives and the radical break with a "complementarity of roles" . . . should be enough to subject the marriage to unbearable pressures. When the function of the wife as provider of childcare and early childhood socialization is diminished as substantially as it is in the families interviewed here, then the fate of the dual-career marriage would seem bleak.[3]

I propose an alternative hypothesis. Rather than assuming that the traditional material exchange between husbands and wives is a necessary element of marital longevity, we might posit that the dissolution of separate spheres ought to give the marital bond a more creative and supportive foundation and encourage those same elements that traditional theories present as essential to marital longevity: intimacy, trust, and nurturance. When the underlying material exchange disappears, these elements no longer disguise in reverent tones the economic dominance of husbands over wives but come to have fuller meaning. In short, a dual-career

---

[3] A number of readers and audiences to whom this research has been presented reacted quite negatively to the strategies some of these dual-career couples adopt in dealing with money, household affairs, and children. Many of these people, including some partners in academic dual-career marriages, objected that separate accounting systems reflect "crass materialism" and a step toward marital dissolution. The vehemence of their reactions reveals first, I would suggest, their understandable ignorance of the circumstances of corporate employment. As the dual-career couples convincingly argue, . . . separate accounts are a standard business practice for higher-level corporate employees—for clothing, entertainment, travel, and so on—and it seems logical to extend this practice into the home. Second, such reactions reveal that money and financial decision making are touchy issues in most marriages. The departure from traditional practice that having separate accounts represents cannot help but highlight the question of money and equity in even the most liberal of households. Finally, such negative reactions demonstrate how deeply the normative model of marriage is ingrained in our consciousness. While not exactly knee-jerk in nature, the facile rejection of the dual-career/separate accounting/hired-labor model of marriage reveals how much we are all influenced by socialization and how difficult it is to question ideological (magical) assumptions and processes (misdirection).

marriage has the potential to be a more rather than a less durable relationship than the normative model.

Lest this proposition be interpreted as utopian, the framework of this question must be emphasized. First, dual-career couples are a special and contingent category of families. They are part of a social and economic elite within a capitalist society, and as such do not represent a model form of marriage.

Second, the concern of dual-career couples for the marital bond—something that family traditionalists certainly would not have expected with women's employment—in some ways shares the contractual character of other kinds of careers. Couples, for example, deal with their individual and shared incomes in a way more reminiscent of a business partnership than of communal enterprises. Although they clearly do not calculate profit and loss, neither do they place as great an emphasis on "ours" as has been the case in traditional marriages. These couples also "subcontract" more and more family services in an effort to sustain the family unit and with it the careers they cherish. Thus, they convert more and more of their lives into commodities (goods and labor), while trying to protect the relationship they have with each other from being dissolved into a monetary exchange. The private purchase and consumption of those commodites allows a degree of intimacy and personal control, which is the saving grace offered by the first two careers. Thus, the dual-career family remains a "haven in a heartless world" . . . only because it has been sufficiently successful in the heartless world to financially afford a haven.

The Marriage License as a Hitting License

Murray A. Straus, Richard Gelles, and Suzanne Steinmetz

Wife-beating is found in every class, at every income level. The wife of the president of a midwestern state university recently asked one of us what she could do about the beatings without putting her husband's career in danger. Japan's former Prime Minister Sato, a winner of the Nobel Peace Prize, was accused publicly by his wife of many beatings in their early married life. Ingeborg Dedichen, a former mistress of Aristotle Onassis, describes his beating her till he was forced to quit from exhaustion. "It is what every Greek husband does, it's good for the wife," he told her.

From *Behind Closed Doors* by Murray A. Straus, Richard J. Gelles and Suzanne K. Steinmetz, published by Doubleday & Company. Copyright © 1980 by Murray A. Straus and Richard J. Gelles. Reprinted by permission. References appearing in the original have been deleted.

What is at the root of such violent attacks? Proverbs such as "A man's home is his castle," go a long way in giving insights into human nature and society. The home belongs to the man. It is the woman who finds herself homeless if she refuses further abuse.

The image of the "castle" implies freedom from interference from outsiders. What goes on within the walls of the castle is shielded from prying eyes. And a modern home, like a medieval castle, can contain its own brand of torture chamber. Take the case of Carol, a Boston woman who called the police to complain that her husband had beaten her and then pushed her down the stairs. The policeman on duty answered, "Listen, lady, he pays the bills, doesn't he? What he does inside of his house is his business."

The evidence we documented . . . suggested that, aside from war and riots, physical violence occurs between family members more often than it occurs between any other individuals. At the same time we also pointed out the limitations of the data. In particular, no research up to now gives information on how often each of the different forms of family violence occurs in a representative sample of American families.

The Over-All Level of Husband-Wife Violence

Violence Rates

A first approach to getting a picture of the amount of violence between 2,143 husbands and wives in this study is to find out how many had engaged in any of the eight violent acts we asked about. For the year we studied this works out to be 16 per cent. In other words, every year about one out of every six couples in the United States commits at least one violent act against his or her partner.

If the period considered is the entire length of the marriage (rather than just the previous year), the result is 28 per cent, or between one out of four and one out of three American couples. In short, if you are married, the chances are almost one out of three that your husband or wife will hit you.

When we began our study of violence in the family, we would have considered such a rate of husbands and wives hitting each other very high. In terms of our values—and probably the values of most other Americans—it is still very high. But in terms of what we have come to expect on the basis of the pilot studies, this is a low figure. *It is very likely a substantial underestimate.*

Later in this chapter we will give the reasons for thinking it is an underestimate. But for now, let us examine the violent acts one by one. This is important if we are to get a realistic picture of the meaning of the overall rates of 28 per cent. One needs to know how much of the violence was slaps and how much was kicking and beating up. This informaiton is given in [Figure] 1.

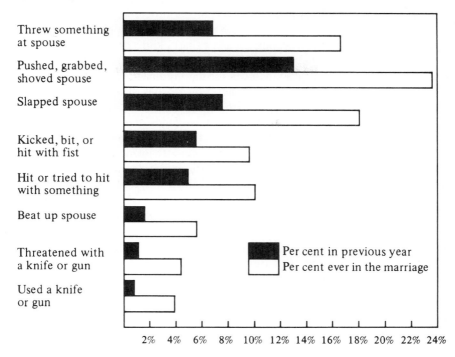

Figure 1   Rate at Which Violent Acts Occurred in the Previous Year and Ever in the Marriage

Slaps, Beatings, and Guns

[Figure] 1 shows that in almost seven of every hundred couples either the husband or the wife had thrown something at the other in the previous year, and about one out of six (16 per cent) had done this at some point in their marriage.

The statistics for *slapping* a spouse are about the same: 7 per cent in the previous year and 18 per cent at some time.

The figures for pushing, shoving, or grabbing during an argument are the highest of any of the eight things we asked about: 13 per cent had done this during the year, and almost one out of four at some time in the marriage.

At the other extreme, "only" one or two out of every hundred couples (1.5 per cent) experienced a *beating-up* incident in the previous year. But a "beating up" had occurred at some time in the marriages of one out of every twenty of the couples we interviewed.

The rates for actually *using a knife or gun* on one's spouse are one out of every two hundred couples in the previous year, and almost one out of twenty-seven couples at some point in the marriage.

We were surprised that there was not a bigger difference between the rate of occurrence for "mild" violent acts (such as pushing and slapping) and the severe acts of violence (such as beating up and using a knife or gun). This is partly because the rates for the more violent acts turned out to be greater than we expected, and partly because the rates for the "ordinary" acts of husband-wife violence were less than expected. Whatever the reasons, it seems that couples are using more than slaps and shoves when violence occurs.

Indeed, the statistics on the number of husbands and wives who had ever "beaten up" their spouses or actually used a knife or gun are astoundingly high. The human meaning of these most extreme forms of violence in the family can be understood better if we translate the percentages into the total number of marriages affected. Since there were about 47 million couples living together in the United States in 1975, the rates just given mean that *over 1.7 million Americans had at some time faced a husband or wife wielding a knife or gun, and well over 2 million had been beaten up* by his or her spouse.

How Accurate Are the Statistics?

It is difficult to know how much confidence to put in these statistics because several different kinds of error are possible. First, these are estimates based on a sample. But the sample is reasonably large and was chosen by methods which should make it quite representative of the U.S. population. Comparisons with characteristics reported in the U.S. census show that this in fact is the case.

Still, there is the possibility of sampling error. So we computed what is known as the "standard error" for each of the rates in [Figure] 1. The largest standard error is for the over-all violence index. Even that is low: there is a 95 per cent chance that the true percentage of couples *admitting to* ever having physically assaulted one another is somewhere between 26.8 and 28.8 per cent of all couples.

"Admitting to" was italicized to highlight a much more serious and more likely source of error, that of an underestimate. The 26.8 to 28.8 per cent figure assumes that everyone "told all." But that is very unlikely. Three of the reasons are:

(1) There is one group of people who are likely to "underreport" the amount of violence. For this group a slap, push, or shove (and sometimes even more severe violence) is so much a normal part of the family that it is simply not a noteworthy or dramatic enough event always to be remembered. Such ommissions are especially likely when we asked about things which had happened during the entire length of the marriage.

(2) At the opposite end of the violence continuum, there is another group who fail to admit or report such acts because of the shame involved if one is the victim, or the guilt if one is the attacker. Such violent attacks as being hit with objects, bitten, beaten up, or attacked with a knife or gun go beyond the "normal violence" of family life and are often unreported.

(3) A final reason for thinking these figures are drastic underestimates lies in the

nature of the sample. We included only couples currently living together. Divorced people were asked only about their present marriage. Since "excessive" violence is often a cause of divorce, the sample probably omits many of the high violence cases.

The sample was selected in this way because a major purpose of the study was to investigate the extent to which violence is related to other aspects of husband-wife interaction. Questions were limited to current marriages because of interview time limits and limits on what people could be expected to remember.

The figures therefore could easily be twice as large as those revealed by the survey. In fact, based on the pilot studies and informal evidence (where some of the factors leading to underreporting were not present), it seems likely that *the true rate is close to 50 or 60 per cent of all couples than it is to the 28 per cent who were willing to describe violent acts to our interviewers.*

Men and Women

Traditionally, men have been considered more aggressive and violent than women. Like other stereotypes, there is no doubt a kernel of truth to this. But it is far from the clear-cut difference which exists in the thinking of most people. This is also the case with our survey. About one out of eight husbands had carried out at least one violent act during the course of a conflict in the year covered by the survey, *and* about the same number of wives had attacked their husbands (12.1 per cent of the husbands versus 11.6 per cent of the wives).

Mutual Violence

One way of looking at this issue is to ask what percentage of the sample are couples in which the husband was the only one to use violence? What per cent were couples in which the only violence was by the wife? And in what percentage did both use violence?

The most common situtaion was that in which both had used violence.

One man, who found himself in the middle of a family battle, reported it this way:

> It started sort of slowly . . . so I couldn't tell for sure if they were even serious. . . . In the beginning they'd push at each other, or shove, like kids— little kids who want to fight but they don't know how. Then, this one time, while I'm standing there not sure whether to stay or go, and them treating me like I didn't exist, she begins yelling at him like she did.
>
> "You're a bust, you're a failure, I want you out of here, I can always get men who'll work, good men, not scum like you." And they're pushing and poking with their hands, like they were dancing. She pushes him, he pushes her, only she's doing all the talking. He isn't saying a word.
>
> Then all of a sudden, she must have triggered off the right nerve because he lets fly with a right cross that I mean stuns. I mean she goes down like a rock! And he's swearing at her, calling her every name in the book. Jesus, I didn't know what the hell to do.

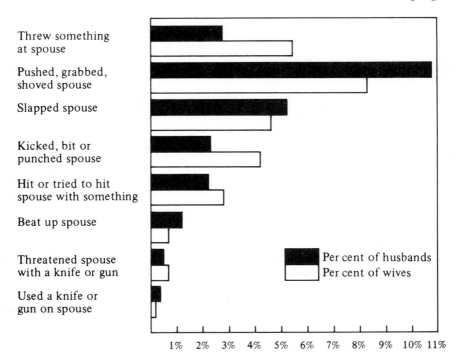

Figure 2   Comparison of Husband and Wife Violence in Previous Year

> What I wanted to do was call the police. But I figured, how can I call the police and add to this guy's misery, because she was pushing him. . . . She was really pushing him. I'd have done something to her myself.

Of those couples reporting any violence, 49 per cent were of situations of this type, where both were violent. For the year previous to our study, a comparison of the number of couples in which only the husband was violent with those in which only the wife was violent shows the figures to be very close: 27 per cent violent husbands and 24 per cent violent wives. So, as in the case of the violence rates, there is little difference between the husbands and wives in this study.

Specific Violent Acts

[Figure] 2 compares the men and women in our study on each of the eight violent acts. Again, there is an over-all similarity. But there are also some interesting differences, somewhat along the lines of the stereotype of the pot- and pan-throwing wife.

> I got him good last time! He punched me in the face and I fell back on the stove.

> He was walking out of the kitchen and I grabbed the frying pan and landed it square on his head. Man, he didn't know what hit him.

The number of wives who threw things at their husbands is almost twice as large as the number of husbands who threw things at their wives. The rate for kicking and hitting with an object is also higher for wives than for husbands. The husbands on the other hand had higher rates for pushing, shoving, slapping, beating up, and actually using a knife or gun.

Wife-Beating—and Husband-Beating

Wife-beating has become a focus of increasing public concern in the last few years. In part this reflects the national anguish over all aspects of violence, ranging from the Vietnam war to the upward surge of assault and murder. Another major element accounting for the recent public concern with wife-beating is the feminist movement. Behind that are the factors which have given rise to the rebirth of the feminist movement in the late 1960s and early 1970s.

What Is Wife-Beating?

To find out how much wife-beating there is, one must be able to define it in a way which can be objectively measured. When this is tried, it becomes clear that "wife-beating" is a political rather than a scientific term. For some people wife-beating refers only to those instances in which severe damage is inflicted. Less severe violence is not considered violence or it is laughed off. A joke one of us heard while driving across northern England in 1974 is no doubt familiar to many readers of this book. It goes like this in the BBC version: One woman asks another why she feels her husband doesn't love her any more. The answer: "He hasn't bashed me in a forthnight." Or take the following letter to Ann Landers:

> *Dear Ann Landers:*
> Come out of the clouds, for Lord's sake, and get down here with us humans. I am sick to death of your holier-than-thou attitude toward women whose husbands give them a well deserved belt in the mouth.
>
> Don't you know that a man can be pushed to the brink and something's got to give? A crack in the teeth can be a wonderful tension-breaker. It's also a lot healthier than keeping all that anger bottled up.
>
> My husband hauls off and slugs me every few months and I don't mind. He feels better and so do I because he never hits me unless I deserve it. So why don't you come off it?—REAL HAPPY.

> *Dear Real Happy:*
> If you don't mind a crack in the teeth every few months, it's all right with me. I hope you have a good dentist.

So a certain amount of violence in the family is "normal violence." In fact, most of the violent acts which occur in the family are so much a part of the way family members relate to each other that they are not even thought of as violence.

At what point does one exceed the bounds of "normal" family violence? When does it become "wife-beating"? To answer this question, we gathered data on a series of violent acts, ranging from a slap to using a knife or gun. This allows anyone reading this book to draw the line at whatever place seems most appropriate for his or her purpose.

Measuring Wife-Beating

This "solution," however, can also be a means of avoiding the issue. So in addition to data on each violent act, we also combined the most severe of these into what can be called a Severe Violence Index. If these are things done by the husband, then it is a "Wife-beating Index." The Wife-beating Index consists of the extent to which the husband went beyond throwing things, pushing or grabbing, and slapping and attacking his wife by kicking, biting, or punching; hitting with some object; beating her up; threatening her with a gun or knife; or using a knife or gun (the last five behaviors in [Figure] 1).

Why limit the Wife-beating Index to "only" the situations where the husband went beyond throwing things, pushing, grabbing, and slapping? Certainly we don't want to imply that this reflects our conception of what is permissible violence. None of these are acceptable for relationships between husband and wife—just as they are unacceptable between student and teacher, minister and parishioner, or colleagues in a department. In short, we follow the maxim coined by John Valusek: "People are not for hitting."

What then is the basis for choosing kicking, biting, or punching; hitting with an object; beating up; threatening with a knife or gun; and using a knife or gun for the Wife-beating Index? It is simply the fact that these are all acts which carry with them a high risk of serious physical injury.

What Percentage Are Beaten?

How many husbands and wives experience the kind of attack which is serious enough to be included in the Wife-beating and Husband-beating Indexes? A remarkably large number. In fact, since our survey produced a rate of 3.8 per cent, this means that about one out of twenty-six American wives get beaten by their husbands every year, or a total of almost 1.8 million per year.

Staggering as are these figures, the real surprise lies in the statistics on husband-beating. These rates are slightly higher than those for wife-beating! Although such cases rarely come to the attention of the police or the press, they exist at all social levels. Here is an example of one we came across:

> A wealthy, elderly New York banker was finally granted a separation from his second wife, 31 years his junior, after 14 years of marriage and physical abuse. According to the presiding judge, the wife had bullied him with hysteria, screaming tantrums and vicious physical violence.
> The husband wore constant scars and bruises. His ear had once been shredded

by his wife with her teeth. She had blackened his eyes, and on one occasion injured one of his eyes so badly that doctors feared it might be lost.

From 4.6 per cent of the wives in the sample admitted to or were reported by their husbands as having engaged in an act which is included in the Husband-beating Index. That works to be about one out of twenty-two wives who attacked their husbands severely enough to be included in this Husband-beating Index. That is over 2 million very violent wives. Since three other studies of this issue also found high rates of husband-beating, some revision of the traditional view about female violence seems to be needed.

How Often Do Beatings Happen?

Let us look at just the couples for which a violent incident occurred during the year previous to our study. Was it an isolated incident? If not, how often did attacks of this kind occur?

It was an isolated incident (in the sense that there was only one such attack during the year) for only about a third of the violent couples. This applies to both wife-beating and husband-beating. Almost one out of five of the violent husbands and one out of eight wives attacked their partner this severely twice during the year. Forty-seven per cent of the husbands who beat their wives did so three or more times during the year, and 53 per cent of the husband-beaters did so three or more times. So, for about half the couples the pattern is that if there is one beating, there are likely to be others—at least three per year! In short, violence between husbands and wives, when it occurs, tends to be a recurrent feature of the marriage.

Was There Ever a Beating?

A final question about how many beatings took place can be answered by looking at what happened over the entire length of the marriage. Did something that can be called a beating *ever* happen in the marriage?

There are several reasons why even a single beating is important. First, even one such event debases human life. Second, there is the physical danger involved. Third is the fact that many, if not most, such beatings are part of a struggle for power in the family. It often takes only one such event to fix the balance of power for many years—or perhaps for a lifetime.

Physical force is the ultimate resource which most of us learn as children to rely on if all else fails and the issue is crucial. As a husband in one of the families interviewed by LaRossa said when asked why he hit his wife during an argument:

> . . . She more or less tried to run me and I said no, and she got hysterical and said, "I could kill you!" And I got rather angry and slapped her in the face three or four times and I said, "Don't you ever say that to me again!" And we haven't had any problem since.

Later in the interview, the husband evaluated his use of physical force as follows:

You don't use it until you are forced to it. At that point I felt I had to do something physical to stop the bad progression of events. I took my chances with that and it worked. In those circumstances my judgment was correct and it worked.

Since greater size and strength give the advantage to men in such situations, the single beating may be an extremely important factor in maintaining male dominance in the family system.

We found that one out of eight couples (12.6 per cent) experienced at least one beating incident in the course of marriage. That is approximately a total of 6 million beatings. However, as high as that figure is, the actual statistics are probably higher. This is because things are forgotten over the years, and also because (as we pointed out earlier) the violent acts in question are only about the current marriage. They leave out the many marriages which ended in divorce, a large part of which were marked by beatings.

Wives and Husbands as Victims

This study shows a high rate of violence by *wives* as well as husbands. But it would be a great mistake if that fact distracted us from giving first attention to wives *as victims* as the focus of social policy. There are a number of reasons for this:

(1) The data in [Figure] 2 shows that husbands have higher rates of the most dangerous and injurious forms of violence (beating up and using a knife or gun).
(2) Steinmetz found that abuse by husbands does more damage. She suggests that the greater physical strength of men makes it more likely that a woman will be seriously injured when beaten up by her husband.
(3) When violent acts are committed by a husband, they are repeated more often than is the case for wives.
(4) The data do not tell us what proportion of the violent acts by wives were in self-defense or a response to blows initiated by husbands. Wolfgang's study of husband-wife homicides suggests that this is an important factor.
(5) A large number of attacks by husbands seem to occur when the wife is pregnant, thus posing a danger to the as yet unborn child. This isn't something that happens only on Tobacco Road:

> The first time Hortense Barber's husband beat her was the day she told him she was pregnant with their first child. "He knocked out my two front teeth and split open my upper lip," the 32 year old honors graduate told a New York Senate Task Force on Women. Later Mrs. Barber's husband regularly blacked her eyes during her pregnancy and threw a knife at her "in jest," cutting her knee.

(6) Women are locked into marriage to a much greater extent than men. Women are bound by many economic and social constraints, and they often have no

alternative to putting up with beatings by their husbands. The situation is similar to being married to an alcoholic. Nine out of ten men leave an alcoholic wife, but only one out of ten women leave an alcoholic husband.

Most people feel that social policy should be aimed at helping those who are in the weakest position. Even though wives are also violent, they are in the weaker, more vulnerable position in respect to violence in the family. This applies to both the physical, psychological, and economic aspects of things. That is the reason we give first priority to aiding wives who are the victims of beatings by their husbands.

At the same time, the violence *by* wives uncovered in this study suggests that a fundamental solution to the problem of wife-beating has to go beyond a concern with how to control assaulting husbands. It seems that violence is built into the very structure of the society and the family system itself. . . . Wife-beating . . . is only one aspect of the general pattern of family violence, which includes parent-child violence, child-to-child violence, and wife-to-husband violence. To eliminate the particularly brutal form of violence known as wife-beating will require changes in the cultural norms and in the organization of the family and society which underlie the system of violence on which so much of American society is based.

Norms and Meanings

Just as we need to know the extent to which violent *acts* occur between husbands and wives, parents and children, and brothers and sisters, it is also important to know how family members feel about intrafamily violence. Just how strongly do they approve or disapprove of a parent slapping a child or a husband slapping a wife? To what extent do people see violence in the family as one of those undesirable but necessary parts of life?

It is hard to find out about these aspects of the way people think about family violence. One difficulty is there are contradictory rules or "norms." At one level there are norms strongly opposed to husbands and wives hitting each other. But at the same time, there also seem to be implicit but powerful norms which permit and even encourage such acts. Sometimes people are thinking of one of these principles and sometimes the other.

Another thing is that violence is often such a "taken for granted" part of life that most people don't even realize there are socially defined rules or norms about the use of violence in the family.

The existence of these implicit norms are illustrated by the case of a husband who hit his wife on several occasions. Each time he felt that it was wrong. He apologized—very genuinely. But still he did it again. The husband explained that he and his wife got so worked up in their arguments that he "lost control." In his mind, it was almost involuntary, and certainly not something he did according to a rule or norm which gives one the right to hit his wife.

But the marriage counselor in the case brought out the rules which permitted him to hit his wife. He asked the husband why, if he had "lost control," he didn't stab his wife! This possibility (and the fact that the husband did not stab his wife despite "losing control") shows that hitting the wife was not just a bubbling over of a primitive level of behavior. Although this husband did not realize it, he was following a behavioral rule or norm. It seems that the unrecognized but operating norm for this husband—and for millions of other husbands—is that it is okay to hit one's wife, but not to stab her.

There is other evidence which tends to support the idea that the marriage license is also a hitting license. For example, "Alice, you're going to the moon," was one of the standard punch lines on the old Jackie Gleason "Honeymooners" skits which delighted TV audiences during the 1950s, and which are currently enjoying a revival. Jokes, plays, such as those of George Bernard Shaw, and experiments which show that people take less severe actions if they think the man attacking a woman is her husband are other signs.

It has been suggested that one of the reasons neighbors who saw the attack didn't come to the aid of Kitty Genovese in the 1964 Queens murder case was because they thought it was a man beating his wife!

Or take the following incident:

> Roy Butler came over to help his bride-to-be in preparations for their wedding, which is why the wedding is off.
>
> Roy, 24, made the mistake of going to a stag party first.
>
> On the way to fiancée Anthea Higson's home, he dropped the wedding cake in the front garden.
>
> In the shouting match that followed, he dropped Anthea's mother with a right cross to the jaw.
>
> Anthea, 21, promptly dropped Roy. She said the wedding was off and she never wanted to see him again.
>
> *"If he had hit me instead of my mother, I probably would have married him all the same,"* [italics added] she said yesterday after a court fined Butler $135 for assaulting Mrs. Brenda Higson.
>
> "But I'm not having any man hitting my mum," Anthea said.

Interesting as are these examples, none of them provide the kind of systematic and broadly representative evidence which is needed. That is what we attempted to get in this study.

Measuring the Meaning of Violence

To find out how our sample felt about violence in the family, we used the "semantic differential" method. For husband-wife violence, we asked subjects to rate the phrase "Couples slapping each other." They were asked to make three ratings: unnecessary . . . necessary; not normal . . . normal; and good . . . bad.

How many of the husbands and wives rated "Couples slapping each other" as "necessary," "normal," or "good"? Over all just under one out of four wives and one out of three husbands (31.3 and 24.6 per cent) saw this type of physical force between spouses as at least somewhat necessary, normal, or good.

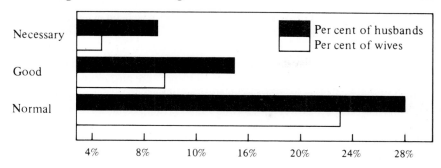

Figure 3   Per Cent of Husbands and Wives Who Rated "A Couple Slapping Each Other" as at Least Somewhat Necessary, Good, or Normal

These statistics are remarkably close to those from a national sample studied by the U.S. Violence Commission. The Violence Commission found that about one quarter of the persons interviewed said they could think of circumstances in which it would be all right for a husband to hit his wife or a wife to hit her husband. This is slightly lower than the percentages for our sample. But if the Violence Commission survey data had been analyzed in the way we examined our data, the results could well have been almost identical.

The separate ratings for violence being necessary, normal, or good are interesting in the contrast they provide with each other and in the way men and women think about violence. On the other hand, there are big differences in the percentage of husbands as compared to wives who could see some situations in which it is necessary for a husband or wife to slap each other (see [Figure] 3). There is also a larger percentage of husbands who could see some situations in which this would not be a bad thing to do. In fact, for both these ratings, twice as many husbands as wives felt this way.

On the other hand, the percentages for the not normal . . . normal rating are particularly interesting because they are larger and because there is little difference between men and women. The figures in the chart show that a large proportion of American husbands and wives see violence as a normal part of married life. It may not be good, and it may not be necessary, but it is something which is going to happen under normal circumstances. The marriage license is a hitting license for a large part of the population, and probably for a much greater part than could bring themselves to rate it as "normal" in the context of this survey.

Summing Up

We are reasonably confident that the couples in the study are representative of American couples in general. But we suspect that not everyone told us about all the violence in his or her family. In fact, the pilot studies and informal evidence suggest that the true figures may be double those based on what people were willing to admit in a mass survey such as this. If this is the case, then about a third of all American couples experience a violent incident every year, and about two thirds have experienced such an incident at least once in the marriage.

Of course, a large part of these "violent incidents" are pushes and slaps, but far from all of them. A large portion are also actions which could cause serious injury or even death. We know from the fact that so many murderers and their victims are husband and wife that this is not just speculation. For the couples in this sample, in fact, almost one out of every twenty-five had faced an angry partner with a knife or gun in hand.

If the "dangerous violence" is not limited solely to use of a knife or gun, and includes everything *more serious* than pushing, grabbing, shoving, slapping, and throwing things, the rate is three times as high. In short, almost one out of every eight couples admitted that at some point in the marriage there had been an act of violence which could cause serious injury.

Another way of grasping this is to compare the rates of wife-beating and husband-beating in our survey with assaults which are reported in official statistics. The Uniform Crime Reports on "aggravated assault" are given in rate per 100,000. But the rates in this chapter are percentages, i.e., rates per 100, not per 100,000.

We can translate the rates for this survey into rates per 100,000 per year. They are 3,800 per 100,000 for assaults on wives, 4,600 for assaults on husbands, and a combined rate of 6,100 per 100,000 couples. Compare this with the roughly 190 per 100,000 aggravated assaults of all kinds known to the police each year.

Of course, many crimes are not reported to the police. So there have been surveys asking people if they were the victims of a crime. The rate of aggravated assault coming out of the National Crime Panel survey is very high: 2,597 per 100,000. But our rate for wife-beating and husband-beating of 6,100 per 100,000 is almost two and a half times higher. Also, since the Uniform Crime Reports, and especially the National Crime Panel data, include many within-family assaults, the amount by which husband-wife assault exceeds any other type of assault is much greater than these rates suggest.

Leaving aside the fact that our figures on husband-wife violence are probably underestimates, and even leaving aside the psychological damage that such violence can produce, just the danger to physical health implied by these rates is staggering. If any other crime of risk to physical well-being involved almost 2 million wives and 2 million husbands per year, plus a much larger amount at some point in the marriage, a national emergency would probably be declared.

Chapter 7

Divorce and Remarriage

The Transformation of Legal Marriage Through No-Fault Divorce

Lenore J. Weitzman and Ruth B. Dixon

Introduction

Divorce and family breakdown constitute one of the major social problems in the United States today. In 1975 alone over 3 million men, women and minor children were involved in a divorce.[1] In the future it is likely that one-third to one-half of all the adults in the United States, and close to one-third of the minor children under 18 will be affected by a divorce or dissolution.[2] These data reflect not only the numerical importance of divorce, but its increased social significance as well. While divorce may have been considered a "deviant family pattern" in the past, it is rapidly becoming accepted as a possible (though not yet probable) outcome of marriage.

Since 1970 there has been a major reform in divorce law which attempts to institutionalize fundamental social changes in family patterns. Commonly referred to as no-fault divorce, this new legislation seeks to alter the definition of marriage, the relationship between husbands and wives, and the economic and social obligations of former spouses to each other and to their children after divorce.

In 1970, California instituted the first no-fault divorce law in the United States. Since then fourteen other states have adopted "pure" no-fault divorce laws[3] and

This article is excerpted from Lenore J. Weitzman, *The Divorce Revolution: The Unexpected Social and Economic Consequence for Women and Children in America* (The Free Press, 1985). It was originally published in its present form in the third edition of *Family in Transition*. Copyright © 1980 by Lenore J. Weitzman and Ruth B. Dixon. Used by permission.

an additional thirteen states have added no-fault grounds to their existing grounds for divorce.[4] No-fault divorce has been praised as the embodiment of "modern" and "enlightened" law, and heralded as the forerunner of future family law in the United States. It has also been strongly attacked for "destroying the family" and for causing irreparable harm to women. This paper aims at analyzing the effects of this new legislation on both marriage and divorce.

The laws governing divorce tell us how a society defines marriage and where it sets the boundaries for appropriate marital behavior. One can generally examine the way a society defines marriage by examining its provisions for divorce, for it is at the point of divorce that a society has the opportunity to reward the marital behavior it approves of, and to punish spouses who have violated its norms.[5] In addition, in virtually all societies which allow divorce, it is assumed that people who were once married continue to have obligations to each other; and these obligations reflect the rights and duties of marriage itself.

This paper is divided into three sections. It begins with a discussion of traditional legal marriage followed by a review of traditional divorce law. The last section examines the aims of the no-fault legislation and its implications for traditional family roles.

Traditional Legal Marriage

The origins of Anglo-American family law[6] may be traced to the tenth or eleventh century, when Christianity became sufficiently influential in Britain to enable the Church to assert its rules effectively. (Clark, 1968:281) Traditionally legal marriage was firmly grounded in the Christian conception of marriage as a holy union between a man and woman. Marriage was a sacrament, a commitment to join together for life: "to take each other to love and to cherish, in sickness and in health, for better, for worse, until death do us part."

The nature of the marital relationship, and the legal responsibilities of the spouses were specified by law—by statute, case law and common law. While a thorough analysis of legal marriage is obviously beyond the scope of this paper (but see Clark, 1968; Kay, 1874; Weitzman, 1979), five important features may be briefly summarized as follows: First, legal marriage was limited to a single man and a single woman; bigamy, polygamy and homosexual unions were prohibited. Second, legal marriage was monogamous. The spouses were to remain sexually faithful to each other and adultery was explicitly prohibited. Third, marriage was for procreation. One of the major objects of matrimony was the bearing and rearing of (legitimate) children. (Reynolds v. Reynolds, 1862)

Fourth, legal marriage established a hierarchical relationship between the spouses: the husband was the head of the family, with his wife and children subordinate to him. The husband's authority was based on the common-law doctrine of coverture which established the legal fiction that a husband and wife took a single legal identity upon marriage—the identity of the husband. At common law a married woman became a *femme covert,* a legal nonperson, under her husband's arm, protection and cover. (Blackstone, 1765)

Although most of the disabilities of coverture were removed by the Married Women's Property Acts in the nineteenth century—the common-law assumption that the husband was the head of the family remained firmly embodied in statutory and case law in the United States. The married woman's subordination was most clearly reflected in rules governing her domicile and name. In both cases the married woman assumed her husband's identity—taking his name and his domicile as her own. This basic assumption of traditional legal marriage has, of course, been challenged in recent years.

The fifth, and most important feature of traditional legal marriage, was its sex-based division of family roles and responsibilities. The woman was to devote herself to being a wife, homemaker and mother in return for her husband's promise of lifelong support. The husband was given the sole responsibility for the family's financial welfare, while he was assured that his home, his children and his social-emotional well-being would be cared for by his wife. Professor Homer Clark, a noted authority on family law, summarizes the legal obligations of the two spouses as follows:

> Specifically, the courts say that the husband has a duty to support his wife, that she has a duty to render services in the home, and that these duties are reciprocal. . . . The husband is to provide the family with food, clothing, shelter and as many of the amenities of life as he can manage, either (in earlier days) by the management of his estates, or (more recently) by working for wages or a salary. The wife is to be mistress of the household, maintaining the home with resources furnished by the husband, and caring for children. A reading of contemporary judicial opinions leaves the impression that these roles have changed over the last two hundred years. (Clark, 1968: 181)

All states, even those with community property systems, placed the burden of the family support on the husband; he was legally responsible for providing necessities for his wife and his children. Similarly, all states made the wife responsible for domestic and child care services: her legal obligation was to be a companion, housewife and mother. As one court enumerated the services a man could legally expect from his wife:

> (she had a duty) to be his helpmate, to love and care for him in such a role, to afford him her society and her person, to protect and care for him in sickness, and to labor faithfully to advance his interest . . . (she must also perform) her household and domestic duties . . . A husband is entitled to the benefit of his wife's industry and economy. (Rucci v. Rucci, 1962: 127)

The wife was also assigned responsibility for child care, both during marriage and after divorce, as the law viewed her as the "natural and proper" caretaker of the young.

While no one would claim that the law was responsible for the traditional division of labor in the family, it did serve to legitimate, sanction, and reinforce these traditional family roles. For example, the law reinforced the wife's subordinate status—and her economic dependency—by defining the husband as the only person who was responsible for (and capable of) supporting the family. (Kay, 1974)

By promising the housewife lifelong support, the law provided a disincentive for women to develop their economic capacity and to work in the paid labor force. In addition, by making them legally responsible for domestic and child care services, it reinforced the primacy of these activities in their lives, leaving them with neither time nor incentive to develop careers outside of the home.

The law similarly reinforced the traditional male role by directing the husband away from domestic and childcare activities. While the law did legitimate the husband's power and authority in the family, it also encouraged a single-minded dedication to work, and to earning a living, for it made it clear that his sole responsibility was his family's economic welfare.

Traditional Divorce Law

Since marriage was regarded as an indissoluble union, it could be ended only by the death of one of the parties. (Rheinstein, 1972) "Divorce, in the modern sense of a judicial decree dissolving a valid marriage, and allowing one or both partners to remarry during the life of the other, did not exist in England until 1857." (Kay, 1970: 221)[7]

A rare exception, originating in the late 17th century, allowed divorce (on the sole ground of adultery) by special act of Parliament. As a practical matter, however, a few of these divorces were granted—and they were available only to the very rich, and to men. (Clark, 1968: 281) The Church also permitted divorce *a mensa et thoro,* literally a divorce from bed and board, which allowed the parties to live apart. But this legal separation did not sever the marital bond.

The Ecclesiastical Courts retained their exclusive jurisdiction over marriage and divorce in England until 1857, when divorce jurisdiction was transferred to the Civil Court System, and divorces were authorized for adultery. But the underlying premise of divorce law remained the same: Marriage was still regarded as a permanent and cherished union which the Church—and then the state—had to protect and preserve. And it was still assumed that the holy bond of matrimony would best be protected by restricting access to divorce. As Clark observed:

> (They believed) that marital happiness is best secured by making marriage indissoluble except for very few causes. When the parties know that they are bound together for life, the argument runs, they will resolve their differences and disagreements and make an effort to get along with each other. If they are able to separate legally upon less serious grounds, they will make no such effort, and immorality will result. (Clark, 1968: 242–43)

It should also be noted that these early divorce laws established a different standard for men and women: "wives . . . could obtain a divorce only if the husband's adultery was aggravated by bigamy, cruelty or incest, while the husband could get his divorce for adultery alone." (Clark, 1969: 282)[8]

Divorce laws in the United States were heavily influenced by the English tradition. In the middle and southern Colonies, divorces were granted by the legislature, and were rare. However, New England allowed divorce more freely. The Protestant doctrines (and the absence of any system of Ecclesiastical Courts) resulted in statutes which authorized divorce for adultery, desertion, and, in some cases, cruelty—sometimes by the courts and sometimes by acts of the Legislature.

Although some diversity in the divorce laws of the states continued, in nineteenth century most states gave the courts the jurisdiction to dissolve marriages on specified grounds (Kay, 1968: 221), and by 1900 most states had adopted what we shall refer to as the four major elements of traditional divorce laws.

First, *traditional divorce law perpetuated the sex-based division of roles and responsibilities in traditional legal marriage.* As we noted above, in legal marriage the woman presumably agreed to devote herself to being a wife, homemaker and mother in return for her husband's promise of lifelong support. Although traditional family law assumed that the husband's support would be provided in a lifelong marriage, if the marriage did not endure, and if the wife was virtuous, she was nevertheless guaranteed alimony—a means of continued support. Alimony perpetuated the husband's responsibility for economic support, and the wife's right to be supported in return for her domestic services. It thus maintained the reciprocity in the legal marriage contract.

Traditional divorce laws also perpetuated the sex-based division of roles with respect to children: the husband remained responsible for their economic support, the wife for their care. All states, by statute or by case law tradition, gave preference to the wife as the appropriate custodial parent after the divorce; and all states gave the husband the primary responsibility for their economic support.

Second, *traditional divorce law required grounds for divorce.* Divorce could be obtained only if one party committed a marital offense, giving the other a legal basis or ground for the divorce. Since marriage was supposed to be a permanent lifelong union, only serious marital offenses such as adultery, cruelty, or desertion could justify a divorce. As Professor Herma Hill Kay explains:

> The state's interest in marital stability, thus delegated to the courts, was to be guarded by the judge's diligence in requiring that evidence clearly established the ground relied on for a divorce, that the defendant had no valid defense to the plaintiff's suit, and that the parties had not conspired to put on a false case. (Kay, 1970: 221)

The standards for judging appropriate grounds also reflected the sex-typed expectations of traditional legal marriage. While the almost ritualistic "evidence" of misbehavior varied from state to state, husbands charged with cruelty were often alleged to have caused their wives bodily harm, while wives charged with cruelty were more typically charged with neglecting their husbands (showing lack of affection, belittling him); or their homes (leaving the home in disarray, neglecting dinner), impuning their husband's self-respect or reputation (denigrating or insulting him in front of business associates or friends); or ignoring their wifely duties (what Clark calls the country club syndrome in which the wife "is entirely preoccupied with club and social life, is extravagant, drinks heavily, and wholly disregards the husband's desires for affection and comfort"). (Clark, 1968: 349)

Cruelty was the most commonly used grounds for divorce followed by desertion, which accounted for less than 18% of all divorces (Jacobson, 1959: 124). Adultery was rarely used outside of New York, where it was the only permissible ground for divorce until 1967. While the standards for desertion also varied from state to state, two sex-based standards were common to most: (1) If a wife refused to live in the domicile chosen by her husband, she was held responsible for desertion in the divorce action. In addition, if the husband moved and she refused to accompany him, *she* was considered to have deserted *him,* since he had the legal right to choose the family home. She would then be the guilty party in the divorce, and that had important economic consequences which are discussed below. Second, a spouse's withdrawal from his or her marital roles might be considered desertion, and the standards for these withdrawals were clearly sex-typed. For example, a wife who showed "lack of affection" for the husband, had a relationship with another man (but did not commit adultery), refused to do housework, and nagged her husband, would be guilty of desertion (see, for example, Anton v. Anton, 1955) but a husband who acted in a similar fashion would not—unless he also stopped supporting his wife financially.

Over time, in actual practice many divorcing couples privately agreed to an uncontested divorce where one party, usually the wife, would take the *pro forma* role of plaintiff. Supported by witnesses, she would attest to her husband's cruel conduct and he would not challenge her testimony. But even if these allegations involved collusion and perjury, as many of them did, the type of behavior reported as grounds for divorce nevertheless reflected what the courts considered "appropriate violations" of the marriage contract. The husband, supposed to support and protect his wife, was sanctioned for nonsupport and physical abuse. The wife, obligated to care for her home and husband, was sanctioned for neglecting her domestic responsibilities.

Third, traditional legal divorce *was based on adversary proceedings.* The adversary process required that one party be guilty, or responsible for the divorce, and that the other be innocent. The plaintiff's success in obtaining a divorce depended on his or her ability to prove the defendant's fault for having committed some marital offense. Divorces had to be "won" by the innocent party against the guilty party. As the Tennessee Supreme Court (Brown v. Brown, 1955: 498) stated "divorce is conceived as a remedy for the innocent against the guilty." If a spouse who was found guilty could prove the other was also at fault, or that the other had colluded in or condoned their behavior, the divorce thus might not be granted in order to punish both parties.

Finally, traditional divorce law *linked the financial terms of the divorce to the determination of fault.* Being found "guilty" or "innocent" in the divorce action had important financial consequences.

For example, alimony, or a "suitable allowance for support and maintenance" could be awarded only to the *innocent* spouse "for his or her life, or for such shorter periods as the courts may deem 'just' as a judgment *against* the guilty spouse." (California Civil Code 139). Thus a wife found guilty of adultery was typically barred from receiving alimony, while a husband found guilty of adultery or cruelty could be ordered to pay for his transgressions with alimony and property. And many attorneys believed that justice was served by using alimony as a lever against a promiscuous husband, or as a reward for a virtuous wife. As Eli Bronstein, a New York matrimonial lawyer, put it: "If a woman has been a tramp, why reward her? By the same token, if the man is alley-catting around town, shouldn't his wife get all the benefits she had as a married woman?" (Wheeler, 1974: 57)

Property awards were similarly linked to fault. In most states, the court had to award more than half of the property to the "innocent" or "injured" party.[9] This standard easily led to heated accusations and counter-accusations of wrongs in order to obtain a better property settlement. (Hogoboom, 1971: 687) It also allowed a spouse who did not want a divorce to use the property award as a lever in the negotiations. In practice, since the husband was more likely to be the party who wanted the divorce, the wife was more likely to assume the role of the innocent plaintiff (Friedman and Percival, 1976: 77); and she was therefore more likely to be awarded a greater share of the property. Of course, the proportion of her share (and the extent of the inequality) was related to both the amount and type of property involved: significantly unequal awards were most likely to occur in cases in which the only family asset was the house, as the (innocent) wife was typically awarded the family home. (Weitzman, Kay & Dixon, 1979)

Custody awards could also be influenced by findings of fault. A woman found guilty of adultery or cruelty might be deprived of her preference as the custodial parent—especially if her behavior indicated that she was an "unfit" mother.[10]

By linking both the granting of the divorce and the financial settlements to findings of fault, the law gave the "aggrieved" spouse, particularly an "innocent" wife who wanted to stay married, a considerable advantage in the financial negotiations. In return for her agreement to the divorce, her husband was typically willing to be the guilty defendant (in a noncontested divorce) and to give her, as the innocent plaintiff, alimony and more than half of the property.

In summary, traditional divorce law helped sanction the spouses' roles and responsibilities in marriage—by both punishment and reward. On the negative side, if a wife was found guilty of adultery, cruelty or desertion, she would have to pay for her wrongdoing by being denied alimony (and sometimes custody and property as well). And if the husband was at fault, he would be "punished" through awards of property, alimony and child support to his ex-wife.

On the positive side, traditional divorce law promised "justice" for those who fulfilled their marital obligations. It guaranteed support for the wife who devoted herself to her family, thus reinforcing the desirability and legitimacy of the wife's role as homemaker, and the husband's role as supporter. And it assured the husband that he would not have to support a wife who betrayed or failed him. Justice in this system was the assurance that the marriage contract will be honored. If not, the "bad" spouse would be punished, the "good" spouse rewarded, and the husband's obligation to support his wife (if she was good) enforced.

No-Fault Divorce

In 1970 California instituted the first law in the Western world to abolish completely any requirement of fault as the basis for marital dissolution. (Hogoboom, 1971) The no-fault law provided for a divorce upon *one* party's assertion that "irreconcilable differences have caused the irremediable breakdown of the marriage." In establishing the new standards for marital dissolution, the California State Legislature sought to eliminate the adversarial nature of divorce and thereby to reduce the hostility, acrimony and trauma characteristics of fault-oriented divorce.

The California no-fault divorce law marked the beginning of a nationwide trend toward legal recognition of "marital breakdown" as a sufficient justification for divorce. The new law not only eliminated the need for evidence of misconduct; it eliminated the concept of fault itself. And it thereby abolished the notion of interpersonal justice in divorce. With this seemingly simple move, the California legislature dramatically altered the legal definition of the reciprocal rights of husbands and wives during marriage and after its dissolution.

Proponents of the divorce law reform had several aims. They sought to eliminate the hypocrisy, perjury and collusion "required by courtroom practice under the fault system" (Kay, 1968: 1223); to reduce the adversity, acrimony and bitterness surrounding divorce proceedings; to lessen the personal stigma attached to the divorce; and to create conditions for more rational and equitable settlements of property and spousal support. (Hogoboom, 1970; Kay, 1970; Krom, 1970) In brief, the new law attempted to bring divorce legislation into line with the social realities of marital breakdown in contemporary society. It recognized that marital conduct and misconduct no longer fit rigid categories of fault. And it eliminated the punitive element of moral condemnation that had pervaded Western thought for centuries.

The no-fault legislation changed each of the four basic elements in traditional divorce law. First, *it eliminated the fault-based grounds for divorce.* No longer did one spouse have to testify to the other's adultery, cruelty or desertion. And no longer were witnesses necessary to corroborate their testimony.

By replacing the old fault-based grounds for divorce with a single new standard of "irreconcilable differences," the legislature sought to eliminate both the artificial grounds for the breakdown of a marriage, and the artificial conception that one party was "responsible" for the breakdown. Further, the criterion of "irreconcilable differences" recognized that whatever the reasons for marital failure, they were best left out of the proceedings because they were irrelevant to an equitable settlement. Now the divorce procedure could begin with a neutral "petition for dissolution," with no specific acts or grounds needed as a justification.

Second, *the new laws eliminated the adversary process.* Divorce reformers believed that at least some of the trauma of a fault-based divorce resulted from the legal process itself, rather than from the inherent difficulties of dissolving a marriage. (See, for example, Rheinstein, 1972.) They assumed that husbands and wives who were dissolving their marriages were potentially "amicable," but that the *legal process generated hostility and trauma* by forcing them to be antagonists. The reformers assumed that if fault and the adversary process were eliminated from the legal proceedings, "human beings who are entitled to divorces could get them with the least possible amount of damage to themselves and to their families" (Proceedings from the California Assembly Committee on the Judiciary, 1964).

Each aspect of the legal process was therefore changed to reflect the new non-adversary approach to divorce: "Divorce" became "dissolution"; "plaintiffs" and "defendants" became "petitioners" and "respondents"; "alimony" became "spousal support"; and the court records read "*in re* the Marriage of Doe" instead of "Doe vs. Doe."[11] Standard printed forms written in plain English replaced the archaic legalistic pleadings. Residence requirements were reduced from one year to six months in the state before filing, and the minimum period between filing and the final decree was shortened from one year to six months. These revisions were designed in part to smooth the progress of a marital dissolution through the courts and to avoid some of the unnecessary legal wrangling and personal hostilities engendered by the adversarial model.

Third, *the financial aspects of the divorce were to be based on equity, equality and economic need* rather than on either fault or sex-based role assignments. Proponents of no-fault divorce contended that it was outmoded to grant alimony and property as a reward for virtue, and to withhold them as punishment for wrongdoing. Instead, they advocated more realistic standards for alimony and property awards—standards based on the spouses' economic circumstances and a new principle of equality between the sexes. They argued that justice for both the wife and husband would be better served by considering their economic situations, rather than by weighing their guilt or innocence. And they believed that men and women should no longer be shackled by the weight of traditional sex roles; new norms were necessary to bring the law into line with modern social reality.

With regard to the new economic criteria for awards, the no-fault law aimed at making the financial aspects of the divorce more equitable to facilitate the post-divorce adjustment of both men and women. Substantively, guidelines for financial settlements were changed to remove evidence of misconduct from consideration. For example, while alimony under the old law could only be awarded to the "injured party," regardless of that person's financial need, under the new law, it was to be based on the financial needs and financial resources of both spouses.

With regard to the new norm of equality between the sexes, the advocates of the divorce law reform pointed to the changing position of women in general, and to their increased participation in the labor force in particular, and urged a reformulation of alimony and property awards which recognized the growing ability of women to be self-supporting. With a reformist zeal they assumed that the employment gains of women had already eliminated the need for alimony as a means of continued support after divorce. Ignoring the fact that even full-time year-round female workers earn less than 60 percent of what men earn, some advocates went so far as to declare that "it does seem somewhat anachronistic, in an era of increasing feminine [sic] equality, that the statutes providing for alimony have remained on the books for as long as they have" (Brody, 1970: 228).

The legislators also challenged the anachronistic assumption that the husband had to continue to support his wife—for life. They pointed to the difficulty that men face in supporting two households if they remarry, and argued that the old law had converted "a host of physically and mentally competent young women into an army of alimony drones who neither toil nor spin and become a drain on society and a menace to themselves." (Hofstadter and Levittan, 1967:55) Thus while the reformers were willing to consider support for the older housewife, they did not believe that the younger housewife deserved continued support; instead they saw her as a potential "alimony drone" who ought to be self-supporting.

Under the new law, California judges setting alimony are directed to consider "the circumstances of the respective parties, including the duration of the marriage, and the ability of the supported spouse to engage in gainful employment without interfering with the interests of the children of the parties in the custody of each spouse." (Civil Code 4801) California's no-fault divorce law is thus typical of new alimony legislation: It is concerned primarily with financial criteria and, while it specifically mentions the custodial spouse and the wife in a marriage of long duration, the thrust of the law is to encourage the divorced woman to become self-supporting (by engaging in gainful employment).

The implicit aim of the new alimony was to encourage (some would say force) formerly dependent wives to assume the responsibility for their own support. With the elimination of fault as the basis for alimony, the new standard explicitly excluded the granting of support awards to women just because they had been wives, or just because their husbands had left them, or just because they had spent years as homemakers. The new law recognized, in theory, the need for transitional support, support for the custodial parent, and support for the older housewife who could not become self-supporting.

Property awards under no-fault are also to be based on equity and equality and are no longer limited to findings of fault. For example, in California the community property *must be divided equally*. [12] Underlying the new law is a conception of marriage as a partnership, with each person having made an equal contribution to the community property and therefore deserving an equal share.

The standards for child custody also reflect the new equality between the spouses. The preference for the mother (for children of tender years) has been replaced by a sex-neutral standard which instructs judges to award custody in the "best interest of the child."[13] Finally, the new law makes both husbands and wives responsible for child support.

Fourth, *no-fault divorce re-defined the traditional responsibilities of husbands and wives by instituting a new norm of equality between the sexes.*

Instead of the old sex-typed division of family responsibilities the new law has attempted to institutionalize sex-neutral obligations which fall equally upon the husband and the wife. No longer is the husband the head of the family—both spouses are now presumed to be equal partners in the marriage. Nor is the husband alone responsible for support, or the wife alone obligated to care for the home and children.

Each of the provisions of the new law discussed above reflect these new assumptions about appropriate spousal roles. The new standards for alimony indicate that a woman is no longer supposed to devote herself to her home and family—rather, she now bears an equal responsibility for her own economic support. For the law has clearly established a new norm of economic self-sufficiency for the divorced woman. Similarly, the new standards indicate that men will no longer be held responsible for their wives' (and ex-wives') lifelong support.

The criterion for dividing property also reflects the new norm of equality between the sexes. There is no preference or protection for the older housewife—or, even for the custodial mother (although some states do have a preference for the custodial parent to retain the family home while the children are living there). Instead, the two spouses are treated equally—each one receives an equal share of the property.

Finally, the expectations for child support are sex-neutral. Both parents are equally responsible for the financial welfare of their children after divorce. What was previously considered the husband's responsibility is now shared equally by the wife.

In summary, traditional divorce law and no-fault reflect two contrasting visions of "justice." The traditional law sought to deliver a moral justice which rewarded the good spouse and punished the bad spouse. It was a justice based on compensation for *past* behavior, both sin and virtue. The no-fault law ignores both moral character and moral history as a basis for awards. Instead it seeks to deliver a fairness and equity based on the financial *needs* and upon equality of the two parties.

The law is based on the assumption that divorced women can be immediately self-supporting. This assumption stands in contrast to the Uniform Marriage and Divorce Act which specifies that the court should consider the time necessary to acquire sufficient education or training to enable the party seeking temporary maintenance to find appropriate employment. Under this provision, a husband whose wife has supported him during his graduate education or professional training may be required to finance her education or training in order to place her in a position more nearly akin to the one she could have achieved. (Kay, 1972) The lack of such provisions in the no-fault divorce laws adopted by most states, such as California, may incur a heavier burden on the wife and make post-divorce adjustment especially difficult for women.

Thus, while the aims of the no-fault laws, i.e. equality and sex-neutrality are laudable, the laws may be instituting equality in a society in which women are not fully prepared (and/or permitted) to assume equal responsibility for their own and their children's support after divorce. Public policy then becomes a choice between temporary protection and safeguards for the transitional woman (and for the older housewife in the transitional generation) to minimize the hardships incurred by the new expectations, versus current reinforcement of the new equality, with the hope of speeding the transition, despite the hardships this may cause for current divorcees.

Endnotes

1. In 1975, for the first time in U.S. history, there were over *one million* divorces in a twelve-month period (Carter and Glick, 1976: 394), and the number of divorces is expected to rise.
2. Preston estimates that 44 percent of all current marriages will end in divorce (Preston, 1974: 435), while the more conservative estimate of Carter and Glick (1976: 396) is that at least one-third of all the first marriages of couples under 30 will end in divorce.
3. As of June, 1976, the fourteen states that adopted "pure" no-fault divorce statutes (in which irretrievable breakdown is the only grounds for the dissolution of the marriage) are Arizona, California, Colorado, Delaware, Florida, Iowa, Kentucky, Michigan, Minnesota, Missouri, Montana, Nebraska, Oregon and Washington.
4. The thirteen states that have added no-fault grounds to their existing fault-based grounds for divorce are Alabama, Connecticut, Georgia, Hawaii, Idaho, Indiana, Maine, Massachusetts, Mississippi, New Hampshire, North Dakota, Rhode Island and Texas. Most of the remaining states have recently added a provision allowing divorce for those "living separate and apart" for a specified period of time, which is an even more modified version of no-fault. Only three states, Illinois, Pennsylvania and South Dakota, retain fault as the *only* basis for divorce (Foster and Freed, 1977, Chart B1).
5. Today more citizens come into contact with the legal system in family law cases than in any other type of litigation (with the possible exception of traffic court) as matrimonial actions now comprise over fifty percent of all civil cases at the trial court level in most cities and states. (Friedman and Percival, 1976: 281–83)
6. We are referring explicitly to divorce, or "the legal termination of a valid marriage," (Clark 1968: 280) as distinguished from an annulment, which is a declaration that a purported marriage has been invalid from its beginning.
7. Adultery remained the only grounds for divorce in England until 1937 when the Matrimonial Causes Act added desertion, cruelty and some other offenses as appropriate grounds for divorce. (Clark, 1968: 282)
8. In contrast, Maxine Virtue's observations of a Chicago court (1956) indicated identical standards for cruelty among husbands and wives. As she notes (Virtue, 1956: 86–89), "The number of cruel spouses in Chicago, both male and female, who strike their marriage partner in the face exactly twice, without provocation, leaving visible marks, is remarkable."
9. Thirty-six states (twenty-eight common-law jurisdictions and eight community property states) allow the court to divide the property upon divorce. (Krause, 1976: 980) The remaining 14 states all have common law property systems which allow each person to retain the property in his or her name. However, there is a considerable impetus for reforms in these states. Legal scholars, such as Foster and Freed, have called the maintenance of the separate property system at the time of divorce obsolete, archaic and shockingly unfair. The strongest argument against it is that "in its

application it ignores the contribution wives make to the family." (Foster and Freed, 1974: 170) This argument has also been the major objection of feminist groups to the common-law property system. For example, the Citizen's Advisory Council on the Status of Women (1974: 6) has advocated the importance of changing the law "to recognize explicitly the contribution of the homemaker . . . and to give courts the authority to divide property (owned by both spouses) upon divorce."

10. Of all the financial aspects of the divorce, only child support was, in theory, unaffected by fault— as it was based on the needs of the children (and the father's financial status).

11. The new language was not always easy to adopt, however. When film star Linda Lovelace was divorced, the newspapers reported that she had "charged her husband with irreconcilable differences."

12. The court may make an unequal award if community property has been deliberately misappropriated, or if immediate equal division will incur an extreme or unnecessary hardship. Property may also be divided unequally in a private agreement between the two parties.

13. In California this was changed in 1972 but was part of the original recommendations from the governor's commission which initiated the no-fault legislation.

References

Anton v. Anton
    1955   49 Del. 431, 118 A.2d 605, (Supp. 1955).
Blackston, William
    1765   Commentaries on the Laws of England.
Brody, Stuart
    1970   "California's Divorce Reform: Its Sociological Implication" Pacific Law Journal, 1.
Brown v. Brown
    1955   198 Tenn. 600, 381 S.W. 2d 492.
Carter, Hugh, and Paul C. Glick
    1970   Marriage and Divorce: A Social and Economic Study. Cambridge, Mass.: Harvard.
    1976   Marriage and Divorce: A Social and Economic Study. Cambridge, Mass.: Harvard (Revised Ed.).
Clark, Homer
    1968   Domestic Relations. St. Paul, Minn.: West.
Citizens' Advisory Council on the Status of Women
    1974   Recognition of Economic Contribution of Homemakers and Protection of Children in Divorce and Practice. Washington, D.C.: U.S. Government Printing Office.
Foster, Henry H., and Doris Jonas Freed
    1974   "Marital Property Reform in New York: Partnership of Co-Equals?" Family Law Quarterly, Vol. 8; pp. 169–205.
    1977   Family Law: Cases and Materials. Boston: Little, Brown (3rd ed.)
Friedman, Lawrence M., and Robert V. Percival
    1976a   "Who Sues for Divorce? From Fault Through Fiction to Freedom." Journal of Legal Studies 5 (1): 61–82.
    1976b   "A Tale of Two Courts: Letigation in Alameda and San Benito Counties." Law and Society Review 10 (2): 267–303.
Hofstadter, Samuel H., and Shirley R. Levittan
    1967   "Alimony—A Reformulation." Journal of Family Law 7:51–60.
Hogoboom, William P.
    1971   "The California Family Law Act of 1970: 18 Months' Experience." Journal of Missouri Bar: 584–589.
Kay, Herma Hill
    1970   A Family Court: The California Proposal in Paul Bohannan (ed.) Divorce and After. Garden City, New York: Doubleday.
    1974   "Sex-Based Discrimination in Family Law" in Kenneth M. Davidson, Ruth G. Ginsburg and Herma Hill Kay, Sex-Based Discrimination Text, Cases and Materials. St. Paul, Minn.: West.

Krause, Harry D.
    1976   Family Law: Cases and Materials. St. Paul, Minn.: West.
Reynolds v. Reynolds
    1862   85 Mass. (3 Allen) 605 (1862).
Rheinstein, Max
    1972   Marriage Stability, Divorce and the Law. Chicago: University of Chicago.
Rucci v. Rucci
    1962   23 Conn. Supp. 221, 181 A.2d 125.
Weitzman, Lenore
    1979   The Marriage Contract. Englewood Cliffs, N.J.: Prentice-Hall.
Weitzman, Lenore, and Ruth B. Dixon
    1976   "The Alimony Myth." Paper read at the meeting of the American Sociological Association.
    1979   "Child Custody Standards and Awards." Journal of Social Issues, Forthcoming.
Weitzman, Lenore J., Herma Hill Kay, and Ruth B. Dixon
    1979   No Fault Divorce: The Impact of Changes in the Law and the Legal Process. California
            Divorce Law Research Project, Center for the Study of Law and Society. University of
            California, Berkeley.
Wheeler, Michael
    1974   No-Fault Divorce. Boston: Beacon Press.

Mothers and Divorce: Downward Mobility

Terry Arendell

[The women in this study*] had assumed that after divorce they would some-how be able to maintain a middle-class life-style for themselves and their children. Those in their twenties and thirties had been confident that they could establish themselves as capable employees and find positions that would provide sufficient incomes. Most of the older women, who had been out of the work force longer, had been less confident about their earning abilities, but they had assumed that the difference between the former family income and their own earnings would be adequately compensated for by court-ordered child support and spousal support payments. In fact, virtually all of the women had assumed that family manage-

*Arendell's study, begun in 1983, is based on interviews with 60 divorced women, ranging in age from 26 to 58, in 8 counties of Northern California. All of the women had custody of children whose ages ranged from 3 to 18. All had lived at a middle-class economic level before the divorce.

ment and parenting efforts, which had kept most of them from pursuing employment and career development while they were married, would be socially valued and legally recognized in their divorce settlements. What had worried them most was not economic difficulty but the possible psychological effects of divorce on themselves and their children. Still, they had believed that they would probably recover from the emotional trauma of divorcing in a matter of months and would then be able to reorganize their lives successfully.

Drastically Reduced Incomes

But even the women who had worried most about how they would manage financially without their husbands' incomes had not imagined the kind of hardship they would face after divorce. All but two of the sixty women had to cope with a substantial loss of family income. Indeed, 90 percent of them (fifty-six out of sixty) found that divorce immediately pushed them below the poverty line, or close to it. As wives and mothers, they had been largely dependent on their husbands, who had supplied the family's primary income.* Without that source of income, they suffered a drastic reduction in standard of living—an experience not shared by their ex-husbands. Like women generally, they were "declassed" by divorce.

The economic decline experienced by these sixty women, all of whom remained single parents, was not temporary. With caution and careful spending, most could meet their essential monthly expenses. But few had any extra money for dealing with emergencies or unexpected demands, and some continued to fall further behind, unable even to pay their monthly bills. One of them, divorced for nearly eight years, described her experience this way:

> I've been living hand to mouth all these years, ever since the divorce. I have no savings account. The notion of having one is as foreign to me as insurance— there's no way I can afford insurance. I have an old pickup that I don't drive very often. In the summertime I don't wear nylons to work because I can cut costs there. Together the kids and I have had to struggle and struggle. Supposedly struggle builds character. Well, some things simply aren't character building. There have been times when we've scoured the shag rug to see if we could find a coin to come up with enough to buy milk so we could have cold cereal for dinner. That's not character building.

Although they had been living for a median period of over four years as divorced single parents, only *nine* of these sixty women had managed to halt the economic fall prompted by divorce; four of these nine had even managed to reestablish a standard of living close to what they had had while married. Thus the remaining majority—fifty-one women—had experienced no economic recovery.

---

*According to Lee Rainwater (1984) and the U.S. Bureau of the Census (1985), the earnings of working married wives contribute only 22 percent of the average family's total income. For this reason, poverty, which occurs in only one of nineteen husband-wife families and in only one of nine families maintained by a single father, afflicts almost one of every three families headed by a woman.

Few had any savings, and most lived from paycheck to paycheck in a state of constant uncertainty. One of them, a woman in her late forties and divorced more than four years, told me:

> I can't go on like this. There's no way. I can manage for another year, maybe a year and a half, but no more. I don't have the stamina. It's not that I don't have a job. My problem is money, plain and simple. That's all that counts in this situation.

This group of recently divorced mothers was by no means unique. All female-headed households experience high rates of economic hardship, and the gap in median income between female-headed families and other types of families has actually widened between 1960 and 1983.* Part of the reason is obvious: certain fixed costs of maintaining a family—such as utility bills and home mortgages or rent—do not change when the family size declines by one, and many other expenses, such as food and clothing, do not change significantly. Additionally, in most cases when the mother obtained employment, it provided a low income that was substantially reduced by new expenses, such as the costs of transportation and child care.†

These women understood how their economic dependency in marriage had contributed to their present economic situation. One of them, who had been married nearly twenty years before divorcing, said:

> Money does wonders in any situation. I'm sure women with more education and better jobs don't have situations quite as desperate as mine. But I quit school when I married and stayed home to raise my children.

Unfortunately, they arrived at such understanding the hard way, through experience. Before divorcing, they had expected to receive "reasonable" child support and had thought they could probably find jobs that paid "reasonable" wages. They had only the vaguest understanding of other women's divorce experiences. Thus two of them said:

> Friends of mine had ended up divorced with children, and they would tell me some of these things. But I had no empathy at all. I might say, "Gee, that doesn't seem fair" or "Gee, that's too bad." But it never *really* hit me how serious it is

---

*Between 1960 and 1983, the median income of female-headed families with no husband present dropped by the following percentages: from 61 to 57 percent of the median income of male-headed families with no wife present, from 43 to 41 percent of the median income of married couples, and from 51 to 38 percent of the median income of married-couple families in which the wife was also employed. In 1983, the median income for female-headed families was $11,484; for male-headed families with no wife present, $20,140; for married-couple families, $26,019; and for married couples in which the wife was employed, $30,340 (U.S. Bureau of the Census, 1985).

†From his Michigan study, David Chambers (1979) concludes that the custodial parent needs 80 percent of the predivorce income to maintain the family's standard of living. The total income of most family units of divorced women and children falls below 50 percent of their former family income. Sweden, in fact, has determined that single-parent families actually need more income than others and provides cash supports that give them incomes comparable to those of two-parent families (Cassetty, 1983a).

until it happened to me. So I think there must be a lot of people out there who don't have the foggiest idea what it feels like.

I had no idea how *much* money it takes. You don't have the [husband's] income, but you still have your family. There's the rub.

Their experiences led them to conclude that in America today, divorced women generally must accept a reduced standard of living. And as women with children, they were keenly aware that only remarriage could offer a quick escape from economic hardship.* A mother of three told me:

I have this really close friend. She was a neighbor and often kept my daughter until I got home from school. She and her husband had two darling little kids. One day he just up and left. Surprised us all—he married his secretary eventually. My friend hadn't worked before, so I helped her get some typing skills. She worked for two weeks and said, "No more." She called me and said, "Well, I'm not going through what you did. I'm getting married." That was like a slap in the face. Gosh, did I look that bad? I started to doubt myself. Was I doing that bad a job? Should I have gone the marriage route? Gone out and gotten a job and then married somebody? I still wonder about that. Things would have been a lot easier financially. The kids would have had a father. And I would have done what society looks at favorably. I don't know. I still don't know what to do.

Economically these women lost their middle-class status, but socially their expectations of themselves and their children remained the same. They still identified with the middle class, but their low incomes prevented them from participating in middle-class activities. This contradiction created many dilemmas and conflicts:

I went to a CETA workshop, and I started crying when all they talked about was how to get a job. A woman came after me in the hallway, and I just bawled. I'd been searching for a job for months. I had a degree and teaching credential, and here I was being told how to fill out a stupid job application. And I had three kids at home that I didn't know how I was going to feed that week and a lovely home I couldn't afford.

I moved here after the divorce because the school had a particularly good program for gifted children. Kids were classed by ability and not just by grade level. So my kid was in a really good spot for what he needed. I didn't realize at the time that I was the only single parent in that group. One reason those kids can achieve at that level is because they have a very stable home life, two parents to work with every child on the enrichment and the projects and the homework. I hate to say this, but it's all socioeconomic. Every kid in there belonged to a high socioeconomic group. Oh, they can rationalize that it's not really like that, but it's completely WASPish, all two-parent families where the mothers don't work. Mothers are available to take kids to music lessons, soccer lessons, gymnastic

---

*Research supports the commonsense belief that the surest way to reverse the economic decline resulting from divorce is to remarry (Sawhill, 1976; Duncan and Morgan, 1974, 1979; Johnson and Minton, 1982). Do women remarry because they conclude, pragmatically, that being a single woman is too costly, for themselves and perhaps also for their children? Would fewer women remarry if they could successfully support themselves? The answers to such questions will have interesting political implications.

lessons, and all of that whenever it's needed. I had to take my son out of that class. I couldn't keep up the level of activity required of the kids and the parents. The gap was growing greater and greater. If I'd lived like this a long time, I might have known how to cope, but this was all new. And it all came down to money.

The women resented their precarious positions all the more because they knew that their former husbands had experienced no loss in class status or standard of living and could have eased their struggles to support the children:

> Five hundred dollars here and there—or taking over the orthodontist's bills— anything like that would have meant a lot. I don't see why this kid should have to live with jaw and tooth problems because I got a divorce. His jaw had to be totally realigned, so it wasn't just cosmetic. His father could easily have paid that monthly [orthodontist] bill and deducted it. That would have made a tremendous difference. But he wouldn't. By making me suffer, he made his child suffer too.

When the children retained some access to middle-class activities through involvement with their fathers, their mothers had ambivalent feelings. They were grateful that their children were not neglected by their fathers and could enjoy some enriching and entertaining activities with them; but they found their former husbands' greater financial resources a painful reminder of how little they themselves could provide. One woman, who had to let her child get free meals through the subsidized school lunch program, despite her many efforts to make more money, told me this:

> His father seldom buys him anything. But his stepmother sometimes does. She can give him all these nice things. She's given him nice books, a stereo headset. I have no idea what her motivation is, but it's a very funny feeling to know that I can't go and buy my son something he would love to have, but this perfect stranger can. And how will that affect my son ultimately? He must know how difficult things are here, and that I'm not deliberately depriving him. But it's kind of ironic—I helped establish that standard of living, but I end up with none of it, and she has full access to it.

Expenses and Economizing

Living with a reduced budget was a constant challenge to most of these women because they had no cushion to fall back on if expenses exceeded their incomes. Their savings were depleted soon after they divorced; only twelve of the sixty women I talked to had enough money in savings to cover a full month's expenses. Most said they had radically cut back their spending. The major expenses after divorce were housing, food, and utilities. The women with young children also had substantial child care expenses, and several had unusually high medical bills that were not covered by health insurance.

Within a short time after their divorces, more than one-third of the women— sixteen women living in homes they owned and seven living in rented places— had to move to different housing with their children in order to reduce their expenses. Two of the women had moved more than four times in the first two years after their divorces, always for financial reasons. During marriage, forty-nine of the sixty women had lived in homes owned with their husbands. After divorce, only nine of them retained ownership of the family home. Of these nine, six were able to acquire ownership by buying out their husbands as part of the community property settlement (five of them only because they were able to get financial assistance from their parents); two retained the home by exchanging other community assets for it; and one received the home according to the dictates of the religion she and her husband shared.

Home ownership brought with it many expenses besides mortgage payments. Several women neglected upkeep and repairs for lack of money. A woman who was in her fifties reported this common dilemma:

> I owe $16,000 on this house. I could get about $135,000 for it, so I have a large equity. But it would have taken all of that to get that condominium I looked at, and my payments would still have been about $400 a month. I don't know how I'll be able to keep up the house, financially or physically. The house needs painting, and I can't keep up the yard work. I'd like to move. I'd like a fresh start. But the kids don't want to move, and I can't imagine how I'll handle all of this once they're gone. When the alimony [spousal support] stops, there'll be no way I can manage a move. I'm stuck here now. The mortgage is really low and the interest is only 5 percent.

Two of the mothers reduced expenses by moving their children from private to public schools. Two others were able to keep their children in private schools only after administrators waived the tuition fees. Seven mothers received financial assistance for preschoolers' child care costs, five from private and two from public agencies. One of these women, who worked full-time, had this to say about her expenses:

> I'm buying this house. I pay $330 a month for it. Child care for my two kids runs to almost $500 a month. Since I bring home only a little more than $900, there's no way I could make it without the child care assistance. There'd be nothing left.

About half of these women had economic situations so dire that careful budgeting was not enough, and they continued to fall further behind economically. Those living close to the margin managed by paying some bills one month and others the next. Their indebtedness increased, and opportunities for reversing the situation did not appear:

> I'm so far in debt. Yes indeed. I keep thinking, why should I worry about the bills? I'll never get out of debt! All I can do is juggle. Without my charge cards, my kids would be bare-assed naked. And school is coming up again. What am I going to do for school clothes? And they've all grown fast this year. . . . I probably owe $3,000 on charge cards, and I still owe rent—I haven't paid this month or last. The landlord I have has been very understanding. He's let us go along as best he can. We've been here four years, and he knows what I'm going through. Over the years, he's given me several eviction notices, but this last time he hired a lawyer and everything. I decided I'd just pitch my tent on the capitol mall in Sacramento and say, "Here I am." I've written my congressman again,

because I qualify for subsidized housing. But it'll take forever to get any action on that.

For many, however, even the persistent realities of economic hardship could not extinguish middle-class hopes:

> My husband liked really good food and always bought lots and the best. So when he left, it was really hard to cut the kids back. They were used to all that good eating. Now there's often no food in the house, and everybody gets really grouchy when there's no food around. . . . I think I've cut back mostly on activities. I don't go to movies anymore with friends. We've lost $150 a month now because my husband reduced the support. It gets cut from activities—we've stopped doing everything that costs, and there's nowhere else to cut. My phone is shut off. I pay all the bills first and then see what there is for food. . . . I grew up playing the violin, and I'd wanted my kids to have music lessons—piano would be wonderful for them. And my older two kids are very artistic. But lessons are out of the question.

Obtaining credit had been a real problem for many, for the reasons given by this woman, who had worked during the marriage while her husband attended school:

> My kids and I were very poor those first years after the divorce. I had taken care of our finances during marriage. But I didn't have accounts in my own name, so I couldn't get credit. I got a job as soon as I could. I was getting $65 a month for child support and paying $175 a month for rent. Between the rent and the child care and the driving to work, I was absolutely broke. I really didn't have enough to live on. I had no benefits either, with my first job. I was living dangerously, and with children. I could barely pay the basic bills. There wasn't enough money for food lots of times. I cried many times because there wasn't enough money. I couldn't get any credit. [When I was married] my husband could get any credit he wanted, but it was on the basis of *my* job, which had the higher income. He couldn't even keep his checkbook balanced, but now I'm the one who can't get credit! It was a hard lesson to learn. Now whenever I get a chance, I tell women to start getting a credit rating.

The woman who told me this, incidentally, had managed to overcome initial impoverishment and gain a middle-class income from her job.

Some women regarded personal possessions such as jewelry, furniture, and cars as things they might sell to meet emergencies or rising indebtedness:

> I sold jewelry to have my surgery, to pay for the part that wasn't covered. I still have some silver, and I have some good furniture, which could probably bring something. That's probably what I'd do in an emergency, sell those things. What else do people do?

Teenaged children helped by earning money through odd jobs and babysitting. Older teenagers changed their college plans, and several entered community colleges instead of universities. One woman's daughter was already in the Navy, pursuing her schooling in languages and working as a translator, and the daughter of another was considering military service as a way of saving money for a college education.

Most women compared their own hardship and forced economizing to the economic freedom enjoyed by their ex-husbands. For example:

> I know my ex-husband goes somewhere almost every weekend, and he usually takes a friend along. I wonder how he can do that. How can he go somewhere every weekend? The only way I could do that is find a rich man! I couldn't possibly work enough hours to pay for that much stuff. I'd be doing well to finance a [twenty-mile] trip to San Francisco!

There were some exceptions to the general pattern of economic decline. Nine of the sixty women had regained some latitude for discretionary spending, though only three of them had managed this economic reversal without help. These nine were a distinct subgroup; the others did not share their higher standards of living or their feelings and approaches to the future. Still, only two of these nine women had not experienced a major decline in income immediately upon divorcing (or separating). One had been living on welfare because her husband's excessive drinking and erratic behavior had prevented him from holding a job; she found employment immediately after separating from him. The other one had been the primary family wage earner during her marriage.* Four of the women whose incomes had dropped significantly had managed to stop and even reverse the economic decline very soon after divorce because they were granted temporary spousal support awards and acquired some money and assets from their community property settlement; two of them, who had been divorced after more than twenty years of marriage, also received substantial amounts of money from their parents. Although these four did not experience the degree of hardship shared by the others, they did not fully recover their formerly high income levels and therefore also had to alter their life-styles. As one of them said:

> Essentially, I took an $80,000 drop in annual income. And I had to borrow again last year. This year I finally sold the house, and that was really the only way I've made it. My change in life-style has been *tremendous*. Just my heating and electricity bill for our home was $350 a month. We just barely got by on $2,000 a month. I stopped buying household things; I stopped buying clothes for myself. And I rented out a room in the house. It was a huge house, and that helped out. I let the cleaning woman and the gardener go. I didn't paint. I let the property taxes go until I sold the house and paid them then. I quit taking trips. This house I'm in now has much lower operating expenses. My son doesn't have the same things he'd had. His grandparents buy most of his shoes and clothes now. He used to have lots and lots, so it's been a change for him.

Of the other five women who succeeded in improving their economic situations after a few years, three did so entirely through their own work efforts, and the other two managed with help from their former husbands—one took in the child

*A recent study by Lee Rainwater (1984:84) shows how economic dependency in a previous marriage makes it difficult for a woman to recover economically from divorce: "By the fourth year that they headed their own families, women who had regular work experience before becoming female heads had family incomes equal to 80 percent of their average family income while a wife. Women who had not worked at all had incomes slightly less than half that of their last married years."

for more than a year while his ex-wife worked at several jobs, and the other accepted a shared parenting arrangement.

Emotional Responses to Economic Loss

None of the nine women who had experienced substantial economic recovery reported suffering serious emotional changes. Forty-four of the others, however, spoke of frequent struggles with depression and despair. Every one of them attributed these intense feelings, which often seemed overwhelming, directly to the financial hardships that followed divorce. This woman spoke for many others in describing the effects that economic loss had had on her:

> I think about money a great deal. It's amazing. I used to get so bored by people who could only talk about money. Now it's all I think about. It's a perpetual thought, how to get money—not to invest, or to save, but just to live. The interesting thing is that you develop a poverty mentality. That intrigues me. I would never have thought that could happen. But if I had had money, several times in the last year I would have fought what was happening to me in a way I no longer think of fighting. You tend to accept what's coming because there's so much you *have* to accept. You get so you accept everything that comes your way. For example, I accepted at first what I was told about treating this cancer on my face: that the only surgery possible would leave my face disfigured with one side paralyzed. I knew it would ruin any possibility of my teaching if they did that to my face, but I would have just accepted it if a friend hadn't gotten me to go to someone else for consultation. I wouldn't have done that on my own. That's not how I would have behaved at other times in my life. I think it must happen to a lot of divorced women. It was only this year that I realized how strange this has become. I'm educated, I've come through a wealthy phase of my life, and now here I am, being shuttled around and not even fighting. It continues to fascinate me. After a while, you develop a begging mentality in which you'd like to squeeze money out of anybody. I guess I'm somewhere in the realm of poverty. I know there are poorer people, but I'm pretty well down near the bottom. If I were to lose this job—which is always possible, there's no security to it—I'd be finished. Finished. I'd lose my house. I'd lose everything. There's no way I could survive.

The first year of divorce was traumatic for most, especially because legal uncertainties were mixed with other fears. A vicious circle was common: anxieties brought sleepless nights, and fatigue made the anxieties sharper. Although economic hardship remained, by the end of the first year most of the women had learned to control some of the anxiety surrounding it.*

Depression overtook a majority of these women at some time or other. Their feelings of despair over financial troubles were worsened by concerns for their children. One of them said:

---

*Various studies argue that the first year or so after divorce is the most stressful and traumatic (Hetherington, Cox, and Cox, 1976; Wallerstein and Kelly, 1979, 1980; Weiss, 1979a, 1979b). Additionally, both Pett (1982) and Buehler and Hogan (1980) found that financial concerns were among the factors that limited divorced mothers' emotional recovery from divorce. None of these studies, however, attempts to distinguish the effects of economic uncertainty from more generalized separation emotions.

> I thought about running away, but who would I have turned my kids over to? I also thought about suicide—especially when the youngest was still a baby and I had so much trouble with child care and it cost me so much. I kept thinking that if I were gone, it would take a major burden off of everybody.

In fact, such despair was a common experience: twenty-six of the sixty women volunteered that they had contemplated suicide at some time after divorce. They mentioned various contributing factors, such as emotional harassment from their husbands and uncertainty about their own abilities and identities, but all said that economic hardship was *the* primary stress that pushed them to the point of desperation.

One mother gave a very detailed account of her experience with suicidal depression, which occurred at a time when she had been barely managing for several months. She would drag herself to work and then collapse in bed when she got home. When she would get out of bed, she told me, the sight of her ten-year-old son sitting in front of the television set, alone in a cold room and eating cold cereal, would send her back to bed, where her exhaustion and despair would be exacerbated by hours of crying. She went on:

> I came home to an empty house that night—it was February. I had gotten my son's father to take him that weekend so I could go to my class—the one about learning to live as a single person again. I'd hoped that by getting some encouragement, I'd be able to pull myself out of this and find a way to make a better living. About eleven o'clock, I just decided this was no way to live. I couldn't take care of this child. I'd gone to Big Brothers, and they wouldn't take him because he had a father. But his father wasn't seeing him. Family Services weren't any help. The woman there did try to help, I think. She cared. But she'd been married more than twenty-five years, and just didn't understand. All I could do in the fifty-minute appointment with her was cry. My attorney wasn't giving me any help or getting me any money. My mother was mad at me—she said it was my fault for leaving my husband.
>
> I just couldn't see it ever being any different, so I decided to kill myself. I'm sure that's not a unique thing. It was the most logical thing in the world. I knew exactly how I was going to do it. I was going to fill the bathtub with warm water and cut my wrists. It would be fine then—that thought was the only thing that made me feel any better. Nothing was as bad as the thought of getting up the next day. So I called my son's father—he was going to bring him back the next day—and I asked him if he thought he could take care of him. I didn't think I gave any evidence [of my feelings] or anything—it wasn't a desperate call for help, or a threatening call, or anything like that, because I'd already made up my mind. I just didn't want him to bring my son in here and find me like that. I wanted him to make some kind of arrangements to take care of him. He didn't say anything on the phone, but in about twenty minutes the doorbell rang. Two young men in blue uniforms were standing there. They wanted to take me to an emergency room. It was a crisis place, they said. They were young and scared themselves and acted like they didn't know what to do.
>
> I guess the shock of realizing how far I'd gone was enough to snap me out of it. I'd spent those twenty minutes [after the phone call] piddling around taking care of some last-minute things, tidying up and so on. It seems that once I made the decision, it gave me such inner peace, such a perfect reconciliation. It seemed the

most logical, practical thing in the world. Then their coming stopped me from doing it. I didn't go with them, but they gave me a phone number and told me there were people there who would come and get me anytime.

I've only recently put into perspective what happened. It wasn't so much my inability to cope as it was the convergence of everything in my situation. That person at Family Services did help, actually, when she pointed out that some people who've never had trouble dealing with anything don't know what else to do when they feel like they can't cope. That fit. I'd never had a crisis I couldn't deal with in some way. I'd gotten myself into bad situations before, but I could always see cause-and-effect relationships, and I'd always felt like I could make some changes right away that would change things in my life. In this case, I couldn't figure anything out. I don't even know how to tell you what I thought.

This woman had been divorced before and had not suffered depression; but she had had no child then, no one else for whom she was responsible.

These women who were new to poverty had no ideas about how to cope in their new situations, and they found little help in the society at large. Some of the most desperate were unable to afford professional counseling. One of them said:

At one point during the eviction, I was getting hysterical. I needed help. So I called a program called Women's Stress. Good thing I wasn't really suicidal, because they kept me on hold a long time. They said, "Well, this program is just for women with an alcohol or drug problem. Does that fit you?" I said, "No, but if I don't get help, it will." They said they'd send me a pamphlet, which they did. It cost twenty-five dollars to join. I never did find any help.

The worst personal pain these women suffered came from observing the effects of sudden economic hardship on their children. Here is one woman's poignant account:

I had $950 a month, and the house payment was $760, so there was hardly anything left over. So there we were: my son qualified for free lunches at school. We'd been living on over $4,000 a month, and there we were. That's so humiliating. What that does to the self-esteem of even a child is absolutely unbelievable. And it isn't hidden: everybody knows the situation. They knew at his school that he was the kid with the free lunch coupons. . . . My son is real tall and growing. I really didn't have any money to buy him clothes, and attorneys don't think school clothes are essential. So he was wearing these sweatshirts that were too small for him. Then one day he didn't want to go to school because the kids had been calling him Frankenstein because his arms and legs were hanging out of his clothes—they were too short. That does terrible things to a kid, it really does. We just weren't equipped to cope with it.

But the need to cut costs—on food, clothing, and activities for the children—was not the only source of pain. Most of the mothers reported that their parenting approaches changed and that their emotions became more volatile, and even unstable, in periods of great financial stress. Mothers who went to work full-time resented the inevitable loss of involvement in their children's lives:

I wish I could get over the resentment. [In the first years after the divorce] I spent half the time blaming myself and the other half blaming their father. Because I was so preoccupied, I missed some really good years with them, doing things I'd looked forward to and wanted to do. Those years are gone now.

Some of the mothers also thought the experience of economic hardship after divorce might eventually affect the society at large, as more and more women and children come to share it. For example:

> It's not just the mother [who's affected]. It's a whole generation of kids who don't even know how to use a knife and a fork, who don't sit at a table to eat, who don't know how to make conversation with people of different ages. There are so many awful possibilities, and it's a whole society that's affected. I'm not talking about people who have lived for years in poverty. We planned and lived one way with no idea of the other reality. Then this harsh reality hits, and everything becomes a question of survival. I think it must be different if that's all you've experienced. At least then your plans fit your responsibilities—that sort of thing. You can't spend your whole day trying to survive and then care anything about what's going on in the world around you. You really can't. . . . Maybe it's going to take 50 percent of the population to be in this shape before we get change. But some of us have to be salvaged, just so we can fight. We can't all be so oppressed by trying to survive that we can't do anything at all.

Although their despair was worsened by concern for their children, it was the children who gave these women their strongest incentive to continue the struggle:

> Sure, I think about suicide. And I'm a smart lady who's been creative and able to do some things to change our situation. But I'm tired—*tired*. And it's real hard. What keeps me alive is my kid. I may be boxed in, but if I give up, what will happen to her? She doesn't deserve that.

Most of these women also admitted to having lost a sense of the future. A fifty-year-old woman, who said she wondered if she would someday become a bag lady, told me:

> That's what I started to say at the beginning—*I don't have a future*. I can sit around and cry about that for a while, but then I have to move on and ask, what am I going to do about it? And there's not much I can do. What career can I start at my age? How do I retrieve all those years spent managing a family?

And another somewhat younger woman said:

> The worst poverty is the poverty of the spirit that sets in when you've been economically poor too long, and it gets to the point where you can't see things turning around.

To avoid this sense of hopelessness, a majority of the sixty women tried not to think about the future and made only short-term plans:

> I learned very quickly that I couldn't think too far into the future or I'd drive myself crazy. The future became, "What will I do next month?" I learned I had to go day to day and just do the best I could. That's been my major technique for coping, and I learned it right away. I've built up some retirement and Social Security through work, thank heavens. But I have to live right now. I just can't

think about the future. The worst that can happen is that the state will take care of me, and I'll end up in a crappy old folks' home. But I don't think about that.

Ten of the sixty women—a unique subgroup—said they had not experienced serious depression or despair after divorce. But the reasons they gave simply reemphasize the central importance of economic loss in the lives of divorced women. Four of these ten had various sources of income that protected them from poverty and enabled them to work actively toward improving their situation. Two of them were using income from the divorce property settlement to attend graduate school, and they hoped to regain their former standard of living by pursuing professional careers. Two were receiving financial support from their parents while they sought employment and planned for the possible sale of their homes as part of the property settlement. The remaining six said they were generally optimistic *in spite of* their poor economic positions. Like the others, they found the financial hardships imposed by divorce surprising and difficult to handle; they simply found these hardships easier to cope with than the despair they had known in their marriages.

In summary, these women discovered that the most important change brought about by divorce was an immediate economic decline, which for most of them had not been reversible. Despite their economizing efforts and dramatically altered life-styles, many of them continued to lose ground financially. In addition, economic circumstances had a powerful effect on their emotional lives. Only a very few escaped feelings of despair and hopelessness. Most found that economic uncertainties fostered depression, discouragement, and despair, and nearly all said they had endured periods of intense anxiety over the inadequacy of their income and its effects on the well-being of their children. Most of them felt trapped in their present circumstances and said they had no sense of the future.

The Impact of Divorce on Children

Susan E. Krantz

Each year, 2 million children are newly introduced to their parents' divorce (Monthly Vital Statistics Report, 1985). It is estimated that by 1990, more than half of all American children under 18 will have experienced a divorce or separation of their natural parents (Hofferth, 1983; Weitzman, 1985).

Divorce changes the lives of children. During a confusing period of high emotional intensity, the child must attempt to understand a complex series of events and to restructure numerous assumptions and expectations about the self, the family, and the future. He or she may be required to leave a familiar school, residence, neighborhood and the social ties established in these places. . . . The child must often assume new household tasks; temporarily receive less support, nurturance, and supervision from one or both parents; and witness the distress of the parents individually and as a couple (Wallerstein & Kelly, 1980).

These events in the child's life raise several questions: First, what are the effects of divorce on the child? Second, how do we explain any undesirable post-divorce reactions of children? The "parental-absence" perspective assumes that negative effects of divorce are related to the breakup of the nuclear family *per se*. The "marital distress" and "economic hardship" perspectives, on the other hand, argue that the effects of divorce on children are not the result of the divorce *per se* but rather stem from other factors, such as the discord between the parents or the low financial status of the custodial parent. The "multiple factor" perspective stresses the multiple and interacting factors that contribute to the effects of divorce on children.

The purposes of this [paper] are to: (1) examine critically the different perspectives on the effects of divorce on children, (2) evaluate the validity of the research procedures in studies of children's post-divorce functioning, (3) review the research findings, and (4) discuss their policy implications.

Differing Perspectives on Divorce and Children

Parental Absence

The "parental absence" view asserts that two parents are necessary for the well-being of a child. The father, who is the absent parent in approximately 90 percent of divorces (Glick, 1979), is thought to be necessary for sex-role socialization,

From S. M. Dornbusch and M. H. Strober, eds., *Feminism, Children, and the New Families* (New York: Guilford, 1988). Reprinted by permission of Guilford Publications, Inc. Cross-references to the parent volume have been omitted.

supervision and discipline. This approach assumes that divorce is harmful because the departure of the father means the loss of a main agent of socialization.

The role of the father, however, may be over-emphasized in the "parent absence" approach. Some fathers in two-parent families are relatively unavailable to their children and so do not perform the functions traditionally attributed to them. According to Szalai et al. (1972), employed fathers living with their children share activities with their children for only two hours per week compared to the five and one-half hours of the employed mother and the 11 hours of homemakers. Blanchard and Biller (1971) found that sons of relatively uninvolved fathers in intact families and boys with absent fathers showed similar academic deficits in comparison to boys with involved fathers in intact families. Thus, the physical absence of the father appears to be no more harmful than his emotional absence, at least with respect to academic performance.

Similarly, the role of other adults may be under-emphasized. It is obvious that the mother plays a crucial role in the socialization of the child. Friends, relatives, teachers, and even heroes of the mass media may also serve as models for the child. Indeed, Aldous (1972) found no differences in the perceptions of young children with absent or present fathers regarding which sex performs conventional sex-typed tasks.

The position that the absence of a parent is harmful to children was dominant in an era when the nuclear family unit was almost unquestioningly valued. More recently, western culture began to move toward a philosophy of individualism and self-fulfillment (Conger, 1981). In this new climate, it is expected that satisfied, fulfilled parents living apart will provide a healthier emotional atmosphere for their children than will dissatisfied, unhappy parents living together. Any negative concommitants of divorce observed in children are attributed not to the divorce itself, but rather to the marital distress or to the economic hardships of divorce.

Marital Distress

Several observers have suggested that the personal or intellectual difficulties among children of divorce are due to the disturbed marital relationship, rather than to the divorce; and that, in fact, divorce can enhance the well-being of children by reducing or eliminating the tension between their parents. Indeed, marital distress has been linked to difficulties in the child's psychosocial functioning, as will be discussed below.

Several assumptions of the "marital distress" view, however, have yet to be examined. The typical assumption that distressed marriages are characterized by open conflict and antagonism overlooks other forms of marital dissatisfaction, such as the gradual and quiet loss of intimacy (Kressel et al., 1980). It is not known whether these other types of distress are as detrimental to children.

Nor should it be assumed that the termination of even a conflict-ridden marriage will be beneficial to the child if the child was not exposed to the conflict.

Wallerstein and Kelly (1980) and Landis (1960) discovered that youngsters who perceived family life as happy and had little awareness of their parents' problems initially reacted to the divorce more intensely than those who had been exposed to their parents' conflict. While the separation of openly hostile parents results in at least some new tranquility in the child's environment, the separation of outwardly compatible parents may produce unexpected difficulties for the child.

The notion that the termination of a distressed marriage will be beneficial to the children is more reasonable, of course, when the divorce serves to remove overt conflict and to foster more satisfactory conditions. However, acrimony between the divorced parents may continue or even intensify after the separation and divorce. Wallerstein and Kelly (1980), for instance, reported continuing conflict between approximately two-thirds of divorced parents at a five-year follow-up; conflict over child support is apparent in many families at a ten-year follow-up (Wallerstein, 1984). A substantial proportion of continuing conflicts are so severe that they must be settled by the courts: Cline and Westman (1971) found that 52 percent of divorces in families with children that were granted in a Wisconsin county required court intervention within two years of the divorce.

To the extent that theorizing about the effects of marital distress on children reflects the recent belief that happier parents raise happier children, it is useful to determine the typical level of custodial parent satisfaction following the divorce. Does divorce produce happier parents? Although divorced persons do not report that they are less satisfied with their lives in comparison to married persons (Haring-Hidore, 1985; Weingarten, 1985), and although divorce may minimize several sources of stress, it often creates new stresses or fails to solve existing problems for the parents. Colletta (1983), Hetherington et al. (1977), McLanahan (1983), Spivey and Shermann (1980), and Weinraub and Wolf (1983) reported that female-headed families experience more chronic life strains, more major stressful life events, or low levels of social and psychosocial support. Stress decreased with time, but women divorced for over six years continued to report somewhat more stress than married women (Spivey & Shermann, 1980). As might be expected, divorced mothers in this stressful situation have negative self-images and negative views about the future (McLanahan, 1983). All too often, these problems are associated with serious emotional disorder: a review by Bloom et al. (1978) found consistent evidence that divorced or separated persons are over-represented among psychiatric inpatients and among victims of suicide, homicide, disease, and even car accidents. Of course, these serious physical and mental health problems among the divorced are not necessarily caused by divorce; rather, the problem may have precipitated the divorce. Nonetheless, it is clear that divorce does not necessarily produce more satisfied parents.

Just as pre-divorce conflict and parental dissatisfaction may lead to disruptions in the child's life, so too do these post-divorce stressors and stress reactions. Although Weinraub and Wolf (1983) found no overall differences between divorced and married mothers in their interactions with their preschoolers, stress is associated with impaired mother-child interactions among both groups of mothers (Weinraub & Wolf, 1983), a lesser quality of life for the children (Morrison, 1983), and difficulties in their social and emotional adjustment (Kurdek & Blisk, 1983; Pett, 1982). Hence, it cannot be assumed that the termination of a distressed marriage will be beneficial to children.

Economic Disadvantage

The "economic disadvantage" explanation of difficulties in children's post-divorce functioning suggests that the substantial differences in the finances of one- or two-parent families, rather than divorce itself, is responsible for any problems suffered by the child. The average 1979 income of divorced women was $12,573 compared to approximately $24,000 for married couples. Whereas 16 percent of all children were living under the poverty line in 1979; a staggering 48.6 percent of children in households headed by women were living in poverty (U.S. Bureau of the Census, 1981). This economic disparity is related to both the higher likelihood of divorce among the poor (Norton & Glick, 1979; Goode, 1956; Ross & Sawhill, 1975) and the drop in the income of mother-headed families following the divorce (Burman & Turk, 1981; Day & Bahr, 1986; Duncan & Morgan, 1976; Jacobs et al., 1986; Hoffman & Holmes, 1976; Kurdek, 1986; Maclean & Eekelaar, 1983; Weitzman, 1985). The "economic disadvantage" view suggests that the overwhelming practical and psychological stresses imposed by poverty can account for any differences in behavior between children in one- or two-parent families.

Although financial hardship appears to be one aspect of divorce which affects children, it is unlikely that financial status can fully account for any increased risks for children following divorce. The children of widows, unlike the children of divorce, do not evidence significantly more aggression and delinquency than do children of intact families (Felner et al., 1981; Rutter, 1971; Zill, 1978) even though the widowed suffer economic hardships almost as severe as the divorced. Shinn (1978) reviewed research showing that children whose fathers were temporarily absent or worked night shifts—yet continued to provide income—scored lower than others on cognitive tests, thereby indicating that children's academic performance may suffer from the father's absence even when his absence does not involve a loss of income. Indeed, Dornbusch et al. (1985) found that parental absence had a greater influence on adolescent deviance than did family income. Both factors have been found to be independently and strongly related to delinquency (Guidubaldi et al., 1983; Willie, 1967).

The financial hardship of custodial parents and their children following divorce plays an important role in the child's well-being, but it is not the only important factor. Efforts of the legislature and the judicial system to reverse their impoverishment and to increase support services (e.g., low-cost, high-quality day care and equal pay for women) are likely to reduce significantly, but not eliminate, the difficulties of these families.

Multiple Factor Perspective

Most contemporary observers believe that children's adjustment following divorce is influenced by numerous interacting factors (Guidubaldi and Cleminshaw, 1985; Jacobs, Guidubaldi and Nastisi, 1986). These factors include characteristics of the child (e.g., age, sex, pre-divorce level of adjustment), the family (e.g., financial status, degree of conflict between the parents, parent-child relationships), and the social environment (e.g., social services, a social support network) (Hetherington, 1979; Longfellow, 1979; Wallerstein & Kelly, 1980; 1984). Cultural values and social policies may also be important for adjustment (Kurdek, 1981). In addition, children influence their own adjustment as they form their own perspective on the divorce. Their perspective on the divorce may then influence their emotional and behavioral reactions (Krantz, Clark, Pruyn, & Usher, 1985; Kurdek, 1981; Longfellow, 1979).

While children are affected by the events and people around them, they in turn affect these events and people (Hetherington, Cox & Cox, 1977; Bell & Harper, 1977), as their anger, cheerfulness, sullenness, cooperativeness, or other emotions and behaviors elicit reactions from others. The nature of the reciprocal influences between the child and other people are constantly changing as the child matures and the others change.

The complexity of this perspective is both a strength and a limitation. It is intuitively compelling that the numerous components of any system—in this case, the family—will affect and be affected by the other components of the system and the culture in which it is imbedded. The difficulties with the study of complex systems include: (1) the limitations in our ability to chart the multiple and reciprocal influences of one factor upon another and (2) the large differences between families in the types of events determining their child's behavior. Because of these complexities, a detailed and clear-cut picture of the effect of divorce on children does not exist and would be difficult to verify if it did.

Research Procedures

Accurate, reliable, and relevant information on children's post-divorce adjustment and the conditions affecting adjustment is essential to the formation of policies that best serve the interests of children and their parents. How much confidence can be placed in the validity of the currently available information?

There are serious limitations to the current information, but contrary to Blechman (1982), the information need not be rejected if conclusions are made cautiously and with full recognition of their limitations. As Emery (1982) noted, the overall trends which emerge from repeated replications are unlikely to be seriously distorted because the different methodological deficiencies are likely to bias the results in different directions. This speculation was supported by Shinn's (1976) report that the overall findings of the more methodologically adequate studies of intellectual performance did not differ substantially from the findings of the seriously flawed research. Hence, this section will detail the major threats to the validity of divorce research, but the review in the next section will include studies which vary in their methodological sophistication. This combination of a discussion of the limitations of the data with a comprehensive review of the findings is intended to encourage the cautious use of the available information.

The following section will describe two of the major challenges to research on divorce and children. First, it is imperative that measurements of children's behavior accurately reflect their actual behavior. Second, we must isolate the conditions presumed to influence behavior from the myriad of other related conditions which may be more important influences on behavior than those targeted in a given study. The current strategies for accomplishing these goals and the threats to the effectiveness of these strategies will be examined.

Validity of the Measurements

Interpretation of the results on divorce and children's adjustment should be interpreted cautiously because a number of biases influence our attempts to assess the child's behavior. First, the information provided by adults about children with divorced parents may reflect the stereotypes of the adults more than the actual behavior of the child. For example, Santrock and Tracy (1978) showed a videotape of an eight-year-old boy to 30 teachers. Some teachers were told that the boy came from a divorced home; others were told that he came from an intact home. The boy was rated happier and better adjusted by the teachers who were told that he came from an intact home in comparison to the teachers who were told that he came from a divorced home.

The high personal involvement of parents and children may also bias their reports. Furey and Forehand (1986) found that the mother's perception of her child's adjustment is related to her relationship with the child's father, and to her personal adjustment. A parent opposed to the divorce or the custody arrangement may be aware only of the difficulties in their child's post-divorce adjustment; the parent who is satisfied with the divorce or custody arrangement may do just the opposite. Fulton (1979) found that the fathers' assessment of the impact of the divorce on their children was more strongly related to the custodial arrangement than it was to any other factor: 45 percent of noncustodial fathers believed that the divorce harmed their children compared to only 29 percent of the custodial fathers. While it is quite possible that children with custodial fathers were, indeed, functioning better than those with custodial mothers[1], it was implied that the

---

[1]If, indeed, children in the custody of their fathers are more well adjusted than those in the custody of their mothers, the representativeness of those in this atypical arrangement must be questioned before concluding that fathers are usually the better parent. Custodial fathers may be unusually involved with their children compared to other divorced fathers; noncustodial mothers may be less interested in or able to have custody compared to other divorced mothers.

difference was in part due to a bias of the custodial father toward self-approval and the bias of noncustodial fathers toward showing disappointment in the performance of their ex-wives.

Even presumably objective records may be biased. Herzog and Sudia (1971), for example, reviewed research suggesting that when compared to adolescents in two-parent homes, those in one-parent homes are arrested for less serious offenses and are more likely to be put on probation or committed to correctional institutions. If arrested at all, adolescents living with two parents are more likely to be released to their parents. Thus, the different delinquency rates of adolescents in one- or two-parent families reported below may reflect the biases of the legal system rather than the behaviors of the youths. It would be a mistake to conclude that divorce is or is not harmful to children if the various measurement procedures were biased in the same direction.

Second, it should be recognized that assessment instruments which purportedly tap some objectively defined behavior are often biased by prevailing cultural norms and values. These values and norms change over time and at any point in time may be disputed. For example, Herzog and Sudia (1971) have criticized the conceptualization of masculinity and femininity used in self-report inventories as outdated and class-related. One such inventory counts the reported desire to race cars or start a fist fight as indicators of masculinity. Boys who do not report a desire to race cars or fight score low on this masculinity scale. Similarly, Hetherington (1972) interpreted girls' physical proximity to boys at a dance and their initiation of dances, touching or other encounters with boys as evidence of the girls' "inappropriate" assertion. These measures tap cultural values as well as child behavior.

Isolating the Determinants of Post-Divorce Functioning

The hypothesized influences on adjustment (e.g., the absence of a parent) are entangled with other related variables. Marital status, for example, is related to the parents' age, socioeconomic status, and incidence of alcoholism, criminality, and promiscuity (McCord, McCord & Thurber, 1962; Zill, 1978). Unless the effects of all of these other variables are controlled, the conclusion that divorce causes psychological difficulties is not warranted: these other variables may be the key determinants of both the child's behavior and also of the parents' marital status. For instance, a father's criminality may influence his son toward delinquency and lead his wife to initiate a divorce; the divorce itself may have little or no effect on the son's delinquency.

Because many studies of the effects of divorce on children do nothing to control for the factors other than marital status which may in part explain the child's behavior, their findings should be intepreted with extreme caution. Other studies use one of three basic methods to examine the effects of marital status apart from the other influences. One method is to form groups of children in one- or two-parent families that are similar in terms of important characteristics such as socioeconomic status (SES). Unfortunately, the divorced tend to cluster at the lower end of any given SES group (Herzog & Sudia, 1971).

A second method matches each divorced person to a nondivorced person with a similar social class level to control for divorced-nondivorced differences within a single social class. Well-matched samples, however, are not representative of the general population (Blechman, 1982): they necessarily contain proportionately more lower-class married individuals and upper-class divorced individuals than are in the general population.

Third, the influence of extraneous factors such as socioeconomic status can be controlled statistically. These computations adjust the data so that the participants in the study are equalized on the factors other than marital status. Once these factors are statistically equalized, the investigator can assess the relationship between marital status and child behavior independently of these other factors. With a few exceptions (Dornbusch et al., 1985; Guidubaldi et al., 1983; Nelson, 1981; Svanum et al., 1982; Willie, 1967; Zill, 1978), however, relatively few studies have used this stringent procedure to isolate divorce from other influences on children's functioning.

The discussion thus far has focused on controls for social class because the "economic hardship" perspective convincingly argues that many childhood difficulties may be explained by the economic troubles of divorced mothers rather than by divorce itself. However, social class is but one of the many factors related to marital status. The ideal study would isolate the effects of marital status from all other related variables.

As noted earlier, biases in the available information are unlikely to distort the conclusions to the extent that the data are (1) repeatedly replicated and (2) biased in different directions. Therefore, the following review will describe the findings that have been repeatedly replicated, regardless of the methodological sophistication of the study. The review will also identify areas where conclusions cannot yet be drawn because of the mixed results thus far available.

Children's Post-Divorce Functioning

Each child is unique, and so the short- and long-term functioning of children after a divorce varies widely. Wallerstein and Kelly (1980), from their observations and interviews with parents and children at three points in time over a five-year period, estimated that approximately one-third of the children emerge from the divorce unscathed and may be even more mature than expected for their age. Another one-third function adequately although they experience some enduring difficulties, and the remaining one-third suffer severe disruptions in their developmental progress. These results must be regarded with caution because the parents may have been drawn to the study in part by the counseling offered and so may over-represent those who are in need of counseling. Caution is also necessary because counseling may (and was certainly intended to) alter the course of adjustment to the divorce. Perhaps most importantly, the conclusions about the children from divorced families were made without the benefit of comparisons with children from two-parent families; hence, it is not known whether the development of children of divorce differs in any significant way from that of other children.

Are there, nonetheless, overall trends in the functioning of children after divorce in comparison to the functioning of children in intact families or in other family arrangements? What particular areas of functioning are most vulnerable to the stresses of divorce? The areas most frequently discussed are intellectual performance, juvenile delinquency and aggression, social and emotional well-being, and cognition and perception.

Intellectual Performance

The majority of studies on intellectual performance report that children in one-parent families (usually the product of divorce) are at a disadvantage, but this finding is far from consistent. Shinn (1978) reviewed 28 methodologically adequate studies of children with an absent parent. Parental absence was associated with disruptions in academic achievement in 16 of these studies: children with absent fathers were up to 1.6 years behind their peers who lived with both parents. Of the remaining 12 studies, 9 found no differences between children with or without a father in the household and 3 found either positive effects of an absent father or mixed positive and negative effects. Interestingly, the proportion of studies showing a link between father absence and intellectual deficits were very similar in 19 additional studies that failed to control for SES.

Several large-scale studies (with 700 to 18,000 subjects sampled from multiple states) completed since Shinn's review also tended to find academic deficits among children of divorce. Four (Brown, 1980; Guidubaldi et al., 1983; Lazarus, 1980; Zakariya, 1982) of five studies found that the academic achievement of children in one-parent families lagged behind those in two-parent families. All but one of these four studies found impairments in academic progress even after controlling for social class. Hence, there is some reason to suspect that the intellectual performance of children in one-parent families is weaker than that of their peers, but definitive conclusions would be premature at this time. . . .

Antisocial Behavior

Based upon parents' and children's reports and upon court and school records, antisocial actions occur more frequently among children of divorce than among a variety of other groups, including children in intact families in the general population (e.g., Brown, 1980; Dornbusch et al., 1985; Hess & Camara, 1979; Hetherington et al., 1978; Lazarus, 1980; McDermott, 1970; Saucier & Ambert, 1983; Zill, 1977), children in intact families in an outpatient mental health facility (Kalter, 1977), and children who experienced the death of a parent (Felner, 1977;

Felner et al., 1975; Felner et al., 1977). Researchers have defined antisocial behavior in many ways: parents' and teachers' reports of fighting and bullying other children, cheating, lying, and stealing (e.g., Zill, 1978); running away from home, truancy, suspension or expulsion from school, smoking, drinking, drug use, and inappropriate sexual behavior (e.g., Brown, 1980; Dornbusch et al., 1985; Kalter, 1977; Lazarus, 1980; Saucier & Ambert, 1983), and contact with the law (e.g., Glueck & Glueck, 1950; Willie, 1967; Dornbusch et al., 1985).

Many of these aspects of antisocial behavior pertain mostly to middle childhood and adolescence, but similar conclusions have been reached about the aggressive behavior of younger children (e.g., Hodges & Bloom, 1984; McDermott, 1967). These findings concerning the antisocial behavior of children of divorce are relatively strong. The strength of the conclusions derives from: (1) the repeated replications of the results; (2) the multiple sites across the nation used in several studies (Dornbusch et al., 1985; Lazarus, 1980; Zill, 1978), which ensured that the results are maximally representative and are not limited to a single school, neighborhood, or city; and (3) the controls for social class in several studies (e.g., Dornbusch et al., 1985; Glueck & Glueck, 1950; Felner, 1977; McDermott, 1970; Willie, 1967; Zill, 1978).

Sex Role Socialization

Sex role socialization can be defined as the acquisition of the goals, values, and behaviors deemed masculine or feminine by a given culture. Sex roles are thought to develop as the child becomes aware of the different physical characteristics of the sexes, adopts the stereotypes linked to those characteristics (Kohlberg, 1966), and imitates the behavior of same-sex models (Mischel, 1970). Will children learn the behaviors considered to be appropriate to their sex in the absence of the same-sex parent?

Reviews by Kohlberg (1966) and Biller (1976) revealed some association between father absence and feminine play preference, feminine self-concepts, lowered aggression, and increased dependency among boys. This association, however, was found only among preschool children. Thus, the absence of the father may slow the development of masculine sex roles but does not appear to be associated with long-term development.

Social and Emotional Functioning

Social and emotional well-being is a broad-band construct which encompasses numerous components of functioning, including interaction with peers; emotional states such as fear, anxiety, and depression; and the capacity to cope with stress or frustration.

The assessment of psychosocial adjustment largely consists of interviews and questionnaires administered to parents, teachers, and children. A few exceptions are the observations by researchers of peer contact and play in preschoolers (e.g.,

Deutsch, 1983; Hetherington et al., 1978). The subjective review and question-naire responses are valuable because the respondents are integral parts of the situation, but biases in their reports are unavoidable. Therefore, the results in this area can be looked at, but their limits must be recognized.

The majority of studies of the social-emotional functioning of children of divorce conclude that they function less smoothly than their peers in intact families. Children in one-parent families show difficulties in their play (Hether-ington et al., 1979); interactions with peers (Felner et al., 1981; Guidubaldi et al., 1983); coping with stress and frustration (Felner et al., 1981; Hess & Camara, 1979; Stolberg & Anker, 1983), and emotional comfort (Hodges et al., 1983). Adolescents of divorced parents also act out sexually (Booth, Brinkerhoff, & White, 1984; Kalter, 1977; Kalter & Rembar, 1981). These difficulties are some-times sufficiently serious to warrant intervention: Guttentag et al. (1980) and Kalter (1977) found that there is a disproportionate number of children of divorced parents in outpatient mental health facilities.

These findings, however, are not uniformly supported: several studies have found no differences between youngsters in one- or two-parent families (Ellison, 1983; Enos & Handal, 1986; Hodges et al., 1979; Raschke & Raschke, 1979; Santrock & Warshak, 1979); mixed results (Hess & Camara, 1979; Slater, 1983); or evidence of better functioning among children of divorce (Deutsch, 1983). In addition, the emotional injuries tend to heal at least to some degree with the passage of time (Wallerstein, 1983b). The typical conclusion is that children of divorce are at risk for social and emotional difficulties. This conclusion holds even if consideration is limited to the disappointingly few studies which have controlled for family relationships (Hess & Camara, 1979), IQ, or SES (Guidubaldi et al., 1983; Kalter, 1977).

Cognition and Perception

On average, children of divorce have a somewhat more negative outlook on their world as compared to children in intact families. They are more likely to evaluate their parents unfavorably (Nunn et al., 1983; Rozendahl, 1983; Warshak & Santrock, 1983) and are more pessimistic about their future in general (Saucier & Ambert, 1982) and their own future marriages in particular (Warshak & Santrock, 1983). As reported by the parent or child, approximately 10 to 30% of youngsters in divorced families perceive rejection from the father, devalue the noncustodial parent, believe that divorce is stigmatized, or predict that they will not marry (Kurdek & Siesky, 1979; 1980; Reinhard, 1977).

Cognitive appraisals of one's world, one's future, and the available coping resources are important because they consistently have been found to be related to coping in children and adults following stressful events (Peterson, Leigh & Day, 1984). As expected, this relationship has also been found among children of divorce. Krantz et al. (1985) found that boys of divorced parents who maintain a positive or balanced evaluation of various divorce situations and were optimistic about their future were more well-adjusted than their negative and pessimistic peers. Their personal adjustment was also related to the number of coping strategies they generated to handle problematic divorce situations.

In summary, children's cognitive appraisals of their family situation are more negative among children of divorce than among children in families that have not experienced divorce. The extent to which children of divorce perceive the divorce situation in a positive or balanced manner is related to their behavioral and emotional adjustment.

Factors Associated with Post-Divorce Adjustment

What aspects of the child, the family, and the divorce situation influence the adjustment of the child in the wake of divorce? The following section describes those aspects that have received the most research attention: age, gender, parental relationship, parent-child relationship, and socioeconomic status. Additional factors (e.g., parental functioning, the pre-divorce adjustment of the child, the family's social support network) may also be important influences on the child's post-divorce adjustment, but the paucity of research on these other factors precludes a review.

Although the various influences on adjustment are discussed separately, they do not act separately. Hodges et al. (1979), Rutter (1979), and Stolberg and Anker (1983) reported that a single stressor did not place the child at risk for disorder, but that problems tended to mount when multiple stressors were present.

Age

Does the child's age influence his or her adjustment to divorce? Investigators agree that children of different ages show qualitatively different types of responses after their parent's separation, but disagree on whether the responses are quantitatively different in terms of their severity.

The qualitative differences between children of different ages are apparent from descriptive accounts of the preschool, middle childhood, and adolescent periods. Preschool children, with their unsophisticated and egocentric forms of reasoning, may blame themselves for the departure of a parent and may interpret this departure as a personal rejection. Associated adjustment problems are usually manifested in disturbed eating, sleeping, play, and toileting (Hetherington et al., 1979; McDermott, 1968; Wallerstein & Kelly, 1975; 1980).

School-age children, by contrast, are sometimes buffeted by loyalty conflicts and may fantasize or actually attempt to reconcile the parents. Adjustment problems at this age are manifested by declines in academic performance or psychosomatic symptoms. Finally, adolescents may be prone to anger and may break the conventions that usually govern aggressive and sexual behavior (Booth et al., 1984; Kalter, 1977; Kalter & Rembar, 1981; Sorosky, 1977; Wallerstein & Kelly, 1974; 1980). Alternatively, growing exposure to the world outside the family and increasing ability to reason sometimes permits enhanced interpersonal sensitivity, maturity, and moral growth (Wallerstein & Kelly, 1980; Weiss, 1979).

The qualitatively different patterns of responses of children of different ages are related to their stage of cognitive and social development at the time of the divorce (Kalter & Rembar, 1981) and at the time of the follow-up assessment. The older child has the opportunity to obtain support outside the home if it is not forthcoming from his or her parents, or to find distractions from the tensions in the home by participating in pleasurable activities. The older child's more complex, abstract reasoning permits him or her to perceive the divorce in ways that differ from those of the younger child (Hetherington, 1980; Kurdek, 1981; Kurdek, Blick & Siesky, 1981; Longfellow, 1979).

There is mixed evidence on whether these qualitative differences between the different age groups are accompanied by differences in the intensity of the symptoms. In Longfellow's (1979) review of 10 studies examining the relationship between age at separation and adjustment, one-half found that preschool children are more adversely affected by their parents' divorce; the remainder found either that middle childhood or adolescence is the most vulnerable period or that adjustment is unrelated to age at the time of separation.

Because these data on the severity of problems at different ages are mixed, it would be premature to conclude that no age group is particularly vulnerable or protected. It may be a mistake to lump together different aspects of children's functioning because the different aspects may become vulnerable or invulnerable at different ages. Three of the five studies which failed to find that preschool children were at greatest risk were studies of intellectual performance. Hence, early separations may be associated with deficits in social and emotional functioning, but not with intellectual functioning. Consistent with this possibility, Hetherington et al. (1979) reviewed research showing that intellectual deficits in the children of divorce are not observed in the preschool years but become increasingly evident with increasing age. Hetherington et al. speculated that the greater abstraction and complexity of test items for older children is more susceptible to interference from the stresses of divorce in comparison to the rote memory, simple vocabulary and sensorimotor tasks given to preschoolers. Further research is needed to determine whether different areas of children's functioning become vulnerable at different ages.

Gender

Most research shows that boys are more vulnerable than girls to divorce-related stresses, and recover from any difficulties more slowly (Guidubaldi et al., 1983; Hess & Camara, 1979; Hetherington et al., 1979; Hodges et al., 1983; Hodges & Bloom, 1984; Krantz et al., 1985; Kurdek & Berg, 1983; McDermott, 1968; Rutter, 1970; Wallerstein & Kelly, 1980; Zakariya, 1982). Wallerstein and Kelly (1980) found that the immediate post-divorce disadvantage of boys was still evident at a five-year follow-up, but had dissipated at least somewhat. The disadvantage of boys, however, is not always found (Deutsch, 1983; Hodges et al., 1978; Pett, 1982; Slater, Stewart & Linn, 1983).

Why are boys more likely than girls to exhibit behavior problems after their parents' divorce? There are several possibilities but no definitive answers. One possibility is that living with the opposite-sex parent is more difficult than living with the same-sex parent (Santrock & Warshak, 1979; Warshak & Santrock, 1983; Hodges & Bloom, 1984). Because the mother is most often the custodial parent, boys are exposed to this relatively difficult situation more often than girls. Alternatively, it has been suggested that boys are more often exposed to parental conflict (Wallerstein & Kelly, 1980). This possibility, however, is inconsistent with the findings that parents report an equivalent degree of fighting in the presence of sons and daughters (Porter & O'Leary, 1980) and that boys did not report a greater awareness of parental fighting than did girls (Emery & O'Leary, 1982). Other speculations are that parents are less supportive of their sons (Hetherington, 1980) and that boys are simply more vulnerable to stress (Rutter, 1970). These possibilities are only speculative; we are not aware of research that substantiates any of the possibilities.

Parental Relationship

The relationship between the parents is thought to be an important determinant of children's reactions to divorce. Parents in a distressed marriage may serve as models for verbal or physical violence and poor communication. Moreover, marital distress may disrupt the parents' ability to provide adequate supervision, discipline, nurturance, and warmth. The parents' conflict may create conflicting loyalties for the child who rightly or wrongly believes that bonds with one parent will provoke anger, hurt, or rejection from the other. When the worth, sanity, intentions, or competence of one parent is attacked by the other in the presence of the child, the maligned parent's ability to function as a parent is undermined.

A number of studies have found that parental conflict is associated with poor child adjustment (Booth et al., 1984; Ellison, 1983; Enos & Handal, 1986; Guidubaldi & Cleminshaw, 1983; Hess & Camara, 1979; Hetherington et al., 1978; Jacobson, 1979; Kurdek & Blisk, 1983; Leupnitz, 1982; Long et al., 1987; Nelson, 1981; Raschke & Raschke, 1979; Rutter, 1971). The association between parental conflict and child functioning is not unique to divorced families: children in distressed two-parent families exhibit problems similar to, or worse than, children in one-parent families (Berg & Kelly, 1979; Nye, 1985; Zill, 1978). These findings that parental conflict is harmful to children are especially important in the context of divorce, however, because of the relatively high likelihood of conflict.

Parent-Child Relationship

Parent-child relationships often deteriorate in the aftermath of divorce. Parents become less available, more demanding, less responsive, and less able to maintain household routines when they must struggle with new emotional and practical burdens (Colletta, 1983; Morrison, 1983; Wallerstein, 1983; Wallerstein & Kelly, 1980). According to Hetherington et al. (1977), mothers become more coercive and fathers become more lax and indulgent; both become less consistent in their discipline. Divorced parents also make less demands for mature behaviors, communicate less effectively, or provide less affection than married parents. Their children are relatively less compliant. Hetherington et al. (1977) found that these differences are most pronounced one year following the divorce; they are still apparent, although to a lesser degree, after two years. Dornbusch et al. (1985) observed that single parents permit earlier autonomy in decision-making by their adolescents within most income and racial groups.

Not surprisingly, less adequate parent-child relationships have consistently been found to be associated with behavior problems in children (Dornbusch et al., 1985; Guidubaldi et al., 1983; Hodges et al., 1983; Hess & Camara, 1979; Pett, 1982; Rutter, 1971; Santrock & Warshak, 1979; Wallerstein & Kelly, 1980). Thus, there is abundant and consistent evidence that (1) parenting among the divorced, especially the newly divorced, is impaired relative to that of married parents, and (2) parenting styles are strongly related to the child's adjustment.

Socioeconomic Status

As in the general population (e.g., Coleman, 1966; Fleisher, 1966; Willie, 1967), the social status of the children of divorce is related to their intellectual performance and other aspects of personal functioning (Desimone-Luis, O'Mahoney & Hunt, 1979; Guidubaldi et al., 1983; Hodges et al., 1979; Pett, 1982; Svanum et al., 1982). Although a few studies did not replicate the greater difficulties of low-socioeconomic-status children (Fulton, 1979; Hetherington, Cox & Cox, 1977; Nelson, 1981), these studies are marred by (1) small samples and/or (2) a range in social class too narrow to permit the detection of an association with children's adjustment. Therefore, it may be concluded that it is very likely—albeit not certain—that children belonging to the lower socio-economic classes after the divorce experience greater personal hardships compared to those in the higher socio-economic classes.

Policy Implications of Research on Divorce and Children

The current review indicates that the psychosocial adjustment of children who have experienced the divorce of their parents is at risk. The evidence on the school performance of children of divorce is equivocal, but it, too, is suggestive of difficulties. Problems are most pronounced in the first two years of divorce, but still can be observed years later. The extent of the youngster's difficulties depends on many factors, including age, sex, parental harmony, parent-child relationships, and socioeconomic class.

These research findings have implications for policy in at least three domains. First, they have important implications for the judicial process. Second, policy-makers must wrestle with questions of providing services to divorcing families to prevent or ameliorate the hardships for children. Finally, the implications for political and organizational issues will be discussed.

Implications for the Judicial Process

Several of the factors shown to be related to child adjustment are strongly influenced by both the process and the outcome of courtroom decisions. Perhaps the most clear-cut outcomes of judicial decisions which influence the child's well-being are the financial consequences of (1) the court's orders concerning the division of property, spousal support, and child support and (2) the enforcement of the support order. . . .

Current norms in support awards typically leave custodial mothers with serious economic hardships. The large discrepancy between the post-divorce financial state of men and women is likely to provoke resentment in women, and, consequently, increased conflict between the former spouses. Indeed, preliminary findings reported by Krantz et al. (in preparation) indicate that the size of the disparity between men's and women's incomes is associated with the number of post-settlement returns to court reported at least two years following the separation. Conflict provoked by a large discrepancy between mothers' and fathers' incomes is likely to be associated with the child's behavior.

In summary, whether the mother's low income is viewed relative to the general population or relative to the father's income, the child suffers. When the mother's income is low relative to the general population, she undergoes numerous stresses which impair her parenting capacities. When the mother's income is low relative to the father's income, conflict often results which is also disruptive for the child. Providing better financial resources for mothers is not a panacea, but this policy change will reduce the mother's level of stress and parental conflict. As a result, the child's well-being is likely to be bolstered.

The custody decision is another important outcome of the judicial process. Because children's adjustment in alternative custody arrangements is beyond the scope of this [paper], the policy implications of research on this topic will not be discussed. The interested reader is referred to Clingempeel and Reppucci (1982).

In addition to re-evaluating the outcomes ordered by the court, it is also important to re-evaluate the processes by which these outcomes are achieved. Although it is becoming increasingly common for states to require mediation of disputes and for attorneys to recommend mediation to their clients as a preferable alterative to a court battle, the adversarial nature of the legal system continues in many domains. Many divorcing couples are reluctant to trust their interests to mediators. Yet the adversarial approach can be harmful to children. For example, a custody dispute can entail attempts by each parent to degrade the other. The parent who can most effectively argue that the other parent is an unfit parent wins the court battle and "wins" the child. To construct a strong argument, the parents often selectively attends to, articulates, and exaggerates the other parent's flaws. This process erodes a more balanced perspective in the parent looking for flaws, antagonizes the maligned parent, elicits counter-charges, and inflames the battle. The child is often aware that a parent is labelled as unfit, uncaring, crazy, or abusive. When the court decides against one parent, its decision may be taken by one or more family members as validation for the argument that the losing parent is, indeed, unfit (Johnston et al., 1983). The heightened parental conflict and associated parent-child tensions emerging from such a battle are harmful to the child and difficult to repair (Buehler, Hogan, Robinson & Levy, 1985/86).

Future policy decisions would serve children best if they supported the development and testing of alternatives to the adversarial system. One trend in this direction is the move of many states toward increasing use of mediation in disputes. Mediation works best when the legitimacy of both parents' interests and the interests of the child are taken into account. Training mediators to be psychologically as well as legally sophisticated may enhance the acceptability of mediation to the divorcing parties and improve the process of dispute settlement.

Implications for Prevention and Remediation

There are numerous ways in which educational, psychological and social services might reduce the harmful influences of divorce on children. High-quality day and evening care would reduce some of the pressure on single working parents. Subgroups at high risk should be identified and educational and psychological services should be provided to prevent difficulties or hasten recovery. For example, parents might be helped to maintain or re-establish consistent supervision and nurturing relationships with their children. Research is needed on the efficacy of various interventions.

Summary

This [paper] examined several perspectives on children's post-divorce functioning, reviewed the literature on children's adjustment, and discussed the policy implications of this review. After examining four perspectives on divorce, the discussion concludes that the complexity of families and of divorce demanded recognition of multiple and interacting factors. The "parent absence" formulation, the "marital distress" and "economic hardship" formulations, each account for some but not all of the findings on children's post-divorce functioning.

The review of research shows that children with divorced parents develop difficulties in some areas of functioning. Disturbances in the ability to cope with stress and in cognitive appraisals of one's world are frequently found. Relationships with peers, teachers, parents, and the community are sometimes aggressive and anti-social in nature. The development of appropriate sex role behaviors may be delayed but resumes its usual course by the early school years. Deficiencies in intellectual functioning are suspected but not demonstrated.

The likelihood that a child will have difficulties depends on a number of factors. Most research shows that girls are more resistant to the stresses of divorce than are boys. There is some tentative evidence that preschool children are more vulnerable than older children to social and emotional difficulties, but less vulnerable to intellectual deficits. The relationship of the parents with each other and with the child is almost uniformly found to be linked to the child's functioning. The data on the socioeconomic status of the divorced parent generally show that low social class handicaps children's post-divorce well-being.

The factors associated with children's post-divorce functioning discussed in this [paper] are limited to those that have been repeatedly investigated. However, other factors are also likely to be important, including psychological problems of the custodial parent, pre-divorce adjustment of the child, availability of support from friends and relatives, frequent changes in residence or household composition, and insufficient community or social support.

The findings presented in this review have important implications for social policy. If financial awards can be made more equitably and enforced more consistently, the improved standard of living would be expected to lead to better parenting and, consequently, better-adjusted children. Improved social services would be another means of improving the living conditions of divorced families. Finally, educational, counseling, and mediation services might help prevent or shorten the period of conflict and emotional trauma experienced by parents and children. The high frequency of divorce makes the need for these changes compelling.

References

Aldous, J. (1972). Children's perceptions of adult role assignment: Father-absence, class, race, and sex influences. *Journal of Marriage and the Family, 34,* 55–65.

Bell, R. Q., & Harper, L. V. (1977). *Child effects on adults.* Hillsdale, N.J.: Erlbaum.

Berg, B., & Kelly, R. (1979) The measured self-esteem of children from broken, rejected and accepted families. *Journal of Divorce, 2,* 363–369.

Biller, H. B. (1976). The father and personality development: Paternal deprivation and sex-role development. In M. E. Lamb (ed.), *The role of the father in child development.* New York: Wiley.

Blanchard, R. W., & Biller, H. B. (1971). Father availability and academic performance among third-grade boys. *Developmental Psychology, 4,* 301–305.

Blechman, E. A. (1982). Are children with one parent at psychological risk? A methodological review. *Journal of Marriage and the Family, 44,* 179–191.

Bloom, B. L., Asher, S. J., & White, S. W. (1978). Marital disruption as a stressor: A review and analysis. *Psychological Bulletin, 85,* 867–894.

Booth, A., Brinkerhoff, D. B., & White, L. K. (1984). The impact of parental divorce on courtship. *Journal of Marriage and the Family, 46,* 85–94.

Brown, B. F. (1980). A study of the school needs of children from one-parent families. *Phi Delta Kappan, 61,* 537–540.

Buehler, C. A., Hogan, M. J., Robinson, B. E., & Levy, R. J. (1985/86). The parental divorce transition: Divorce-related stressors and well-being. *Journal of Divorce, 9,* 61–81.

Bureau of Labor Statistics. (1968). U.S. Department of Labor, Bulletin No. 1570-2.

Burman, W. H., & Turk, D. C. (1981). Adaptation to divorce problems and coping strategies. *Journal of Marriage and the Family, 43*, 179–189.

Cline, D. W., & Westman, J. C. (1971). The impact of divorce on the family. *Child Psychiatry and Human Development, 2*, 78–83.

Clingempeel, W. G., & Reppucci, N. D. (1982). Joint custody after divorce: Major issues and goals for research. *Psychological Bulletin, 91*, 102–107.

Cohen, S., & Katzenstein, M. F. (Forthcoming). The war over the family is not over the "family." In S. M. Dornbusch & M. H. Strober (eds.), *Feminism, children and the new families*. New York: Guilford Press.

Coleman, J. S. (1966). *Supplemental appendix to the survey on equality of educational opportunity*. Washington, D.C.: U.S. Government Printing Office.

Colletta, N. D. (1979). The impact of divorce: Father absence of poverty. *Journal of Divorce, 3*, 27–35.

Colletta, N. D. (1983). Stressful lives: The situation of divorced mothers and their children. *Journal of Divorce, 6*, 19–31.

Conger, J. J. (1981). Freedom and commitment: Families, youth and social change. *American Psychologist, 36*, 1475–1486.

Day, R. D., & Bahr, S. J. (1986). Income changes following divorce and remarriage. *Journal of Divorce, 9*, 75–88.

Desimone-Luis, J., O'Mahoney, K., & Hunt, D. (1979). Children of separation and divorce: Factors influencing adjustment. *Journal of Divorce, 3*, 37–42.

Deutsch, F. (1983). Classroom social participation of preschoolers in single-parent families. *Journal of Social Psychology, 119*, 77–84.

Dornbusch, S. M., Carlsmith, J. M., Bushwall, S. J., Ritter, R. L., Leiderman, H., Hastorf, A. H., & Gross, R. T. (1985). Single parents, extended households, and the control of adolescents. *Child Development, 56*, 326–341.

Duncan, G. J., & Morgan, J. N. (1976). Introduction, overview, summary and conclusions. In G. J. Duncan & J. N. Morgan (eds.), *Five thousand American families: Patterns of economic progress*. Ann Arbor, Mich.: University of Michigan, Institute of Social Research.

Ellison, E. (1983). Issues concerning parental harmony and children's psychosocial development. *American Journal of Orthopsychiatry, 53*(1).

Emery, R. E. (1982). Interparental conflict and the children of discord and divorce. *Psychological Bulletin, 92*, 310–330.

Emery, R. E., & O'Leary, K. D. (1982). Children's perceptions of marital discord and behavior problems of boys and girls. *Journal of Abnormal Child Psychology, 10*, 11–24.

Enos, D. M., & Handal, P. J. (1986). The relation of parental marital status and perceived family conflict to adjustment in white adolescents. *Journal of Consulting and Clinical Psychology, 54*, 820–824.

Felner, R. D., Ginter, M. A., Boike, M. F., & Cowen, E. L. (1981). Parental death or divorce and the school adjustment of young children. *American Journal of Community Psychology, 9*, 181–191.

Felner, R. D., Stolberg, A., & Cowen, E. L. (1975). Crisis events and school mental health referral patterns of young children. *Journal of Consulting and Clinical Psychology, 43*, 305–310.

Fleisher, B. M. (1966). The effect of income on delinquency. *American Economic Review, 56*, 118–137.

Fulton, J. A. (1979). Parental reports of children's post-divorce adjustment. *Journal of Social Issues, 35*, 126–139.

Furey, W. M., & Forehand, R. (1986). What factors are associated with mother's evaluations of their clinic-referred children? *Child and Family Behavior Therapy, 8*, 21–42.

Glick, P. O. (1979). Children of divorced parents in demographic perspective. *Journal of Social Issues, 35*, 170–182.

Glueck, S., & Glueck, E. (1950). *Unraveling juvenile delinquency*. Cambridge, Mass.: Harvard University Press.

Goode, W. J. (1956). *After divorce*. New York: Macmillan.

Guidubaldi, J., & Cleminshaw, H. K. (1983). *Impact of family support systems on children's academic and social functioning after divorce*. Paper presented at the Annual Convention of the American Psychological Association, Anaheim, Calif.

Guidubaldi, J., Cleminshaw, H. K., Perry, J. D., & McLoughlin, C. S. (1983). The impact of parental divorce on children: Report of the nationwide NASP study. *School Psychology Review, 12*(3), 300–323.

Guidubaldi, J., & Cleminshaw, H. K. (1985). Divorced family health and child adjustment. *Family Relations, 34,* 35–41.

Guttentag, M., Salasin, S., & Belle, D. (1980). *The mental health of women.* New York: Academic Press.

Haring-Hidore, M., Stock, W. A., Okun, M. A., & Witter, R. A. (1985). Marital status and subjective well-being: A research synthesis. *Journal of Marriage and the Family, 47,* 947–953.

Herzog, E., & Sudia, E. (1971). *Boys in fatherless families.* Washington, D.C.: Government Printing Office.

Hess, R. D., & Camara, K. A. (1979). Post-divorce family relationships as mediating factors in the consequences of divorce for children. *Journal of Social Issues, 35,* 79–96.

Hetherington, E. M. (1972). Effects of father absence in adolescent daughters. *Developmental Psychology, 7,* 313–326.

Hetherington, E. M. (1979). Divorce: A child's perspective. *American Psychologist, 34,* 851–858.

Hetherington, E. M., Cox, M., & Cox, R. (1977). Beyond father absence: Conceptualization of the effects of divorce. In E. M. Hetherington & R. D. Parke (eds.), *Contemporary readings in child psychology.* New York: McGraw-Hill.

Hetherington, E. M., Cox, M., & Cox, R. (1978). The aftermath of divorce. In J. H. Stevens & M. Matthews (eds.), *Mother-child; father-child relations.* Washington, D.C.: National Association for the Education of Young Children.

Hetherington, E. M., Cox, M., & Cox, R. (1979). Play and social interactions in children following divorce. *Journal of Social Issues, 35,* 26–49.

Hodges, W. F., & Bloom, B. L. (1984). Parent's report of children's adjustment to marital separation: A longitudinal study. Journal of Divorce, 8.

Hodges, W. F., Buchsbaum, H. H., & Tierney, C. W. (1983). Parent-child relationships and adjustment in preschool children in divorced and intact families. *Journal of Divorce, 7,* 43–57.

Hodges, W. F., Weschler, R. C., & Ballantine, C. (1979). Divorce and the preschool child: Cumulative stress. *Journal of Divorce, 3,* 55–68.

Hofferth, S. (1983). *Updating children's life course.* Washington, D.C.: National Institute of Child Health and Human Development, Center for Population Research.

Hoffman, S., & Holmes, J. (1976). Husbands, wives, and divorce. In G. J. Duncan & J. N. Morgan (eds.), *Five thousand American families: Patterns of economic progress.* Ann Arbor, Mich.: University of Michigan, Institute for Social Research.

Jacobs, N. L., Guidubaldi, J., & Nastasi, B. (1986). Adjustment of divorced family day care children. *Early Childhood Research Quarterly, 1,* 361–378.

Jacobson, D. S. (1979). The impact of marital separation/divorce on children: Interpersonal hostility and child adjustment. *Journal of Divorce, 2,* 3–19.

Johnson, W. D., & Minton, M. H. (1982). The economic choice in divorce: Extended or blended family. *Journal of Divorce, 6,* 101–113.

Johnston, J. R., Campbell, L. E. G., & Tall, M. C. (1983). *The reconstruction of spousal identities after divorce—Its role in post-divorce disputes.* Paper presented at the 54th Annual Meeting of the Sociological Association, San Jose, Calif.

Kalter, N. (1979). Children of divorce in an outpatient psychiatric population. *American Journal of Orthopsychiatry, 46,* 20–32.

Kalter, N., & Rembar, J. (1981). The significance of a child's age at the time of parental divorce. *American Journal of Orthopsychiatry, 51,* 85–100.

Kohlberg, L. (1966). A cognitive-development analysis of children's sex-role concepts and attitudes. In E. Maccoby (ed.), *The development of sex differences.* Berkeley, Calif.: Stanford University Press.

Krantz, S. E., Clark, J., Pruyn, J., & Usher, M. (1985). Cognition and adjustment among children of separation and divorce. *Cognitive Therapy and Research, 9.*

Krantz, S. E., Johnston, J. R., Gonzalez, R., & Clark, J. (1985, in preparation). *Predictors of long-term post-divorce conflict.*

Kressel, K., Jaffee, N., Tuchman, B., Watson, C., & Deutsch, M. (1980). A typology of divorcing couples: Implications for mediation and the divorce process. *Family Process, 19,* 101–116.

Kurdek, L. A. (1981). An integrative perspective on children's divorce adjustment. *American Psychologist, 36,* 856–866.

Kurdek, L. A., Blisk, D., & Siesky, A. E. (1981). Effects of divorce on children. *Journal of Divorce, 4*, 85–99.

Kurdek, L. A., & Berg, B. (1983). Correlates of children's adjustment to their parents' divorces. In L. A. Kurdek (ed.), *Children and divorce*. San Francisco: Jossey-Bass.

Kurdek, L. A., & Blisk, D. (1983). Dimensions and correlates of mother's divorce experiences. *Journal of Divorce, 6*, 1–24.

Kurdek, L. A. (1986). Custodial mothers' perceptions of visitation and payment of child support by non-custodial fathers in families with low and high levels of preseparation interpersonal conflict. *Journal of Applied Developmental Psychology, 7*, 301–323.

Landis, J. (1960). The trauma of children when parents divorce. *Marriage and Family Living, 22*, 7–13.

Lazarus, M. (1980). One-parent families and their children. *Principal, 60*, 31–37.

Levy-Shiff, R. (1982). The effects of father absence on young children in mother-headed households. *Child Development, 53*, 1400–1405.

Long, N., Forehand, R., Fauber, R., & Brady, R. H. (1987). Self-perceived and independently observed competence of young adolescents as a function of parental conflict and recent divorce. *Journal of Abnormal Child Psychology, 15*, 15–27.

Longfellow, C. (1979). Divorce in context: Its impact on children. In G. Levinger & O. Moles (eds.), *Divorce and separation: Context, causes and consequences*. New York: Basic Books.

Lowenstein, J. S., & Koopman, E. J. (1978). A comparison of the self-esteem between boys living with single-parent mothers and single-parent fathers. *Journal of Divorce, 2*, 195–208.

Maclean, M., & Eekelaar, J. (1983). *Children and divorce: Economic factors*. Oxford, England: Centre for Socio-legal Studies.

McCord, J., McCord, W., & Thurber, E. (1962). Some effects of paternal absence on male children. *Journal of Abnormal and Social Psychology, 64*, 361–369.

McDermott, J. F. (1968). Parental divorce in early childhood. *American Journal of Psychiatry, 124*, 1424–1432.

McDermott, J. F. (1970). Divorce and its psychiatric sequelae in children. *Archives of General Psychiatry, 23*, 421–427.

McLanahan, S. S. (1983). Family structure and stress: A longitudinal comparison of two-parent and female-headed families. *Journal of Marriage and the Family, 45*, 347–357.

Meyer, H. (Forthcoming). The state, and the institutionalization of the relations between women and children. In S. M. Dornbusch & M. H. Strober (eds.), *Feminism, children and the new families*. New York: Guilford Press.

Mischel, W. (1970). Sex-typing and socialization. In P. H. Mussen (ed.), *Carmichael's manual of child psychology*. New York: John Wiley and Sons.

Monthly Vital Statistics Report. (1985). Vol. *3*(11), Supplement 1. National Center for Health Statistics. *U.S. Government Printing Office*.

Morrison, A. L., et al. (April, 1983). *A prospective study of divorce and its relationship to family functioning*. Paper presented at the Biennial Meeting of the Society for Research in Child Development, Detroit, Mich.

Nelson, G. (1981). Moderators of women's and children's adjustment following parental divorce. *Journal of Divorce, 4*, 71–83.

Norton, A. J., & Glick, P. C. (1979). Marital instability in America: Past, present and future. In G. Levinger & O. C. Moles (eds.), *Divorce and separation: Context, causes and consequences*. New York: Basic Books.

Nunn, G. D., Parish, T. S., & Worthing, R. J. (1983). Perceptions of personal and familial adjustment by children from intact, single parent, and reconstituted families. *Psychology in the Schools, 20*(2).

Nye, F. E. (1957). Child adjustment in broken and unhappy unbroken homes. *Marriage and Family Living, 19*, 356–361.

O'Reilly, B. (1983). *Where equal opportunity fails: Corporate men and women in dual-career families*. Unpublished doctoral dissertation, Stanford University.

Peterson, G. W., Leigh, G. K., & Day, R. D. (1984). Family stress theory and the impact of divorce on children. *Journal of Divorce, 7*, 1–20.

Pett, M. G. (1982). Correlates of children's social adjustment following divorce. *Journal of Divorce, 5*(4), 25–39.

Porter, B., & O'Leary, K. D. (1980). Marital discord and childhood behavior problems. *Journal of Abnormal Child Psychology, 80*, 287–295.

Raschke, H. J., & Raschke, V. J. (1979). Family conflict and children's self-concepts: A comparison of intact and single-parent families. *Journal of Marriage and the Family, 41,* 367–373.

Ross, H. L., & Sawhill, I. V. (1975). *Time of transition: The growth of families headed by women.* Washington, D.C.: Urban Institute.

Rutter, M. (1970). Sex differences in response to stress. In E. J. Anthony & C. Koupernik (eds.), *The child in his family.* New York: Wiley.

Rutter, M. (1971). Parent-child separation: Psychological effects on the children. *Journal of Child Psychology and Psychiatry and Allied Disciplines, 12,* 233–260.

Rutter, M. (1979). Maternal deprivation, 1972-1978: New findings, new concepts, new approaches. *Child Development, 50,* 283–305.

Santrock, J. W., & Tracy, R. L. (1978). Effects of children's family structure status on the development of stereotypes by children. *Journal of Educational Psychology, 70,* 754–757.

Santrock, J. W., & Warshak, R. A. (1979). Father custody and social development in boys and girls. *Journal of Social Issues, 35,* 112–125.

Saucier, J. F., & Ambert, A. M. (1982). Parental marital status and adolescents' optimism about their future. *Journal of Youth and Adolescence, 11*(5), 345–354.

Shinn, M. (1978). Father absence and children's cognitive development. *Psychological Bulletin, 85,* 295–324.

Slater, E. J., Stewart, K. J., & Linn, M. W. (1983). The effects of family disruption on adolescent males and females. *Adolescence, 18,* 931–942.

Sorosky, A. D. (1977). The psychological effects of divorce on adolescents. *Adolescence, 45,* 123–136.

Spivey, P. B., & Sherman, A. (1980). The effects of time lapse on personality characteristics and stress of divorced women. *Journal of Divorce, 4,* 49–59.

Stolberg, A. L., & Anker, J. M. (1983). Cognitive-behavioral changes in children resulting from parental divorce and consequent environmental changes. *Journal of Divorce, 7*(2), 231–241.

Svanum, S., Bringle, R. G., & McLaughlin, J. E. (1982). Father absence and cognitive performance in a large sample of six- to eleven-year-old children. *Child Development, 53,* 136–143.

Szalai, A., Converse, P. E., Feldheim, P., Scheuch, E. K., & Stone, P. J. (eds.). (1972). *The use of time: Daily activities of urban and suburban populations in twelve countries.* The Hague, The Netherlands: Mouton.

U.S. Bureau of the Census. (1981). *Statistical Abstract of the United States: 1981.* (102nd ed.). Washington, D.C.: Government Printing Office.

Wallerstein, J. S. (1983a). Children of divorce: Stress and developmental tasks. In N. Garmezy & M. Rutter (eds.), *Stress, coping and development in children.* New York: McGraw-Hill.

Wallerstein, J. S. (1983b). The psychological tasks of the child. *American Journal of Orthopsychiatry, 53,* 230–243.

Wallerstein, J. S. (1984). Children of divorce: Preliminary report of a ten-year follow-up of young children. *American Journal of Orthopsychiatry, 54*(3), 444–498.

Wallerstein, J. S., & Kelly, J. B. (1974). The effects of parental divorce: The adolescent experience. In E. J. Anthony & C. Koupernik (eds.), *The child in his family: Children at psychiatric risk.* New York: Wiley.

Wallerstein, J. S., & Kelly, J. B. (1975). The effects of parental divorce: Experiences of the pre-school child. *Journal of the American Academy of Child Psychiatry, 14,* 600–616.

Wallerstein, J. S., & Kelly, J. B. (1980). *Surviving the break-up: How children and parents cope with divorce.* New York: Basic Books, Inc.

Weingarten, H. R. (1985). Marital status and well-being: A national study comparing first-married, currently divorced and remarried adults. *Journal of Marriage and the Family, 47,* 653–661.

Weinraub, M., & Wolf, B. M. (1983). Effects of stress and social supports on mother-child interaction in single- and two-parent families. *Child Development, 54,* 1297–1311.

Weiss, R. S. (1979). Growing up a little faster: The experience of growing up in a single-parent household. *Journal of Social Issues, 35,* 97–111.

Weitzman, L. J. (1981). The economics of divorce: Social and economic consequences of property, alimony, and child support awards. *University of California, Los Angeles, Law Review, 28,* 1181–1268.

Weitzman, L. J. (1985). *The divorce revolution: The unexpected social and economic consequences for women and children in America.* New York: The Free Press.

Willie, C. N. (1967). The relative contribution of family status and economic status to juvenile delinquency. *Social Problems, 14*, 326–334.

Zakariya, S. B. (1982). Another look at the children of divorce: Summary report of the study of school needs of one-parent children. *Principal, 62*, 34–37.

Zill, N. (1978). *Divorce, marital happiness, and the mental health of children: Findings from the FDC national survey of children.* Prepared for the NIMH workshop on Divorce and Children, Bethesda, Md.

The Remarriage Transition

Constance R. Ahrons and Roy H. Rodgers

The family change process set in motion by one marital disruption boggles one's mind. It frequently requires complex computation to chart and undertand the kinship relationships. Even though the current remarriage rates show a continuing decline . . . , the vast majority of divorced families will move through the series of stressful transitions and structural changes brought about by the expansion of the family postdivorce. The structural changes in remarriage give rise to a host of disruptions in roles and relationships, and each transition may be mastered with varying amounts of stress and turmoil.

Projections from the current trends indicate that between 40 and 50 percent of the children born in the 1970s will spend some portion of their minor years in a one-parent household. Given the current remarriage rates it is also projected that approximately 25 to 30 percent of American children will live for some period of time in a remarried household. Although we do not have as adequate cohabitation information as we would like, we can assume that many of these children will also live for some period of time in a cohabiting household, which may or may not become a remarriage household. This means that at least 25 to 30 percent of the children will have more than two adults who function simultaneously as parents. Rates of redivorce are also increasing, resulting in even more complex kinship structures.

Consider the following case example of the Spicer/Tyler/Henry binuclear family. . . .

When Ellen was eight and David ten, their parents separated. They continued to live with their mother, Nancy, spending weekends and vacations with their father, Jim. Two years after the divorce their father married Elaine, who was the custodial parent of her daughter, Jamie, aged six. Ellen and David lived in a one-parent household with their mother for three years, at which time their mother remarried. Their new stepfather, Craig, also had been divorced, and he was the joint-custodial parent of two daughters, aged six and 11. His daughters spent about ten days each month living in his household. Within the next four years, Ellen and David's father and stepmother had two children of their own, a son and a daughter.

When Ellen and David are 15 and 17, their family looks like this: They have two biological parents, two stepparents, three stepsisters, a half-brother and a half-sister. Their extended family has expanded as well: They have two sets of step-grandparents, two sets of biological grandparents, and a large network of aunts, uncles, and cousins. In addition to this complex network of kin, they have two households of "family." . . .

Binuclear Family Reorganization Through Expansion: An Overview

The expansion of the binuclear family through remarriage involves the addition of new family members in all three generations. The recoupling of one of the former spouses requires another reorganization of the former spouse subsystem and each of the parent-child subsystems; a recoupling of the other former spouse requires still another reorganization of the whole system. Each of these transitions has the potential of being highly stressful for family members. The way in which the family reorganizes itself will determine whether the binuclear family emerges as a functional or dysfunctional system. . . .

We are very much hindered by the inadequacy of current language in our discussion of the binuclear family in remarriage. For most of the relationships between family members in this expanded system there are no formal labels or role titles. What does one call one's former mate's new spouse? Or the children or parents of the new mate who have a relationship with one's child? Even the former spouse relationship has no current title, which requires that we continue to speak of it as a past relationship. Although ex-spouses with children may refer to each other as "my daughter's (or son's) father (or mother)," this does not capture the ongoing nonparental relationship between the divorced couple. So, of necessity, as we struggle to analyze some of the components of this complex system, our language suffers from being cumbersome and we will occasionally resort to inadequate terms that have emerged in the process of studying these families.

Former Spouse Subsystem

The former spouse relationship, with its many possible relational variations, becomes even more complex when one or both partners remarry. The timing of the remarriage further complicates the dynamics of this highly ambiguous post-divorce relationship. In McCubbin and Patterson's theoretical formulation of the pathways and mediating factors leading from stress to crisis, accumulating stressors, or "pileup," increase the potential for crisis. Consequently, if one of the ex-spouses remarries before the binuclear family has adequate time to establish new patterns for its reorganized structure, the potential for dysfunctional stress is high. Given the statistic that about 62 percent of men and 61 percent of women remarry within two years after divorce . . . , many families will experience the added stress of incorporating new family members in the midst of struggling with the complicated changes produced by the divorce.

Even if remarriage is delayed until the divorced family has had sufficient time to reorganize and stabilize, shifting of roles and relationships is necessary when a new member is introduced into the family system by remarriage. The family has to struggle with the role of the new family member while allegiances, loyalties and daily relationship patterns undergo transition. For many families, just as they are adjusting to one new member, the other ex-spouse remarries, which causes another transition requiring a shift in the family's tentative equilibrium. The length of time between one ex-spouse's remarriage and the second remarriage will influence the severity of stress experienced by all family members as they are required once again to cope with reorganization.

For the single ex-spouse, the remarriage of a former mate irrespective of the timing, may stimulate many of the feelings unresolved in the emotional divorce. If there are any lingering fantasies of reconciliation, the remarriage brings the sharp reality that reunion is no longer a possibility. It is not unusual for the single ex-spouse to feel a temporary loss of self-esteem as he or she makes comparisons to the new partner. Feelings of jealousy and envy are normal, even for those who thought they had worked through these feelings at the time of the divorce. Seeing an ex-spouse "in love" with someone else often rekindles the feelings of the early courtship and romantic phase of the first married relationship and a requestioning of the reasons for divorce. For a single ex-spouse who did not want the divorce, the remarriage has the potential of creating a personal crisis that closely resembles the experiences of the divorce. But even for those ex-spouses who may have initiated the divorce, the remarriage usually stimulates old feelings and resentments.

> *Nancy:* When Jim told me he was getting married I reacted with a cutting comment, saying I hoped she was better prepared for long evenings alone than I was. But what I was really scared about was that he would be different with her than he was with me. What if he had *really* changed? I realized that I wanted his marriage to fail. Then I would know that I was right in divorcing him.

Jim's remarriage resulted in Nancy's returning to therapy to work through many of the unresolved issues of the divorce. Jim's new wife was younger than Nancy and had one child by a previous marriage. Nancy and Jim had become cooperative colleagues in their divorced parenting relationship and she was fearful that she would have to give up many of the conveniences of their shared parenting as Jim took on the responsibilities of a new family.

The remarriage of one or both of the former spouses might be expected to decrease the amount of coparenting between former spouses, since a person involved in a new relationship may have less time to spend, or interest in, relating to his or her former spouse, or may perhaps feel pressure from the new spouse to decrease his or her involvement with the first spouse. For Jim, the conflicts were many.

> *Jim:* When Elaine and I decided to get married I felt guilty and like I needed to tell Nancy immediately. I dreaded telling her. When I did tell her she didn't say much but I knew she was feeling upset. I wanted the kids to be part of the wedding and I knew Nancy was going to feel jealous and left out. I'd feel much better if she had someone else in her life. Elaine's relationship with her ex-husband is nothing like my relationship with Nancy and she didn't understand my wanting to ease Nancy's pain by not flaunting my new life at her.

Jim's marriage to Elaine initiates a complex cycle of changes for all participants. Nancy needs to adjust to Jim's sharing of his life with a new partner and a child, while both Jim and Elaine need to cope with two ex-spouses who will continue to be part of their future lives. Six months after Jim's marriage to Elaine, Nancy summarized it this way:

> *Nancy:* Things have changed a lot since Jim remarried. He's less willing to accommodate when I need to change plans around the kids. He always has to check with Elaine first. I really resent that—the kids should come first. I invited Jim to Ellen's birthday party but he couldn't come because of plans he had made with Elaine and her child. And I feel uncomfortable calling him at home about anything. Elaine usually answers the phone and I feel like she's listening the whole time. Jim has asked to take the kids on a week's vacation to visit Elaine's parents over Easter. I know it's his time with the kids but I think he should give them some special time and not make them spend it with Elaine's family.

For Nancy it is difficult for her to see her children's family extending to include more members not directly related to her. And in these early stages of his remarriage Jim is having difficulty coping with the conflicting demands that his increasing family membership causes.

> *Jim:* I knew Nancy would be upset about our plans for the Easter vacation. Sometimes I wish I could just go off with the kids skiing like we did the first year after the divorce, but I know Elaine wants to visit her parents. There's no way I can please everyone.

Nancy and Jim's relationship is in the process of undergoing considerable change. They talk less frequently and anger sparks up more often now as they try to make decisions about the kids. Jim feels more anger at Nancy now because she is "not understanding" his new responsibilities, and Nancy feels more anger as she has less access to Jim. They are traveling the bumpy road of this transition as they redefine their relationship again, dealing with the changes brought about by Elaine's entry into the family system.

In Ahrons' Binuclear Family Study a deterioration in coparental relations after remarriage did occur among the respondents. This was especially true if only the husband had remarried. For instance, the number and frequency of childrearing activities shared between the former spouses were highest where neither partner had remarried and lowest if only the husband had remarried. The amount of support in coparental interaction was highest and conflict lowest where neither partner had remarried, while conflict was highest and support lowest if only the husband had remarried. Also, if neither former spouse had remarried, they were most likely to spend time together with each other and their children, and least likely if only the husband had remarried. . . .

Remarried Couple Subsystem

The transition to remarriage after a divorce of one or both partners is markedly different from the transition to a first marriage. Not only do the new spouses bring their families of origin into their extended system, but they also have relationships with their first married families which need to be integrated in some way. Remarried couples overwhelmingly report that they are unprepared for the complexities of remarried life. Their model for remarriage is often based on a first marriage model. In contrast to the relatively impermeable boundary that surrounds a nuclear family, permeable boundaries are needed in households within the binuclear family system. These facilitate the exchange of children, money, and decision-making power. If one of the partners has not been previously married, he or she is particularly vulnerable to the dream of the ideal traditional family. . . .

When Elaine and Jim decided to get married, they talked about their divorce histories and their current relationships with their ex-spouses and brought their respective children together for brief periods of time. They fantasized about their plans for blending their family and perhaps adding a new child of their own to the picture. Although they were both aware of some potential problems, they felt able to cope because of the strong bond they had developed between themselves. But as they actually made the transition to remarriage many of the problems created more stress than they had anticipated.

> *Elaine:* When Jim and I decided to get married I was surprised by his feeling guilty about Nancy. I didn't have any of those feelings about my ex, Tom. When Tom remarried last year it didn't make much difference in my life. He hadn't seen much of Jamie anyway and he just saw her less after he remarried. It was a relief not to have much to do with him. So, after living alone with Jamie for three years, I was really excited to have a family again and give Jamie more of a dad. But it's not working out that way. Jamie is angry a lot about not having time alone with me, which ends up with Jim and me fighting a lot. Jim feels badly about not spending enough time with his kids and when the kids are together, it just seems to be everyone fighting over Jim. And I feel resentful at not having enough time alone with Jim. Between every other weekend with his kids and the long hours we both work we never seem to have time alone together. Last Friday we were finally spending an evening all alone and, just as I was putting dinner on the table, Nancy called. Jim and I spent the next two hours talking about Nancy. It ended up spoiling our whole evening.

Elaine's feelings are not uncommon for second spouses within a complex binuclear family. The stresses of accommodating the existing bonds of first married relationships into the new stepfamily subsystem often turn the traditional "honeymoon stage" of marriage into an overwhelming cast of characters who share the marital bed. The reorganization required in moving from a one-parent household to a two-parent one often involves more adjustment than the single parent expected. Roles and relationships require realignment and the addition of a new person in some type of parent role is stressful for all the family participants. A frequent complaint in new remarriages is the lack of time and privacy for the newly remarried partners. Jim expressed his disillusionment this way:

> *Jim:* Maybe we shouldn't have gotten married. When we were dating we made time for each other and spent many days and evenings enjoying things together. But after we got married Elaine felt guilty leaving Jamie with her mother or a babysitter very often. Jamie is very demanding—she always seems to want Elaine to do something for her. And Elaine can't seem to say no. Whenever I try to suggest to Elaine that Jamie should learn to play alone more, Elaine seems to get moody and quiet. Her resentment of the time I spend with my kids is hard for me to deal with. Sometimes I think she wishes I would stop seeing them or see them as little as Tom sees Jamie.

When the remarriage partners have been previously married, it is difficult for them not to compare their respective relationships with their ex-spouses. Their own former spouse relationship becomes the model for their new spouse's former spouse relationship. Elaine's expectation that Jim would have a similar relationship with Nancy as she had with Tom was shattered as she realized that Nancy was still very much a part of Jim's life.

The rise of dual-career marriages has resulted in a time problem for first marriages which is only exacerbated in the dual career remarriage. Add to this children and an ex-spouse or two and the issue of time becomes a very real problem. The usual marital issues of power and regulation of distance and intimacy are multiplied in the complex binuclear family. . . .

As with divorce, and with marriage as well, the first year of remarriage has the most potential for crisis. The rate for divorce after remarriage is even higher than that for divorce in first marriages. Glick calculates that 54 percent of women and 61 percent of men who remarry will divorce. The timing of redivorce also differs from that of a first divorce. Remarriages have a 50 percent greater probability of redivorce in the first five years than first marriages.

Current empirical work also suggests that remarriage satisfaction is highly dependent on stepparent-stepchild relationships. How the crises are handled by the remarriage pair will depend on many past experiences and will define the future functioning of the family. Over time, and perhaps with some professional help, Elaine and Jim may be able to find ways to cope with their overcrowded lives. They will need to devise ways to protect and nourish their relationship without damaging the existing parent-child bonds. This will require developing a new model of familying which includes more flexibility, compromise, and fluidity of boundaries than they may have expected originally. . . .

Sibling Subsystems: Step and Half

The child development literature notes the stresses of adding children to the family with its normalizing of "sibling rivalry." In the remarriage family with children of both partners, the joining of the new sibling subsystems is a difficult transition for the children—acquiring an "instant sibling" can pose a threat to even the most secure child. The new remarriage partners have their marriage at stake and, therefore, need their respective children to like each other. Given a host of factors, such as the age and temperament of the children, the blending of two households of unrelated children requires major adjustments. Few newly blended families resemble the "Brady Bunch," but many have this as their model for this transition!

The usual competitive struggles among siblings often become major battles in remarried families, as children must adapt to sharing household space and parental time with new siblings. . . . [T]he remarriage of Ellen and David's father included a new "kid sister" for them. That was followed a year later by their mother's remarriage, which included two more "kid sisters" who shared their home with them for one-third of every month. And, a few years down the line, they had to incorporate two half siblings when their father and stepmother had a son and a daughter. . . .

Empirical research on the effects of remarriage on children is not as easily summarized as the literature on the effects of divorce. Although research is steadily increasing, we still lack major longitudinal studies identifying the stresses and developmental phases of adding new members to the binuclear family. And sibling relationships in binuclear families have been a sadly neglected area of study. But it is our guess that for many children the transition to remarriage is more stressful than the transition to divorce. The addition of new family members can also mean more loss than gain for many children—if not permanent losses, then at least temporary relationship loss in the transition period. The changes children need to make when a parent inherits new children as part of his or her remarriage are numerous and difficult. And the newly remarried parent, who so frequently feels overwhelmed, may have her or his energies absorbed more in the new mate than in facilitating the child's transition.

Mother/Stepmother—Father/Stepfather Subsystems

Now we are faced with describing baffling relationships with a wordiness created by our current language deficits. We are hampered further in our efforts by the lack of clinical or empirical research on these relationships. Nevertheless, we will attempt here to describe some of the stressful aspects of these relationships, which form such an integral part of the remarriage transition.

In fact, these first and second spouses do have some bearing on each other's lives. For some second spouses, the "ghost" of the first spouse is ever present. For many, the first spouse can be an unwanted interloper, creating conflict between the remarriage pair. In other remarriage couples the first spouse is a uniting force on whom the new spouses place blame for all the problems of a dysfunctional family. This type of scapegoating is the subject of much humor and provides the basis for many of the prevalent negative stereotypes of this relationship.

Obviously, even in one family system, the relationships between current and former spouses can be quite different, depending on the type of relationship between the former spouse pairs and all the individual personalities. . . .

The possibilities and complexities in these types of relationships are vast, and our knowledge of them is almost nonexistent. But clearly the type of relationship style adopted by the former spouses is a major factor determining the relationship between first and second spouses. In many remarried binuclear systems the former spouse relationship is likely to diminish in importance over time, especially when there are no minor children to bind the parents together. As this happens, the need for first and second spouses to relate also diminishes. . . .

Functional and Dysfunctional Remarriage Relationships

Our definition of functional and dysfunctional systems in remarriage is very similar to that of functional and dysfunctional divorces. . . . Developing new roles and relationships in remarriage which take into account the existence and losses of divorced family relationships is critical to enhancing remarried family functioning. The addition of new family members can result in dysfunctional binuclear family systems if prior kin relationships are severed. If remarriage subsystems try to model nuclear families—that is, if they insist upon "instant" family and try to establish traditional parenting roles—they will experience resistance and distress. A functional binuclear family system needs to have permeable boundaries which permit children and adults to continue prior family relationships while slowly integrating the new remarried subsystem. This, of necessity, causes transitory stresses and strains created by the conflict between new and old alliances. Remarriage is still another transition, with even more possibilities for stress than divorce.

As we emphasized in the divorce transition, the clear delineation of boundaries is critical to successful functioning. The remarried husband coparent, for example, must clarify his role vis-à-vis his biological and stepchildren, and his first and second spouses. He and his ex-spouse need to renegotiate what is appropriate and inappropriate in his continuing role as coparent. Coparenting agreements that may have been satisfactory prior to his remarriage are likely to have implications for his current spouse. For example, if it has been agreed that he needs to spend more time with his eight-year-old son, who wants and needs his father's attention, this takes time away from his marriage. His responsibilities as a parent and his spousal responsibilities come into conflict. This can be exacerbated by opinions expressed by his current partner that the "boy is spoiled and demanding and needs to learn that his father can't always be there." Or she may feel that the former spouse is using the child as a way of hanging on to her ex-husband. And, of course, she may also be concerned about the time taken away from her and the children she has brought to this new marriage. But the new partner must also be sensitive to the degree that expression of such thoughts violates important boundaries between the new marriage and the old.

While he will be wise not to pass these opinions of his new partner on to the former spouse (these are clearly outside the boundaries of the former spouse relationship), unless the husband coparent is able to deal effectively with his ex-spouse around these conflicting pressures, crisis may result. His former wife may see him as withdrawing from the coparental relationship they have agreed upon. And she, not having remarried, may have a renewed sense of abandonment resulting from the remarriage of her former spouse. Given their agreements concerning coparenting, she has legitimate call upon her former spouse. At the same time, the remarried spouse has equally legitimate expectations related to their marriage. Without explicit negotiation of arrangements and reasonable expectations from both sides, thus establishing clear boundaries for his actions in both subsystems, he is destined to fall short in both.

The single former spouse also may experience considerable distress in adjusting to the expanded system. Noncustodial parents will feel some resentment at losing some of their former responsibilities in both division of labor and decision-making. They may also feel that the new spouse interferes in their relationship with the former spouse and their children. A custodial parent, usually the mother, will often experience a loss of services when her former spouse remarries. She may no longer be able to call on him for help, as many of her demands—except as they are related to the coparenting relationship—begin to fall outside the legitimate boundaries of the former spouse relationship. Clearly, agreements and court orders with respect to financial child support are legitimate. However, expectations that the former husband will perform repairs or maintenance on the home of the former spouse may have to be rejected. This may be difficult, since that home is likely to be his former home, in which he may feel some residual investment, and in some cases may still retain some financial investment. However, resistance from the new partner to continuing such tasks is likely to severely restrict any such activity. All of this may be softened or made more difficult, depending upon the kind of postdivorce relationship style which has developed.

Remarriage restructures the division of labor developed in the postdivorce reorganization. New spouses of custodial parents take on many of the day-to-day responsibilities for care of children and household tasks formerly handled alone by the custodial parent or carried out by one of the children from time to time. As we have seen, this may lead to some genuine friction, as children resent the new stepparent's "taking over" or displacing them in some valued responsibility. If the new spouse attempts to assume responsibilities which the noncustodial parent may have continued, this is another source of potential stress. The former spouse may resent it, the stepchildren may resent it, and even the new spouse may have difficulty in accepting it.

Decision-making and the power structure implications carry similar potential stress. This will be especially true around decisions concerning the stepchildren, but may be true in other areas as well. If a new spouse has been used to having his or her former spouse participate and be involved in decisions concerning the children, the new spouse can easily be seen as "interfering," both by the other biological parent and the child. For example, as we have seen in the case presented in this chapter, Nancy resented Elaine's parenting involvement.

The style of the postdivorce ex-spouse relationship may either ease these adjustments, as with the perfect pals and cooperative colleagues, or make them more difficult, as with angry associates or fiery foes. If former spouses are insecure and competitive about their parenting relationships with their children, as is common between angry associates and fiery foes, the addition of a new parent figure will intensify those feelings during the transition. An ex-spouse may feel threatened by the "new family" of the remarried spouse, anticipating that the children will prefer this new household to the one-parent household where they currently live.

When parents—both biological and step—are unclear about their roles, children are likely to use the ambiguity to manipulate the new stepparent, their custodial parent, and the noncustodial parent. During the early stages of the remarriage transition it is not unusual for children to play one parent off against another for some personal gain. For example, in the Spicer-Tyler-Henry family, Ellen, after spending a weekend at her father's house, might very well tell her mother that Elaine, her new stepmother, "lets me watch TV until 10 p.m." Ellen's hope, of course, is that her mother will respond by permitting her to stay up later than her usual bedtime. Sometimes, new stepparents will be more lenient with their stepchildren in the hopes of being liked and accepted by them. Consciously, or perhaps unconsciously, the new stepparent is competing with the other biological parent for the child's affections.

Although former spouses may have worked out consistent rules for discipline, etc., during the divorce transition, these are likely to need renegotiation when a new parent enters the family. Only now, the renegotiation is more complicated, as three parents become part of the process instead of the original two. And if the other ex-spouse remarries, there may be a replay of some of the issues as the system accommodates to a fourth parent. As we noted earlier, however, this may be an easier transition. Not only are the parents familiar now with many of the problems of adjustment but the system itself is in better balance. There are now two stepfamily households, with each biological parent having an ally.

The remarried binuclear family faces a unique problem in controlling intimacy in the family. Incest taboos, which are assumed between blood kin in first marriage nuclear families (though, as is now being revealed, more often violated than many have known), become an important issue. The function of such taboos, of course, is to maintain unambiguous and appropriate intimate relationships in families. The potential for sexual feelings and possible abuse between non-blood parents and children, as well as between adolescent stepsiblings, is high. Therefore, establishment of clearly defined boundaries in this highly charged emotional area is essential.

A situation observed by one of the authors in family therapy illustrates how dysfunctional failure to establish such boundaries can be. In the course of the session, an adolescent stepdaughter revealed that she had been sexually involved with the son of her stepfather, i.e., her stepbrother. There were indications that this involvement was involuntary on her part. The mother of the young woman became very angry. At this point, the two biological daughters of the stepfather, who no longer lived in the household, confronted their stepmother with their sexual experiences some years before with her son—their stepbrother. They were extremely angry with the stepmother for not having the same reactions to their experiences, of which they believed the stepmother to be aware. These revelations, of course, provided some understanding of the kinds of conflicts in this stepfamily that had prompted the request for therapeutic treatment. The issues extended far beyond the matter of sexual abuse to include the entire range of emotional relationships which had developed in this remarried family over several prior years. Failure to have defined appropriate intimacy boundaries in the reorganization of this binuclear family had contributed to an extremely dysfunctional situation.

Relationships with extended kin find new stresses facing them upon the remarriage of one or both ex-spouses. Children may be particularly puzzled by suddenly finding their access to one set of grandparents or a favored aunt or uncle severely restricted or cut off. The nature of those relationships may also be changed, even if they are continued, by the inability of the extended kin to keep their feelings about the ex-spouse from contaminating their interactions with the children. Further, the introduction of new extended kin can also be confusing and stress-producing for children.

The new relationships with the spouse's extended family are not of the same character as those of first married couples. They often carry residual elements from the former marriage, particularly since these are not just in-laws, but also grandparents, uncles, and aunts. In addition, in many cases there are also associations to be worked out with the former spouse of the new partner. Until new relationships with extended family are established, they tend to be mediated through the new marital relationship.

Conclusion

. . . The study of even one remarried subsystem alone presents sufficient complexities to cause many social scientists to return to studying individuals rather than family systems. Our lack of both language and analytic tools, as well as the difficulties in conceptualizing the totality of these complex systems, creates frustration in both the writer and the reader.

All of this brings into sharp relief the importance of developing a new set of meanings for the relationships between former spouses, with the new spouse, between former and current spouses, between stepparents and stepchildren, between step and half siblings, and with extended kin. If the expanded binuclear family structure is to survive and function in an effective manner, then all parties must develop clear understandings of what these meanings are in the new remarriage situation. These meanings are most likely to center on the coparenting responsibilities that the ex-spouses share, but they go well beyond this.

Clearly delineating a precise definition of functional and dysfunctional remarriage binuclear families is not possible, given our current lack of knowledge. Although we can comfortably conclude that remarriage subsystems must be open systems with permeable boundaries, we cannot say what degree of openness is optimal. Remarriage subsystems need to be able to develop their own sense of connectedness and independence, while simultaneously functioning as interdependent units. Stepparents have a confusing and difficult role. In most families they need to develop new parenting type roles that supplement, rather than replace, biological parents. And they need to do so expecting resistance and a long developmental process of integration. What is required is a new model of familying that encompasses an expanded network of extended and quasi-kin relationships.

4

Children in the Family

Introduction

Chapter 8   Children

Chapter 9   Parents

Introduction

No aspect of childhood seems more natural, universal, and changeless than the relationships between parents and children. Yet the historical evidence reveals major changes in the conceptions of childhood and adulthood and in the psychological relationships between children and parents. Emotional bonds between parents and children have always existed. Before the eighteenth century, however, parents were not expected to emphasize these bonds or the value of children as unique individuals. Parents and children were bound together by economic necessity: children were a necessary source of labor in the family economy and a source of support in old age. Still, children were sometimes born when another mouth to feed threatened the survival of the family. Today, almost all children are economic liabilities. But they now have profound emotional significance. Parents hope offspring will provide intimacy, even genetic immortality.

As Viviana A. Zelizer observes in her article here, today's children have become economically worthless but emotionally "priceless." Zelizer's study of changing adoption practices over the last century reveals dramatic shifts in the economic and emotional significance of children. In the nineteenth century, foster parents provided homes for children in exchange for their labor. Whereas older children, especially boys, were preferred, there was no demand for babies, and mothers of unwanted infants had to abandon them, leave them in foundling homes, or else pay for their board and care at so-called "baby farms." By the 1930s, however, the sentimental value of children had increased. Adoptive parents wanted babies, especially girls, and older children became hard to place. In the 1980s the growing emotional value of children led to the phenomena of surrogate motherhood, *in vitro* fertilization, and other new birth technologies.

In her article on infertility, Charlene E. Miall reinforces Zelizer's argument about the enormous significance of children in contemporary American society. The pain and stigma of infertility today undermine the fashionable view that America is a nation of narcissists fleeing from attachment and commitment. Far from celebrating their freedom from the burdens of parenthood, Miall's subjects are more likely to view their plight as "the worst thing that ever happened to us." Miall finds that despite declining birthrates, traditional fertility norms persist: all married couples are expected to want to have children, and to have them. Thus, childlessness is a form of deviant behavior. To be infertile is to have a stigma—a discrediting attribute—that profoundly affects one's identity and relations with other people.

According to current estimates cited by Miall, the problem of infertility affects between 10 and 20 percent of couples. It is one of the factors behind the rise of surrogate motherhood and the new reproductive technologies. A quotation cited in the article by Herma Hill Kay here states the possibilities of the new methods: "It is now technically possible to take sperm from any fertile male, an egg from any fertile female, join them by the *in vitro* fertilization process, and implant the resulting embryo into any womb. After birth the child can be raised by any set of adults who may or may not have been participants in the child's conception or birth" (O'Rourke, cited in Kay, this volume, p. 405–406). Thus, these new techniques not only separate the biological from the social aspects of parenthood, as adoption has always done, but also separate biological processes that used to be "naturally" linked together—intercourse and fertilization, bearing a child and being its genetic mother.

The new reproduction technologies obviously raise profound moral, legal, psychological, and social policy questions. In her article, Kay examines a number of these issues. She focuses on the celebrated Baby M case, probably the most famous custody case since the judgment of Solomon. This case aroused passionate debates that still remain unresolved. Should surrogate motherhood contracts be legally enforceable? Should the surrogate mother be allowed to change her mind and keep the child? Does the wife have to be infertile? For many people, the Baby M case raised the fear that middle-class women will eventually employ poor women as breeders of their own genetic children. The Sterns, the childless couple who hired Mary Beth Whitehead as a surrogate mother, were not infertile. Rather, Mrs. Stern, who suffered from a mild case of multiple sclerosis, feared that pregnancy might endanger her health. The central legal issue of the case, however, was the custody dispute between the Sterns and Whitehead. How can the "best interests of the child" standard be applied to such cases? After examining the complexities the new biology introduces into family law, Kay concludes with the reminder that an infant born as the result of a surrogate parenting agreement has the same human and developmental needs as other infants.

Children and Parents

No matter how eagerly the first child is awaited, becoming a parent is usually experienced as one of life's major "normal" crises. In her now classic article on the transition to parenthood, reprinted here, Alice Rossi explains why. Since Rossi's article first appeared over two decades ago, a large research literature has developed, most of which supports her view of the transition to parenthood as crisis.

Parenthood itself has changed since Rossi wrote, as increasing numbers of men have reached out for greater involvement in the lives of their children. Mothers are still the principal nurturers and caretakers of their children, but the norms of parenthood have shifted somewhat—as the growing use of the term "parenting" suggests. Robert Fein's article here describes how views of fatherhood in the research literature are changing along with the behavior of fathers and children in real life.

Until recently, a father could feel he was fulfilling his parental obligations merely by supporting his family. He was expected to spend time with his children when his work schedule permitted, to generally oversee their upbringing, and to discipline them when necessary. Even scholars of the family and of child development tended to ignore the role of the father except as breadwinner and role model. His family participation did not call for direct involvement in the daily round of childrearing, especially when the children were babies. By contrast, scholars expressed the extreme importance of the mother and the dangers of maternal deprivation. Today, however, the role of father is beginning to demand much more active involvement in the life of the family, especially with regard to childrearing. Countering this trend, however, is the rising divorce rate of recent years, which for many children means a greatly reduced amount of life with father.

Single Mothers

The rise in the divorce rate is one reason for the dramatic increase in single-parent families since the 1970s. The vast majority of single-parent families are headed by women, and as Martha T. Mednick observes in her article here, the term "feminization of poverty" was coined to describe this segment of the population. Mednick reviews and criticizes current research on single mothers from the point of view of the mothers themselves. In the past, the single-parent family was treated as a pathological family type that had a uniform set of bad effects. Today many researchers recognize that single mothers are a diverse group and that single motherhood need not inevitably lead to negative personal or social consequences. For example, much of the depression and stress experienced by these women may be due to poverty rather than single-parent status per se. But poverty is not the only problem that confronts single mothers. Having to take over the traditionally male role of supporting and heading the family may be incongruent with assumptions about women's roles. Further, raising children as a single mother can be stressful, especially if the children are boys. Finally, even though this family form is more accepted than it used to be, the assumption that nuclear family is the "hallmark of normality" still affects research as well as the mothers themselves.

Child Abuse

While the stable two-parent family remains the ideal norm, marital conflict and divorce can be understood as one of the hazards of family life—a "normal" problem. Child abuse, by contrast, seems to be a violation of the very nature of family bonds. Yet as researchers have discovered, most child abusers are not pathological monsters, and most incidents of child abuse seem to be an exaggeration of everyday family life, rather than something apart from it. The line between "normal" punishment and abuse is sometimes hard to draw.

Although the idea of battered child thus suggests a physical phenomenon, child abuse is, according to the reprinted selection by Eli H. Newberger and Richard Bourne, a social phenomenon created and shaped through the definitions applied by clinicians and other professionals—often more to the advantage of their own interests than to the benefit of the clients they are supposed to serve. Children are frequently battered in our society. Reprehensible battering or "abuse" is a label, perhaps well deserved, but one that varies with such factors as social class, ethnicity, and professional intervention.

Chapter 8

Children

Pricing the Priceless Child:
From Baby Farms to Black-Market Babies

Viviana A. Zelizer

In 18th-century rural America, as in many older rural cultures, the birth of a child was welcomed as the arrival of a future laborer and as security for parents later in life. Today's children, on the other hand, are worthless to their parents in economic terms, but in sentimental value they are "priceless."

Although this transformation has been gradual and has occurred at different times among different classes in the population, the most profound changes took place between the 1870s and the 1930s. At the beginning of this period, rapid industrialization was introducing new occupations for poor children and working-class urban families depended on their wages. In the new century, however, child labor laws and compulsory education began to take effect, and by the 1930s, even lower-class children had joined the nonproductive world of childhood.

To be sure, child labor did not magically and totally vanish. In the 1920s and 1930s, some children under 14 still worked in rural areas and in street trades. Moreover, the Great Depression temporarily restored the need for a useful child even in some middle-class households. But the overall trend was unmistakable. In the first three decades of the 20th century, the economically useful child became both numerically and culturally an exception.

One aspect of this transformation, which also reflected the changing roles of women, occurred in the "exchange" value of children. In the 19th-century boarding out system, foster parents provided child care in exchange for child labor, and older boys were in great demand. After the 1920s, however, adoptive parents were only interested in (and willing to wait several years for) a blue-eyed baby or a cute two-year-old curly-haired girl. While 19th-century mothers were forced to pay to get rid of a baby, by the 1930s unwanted babies were selling for $1000 or more. In the 1980s, advancing technology joined with the growing sentimental value of the economically worthless child to create the new phenomenon of "surrogate motherhood."

The 19th-Century Approach to Substitute Parenting

The legitimacy of child labor was essential to early 19th-century substitute care arrangements. In exchange for board, clothing, and some education, children were expected to assist the foster household in a variety of tasks. It was considered a fair bargain. After all, if children worked for their own parents, why not work for surrogate caretakers?

The tradition had been established in colonial times with the widespread system of apprenticeship. Seventeenth-century parents placed their children with neighbors, relatives, and sometimes even strangers to learn a skilled trade. While for some it was an instructional and elective indenture, for poor and dependent children it was the only way to secure a home.

Even when they were institutionalized in alms-houses and, after the 1830s, in orphanages, children's value as laborers determined the nature of their placement. They were expected to subsidize their stay by contributing with their work to the support of the asylum, and after they reached the age of 12 or 14 were placed out as workers in foster families.

The most renowned 19th-century program of placing children in family homes was directly contingent on children's economic usefulness. In 1854 the New York Children's Aid Society began sending needy city children to rural homes in the midwest and upstate New York. It was hoped that families would welcome the children as working family members rather than as cheap laborers, but the children's work contribution was never in dispute. Poor urban families used the Society as a quasi-employment agency, surrendering custody of their children to meet their need for jobs. Thus the system served not only the interests of employers but those of at least a segment of the children placed. The useful child—generally older than ten, and a boy—found a legitimate place in the foster household economy no less than in his own working-class family.

If a working child in the 19th century was an asset, an infant was a liability. Unwanted babies, or those whose parents could not afford to keep them, were more likely to die than be adopted. Faced with almost insurmountable social and economic pressures, single, widowed, or deserted mothers had few options. Abortion was not only expensive, but required connections, especially after the 1860s when it became an increasingly illegitimate and illegal practice. The few jobs available to women with children did not pay a living wage. Unprotected by insurance, and without the support of adequate public relief or private programs, many lower-class women abandoned their babies soon after birth in public places or in a foundling asylum.

Baby farmers offered an alternative to those who could afford their fee. These usually middle-aged women built a profitable enterprise by boarding mostly illegitimate babies. With high rates of mortality, the turnover was quick and business brisk. For fifty dollars, perhaps, mothers were relieved of responsibility and assured of confidentiality. The terms usually included the child's eventual adoption into a good home, but this prospect was seldom fulfilled. As a 1910 investigation discovered, the baby farm "swarms with children whose numbers are added to weekly. Always they come and come, and rarely . . . are they carried away."[1]

A Proper Home for the Sacred Child: Revising the Adoption Contract

Once the useful child was defined as a social problem, traditional solutions for the care of dependent children became untenable. Seeking a destitute child for its labor, or taking in a homeless baby for the sake of a cash bonus equally transgressed the new sentimental value of children. Child welfare workers sought to replace mercenary foster parenting of any kind with a new approach to adoption more suitable for the economically "useless" child. In 1909, the White House Conference on Children officially declared foster homes the "best substitute for the natural home."

As the concept of home care gained increasing recognition, it became imperative to rethink carefully children's proper place in the foster home. Prospective adopters were duly warned that raising a useless child was an expensive commitment, but one which new intangible benefits would make worthwhile.

Challenging the established exchange of child labor for child care was often a frustrating effort. But traditional solutions to substitute parenting were not maintained, as child welfare workers supposed, simply by the individual selfishness of foster parents or even the material greediness of baby farmers. Instead, the shift to sentimental adoption was obstructed by the continuing legitimacy of children's usefulness. For working-class families, taking in a child was justified only if he or she paid its way with some form of work. For child-placing agencies, it was essential to determine at what point the foster child ceased being a family member to become the family's servant.

As in natural families, the relationship of foster children to work and money was transformed in the 20th century. New educational guidelines replaced earlier economic criteria. Child work became acceptable only as part of an "educational program." Child money was a means to teach children how to save and how to spend. While some natural mothers "paid" their children for performing household duties, most experts discouraged foster parents from paying a child for "his share of the routine household chores as would be performed as a matter of course by their own children."[2]

Boarding Homes: A Controversial "Dowry" for Useless Children

In the late 1860s, the Massachusetts State Board of Charities pioneered the concept of paying foster parents for the care of a child. These subsidized boarding homes stood at the crossroads between instrumental and sentimental adoption. Initially, boarding homes complemented the customary exchange of child labor for child care by financing primarily those unable to fulfill the traditional contract, especially small children, or sickly or troublesome ones.

But boarding homes also played a key role in the breakup of 19th-century fostering practices. Paid parenting presented the perfect alternative to working homes, especially for children between the ages of seven and eleven—too young to be placed as workers, yet too old to be adopted as "pets and means of amusement."[3] Boarding homes offered this in-between age group a substitute for the traditional indenture or free working home, thereby assuring them a prolonged period of "uselessness." With some luck, it was even possible that a proper "dowry" would provide children with a passport to sentimental adoption.

Yet for its critics, the monetization of child care was a dangerous new variant of the instrumental approach to substitute parenting. Despite every effort to depict boarding as a task of love and regardless of the individual motivations of foster parents, the contractual arrangement by which families received a fee for the care of a child defined their task as partly commercial. Therefore, while boarding homes had an important part in the transition from instrument to sentimental adoption, paid parenting remained an ambivalent occupation.

Blue-Eyed Babies and Golden-Haired Little Girls: The Sentimental Value of a Priceless Child

In the 1920s and 1930s, sentimental adoption made sympathetic headlines as it rapidly displaced earlier instrumental fostering arrangements. A new consensus was reached. The only legitimate rewards of adoption were emotional, "an enlargement of happiness to be got in no other way."[4]

Legal adoption, rare in the 19th century, became increasingly popular, and the problem soon became that of finding enough children for childless homes. The quest for a child to love turned into a glamorous and romanticized search as a number of well-known entertainment and political figures proudly and publicly joined the rank of adoptive parents: Al Jolson, Gracie Allen and George Burns, Mayor LaGuardia, Babe Ruth, and Eddie Rickenbacker, among others, announced their decision to adopt a child.

While the most well-known incidents were exceptions, the social class of adoptive parents was indeed undergoing change. A comparison by the New York State Charities Aid Association of the occupations of 100 foster fathers between 1898 and 1900 with the same number of fathers in the period between 1920 and 1921, found that nearly three-quarters of the first group were in skilled, semiskilled, or unskilled labor, or in farming, while in the latter period there was a predominance of men in business and office work.

Sentimental adoption created an unprecedented demand for children under three, especially for infants. While the economically "useless" 19th-century baby had to be protected because it was unwanted, the priceless 20th-century baby "needs protection as never before . . . [because] too many hands are snatching it."[5]

The priceless child was judged by new criteria: physical appeal and personality replaced earlier economic yardsticks, and the greatest demand was for little girls. In the 1920s, wealthy Americans even imported their "English rose" golden-haired baby girls from London.

Considering the widespread parental preference for a male first-born child, the popularity of adopted daughters was puzzling. Parents, suggested one adoption agency in 1916, "seem to feel that a girl is easier to understand and to rear, and they are afraid of a boy . . ."[6] It was not the innate smiling expertise of females, but established cultural assumptions of women's superior emotional talents which made girls so uniquely attractive for sentimental adoption.

The new appeal of babies was further enhanced by the increasing acceptance, in the 1920s, of environmental theories of development. Couples considering adoption were now reassured that "heredity has little or nothing to do with our characters. It is the environment that counts . . ."[7] Intelligence tests and improved methods of determining children's physical health reduced the "old prejudice against thrusting one's hand in a grab-bag, eugenically speaking, and breeding by proxy."[8]

Ironically, as the priceless child displaced the useful child, the dangers of adoption shifted from economic to emotional hazards; the previously exploited little laborer risked becoming a "pretty toy." If child-placing agencies were less often confronted by requests for a sturdy working child, they now faced new expectations, as in the couple who applied to the New York State Charities Aid Association for a three-month-old baby "who could eventually go to Princeton."[9]

Black-Market Babies: The Price of a Priceless Child

The sentimentalization of adoption had an unanticipated and paradoxical effect: because 20th-century adoptive parents were willing to pay to obtain an infant, "baby traffickers" made money not only from the surrender of babies, but by then selling them to their new customers. As a result, the value of a priceless child became increasingly monetized and commercialized.

Commercial child placement emerged as a significant social problem in the 1920s in large part because it violated new professional standards in adoption. Without proper supervision by a licensed child-placing agency, adoption could be dangerous both for children and their adoptive parents. Yet, despite increased public regulation of child care and the multiplication of adoption laws, including stricter licensing of boarding homes and new laws against adoption by advertisement, informal child placement persisted. Independent adoptions were often arranged by well-intentioned intermediaries, without involving profit. But in many cases, middlemen built a lucrative business by "bootlegging" babies.

Harshly denounced as an "iniquitous traffic in human life," and a "country-wide shame," the black market in babies flourished in the 1930s and 1940s.[10] As demand for adoptable children grew, the traffic in infants reached a new third stage. It was now a seller's market. The mother of an unwanted child no longer needed to pay to dispose of her baby. Instead, entrepreneurial brokers approached her, offering to pay medical and hospital expenses and often a bonus in exchange for her baby. (Even in independent placements arranged without profit, it became common practice to pay the hospital and medical expenses of the natural mother.) In 1955, a Congressional investigation conducted by Senator Estes Kefauver pronounced baby selling a national social problem, and Senate Committee hearings revealed that the price of a black market baby could be as much as $10,000.

The money value of infants was partly determined by a reduced supply. As the dramatic decline in the national birthrate, which began early in the 19th century, continued into the 1930s, fewer babies were available for adoption. In addition, after 1911, the mothers' pension movement allowed widows, and in some cases deserted wives or mothers whose husbands were handicapped, or in prison, to keep their children. Reformers also encouraged unmarried mothers to keep their babies. As a result, the supply of adoptable infants shrank, and the waiting lists of adoption agencies grew longer. Unwilling to wait two or more years for a child, and impatient with the increasingly restrictive standards set by agencies, parents turned to the black market.

But scarcity alone cannot determine value. A reduced supply raised the price of babies only because there was a growing number of enthusiastic buyers for white, healthy infants. In sharp contrast, older children found few customers. Deprived of their former labor value, they were excluded from the new emotional market. Therefore, while the agencies' waiting lists for babies had the names of hundreds of impatient parents, it was virtually impossible to find homes for children older than six, who had become both economically and sentimentally "useless."

Pricing the Priceless: The Special Market for Children

As the market for child labor disappeared, and the market price developed for children's new sentimental value, an apparently profound contradiction was created: between a cultural system that declared children priceless emotional assets, and a social arrangement that treated them as "cash commodities."[11] In the view of some economists, this persistent conflict should be resolved in favor of the market: "The baby shortage and black market are the result of legal restrictions that prevent the market from operating freely in the sale of babies as of other goods. This suggests as a possible reform simply eliminating these restrictions."[12]

But a "free" independent market for babies is a theoretical illusion: cultural constraints cannot be simply dismissed as obsolete. From the start, the baby market was shaped by the cultural definition of children as priceless. The black market is unacceptable because it treats children in the same manner used for less sacred commercial products: "If [baby brokers] were not selling babies, they would be selling whatever else was hot and produce a profit."[13]

Today black market practices are illegal, yet a different kind of market exists which is, in most cases, legal and compatible with sentimental adoption. In this "gray market," placements are arranged "without profit by well-meaning parents, friends, relatives, doctors and lawyers."[14] Professional fees for legal or medical services are acceptable; not only do most adoption experts support the right to collect "reasonable fees for professional services," but certain statutes specifically allow legal fees and compensation for the mother's medical expenses. Thus, while the black market is defined as a degrading economic arrangement, a modified, legitimate market exists for the exchange of children.

Adoption fees also constitute a separate market. From the start, agencies sought to define their work as consistent with sentimental adoption. Until the 1940s, only "gratitude donations" were accepted from adoptive parents. The boundary between adoption and purchase was preserved by defining the money as an elective gift, not a price. The shift from donations to fees was, therefore, a sensitive matter.

The uniqueness of a market involving children is also apparent in their "rental." Even after the 1930s, when boarding homes increasingly became the preferred method for temporary care of dependent children, the early dilemmas of paid parenting remained unsolved. Traditionally low board payments, besides being economical for the agency, were seen as certifying the altruism of boarding mothers.

The "gray market," adoption fees, and board payments illustrate some of the cultural contours of the modern adoption market. Even baby selling is justified by criteria other than profit, with payments legitimized as symbolic expressions of sentimental concern. Pricing the priceless child is a unique commercial venture.

References

1. Mary Boyle O'Reilly, "The Daughters of Herod," *New England Quarterly* 43 (Oct.1910): 144–5.
2. *The ABC of Foster-Family Care for Children*, U.S. Children's Bureau Publication No. 216, 1933.
3. Herbert W. Lewis, "Terms on Which Children Should be Placed in Families," *Proceedings of the 21st National Conference of Charities and Correction*, 1894, pp. 141–2.
4. *New York Times*, Oct. 25, 1926, p. 18.
5. Spence Alumnae Society, *Annual Report*, 1916, p. 37.
6. Ibid., p. 38.
7. Josephine Baker, "Choosing a Child," *Ladies Home Journal*, 41 (Feb. 1924): 36.
8. Robert Grant, "Domestic Relations and the Child," *Scribner's Magazine* 65 (May 1919): 527.
9. *New York Times*, May 8, 1927, VII, p. 14.
10. Vera Connolly, "Bargain-Counter Babies," *Pictorial Review* 38 (Mar. 1927), p. 96.
11. Mona Gardner, "Traffic in Babies," *Collier's* 104 (Sept. 16, 1939): 43.
12. Elisabeth M. Landes and Richard A. Posner, "The Economics of the Baby Shortage," *7 Journal of Legal Studies* 339 (June 1978).

13. Statement by Joseph H. Reid, Executive Director, Child Welfare League of America, in Hearings
    Before the Subcommittee on Children and Youth of the Committee on Labor and Public Welfare,
    94th Congress, 1st Session (1975), p. 19.
14. "Moppets on the Market: The Problem of Unregulated Adoptions," 59 *Yale Law Journal* (1950),
    p. 715.

The Stigma of Involuntary Childlessness*

Charlene E. Miall

The United States and Canada are still strongly pronatalistic societies despite long-term declines in their birth rates and average family size. Two traditional fertility norms continue to be widely accepted in North America: (1) all married couples should reproduce and (2) all married couples should *want* to reproduce (Veevers, 1980:3, emphasis added). It is within this context that Veevers (1972) conceptualizes childlessness—whether voluntary or involuntary—as a form of deviant behavior in marriage, a violation of prevailing norms of acceptable conduct. When cultural norms and values encourage reproduction and celebrate parenthood, childlessness becomes a potentially stigmatizing status which can adversely affect the identities and interpersonal relationships of married persons.

Previous sociological investigations have focused on the impact of stigmatization on couples who are voluntarily childless or "childless by choice" (see Veevers, 1979, 1980, 1983). However, with only a few exceptions, sociologists have overlooked the experiences of those who are involuntarily childless through subfecundity or infertility (see Humphrey, 1969; Kirk, 1964; Matthews and Martin Matthews, 1986; Miall, 1984, 1985). Although infertility has been the subject of demographic, clinical, and autobiographical works, systematic research is lacking on personal and social reactions to involuntary childlessness as a deviant status. In this paper, I address this deficit in the sociological literature by presenting evidence from a study of 71 involuntarily childless women. Following a brief discussion of some crucial analytical issues for sociological research on involuntary childlessness, I show how these women perceive their own or their spouse's "problem" and analyze their stategies for managing its potentially stigmatizing implications in interaction with others.

*This is a revision of a paper presented at the 1983 annual meetings of the Canadian Sociology and Anthropology Association, British Columbia. Thanks to Fred Elkin, Ray Morris, Judith Posner, Bill Shaffir, and the anonymous reviewers for their comments. The research was supported by grants from the Social Sciences and Humanities Research Council of Canada and from the Government of Ontario.

Involuntary Childlessness: Analytical Distinctions

Estimates indicate that from one in five (Burgwyn, 1981; Kraft et al., 1980) to one in 10 couples (Mosher, 1982) may be involuntarily childless—that is, infertility affects their relationship.[1] Within western nations infertility is usually estimated to occur in 10 to 15 percent of the population (Benet, 1976; Menning, 1975; National Center for Health Statistics, 1985).[2] Generally, medical researchers distinguish between *primary* infertility and *secondary* infertility. Couples are considered to have primary infertility if they fail to conceive after one year of regular intercourse without contraception and if conception has never occurred before. Couples are considered to have secondary infertility if they fail to conceive following one or more births, or, following conception, fail to carry pregnancy to term (McFalls, 1979).

Involuntary childlessness can be conceptualized as a form of physical disability. It is a chronic condition that meets biopsychological, social role, and legal criteria for disability.[3] Most cases of involuntary childlessness are medically diagnosed as the consequence of some form of physical impairment—for example, there may be disease-related or genetic malformations of the male or female reproductive organs. Certain forms of involuntary childlessness may be related to psychological factors, although the numbers so afflicted appear small (Weinstein, 1962). Involuntary childlessness also meets a social role definition of disability (Nagi, 1966) in that couples are prevented from reproducing, a social role expectation that has great revelance in western society. Finally, involuntary childlessness is treated legally as a form of disability. For example, many adoption agencies in the United States and Canada require documented proof of infertility in a relationship before they will accept adoption applications for infants. Unlike visible disabilities like paralysis or disfigurement, involuntary childlessness is a *discreditable* or potentially stigmatizing attribute in that it is not readily apparent (Goffman, 1963). However, involuntary childlessness is similar to other disabilities which are viewed as *accidental* (Lorber, 1967:303) or *involuntary* deviance (Birenbaum and Sagarin, 1976:35). It is usually not motivated, and is typically associated with "contingencies of inheritance, accidents of infection and trauma" (Freidson, 1966:81).

[1] Unless otherwise noted, the terms "infertility" and "involuntary childlessness" are used synonymously.

[2] Estimates range between 5 and 30 percent of the population (Kraft et al., 1980; McFalls, 1979). The lack of consensus on the prevalence of infertility results from differing definitions of infertility, the varying periods of time over which it is studied, and a failure to distinguish analytically between voluntarily and the involuntarily childless (McFalls, 1979; Rao, 1974). However, infertility appears to be increasing (Curran, 1980; Mosher, 1982). Reasons offered for the increase include rising rates of gonorrhea and pelvic inflammatory disease, intentional postponement of childbearing to an age where fertility diminishes, sepsis after abortion, coerced sterilization, and increasing exposure to chemical toxins (Curran, 1980; Menning, 1981; Zimmerman, 1982).

[3] In the literature on health and rehabilitation (Nagi, 1966; Sussman, 1977), a distinction is made between illness or sickness (acute or short-term episodes or diseases) and disability or impairment (chronic or long-term episodes or diseases).

The literature on childlessness distinguishes between voluntary and involuntary childlessness regardless of the physical status of the individuals concerned. Two separate components are involved in this distinction: "the physical capacity to procreate and the psychic wish to do so" (Veevers, 1979:3). From a social psychological viewpoint, the essential component in defining persons as involuntarily childless is not their biological status as fertile or infertile, but their psychological preference to procreate and their inability in present circumstances to do so. For example, although only one partner in a relationship might be diagnosed as infertile, both partners would be considered involuntarily childless if they had a conscious desire to procreate but were unable to do so. Similarly, the same couple would be considered voluntarily childless if their psychological preference was not to procreate and they subsequently avoided or rejected the parenthood role (Veevers, 1979).

Pronatalism and Social Definitions of Childlessness

Involuntary childlessness can be a devastating blow to some individuals (Kraft et al., 1980; Menning, 1977; Pfeffer and Woollett, 1983; Zimmerman, 1982). The negative impact of involuntary childlessness is undoubtedly related to the pronatalistic views of marriage that pervade western society. Indeed, contemporary endorsement of the fertility norms of having and wanting children transcends sex, age, race, religion, ethnic, and social class divisions in North America (Pohlman, 1969, 1974; Russo, 1976; Veevers, 1980, 1983).[4] This commitment to parenthood in western society has been attributed to the Judaeo-Christian tradition which sees children as blessings from heaven and barrenness as a curse or punishment (Burgwyn, 1981; McFalls, 1979; Pohlman, 1970).[5] Like leprosy and epilepsy, infertility bears an ancient social stigma.

Women in particular may be seriously affected by childlessness (Russo, 1976; Veevers, 1972). Our social and cultural institutions continue to emphasize the importance of motherhood for the female role (Broverman et al., 1972; Fox et al.,

---

[4] Pronatalism loosely means "any attitude or policy that is 'pro-birth', that encourages reproduction, that exalts the role of parenthood" (Peck and Senderowitz, 1974:1). Veevers (1979) has observed that permanent voluntary childlessness is characteristic of only about 5 percent of married couples. More recently, Rossi (1984) has noted only a slight increase in voluntary childlessness with fewer than 10 percent of young women entering adulthood with no expectation or desire for children. Given the trend toward postponement of childbearing until women are over 30, this figure may overestimate the percentage of women who initially report a desire to remain childless but who later decide to have children. For a more detailed discussion of pronatalism and the relevance of fertility and reproduction for western society in general, and for women in particular, see Peck and Senderowitz (1974) and Veevers (1980).

[5] Cultural evaluations of fertility and infertility are reflected in everyday speech—for example, a fertile mind, pregnant with hope, and a fruitful enterprise versus fruitless labors, a sterile approach, and barren soil (Burgwyn, 1981:92; Veevers, 1972:576–77). Indeed, the medical terminology used to describe some reproductive disorders is revealing: hostile vagina, hostile cervical mucus, blighted ovum, incompetent or competent cervix, and incompetent or competent spermatozoa (Burgwyn, 1981).

1982; Russo, 1976; Veevers, 1980). In the clinical literature, women's sexual and psychological adjustment is tied to childbearing (Pohlman, 1970; Rossi, 1977). Although less is written about the importance of fatherhood to men, the announcement of the pregnancy of the wife is usually considered a sign of virility in the husband. However, the failure to reproduce is likely to be attributed to some problem in the woman (Veevers, 1972:577).

Individuals usually learn that they are infertile or involuntarily childless later in life, after they are married with presumably well-established adult identities. Given pronatalistic attitudes, a significant part of this identity for men and women probably revolves around the expectation of conceiving, bearing, and rearing children. The awareness that one is infertile therefore, may have profound consequences for the social identity and behavior of the actor.

Although the social context strongly suggests that involuntarily childless individuals, and particularly women, are subject to stigmatization, there has been no empirical research on this issue. Therefore, in this paper, I explore the perceptions of involuntarily childless women to determine if they view infertility as a stigmatizing or discreditable attribute. I use the following criteria to determine if respondents are involuntarily childless: the demonstration of infertility in the presently contracted marriage, and the absence of biologically-related offspring on either side from previous marriages or relationships. In addition, I examine the ways in which involuntarily childless women handle this attribute in interaction with others. I consider the extent to which these information management strategies reflect those observed by Schneider and Conrad (1980) in their study of individuals who possess another discreditable attribute—epilepsy.

In addition, I examine fertile women who are married to husbands with documented infertility. I consider these women to be involuntarily childless because they desire to bear children but are unable, in present circumstances, to do so. However, if these women share the stigma of infertility, it is in the sense of possessing a *courtesy stigma* (Birenbaum, 1975:348; Goffman, 1963)—that is, their stigma is based on their association with someone who has a stigmatizing attribute, and not on their own personal attributes. I am particularly interested in whether there are discernible differences in perceptions of infertility and use of information management strategies between the physically infertile, and the physically fertile who are childless. It seems likely that involuntarily childless women whose stigma is based on their association with someone who is infertile, rather than on a personal physical attribute, are less sensitive to its discrediting implications.

Method

I began my research with the aim of comparing reactions of men and women to their involuntary childlessness. However, I was unable to obtain a sample of men sufficient for this comparative approach. Indeed, in order to recruit female respondents, I was obliged to use a snowball sampling technique. The difficulty that I had in obtaining a sample of infertile individuals who would participate in my study reflects the sensitivity and secrecy that surround the problem of infertility. Volunteers were recruited through social work agencies, adoptive parent groups, and through other research participants. Therefore I do not claim that my results are statistically representative of all involuntarily childless women.

I conducted a pre-tested, standardized, open-ended interview (Patton, 1980) with 30 involuntarily childless women. In addition, 41 involuntarily childless women completed a questionnaire identical to the interview schedule.[6] Questions were based on previous research on infertility, over one-and-a-half years of participant observation in an infertility self-help group, discussions with infertile individuals in the community, and popular anecdotal literature on infertility. The interviews lasted from two-and-one-half to four hours. The women in this sample ranged in age from 25 to 45. Most of them were well-educated, from middle- to upper-middle class backgrounds, white, and Protestant (16 respondents were Jewish). Twelve respondents were fertile themselves but married to infertile men—that is, they shared a courtesy stigma.

Perceptions of Involuntary Childlessness

The Stigma Potential of Infertility

In this study, I regarded actors' definitions or constructions of the personal meanings of infertility as important. Nearly all the respondents categorized infertility as something negative, as representing some sort of failure, or an inability to work normally. In addition, women experiencing or sharing infertility regarded it as a discreditable attribute—that is, most were concerned that an awareness of problems with fertility would cause others to view them in a new and damaging light (see Miall, 1985). One woman summed it up for most respondents:

> We expected things to work out. We led the golden lives until this happened to us. It's the worst thing that ever happened to us. My husband and I are high achievers. We work together and it works out. Therefore, it's even harder for us to accept this because we don't have control over something that's so easy for other people.

These respondents often became aware of possible infertility before they consulted a physician. For example, many women became suspicious when they failed to conceive after six months or a year without birth control. The majority of these women secretly arranged to visit a doctor or a fertility clinic to avoid public awareness of difficulty. Some respondents found it difficult to express a reason for their secretive behavior. Often the statements "It's a private matter," or "It's nobody's business" were offered as rationales. As one respondent put it:

---

[6] In many instances, volunteers refused to be interviewed but offered to fill in a questionnaire anonymously. Although quotes in the text are taken from interview data only, they reflect the sentiments expressed in the questionnaire responses.

> Well we just didn't discuss it. I mean we've never even discussed it with my husband's mother. I don't believe that it's anyone's business but ours. It's a personal thing.

On the other hand, most respondents expressed the sentiment that the admission of possible problems with infertility was in some way an admission of failure, which in turn might have serious consequences for the person doing the disclosing. One woman felt that admitting to possible problems with reproduction was

> an admission that you're not a whole person . . . either sexually or anatomically or both. That there's something wrong and I guess reproduction, the ability to reproduce strikes at the very essence of one's being.

Another woman spoke of trying to protect parents from unnecessary concern:

> We kept it very private. Even our parents didn't know. We didn't want people worrying before we knew what the result was. We never told anybody we had problems conceiving until the end [when permanent infertility was confirmed].

In fact, nearly all the respondents in the study experienced feelings of anxiety, isolation, and conflict as they explored the possibility of personal infertility. Most were concerned that an awareness of their infertility problems would cause others to view them in a new and damaging light. As one respondent put it:

> I do believe it lessens you in some people's eyes, makes you different and possibly even morally suspect like God is punishing you or something. Somehow infertility lessens your accomplishments for some people.

When respondents did tell others of their decision to seek help, the people they told were usually medical personnel, had experienced reproductive problems themselves, or already knew either of the decision to start a family or of difficulties with previously announced, but ultimately unsuccessful, pregnancies. However, most of the respondents did not inform others of problems they were having.

In order to explore the implications of "courtesy stigma" for fertile women with infertile husbands, I compared their perceptions and initial responses to the possibility of personal infertility to those of the other women. No discernible differences emerged, either in their definitions of infertility or in their initial responses to the realization of possible infertility. In all cases, these women defined infertility as a discreditable or negative attribute, were the first to approach a doctor or clinic for help, and told no one of their decision to do so. This observation supports the contention that failure to conceive is perceived, at least initially, as the woman's problem.

Initial Disclosure Patterns

Following a diagnosis of possible reproductive problems, nearly half the physically infertile women found it difficult to disclose to their families and friends that they were having problems. These respondents linked the difficulty in telling others to personal feelings of inadequacy and shame.[7] Indeed, all the infertile respondents spoke of a personal sense of failure associated with their involuntary childlessness, a perception reflected in the observations contained in self-help and anecdotal literature on infertility (Menning, 1977; Pfeffer and Woollett, 1983).[8] As one infertile woman observed:

> You have to admit failure to some extent. . . . It's the business of having to admit some problem or abnormality; this business of feeling like some sort of freak.

However, several respondents also indicated that they had difficulty in revealing their infertility to their families because they anticipated serious consequences for the persons being told.

> I had difficulty telling family and only confided in a few close friends. I didn't want to tell my family because I knew they'd worry and be quite upset.

Many respondents revealed infertility problems only at the time they applied for adoption. In fact, disclosure of the intention to adopt amounted to an admission of infertility and was often accompanied by a desire for secrecy.

> We only told people once. In fact we made some calls. . . . We needed some references [to adopt] so we had to pick three people but very very close friends and they were also people that we felt we could really trust not to talk about it.

In three interviews, respondents claimed that they had never discussed their infertility with anyone but their doctors and their social worker at the adoption agency. One woman, who learned of her infertility through a previous marriage, expressed the fear she felt about disclosing it to her new husband prior to their marriage:

> I went through agony when we were going out because I was afraid to tell my husband about my infertility. When he did ask me to marry him, I went through a long period when I wouldn't tell him. I'd just say we can't get married and so on. I did my years in hell.

Overall, more than half the infertile respondents indicated that they hesitated in telling others. Two-thirds engaged in some sort of information management—that is, they admitted that they did not always reveal the exact details of their condition—and nearly one-third admitted giving inaccurate answers to questions about their childlessness.

The responses of women with infertile husbands indicate that they were partic-

[7] Women who found it easy to disclose their infertility were those who initially announced their intention to start a family and then were unable to do so; who were open about problems from the beginning; or whose infertility became obvious without formal disclosure because of repeated miscarriages or a hysterectomy.

[8] Responses to a series of questions on commitment to motherhood revealed that these women strongly valued this status, a value which probably contributed to their perception of infertility as stigmatizing.

ularly likely to find it difficult to tell family and friends that they were having fertility problems in their relationship. In addition, they were more likely to give inaccurate answers to others' questions about their childlessness. However, as expected, they were less likely to feel as personally stigmatized as did the infertile respondents.

In view of these findings, it could be argued that women with a courtesy stigma find it more difficult to tell family and friends of their problem precisely because of the nature of the infertility. Women with reproductive disorders for example, may have miscarriages or other obvious signs of reproductive difficulty. A general awareness of this difficulty may preclude the need to announce formally and irrevocably their problems with the reproductive process. Women whose husbands have low or non-existent sperm counts (the most probable cause of male infertility) are not likely to conceive. This lack of observable reproductive difficulty may make it easier in the short term for these women to avoid the appearance of having fertility problems, but harder in the long term to disclose the difficulty.

It could also be argued that women with a courtesy stigma have more difficulty telling others because of the greater perceived stigma associated with male infertility. I found that nearly two-thirds of the infertile respondents and over half the courtesy stigma respondents felt that male infertility is viewed more negatively than female infertility. These respondents considered male infertility more discrediting to masculinity than female infertility to femininity, and associated male infertility with impotence or a lack of virility. As one courtesy stigma respondent put it:

> Somehow it's just a medical problem for her but a real assault on his masculinity to the man. . . . It's often wrongly thought to be associated with impotence.

Whereas infertile women may have difficulty telling others of their childlessness because of personal feelings of shame or stigma, women with an infertile husband may have difficulty because of the perceived need to protect their partner from the even greater stigma associated with male sexual dysfunction. As one such respondent observed:

> It was difficult to tell his family because I know he felt bad because he thought he was failing me and it was also kind of a slap in the eye because of his manhood you know but obviously it doesn't affect anything.

While nearly two-thirds of the infertile women expressed feelings of openness, warmth, and understanding toward other infertile individuals, only 17 percent of the women with a courtesy stigma felt this kind of rapport. As I expected, the women with a courtesy stigma were much less likely to identify themselves with other infertile individuals. Indeed, they strongly distinguished themselves from women with "real" fertility problems.[9] As one woman put it:

[9] For a detailed discussion of how involuntarily childless respondents categorized one another on the basis of reproductive disorder, see Miall (1985).

> I'm one of those couples where it's the husband who has the infertility problem. Mostly I've met women who have fertility problems. Thank God I'm not one of them. When I see what they've been through; when I hear the stories. I don't know if eventually one gets reconciled but thank God I missed all that.

Thus courtesy stigma respondents seemed less concerned about their own personal "inadequacy" as childless and more concerned with the difficulty of managing information about their husbands' infertility.

The possibility of conceiving children may also have lessened feelings of stigmatization. Presumably, courtesy stigma women could make use of artificial insemination or leave an infertile marriage if they chose to bear a child, an option not available to infertile women. As Goffman (1963:107) oberved, "the more allied the individual is with normals, the more he will see himself in nonstigmatic terms." [10]

Involuntary Childlessness and Information Management

Nearly two-thirds of all respondents indicated that they engaged in some form of information control about their childlessness. To isolate patterns of behavior surrounding involuntary childlessness, I asked respondents about their patterns of disclosure and about the techniques they used to handle situations and persons likely to make them feel uncomfortable. Although variations emerged, the strategies used by these women to handle information about infertility closely resembled those observed by Schneider and Conrad (1980) in their study of epilepsy. These strategies included: (1) selective concealment; (2) therapeutic disclosure; and (3) preventive disclosure. In addition, I found evidence of deviance avowal, and a strategy of practiced deception. [11]

Infertility and Selective Concealment

In their research, Schneider and Conrad (1980) focused on the metaphor of being either in or out of the closet with a discreditable attribute. Questioning the utility of this metaphor for discreditable attributes for which there is no alternate new or proud identity, Schneider and Conrad (1980:42) concluded that the closet metaphor needs to be extended "to incorporate the complex reality of how people very selectively disclose or withhold discreditable evidence about themselves."

In this study, respondents displayed patterns of selective concealment even in those instances when secrecy was the major strategy for handling the discovery of infertility in the relationship. For example, respondents who told no one of their

---

[10] The lack of rapport with infertile women noted by courtesy stigma respondents may also have stemmed from their perception of not being really accepted or understood by infertile women as "sharing their fate."

[11] All the strategies presented here can be considered forms of "disclosure etiquette" or formulas for admitting a failing (Goffman, 1963:101). Unless otherwise noted, they apply equally to infertile and to courtesy stigma respondents.

decision to seek help, or of their status as involuntarily childless, nevertheless conveyed concern about the infertility in the relationship to medical personnel and, later, to adoption workers. Apart from these disclosures to professionals, nearly all the respondents decided whether to conceal or disclose their infertility based on their perception of others as genuine or trustworthy. They learned to judge or recognize people who might make them feel uncomfortable about their childlessness and to avoid them. As one woman put it:

> I find you have to avoid certain people. You learn to pick up on those people. . . . I've always had a sort of sixth sense but it's just really become attuned.

When it was not possible to avoid contacts with such people, respondents used the strategy of concealment in conversation by avoiding or changing sensitive subjects. For instance, one respondent described her efforts to "pass" as normal as follows:

> On occasion at parties, I've tried to avoid the topic. Even though no one has done anything that might upset me, I believe in being prepared for the possibility of it happening. My whole approach is to be as low key as possible, not to get excited, to show we are normal.

However, respondents often made selective disclosures to others to test their reactions. These reactions contributed to the evolution of other strategies or to the continued use of selective disclosure or secrecy in the face of negative responses (see Schneider and Conrad, 1980:39). Thus the discovery of infertility in the relationship was initially marked by a desire for secrecy which lessened over time and was replaced by some form of disclosure for therapeutic or preventive reasons.

Therapeutic Disclosure

Therapeutic disclosure can be defined as the selective disclosure of the discreditable attribute to others in order to enhance self-esteem or to renegotiate personal perceptions of stigma. Infertile respondents used therapeutic disclosure more often than courtesy stigma respondents. Typically, such disclosures were made to family, close friends, or other infertile people. As one woman revealed, disclosure to her family was cathartic:

> Initially I felt uncomfortable until I sat down and talked about it with my husband and my family, about how I felt I was failing. Then I felt better for having gotten it all out.

Therapeutic disclosure also allowed for renegotiation of the negative meanings attached to infertility. One woman who had experienced several miscarriages observed that talking with her friends allowed her to put her own infertility in perspective:

> One thing I always tell people to do is to talk to their women friends if they are

having trouble conceiving or miscarrying because I learned something I didn't know; that almost every woman I knew had at least one miscarriage and it was very supportive having friends say, "Look I lost a kid too" because it's not the kind of thing that people tell you.

Generally, infertile women perceived the disclosure of infertility as most therapeutic when done with other infertile couples. However, disclosure to non-supportive audiences was also considered therapeutic by some respondents:

There was a lot of stammering going on and they just didn't know how to react and maybe it was a little unfair on our part. In a couple of situations we just blurted it out and I don't think we did it very well. And yet everytime we talked about it we felt better. Sometimes we imposed on people by telling them.

The perception of disclosure to a nonsupportive audience as therapeutic represents a departure from Schneider and Conrad's (1980) emphasis on supportive audiences and highlights the importance of actor definitions. It suggests that stigmatized individuals may use their attribute to gain control of the situation by deliberately shocking their "normal" audience.

To sum up, infertile women used therapeutic disclosure as a strategy to relieve anxiety, to restore self-esteem, and to renegotiate personal perceptions of infertility as discreditable. Indeed, several respondents observed that the ability to reveal infertility at all was suggestive of the beginning of adjustment to the possession of a stigmatizing attribute.

Preventive Disclosure

Preventive disclosure can be defined as the selective disclosure to others of the discreditable attribute, with a view to influencing others' actions or ideas about oneself, or about infertility in general (see Schneider and Conrad, 1980:40). Respondents using this strategy anticipated that their childlessness would become known at some future date to the people with whom they were interacting. In order to influence others' perceptions of them, respondents used such devices as the medical disclaimer (Hewitt and Stokes, 1978), deviance avowal, and practiced deception.

The use of a *medical disclaimer* involves the presentation of a "blameless, beyond-my-control medical interpretation . . . to reduce the risk that more morally disreputable interpretations might be applied by naive others" who become aware of a discreditable attribute (Schneider and Conrad, 1980:41). Several infertile women revealed their infertility by using the medical analysis of their condition to avoid greater perceived negative consequences. As one woman observed:

Because of the nature of our infertility problem, it was a medically open and shut case. . . . There was an anatomical deficit in that I'd had my tubes taken out. . . . So when people would say to me, "Well maybe there's artificial insemination," I would say, "There's no medical way." If the reason is not an anatomical reason or a reason for which they can't find a reason, I think people

> will chime in with "Well maybe you're not doing it right" and you don't want to leave yourself open to that.

In addition, respondents who were able to do so would reveal their infertility as an uncontrollable side effect of another medical condition, such as diabetes or kidney disease, so that reproductive disorder was not the main issue. This use of medical disclaimers indicates that medical definitions are widely accepted as legitimate accounts for a potentially stigmatizing problem.

Schur (1979:261) has argued that "individuals sometimes find 'identification with a deviant role' to be the lesser of two evils and may therefore consciously incur negative labeling."[12] In adopting the strategy of *deviance avowal,* individuals actively seek or acquiesce to a deviant label. I found evidence of two forms of deviance avowal among these women. First, women with a courtesy stigma took responsibility for the infertility of their husbands; and, second, women related their infertility to avoid the negative perceptions associated with being childless by choice.

All the courtesy stigma respondents admitted to accepting readily others' perceptions of them as responsible for the couple's infertility. This deviance avowal differentiated the courtesy stigma women from the other respondents who attempted, for the most part, to avoid designations of infertility or to renegotiate infertility as a discreditable attribute. As one woman observed:

> There have been instances where we've been where someone will say, "Oh well, she can't have a baby" and I just leave it at that. I wouldn't say, "It's not me, it's him." Not that my husband would want me to hide the fact but I just don't see any point in getting into that.

The willingness to accept perceived responsibility for the infertility appeared to be aimed at avoiding the more negative implications of male infertility.[13] As one courtesy stigma respondent humorously noted:

> When I tell them we can't have children, I generally try to leave the impression that it's me. I may mutter "Tubes you know" or "Faulty plumbing." I think it's easier for me to go with that than to deal with the idea that maybe my husband "can't get it up."

Several respondents in this study also revealed their infertility to avoid the more negative connotations of being falsely accused of voluntary childlessness. For example, women who were reluctant to tell others of their infertility problems were hurt and frustrated when others assumed that they did not want children.

> I know at one point I overheard someone saying, "Oh, they're too selfish, they're

---

[12] For example, although they did not label it as such, Schneider and Conrad (1980:41) wrote of a man using deviance avowal as a device for preventive disclosure. The man in question disclosed his epilepsy to deflect others' complaints about his alcoholism.

[13] These perceptions of male infertility cannot be confirmed by this study. Further research is needed to determine whether men feel more stigmatized than women, and whether men with a courtesy stigma would take the blame to protect their wives.

too interested in going on fancy holidays. Material things, that's why they're not having children." It was so untrue and it hurt.

Veevers (1979:4–5) argues that the childless by choice are more likely to be stigmatized than the infertile: "The subfecund may be considered unfortunate and hence deserving of sympathy, but the voluntarily childless are considered immoral and hence deserving of censure" (also see Calhoun and Selby, 1980). The involuntarily childless women in this study appeared to regard voluntary childlessness as more stigmatizing given their own efforts to renegotiate their childlessness from deliberate to involuntary—a strategy also employed by voluntarily childless individuals (Veevers, 1980).

Practiced deception differs from concealment in that respondents readily admit to being infertile. However, they distort or alter the circumstances contributing to their childlessness. Practiced deception can also be distinguished from deviance avowal. In practiced deception, *both* members of the infertile dyad accept responsibility for the infertility—whether it's true or not—while deviance avowal involves one member who accepts sole responsibility for infertility caused by the other member of the dyad.

Practiced deception in revealing infertility was apparently used to enhance self-esteem. Most respondents who employed this strategy *rehearsed* it beforehand. This rehearsal in the dyad is similar to "coaching" noted by Schneider and Conrad (1980:36) wherein stigma coaches—for example, parents, friends, professionals, or other epileptics—taught epileptics to conceal or reveal their attribute. However, practiced deception differs from coaching in that it appears to be created solely through a process of interaction within the infertile dyad; that is, no others appear involved in the decision to reveal or conceal the attribute. As one woman solely responsible for the couple's infertility revealed:

> My husband and I actually discussed how we would respond to others after we got the classic question from the first person we told [his mother], "Whose fault is it?" We agreed to present it as a joint problem of trifling proportions individually but enough to ensure that we as a couple would not be able to have our own children. We left them with the suspicion that with someone else we could. Love keeps us together see?

Most other respondents who provided inaccurate answers presented their infertility as a joint problem:

> We fudge the issues and pretend that it's both of us. Usually by fudging the issue you never give a clear answer. I don't think that it's any of their business.

Indeed, the practiced deception by performance teams (Goffman, 1959:91) extended, on occasion, to self-help group meetings wherein participants avoided revealing whose condition was contributing to the infertility. In addition to enhancing self-esteem, preventive disclosure may also have been a way of testing acquaintances who had the potential to become good friends, or a way of preventing a loss of self-esteem if the infertility was discovered by these acquaintances later.

In many instances, couples progressed from one strategy to another as they managed information. Specifically, respondents appeared to move from a strategy of early selective concealment to disclosure for therapeutic or preventive reasons. Respondents appeared to link up this progression to increased adjustment to childlessness. As one respondent put it:

> I don't think at first that there is much that can be done other than to listen if people want to talk. Often I find though that people only want to talk about it when they are, so to speak, on the mend. They are coming to terms with their infertility. . . . Until you start to accept it, you may avoid that kind of thing [talking] like the plague.

Similarly, another respondent noted that participation in self-help groups could be difficult because:

> You run into problems there in that they [other infertile couples] might not be at the same stage and you've got to be very careful about that. You don't want to frighten them off if you've already gone through a stage and are more open than them.

Although progression appears linked to increased adjustment, it may also reflect audience responses to the revelation of infertility. As others' reactions were tested through selective disclosures, these reactions prompted the use of other strategies or continued secrecy in the face of negative responses.[14]

Discussion and Conclusions

This study demonstrates the relevance of pronatalistic social values for the personal adjustment and self-definition of involuntarily childless women. In particular, it presents the first sociological comparison of the experiences of women who are physically infertile with those of childless women who share a courtesy stigma. While I found that physically infertile women feel more stigmatized, women with a courtesy stigma more actively manage information to protect their husbands from the stigma associated with sexual dysfunction.

My results also offer new insight into the various strategies that people use to manage potentially stigmatizing information. Although the strategies employed by these women were similar to those observed by Schneider and Conrad (1980) in their study of epilepsy, some important differences were evident. First, respondents perceived therapeutic disclosure to be beneficial even when the audience was unsupportive. Second, I explicitly conceptualized and documented the use of deviance avowal as a device for preventive disclosure. Although Turner (1972:320) noted that deviance avowal is less common than deviance disavowal, evidence for its use among women with a courtesy stigma in this study contributes

[14] Notably, nearly all the respondents could provide detailed instances of informal labeling in which real or perceived negative consequences followed from the disclosure of infertility (see Miall, 1985).

to an understanding of the deviant actor "as an active and sometimes initiating partner in the social exchanges through which deviant and conforming roles are allocated." Finally, I found that respondents used practiced deception as a strategy to enhance self-esteem and to influence others' perceptions of them, a process not noted in Schneider and Conrad's work.

The personal possession or secret sharing of infertility has profound consequences for the social identity and behavior of actors. For example, respondents generally engaged in self-diagnosis of a potential problem with the reproductive process. Most of them remained secretive as they explored the possibility that they or their spouses might be infertile. In the majority of cases, initial visits to a doctor or a fertility clinic were arranged in such a way as to avoid public awareness of difficulty. Given this kind of secretive behavior, it is reasonable to conclude that the women expected some negative or devaluing response, at the very least, if their difficulty became known (Goode, 1981). Indeed, most respondents linked their secretive behavior to a fear that awareness of a problem with fertility would cause others to view them in a new and damaging light.

In addition, respondents themselves categorized infertility as discreditable, as something negative, as representing some sort of failure. Most discussed experiences of anxiety, isolation, and conflict as they privately explored the possibility of personal infertility. Indeed, to avoid feelings of personal inadequacy, many of the respondents excluded themselves from gatherings such as baby showers or avoided their pregnant friends *prior to* the revelation of involuntary childlessness.

Versions of labeling theory that focus on *social reactions* to deviance cannot adequately account for this self-isolation behavior. Instead, the personal and social experiences of these involuntarily childless women reflect a process that has received relatively little attention in empirical work on deviance and disability— *self-labeling*. Self-labeling or self-identification has been conceptualized as the perception of stigma by *hidden* or *secret* deviants. Self-labeling occurs when individuals recognize that other people may label their particular attributes as discrediting or deviant if they learn of them (Lorber, 1967; Rotenberg, 1974; Sagarin and Kelly, 1980; Sawchuk, 1974; Schur, 1979). When an actor is aware of the discreditable nature of an attribute prior to a formal or informal devaluating response, it is probably because he or she has learned the normative social meanings accompanying the attribute (Gibbs, 1972; Hawkins and Tiedeman, 1975:255; Plummer, 1979:96). Therefore, the concept of self-labeling not only emphasizes the importance of primary deviance and the normative order for self-definitions of discreditability, but also the contributions of the actor's perceptions, interpretations, and behavior to this definitional process.

My findings strongly suggest that a complete appreciation of the evolution of a deviant identity must include an analysis of the intricate interplay between self-labeling and the perceived disapproval and rejection by social audiences. Indeed, the apparent existence of a self-labeled, discreditable identity in the absence of visible deviant behavior offers additional support for the concept of deviance as an inner essence which can exist independent of behavior (Katz, 1972; Petrunik and

Shearing, 1983). In addition, this study clearly demonstrates the interpretive nature of the interactional sequence. Specifically, my evidence indicates that the emergence of a discreditable identity involves actors' use of generalized normative perspectives to interpret their attribute. In addition, actors' interpretations of encounters with others and their evaluations of social audiences affect the strategies they employ to negotiate more positive labels.

Future research on involuntary childlessness should focus on the process whereby infertile couples come to acknowledge their possible infertility. Are the social responses within the dyad as important for this process as are self-labeling and broader normative perspectives. The use of deviance avowal by courtesy stigma respondents and the collaborative strategy of practiced deception suggest that future research is needed on dyadic interaction and the social construction of infertile identities.[15]

In addition, further research is needed on the relevance of medical diagnosis and treatment to the emergence of infertility as a discreditable attribute. The medical diagnosis of infertility takes place over an extended period of time and involves the use of numerous tests and treatments to pinpoint possible problems with the reproductive process. Indeed, medical personnel rarely make a final diagnosis of absolute sterility or permanent infertility; hence, couples in self-help groups frequently complain about the difficulty of deciding (1) when to stop testing and treatment; (2) when to accept the possibility of a permanent childless condition; and (3) when to reveal it to others. Research should examine how this process relates to the emergence of a discreditable infertile identity.

Finally, future research should also focus on men's personal experiences of infertility. Although involuntary childlessness is often perceived as the woman's problem, the respondents in this study considered male infertility more stigmatizing than female infertility. We need to learn more about how husbands and wives individually and jointly deal with the stigma of involuntary childlessness.

References

Benet, Margaret
  1976   The Character of Adoption. London: Cox and Wyman.
Birenbaum, Arnold
  1975   "On managing a courtesy stigma." Pp. 347–57 in Frank Scarpitti and Paul McFarland (eds.), Deviance: Action, Reaction, Interaction. Reading, MA: Addison-Wesley.
Birenbaum, Arnold and Edward Sagarin
  1976   Norms and Human Behavior. New York: Praeger.
Broverman, Inge, Susan Vogel, Donald Broverman, Frank Clarkson and Paul Rosenkrantz
  1972   "Sex role stereotypes: a current appraisal." Journal of Social Issues 28:59–78.
Burgwyn, Diana
  1981   Marriage Without Children. New York: Harper and Row.
Calhoun, Lawrence and James Selby
  1980   "Voluntary childlessness, involuntary childlessness, and having children: a study of social perceptions." Family Relations 29:181–83.

[15] For a discussion of the theoretical relevance for infertile couples of the social construction of identity, see Matthews and Martin Matthews (1986).

Curran, James
   1980   "Economic consequences of pelvic inflammatory disease in the United States." American
          Journal of Obstetrics and Gynecology 138:848–51.
Fox, Greer, Bruce Fox and Katherine Frohardt-Lane
   1982   "Fertility socialization: the development of fertility attitudes and behavior." Pp. 19–49 in
          Greer Fox (ed.), The Childbearing Decision: Fertility Attitudes and Behavior. Beverly Hills,
          CA: Sage.
Freidson, Eliot
   1966   "Disability as social deviance." Pp. 71–99 in Marvin Sussman (ed.), Sociology and
          Rehabilitation. Washington, D.C.: American Sociological Association.
Gibbs, Jack
   1972   "Issues in defining deviant behavior." Pp. 39–68 in Robert Scott and Jack Douglas (eds.),
          Theoretical Perspectives on Deviance. New York: Basic Books.
Goffman, Erving
   1959   The Presentation of Self in Everyday Life. New York: Doubleday.
   1963   Stigma. Englewood Cliffs, NJ: Prentice-Hall.
Goode, Erich
   1981   "Deviance, norms, and social reaction." Deviant Behavior 3:47–53.
Hawkins, Richard and Gary Tiedeman
   1975   The Creation of Deviance. Columbus, OH: Charles G. Merrill.
Hewitt, John and Randall Stokes
   1978   "Disclaimers." Pp. 308–19 in Jerome Manis and Bernard Meltzer (eds.), Symbolic Interac-
          tionism, 3rd edition. Boston: Allyn and Bacon.
Humphrey, Michael
   1969   The Hostage Seekers. London: Longmans.
Katz, Jack
   1972   "Deviance, charisma, and rule-defined behavior." Social Problems 20:186–202.
Kirk, David
   1964   Shared Fate. Toronto: Collier-Macmillan.
Kraft, Adrienne, Joseph Palombo, Dorena Mitchell, Catherine Dean, Steven Meyers and Anne
Wright-Schmidt
   1980   "The psychological dimensions of infertility." American Journal of Orthopsychiatry
          50:618–28.
Lorber, Judith
   1967   "Deviance as performance: the case of illness.: Social Problems 14:302–10.
McFalls, Joseph
   1979   Psychopathology and Sub-Fecundity. New York: Academic Press.
Matthews, Ralph and Anne Martin Matthews
   1986   "Infertility and involuntary childlessness: the transition to non-parenthood." Journal of
          Marriage and the Family 48: In press.
Menning, Barbara
   1975   "The infertile couple: a plea for advocacy." Child Welfare 54:454–60.
   1977   Infertility: A Guide for the Childless Couple. Englewood Cliffs, NJ: Prentice-Hall.
   1981   "In defense of in vitro fertilization." Pp. 263–67 in Helen Holmes, Betty Hoskins and
          Michael Gross (eds.), The Custom-Made Child. Englewood Cliffs, NJ: Humana Press.
Miall, Charlene
   1984   "Women and involuntary childlessness: perceptions of stigma associated with infertility and
          adoption." Unpublished Ph.D. dissertation, York University, Toronto, Ontario, Canada.
   1985   "Perceptions of informal sanctioning and the stigma of involuntary childlessness." Deviant
          Behavior 6:383–403.
Mosher, William
   1982   "Infertility trends among U.S. couples: 1965–1976." Family Planning Perspectives 14:-
          22–27.
Nagi, S.
   1966   "Some conceptual issues in disability and rehabilitation." Pp. 100–13 in Marvin Sussman
          (ed.), Sociology and Rehabilitation. Washington, D.C.: American Sociological Association.
National Center for Health Statistics
   1985   "Fecundity and infertility in the United States, 1965–82." Advance Data From Vital and

Health Statistics. No. 104. DHHS Pub. No. (PHS) 85–1250. Public Health Service. Hyattsville, MD, February 11, 1985.

Patton, Michael
  1980   Qualitative Evaluation Methods. Beverly Hills, CA: Sage.
Peck, Ellen and Judith Senderowitz (eds.)
  1974   Pronatalism: The Myth of Mom and Apple Pie. New York: Thomas Y. Crowell.
Petrunik, Michael and Clifford Shearing
  1983   "Fragile facades: stuttering and the strategic manipulation of awareness." Social Problems 31:125–38.
Pfeffer, Naomi and Anne Woollett
  1983   The Experience of Infertility. London: Virago.
Plummer, Kenneth
  1979   "Misunderstanding labeling perspectives." Pp. 85–121 in David Downes and Paul Roch (eds.), Deviant Interpretations. Oxford: Martin Robertson and Company.
Pohlman, Edward
  1969   The Psychology of Birth Planning. Cambridge, MA: Schenkman.
  1970   "Childlessness: intentional and unintentional." Journal of Nervous and Mental Disease 151:2–12.
  1974   "Motivations in wanting conceptions." Pp. 159–90 in Ellen Peck and Judith Senderowitz (eds.), Pronatalism: The Myth of Mom and Apple Pie. New York: Thomas Y. Crowell.
Rao, S. L. N.
  1974   "A comparative study of childlessness and never-pregnant status." Journal of Marriage and the Family 36:149–57.
Rossi, Alice
  1977   "A biosocial perspective on parenting." Dedaelus 106:1–31.
  1984   "The presidential address: gender and parenthood." American Sociological Review 49:-1–19.
Rotenberg, Mordechai
  1974   "Self-labeling: a missing link in the societal reaction theory of deviance." Sociological Review 22:335–54.
Russo, Nancy
  1976   "The motherhood mandate." Journal of Social Issues 32:143–79.
Sagarin, Edward and Robert Kelly
  1980   "Sexual deviance and labeling perspectives." Pp. 347–79 in Walter Gove (ed.), The Labeling of Deviance, 2nd edition. Beverly Hills, CA: Sage.
Sawchuk, Peter
  1974   "Becoming a homosexual." Pp. 233–45 in Jack Haas and Bill Shaffir (eds.), Decency and Deviance. Toronto: McClelland and Stewart.
Schneider, Joseph and Peter Conrad
  1980   "In the closet with illness: epilepsy, stigma potential and information control." Social Problems 28:32–44.
Schur, Edwin
  1979   Interpreting Deviance: A Sociological Introduction. New York: Harper and Row.
Sussman, Marvin
  1977   "Dependent disabled and dependent poor: similarity of conceptual issues and research needs." Pp. 247–59 in Joseph Stubbins (ed.), Social and Psychological Aspects of Disability. Baltimore, MD: University Park Press.
Turner, Ralph
  1972   "Deviance avowal as neutralization of commitment." Social Problems 19:308–21.
Veevers, Jean
  1972   "The violation of fertility mores: voluntary childlessness as deviant behaviour." Pp. 571–92 in Craig Boydell, Carl Grindstaff and Paul Whitehead (eds.), Deviant Behaviour and Societal Reaction. Toronto: Holt, Rinehart and Winston.
  1979   "Voluntary childlessness: a review of issues and evidence." Marriage and Family Review 2:1–26.
  1980   Childless by Choice. Toronto: Butterworth.
  1983   "Researching voluntary childlessness: a critical assessment of current strategies and find-

ings." Pp. 75–96 in Eleanor Macklin and Roger Rubin (eds.), Contemporary Families and Alternative Lifestyles. Beverly Hills, CA: Sage.
Weinstein, Eugene
  1962 "Adoption and infertility." American Sociological Review 27:408–12.
Zimmerman, Shirley
  1982 "Alternatives in human reproduction for involuntary childless couples." Family Relations 31:233–41.

Reproductive Technology and Child Custody

Herma Hill Kay

Introduction: New Reproductive Technology Produces New Legal Issues

The rapid growth of reproductive technology has forced family law . . . to confront new and difficult questions. We are all familiar with the centuries-old problem of identifying the father of a child, but now we are confronted with the necessity of identifying the mother as well. One of the pressing legal questions raised by the new reproductive technology is to decide who among several possible women is the child's mother. A less-frequently discussed question . . . is how the child's caregivers should be chosen from among several available sets of parents.

The bare outlines of the medical technology were sketched by Professor John Robertson in 1983:[1]

> Scientists did not even observe the union of human sperm and ovum through a microscope until 1944. In the years since then, however, science has made major [advances] in reproductive physiology, human genetics, embryology, and obstetrics. Medical practitioners can now stimulate ovulation, extract the eggs, fertilize them outside the body, and implant the embryo in the uterus of the egg donor or another. They can observe the fetus directly throughout most of the pregnancy; they can diagnose and treat its diseases in utero; and they can even remove it temporarily for treatment. . . .

Or, to put the matter in less scientific terms, as O'Rourke does,[2]

> It is now technically possible to take sperm from any fertile male, an egg from any fertile female, join them by the *in vitro* fertilization process, and implant the resulting embryo into any womb. After birth the child can be raised by any set of

From "Child Custody Litigation Arising From Surrogate Parenting Agreements: A Family Law Perspective on the 'Baby M' Case," *The Boalt Hall Transcript*, Vol. 20, No. 2. Reprinted by permission. Portions of the original have been omitted.

adults who may or may not have been participants in the child's conception or birth.

The scenario may be as simple as sperm from Mr. Jones being joined in a petri dish with an egg from Mrs. Jones, who carries it and gives birth, and then the Joneses raise their child. It may be as complicated as a sperm from an anonymous party A being joined to an egg from party B, the gestation being provided by party C, and the child being raised by parties D and E.

The new reproductive technology is available all over the world, and people with fertility problems were the first to take advantage of it. Their use of the medical technology has given rise to legal problems in several countries. The following are some illustrative cases.

- In 1981, a married couple from Los Angeles, California, Mario and Elsa Rios, sought the help of specialists at the Queen Victoria Medical Center in Melbourne, Australia. Mr. Rios, aged 50, was infertile. His wife, aged 37, was fertile. An anonymous sperm donor from Melbourne gave sperm that was used to artificially inseminate three eggs taken from Mrs. Rios. One of the resulting embryos was implanted in the body of Mrs. Rios; the other two embryos were frozen for possible future use. Mrs. Rios subsequently had a miscarriage. Before she could return to Melbourne for another implantation, she and her husband died in a plane crash in Chile. They died intestate, leaving an estate worth approximately $8 million. On June 18, 1984, the media discovered that the two frozen embryos existed, and raised the question whether they had a legal right to be implanted in a surrogate mother and to inherit the estate if born alive.[3]
- In 1983, an anonymous American couple in their 30s wanted to have a child despite the wife's infertility. The husband, Mr. A., entered into a contract with an American agency that undertook to locate a woman who would be impregnated with his sperm and produce a child for him and Mrs. A to raise. The agency located a surrogate mother, Kim Cotton, through an agency in England. In 1984, Mr. A traveled to England in order to provide semen for insemination of Ms. Cotton. He produced the semen, gave it to a nurse, and it was introduced into the surrogate mother. The father and the mother did not meet each other, and have not met each other. The baby was born on January 4, 1985. Kim Cotton voluntarily relinquished all parental rights to the child, as she had agreed to do, and has not seen the baby since its birth. A local authority charged with the welfare of children, the London Borough of Barnet, applied for a place of safety order. Pursuant to the order, the baby remained in the hospital pending an inquiry by the social services department. According to Professor M. D. A. Freeman,[4]

> It is no overstatement to describe what then happened as a "moral panic." . . . Kim Cotton, the surrogate mother at the centre of the storm, overnight became a "folk-devil," a "visible reminder of what we should not be."

- In 1984, a young widow in France brought suit against the *Centre d'Etude et de Conservation du Sperme* of the Bicentre. The Centre possessed sperm previously donated by her deceased husband for experimental purposes. She wanted to use his sperm to conceive a child. The Centre refused to inseminate her, or to make the sperm available to her.[5]

- In 1985, the Berlin Court of Appeal dealt with the following case: A and B, a married couple, were unable to have a child because of the wife's infertility. A married woman, C, agreed to be inseminated with A's sperm. C's husband also agreed to the procedure. Both couples agreed that the child would be adopted by A and B. Under the law of the Federal Republic of Germany, the consent of C and D to the adoption was not possible until eight weeks after the child was born. C and D refused to carry out the agreement, and A brought suit to have the child declared his illegitimate child.[6]

- In another case from Germany arising in December 1985, a sperm donor brought suit to obtain the return of 27,000 DM he had paid to a married woman to be artificially inseminated with his sperm. He and she had agreed that the child would be raised by the sperm donor and his wife. It turned out that the child was not that of the sperm donor, but rather that of the woman's husband.[7]

- In April, 1986, the first child bred by implanting a fertilized ovum into a surrogate carrier was born in Detroit, Michigan. The 22-year-old surrogate mother received a fee for bearing the child. The attorney representing the genetic parents, Noel Keane, brought suit on behalf of the egg donor to establish her maternity of the child.[8]

- On March 27, 1986, the child known as "Baby M" in the American media was born in New Jersey. Baby M had been conceived by Mary Beth White-head, a married woman with two teen age children, using the sperm of William Stern, a childless married man whose wife, Elizabeth Stern, did not wish to become pregnant because she feared that a pregnancy would exacer-bate her multiple sclerosis. The parties signed a contract, called a "Surrogate Parenting Agreement," on February 6, 1985. The contract provided in part that Mrs. Whitehead would attempt to conceive a child using Mr. Stern's sperm; that upon conception, she would carry the child to term; that she would deliver the child and surrender the child to the Sterns. It was also agreed that Mr. Stern's name would appear on the birth certificate: that he had the right to name the child; and that Mrs. Whitehead would submit to a psychiatric evaluation. Mrs. Whitehead further agreed to undergo amniocen-tesis during the pregnancy, and to abort the child at Mr. Stern's request if that test indicated that the child had a genetic or congenital abnormality. She agreed not to abort the child for any other reason. Mr. Stern agreed to pay all of the medical and dental expenses incurred by Mrs. Whitehead as a result of the pregnancy, and in addition to pay her a fee of $10,000. Mrs. Whitehead acknowledged that relinquishing her parental rights was in the child's best interests. Mr. Stern agreed to assume legal responsibility for the child if it was born with genetic or congenital abnormalities. Mr. Whitehead acknowledged that he refused to consent to his wife's artificial insemination, thus ruling him out as the child's legal father pursuant to New Jersey law. Mrs. Stern was not a party to the contract, although it was anticipated that she would adopt the child after its birth.

The Sterns located the Whiteheads through the services of the Infertility Center of New York. Mrs. Whitehead had responded to an advertisement in a newspaper placed by ICNY for surrogate parents. She had been accepted into the program in April, 1984, after undergoing psychological testing and an interview to determine her suitability as a potential surrogate mother. She had tried unsuccessfully to conceive a child for another couple in 1984.

The Sterns and the Whiteheads met in person to discuss the proposed surrogacy arrangement. At the conclusion of the meeting, they agreed that Mrs. Whitehead would attempt to conceive a child using Mr. Stern's sperm, and that the child would be raised by the Sterns. Mr. Stern and Mrs. Whitehead signed the Surrogate Parenting Agreement on February 6, 1985. Thereafter, Mrs. Whitehead was inseminated with Mr. Stern's seminal fluid nine times before she conceived in July, 1985.

After Baby M was born on March 7, 1986, the Whiteheads failed to follow the terms of the Surrogate Parenting Agreement. Thus, Mr. Whitehead, not Mr. Stern, was named the father on the child's birth certificate. Mrs. Whitehood took the baby home with her, and gave up the child to the Sterns on March 30 at her home. After passing a restless night, she visited the baby at the Stern's home on March 31. They agreed to allow her to keep the baby for a week; Mrs. Whitehead agreed to return Baby M at that time. Instead, she and Mr. Whitehead left New Jersey, taking Baby M with them to Florida. After a brief return to New Jersey, they left again with the baby for Florida, where Mrs. Whitehead's parents lived. The Whiteheads disappeared with the baby for nearly three months. During this period, on May 5, 1986, Mr. and Mrs. Stern filed a . . . complaint in the New Jersey Superior Court for Bergen County . . . seeking enforcement of the Surrogate Parenting Agreement, compelling surrender of the baby to the Sterns, restraining the Whiteheads from interfering with the Sterns' custody of the baby, terminating Mrs. Whitehead's parental rights, and adoption of the baby by Mrs. Stern. Later in July, the Whiteheads reappeared in Florida. The Florida authorities took possession of Baby M at her maternal grandmother's home on July 31, 1986, and gave her to the Sterns. Ultimately, all parties began litigation of their respective legal claims to Baby M in the New Jersey court.[9]

As the *Baby M* case shows, the new reproductive techniques are not limited to persons who are infertile. Mrs. Stern was fully fertile, but chose not to risk debilitating illness by becoming pregnant. The new technology is also attractive to individuals who choose alternative family forms. Thus, Sheila O'Rourke notes that[10]

A more controversial consequence is the use of alternative methods of reproduction by a growing number of individuals to create families by choice outside the traditional heterosexual nuclear family model. In particular, many unmarried women, heterosexual and lesbian, are choosing to bear children and raise them either alone or with other women.

Still more controversial, although as yet discussed only in terms of hypothetical cases, is the use of a surrogate to bear the genetic child of a woman who is herself fertile and capable of childbearing, but who wishes to avoid the inconvenience of pregnancy. This possibility seems to conjure up pictures of middle-and-upper class women exploiting poor and lower class women by paying them to become breeders of babies. It also has racial overtones, for as O'Brien points out,[11]

[When] the "raw" material is supplied by the commissioning parents, the race and intelligence of the gestator would be irrelevant. Thus, ethnically and mentally disadvantaged women, who already comprise a large measure of the class of indigent women, would join what one commentator has styled a "caste of child-bearers."

Given the wide range of possible applications and the controversy surrounding the new reproductive technology, it is not surprising that the cases cited earlier have come to very different conclusions. Here is how they were decided.

The Australian frozen embryos were the subjects of both a special committee report and special legislation. The Waller Committee Report, *On the Disposition of Embryos Produced by In Vitro Fertilization,* was released in mid-August, 1984. It concluded that the stored embryos did not possess legal rights to be born alive, or to claim inheritance, and went on to say that if "by mischance or for any other reason, an embryo is stored which cannot be transferred as planned, and no agreed provision has been made at the time of storage . . . the embryos shall be removed from storage." In disregard of this recommendation, however, the legislature in the State of Victoria enacted a special provision directing that an attempt be made to have the embryos implanted in a surrogate. The provision also indicates that if they are born alive, they should be placed for adoption. This course of action would presumably terminate any right they might have to claim an inheritance from the Rio's estate, since they would become the children of the adoptive parents. As of August 19, 1985, however, the frozen embryos remained in storage at the Queen Victoria Medical Center in Melbourne.

In the English case, *In re C,* [1985] FLR 846, the London Borough of Barnet completed its inquiries and supported the application of Mr. and Mrs. A that the child be given into their care and custody. Judge Latey agreed, and committed the care and control of the baby to the A's, giving them permission to take her to live with them outside the jurisdiction (conditioned on their undertaking to return the child to the jurisdiction should the court so order). The public outcry surrounding the case, however, prompted the Government to propose a Bill, the Surrogacy Arrangements Act, that was enacted in July 1985. The Act is directed toward commercial surrogacy agencies. It prohibits the recruitment of women as surrogate mothers and the negotiation of surrogacy arrangements by agencies acting on a commercial basis. It also prohibits advertising of or for surrogacy services. Both surrogates and commissioning parents are exempt from criminal liability. Thus, as M. D. A. Freeman points out, "A man who negotiates directly with a potential surrogate and offers her a fee does not commit a crime. He must, however, negotiate without the benefit of paid professional advice or assistance, for the lawyer or doctor who assists any such arrangement or counsels either party to it would commit an offense." Freeman further notes that the public debates on the Act "pander to moral populism." For example, Harry Greenaway, M.P. declaimed that the Bill "rightly outlaws the hell and wickedness that exists in America—where women are exploited and handled in an undignified manner for gain."[12]

In France, according to Professor Rubellin-Devichi,[13] the law governing paternity provides for a child

> born of a surrogate mother to be designated as the child of the man who provided the sperm. It also provides that the mother has a choice as to whether to keep the child or not. Since human beings cannot be traded, the agreement between the infertile couple and the surrogate mother cannot be enforced. Under French law, surrogacy agencies are open to prosecution as are infertile couples who use them and surrogates or would-be surrogates who offer their services to them. This is yet another subject on which there is divided opinion.

The Berlin Court of Appeal, in the case of the married surrogate and her husband who refused to relinquish the child to the sperm donor and his wife, held that the donor had no standing to contest the child's paternity. The Court further held that the legal parents, the surrogate mother and her husband, were not to be legally regarded as unsuitable for the care and upbringing of the child because of the circumstances that led to its birth. The Regional Appeal Court of Hamm ruled that the sperm donor could recover his money from the surrogate whose child turned out to be fathered by her husband rather than the donor. According to Professor Frank, the court reasoned that the contract was *contra bonos mores* and void, since its "manifest treatment of the child as merchandise offended the basic legal and moral order."[14]

The Detroit circuit court judge in the case of *Smith v. Jones* held that the donor of the ovum, rather than the surrogate carrier, was the legal mother of the child.

In the *Baby M* case, Judge Sorkow upheld the Surrogate Parenting Agreement as valid, and ordered that it be specifically enforced. He granted permanent custody of Baby M to her father, William Stern, and terminated all parental rights to Mary Beth Whitehead. In a separate proceeding held in his chambers immediately after he handed down the judgment, Judge Sorkow granted Elizabeth Stern's petition to adopt Baby M. Judge Sorkow's judgment has been appealed to the New Jersey Supreme Court. . . .

The Baby M Case as a Study in Child Custody Litigation

The "Best Interests of the Child" Standard

The *Baby M* case raises profound questions of ethics and legal policy. It also raises tough legal questions in the fields of contracts, family law, and sex-based discrimination.[15] In what follows, I will leave aside most of those thorny problems in order to concentrate on some family law issues. In particular, I will focus on the use of the best interests standard in the *Baby M* case and offer some suggestions about modifying that standard if it is to be used to decide child custody disputes in the context of surrogate parenting agreements.

It is striking that both the English judge in *In re C* and the American judge in *Baby M* phrased the ultimate legal issue as one of determining the best interests of the child. Judge Latey noted that

> First and foremost . . . is what is best for the child or children conceived. That and nothing else. Plainly, the methods used to produce a child as this baby has been, and the commercial aspects of it, raise difficult and delicate problems of ethics, morality and social desirability. . . .
>
> In my judgment, however, [these problems] are not relevant. The baby is here. All that matters is what is best for her now that she is here and not how she arrived.

Judge Sorkow began his opinion with this sentence: "[t]he primary issue to be determined by this litigation is what are the best interests of a child until now called 'Baby M.' All other concerns raised by counsel constitute commentary."

It is not entirely clear, however, how the best interests standard should be applied in litigation arising from surrogate parenting agreements. The best interests standard was originally developed to resolve disputes over children between natural parents who had been married to each other and who were obtaining a divorce. Even in that context, it was not at first the primary standard used to decide contested cases. As between parents, both of whom were fit custodians, a "maternal preference" applied in cases involving young children. The preference for mothers as custodians of young children was so prevalent that, as a practical matter, fathers rarely were able to obtain custody of their children unless they could show that the mother was unfit. If the maternal preference was not applicable, the best interests standard came in to play as a residual test. Most cases, however, were resolved by the maternal preference.

The family law reforms stimulated by the desire to obtain equality between women and men have greatly weakened the maternal preference. In some states, such as California, the statutory priority accorded the mother was repealed. In other states, the maternal preference was held to be a violation of equal protection or equal rights clauses in federal or state constitutions. The best interests standard was moved to highest priority as the basic test for determining the custody of children. Once the best interests standard became the primary test, however, scholars as well as judges and lawyers quickly became aware that it gave no clear or definite guidance about how a particular case should be decided.[16] Not surprisingly, the present thrust in statutory reform appears to lie in devising ways to make the vague best interests standard more concrete. The Uniform Marriage and Divorce Act, and most of the current state statutes, now contain lists of factors that the judge should consider in awarding custody. In addition, other standards have been developed to guide the decision. These include the effort to identify the "primary nurturing parent"[17] and the admonition to rest content with the "least detrimental alternative"[18] rather than continue the hopeless search for a "best" solution.

Even when it is used in divorce custody cases, the best interests standard has proven unpredictable. But when that standard is used in a custody dispute between a natural father whose sperm has been donated to a natural mother for her impregnation, or between a sperm donor, an egg donor, and the gestational surrogate carrier, the context of the case makes the best interests test virtually unrecognizable. In my view, because of the factual differences between divorce custody cases and surrogate parenting cases, the best interests standard may be inappropriate for the latter cases. At the very least, it must be modified to fit the different circumstances those cases present.

The Special Circumstances of Custody Litigation in Surrogate Parenting Cases

Surrogate reproduction is unique. It resembles adoption in that a parent (usually the mother) surrenders a child for upbringing by others. In most adoption cases, however, the child is not genetically related to the adoptive father. Nor did the mother become pregnant pursuant to a prior agreement that she would surrender the child to the caretaking family. Surrogate reproduction also resembles the situation of illegitimate children, in that the mother and father are not married to each other. But in most cases of illegitimacy, there has been at least a sexual union between the natural parents, and frequently they have lived together in nonmarital cohabitation.

Surrogate reproduction cases differ from these two similar kinds of cases, and from the typical divorce child custody case, in at least three ways, all relevant to the custody decision. These differences are as follows:

1. Although the contesting parties are the child's natural parents, or the child's gestational carrier, they have not had sexual relations with each other, have not lived together and may not have met each other in person. The contesting parties have not participated jointly in the child's care and nurturance, nor do they expect to do so in the future.
2. The litigation over the child's custody, if it occurs at all, is likely to begin early

in the child's life. In the Michigan case, *Smith v. Jones,* the litigation was commenced before the child was born.
3. The natural parents, or the natural parents and the surrogate carrier, may come from different countries, from different social classes, or from different races. There has been no "mate selection" between the adults that anticipated a sexual, marital, or cohabiting relationship in which these differences, had they existed, would have been considered and accepted or rejected.

These three characteristics of surrogate parenting cases suggest that several constraints limit the custody determination in such cases. These constraints are as follows:

1. Except in rare cases, joint custody will probably not be an appropriate disposition. Joint custody has developed in the context of divorce custody cases. In its broadest sense, joint custody means shared physical and legal custody between two parents who have had a previous family relationship with the child. Ideally, joint custody arises from an agreement betwen the separating parents to continue the shared parenting they had experienced during their lives with each other and the child. The goal of joint custody is to preserve the child's relationship with both parents. In the case of surrogate parenting, however, the natural parents have not shared the daily responsibilities of child care. They have no past caring experience upon which they can build a future shared parenting relationship.
2. It follows that sole custody in one set of parents will probably be the preferred outcome in surrogate parenting custody cases. If the custody litigation has begun early in the child's life, however, the sole custodian cannot be chosen on the basis of which parent is the "psychological parent" or the "primary nurturing parent." If we reject the claim that the natural mother or the surrogate gestational carrier should be given priority because she carried the child during the pregnancy as inconsistent with the goal of equality between men and women, that means of choosing the custodian is also foreclosed.
3. The best interests test will have to be applied without its customary mooring in a prior parental relationship between the contesting parties and the child. In this situation, the temporary custody decision may in practice be determinative of the outcome. If the child is left in the temporary custody of one of the competing parents, with limited visitation to the other parent, and if the litigation is time-consuming, the child will form an affectionate bond with the temporary custodians. The existence of that relationship, if it is a warm and loving one, may in itself be a persuasive reason motivating the trial court judge to grant permanent custody to the temporary custodians.
4. In the absence of a past or current family relationship between the child and one set of potential custodians, the judge may tend to rely more heavily on the opinion of expert witnesses about the child's best interests than is ordinarily the

case in divorce custody litigation. The best interests standard may in the process lose some of its individualized focus on the particular child and adults before the court, and take account instead of material factors, such as the relative economic and social standing of the competing parties, that would benefit any child.

I turn now to a discussion of the *Baby M* case in light of these observations about the best interests standard.

Application of the Best Interests Standard in the *Baby M* Case

Judge Sorkow used the best interests standard in a unique way in the *Baby M* case. His use of the standard grew out of the way he characterized the case. To the judge, the *Baby M* case was not a family law case; it was a contract case. As Judge Sorkow put the matter in the opening paragraph of his opinion,

> [w]e need to determine if a unique arrangement between a man and a woman, unmarried to each other, creates a contract. If so, is the contract enforceable; and if so, by what criteria, means and manner. . . .

The structure of Judge Sorkow's opinion followed his view of the case. First, he decided that the Surrogate Parenting Agreement was valid and should be enforced. He then turned to a choice of the appropriate remedy for breach of the contract. Only then did he enlist the aid of the best interests standard: it was relevant only because of the unique subject matter of the contract. He noted that

> [a]t this point the court would enter its order for specific performance,* but an additional inquiry is necessary. Since we here deal with a human life of only one year, since we treat with. . . "the most precious and unique thing on this earth, a small, vulnerable and lovable child," it is required that inquiry must be made to determine if the result of such an order for specific performance would be in the child's best interest. This court holds that whether there will be specific performance of this surrogacy contract depends on whether doing so is in the child's best interest. . . .

This way of introducing the best interest standard gives it a negative cast. It is almost as if the finding that the contract is valid creates a presumption favoring the outcome agreed to in the contract: custody in Mr. Stern and his wife. The best interests standard could overcome that contract provision and lead to an award of custody to Mrs. Whitehead and her husband only if it could be shown that custody in the Sterns would not be in the child's best interest. Such a negative showing, of course, would be difficult to make in any case where both contestants are fit custodians. In the context of a case responsive to the constraints outlined above, such a negative showing proved impossible for the Whiteheads to make.

The *Baby M* case was a remarkable example of the American method of adversary litigation. . . . Judge Sorkow was both the finder of fact and the

*[As provided in the contract, deliver the child.]

lawgiver. The trial itself consumed six weeks of courtroom time. Twenty-eight witnesses, in addition to the parties, testified. Fifteen of these witnesses were expert witnesses who testified on various issues. Of the fifteen, eleven were mental health professionals: six psychiatrists, two psychologists, two social workers, and one pediatrician. The other four experts were medical witnesses who testified concerning Mrs. Stern's multiple sclerosis. Both sets of contestants were represented by teams of three lawyers each; in addition, Judge Sorkow appointed a guardian ad litem to represent Baby M.

Judge Sorkow reviewed the testimony of the eleven expert witnesses. He adopted for his own use a nine-point test offered by Dr. Salk, who had testified on behalf of the Sterns, to assess the best interests of the child. Dr. Salk's nine points, rephrased by Judge Sorkow, were as follows:

1. Was the child wanted and planned for?
2. What is the emotional stability of the people in the child's home environment?
3. What is the stability and peacefulness of the families?
4. What is the ability of the respective adults to recognize and respond to the child's physical needs?
5. What are the family attitudes toward education and their motivation to encourage curiosity and learning?
6. What is the ability of the adults to make rational judgments?
7. What is the capacity of the adults to instill positive attitudes about matters concerning health?
8. What is the capacity of the adults in the baby's life to explain the circumstances of origin with least confusion and greatest emotional support?
9. Which adults would better help the child cope with her own life?

As Dr. Salk had used these nine points, they all identified the Sterns as the preferable custodians. Judge Sorkow came to the same conclusion.

> This court is satisfied by clear and convincing proof that Mr. and Mrs. Stern wanted and planned for this child. They intended to be parents of the child. They have a strong and mutually supportive relationship wherein each respects the other and there is a balancing of obligations. There is proof of a successful cooperative parenting effort. The Sterns have a private, quiet and unremarkable life which augurs well for a stable household environment. Mr. and Mrs. Stern show sensitivity to the child's physical and emotional needs. They would be supportive of education and have shown, at least in their own lives, a motivation for learning. It can be concluded that they would initiate and encourage intellectual curiosity and learning for the child. They have shown an ability to make rational judgments in the face of the most trying emotional circumstances. They have obeyed the law. With the health and medical education of Mrs. Stern and the scientific training of Mr. Stern, the child's health will not be jeopardized. Mr. and Mrs. Stern have presented as credible, sincere and truthful people. They have expressed a willingness and a history of obtaining professional help to address the child's unique problems. Finally, they have shown no difficulty in coping with crisis. It may be anticipated that because the child is unique and at risk,

crisis for the next several years will be part of their lives. Mr. and Mrs. Stern have shown an ability to deal with such exigencies. It is for all these reasons, it is because of all of the facts found by this court as the trier of fact that we find by clear and convincing evidence, indeed by a measure of evidence reaching beyond reasonable doubt that Melissa's best interest will be served by being placed in her father's sole custody.

These factors, as applied by Judge Sorkow, tend to favor the couple who are better educated, more affluent, and more socially acceptable. In surrogate parenting cases, given the characterics described above, that couple will usually be the sperm donor and his wife. If that couple can in addition rely on a presumption arising from the surrogate contract favoring their custody, the best interests standard will simply confirm the agreed-upon contractual disposition in virtually every case.

Before we conclude, however, that it follows that the best interests standard is not appropriate for surrogate parenting cases because it is too outcome-derivative, we should briefly inquire how the standard might have worked had it been used in tandem with the presumption arising from the finding that the contract was valid. That inquiry begins with a recognition that the *Baby M* case exhibits the three characteristics of surrogate parenting arrangements identified above:

1. The Sterns sought the help of Mrs. Whitehead because Mrs. Stern feared that a pregnancy would be dangerous to her health. Mr. Stern was the sole survivor of his family line, and he preferred a genetic child to an adoptive child. At any event, the Sterns would not have been viewed by adoption agencies as an "ideal" adoptive couple. They were older than most prospective adoptive couples—both were past 35—and they were of different religious backgrounds. It is unlikely that they would have been able to obtain an infant for adoption. The relationship between the Sterns and the Whiteheads was initiated by an agency. Unlike the English *Baby C* case, the Sterns and Whiteheads met in person to discuss the contract, and kept in touch during Mrs. Whitehead's pregnancy.
2. Litigation over Baby M's custody began on May 5, 1986, nine weeks after her birth. She spent the first three months of life with the Whiteheads in Florida. She came to live with the Sterns on July 31, 1986, and has lived with them continuously since that time. Her age at the time the New Jersey Supreme Court hear[d] argument in the case in September, 1987, [was] approximately 16 months.
3. Although both the Sterns and Whiteheads live in New Jersey, they have very different socio-economic backgrounds. The Whiteheads separated in August 1987, but at the time of trial they lived in a working class neighborhood in Ocean County. They were married when Mary Beth was 16 and Richard was 24 years old. He works as a truck driver. He has had problems with alcohol abuse. Mrs. Whitehead does not work outside the home. They have two children, a boy aged 12 and a girl aged 11. They did not plan to have any other

children at the time Mrs. Whitehead entered into the Surrogate Parenting Agreement. The Sterns met when both were attending graduate school at the University of Michigan. William is a biochemist; Elizabeth is a pediatrician. They live in a middle-class neighborhood in Bergen County.

Just as the three characteristics of surrogate parenting cases apply to the *Baby M* case, so do the constraints identified above limit the possible options for disposition of the case. Thus, only one of the eleven mental health experts suggested that joint custody was a possibility. Dr. Harold Koplewicz, a psychiatrist who testified for the Whiteheads, made that recommendation accompanied by the opinion that the parties should be able to deal with each other after approximately six months of court-ordered family therapy. Judge Sorkow rejected this recommendation, indicating that he did not believe the parties would be able to overcome the rancor they felt for each other and work together in a shared parenting relationship.

Judge Sorkow chose the other alternative—sole custody in one parent—and, as we have seen, identified the father as the most appropriate custodian. That choice is consistent with the fact that the child had been living with the Sterns for eight months prior to the decision, and had formed an attachment to them as her parents. Mrs. Whitehead's limited visitation rights—two hours of supervised visitation twice a week—could not afford her the same opportunity to interact with the child that the Sterns enjoyed. Judge Sorkow had granted temporary custody of Baby M to the Sterns on May 5, 1986, the day on which the litigation was commenced and the day before the Whiteheads took the baby and left for Florida. That temporary custody order may yet determine the final disposition of the case.

The best interests standard, applied without regard to the surrogate parenting contract, thus probably supports the decision that custody in the Sterns is in the child's best interests. The psychological factors that link the baby to the Sterns as her primary caretakers point in that direction, as do the more objective factors of their greater material ability to provide for her needs as she matures to womanhood. This outcome might not have been so clear, however, if the court had left Baby M in the custody of the Whiteheads pending trial. The emotional and psychological factors then might point more strongly to the mother as sole custodian, with the Sterns being forced to rely more heavily on their superior economic and social situation. The case would then have been harder for the court to decide. Under those circumstances, the best interests standard would have been no more determinative than it is in most divorce custody cases. Rather than offering an optimal solution in surrogate parenting cases, the best interests standard provides no more than a convenient way of organizing the facts. Under such circumstances, each custody decision will be an ad hoc determination that is heavily dependent on the judge's point of view.

Conclusion

The new reproductive technology has raised challenging questions in many areas of law and morality. When its use generates a child custody dispute between two persons who are the natural parents of a child, however, the ultimate focus of the family law practitioner and scholar alike turns to the child's future rather than her parents' past interaction. Judge Latey grasped the essential point when he said, "The baby is here. All that matters is what is best for her now that she is here and not how she arrived."

The message of this brief exploration has been to question the automatic use of the traditional best interests of the child standard to serve as a vehicle for addressing Judge Latey's implicit question. If the best interests standard, when applied to surrogate parenting cases, will favor the sperm donor and his wife if used in conjunction with a presumption in their favor arising from the contract, or will favor the natural parent who is chosen as the child's temporary custodian pending litigation, then it may not be adequate to encompass the various competing factors involved. This criticism, however, may not go beyond that of others who have called attention to the deficiencies of the best interests standard. The challenge for all of us who work in this field is to try to develop a more sensitive standard that can be used in the majority of litigated cases with some confidence that the results produced are sound.[19] If that object can be achieved in a way that lessens the cost of hiring dozens of expert witnesses, so much the better. Alternatively, if the use of alternative methods of dispute resolution, such as mandatory mediation in contested custody cases, can produce settlements that do not themselves threaten the child's future, some progress will have been made. Above all, however, we cannot lose sight of the fact that an infant born as the result of a surrogate parenting agreement has the same human and developmental needs as any other infant. The task for family lawyers is to be guided by that recognition in devising new laws to accommodate the new biology.

References

1. Robertson, *Procreative Liberty and the Control of Conception, Pregnancy, and Childbirth,* 69 Va. L. Rev. 405, 407 (1983).
2. O'Rourke, *Family Law in a Brave New World: Private Ordering of Parental Rights and Responsibilities for Donor Insemination,* 1 Berkeley Wom. L.J. 140, 140 (1985) [quoting *Infertility: The Great Debate,* Stanford Magazine 28 (Winter 1984).]
3. Smith, *Australia's Frozen "Orphan" Embryos: A Medical, Legal and Ethical Problem,* 24 J. Fam. L 27 (1985–86).
4. Freeman, *After Warnock–Wither the Law?,* 39 Curr. Leg. Prob. 33, 38 (1986).
5. Rubellin-Devichi, *France: The Reform Wagon Rolls Again,* 25 J. Fam. L. 127, 131–32 (1986–87).
6. Frank, *Federal Republic of Germany: Accommodating to Social Change After the Major Reforms,* 25 J. Fam. L. 103, 106–08 (1986–87).
7. *Ibid.*
8. O'Brien, *The Itinerant Embryo and the Neo-Nativity Scene: Bifurcating Biological Maternity,* 1987 Utah L. Rev. 1, 11–12, 15–16 (1987).
9. *In re Baby M,* N.J. Superior Court, Chancery Division, Bergen County, No. FM-25314-86E, 3/31/87 [the discussion of this case is taken from the reported opinion in 13 Family Law Reporter 2001 (April 7, 1987)].
10. O'Rourke, *supra* note 2, at 141.
11. O'Brien, *supra* note 8, at 30–31.

12. Freeman, *supra* note 4, at 38–39.

13. Rubellin-Devichi, *supra* note 5, at 132.

14. Frank, *supra* note 6, at 108.

15. The literature is voluminous. Some recent examples include two student notes, 99 Harv. L. Rev. 1936 (1986) and 96 Yale L. L. 187 (1986). See also, for a provocative application of a broader thesis to the situation of surrogate parenting agreements, Radin, *Market-Inalienability,* 100 Harv. L. Rev. 1849, 1928–36 (1987).

16. See, e.g. Elster, *Solomonic Judgments: Against the Best Interest of the Child,* 54 U. Chi. L. Rev. 1 (1987); Mnookin, *Child-Custody Adjudication: Judicial Functions in the Face of Indeterminacy,* 39 L. & Contemp. Prob. 226 (1975).

17. Neeley, *The Primary Caretaker Rule: Child Custody and the Dynamics of Greed,* 3 Yale L. & Pub. Pol. Rev. 168 (1984).

18. J. Goldstein, A. Freud, & A. Solnit, BEYOND THE BEST INTERESTS OF THE CHILD 53–64 (Free Press Paperback 1973).

19. See e.g., Elster, *supra* note 16; Chambers, *Rethinking the Substantive Rules for Custody Disputes in Divorce,* 83 Mich. L. Rev. 477 (1984).

Chapter 9

Parents

Transition to Parenthood

Alice S. Rossi

From Child to Parent: An Example

What is unique about this perspective on parenthood is the focus on the adult parent rather than the child. Until quite recent years, concern in the behavioral sciences with the parent-child relationship has been confined almost exclusively to the child. . . .

The very different order of questions which emerge when the parent replaces the child as the primary focus of analytic attention can best be shown with an illustration. Let us take, for our example, the point Benedek makes that the child's need for mothering is *absolute* while the need of an adult woman to mother is *relative*. From a concern for the child, this discrepancy in need leads to an analysis of the impact on the child of separation from the mother or inadequacy of mothering. Family systems that provide numerous adults to care for the young child can make up for this discrepancy in need between mother and child, which may be why ethnographic accounts give little evidence of postpartum depression following childbirth in simpler societies. Yet our family system of isolated households, increasingly distant from kinswomen to assist in mothering, requires that new mothers shoulder total responsibility for the infant precisely for that stage of the child's life when his need for mothering is far in excess of the mother's need for the child.

From the perspective of the mother, the question has therefore become: what does maternity deprive her of? Are the intrinsic gratifications of maternity sufficient to compensate for shelving or reducing a woman's involvement in nonfamily

From *Journal of Marriage and the Family,* Vol. 30 (February 1968), pp. 26–39. Copyright 1968 by the National Council on Family Relations, 1910 West County Road B, Suite 147, St. Paul, MN 55113. Reprinted by permission.

interests and social roles? The literature on maternal deprivation cannot answer such questions, because the concept, even in the careful specification Yarrow has given it, has never meant anything but the effect on the child of various kinds of insufficient mothering. Yet what has been seen as a failure or inadequacy of individual women may in fact be a failure of the society to provide institutionalized substitutes for the extended kin to assist in the care of infants and young children. It may be that the role requirements of maternity in the American family system extract diversified interests and social expectations concerning adult life. Here, as at several points in the course of this paper, familiar problems take on a new and suggestive research dimension when the focus is on the parent rather than the child. . . .

Parsons' analysis of the experience of parenthood as a step in maturation and personality growth does not allow for negative outcome. In this view either parents show little or no positive impact upon themselves of their parental-role experiences, or they show a new level of maturity. Yet many women, whose interests and values made a congenial combination of wifehood and work role, may find that the addition of maternal responsibilities has the consequence of a fundamental and undesired change in both their relationships to their husbands and their involvements outside the family. Still other women, who might have kept a precarious hold on adequate functioning as adults had they *not* become parents, suffer severe retrogression with pregnancy and childbearing, because the reactivation of older unresolved conflicts with their own mothers is not favorably resolved but in fact leads to personality deterioration and the transmission of pathology to their children.

Where cultural pressure is very great to assume a particular adult role, as it is for American women to bear and rear children, latent desire and psychological readiness for parenthood may often be at odds with manifest desire and actual ability to perform adequately as parents. Clinicians and therapists are aware, as perhaps many sociologists are not, that failure, hostility, and destructiveness are as much a part of the family system and the relationships among family members as success, love, and solidarity are. . . .

Role-Cycle Stages

A discussion of the impact of parenthood upon the parent will be assisted by two analytic devices. One is to follow a comparative approach, by asking in what basic structural ways the parental role differs from other primary adult roles. The marital and occupational roles will be used for this comparison. A second device is to specify the phases in the development of a social role. If the total life span may be said to have a cycle, each stage with its unique tasks, then by analogy a role may be said to have a cycle and each stage in that role cycle to have its unique tasks and problems of adjustment. Four broad stages of a role cycle may be specified:

1. Anticipatory Stage

All major adult roles have a long history of anticipatory training for them, since parental and school socialization of children is dedicated precisely to this task of producing the kind of competent adult valued by the culture. For our present purposes, however, [we use] a narrower conception of the marital role, pregnancy in the case of the parental role, and the last stages of highly vocationally oriented schooling or on-the-job apprenticeship in the case of an occupational role.

2. Honeymoon Stage

This is the time period immediately following the full assumption of the adult role. The inception of this stage is more easily defined than its termination. In the case of the marital role, the honeymoon stage extends from the marriage ceremony itself through the literal honeymoon and on through an unspecified and individually varying period of time. Raush has caught this stage of the marital role in his description of the "psychic honeymoon": that extended postmarital period when, through close intimacy and joint activity, the couple can explore each other's capacities and limitations. I shall arbitrarily consider the onset of pregnancy as marking the end of the honeymoon stage of the marital role. This stage of the parental role may involve an equivalent psychic honeymoon, that post-childbirth period during which, through intimacy and prolonged contact, an attachment between parent and child is laid down. There is a crucial difference, however, from the marital role in this stage. A woman knows her husband as a unique real person when she enters the honeymoon stage of marriage. A good deal of preparatory adjustment on a firm reality base is possible during the engagement period which is not possible in the equivalent pregnancy period. Fantasy is not corrected by the reality of a specific individual child until the birth of the child. The "quickening" is psychologically of special significance to women precisely because it marks the first evidence of a real baby rather than a purely fantasized one. On this basis alone there is greater interpersonal adjustment and learning during the honeymoon stage of the parental role than of the marital role.

3. Plateau Stage

This is the protracted middle period of a role cycle during which the role is fully exercised. Depending on the specific problem under analysis, one would obviously subdivide this large plateau stage further. For my present purposes it is not necessary to do so, since my focus is on the earlier anticipatory and honeymoon stages of the parental role and the overall impact of parenthood on adults.

4. Disengagement-Termination Stage

This period immediately pecedes and includes the actual termination of the role. Marriage ends with the death of the spouse or, just as definitively, with separation and divorce. A unique characteristic of parental-role termination is the fact that it is not closely marked by any specific act but is an attenuated process of termination with little cultural prescription about when the authority and obligations of a parent end. Many parents, however, experience the marriage of the child as a psychological termination of the active parental role.

Unique Features of Parental Role

With this role-cycle suggestion as a broader framework, we can narrow our focus to what are the unique and most salient features of the parental role. In doing so, special attention will be given to two further questions: (1) the impact of social changes over the past few decades in facilitating or complicating the transition to and experience of parenthood and (2) the new interpretations or new research suggested by the focus on the parent rather than the child.

1. Cultural Pressure to Assume the Role

On the level of cultural values, men have no freedom of choice where work is concerned: They must work to secure their status as adult men.

The equivalent for women has been maternity. There is considerable pressure upon the growing girl and young woman to consider maternity necessary for a woman's fulfillment as an individual and to secure her status as an adult.*

This is not to say there are no fluctuations over time in the intensity of the cultural pressure to parenthood. During the depression years of the 1930s, there was more widespread awareness of the economic hardships parenthood can entail, and many demographic experts believe there was a great increase in illegal abortions during those years. Bird has discussed the dread with which a suspected pregnancy was viewed by many American women in the 1930s. Quite a different set of pressures were at work during the 1950s, when the general societal tendency was toward withdrawal from active engagement with the issues of the larger society and a turning in to the gratifications of the private sphere of home and family life. Important in the background were the general affluence of the period and the expanded room and ease of child rearing that go with suburban living. For the past five years, there has been a drop in the birth rate in general, fourth and higher-order births in particular. During this same period there has been increased

---

*The greater the cultural pressure to assume a given adult social role, the greater will be the tendency for individual negative feelings toward that role to be expressed covertly. Men may complain about a given job, not about working per se, and hence their work dissatisfactions are often displaced to the nonwork sphere, as psychosomatic complaints or irritation and dominance at home. An equivalent displacement for women of the ambivalence many may feel toward maternity is to dissatisfactions with the homemaker role.

concern and debate about women's participation in politics and work, with more women now returning to work rather than conceiving the third or fourth child.*

2. Inception of the Parental Role

The decision to marry and the choice of a mate are voluntary acts of individuals in our family system. Engagements are therefore consciously considered, freely entered, and freely terminated if increased familiarity decreases, rather than increases, intimacy and commitment to the choice. The inception of a pregnancy, unlike the engagement, is not always a voluntary decision, for it may be the unintended consequence of a sexual act that was recreative in intent rather than procreative. Secondly, and again unlike the engagement, the termination of a pregnancy is not socially sanctioned, as shown by current resistance to abortion-law reform.

The implication of this difference is a much higher probability of unwanted pregnancies than of unwanted marriages in our family system. Coupled with the ample clinical evidence of parental rejection and sometimes cruelty to children, it is all the more surprising that there has not been more consistent research attention to the problem of *parental satisfaction,* as there has for long been on *marital satisfaction* or *work satisfaction.* Only the extreme iceberg tip of the parental satisfaction continuum is clearly demarcated and researched, as in the growing concern with "battered babies." Cultural and psychological resistance to the image of a nonnurturant woman may afflict social scientists as well as the American public.

The timing of a first pregnancy is critical to the manner in which parental responsibilities are joined to the marital relationship. The single most important change over the past few decades is extensive and efficient contraceptive usage, since this has meant for a growing proportion of new marriages, the possibility of and increasing preference for some postponement of childbearing after marriage. When pregnancy was likely to follow shortly after marriage, the major transition point in a woman's life was marriage itself. *This transition point is increasingly the first pregnancy rather than marriage.* It is accepted and increasingly expected that women will work after marriage, while household furnishings are acquired and spouses complete their advanced training or gain a foothold in their work. This provides an early marriage period in which the fact of a wife's employment presses for a greater egalitarian relationship between husband and wife in decision-making, commonality of experience, and sharing of household responsibilities.

The balance between individual autonomy and couple mutuality that develops during the honeymoon stage of such a marriage may be important in establishing a

---

*When it is realized that a mean family size of 3.5 would double the population in 40 years, while a mean of 2.5 would yield a stable population in the same period, the social importance of withholding praise for procreative prowess is clear. At the same time, a drop in the birth rate may reduce the number of unwanted babies born, for such a drop would mean more efficient contraceptive usage and a closer correspondence between desired and attained family size.

pattern that will later affect the quality of the parent-child relationship and the extent of sex-role segregation of duties between the parents. It is only in the context of a growing egalitarian base to the marital relationship that one could find, as Gavron has, a tendency for parents to establish more barriers between themselves and their children, a marital defense against the institution of parenthood as she describes it. This may eventually replace the typical coalition in more traditional families of mother and children against husband-father. . . .

There is one further significant social change that has important implications for the changed relationship between husband and wife: the increasing departure from an old pattern of role-inception phasing in which the young person first completed his schooling, then established himself in the world of work, then married and began his family. Marriage and parenthood are increasingly taking place *before* the schooling of the husband, and often of the wife, has been completed. An important reason for this trend lies in the fact that, during the same decades in which the average age of physical-sexual maturation has dropped, the average amount of education which young people obtain has been on the increase. Particularly for the college and graduate or professional school population, family roles are often assumed before the degrees needed to enter careers have been obtained. . . .

The major implication of this change is that more men and women are achieving full status in family roles while they are still less than fully adult in status terms in the occupational system. Graduate students are, increasingly, men and women with full family responsibilities. Within the family many more husbands and fathers are still students, often quite dependent on the earnings of their wives to see them through their advanced training. No matter what the couple's desires and preferences are, this fact alone presses for more egalitarian relations between husband and wife, just as the adult family status of graduate students presses for more egalitarian relations between students and faculty.

3. Irrevocability

If marriages do not work out, there is now widespread acceptance of divorce and remarriage as a solution. The same point applies to the work world: we are free to leave an unsatisfactory job and seek another. But once a pregnancy occurs, there is little possibility of undoing the commitment to parenthood implicit in conception except in the rare instance of placing children for adoption. We can have ex-spouses and ex-jobs but not ex-children. This being so, it is scarcely surprising to find marked differences between the relationship of a parent and one child and the relationship of the same parent with another child. If the culture does not permit pregnancy termination, the equivalent to giving up a child is psychological withdrawal on the part of the parent.

This taps an important area in which a focus on the parent rather than the child may contribute a new interpretive dimension to an old problem: the long history of interest, in the social sciences, in differences among children associated with their sex-birth-order position in their sibling set. . . .

Some birth-order research stresses the influence of sibs upon other sibs, as in Koch's finding that second-born boys with an older sister are more feminine than second-born boys with an older brother. A similar sib-influence interpretation is offered in the major common finding of birth-order correlates, that sociability is greater among last-borns and achievement among first-borns. It has been suggested that last-borns use social skills to increase acceptance by their older sibs or are more peer-oriented because they receive less adult stimulation from parents. The tendency of first-borns to greater achievement has been interpreted in a corollary way, as a reflection of early assumption of responsibility for younger sibs, greater adult stimulation during the time the oldest was the only child in the family, and the greater significance of the first-born for the larger kinship network of the family.

Sociologists have shown increasing interest in structural family variables in recent years, a primary variable being family size. . . . The question posed is: what is the effect of growing up in a small family, compared with a large family, that is attributable to this group-size variable? Unfortunately, the theoretical point of departure for sociologists' expectations of the effect of the family-size variables is the Durkheim-Simmel tradition of the differential effect of group size or population density upon members or inhabitants. In the case of the family, however, this overlooks the very important fact that family size is determined by the key figures *within* the group, i.e., the parents. To find that children in small families differ from children in large families is not simply due to the impact of group size upon individual members but to the very different involvement of the parent with the children and to relations between the parents themselves in small versus large families.

An important clue to a new interpretation can be gained by examining family size from the perspective of parental motivation toward having children. A small family is small for one of two primary reasons: either the parents wanted a small family and achieved their desired size, or they wanted a large family but were not able to attain it. In either case, there is a low probability of unwanted children. Indeed, in the latter eventuality they may take particularly great interest in the children they do have. Small families are therefore most likely to contain parents with a strong and positive orientation to each of the children they have. A large family, in contrast, is large either because the parents achieved the size they desired or because they have more children than they in fact wanted. Large families therefore have a higher probability than small families of including unwanted unloved children. Consistent with this are Nye's finding that adolescents in small families have better relations with their parents than those in large families, and Sears and Maccoby's finding that mothers of large families are more restrictive toward their children than mothers of small families.

This also means that last-born children are more likely to be unwanted than first- or middle-born children, particularly in large families. This is consistent with what is known of abortion patterns among married women, who typically resort to abortion only when they have achieved the number of children they want or feel they can afford to have. Only a small proportion of women faced with such unwanted pregnancies actually resort to abortion. *This suggests the possibility that the last-born child's reliance on social skills may be his device for securing the attention and loving involvement of a parent less positively predisposed to him than to his older siblings.*

In developing this interpretation, rather extreme cases have been stressed. Closer to the normal range of families in which even the last-born child was desired and planned for, there is still another element which may contribute to the greater sociability of the last-born child. Most parents are themselves aware of the greater ease with which they face the care of a third fragile newborn than the first; clearly parental skills and confidence are greater with last-born children than the first-born children. But this does not mean that the attitude of the parent is more positive toward the care of the third child than the first. There is no necessary correlation between skills in an area and enjoyment of that area. Searls found that older homemakers are *more* skillful in domestic tasks but experience *less* enjoyment of them than younger homemakers, pointing to a declining euphoria for a particular role with the passage of time. In the same way, older people rate their marriages as "very happy" less often than younger people do. It is perhaps culturally and psychologically more difficult to face the possibility that women may find less enjoyment of the maternal role with the passage of time, though women themselves know the difference between the romantic expectation concerning child care and the incorporation of the first baby into the household and the more realistic expectation and sharper assessment of their own abilities to do an adequate job of mothering as they face a third confinement. Last-born children may experience not only less verbal stimulation from the parents than first-born children but also less prompt and enthusiastic response to their demands—from feeding and diaper changes as infants to requests for stories read at three or a college education at eighteen—simply because the parents experience less intense gratification from the parent role with the third child than they did with the first. The child's response to this might well be to cultivate winning, pleasing manners in early childhood that blossom as charm and sociability in later life, showing both a greater need to be loved and greater pressure to seek approval.

One last point may be appropriately developed at this juncture. Mention was made earlier that for many women the personal outcome of experience in the parent role is not a higher level of maturation but the negative outcome of a depressed sense of self-worth, if not actual personality deterioration. There is considerable evidence that this is more prevalent than we recognize. On a qualitative level, a close reading of the portrait of the working-class wife in Rainwater, Newsom, Komarovsky, Gavron, or Zweig gives little suggestion that maternity has provided these women with opportunities for personal growth and development. So, too, Cohen notes with some surprise that in her sample of middle-class educated couples, as in Pavenstadt's study of lower-income women in Boston, there were more emotional difficulties and lower levels of maturation among multiparous women than primiparous women. On a more extensive sample basis, in Gurin's survey of Americans viewing their mental health, as in Bradburn's reports on happiness, single men are less happy and less active than single women, but among the married respondents the women are unhappier, have more problems, feel inadequate as parents, have a more negative and passive outlook on life, and show a more negative self-image. All of these characteristics increase with age among men. While it may be true, as Gurin argues, that women are more introspective and hence more attuned to the psychological facets of experience than men are, this point does not account for the fact that the things which the women report are all on the negative side; few are on the positive side, indicative of euphoric sensitivity and pleasure. The possibility must be faced, and at some point researched, that women lose ground in personal development and self-esteem during the early and middle years of adulthood, whereas men gain ground in these respects during the same years. The retention of a high level of self-esteem may depend upon the adequacy of earlier preparation for major adult roles in the occupational system, as it does for those women who opt to participate significantly in the work world. Training in the qualities and skills needed for family roles in contemporary society may be inadequate for both sexes, but the lowering of self-esteem occurs only among women because their primary adult roles are within the family system.

4. Preparation for Parenthood

Four factors may be given special attention on the question of what preparation American couples bring to parenthood.

(a) Paucity of preparation. Our educational system is dedicated to the cognitive development of the young, and our primary teaching approach is the pragmatic one of learning by doing. How much one knows and how well he can apply what he knows are the standards by which the child is judged in school, as the employee is judged at work. The child can learn by doing in such subjects as science, mathematics, art work, or shop, but not in the subjects more relevant to successful family life: sex, home maintenance, child care, interpersonal competence, and empathy. If the home is deficient in training in these areas, the child is left with no preparation for a major segment of his adult life. A doctor facing his first patient in private practice has treated numerous patients under close supervision during his internship, but probably a majority of American mothers approach maternity with no previous child-care experience beyond sporadic baby-sitting, perhaps a course in child psychology, or occasional care of younger siblings.

(b) Limited learning during pregnancy. A second important point makes adjustment to parenthood potentially more stressful than marital adjustment. This is the lack of any realistic training for parenthood during the anticipatory stage of pregnancy. By contrast, during the engagement period preceding marriage, an individual has opportunities to develop the skills and make the adjustments which

ease the transition to marriage. Through discussions of values and life goals, through sexual experimentation, shared social experiences as an engaged couple with friends and relatives, and planning and furnishing an apartment, the engaged couple can make considerable progress in developing mutuality in advance of the marriage itself. No such headstart is possible in the case of pregnancy. What preparation exists is confined to reading, consultation with friends and parents, discussions between husband and wife, and a minor nesting phase in which a place and the equipment for a baby are prepared in the household.*

(c) Abruptness of transition. Thirdly, the birth of a child is not followed by any gradual taking on of responsibility, as in the case of a professional work role. It is as if the woman shifted from a graduate student to a full professor with little intervening apprenticeship experience of slowly increasing responsibility. The new mother starts out immediately on 24-hour duty, with responsibility for a fragile and mysterious infant totally dependent on her care.

If marital adjustment is more difficult for very young brides than more mature ones, adjustment to motherhood may be even more difficult. A woman can adapt a passive dependence on a husband and still have a successful marriage, but a young mother with strong dependency needs is in for difficulty in maternal adjustment, because the role precludes such dependency. This situation was well described in Cohen's study in a case of a young wife with a background of coed popularity and a passive dependent relationship to her admired and admiring husband, who collapsed into restricted incapacity when faced with the responsibilities of maintaining a home and caring for a child.

(d) Lack of guidelines to successful parenthood. If the central task of parenthood is the rearing of children to become the kind of competent adults valued by the society, then an important question facing any parent is what he or she specifically can do to create such a competent adult. This is where the parent is left with few or no guidelines from the expert. Parents can readily inform themselves concerning the young infant's nutritional, clothing, and medical needs and follow the general prescription that a child needs loving physical contact and emotional support. Such advice may be sufficient to produce a healthy, happy, and well-adjusted preschooler, but adult competency is quite another matter.

In fact, the adults who do "succeed" in American society show a complex of characteristics as children that current experts in child-care would evaluate as "poor" to "bad." Biographies of leading authors and artists, as well as the more rigorous research inquiries of creativity among architects or scientists, do not portray childhoods with characteristics currently endorsed by mental-health and child-care authorities. Indeed, there is often a predominance of tension in childhood family relations and traumatic loss rather than loving parental support,

---

*During the period when marriage was the critical transition in the adult woman's life rather than pregnancy, a good deal of anticipatory "nesting" behavior took place from the time of conception. Now more women work through a considerable portion of the first pregnancy, and such nesting behavior as exists may be confined to a few shopping expeditions or baby showers, thus adding to the abruptness of the transition and the difficulty of adjustment following the birth of a first child.

intense channeling of energy in one area of interest rather than an all-round profile of diverse interests, and social withdrawal and preference for loner activities rather than gregarious sociability. Thus, the stress in current childrearing advice on a high level of loving support but a low level of discipline or restriction on the behavior of the child—the "developmental" family type as Duvall calls it—is a profile consistent with the focus on mental health, sociability, and adjustment. Yet, the combination of both high support and high authority on the part of parents is most strongly related to the child's sense of responsibility, leadership quality, and achievement level, as found in Bronfenbrenner's studies and that of Mussen and Distler.

Brim points out that we are a long way from being able to say just what parent-role prescriptions have what effect on the adult characteristics of the child. We know even less about how such parental prescriptions should be changed to adapt to changed conceptions of competency in adulthood. In such an ambiguous context, the great interest parents take in school reports on their children or the pediatrician's assessment of the child's developmental progress should be seen as among the few indices parents have of how well *they* are doing as parents.

Research on Fathering:
Social Policy and an Emergent Perspective

Robert A. Fein

Discussion of fathering is becoming fashionable. Social scientists, family life educators, clinicians, and parents have begun a long-overdue assessment of the problems and possibilities of relationships between fathers and children. Increasingly, dogmas and conventional wisdoms that have guided and defined those relationships are being scrutinized—and found wanting. Rather than sit by the sidelines or serve as mothers' helpers, men are being urged to participate in the lives of their children, from conception on. And apparently increasing numbers of men are reaching out for more sustaining relationships with the young in their lives.

Changes in social norms which foster re-evaluation of fathering and relationships between men and children deserve support. But to affect relations between fathers and children (and family lives in general), examination of fathering should occur within the context of social policy, with an appreciation of the multitude of social forces that impinge on the daily behaviors of children and parents. As Kamerman and Kahn (1976) note, American social policies concerning families,

From *Journal of Social Issues* Vol. 34, No. 1 (1978), pp. 122–135. Copyright 1978 by the Society for the Psychological Study of Social Issues. Reprinted by permission.

which have been implicit and unexamined for years, are being made explicit, with attention given to government and business programs which affect the lives of men, women, and children.

Research concerning fathers has occurred within the context of social stereotypes and norms of American society. This paper begins with a description of the two major perspectives on fathering of the past 25 years, a *traditional* view and a *modern* view, then charts some recent developments in research on fathering which may be seen as constituting an *emergent* perspective. The paper concludes by suggesting that the time is ripe for social scientists to contribute to the development of policies that support family life.

The Traditional Perspective

The major image of the father role in the traditional perspective is the aloof and distant father. English's (1954) description exemplified how the father role was viewed.

> Traditionally, Father has been looked on as the breadwinner. In times past, so much of his time and energy was used in this role that at home he was thought of as taciturn and stern, albeit kind. He was respected but feared by his children who never learned to know him very well. He accepted the fact that he earned the money and Mother cared for the home and raised the children. (p. 323)

In the traditional perspective, a father cares for his children primarily by succeeding in the occupational arena. At home, father's job is to provide for his family so that mother can devote herself to the care of the children (Bowlby, 1951). In this view, men offer companionship and emotional support to their spouses and have relatively little direct involvement with the children. It is worth observing that Bowlby (and others in the psychoanalytic tradition) saw no direct caring role for fathers with infants and young children. Men, while symbolically important to children as close-to-home models of power and authority, were supposed to have little to do with the actual parenting of the young.

In sociology, Parsons and Bales (1955) presented the traditional perspective on men in the family: the instrumental/expressive dichotomy. Men were seen as responsible for the family's relationships with the outside world (primarily the world of work), whereas women were the primary "givers of love" at home.

The traditional perspective on fathering generally conformed to social ideals and realities of the late 1940s and 1950s. Relatively few women were in the paid labor force more than temporarily, and of these women only a small percentage were mothers with young children. Mothers stayed home and fathers went out to work. The husband-breadwinner/wife-homemaker nuclear family was the norm, both in a statistical sense and in the social values of the time.

But there were occasional commentators in the 1950s who noted that norms of American society might change to permit different patterns of childrearing. One such observer was psychiatrist Irene Josselyn:

> As long as men are seen as animated toys, mothers' little helpers, or powerful
> ogres who alone mete out rewards and punishment, the role of men in the family
> structure will be boring and/or depreciating. Being frustrated in their attempt to
> find gratification of their fatherliness, and dissatisfied with the watered-down
> expression of themselves in the home, they will continue to seek release by
> diverting their available free energy into channels in which they feel more
> adequate, with a resultant overinvestment in the gratification they attain from
> activities away from the home. . . . For the sake of the child and the father we
> should learn a great deal more of the deeper, subtler meanings of the poten-
> tialities in the father-child relationship. (1956, p. 270)

The Modern Perspective

The 1960s saw a major increase in the attention given to fathers by social
scientists. Whereas the traditional view of fathering assumed that if men successfully fulfilled head of household, provider roles and mothers carried out their
expressive responsibilities, children would be socialized successfully into adult
roles, the modern perspective on fathering assumed that children (especially boys)
were vulnerable in their psychosocial development (Biller, 1971).

Some 1950s researchers (such as Aberle & Naegele, 1956) had pointed toward
the modern perspective by suggesting that fathers inculcated attitudes and behaviors that their children needed for educational and vocational attainment. In the
1960s, spurred by a concern for child development, a number of researchers
turned to fathering. For example, John Nash (1965) published "The Father in
Contemporary Culture and Current Psychological Literature," in which he concluded that most psychologists had mistakenly assumed that fathers were unimportant in childrearing. Apparently, questioning dominant assumptions about
childrearing was risky, for Nash concluded his paper was a "disclaimer":

> This paper is not to be interpreted as an attack on motherhood, but merely as a
> suggestion that there are other aspects to parent-child relationships than those
> included in the widely discussed interaction between mother and child. (p. 292)

It is important to note that research within the modern perspective on fathering
saw successful child development as a goal of fathering. Three child development
outcomes were emphasized: (a) achievement of socially appropriate sex-role
identity (masculinity and femininity), (b) academic performance, and (c) moral
development (often measured as the absence of delinquency). Researchers attempted to study these outcomes by attending to families without fathers, so-
called "father-absent" families. Studies of father-absent children, particularly
boys (reviewed, for example, in Biller, 1974), suggested that children without
fathers had significantly more difficulty in the development of sex-role identity, in
academic achievement, and in moral development and behavior. Since achievement in these areas was viewed as essential for interpersonal adjustment and life
success, boys in father-absent families were considered to be at risk.

Whereas the traditional perspective was supportive of social policies designed to maintain the instrumental/expressive dichotomy, the modern perspective on fathering paralleled attention to policies that appeared to decrease the opportunities for children to interact with their fathers. For example, the Aid to Families with Dependent Children (AFDC) program in most circumstances provided lower benefits for families with an adult male in the household compared to those without an adult male. Concern about the development of children in fatherless families gradually became coupled with concern that AFDC appeared to provide incentives for families to exclude fathers. Such concern was highlighted in debates over the "Moynihan Report" (Rainwater & Yancy, 1967), which argued that black family structure was predominantly matriarchal and was a significant factor in maintaining high levels of black male unemployment. The implication of this debate was that young black males suffered from the absence of male role models (fathers) which contributed to their having higher unemployment levels than other segments of the population.

Concerned about claims of researchers who compared father-absent and father-present families (researchers who suggested that boys from father-absent families were more prone to fail in sex-role identity and academic attainments and were more likely to engage in antisocial behaviors), Herzog and Sudia (1968, 1972, 1974) reviewed the father-absent literature and argued that researchers had not demonstrated that boys in father-absent families were consistently different from boys in father-present families.

Herzog and Sudia's review of the research suggested:

(a) that father absence in itself is not likely to depress school performance;
(b) that there might be a slightly greater likelihood of a boy in a father-absent family engaging in delinquent behavior, but even if statistically more likely, the difference would be so small that it would not be practically important; and
(c) that there is no solid research support for the thesis that a resident father is the only source of masculine identification or that the absence of a father from the home necessarily affects a boy's masculine identity.

They noted that many studies which had reported differences between boys in father-absent and father-present families had failed to account for the power of social class, which when statistically controlled removed the differences.

To account for possible differences in some areas between father-absent and father-present families, Herzog and Sudia suggested that key factors might be the additional stresses on families attendant on the loss of a father rather than the absence of the father per se. Writing about the use of masculinity-femininity scales, the authors noted that these scales "add up to dubious definitions of adequate masculinity and femininity," and that a study of the items suggested that Stalin or Al Copone would look better on the scales than Abraham Lincoln or Martin Luther King (Herzog & Sudia, 1972, pp. 177–178).

While most researchers in the modern perspective dwelt on father-absent families, some attempted to study families with fathers present. Mussen and his colleagues conducted a number of studies which suggested that father's nurturance as perceived by the child was a key factor in the development of sex-role identity (reviewed in Mussen, 1969). However, Mussen and his colleagues did not actually observe fathers. Radin (1972, 1973) suggested that paternal nurturance is an antecedent of intellectual functioning in 4- and 5-year-old boys. While her research dealt only with child outcomes, the attention to cognitive development and her effort to observe father-child interaction were significant advances over previous studies.

While from the point of view of contemporary values the modern perspective on fathering represented an improvement on the traditional (in that the modern view focused attention on child development and on the idea that fathers' behaviors influenced their children), some of the assumptions of the modern perspective have been criticized recently. For example, the nature and desirability of sex-role identity, as measured by masculinity scales, has come under question and attack (Pleck, 1975). Researchers like Kotelchuck (1976) and Pederson (1976) highlight the fact that there were relatively few studies of actual fathering behavior by researchers in the modern perspective.

The Emergent Perspective

What I am calling the *emergent* perspective on fathering proceeds from the notion that men are psychologically able to participate in a full range of parenting behaviors, and furthermore that it may be good both for parents and children if men take active roles in childcare and childrearing. While some research in the emergent perspective focuses on effects on the child, analysis has begun to examine the impact of father-children relationships on all members of the family. Researchers are exploring the idea that children's lives are enhanced by the opportunity to develop and sustain relationships with adults of both sexes. Issues of adult development are under consideration, including the idea that opportunity to care for others, including and especially children, can be a major factor in adult well-being.

The emergent perspective on fathering is androgynous in assuming that the only parenting behaviors from which men are necessarily excluded by virtue of gender are gestation and lactation. Arguments suggesting that men are inherently limited in child-rearing capacity have drawn on studies of infrahuman animal species which suggested that parenting behaviors by males are rare. Howells (1971), reviewing these data, suggests that "the main lesson to be found from the study of the care given to young animals is that nature is flexible" (p. 128). There are examples of male animal behavior which can be seen as parental and nurturant. For one, the male stickleback builds a nest, receives eggs from females, fertilizes them, cares for them, and brings up the young. The males of some catfish carry eggs in their mouths until they hatch; "when danger threatens, *he* holds his mouth open so that the frightened youngsters can dash into it to safety" (Howells, 1971, p. 130). Data from infrahuman animal species can refute biologically-based arguments of major inherent limitations in human male parenting capabilities.

In psychology, innovative research on fathering is developing in five areas:

(a) fathers' experience before, during, and after the birth of children;
(b) fathers' ties with newborns and infants;
(c) the development and nature of bonds between young children and fathers;
(d) fathers in nontraditional childcare arrangements; and
(e) effects of parenting experiences on fathers.

While there are overlaps in these categories, each contributes an important focus to the development of the emergent perspective.

Entering Parenthood

Several studies in the 1970s have employed models of male parenting that assume that men are able to participate in pregnancy and childbirth. Influenced by media accounts of men who participated in delivery and by the popularity of childbirth education programs (Wapner, 1976), researchers have compared experiences of men who participated in childbirth education courses with men who did not and have described experiences of men who shared labor and delivery experiences with their wives. Cronenwett and Newmark (1974) gave a questionnaire to 152 fathers and found that fathers who attended childbirth preparation classes and/or the birth rated their overall experience during childbirth and the experience of their wives significantly higher than other men. Interestingly, there were no differences on infant-related items reported between fathers who attended classes and/or the birth and men who did not. Fein (1976) found that effective postpartum adjustment in men was related to development of a coherent fathering role. Interviews with 30 middle-income couples suggested that neither the women nor the men were particularly well prepared for the practical realities of parenting, with men's lack of experience in part a result of social attitudes that have assumed that boys and young men have little interest or aptitude to learn about children and childcare. Reiber (1976) studied nine couples before and after the birth of a child and noted that the fathers were interested in being nurturers and the men appeared to be involved in caring for their babies to the extent that their wives allowed them to be. Manion (1977), in a correlational study of 45 first-time fathers several weeks after the birth of their children, found that although fathers were seldom included in postpartum hospital instruction about childcare, men did become involved in providing care for their infants. Men who remembered their parents as nurturant tended to be more active in childcare than other men. Fathers who had a higher degree of involvement in the birth had a higher degree of involvement in childcare activities.

Ties with Newborns and Infants

Parke and Savin (1976) recently summarized the traditional view of fathers' roles in infancy:

1. Fathers are uninterested in and uninvolved with newborn infants.
2. Fathers are less nurturant toward infants than mothers.
3. Fathers prefer noncaretaking roles and leave the caretaking up to mothers.
4. Fathers are less competent than mothers to care for newborn infants. (p. 365)

Research about father-infant relationships is questioning the credibility of these assumptions. Greenberg and Morris (1974) gave a written questionnaire to 30 first-time fathers who had either attended the births of their babies or who had been shown their babies shortly after birth. In addition, a series of interviews was conducted with half the sample. The researchers noted that fathers enjoyed looking at their babies, reported a desire for and pleasure in physical contact with the newborns, and were aware of unique features and characteristics of their babies. Many fathers were surprised at the impact their contact with the baby had on them. Greenberg and Morris suggested that fathers begin developing a bond to their newborns within three days after birth and called this phenomenon "engrossment."

Parke and O'Leary (1976) observed men interacting with their newborns. Fathers were seen to be active with their infants, being more likely to touch and rock their infants when alone than with the mother. In one of their studies, the researchers compared fathers of different social classes and found that "high interaction fathering" occurred across socioeconomic class lines. Parke and O'Leary suggested that early contact with infants may be important for the development of father-child bonds, raising questions about the thresholds of paternal responsivity to infants.

Bonds Between Young Children and Fathers

Given the power and primacy of cultural assumptions about mother-child bonds, only in the last decade have researchers begun to look carefully at the relationships men establish with their young children. Yogman, Dixon, Tronick, Adamson, Als, and Brazelton (Note 1) found that infants responded differentially to their fathers compared to strangers by four weeks of age, even when the fathers were not their primary caretakers. Kotelchuck (Note 2, 1976), in an observational study of 144 children, found that children responded to both fathers and mothers more than to strangers. While the child's parental preferences at 18 months of age were strongly related to parental involvement in the home, Kotelchuck concluded that the overall lack of mother-father differences in terms of children's observed behaviors suggested that neither the quality of parent-child interaction nor specific caretaking practices are critical issues in formation of a relationship. His study strongly suggested that young children form significant relationships with their fathers.

Cohen and Campos (1974), attempting to measure both attachment behaviors of young children and distress indicators, concluded that fathers were more powerful elicitors of attachment behaviors than strangers, but that mothers were superior to fathers as elicitors of these behaviors. There were no differences between fathers and mothers in eliciting distress vocalization. Lamb and Lamb (1976), reviewing the literature on the development of father-child bonds, concluded that fathers are salient figures in the lives of their children from infancy on. These researchers suggested that the family should be seen as a complex system in which all persons (including infants) influence and are affected by all.

Nontraditional Childcare Arrangements

Responding to changes in family and marital patterns in the United States, a number of social scientists have begun to study fathers who parent outside of the context of the husband-provider/wife-homemaker nuclear family. Separated fathers, widowed fathers, divorced fathers, unmarried fathers, adopting fathers, and stepfathers are recent subjects of study.

Hetherington, Cox, and Cox (1976) studied 96 families, comparing relationships in divorced familes with those in intact families. Two years after their divorces, fathers in this group were seen as influencing their children significantly less than the fathers in intact families. Noting that divorced fathers in their sample generally left the home, the children remaining with the mother, Hetherington et al. report that divorced men complained of being rootless, with separation inducing great feelings of loss, particularly with regard to feelings about their children.

Finkelstein-Keshet (1977), studying the coping strategies of fathers following marital separation, found that for some men the opportunity to care for their children became the basis of a major life reorganization. Levine (1976), in a book about varieties of fathering, reported on single men who adopt children, men who share childcare on an equal basis with their wives, and men who become primary parents of their children. His study suggested that a wide variety of fathering roles is practiced in the United States. Rallings (1976), noting that step-fathering has been an understudied phenomenon, suggested that since 15% of all children under age 18 were living with a divorced parent (in 1970), and since courts were more likely to give custody to a mother than to a father, and since remarriage rates have been high, it is likely that there are several million children now living with stepfathers.

Effects of Parenting on Fathers

How men respond to and are affected by the children in their lives is a key area of the emergent perspective on fathering. While novels and popular magazines have presented personal accounts, there has been little systematic exploration of the fathering experience. The clinical literature that exists in this area (see Fein, 1976, and Earls, 1976, for reviews) highlights pathological experiences, with titles such as "Pregnancy as a Precipitant of Mental Illness in Men" (Freeman, 1951), "Fatherhood as a Precipitant of Mental Illness" (Wainwright, 1966), and "Paranoid Psychoses Associated with Impending or Newly Established Father-hood" (Retterstoll, 1968). Researchers in the four other areas discussed above occasionally touch on aspects of male parenting development—noting, for example, that men may be profoundly affected by participating in childbirth, by holding their newborns, by caring regularly for their toddlers, by becoming primary parents for adolescent children—but there is a need for systematic research. These questions gain importance when placed next to survey data that suggest that a large number of men feel that the trait "able to love" is not highly characteristic of themselves (Tavris, 1977).

The Emergent Perspective and Social Policy

The emergent perspective on fathering both proceeds from and leads to differ-ent social policy considerations than either traditional or modern ideologies of fathering. For one thing, the emergent perspective seeks to deal with the reality that increasing numbers of women are entering the paid labor force. A perspective on fathering that accepts the possibility that significant numbers of men can be effective nurturers of children may provide some relief from burdensome debates of the "should mothers mother or should mothers work?" variety (Rowe, 1976). If fathers are seen as able to care for their young, from a social policy perspective the question of childcare becomes one of family support: How can families be aided to carry out their childrearing and paid employment responsibilities? For example, an emergent perspective on fathering suggests attention to parental leave rather than maternity leave, to examination of the ways in which personnel and employment practices and policies affect the options of women and men both to care for their children and to provide economically for their families (Levine, 1977).

The idea of equal parenting, consistent with an emergent perspective on fathering, is receiving attention in discussions of family support. Sweden, several years ahead of the United States in these debates, embarked in the 1960s on a policy to support women to have a full range of options in paid employment. Premised on the ideal of equality, the Swedish program to support women in paid employment was concerned also with developing men's opportunities to partici-pate in home life (Palme, 1972). To these ends, Sweden has enacted programs which allow men and women to care for children at home in the months after their birth and to be compensated at 90% of pre-birth salaries. Furthermore, men and women have the same right to stay home from work if the children are sick. Data from Sweden indicate that only one to two percent of fathers of newborn children took advantage of the new policy during the first year after it was enacted into law, but the figure rose to six percent the second year (Liljestrom, 1977).

It would be naive to suggest that the emergent perspective on fathering will provide full answers to complicated questions concerning the relationship between family life and work life in the United States. Liljestrom suggests that, for Swedish society, it would be foolhardy to imagine that fathers should seek to emulate the role of yesterday's mothers and points to the need to think about the implications of equal parenting:

> The time is ripe for retesting our notions about the meaning of parenthood. Perhaps future parents will live in more open families, where it is easier for the adults to coordinate parenthood with work and public affairs interests and where the children are surrounded by a network of adult contacts. Otherwise, how will we be able to solve the conflicts between the roles of parents and other adult life roles? (1977, p. 77)

The new perspective calls attention to issues of equal parenting. That there may indeed be a need for such discussion in the United States is highlighted by a front-page *New York Times Book Review* article on Selma Fraiberg's 1977 book, *Every Child's Birthright: In Defense of Mothering*. Describing the debate about family policy in the United States, the reviewer, Kenneth Keniston, comments on widespread concerns that maternal employment has resulted in inadequate care for many children. While noting that research has not supported a linkage between maternal employment and negative child outcomes (such as failure to thrive in infancy or criminality in adulthood), and arguing that children have a right to be nurtured, Keniston, amazingly, does not once mention fathers as a part of the solution to these problems (Keniston, 1977). In ignoring almost one-half of potential childcarers (men), Keniston may be seen as writing from the traditional perspective of fathering. The exclusion of fathers in a consideration of the needs of children and families would appear to underscore the need for a new perspective.

It seems increasingly clear that the next several years will witness considerable discussion and debate about parenting, family life, and work in the United States. I have tried to suggest that social scientists have tended to lag behind or at best run parallel to debates about social values and policies concerning parenting and fathering. Both the traditional and the modern perspectives of fathering have limited usefulness in a society marked by increasing levels of female paid employment and growing concerns about the care of children. Forthcoming debates on family life will provide opportunities for social scientists to contribute to the formation of policies that will affect millions of American parents and children. Given the importance of these issues, attention to an emergent perspective of fathering appears timely and prudent.

Reference Notes

1. Yogman, M. W., Dixon, S., Tronick, E., Adamson, L., Als, H., & Brazelton, T. B. *Development of infant social interaction with fathers.* Paper presented at the meeting of the Eastern Psychological Association, New York, April 1976.

2. Kotelchuck, M. *The nature of the infant's tie to his father.* Paper presented at the meeting of the Society for Research in Child Development, Philadelphia, 1973.

References

Aberle, D., & Naegele, K. Father's occupational role and attitudes toward children. *American Journal of Orthopsychiatry,* 1956, *22,* 366–378.

Biller, H. B. *Father, child, and sex role.* Lexington, MA: D. C. Heath, 1971.

Biller, H. B. *Paternal deprivation.* Lexington, MA: D. C. Heath, 1974.

Bowlby, J. *Maternal care and mental health.* Geneva: World Health Organization, 1951.

Cohen, J. J., & Campos, J. J. Father, mother, and stranger as elicitors of attachment behaviors in infancy. *Developmental Psychology,* 1974, *10,* 146–154.

Cronenwett, L. R., & Newmark, L. L. Father's responses to childbirth, *Nursing Research,* 1974, *23,* 210–217.

Earls, F. The fathers (not the mothers): Their importance and influence with infants and young children. *Psychiatry,* 1076, *39,* 209–226.

English, O. S. The psychological role of the father in the family. *Social Casework,* 1954, pp. 323–329.

Fein, R. A. Men's entrance to parenthood. *The Family Coordinator,* 1976, *25,* 341–350.

Finkelstein-Keshet, H. *Marital separation and fathering.* Unpublished doctoral dissertation, University of Michigan, 1977.

Freeman, T. Pregnancy as a precipitant of mental illness in men. *British Journal of Medical Psychology,* 1951, *24,* 49–54.

Greenberg, M., & Morris, N. Engrossment: The newborn's impact upon the father. *American Journal of Orthopsychiatry,* 1974, *44,* 520–531.

Herzog, E., & Sudia, C. Fatherless homes. *Children,* 1968, pp. 177–182.

Herzog, E., & Sudia, C. Families without fathers. *Childhood Education,* 1972, pp. 175–181.

Herzog, E., & Sudia, C. Children in fatherless families. In E. M. Hetherington & P. Ricciuti (Eds.), *Review of child development research* (Vol. 3). Chicago: University of Chicago, 1974.

Hetherington, E. M., Cox, M., & Cox, R. Divorced fathers. *The Family Coordinator,* 1976, *25,* 417–428.

Howells, J. G. Fathering. In J. G. Howells (Ed.), *Modern perspectives in child psychiatry.* New York: Bruner-Mazel, 1971.

Josselyn, I. M. Cultural forces, motherliness and fatherliness. *American Journal of Orthopsychiatry,* 1956, *26,* 264–271.

Kamerman, S. B., & Kahn, A. J. Explorations in family policy. *Social Work,* 1976, *21,* 181–186.

Keniston, K. First attachments. (Review of *Every child's birthright: In defense of mothering* by S.Fraiberg.) *The New York Times Book Review,* December 11, 1977, pp. 1:40–41.

Kotelchuck, M. The infant's relationship to the father: Experimental evidence. In M. E. Lamb (Ed.), *The role of the father in child development.* New York: Wiley, 1976.

Lamb, M. E., & Lamb, J. E. The nature and importance of the father-infant relationship. *The Family Coordinator,* 1976, *25,* 379–386.

Levine, J. *Who will raise the children? New options for fathers (and mothers).* New York: Lippincott, 1976.

Levine, J. Redefining the child care "problem"—Men as child nurturers. *Childhood Education,* November/December 1977, pp. 55–61.

Liljestrom, R. The parent's role in production and reproduction. *Sweden Now,* 1977, *11,* 73–77.

Manion, J. A study of fathers and infant caretaking. *Birth and the Family Journal,* 1977, *4,* 174–179.

Mussen, P. Early sex-role development. In D. Goslin (Ed.), *Handbook of socialization theory and research,* New York: Rand McNally, 1969.

Nash, J. The father in contemporary culture and current psychological literature. *Child Development,* 1965, *36,* 261–297.

Palme, O. The emancipation of man. *Journal of Social Issues,* 1972, *28*(2), 237–246.

Parke, R. D., & O'Leary, S. E. Father-mother-infant interaction in the newborn period. In K. Riegel & J. Meacham (Eds.), *The developing individual in a changing world.* The Hague: Mouton, 1976.

Parke, R. D., Savin, D. B. The father's role in infancy: A re-evaluation. *The Family Coordinator,* 1976, *25,* 365–372.

Parsons, T., & Bales, R. F. *Family, socialization, and interaction process.* Glencoe, IL: The Free Press, 1955.

Pederson, F. Does research on children reared in father-absent families yield information on father influences? *The Family Coordinator,* 1976, *25,* 459–464.

Pleck, J. H. Masculinity-femininity: Current and alternate paradigms. *Sex Roles,* 1975, *1,* 161–178.

Radin, N. Father-child interaction and the intellectual functioning of four-year-old boys. *Developmental Psychology,* 1972, *6,* 353–361.

Radin, N. Observed paternal behaviors as antecedents of intellectual functioning in young boys. *Developmental Psychology,* 1973, *8,* 369–376.

Rainwater, L., & Yancy, W. L. *The Moynihan report and the politics of controversy.* Cambridge, MA: MIT Press, 1967.

Rallings, E. M. The special role of stepfather. *The Family Coordinator,* 1976, *25,* 445–450.

Reiber, V. D. Is the nurturing role natural to fathers? *American Journal of Maternal Child Nursing,* 1976, *1,* 366–371.

Retterstol, N. Paranoid psychoses associated with impending or newly established fatherhood. *Acta Psychiatrica Scandinavica,* 1968, *44,* 51–61.

Rowe, M. O. That parents may work and love and children may thrive. In N. B. Talbot (Ed.), *Raising children in modern America.* Boston: Little, Brown, 1976.

Tavris, C. Men and women report their views on masculinity. *Psychology Today,* 1977, *10,* 34–43.

Wainwright, W. Fatherhood as a precipitant of mental illness. *American Journal of Psychiatry,* 1966, *123,* 40–44.

Wapner, J. The attitudes, feelings and behaviors of expectant fathers attending Lamaze classes. *Birth and the Family Journal,* 1976, *3,* 5–14.

Single Mothers:
A Review and Critique of Current Research

Martha T. Mednick

The single mother of minor children has been a subject of considerable public attention since the early 1970s. This group of women was then recognized as a growing segment of the population, and one that would continue to grow. Now, in the mid-1980s, this forecast has been proven correct, and public discussion has focused on the impoverished condition of women raising young children alone. Indeed, the term "feminization of poverty" was coined to characterize this group (Pearce, 1978).

The problems encountered by these women constitute a social issue that needs constructive study by applied social psychologists. My purpose in this [paper] is to set a direction for such work by critically reviewing the psychological research on divorced, separated, or never-married women who are raising one or more children on their own. I have excluded studies of teenage pregnancy, of divorce process and trauma, and ones that examine only effects on children.

From *Family Processes and Problems: Social Psychological Aspects, (Applied Social Psychology Annual 7).* Copyright 1987 by the Society for the Psychological Study of Social Problems, Inc. Reprinted by permission of Sage Publications, Inc. Cross-references to within the original have been omitted.

Table 1.   Percentage of Female Householders Below the U.S. Poverty
Level, 1981

Ethnicity and employment status	Number of children under age 18			
	Zero	*One*	*Two*	*Three*
White female head	12.7%	31.3%	38.8%	58.8%
no earners	26.9	86.0	89.1	92.9
head only earner	11.5	25.1	27.3	47.5
Black female head*	35.8	45.1	61.2	72.6
no earners*	66.2	88.7	96.0	97.7
head only earner*	37.1	26.4	42.1	57.2
Hispanic female head	30.5	47.8	60.1	76.8
no earners	64.3	—	—	—
head only earner	25.0	30.4	—	—

Source: U.S. Commission on Civil Rights (1983, p. 3).
— Base less than 75,000.
*It is possible for the overall poverty rate for all black female-headed households to be lower than the poverty rate for black female-headed households where the head is the only earner because some such households have two or more adult earners.

This review of the research of the past decade begins with demographics that give a sense of the dimensions of the problem. I then discuss the values that have framed the research in this area. Next is a review and critique of the research, and, finally, conclusions, some suggestions for future work, and a comment on public policy.

A Demographic Frame of Reference

Incidence and Economic Status

Reports based on the 1980 census, as well as on subsequent counts and projections, show a marked increase in the number and proportion of single mothers heading their own households.[1] In 1970, the percentage of female-headed households was 8.7%; by 1983, it was 11.3%. More pertinent is the fact that, by 1981, 18.8% of all families with minor children were female-headed. For blacks the rates were higher; by 1981, 47.5% of black families with minor children present were headed by women, up from 30.6% in 1970 (U.S. Commission on Civil Rights, 1983). Female-headed families and the millions of children living in these families became progressively poorer, even as the economy improved. In 1980, about 40% of single mothers were below national poverty levels; by 1983, this figure had increased to 47% (U.S. Commission on Civil Rights, 1983).

Single mothers tend to be in and out of the labor force and are more subject to unemployment and underemployment. Even with full-time employment, women

Table 2.   Median Family Income, by Race and Type of Family

Type of family	$ 1970	$ 1981	% Increase 1970–1981
Husband-wife families	$10,516	$25,065	138%
wife in labor force	12,276	29,247	138
Female householder, no husband present	5,093	10,960	115
Male householder, no wife present	—	19,889	—
White Families			
Husband-wife families	10,723	25,474	138
wife in labor force	12,543	29,713	137
Female householder, no husband present	5,754	12,508	117
Male householder, no wife present	—	20,421	—
Black Families			
Husband-wife families	7,816	19,624	151
wife in labor force	9,721	25,040	158
Female householder, no husband present	3,576	7,506	110
Male householder, no wife present	—	14,489	—

Source: U.S. Commission on Civil Rights (1983, p. 6).

heading their own families have a poverty rate that is two and one-half times that of two-parent families; and part-time and unemployed women workers are even worse off.

Family poverty rates by ethnicity, employment status, and family size are presented in Table 1. The negative impact of the presence of children, and of being black or Hispanic, on women's economic status is profound. Table 2 compares family income for various family structures and employment patterns in 1970 and 1981 and shows the impoverishing effects of being a female head of household. Black women in this category are particularly disadvantaged.

For many women, full-time employment does not raise their economic status much, if any, above the level of poverty, because women's work does not provide an income at all comparable to men's work. This is due to a multiplicity of factors, including occupational sex segregation, sex discrimination, poor education and training, sex role stereotyping, and the general devaluation of women's work (Mednick, 1982). "Employment is generally considered the key to economic independence in our society, but it does not unlock the door for many women" (U.S. Commission on Civil Rights, 1983)—a fact that has a particularly strong impact on the situation of the single mother.

Family and Motherhood Values

The values that have typically framed research in this area are that legitimate power and authority are the father's role, that the husband should be the sole or major economic provider, that marriage and family life must be structured in terms of separate roles and activities with a strict and proper division of labor, that all other family forms are deviant, and that single mothers are in a transitional state anyway.

The biasing effect of such values on the research on single mothers was delineated in an important review by Brandwein, Brown, and Fox (1974). Their search of the psychological, sociological, and social welfare literature revealed the limitations imposed by the assumption that the single-mother family form is deviant and pathological, and they concluded that more had been revealed about the effects of stigmatization than about the female-headed families under study. The corpus of work they reviewed had overlooked economic issues, the nature and effect of the authority shift from fathers to mothers, and the extent to which mothers' increased responsibilities and stress might be the important determinants of familial well-being.

Are Single Mothers in Transition?

Another part of the ideology that influenced earlier work was the view that the single-mother status is a transitional one (e.g., Ross & Sawhill, 1975). The impact of this view began with sample characteristics: Rarely was information provided about how long the subjects had been single, and there was almost no longitudinal research. Studies of effects of divorce and postdivorce adjustment typically covered only one or two years, as it was assumed that the effects of divorce trauma are over by then and that most women remarry. However, only longitudinal studies can address the vital question of how various single mothers manage their work and family lives during the entire course of their childrearing years.

Review of the Research

Some Methodological and Conceptual Concerns

In the past, the mere fact of single status was treated as though it invariably produced a particular kind of experience that accounted for differences observed between single and married parents. The experience itself was rarely studied. Newer studies have begun to show that this is a heterogeneous population, with various types of single mothers. For example, race, culture, and class all affect the meaning and consequences of single parenthood, but such subgroups have been largely unstudied. It is only in recent years that nonracist and nonsexist writing about the black family has begun to appear at all (Carr, 1982; Engram, 1982;

McAdoo, 1981), and most of the studies reviewed herein are of majority women. The exceptions are noted below.

Another problem is that the research is mainly about divorced and separated mothers; the never-married are rarely studied except as teenagers. It may seem reasonable to assume that, aside from the trauma of divorce and separation per se, many of the issues and problems of solo parenting are very similar for these different groups, but we do not really know the extent of generalizability. The research reviewed herein includes a few studies of different types of single-mother families, but most research was not designed to make comparison possible, so differential conclusions cannot be reached.

There is now less focus on deviant and clinical populations of single mothers (Belle, 1982; Kohen, Brown, & Feldberg, 1979). More studies have looked at women as they function in the community, and also at ones who have been in this status for longer than a year or two. There are still few efforts to look at families longitudinally, although several studies have been intensive and have extended over a brief period (Belle, 1982; Colletta, 1978). Finally, as will be seen, very little of the research is programmatic, nor has any of it been stimulated by systematic application of psychological theory.

Depression and Stress

Depression and stress are central to many of these women's lives, particularly for those who are poor (Belle, 1982; Pearlin & Johnson, 1977). Depression is the number one mental health problem for women under 45 (Merekengas, 1985; Walker, 1982). Various levels of depression, feelings of guilt and worthlessness, helplessness, despair, retarded activity, and change in eating or sleeping patterns were found by Belle and her colleagues (1982) in their study of poor women, two-thirds of whom were single parents. This depression apparently was caused by impoverishment and powerlessness, rather than marital status per se. The women viewed the mental health establishment as no real help, and the help they did receive appeared to reinforce self-blame, hardly a way out of depression (Belle & Dill, 1982). Similar findings were reported by Verbrugge (cited by Sales & Frieze, 1984), who found that role reduction and lack of control over life situations led to poor health and to depression.

It is hardly surprising that money problems have been found to be stressors (Pett, 1982). Keith and Schafer (1982) found that depression, even for employed divorced women, was linked to a low income level. Colletta (1979) compared the stress levels of low- and middle-income employed single mothers of preschoolers. These women reported many more areas of stress than a married control group, but income level made an impressive difference in their reported amount and source of stress and in the general quality of their lives. The single women with more income, even though it was an amount that hardly lifted them above the poverty level, said that they were very satisfied with their work and reported less stress than the low-income group.

Bould (1977) found that level of personal control was related to income. She studied a sample of families for whom single-mother status was a relatively permanent condition and who had had some time to adjust financially and psychologically. She found that the extent to which their income was controllable, stable, and free of stigmatization was more strongly predictive of level of personal control than was amount of income. "The mother who fully assumed both roles and earned her family's support was more likely to be better off than the mother who stayed home" (p. 348). This conclusion held for the black as well as the white women in her sample. Other investigators have reported that single mothers feel relatively powerless (Smith, 1980), a finding that suggests why welfare in its present form has negative personal consequences. Marshall (1985) reported that poor women typically consider all other alternatives before turning to AFDC welfare support.

Sense of control over income and feelings of efficacy as self-supporters have been found to be significant predictors of life satisfaction and absence of stress (Colletta, 1979; Kazak & Linney, 1983; Makosky, 1982; McAdoo, 1983; Ritchie, 1980). Kohen et al. (1979), in an intensive qualitative study, found that a sense of power and authority in her own domain was a positive factor for the female head of household.

The Michigan Panel Study of Income Dynamics longitudinal data were used by McLanahan (1983) to study the relationship of stress and family structure.[2] Three types of stress—the presence of chronic life strains, the occurrence of major life events, and the absence of social and psychological supports—were compared in male-headed and single-parent families. There was a higher incidence of major life events for single than for married families. These included decrease in family income, voluntary and involuntary job changes, household moves, and illness. McLanahan also found striking differences in amount of psychological support, with single mothers reporting much lower levels; in addition, they had lower self-esteem, lower feelings of efficacy, and greater pessimism. Furthermore, as the years passed, stressful life events increased, most notably after three years. Black women were more likely than white women to remain single, as were those who were less educated, illustrating the greater vulnerability of these groups.

The stress of life conditions as well as of life events was examined by Makosky (1982) as part of the Harvard Stress and Families Project (Belle, 1982). To a standard life-events survey, she added items germane to women's lives, such as rape, having an abortion, change in childcare arrangements, and going on welfare. The Revised Life Events Measure produced a life-events score for this sample that was significantly higher than any previously reported score. In addition, life conditions, such as low and unpredictable income, especially when these had been experienced for the previous two years, were found to be more predictive of stress, depression, anxiety, and poor self-esteem than were life events.

The loosely related group of studies that have looked at determinants of stress and depression indicate that, although single mothers are at risk, some experience positive outcomes. The favorable outcomes seem to relate to level of income and to other conditions that allow them to reduce the sense of powerlessness and increase areas of control in their lives.

Social Supports and Social Networks

Available help from relatives reduces the effects of stressors on single-mother families (Giovanni & Billingsley, cited by McAdoo, 1985). However for divorced single mothers, under some circumstances, support may also have negative consequences. Belle and her colleagues (1982) found that for low-income mothers, "social ties proved to be a two-edged sword, associated with important forms of assistance and emotional support and yet also associated with worries, upset and concern" (p. 142). Belle attributed part of the strain to the unalterable dependency involved. Thus, to the extent that low-income women must depend on relatives for support, she argued, they find such support to be a source of stress as well. If relatives and friends are supportive emotionally as well as materially, their presence and proximity do have a positive effect; but otherwise, such social ties can cause additional stress.

Colletta (1979) found that low-income mothers' satisfaction with support was related to their perceptions of need and of amount of stress in their lives, rather than to amount of support per se. Perceived support from community services was greater for these women than perceived social support; they especially appreciated help with daily coping and with finances.

Other studies of single mothers have found that perceived size of and satisfaction with their social network and social support predicts their social adjustment (Pett, 1982), but not maternal role satisfaction (Bowen, 1982). McLanahan, Wedemeyer, and Adelberg (1981) reported on the varied nature of networks and supports. Weinraub and Wolf's (1983) study of middle-class families concluded that single mothers were more socially isolated, received less emotional support, and had less stable social networks than their married counterparts. But support availability enhanced parental effectiveness, regardless of marital status.

Eger, Sarkissian, Brady, and Hartmann (1985) found that mothers living in an isolated Australian suburb, whether single or not, were depressed, passive, and had low self-esteem. The creation of a political-action support network radically changed the quality of life and level of psychological well-being for women in this study.

In sum, studies of social support and social networks appear to point to their generally positive features, although the type of support and extent of control over the process make a difference in their effects. . . .

Work and the Single Parent

The consistent association of income level with indicators of well-being, satisfaction, and lack of depression or stress is, as we have seen, moderated by psychological factors, most notably controllability, stability, and feelings of self-sufficiency. As the best way to be in control of the source of one's income and to feel self-sufficient is to have good employment, we should look next at studies that have examined work issues and the single mother.

The economic consequences of mothers being single, or of leaving a marriage, and the effect of welfare on labor-market behavior and marital stability have been of great concern, especially to economists, demographers, and other social researchers with an interest in public policy (Danziger, Jakobson, Schwartz, & Smolensky, 1982; Hoffman, 1977; Levitan & Belous, 1981; Mudrick, 1978; Schorr & Moen, 1984). Few of these economic studies raise psychological questions about work, but they contain some striking findings, such as that women chose work over welfare (Hoffman, 1977), and that 80% of the divorced and separated women in the Michigan Panel Study sample were employed, a figure that was similar for white and black respondents. The significance of work was also stressed by Bergmann and Roberts (1984), who developed a model that predicted that women would be less likely to be on AFDC and more likely to work if the federal government enforced fathers' child support payments. In their view, the enactment of such government enforcement in 1985 is important because it recognizes that fathers, as well as mothers, have economic responsibility for their children.

The conclusion that a *predictable* source of income and meaningful work lead to positive mental health consequences for single mothers is unavoidable. Yet apart from effects of level and source of income, we know very little about the meaning of work for single mothers. We have little idea how the kind of work, structure of worklife patterns, motivation, aspiration, or satisfaction on the job relate to the quality of their lives. Although many investigators have indicated that their women respondents were employed, detailed questions about psychological aspects of their work have rarely been asked. . . .

Tebbets (1982), as part of the aforementioned Harvard Stress and Families Project (Belle, 1982), found that even its sample of poor women had great interest and involvement in their work. Their work patterns varied; participation was tied to timing of births and number of children, and past and current work status was contingent upon other life commitments and experiences. For instance, women were more likely to be working currently if they were older when they had their first child, if they had fewer children, fewer preschoolers, and higher levels of education. Work was important for their emotional as well as financial health. Women who had held more jobs, had worked more in recent years, or were currently working were less depressed than those who wanted to work but were unemployed. Sales and Frieze (1984) stressed the positive consequences of work, especially for mothers of young children. These women were found to be less depressed and less lonely if they had employment outside the home (Stewart & Salt, 1981, cited by Sales & Frieze, 1984).

Other studies have found that single mothers thrive in rewarded and rewarding work roles in spite of their other life problems. Baruch et al. (1984) found employment to be good for women's sense of well-being and life satisfaction. The single parents in their study—in spite of great role overload and role conflict— were as satisfied with life as married women were. Monaghan-Leckband's (1978) single mothers, who reported role conflict in relation to "instrumental leadership of the family," did not report that work was a source of such strain. Although employed single mothers were found by Keith and Shafer (1982) to be depressed by work-family role strain, assistance with domestic tasks and childcare served as buffers.

Kazak and Linney (1983) reported that the "self-supporter" role is an important factor in level of life satisfaction of employed divorced mothers of minor children. The length of time since divorce enhanced this relationship; for those divorced more than three years, the self-supporter role was a more potent contributor to reported life satisfaction than either parenting or social roles.

Yet there are work circumstances that are stressful. McAdoo (1985) found, for employed black single mothers with a modal income at the poverty level, that work was a source of stress. Specifically, the mother role and work role were often reported as being in conflict. However, the stress level was reduced when mothers used a coping style that involved a redefinition of employers' expectations (e.g., refusing to work overtime because a child had to be picked up from daycare by a certain time). This method of coping, which increased level of control over a particular condition, was more effective than coping that involved relinquishing one of the roles (see also Harrison & Minor, 1982).

In a major survey of employed working mothers, Michelson (1983) found that mothers who felt that they had been forced into full-time employment were tense and unhappy. For others, tensions were due to the logistics of getting to work and of arranging for childcare. Time-pressure stress was found to be less for single mothers *"due to the absence of demands from a spouse"* (italics added, p. xi); and even with greater daily household responsibility and less relative overall satisfaction than married women, their self-image still benefited from employment.

Baruch et al. (1983) found, for the middle-class single mothers they studied, that amount of money earned and how well a woman felt she could support herself were important determinants of well-being. These women felt their careers and education had benefited by their divorce, and their employment appeared to buffer stress. Although concerned about loneliness and social isolation, they were positive about themselves in terms of mastery, growth in skills, and competence.

In sum, these few studies show how single mothers can benefit from having meaningful work, even though their daily life may become more complex and strained.

Gender Roles

Most of the research we have been discussing indirectly touches on gender roles, yet few studies have directly assessed single mothers' views about such roles or about gender identity.

Expectations about marital roles were examined by Ganvold, Pedler, and Schellie (1979) in a study of employed women. They found that egalitarian marriage role expectations were related to high acceptance of self and low levels of social anxiety for single mothers. Wedemeyer and Johnson (1982), studying gender role beliefs and post-divorce adjustment, found that traditional views generally prevailed. Thus, custodial mothers were more interested in their children than their work, whereas the reverse held for custodial fathers. Yet the women derived pleasure from the autonomy that work provided, even in the face of reduced financial circumstances.

Autonomy, authority, and power are not congruent with traditional family roles for women, yet these characteristics have been cited as an important source of positive feelings for single mothers (Baruch et al., 1983; Belle, 1982; Kohen et al., 1979; Ritchie, 1980; Weiss, 1979). As mentioned earlier, Kazak and Linney (1983) found that perceived competence as a self-supporter was a stronger predictor of life satisfaction than perceived competence in the parenting role. At the same time, the self-supporter role was also an area of low perceived competence, reflecting the fact that the role of economic provider was not traditional for these women and was therefore fraught with concerns. Still, as one of Baruch et al.'s (1983) single mothers stated, "There's one thing for sure. Every woman has to think absolutely like a man. She has to be prepared to support herself and others because the reality is that we still have the babies—and we will have to be able to support ourselves" (p. 198).

My search unearthed only two reports that applied the much-studied concept of androgyny. Custodial mothers of children aged 10–19 were more likely to be androgynous on the Bem Sex Role Inventory (BSRI) than a college student normative group, and were more likely to score high on the BSRI masculinity scale than married mothers. The researchers suggested that the demands of single-parent functioning may explain these scores (Kundek & Siesky, 1980). An androgynous self-concept was found to be related to the role satisfaction of single mothers by Ballard (1981).

Carr (1982), as part of a study of the development of achievement motivation in young black children, found that black single mothers, regardless of class, were more likely to report atypical sex-role socialization of their children than were married mothers. Mothers of boys reported more conventional attitudes than mothers of girls.

These issues are significant because the struggle with the common assumptions about legitimate power in the family and in relation to society is a central task for these women, one that involves serious incongruence with women's sex role stereotyping. Typically, society perceives women to be

> deficient in those qualities that are required for leadership . . . such as . . . rational thinking, assertiveness, competitiveness and aggression. . . . Such an ideology supports the relegation of women to supportive roles and creates negative expectations of their abilities to function in circumstances requiring . . . "male qualities." (Engram, 1982, p. 73)

Single mothers are probably particularly undermined by gender role expectations, and these issues have hardly been touched.

Parenting Role

Colletta (1979) found single mothers of sons or of two children to be the most stressed in her sample. The debilitating effect of boys on solo mothers has also been reported by Hetherington, Cox, and Cox (1979), who showed that recently divorced mothers of boys were less in control of the children's behavior than were girls' mothers or married mothers. They summarized,

> The divorced mother is harassed by her children, particularly her sons. . . . Her children in the first year don't obey, affiliate or attend to her. . . . The aggression of boys with divorced mothers peaks at one year (after divorce) . . . then drops significantly, but it is still higher than that of boys in intact families at two years. (p. 35)

These authors speak of the role of divorced mothers as being intrinsically that of victim, particularly when there are problems and a consequent loss of control over outcomes.

Draper's (1982) study examining personal locus of control has some bearing on this. He found that older single mothers with several children, including a son under three years of age, were more external than married mothers or than single mothers of girls. He speculated that boys' aggressivity may affect the mothers' emotional well-being and that son-rearing is thus harder than daughter-rearing. He further suggested that fathers are needed to check their sons' aggression. Hetherington et al. (1979) cite a study by Patterson that suggests an alternative explanation, one less rooted in gender-based beliefs about boys' immutable aggressivity and mothers' inability to "check it." Patterson found that mothers and children get involved in a vicious cycle of coercion:

> The lack of management skills of the mother accelerates the child's aversive behavior, of which she is the main instigator and target. This is reciprocated by increased coercion in the mother's parenting behavior and induces feelings of helplessness, depression, anger, and self-doubt in the mother. (Hetherington et al., 1979, p. 121)

These authors tested the Patterson hypothesis with their mothers and found that children's behavior, especially sons' aggression, resulted in more trait and state anxiety, low feelings of competence, low self-esteem, depression, and feelings of external control.

There is some evidence that mothers are rewarded less by their children than are fathers. Ambert (1982) found that children differ in their attitude about custodial mothers and fathers and are much more likely to express appreciation of fathers than of mothers.

The hopeful view that stress in parenting is not inevitable and that it subsides over time was emphasized by Kohen et al. (1979). They concluded that for their sample, the conflict-free nature of the divorced mother's authority in the family had led to improved mother-child relationships.

In spite of increased and changed responsibilities and the need to manage parenting in a nontraditional manner, single parents like being parents, are generally satisfied, and feel competent (Baruch et al., 1983; Belle, 1982; Kazak & Linney, 1983; Kohen et al., 1979; Weiss, 1979). A study by Fine et al. (1985) compared maternal satisfaction for different groups of employed mothers. On their Reactions to Motherhood Scale, they found that white single mothers were less satisfied with their motherhood experience than black single mothers or married mothers; their study was unenlightening about why this might be, but it should be noted that the general level of satisfaction was high.

These studies provide a few ideas about single mothering, but much more research is needed. A recent reviewer of family interaction research noted that no studies have compared time spent with children in two-parent and single-parent families. Her radical suggestion that children get more undivided attention in single-parent households, and may therefore do better, remains a hypothesis that begs to be tested (Scarr, 1984).

Another virtually untested set of questions concerns the effects of societal prejudice upon the single mother's role as a parent. Even though stigmatization is on the decline (Baruch et al., 1983; Weiss, 1979), the poor women interviewed by Belle (1982) and Colletta (1979) spoke of problems with bias in the social system. Work by Santrock and Tracy (1978) suggests that this perception may be based on reality. They had teachers view videotapes of the social interactions of an eight-year-old boy. His behavior was rated less positively when the teachers were told he was from a single-parent home than when he was described as being from a two-parent home. A question that must also be asked is how mothers, who must deal with teachers and other school authorities, are affected by the messages they receive in such contacts. Social psychologists who study attitudes, prejudice, stigma, and discrimination can play an important role here. The hypothesis that, like sexism and racism, dogmas of motherism and familism create hostile social environments for single mothers, and add to the mentally unhealthy and uncontrollable character of their lives, needs to be tested.

Conclusions

The past decade has produced research that reflects changing beliefs and values about single mothers, and investigators with nontraditional views about women's place and the meaning of family have made a contribution. Studies have moved from assumptions about deviant family forms and psychopathology to consideration of the hypothesis that good adjustment, well-being, and satisfaction with life are possible for single mothers. Furthermore, the determinants of good outcomes are being explored (Belle, 1982; Kohen et al., 1979). Recognition that many of these women are not in a transition stage, and that they are not one homogeneous group, has also had an impact. The category "female single parent" is now less likely to be confounded with other person variables, such as race and class. This unconfounding has led to new interpretations, as when depression or stress is understood as the result of poverty and all of its concomitants, rather than simply being due to single-parent status per se (Belle, 1982; Colletta, 1978). We also know there are many other sources of variation in single mothers' adjustment, such as coping styles (Belle, 1982; Harrison & Minor, 1982; McAdoo, 1985), life conditions (Makosky, 1982), and type and source of social support networks.

Yet social and personal views about gender roles and gender identity are deeply embedded and continue to affect what is studied. For instance, although a number of studies have found that good employment enhances well-being and that the meaning of work in single mothers' lives is an important factor in adjustment, relatively few studies have considered work and work attitudes as an important class of psychological variables, nor has any research attention been paid to the possibility that under some circumstances women will choose single-mother status as a positive alternative. It appears that gender role assumptions, especially about "mother at home," "husband as economic provider," and "nuclear family as the hallmark of normalcy," are still affecting research approaches. Nevertheless, research on parenting has finally begun to move to a new and more differentiated set of questions about sex-role socialization, about the effects of mothers and children on each other, about differences in the mothering of boys and girls, and about parenting efficacy and authority.

The future agenda of psychological study of the family must, of course, include the single-mother family form. This review has suggested that at least a portion of such work should be planned as a systematic exploration of the usefulness of control, efficacy, and gender-role concepts in explaining outcomes in two major role areas, that of parent and of self-supporter. Adequate research on single mothers demands methodology and conceptualizations that take account of the social context in which single mothers live.

Policy Implications

Finally, we should remember that research on single mothers had important public policy implications; it does not take place in a social vacuum. Schorr and Moen (1984) showed how public policy about single mothers has been shaped by the same biases that have affected the research. Thus, AFDC and workfare programs for the poor (mothers) are also grounded in the assumption that women's place is in the home and that families should be kept intact or reconstituted. As we have seen, the reality for many women, especially for those over 30 and for black women, is that remarriage is unlikely. Such policies also ignore the idea that, given a real choice economically, many women would not choose to remarry.

The research and findings based on alternative assumptions about the family can direct a search for alternative policy recommendations. The recognition that single motherhood is a fact of life and not necessarily one with negative personal or social consequences has already affected recent research on single mothers. It should be brought to bear more fully in future work, and it may perhaps lead to more appropriate policy recommendations.

Notes

1. A family household is defined by the U.S. Census Bureau as one that has two or more related persons, one of whom owns or rents the living quarters. A female-headed household is so designated when there is no husband present (U.S. Department of Commerce, 1983, p. 1). In this [paper], we are concerned with female-headed households with minor children present.
2. The Michigan Panel Study data used in this way must be interpreted with caution, as only men were interviewed in the first round.

References

Ambert, A. (1982). Differences in children's behavior toward custodial mothers and custodial fathers. *Journal of Marriage and the Family, 44,* 73–86.

Ballard, B. (1981). *Role satisfaction of divorced mothers in single parent families as a function of social networks and sex-role orientation.* Unpublished doctoral dissertation, California School of Professional Psychology, Berkeley.

Baruch, G., Barnett, R., & Rivers, C. (1983). *Lifeprints: New patterns of love and work for today's women.* New York: McGraw-Hill.

Belle, D. (1982). *Lives in stress: Women and depression.* Beverly Hills, CA: Sage.

Belle, D., & Dill, D. (1982). Research methods and sample characteristics. In D. Belle (Ed.), *Lives in stress: Women and depression.* Beverly Hills, CA: Sage.

Bergmann, B. R., & Roberts, M. D. (1984). *Income for the single parent: Work, child support, and welfare* (Working paper 84–12). Department of Economics, University of Maryland.

Bould, S. (1977). Female-headed families: Personal fate control and the provider role. *Journal of Marriage and the Family, 39,* 339–349.

Bowen, G. L. (1982). Social networks and the maternal role satisfaction of formerly-married mothers. *Journal of Divorce, 5,* 77–85.

Brandwein, A., Brown, A., & Fox, M. (1974) Women and children last: The social situation of divorced mothers and their families. *Journal of Marriage and the Family, 36,* 498–514.

Burlage, D. (1978). *Divorced and separated mothers: Combining the responsibilities of breadwinning and child rearing.* Unpublished doctoral dissertation, Harvard University.

Carr, P. (1982). *Family background and the socialization of achievement motivation in girls and boys.* Unpublished doctoral dissertation, Howard University.

Colletta, N. D. (1979). The impact of divorces: Father absence or poverty. *Journal of Divorce, 3,* 27–34.

Danziger, S., Jakubson, G., Schwartz, S., & Smolensky, E. (1982). Work and welfare as determinants of female poverty and household headship. *Quarterly Journal of Economics,* 320–334.

Draper, T. W. (1982). Sons, mothers, and externality: Is there a father effect? *Child Study Journal, 12,* 271–280.

Eger, R., Sarkissian, W., Brady, D., & Hartmann, L. (1985). Reviewing the Australian suburban dream: A unique approach to neighborhood change with the family support scheme. In M. Safir, M. T. Mednick, D. Izraeli, J. Bernard (Eds.), *Women's worlds: From the new scholarship.* New York: Praeger.

Engram, E. (1982). *Science, myth, reality: The black family in one-half century of research.* Westport, CT: Greenwood.

Fine, M. A., Schwebel, A. I., & Myers, C. J. (1985). The effects of world view on adaption to single parenthood among middle-class women. *Journal of Family Issues, 6,* 107–127.

Granvold, D. K., Pedler, C. M., & Schellie, S. G. (1979). A study of sex role expectancy and female post divorce adjustment. *Journal of Divorce, 2,* 283–293.

Harrison, A. O., & Minor, J. H. (1982). Interrole conflict, coping strategies, and role satisfaction among single and married employed mothers. *Psychology of Women Quarterly, 6,* 354–360.

Hetherington, E. M., Cox, M., & Cox, R. (1979). Stress and coping in divorce: A focus on women. In J. Gullahorn (Ed.), *Psychology and women in transition.* Washington, D.C.: Winston.

Hoffman, S. (1977). Marital instability and the economic status of women. *Demography, 14,* 67–76.

Kazak, A. E., & Linney, J. A. (1983). Stress, coping, and life-changes in the single-parent family. *American Journal of Community Psychology, 11,* 207–220.

Keith, P. M., & Schafer, R. B. (1982). A comparison of depression among employed single-parent and married women. *Journal of Psychology, 110,* 239–247.

Kohen, J. A., Brown, C. A., & Feldberg, R. (1979). Divorced mothers: The costs and benefits of family controlling. In G. Levinger & O. C. Moles (Eds.), *Divorce and separation.* New York: Basic Books.

Kundek, C. A., & Siesky, A. E., Jr. (1980). Sex role self-concepts of single divorced parents and their children. *Journal of Divorce, 3,* 249–261.

Levitan, S., & Belous, R. S. (1981). *What's happening to the American family?* Baltimore: Johns Hopkins University Press.

Makosky, V. P. (1982). Sources of stress: Events or conditions? In D. Belle (Ed.), *Lives in stress: Women and depression.* Beverly Hills, CA: Sage.

Marshall, N. (1985, March). *Welfare mothers.* Paper presented at Henry A. Murray Research Center, Radcliffe College.

McAdoo, H. P. (1981). *Black families.* Beverly Hills, CA: Sage.

McAdoo, H. P. (1985, May). *Stress levels and coping strategies used by single mothers.* Paper presented at Radcliffe College Conference on Women's Mental Health in Social Context.

McLanahan, S. S. (1983). Family structure and stress: A longitudinal comparison of two-parent and female-headed families. *Journal of Marriage and the Family, 45,* 347–357.

McLanahan, S. S., Wedemeyer, N. V., & Adelberg, T. (1981). Network structure, social support and psychological well-being in the single parent family. *Journal of Marriage and the Family, 43,* 601–612.

Mednick, M. T. (1982). Women and the psychology of achievement: Implications for personal and social change. In J. H. Bernardin (Ed.), *Women in the work force.* New York: Praeger.

Merekengas, K. (1985, May). *Sex differences in depression.* Paper presented at Radcliffe College Conference on Women's Mental Health in Social Context.

Michelson, W. (1983). *The logistics of maternal employment: Implications for women and their families* (Child in the City Report No. 18). Toronto: Ministry of National Health and Welfare.

Monaghan-Leckband, K. (1979). *Role adaptations of single parents: A challenge of the pathological view of male and female single parents.* Unpublished doctoral dissertation. New York University.

Mudrick, N. R. (1978). Note on policy and practice: The use of AFDC by previously high and low income households. *Social Service Review,* 107–115.

Pearce, D. (1978). The feminization of poverty: Women, work and welfare. *Urban and Social Change, 2,* 24–36.

Pearlin, L. T., & Johnson, J. (1977). Marital status, life strains, and depression. *American Sociological Review, 42,* 704–715.

Pett, M. G. (1982). Predictors of satisfactory social adjustment of divorced single parents. *Journal of Divorce, 5,* 1–17.

Ritchie, J. (1980). Characteristics of a sample of solo mothers. *New Zealand Medical Journal,* 349–352.

Ross, H. C., & Sawhill, I. V. (1975). *Time of transition: The growth of families headed by women.* Washington, D.C.: Urban Institute.

Sales, E., & Frieze, I. H. (1984). Women and work: Implications for mental health. In L. E. Walker (Ed.), *Women and mental health policy.* Beverly Hills, CA: Sage.

Santrock, J. W., & Tracy, R. L. (1978). The effects of children's family structure status on the development of stereotypes by teachers. *Journal of Education Psychology, 70,* 754–757.

Scarr, S. (1984). *Mother care, other care.* New York: Basic Books.

Schorr, A. C., & Moen, P. (1984). The single parent and public policy. In P. Voydanoff (Ed.), *Work and family: Changing roles of men and women.* Palo Alto, CA: Mayfield.

Smith, M. J. (1980). The social consequences of single parenthood: A longitudinal perspective. *Family Relations, 29,* 75–81.

Tebbets, R. (1982). Work: Its meaning for women's lives. In D. Belle (Ed.), *Lives in stress: Women and depression.* Beverly Hills, CA: Sage.

U.S. Commission on Civil Rights. (1983). *A growing crisis: Disadvantaged women and their children.* Washington, D.C.: Clearinghouse Publications.

U.S. Department of Commerce, Bureau of the Census. (1983). *Households, families, marital status and living arrangements* (Series P-20, no. 382). Washington, D.C.: Author.

Walker, L. E. (1984). *Women and mental health policy.* Beverly Hills, CA: Sage.

Wedemeyer, N. V., & Johnson, J. M. (1982). Learning the single-parent role: Overcoming marital-role influence. *Journal of Divorce, 5,* 41–53.

Weinraub, M., & Wolf, B. M. (1983). Effects of stress and social supports on mother-child interactions in single- and two-parent families. *Child Development, 54,* 1297–1311.

Weiss, R. S. (1979). *Going it alone: The family life and social situation of the single parent.* New York: Basic Books.

The Medicalization and Legalization of Child Abuse

Eli H. Newberger and Richard Bourne

Child abuse has emerged in the last fifteen years as a visible and important social problem. Although a humane approach to "help" for both victims of child abuse and their families has developed (and is prominently expressed in the title of one of the more influential books on the subject[29]), a theoretical framework to integrate the diverse origins and expressions of violence toward children and to inform a rational clinical practice does not exist. Furthermore, so inadequate are the "helping" services in most communities, so low the standard of professional action, and so distressing the consequences of incompetent intervention for the family that we and others have speculated that punishment is being inflicted in the guise of help.[3, 28]

What factors encourage theoretical confusion and clinical inadequacy? We propose that these consequences result, in part, from medical and legal ambiguity concerning child abuse and from two fundamental, and in some ways irreconcilable, dilemmas about social policy and the human and technical response toward families in crisis. We call these dilemmas *family autonomy versus coercive intervention* and *compassion versus control.*

This paper will consider these dilemmas in the context of a critical sociologic perspective on child abuse management. Through the cognitive lens of social labeling theory, we see symptoms of family crisis, and certain manifestations of childhood injury, "medicalized" and "legalized" and called "child abuse," to be diagnosed, reported, treated, and adjudicated by doctors and lawyers, their constituent institutions, and the professionals who depend on them for their social legitimacy and support.

From the *American Journal of Orthopsychiatry,* Vol. 48, No. 4 (October1978), pp. 593–607.

We are mindful, as practitioners, of the need for prompt, effective, and creative professional responses to child abuse. Our critical analysis of the relationship of professional work to the societal context in which it is embedded is meant to stimulate attention to issues that professionals ignore to their and their clients' ultimate disadvantage. We mean not to disparage necessary efforts to help and protect children and their families.

How children's rights—as opposed to parents' rights—may be defined and protected is currently the subject of vigorous, and occasionally rancorous, debate.

The *family autonomy* vs. *coercive intervention* dilemma defines the conflict central to our ambiguity about *whether* society should intervene in situations of risk to children. The traditional autonomy of the family in rearing its offspring was cited by the majority of the U.S. Supreme Court in its ruling against the severely beaten appellants in the controversial "corporal punishment" case *(Ingraham* vs. *Wright et al.).*[25] The schools, serving *in loco parentis,* are not, in effect, constrained constitutionally from any punishment, however cruel.

Yet in California, a physician seeing buttock bruises of the kind legally inflicted by the teacher in the Miami public schools risks malpractice action if he fails to report his observations as symptoms of child abuse *(Landeros* vs. *Flood).*[32] He and his hospital are potentially liable for the cost of the child's subsequent injury and handicap if they do not initiate protective measures.[7]

This dilemma is highlighted by the recently promulgated draft statute of the American Bar Association's Juvenile Justice Standards Project, which, citing the low prevailing quality of protective child welfare services in the U.S., would sharply *restrict* access to such services.[28] The Commission would, for example, make the reporting of child neglect discretionary rather than mandatory, and would narrowly define the bases for court jurisdiction to situations where there is clear harm to a child.

Our interpretation of this standard is that it would make matters worse, not better, for children and their families.[3] So long as we are deeply conflicted about the relation of children to the state as well as to the family, and whether children have rights independent of their parents', we shall never be able to articulate with clarity *how* to enforce them.

The *compassion* vs. *control* dilemma has been postulated and reviewed in a previous paper,[47] which discussed the conceptual and practical problems implicit in the expansion of the clinical and legal definitions of child abuse to include practically every physical and emotional risk to children. The dilemma addresses a conflict central to the present ambiguity about *how* to protect children from their parents.

Parental behavior that might be characterized as destructive or criminal were it directed towards an adult has come to be seen and interpreted by those involved in its identification and treatment in terms of the psychosocial economy of the family. Embracive definitions reflect a change in the orientation of professional practice. To the extent to which we understand abusing parents as sad, deprived, needy human beings (rather than as cold, cruel murderers) we can sympathize with their plight and compassionately proffer supports and services to aid them in their struggle. Only with dread may we contemplate strong intervention (such as court action) on the child's behalf, for want of alienating our clients.

Notwithstanding the humane philosophy of treatment, society cannot, or will not, commit resources nearly commensurate with the exponentially increasing number of case reports that have followed the promulgation of the expanded definitions. The helping language betrays a deep conflict, and even ill will, toward children and parents in trouble, whom society and professionals might sooner punish and control.

We are forced frequently in practice to identify and choose the "least detrimental alternative" for the child[21] because the family supports that make it safe to keep children in their homes (homemakers, child care, psychiatric and medical services) are never available in sufficient amounts and quality.

That we should guide our work by a management concept named "least detrimental alternative" for children suggests at least a skepticism about the utility of these supports, just as the rational foundation for child welfare work is called into question by the title of the influential book from which the concept comes, *Beyond the Best Interests of the Child.*[21] More profoundly, the concept taps a vein of emotional confusion about our progeny, to whom we express both kindness and love with hurt.

Mounting attention to the developmental sequelae of child abuse[16, 33] stimulates an extra urgency not only to insure the physical safety of the identified victims but also to enable their adequate psychological development. The dangers of child abuse, according to Schmitt and Kempe in the latest edition of the Nelson Textbook of Pediatrics,[53] extend beyond harm to the victim:

> If the child who has been physically abused is returned to his parents without intervention, 5 per cent are killed and 35 per cent are seriously reinjured. Moreover, the untreated families tend to produce children who grow up to be juvenile delinquents and murderers, as well as the batterers of the next generation.

Despite the speculative nature of such conclusions about the developmental sequelae of child abuse,[6, 10, 11] such warnings support a practice of separating children from their natural homes in the interest of their and society's protection. They focus professional concern and public wrath on "the untreated families" and may justify punitive action to save us from their children.

This professional response of control rather than of compassion furthermore generalizes mainly to poor and socially marginal families, for it is they who seem preferentially to attract the labels "abuse" and "neglect" to their problems in the public settings where they go for most health and social services.[36] Affluent families' childhood injuries appear more likely to be termed "accidents" by the private practitioners who offer them their services. The conceptual model of cause and effect implicit in the name "accident" is benign: an isolated, random event rather than a consequence of parental commission or omission.[37, 38]

Table 1.   Dilemmas of Social Policy and Professional Response

Response	Family autonomy	versus	Coercive intervention
Compassion ("support")	1. Voluntary child development services 2. Guaranteed family supports: e.g., income, housing, health services		1. Case reporting of family crisis and mandated family intervention 2. Court-ordered delivery of services
Versus			
Control ("punishment")	1. "Laissez-faire": No assured services or supports 2. Retributive response to family crisis		1. Court action to separate child from family 2. Criminal prosecution of parents

Table 1 presents a graphic display of the two dilemmas of social policy (*family autonomy* vs. *coercive intervention*) and professional response (*compassion* vs. *control*). The four-fold table illustrates possible action responses. For purposes of this discussion, it is well to think of "compassion" as signifying responses of support, such as provision of voluntary counseling and child care services, and "control" as signifying such punitive responses as "blaming the victim" for his or her reaction to social realities[49] and as the criminal prosecution of abusing parents.

Child Abuse and the Medical and Legal Professions

The importance of a technical discipline's conceptual structure in defining how it approaches a problem has been clearly stated by Mercer:[34]

> Each discipline is organized around a core of basic concepts and assumptions which form the frame of reference from which persons trained in that discipline view the world and set about solving problems in their field. The concepts and assumptions which make up the perspective of each discipline give each its distinctive character and are the intellectual tools used by its practitioners. These tools are incorporated in action and problem solving and appear self-evident to persons socialized in the discipline. As a result, little consideration is likely to be given to the social consequence of applying a particular conceptual work to problem solving.

> When the issues to be resolved are clearly in the area of competence of a single discipline, the automatic application of its conceptual tools is likely to go unchallenged. However, when the problems under consideration lie in the interstices between disciplines, the disciplines concerned are likely to define the situation differently and may arrive at differing conclusions which have dissimilar implications for social action.

What we do when children are injured in family crises is shaped also by how our professions respond to the interstitial area called "child abuse."

"Medicalization"

Though cruelty to children has occurred since documentary records of mankind have been kept,[9] it became a salient social problem in the United States only after the publication by Kempe and his colleagues describing the "battered child syndrome."[30] In the four-year period after this medical article appeared, the legislatures of all 50 states, stimulated partly by a model law developed under the aegis of the Children's Bureau of the U.S. Department of Health, Education, and Welfare, passed statutes mandating the identification and reporting of suspected victims of abuse.

Once the specific category "battered child syndrome" was applied to integrate a set of medical symptoms, and laws were passed making the syndrome reportable, the problem was made a proper and legitimate concern for the medical profession. Conrad has discussed cogently how "hyperactivity" came officially to be known and how it became "medicalized."[5] Medicalization is defined in this paper as the perception of behavior as a medical problem or illness and the mandating or licensing of the medical profession to provide some type of treatment for it.

Pfohls[41] associated the publicity surrounding the battered child syndrome report with a phenomenon of "discovery" of child abuse. For radiologists, the potential for increased prestige, role expansion, and coalition formation (with psychodynamic psychiatry and pediatrics) may have encouraged identification and intervention in child abuse. Furthermore,

> . . . the discovery of abuse as a new "illness" reduced drastically the intra-organizational constraints on doctors' "seeing" abuse . . . Problems associated with perceiving parents as patients whose confidentiality must be protected were reconstructed by typifying them as patients who needed help . . . The maintenance of professional autonomy was assured by pairing deviance with sickness . . .

In some ways, medicine's "discovery" of abuse has benefited individual physicians and the profession.

> One of the greatest ambitions of the physician is to discover or describe a "new" disease or syndrome.[24]

By such involvement the doctor becomes a moral entrepreneur defining what is normal, proper, or desirable; he becomes charged "with inquisitorial powers to discover certain wrongs to be righted."[24] New opportunities for the application of traditional methods are also found—for example, the systematic screening of suspected victims with a skeletal X-ray survey to detect previous fractures, and the recent report in the neurology literature suggesting the utility of diphenylhydantoin* treatment for child abusing parents.[46]

---

*Dilantin, a commonly-used seizure suppressant.

Pfohl's provocative analysis also took note of some of the normative and structural elements within the medical profession that appear to have reinforced a *reluctance* on the part of some physicians to become involved: the norm of confidentiality between doctor and patient and the goal of professional autonomy.[41] For many physicians, child abuse is a subject to avoid.[50]

First, it is difficult to distinguish, on a theoretical level, corporal punishment that is "acceptable" from that which is "illegitimate." Abuse may be defined variably even by specialists, the definitions ranging from serious physical injury to nonfulfillment of a child's developmental needs.[12, 19, 30]

Second, it is frequently hard to diagnose child abuse clinically. What appears on casual physical examination as bruising, for example, may turn out to be a skin manifestation of an organic blood dysfunction, or what appear to be cigarette burns may in reality be infected mosquito bites. A diagnosis of abuse may require social and psychological information about the family, the acquisition and interpretation of which may be beyond the average clinician's expertise. It may be easier to characterize the clinical complaint in terms of the child's medical symptom rather than in terms of the social, familial, and psychological forces associated with its etiology. We see daily situations where the exclusive choice of medical taxonomy actively obscures the causes of the child's symptom and restricts the range of possible interventions: examples are "subdural hematoma," which frequently occurs with severe trauma to babies' heads (the medical name means collection of blood under the *dura mater* of the brain), and "enuresis" or "encopresis" in child victims of sexual assault (medical names mean incontinence of urine or feces).

Third, child abuse arouses strong emotions. To concentrate on the narrow medical issue (the broken bone) instead of the larger familial problem (the etiology of the injury) not only allows one to avoid facing the limit of one's technical adequacy, but to shield oneself from painful feelings of sadness and anger. One can thus maintain professional detachment and avert unpleasant confrontations. The potentially alienating nature of the physician-patient interaction when the diagnosis of child abuse is made may also have a negative economic impact on the doctor, especially the physician in private practice.

"Legalization"

The legal response to child abuse is triggered by its medicalization. Child abuse reporting statutes codified a medical diagnosis into a legal framework which in many states defined official functions for courts. Immunity from civil liability was given to mandated reporters so long as reports were made in good faith; monetary penalties for failure to report were established; and familial and professional-client confidentiality privileges, except those involving attorneys, were abrogated.

Professional autonomy for lawyers was established, and status and power accrued to legal institutions. For example, the growth in the number of Care and

Protection cases* before the Boston Juvenile Court "has been phenomenal in recent years . . . four cases in 1968 and 99 in 1974, involving 175 different children."[44] Though these cases have burdened court dockets and personnel, they have also led to acknowledgement of the important work of the court. The need for this institution is enhanced because of its recognized expertise in handling special matters. Care and Protection cases are cited in response to recommendations by a prestigious commission charged with proposing reform and consolidation of the courts of Massachusetts. Child protection work in our own institution would proceed only with difficulty if access to the court were legally or procedurally constrained. Just as for the medical profession, however, there were normative and structural elements within law which urged restraint. Most important among them were the traditional presumptions and practices favoring family autonomy.

If individual lawyers might financially benefit from representing clients in matters pertaining to child abuse, they—like their physician counterparts—were personally uncertain whether or how to become involved.

> Public concern over the scope and significance of the problem of the battered child is a comparatively new phenomenon. Participation by counsel in any significant numbers in child abuse cases for juvenile or family courts is of even more recent origin. It is small wonder that the lawyer approaches participation in these cases with trepidation.[26]

Lawyers, too, feel handicapped by a need to rely on concepts from social work and psychiatry and on data from outside the traditional domain of legal knowledge and expertise. As counsel to parents, lawyers can be torn between advocacy of their clients' positions and that which advances the "best interest" of their clients' children. As counsel to the petitioner, a lawyer may have to present a case buttressed by little tangible evidence. Risk to a child is often difficult to characterize and impossible to prove.

Further problems for lawyers concerned with child abuse involve the context of intervention: whether courts or legislatures should play the major role in shaping practice and allocating resources; how much formality is desirable in legal proceedings; and the propriety of negotiation as opposed to adversary confrontation when cases come to court.

Conflicts Between Medical and Legal Perspectives

Despite the common reasons for the "medicalization" and the "legalization" of child abuse, there are several areas where the two orientations conflict:

1. *The seriousness of the risk.* To lawyers, intervention might be warranted only when abuse results in serious harm to a child. To clinicians, however, *any*

---

*Care and Protection cases are those juvenile or family court actions which potentially transfer, on a temporary or permanent basis, legal and/or physical custody of a child from his biological parents to the state.

inflicted injury might justify a protective legal response, especially if the child is very young. "The trick is to prevent the abusive case from becoming the terminal case."[14] Early intervention may prevent the abuse from being repeated or from becoming more serious.

2. *The definition of the abuser.* To lawyers, the abuser might be defined as a wrongdoer who has injured a child. To clinicians, both the abuser and child might be perceived as victims influenced by sociological and psychological factors beyond their control.[17, 35]

3. *The importance of the abuser's mental state.* To lawyers, whether the abuser intentionally or accidentally inflicted injury on a child is a necessary condition of reporting or judicial action. So-called "accidents" are less likely to trigger intervention. To clinicians, however, mental state may be less relevant, for it requires a diagnostic formulation frequently difficult or impossible to make on the basis of available data. The family dynamics associated with "accidents" in some children (*e.g.*, stress, marital conflict, and parental inattention) often resemble those linked with inflicted injury in others. They are addressed with variable clinical sensitivity and precision.

4. *The role of law.* Attorneys are proudly unwilling to accept conclusions or impressions lacking empirical corroboration. To lawyers, the law and legal institutions become involved in child abuse when certain facts fit a standard of review. To clinicians, the law may be seen as an instrument to achieve a particular therapeutic or dispositional objective (*e.g.*, the triggering of services or of social welfare involvement) even if, as is very often the case, the data to support such objectives legally are missing or ambiguous. The clinician's approach to the abuse issue is frequently subjective or intuitive *(e.g., a feeling that a family is under stress or needs help, or that a child is "at risk")*, while the lawyer demands evidence.

Doctoring and Lawyering the Disease

These potential or actual differences in orientation notwithstanding, both medicine and law have accepted in principle the therapeutic approach to child abuse.

To physicians, defining abuse as a disease or medical syndrome makes natural the treatment alternative, since both injured child and abuser are viewed as "sick"—the one, physically, the other psycholgically or socially. Therapy may, however, have retributive aspects, as pointed out with characteristic pungency by Illich:[24]

> The medical label may protect the patient from punishment only to submit him to interminable instruction, treatment, and discrimination, which are inflicted on him for his professionally presumed benefit.

Lawyers adopt a therapeutic perspective for several reasons. First, the rehabilitative ideal remains in ascendance in criminal law, especially in the juvenile and family courts which handle most child abuse cases.[1]

Second, the criminal or punitive model may not protect the child. Parents may hesitate to seek help if they are fearful of prosecution. Evidence of abuse is often insufficient to satisfy the standard of conviction "beyond all reasonable doubt" in criminal proceedings. An alleged abuser threatened with punishment and then found not guilty may feel vindicated, reinforcing the pattern of abuse. The abuser may well be legally freed from any scrutiny, and badly needed social services will not be able to be provided. Even if found guilty, the perpetrator of abuse is usually given only mild punishment, such as a short jail term or probation. If the abuser is incarcerated, the other family members may equally suffer as, for example, the relationship between spouses is undercut and child-rearing falls on one parent, or children are placed in foster home care or with relatives. Upon release from jail, the abuser may be no less violent and even more aggressive and vindictive toward the objects of abuse.

Third, the fact that child abuse was "discovered" by physicians influenced the model adopted by other professionals. As Friedson[15] noted:

> Medical definitions of deviance have come to be adopted even where there is no reliable evidence that biophysical variables "cause" the deviance or that medical treatment is any more efficacious than any other kind of management.

Weber, in addition, contended that "status" groups (e.g., physicians) generally determine the content of law.[45]

The Selective Implementation of Treatment

Medical intervention is generally encouraged by the Hippocratic ideology of treatment (the ethic that help, not harm, is given by practitioners), and by what Scheff[52] called the medical decision rule: it is better to wrongly diagnose illness and "miss" health than it is to wrongly diagnose health and "miss" illness.

Physicians, in defining aberrant behavior as a medical problem and in providing treatment, become what sociologists call agents of social control. Though the technical enterprise of the physician claims value-free power, socially marginal individuals are more likely to be defined as deviant than are others.

Characteristics frequently identified with the "battered child syndrome," such as social isolation, alcoholism, unemployment, childhood handicap, large family size, low level of parental educational achievement, and acceptance of severe physical punishment as a childhood socializing technique, are associated with social marginality and poverty.

Physicians in public settings seem, from child abuse reporting statistics, to be more likely to see and report child abuse than are those in private practice. As poor people are more likely to frequent hospital emergency wards and clinics,[36] they have much greater social visibility where child abuse is concerned than do people of means.

The fact that child abuse is neither theoretically nor clinically well defined increases the likelihood of subjective professional evaluation. In labeling theory, it is axiomatic that the greater the social distance between the typer and the person singled out for typing, the broader the type and the more quickly it may be applied.[48]

In the doctor-patient relationship, the physician is always in a superordinate position because of his or her expertise; social distance is inherent to the relationship. This distance necessarily increases once the label of abuser has been applied. Importantly, the label is less likely to be fixed if the diagnostician and possible abuser share similar characteristics, especially socioeconomic status, particularly where the injury is not serious or manifestly a consequence of maltreatment.

Once the label "abuser" is attached, it is very difficult to remove; even innocent behavior of a custodian may then be viewed with suspicion. The tenacity of a label increases in proportion to the official processing. At our own institution, until quite recently, a red star was stamped on the permanent medical record of any child who might have been abused, a process which encouraged professionals to suspect child abuse (and to act on that assumption) at any future time that the child would present with a medical problem.

Professionals thus engage in an intricate process of selection, finding facts that fit the label which has been applied, responding to a few deviant details set within a panoply of entirely acceptable conduct. Schur[55] called this phenomenon "retrospective reinterpretation." In any pathological model, "persons are likely to be studied in terms of what is 'wrong' with them," there being a "decided emphasis on identifying the characteristics of abnormality;" in child abuse, it may be administratively impossible to return to health, as is shown by the extraordinary durability of case reports in state central registers.[58]

The response of the patient to the agent of social control affects the perceptions and behavior of the controller. If, for example, a child has been injured and the alleged perpetrator is repentant, a consensus can develop between abuser and labeler that a norm has been violated. In this situation, the label of "abuser" may be less firmly applied than if the abuser defends the behavior as proper. Support for this formulation is found in studies by Gusfield,[22] who noted different reactions to repentant, sick, and enemy deviants, and by Piliavin and Briar,[42] who showed that juveniles apprehended by the police receive more lenient treatment if they appear contrite and remorseful about the violations.

Consequences of Treatment for the Abuser

Once abuse is defined as a sickness, it becomes a condition construed to be beyond the actor's control.[39] Though treatment, not punishment, is warranted, the *type* of treatment depends on whether or not the abuser is "curable," "improvable," or "incurable," and on the speed with which such a state can be achieved.

To help the abuser is generally seen as a less important goal than is the need to protect the child. If the abusive behavior cannot quickly be altered, and the child remains "at risk," the type of intervention will differ accordingly (*e.g.*, the child may be more likely to be placed in a foster home). The less "curable" is the abuser, the less treatment will be offered and the more punitive will society's response appear. Ironically, even the removal of a child from his parents, a move nearly always perceived as punitive by parents, is often portrayed as helpful by the professionals doing the removing ("It will give you a chance to resolve your own problems," etc.)

Whatever the treatment, there are predictable consequences for those labeled "abusers." Prior to diagnosis, parents may be afraid of "getting caught" because of punishment and social stigma. On being told of clinicians' concerns, they may express hostility because of implicit or explicit criticism made of them and their child-rearing practices yet feel relief because they love their children and want help in stopping their destructive behavior. The fact that they see themselves as "sick" may increase their willingness to seek help. This attitude is due at least in part to the lesser social stigma attached to the "sick," as opposed to the "criminal" label.

Socially marginal individuals are likely to accept whatever definition more powerful labelers apply. This definition, of course, has already been accepted by much of the larger community because of the definers' power. As Davis[8] noted:

> The chance that a group will get community support for its definition of unacceptable deviance depends on its relative power position. The greater the group's size, resources, efficiency, unity, articulateness, prestige, coordination with other groups, and access to the mass media and to decision-makers, the more likely it is to get its preferred norms legitimated.

Acceptance of definition by child abusers, however, is not based solely on the power of the labelers. Though some might consider the process "political castration,"[43] so long as they are defined as "ill" and take on the sick role, abusers are achieving a more satisfactory label. Though afflicted with a stigmatized illness (and thus "gaining few if any privileges and taking on some especially handicapping new obligations"[15]) at least they are merely sick rather than sinful or criminal.

Effective social typing flows down rather than up the social structure. For example, when both parents induct one of their children into the family scapegoat role, this is an effective social typing because the child is forced to take their definition of him into account.[48] Sometimes it is difficult to know whether an abusive parent has actually accepted the definition or is merely "role playing" in order to please the definer. If a person receives conflicting messages from the same control agent (*e.g.*, "you are sick and criminal") or from different control agents in the treatment network (from doctors who use the sick label, and lawyers who use the criminal), confusion and upset predictably result.[56]

As an example of how social definitions are accepted by the group being defined, it is interesting to examine the basic tenets of Parents Anonymous, which began as a self-help group for abusive mothers:

> A destructive, *disturbed* mother can, and often does, produce through her actions

> a physically or emotionally abused, or battered child. Present available *help* is limited and/or expensive, usually with a long waiting list before the person requesting help can actually receive *treatment* . . . We must understand that a problem as involved as this cannot be *cured* immediately . . . the problem is *within us* as a parent . . .[29] [emphases added]

To Parents Anonymous, child abuse appears to be a medical problem, and abusers are sick persons who must be treated.

Consequences of Treatment for the Social System

The individual and the social system are interrelated; each influences the other. Thus, if society defines abusive parents as sick, there will be few criminal prosecutions for abuse; reports will generally be sent to welfare, as opposed to police, departments.

Since victims of child abuse are frequently treated in hospitals, medical personnel become brokers for adult services and definers of children's rights. Once abuse is defined, that is, people may get services (such as counseling, child care, and homemaker services) that would be otherwise unavailable to them, and children may get care and protection impossible without institutional intervention.

If, as is customary, however, resources are in short supply, the preferred treatment of a case may not be feasible. Under this condition, less adequate treatment stratagems, or even clearly punitive alternatives, may be implemented. If day care and competent counseling are unavailable, court action and foster placement can become the only options. As Stoll[56] observed,

> . . . the best therapeutic intentions may be led astray when opportunities to implement theoretical guidelines are not available.

Treating child abuse as a sickness has, ironically, made it more difficult to "cure." There are not enough therapists to handle all of the diagnosed cases. Nor do most abusive parents have the time, money, or disposition for long-term therapeutic involvement. Many, moreover, lack the introspective and conceptual abilities required for successful psychological therapy.

As Parents Anonymous emphasizes, abuse is the *abuser's* problem. Its causes and solutions are widely understood to reside in individuals rather than in the social system.[5, 17] Indeed, the strong emphasis on child abuse as an individual problem means that other equally severe problems of childhood can be ignored, and the unequal distribution of social and economic resources in society can be masked.[20] The child abuse phenomenon itself may also increase as parents and professionals are obliged to "package" their problems and diagnoses in a competitive market where services are in short supply. As Tannenbaum[57] observed in 1938:

> Societal reactions to deviance can be characterized as a kind of "dramatization of evil" such that a person's deviance is made a public issue. The stronger the

reaction to the evil, the more it seems to grow. The reaction itself seems to generate the very thing it sought to eliminate.

Conclusion

Dispelling the Myth of Child Abuse

As clinicians, we are convinced that with intelligence, humanity, and the application of appropriate interventions, we can help families in crisis.

We believe, however, that short of coming to terms with—and changing—certain social, political, and economic aspects of our society, we will never be able adequately to understand and address the origins of child abuse and neglect. Nor will the issues of labeling be adequately resolved unless we deal straightforwardly with the potentially abusive power of the helping professions. If we can bring ourselves to ask such questions as, "Can we legislate child abuse out of existence?" and, "Who benefits from child abuse?", then perhaps we can more rationally choose among the action alternatives displayed in the conceptual model (Table 1).

Although we would prefer to avoid coercion and punishment, and to keep families autonomous and services voluntary, we must acknowledge the realities of family life and posit some state role to assure the well-being of children. In making explicit the assumptions and values underpinning our professional actions, perhaps we can promote a more informed and humane practice.

Because it is likely that clinical interventions will continue to be class and culture-based, we propose the following five guidelines to minimize the abuse of power of the definer.

1. *Give physicians, social workers, lawyers, and other intervention agents social science perspectives and skills.* Critical intellectual tools should help clinicians to understand the implications of their work, and, especially, the functional meaning of the labels they apply in their practices.

   Physicians need to be more aware of the complexity of human life, especially its social and psychological dimensions. The "medical model" is not of itself inappropriate; rather, the conceptual bases of medical practice need to be broadened, and the intellectual and scientific repertory of the practitioner expanded.[12] Diagnostic formulation is an active process that carries implicitly an anticipation of intervention and outcome. The simple elegance of concepts such as "child abuse" and "child neglect" militate for simple and radical treatments.

   Lawyers might be helped to learn that, in child custody cases, they are not merely advocates of a particular position. Only the child should "win" a custody case, where, for example, allegations of "abuse" or "neglect," skillfully marshalled, may support the position of the more effectively represented parent, guardian, or social worker.

2. *Acknowledge and change the prestige hierarchy of helping professions.* The workers who seem best able to conceptualize the familial and social context of problems of violence are social workers and nurses. They are least paid, most overworked, and as a rule have minimal access to the decision prerogatives of medicine and law. We would add that social work and nursing are professions largely of and by women, and we believe we must come to terms with the many realities—including sexual dominance and subservience—that keep members of those profession from functioning with appropriate respect and support. (We have made a modest effort in this direction at our own institution, where our interdisciplinary child abuse consultation program is organized under the aegis of the administration rather than of a medical clinical department. This is to foster, to the extent possible, peer status and communication on a coequal footing among the disciplines involved—social work, nursing, law, medicine, and psychiatry.)

3. *Build theory.* We need urgently a commonly understandable dictionary of concepts that will guide and inform a rational practice. A more adequate theory base would include a more etiologic (or causal) classification scheme for children's injuries, which would acknowledge and integrate diverse origins and expression of social, familial, child developmental, and environmental phenomena. It would conceptualize strength in families and children, as well as pathology. It would orient intervenors to the promotion of health rather than to the treatment of disease.

   A unified theory would permit coming to terms with the universe of need. At present, socially marginal and poor children are virtually the only ones susceptible to being diagnosed as victims of abuse and neglect. More affluent families' offspring, whose injuries are called "accidents" and who are often unprotected, are not included in "risk" populations. We have seen examples of court defense where it was argued (successfully) that because the family was not poor, it did not fit the classic archetypes of abuse or neglect.

   The needs and rights of all children need to be spelled out legally in relation to the responsibilities of parents and the state. This is easier said than done. It shall require not only a formidable effort at communication across disciplinary lines but a serious coming to terms with social and political values and realities.

4. *Change social inequality.* We share Gil's[20] view that inequality is the basic problem underlying the labeling of "abusive families" and its consequences. Just as children without defined rights are *ipso facto* vulnerable, so too does unequal access to the resources and goods of society shape a class hierarchy that leads to the individualization of social problems. Broadly-focused efforts for social change should accompany a critical review of the ethical foundations of professional practice. As part of the individual's formation as doctor, lawyer, social worker, or police officer, there could be developed for the professional a notion of public service and responsibility. This would better enable individuals to see themselves as participants in a social process and to

perceive the problems addressed in their work at the social as well as the individual level of action.

5. *Assure adequate representation of class and ethnic groups in decision-making forums.* Since judgments about family competency can be affected by class and ethnic biases, they should be made in setting where prejudices can be checked and controlled. Culture-bound value judgments in child protection work are not infrequent, and a sufficient participation in case management conferences of professionals of equal rank and status and diverse ethnicity can assure both a more appropriate context for decision making and better decisions for children and their families.

References

1. Allen, F. 1964. The Borderland of Criminal Justice. University of Chicago Press, Chicago.
2. Becker, H. 1963. Outsiders: Studies in the Sociology of Deviance. Free Press, New York.
3. Bourne, R. and Newberger, E. 1977. 'Family autonomy' or 'coercive intervention?' ambiguity and conflict in a proposed juvenile standard on child protection. Boston Univ. Law Rev. 57(4):670–706.
4. Omitted.
5. Conrad, P. 1975. The discovery of hyperkinesis: notes on the medicalization of deviant behavior. Soc. Prob. 23(10):12–21.
6. Cupoli, J. and Newberger, E. 1977. Optimism or pessimism for the victim of child abuse? Pediatrics 59(2):311–314.
7. Curran, W. 1977. Failure to diagnose battered child syndrome. New England J. Med., 296(14):795–796.
8. Davis, F. 1975. Belief, values, power and public definitions of deviance. *In* The Collective Definition of Deviance, F. Davis and R. Stivers, eds. Free Press, New York.
9. Demause, L., ed., 1974. The History of Childhood. Free Press, New York.
10. Elmer, E. 1977. A follow-up study of traumatized children. Pediatrics 59(2):273–279.
11. Elmer, E. 1977. Fragile Families, Troubled Children. University of Pittsburgh Press, Pittsburgh.
12. Engel, G. 1977. The need for a new medical model: a challenge for biomedicine. Science 196(14):129–136.
13. Fontana, V. 1964. The Maltreated Child: The Maltreatment Syndrome in Children. Charles C. Thomas, Springfield, Ill.
14. Fraser, B. 1977. Legislative status of child abuse legislation. *In* Child Abuse and Neglect: the Family and the Community, C. Kempe and R. Helfer, eds. Ballinger, Cambridge, Mass.
15. Freidson, E. 1970. Profession of Medicine: A Study of the Sociology of Applied Knowledge. Dodd, Mead, New York.
16. Galdston, R. 1971. Violence begins at home. J. Amer. Acad. Child Psychiat. 10(2):336–350.
17. Gelles, R. 1973. Child abuse as psychopathology: a sociological critique and reformulation. Amer. J. Orthopsychiat. 43(4):611–621.
18. Gelles, R. 1978. Violence toward children in the United States. Amer. J. Orthopsychiat. 48(4):580–592.
19. Gil, D. 1975. Unraveling child abuse. Amer. J. Orthopsychiat. 45(4):346–356.
20. Gil, D. 1970. Violence Against Children. Harvard University Press, Cambridge, Mass.
21. Goldstein, J., Freud, A. and Solnit, A. 1973. Beyond the Best Interests of the Child. Free Press, New York.
22. Gusfield, J. 1967. Moral passage: the symbolic process in public designations of deviance. Soc. Prob. 15(2):175–188.
23. Hyde, J. 1974. Uses and abuses of information in protective services contexts. *In* Fifth National Symposium on Child Abuse and Neglect. American Humane Association, Denver.
24. Illich, I. 1976. Medical Nemesis: The Expropriation of Health. Random House, New York.
25. *Ingraham v. Wright.* 1977. 45 LW 4364 U.S. Supreme Court.

26. Isaacs, J. 1972. The role of the lawyer in child abuse cases. *In* Helping the Battered Child and His Family, R. Helfer and C. Kempe, eds. Lippincott, Philadelphia.
27. Joint Commission on the Mental Health of Children. 1970. Crisis in Child Mental Health. Harper and Row, New York.
28. Juvenile Justice Standards Project. 1977. Standards Relating to Abuse and Neglect. Ballinger, Cambridge, Mass.
29. Kempe, C. and Helfer, R., eds. 1972. Helping the Battered Child and His Family. Lippincott, Philadelphia.
30. Kempe, C. et al. 1962. The battered child syndrome. JAMA 181(1):17–24.
31. Kittrie, N. 1971. The Right To Be Different. Johns Hopkins University Press, Baltimore.
32. *Landeros v. Flood*. 1976. 131 Calif. Rptr 69.
33. Martin, H., ed. 1976. The Abused Child: A Multidisciplinary Approach to Developmental Issues and Treatment. Ballinger, Cambridge, Mass.
34. Mercer, J. 1972. Who is normal? two perspectives on mild mental retardation. *In* Patients, Physicians and Illness (2nd ed.), E. Jaco, ed. Free Press, New York.
35. Newberger, E. 1975. The myth of the battered child syndrome. *In* Annual Progress in Child Psychiatry and Child Development 1974, S. Chess and A. Thomas, eds. Brunner Mazel, New York.
36. Newberger, E., Newberger, C. and Richmond, J. 1976. Child health in America: toward a rational public policy. Milbank Memorial Fund Quart./Hlth. and Society 54(3):249–298.
37. Newberger, E. and Daniel, J. 1976. Knowledge and epidemiology of child abuse: a critical review of concepts. Pediat. Annuals 5(3):15–26.
38. Newberger, E. et al. 1977. Pediatric social illness: toward an etiologic classification. Pediatrics 60(1):178–185.
39. Parsons, T. 1951. The Social System. Free Press, Glencoe, Ill.
40. Paulsen, M. 1966. Juvenile courts, family courts, and the poor man. Calif. Law Rev. 54(2):-694–716.
41. Pfohl, S. 1977. The 'discovery' of child abuse. Soc. Prob. 24(3):310–323.
42. Piliavin, I. and Briar, S. 1964. Police encounters with juveniles. Amer. J. Sociol. 70(2):206–214.
43. Pitts, J. 1968. Social control: the concept. *In* The International Encyclopedia of the Social Sciences 14:391. Macmillan, New York.
44. Poitrast, F. 1976. The judicial dilemma in child abuse cases. Psychiat. Opinion 13(1):22–28.
45. Rheinstein, M. 1954. Max Weber on Law in Economy and Society. Harvard University Press, Cambridge, Mass.
46. Rosenblatt, S., Schaeffer, D. and Rosenthal, J. 1976. Effects of diphenylhydantoin on child abusing parents: a preliminary report. Curr. Therapeut. Res. 19(3):332–336.
47. Rosenfeld, A. and Newberger, E. 1977. Compassion versus control: conceptual and practical pitfalls in the broadened definition of child abuse. JAMA 237(19):2086–2088.
48. Rubington, E. and Weinberg, M. 1973. Deviance: The Interactionist Perspective (2nd ed.). Macmillan, New York.
49. Ryan, W. 1971. Blaming the Victim. Random House, New York.
50. Sanders, R. 1972. Resistance to dealing with parents of battered children. Pediatrics 50(6):-853–857.
51. Scheff, T. 1966. Being Mentally Ill: A Sociological Theory. Aldine, Chicago.
52. Scheff, T. 1972. Decision rules, types of error, and their consequences in medical diagnosis. *In* Medical Men and Their Work, E. Freidson and J. Lorber, eds. Aldine, Chicago.
53. Schmitt, B. and Kempe, C. 1975. Neglect and abuse of children. *In* Nelson Textbook of Pediatrics (10th ed.), V. Vaughan and R. McKay, eds. W. B. Saunders, Philadelphia.
54. Schrag, P. 1975. The Myth of the Hyperactive Child. Random House, New York.
55. Schur, E. 1971. Labeling Deviant Behavior. Harper and Row, New York.
56. Stoll, C. 1968. Images of man and social control. Soc. Forces 47(2):119–127.
57. Tannenbaum, F. 1938. Crime and the Community. Ginn and Co., Boston.
58. Whiting, L. 1977. The central registry for child abuse cases: rethinking basic assumptions. Child Welfare 56(2):761–767.

5

A Wider Perspective

Introduction

During the 1950s and 1960s, family scholars and the mass media presented an image of the typical, normal, or model American family. It included a father, a mother, and two or three children who lived a middle-class existence in a single-family home in an area neither rural nor urban. Father was the breadwinner, and mother was a full-time homemaker. Both were, by implication, white.

No one denied that many families and individuals fell outside the standard nuclear model. Single persons, one-parent families, two-parent families in which both parents worked, three-generation families, and childless couples abounded. Three- or four-parent familes were not uncommon, as one or both divorced spouses often remarried. Many families, moreover, neither white nor well-off, varied from the dominant image. White and seemingly middle-class families of particular ethnic, cultural, or sexual styles also differed from the model. The image scarcely reflected the increasing ratio of older people in the postfamily part of the life cycle. But like poverty before its "rediscovery" in the mid-1960s, family complexity and variety existed on some dim fringe of semi-awareness.

When noticed, individuals or families departing from the nuclear model were analyzed in a context of pathology. Studies of one-parent families or working mothers, for example, focused on the harmful effects to children of such situations. Couples childless by choice were assumed to possess some basic personality inadequacy. Single persons were similarly interpreted, or else thought to be homosexual. Homosexuals symbolized evil, depravity, and degradation.

As Marvin Sussman (1971) noted early on, "This preoccupation with the model nuclear family pattern and efforts to preserve it at all costs prevented sociologists from describing what was becoming obvious to non-sociological observers of the American scene: a pluralism in family forms existing side by side with members in each form having different problems to solve and issues to face" (p. 42). Curiously, although social scientists have always emphasized the pluralism of American society in terms of ethnic groups, religion, and geographic region, the concept of pluralism had rarely been applied to the family.

What we are actually witnessing today is not so much new forms of family living as a new way of looking at alternative family patterns that have been around for a long time. Even the flowering of communal living experiments in America during the late 1960s was not something new under the sun but rather the revival of an old American tradition. But while communes were being developed, nuclear family ideology was challenged on other grounds. Blacks challenged the validity of the white middle-class family as a model for all groups in society; the population explosion made singleness, childlessness, and even homosexuality seem to be adaptive responses to a pressing social problem; the women's movement challenged the traditional roles of wife and mother and argued for the validity of singleness, childlessness, unwed motherhood, homosexuality, and even celibacy.

Our selections here are intended to reflect this diversity and the increasingly bitter controversies surrounding it. The article by Robert Staples and Alfredo Mirandé reviews the literature of the past decade in terms of classical theoretical controversies about the nature of minority families. For example, does research suggest that the black family should be viewed primarily as culturally deviant (pathological), culturally equivalent (middle class), or culturally variant (unique, legitimate)? What is the history of, contemporary evidence for, and future of each of these perspectives? Should the machismo of the Chicano father be mainly interpreted as representing power, control, and violence? Or is a more benevolent interpretation, stressing honor, respect, and dignity, supported by the research evidence? Staples and Mirandé also review the sparser literature on Asian-American and Native American families.

In a related article, actually a chapter from William Julius Wilson's book *The Truly Disadvantaged,* Wilson, with Kathryn Neckerman, explores the relationship between poverty and family structure in the light of Wilson's more general argument that recent increases in social dislocation in the ghetto underclass defy simple explanation. Such increases are explained neither by racism nor by racial discrimination, as some left analysts have contended; nor are they explained by ghetto culture or the liberal welfare state, as conservative scholars have suggested. This problem—and its impact on the black family—is attributable instead to shifts in the American economy that have generated black joblessness, as well as minority migration patterns and age and class transformation of the inner city. Wilson concludes that, from a public policy perspective, the number one priority for enhancing the status of poor black families is to heighten employment opportunities for inner-city males.

We also examine the impact of "the revolution in longevity," as Matilda White Riley calls it in the selection we reprint here. During this century, life expectancy has risen from under 50 to over 70 years of age—and is continually rising. This sharp increase in life expectancy is accompanied by a greatly expanded kinship structure persisting through time. People used to have lots of relatives, and they didn't live so long. Now people begin with smaller families, but these persist and accrete through marriage, procreation, and remarriage. Kinship structures used to look like short, stubby, ephemeral bushes. Now they have sprouted into long, slender trees, with many branches. Riley argues optimistically that the new kinship structure offers more choice for selecting relationships individuals deem more significant.

How should we think about different visions of the family? This is the question addressed by the articles in our final chapter. We call it "The Politics of the

Family" because we recognize that change in the family, like all social change, is predicated on visions of the good society and the power to enforce those moral assessments.

The first two selections in Chapter 11 suggest that the future of the institution of the family will depend on the outcome of debates between those holding key moral and political definitions and quite different world views. For example, the the abortion debate, argues Kristin Luker in the first selection, is not so much about the fate of the embryo as about the meaning of women's lives. Working women who are educated, affluent, and liberal tend to be "pro-choice." "Pro-life" women, by contrast, have already arranged their lives to support traditional concepts of women as wives and mothers. Thus, pro-life and pro-choice women live in different evaluative worlds that offer different and conflicting definitions of motherhood—and public policy.

Such opposing definitions have emerged in the 1980s as major and bitterly fought controversies. The acceptance or rejection of homosexuality is an issue closely related to abortion. Both have to do with interpretations of the right to privacy under the Constitution. From the perspective of constitutionally protected privacy, both issues can be seen as involving the rights of human beings to make decisions about their bodies, without government sanctions limiting their choice—whether, in the one instance, to abort a pregnancy, and, in the other, to engage in intimate sexual conduct with persons of the same sex.

The abortion decision in *Roe v. Wade* 410 U.S. 113 (1973) is actually quite complicated, because the U.S. Supreme Court there recognized a compelling state interest in preserving the life of the fetus once it is "viable," that is, capable of surviving outside the uterus with artificial aid. However, the Court basically recognized that a woman's right to decide whether to end her pregnancy is a fundamental right of privacy that cannot be interfered with in any way, unless a state can show a compelling interest. During the first trimester of pregnancy, the only compelling interest the state may assert is that the abortion be performed by a licensed physician. Later in pregnancy, the state has a compelling interest in the mother's health that permits it to institute further requirements—such as that the abortion be performed in a hospital, or only after approval of another doctor or committee. Still later, once the fetus is "viable," the state's interest in preserving the life of the fetus becomes compelling, and the state then enjoys greater discretion to limit a pregnant woman's decision to abort. For example, it may permit abortion if the woman's life or health is endangered by continuation of the pregnancy.

When an individual or a class of individuals is found to have a constitutionally protected right, a state cannot enforce a law, even though it has been passed by a majority. Until as late as 1967, for example, a number of states, particularly in the South, still maintained laws forbidding "miscegenation," that is, the marriage of people of different races. In *Loving v. Virginia* 388 U.S.1 (1967), the U.S. Supreme Court held that the right to marry was a basic civil right and therefore held unconstitutional a white supremacist Virginia law that made it illegal "for any white person in the State to marry any save a white person, or a person with no other admixture of blood than white and American Indian."

The case we reprint here, *Bowers v. Hardwick* 106 S. Ct. 2841 (1986), is the most recent one, and limits the constitutional right to privacy. The case arose when Atlanta police officers arrested Michael Hardwick on August 3, 1982, for committing an act of sodomy with a consenting adult male in Mr. Hardwick's bedroom. Mr. Hardwick did not deny that the act occurred. On the contrary, not only did he admit the act, he brought suit to test its constitutionality, even though the District Attorney had dropped the charges. Mr. Hardwick argued that—despite the fact that he no longer faced criminal prosecution, conviction, and punishment—he had standing to sue because he was a practicing homosexual and would commit further acts in violation of Georgia's allegedly unconstitutional anti-sodomy statute. The case made its way through the courts until 1986, when the Supreme Court, in a 5-4 decision, held that the statute was constitutional.

Especially interesting about this case are its jurisprudential and sociological implications. In terms of jurisprudence, the majority upheld the statute in the interests of judicial restraint. Thus, the Court declined to overrule the legislature, because as an elected body the legislature represents and understands the values of the people. But that cannot be the entire answer, because in previous cases the Court had overturned legislation regulating intimate conduct on grounds that a constitutional right to privacy trumps laws interfering with decisions to use contraceptives, to decline to procreate, or to marry regardless of the race of the partners. So the Court had to distinguish this case, and that it did on essentially sociological grounds, namely, that centuries of law and moral teaching have found homosexual sodomy to be impermissible. The majority drew the Durkheimian line of the boundaries of permissible behavior. As Justice Burger says in his concurring opinion, "To hold that the act of homosexual sodomy is somehow protected as a fundamental right would be to cast aside millennia of moral teaching—that is, to find a right to privacy in this instance would be to undermine the moral basis of the community.

By contrast, the dissent in *Bowers* employs a quite different interpretation of community. Written by Justice Blackmun, who was sorely distressed by the majority opinion (he made the unusual gesture of reading his dissenting opinion aloud in the Court proceedings), the dissent envisions tradition as protecting "a private sphere of individual liberty . . . largely beyond the reach of government." Central to this concept of liberty is the ability to "define one's identity" and to seek "emotional enrichment" through "close ties with others." To Blackmun, society does not require such clear moral boundaries. On the contrary, he envisions different kinds of societies—those valuing conformity in expressions of intimate conduct, and those valuing diversity—and concludes by writing: "I can only hope that . . . the Court soon will reconsider its analysis and conclude that depriving individuals of the right to choose for themselves how to conduct their intimate relationships poses a far greater threat to the values most deeply rooted in our Nation's history than tolerance of nonconformity could ever do."

How we interpret the family sociologically likewise depends upon our vision of the historical values of the institution of the family. Was it ever actually a haven in a heartless world, and is it presently falling apart, as suggested in the selection by Christopher Lasch? Or is it here to stay as a changing institution, as the famous assessment of Mary Jo Bane reprinted here suggests?

The move from traditional marriage norms to relationships based on personal psychological gratification is the concern of the article by Robert N. Bellah, Richard Madsen, William M. Sullivan, Ann Swidler, and Steven M. Tipton. The authors argue that if love and marriage are based primarily on concerns for self, they may be unable to fulfill what the authors consider to be the older social function of marriage—the formation of stable, committed relationships that tie the married couple to the larger society.

In actuality, the more traditional conceptions of the family have been questioned by family sociologists and historians for the past two decades. Research has challenged the popular assumption that the extended family or the three-generational household was ever the norm in American or western European society. The myth of the large kin group living happily on the grandparents' farm has repeatedly been laid to rest by sociologists and historians. Still, it lives on in the minds of many. Confronted with the different problems raised by a modern aging population, it is easy to yearn for some golden era of the past when the old lived happily in the bosom of the family. Yet there is little evidence that such a golden era ever existed. Even when old people and young people lived together, their lives were not necessarily idyllic (Kent, 1965).

Traditional conceptions of the family are questioned in our final selection, by Francesca M. Cancian. Writing as a critic of such theorists as Robert Bellah and Christopher Lasch (included in this collection), Cancian disagrees with their interpretation of the family. She argues that the debate over the family is really grounded in a set of values—much like those that distinguish the majority and dissenting opinions in *Bowers v. Hardwick*. For her the issue is not what is necessary for the family but rather which values are stressed in considering the institution. Thus, the issue is grounded in whether we value traditional role definitions of gender and authority, or prefer to stress the part the family plays in encouraging self-development, downplaying traditional gender roles and offering personal freedom for intimate relations.

We envision family life as falling short of the traditional ideals ascribed to it, because families are not isolated havens set off from the surrounding society. In societies marked by scarcity, insecurity, inequalities of goods and power, anxiety over status, fear, and hatred, family life will bear the impact of these qualities. The family in a malfunctioning society is usually part of the problem.

Chances are that, even in a relatively untroubled society, family life will still be problematic because of the special psychology of close relationships. The family, as one writer put it, is where you are dealing with life and death voltages. No matter what form the family takes, the distinctive intimacy and commitment of family life provide the source of both the joy and the torment to be found there.

Still, it is important to note that whatever form the family takes, it is not self-sufficient, insulated from society. If the nation goes to war, family lives are disrupted. When a provider—father, mother, brother—is unemployed, everybody in the family is affected.

As we move toward the future, an informed public policy would require that full recognition be given to the complexity and variety of forms and life-styles the family and other intimate environments can take. This is not to suggest that the nuclear family is going to disappear, nor should it. Nevertheless the traditional, one-earner, one-and-only-marriage family of husband, wife, and children now accounts for a minority of American families. Even where the traditional nuclear family still reigns, changes in the ecology and organization of domestic work could ease the strain on that venerable institution as well as on the single person. The trick, of course, is to maintain a philosophy of public policy that seeks to provide facilitative communal arrangements while avoiding the temptation to intrude on private lives. In any case, public policy should be based on the reality of variation rather than on unrealistic visions of an outmoded orthodoxy.

References

Kent, Donald, P. "Aging: Fact or Fancy." *The Gerontologist,* Vol. 5, No. 2 (June 1965), pp. 51–56.
Sussman, Marvin B. 1971. "Family Systems in the 1970s: Analysis, Policies, and Programs." *Annals of the American Academy of Political and Social Science*, Vol. 396.

Chapter 10

Variation in Family Experience

Racial and Cultural Variations Among American Families: A Decennial Review of the Literature on Minority Families

Robert Staples and Alfredo Mirandé

As an institution the family continues to be a subject of intense and controversial public concern. This interest is generated, in part, by the lack of consensus on what its form and function should be. In the case of minority groups, the controversy is heightened by their depiction in the literature and an ongoing debate over how their family lifestyle relates to the larger society. Before examining how this issue was expressed in the family literature of the seventies, it is necessary to place some parameters around our definition of minorities. Too global a definition of "minority" militates against the purpose and scope of this decade review. Hence, those groups of interest are any collectivity whose membership is derived from a shared racial identity, with high visibility in the society and a devalued social status: *i.e.,* Asians, blacks, Chicanos and Native Americans.

Given the American commitment to the concept of a melting pot (*i.e.,* the blending of diverse racial and ethnic groups into a standard prototype), there should be no need to study minority families separately. However, that ideal has never been translated into reality. Instead, we have what Gordon (1964) has described as "Anglo conformity": an assumption of the superiority of Anglo-Saxon culture and the devaluation of all other forms. This conflict between the melting pot theory and the dictates of Anglo conformity is expressed nowhere better than in the family literature on minorities. Thus, this decade review is more

From the *Journal of Marriage and the Family,* Vol. 42, No. 4 (November 1980), pp. 157–173. Copyright 1980 by the National Council of Family Relations, 1910 West County Road B, Suite 147, St. Paul, MN 55113. Reprinted by permission.

than an assessment of basic theory and research, it is also part of an ongoing debate about ideology and its role in the conceptualization of minority-family lifestyles.

The role of ideology is not unique to the field of the family or racial minorities. Under the rubric of the sociology of knowledge, it has been asserted that the social location of the individual within a given society will influence the knowledge he possesses (Mannheim, 1936). Since the study of minority families has been dominated by white, middle-class males, a debate centering around the "insider-outsider thesis" has arisen (Merton, 1972; Staples, 1976a). One side contends that indigenous minorities possess a special capacity for understanding the behavior of their group, while the other side contends that the use of objective scientific methods nullifies the racial membership of the investigator as a significant factor. Those holding the latter view often choose to conceptualize the whole issue as a conflict between ideology and science (Dennis, 1976).

The argument is compounded by the division of minority family researchers into empiricists and nonempiricists. Many minority researchers have used the essay and qualitative analysis as their main tool in understanding minority families. In part, this is due to a desire for a broader understanding of the behavioral processes that animate the family life of American minorities. Since white males dominate the quantitative studies of minority families, they have often discredited their minority counterparts with the charge of being polemicists and substituting speculation and ideology for objective data. The white male's claim to a monopoly on objectivity is countered by Myrdal's (1944:1041) contention that "biases in social science cannot be erased simply by 'keeping to the facts' and by refined methods of statistical treatment of the data." Facts, he notes, and the "handling of data sometimes show themselves even more pervious to tendencies toward bias than does pure thought."

Questions of objectivity versus ideology would be beyond cavil were it not for the fact that for a very long time, minority families were treated pejoratively in the family literature. At the end of the sixties, the consensus was that minority families were negatively different from the middle-class Anglo family system. The source and nature of their deviance was never agreed upon beyond the fact that they generally constituted dysfunctional units and represented barriers to their group's mobility (Staples, 1971). Part of the problem in understanding minority families was the failure of researchers to distinguish between factors of class and culture in their family lifestyles. This also represented a methodological flaw. In an analysis of empirical research in the *Journal of Marriage and the Family* during the period of 1959 to 1968, it was found that only 7 percent of the *Journal's* articles reported on lower-class populations. In contrast, almost all the research on minority families, in the same period, had lower-class groups as the subject population (Lieberman, 1973:18).

While lower-class minority families were often compared to middle-class white families and found wanting, a central question persisted. That question might be best framed as: What is the relationship of the family to the larger society? Does the family simply respond passively to the forces it encounters or is it a unit that acts as a conduit for the mobility of its individual members? In other words, does the family structure determine social achievement or does social achievement influence the form of the family? Belief in the determinancy of family structure on social achievement was the prevalent position in the study of minority families for many years. It was this underlying attitude which gave the study of minority families more than theoretical implications. Since research findings can be and are translated into public policy that, in turn, impacts on the life chances of minority individuals, the study of minority families becomes extremely consequential. Thus, it is imperative that all views be given a fair hearing in the family literature.

The Black Family

At the end of the sixties, controversy was still raging over the Moynihan (1965) report. Moynihan's assertion that "at the root of the deterioration of Black society was the deterioration of the Black family" stimulated a plethora of theory and research. Over 50 books and 500 articles related to the black family were published in the last decade. That 10-year period produced five times more black family literature than had been produced in all the years prior to 1970. In the early stages of the decade, such research was primarily in response to the work of Frazier (1939), Moynihan (1965), and Rainwater (1966), who had uniformly depicted the lower-class black family as pathological. Subsequently, however, the researchers expanded into studies of the black family as an autonomous unit.

Along with the expansion of black family research came the development of new theoretical constructs. Allen (1978) has identified three ideological perspectives in research done on the black family: the *cultural deviant* approach; the *cultural equivalent* approach; and the *cultural variant* approach. The cultural deviant approach viewed black families as pathological. The cultural equivalent perspective conferred a legitimacy upon black families as long as their family lifestyles conformed to middle-class family norms. The cultural variant orientation depicted black families as different, but functional, family forms. In an analysis of the treatment of black families in the research literature between 1965 and 1979, Haynes and Johnson (1980) discovered that, in the seventies, the literature shifted dramatically from the cultural deviant to the cultural equivalent perspective. The cultural variant perspective, which views the black family as a culturally unique, legitimate unit, continues to be underrepresented in mainstream journals. In fact, only in the predominantly black journals and in the special issue of the *Journal of Marriage and the Family* on the black families does a cultural variant perspective prevail. These journals account for 74 percent of the articles published on the black family using such a perspective.

Theory

Since research on black families has [as] its dominant orientation the cultural equivalent approach, it would appear that the assimilation model guides most of the empirical studies. However, it remains the case that much research on the family is atheoretical. In the last decade, two new theoretical constructs were applied to the study of black families. The first and most common one is called the "Africanity" model. The underlying tenets of this model are that African traits were retained and are manifested in black styles of kinship patterns, marriage, sexuality, and childrearing, etc. (Staples, 1974; Nobles, 1978). While it is an axiom of human existence that no group loses all of its cultural heritage, the precise locus of African traits in black family lifestyles remains an empirical question. It is possible that the Africanisms that exist are so fused with American traits that it is impractical to seek specific behavioral patterns, values, and structural features that are uniquely African in origin. At this juncture the model remains on an abstract level, untested by any systematic research.

Another conceptual model applied to the study of black families is the "internal colonialism" approach. It has the advantage of bridging the cultural equivalent and cultural variant perspectives. By using the colonial analogy, it assumes that racial domination by outsiders can create weaknesses in a group's family structure while acknowledging the existence of functional elements in its family system (Lieberman, 1973; Staples, 1978a). Research using this model has been slow in emerging, partly due to the problem of operationalizing the concept of internal colonialism with the kind of data readily available to social scientists. At this point in time, most of the works using this model have been theoretical essays or research which have used the colonial analogy in a serendipitous manner (Staples, 1976b).

Historical Research

Surprisingly, the most groundbreaking research on black families was conducted by historians. For years, the works of Frazier (1939) and Elkins (1968) had been accepted as the definitive history of black families and posited as a causal explanation of their contemporary condition. Based on traditional historical methods, using plantation records and slaveowner testimony, both men reached the conclusion that the family was destroyed under slavery and the culture of the slaves was decimated. The first historian to challenge that thesis was Blassingame (1572), whose use of slave narratives indicated that in the slave quarters black families did exist as functioning institutions and role models for others. Moreover, strong family ties persisted in the face of the frequent breakups deriving from the slave trade. To further counteract the Frazier/Eluins thesis, Fogel and Engerman (1974) used elaborate quantitative methods to document that slaveowners did not separate a majority of the slave families. Their contention, also controversial, was that the capitalistic efficiency of the slave system meant it was more practical to keep slave families intact.

Continuing in the vein of revisionist historical research, Genovese (1974) used a mix of slaveholders' papers and slave testimony. Still, he concluded that black culture, through compromise and negotiation between slaves and slaveowners, did flourish during the era of slavery. Within the context of slavery, there was a variety of socially approved and sanctioned relationships between slave men and women. The alleged female matriarchy that was extant during that era is described by Genovese as a closer approximation to a healthy sexual equality than was possible for whites. It was the landmark study of Gutman (1976), however, that put to rest one of the most common and enduring myths of black families. Using census data for a number of cities between 1880 and 1925, he found that the majority of blacks, of all social classes, lived in nuclear families. Through the use of plantation birth records and marriage applications, he concluded that the biparental household was the dominant form during slavery. More important than Gutman's compelling evidence that slavery did not destroy the black family was his contention that their family form in the past era had evolved from family and kinship patterns that had been given birth under slavery, a cultural form that was a fusion of African and American traits.

Social historians and historical demographers also made contributions to our understanding of black family history. Furstenberg and his colleagues (1975) investigated the origin of the female-headed black family and its relationship to the urban experience. Basing their analysis on samples from the decennial federal population manuscript schedulers for the period from 1850 to 1880, they found that blacks were only slightly less likely to reside in nuclear households than were native whites and immigrants to Philadelphia. While these historical works have, in combination, challenged the Moynihan view that slavery created the conditions for black family disorganization, the prevalence of marital breakups at the hands of slaveowners means that many marriages were not that stable. Even the use of slave accounts does not eliminate bias in slave history. Many of the slave narratives were edited by Northern abolitionists and they constitute the reports of highly literate slaves.

Macrosociological Studies

The studies which focused on generalized aspects of the black family shared certain commonalities. Most of them were responding to the Moynihan thesis about the instability of black families. Additionally, they attempted to delineate the structure and function of black families. The goals may have been similar, but the perspectives, again, fell into one of Allen's (1978) typologies. Studies by Heiss (1975), Scanzoni (1971), and Willie (1976) would belong in the cultural equivalent category. Both Heiss and Scanzoni used quantitative analysis to illustrate that black families are stable, egalitarian, and functional units. They reached this conclusion by delineating how well black families meet the white, middle-class family ideal. Willie used qualitative analysis and examined a variety of black families. The poor black families were still depicted as less than healthy units. Hill's (1972) study of the strengths of black families would fall somewhere in a middle ground. Through the use of census data he demonstrated that black families, like white families, adhere to such sacrosanct American values as strong work, achievement, and religious orientations. Conversely, he stressed the more unique traits of strong kinship bonds and role flexibility, although he did not link them to an autonomous cultural system.

An ongoing debate in black family studies revolves around the appropriate unit of analysis. A number of scholars have contended that the functions of the black family are carried out by the extended, rather than the nuclear, family unit. A number of studies have used the extended family as the focus of research (Aschenbrenner, 1975; Martin and Martin, 1978; McAdoo, 1978a; Shimkin *et al.*, 1978; Stack, 1974). Basically, they have delineated the use of kinship ties, both genealogical and fictive, as a resource for carrying out the functions of role modeling, socialization, mutual aid, and other support functions. The research by McAdoo (1978a) is especially significant because it illustrated that extended family ties transcend class boundaries. Her study of middle-class black families demonstrated that the kinship-help pattern remains strong after individuals have achieved mobility within the larger society.

Nevertheless, the viability of kinship networks must be questioned. First, there are indications that they are statistically a declining form. The number of blacks in each household decreased in the last decade (Bianchi and Farley, 1979). Young females who bear children out-of-wedlock are more likely to move into their own household rather than become part of an extended family network (Bianchi and Farley, 1979). Moreover, as Stack (1974) has noted, kinship ties can militate against stable marital unions. The woman in a stable conjugal relationship uses her resources for her nuclear family, not her kinsmen. Thus, the kinsmen have vested interest in discouraging the development of stable nuclear families. We might also raise the question of how compatible kinship ties are with an indus-trialized society for some individuals. While it may facilitate mobility in some cases, it may impede it in others. The Parsonian (Parsons and Bales, 1955) notion that the extended family was supplanted by the nuclear family in order to create a mobile work force may have some validity. Individuals tied to an extended kinship system are also chained to the same geographical locale, which impairs the capacity to respond to different and better job opportunities.

Sex Roles

The burgeoning of the women's liberation movement gave rise to a number of books on black women. In the main, they were nonempirical works which focused on the role of black women in their community and the larger society (Cade, 1970; Staples, 1973; Noble, 1978; Rose, 1980). Among the better books was the study by Ladner (1971) of black teenage females growing up in a low-income urban community. Through the use of systematic open-ended interviews, participatory observation, and her own experiences, she explored how these young women coped with the forces of poverty and maintained a sense of positive identity. Many of the books on black women emphasized that while they were strong, due to the need to face adverse forces in the society, they were not overbearing matri- archs. At the end of the decade, a young black feminist broke ranks with her more conciliatory sisters and issued a broadsided attack on black male chauvinism in the black community (Wallace, 1979). It is possible that her book was the harbinger of the eighties and future literature on black sex roles will contain a feminist ideology.

The Family Life Cycle

Other than fertility behavior and child socialization processes, the black family life cycle remains a largely neglected part of black family studies. The few studies of black dating and sexual behavior suggest a convergence of black and white behavioral modalities (Dickinson, 1975; Christensen and Johnson, 1978; Staples, 1978b; Porter, 1979). Almost all of the studies have used biracial comparisons and there has yet to be developed a systematic analysis of black dating and sexual codes. Mate selection norms and processes are equally ignored in the black family literature, despite the large proportion of unmarried blacks in our midst (Staples, in press). Perhaps it is the fact that the majority of adult blacks are unmarried that accounts for the paucity of research on black marriages and divorces (Chavis and Lyles, 1975; Hampton, 1979). At any rate, all we know is that the divorce rate for blacks increased by 130 percent in the last decade (U.S. Bureau of the Census, 1979). While there were few studies on interracial marriages, there were an abundance of books and articles on interracial marriages produced in the last decade (Henriques, 1975; Stember, 1976; Porterfield, 1977). Many of them were written in an *ad hominem* fashion and concluded that black/white marriages were problematic but viable. Heer's (1974) more careful analysis of census data documents the sharp increase in black male/white female pairings and the fairly high rate of dissolution of such unions.

Studies of childbearing and rearing practices in the black community reflect the same convergence of black and white behavior. The fertility rate of married black women declined at a slightly higher rate than did that of white women, with college educated black women continuing to have the lowest fertility rate of all groups (Farley, 1970; Kiser, 1970). The biggest racial difference in fertility rates continued to be out-of-wedlock births occurring to black females. More than half of all black births now occur out-of-wedlock (Bianchi and Farley, 1979). In part, the increase in out-of-wedlock births is due to the decline in fertility rates among married black women. Many of the unwed mothers are teenagers and we have little in the way of research to inform us as to how their children are being reared. There are indications that the informal adoption practices (Hill, 1977) of black families are no longer prevalent (Bianchi and Farley, 1979). Childrearing practices, in general, tend to be similar for black and white parents as does the level of the child's self-esteem (Halpern, 1973; Silverstein and Krate, 1975).

Summary

The past decade has witnessed a basic transformation in ideology and research on the black family. Prior to the seventies, the common wisdom was that black families, in comparison to middle-class white families, were dysfunctional units which could not carry out the normative functions ascribed to that institution. During the last decade, the research emphasis shifted to the investigation of stable black families and their conformity to middle-class family norms. However, it was in this same decade that the economic gains that blacks accrued were translated in greater family stability for many, again raising the question of the relationship between black family stability and changes in the larger society. Another question concerns the interaction between cultural values and family organization; this has to be systematically examined by the proponents of the "Africanity" and "colonial" models. Finally, it would appear that we may need to go back to the drawing board on black family research. Based on the latest census data (U.S. Bureau of the Census, 1979), there has been a dramatic increase in teenage pregnancies, out-of-wedlock births, single-parent households, and marital dissolution among blacks of all social classes. Since these changes parallel changes in white families during the same period, it may presage a need to undergo a revolution in theory and research on the family as a viable institution for all groups in society.

The Chicano Family

The last decade has witnessed a proliferation of research and writing on the Chicano family.[1] Prior to this time, social scientists demonstrated an intense interest in the Chicano family and generalizations concerning it abounded, but such generalizations were typically based on either meager or nonexistent data (Mirandé, 1977:747; Kagan and Valdez, in press). In 1970, Miguel Montiel wrote an excellent critique of Mexican American family studies entitled "Social Science Myth of the Mexican American Family." At the risk of oversimplification, it seems fair to say that the bulk of research at the end of the previous decade could be characterized not only as negative and pejorative, but as lacking in empirical support. Montiel (1970:62) has noted that such studies were based on a pathological model which "is inherently incapable of defining normal behavior and thus automatically labels all Mexican American people as sick—*only in degree of sickness do they vary.*"

During the late 1960s and early 1970s a number of Chicano scholars sought to refute many of the stereotypes and myths perpetrated by pathological studies and

[1]There were only 17 articles on Hispanic families between 1950 and 1959, 57 in the following decade, and 155 in the past decade (Padilla *et al.*, 1978).

to present a more sympathetic "inside" view of *la familia*. These sympathetic studies served as an important corrective; however, in their eagerness to counter negative perspectives, they tended to present an idealized and romanticized conception of the Chicano family. More recently, a body of research has emerged that is sympathetic to Chicanos and the nuance of Chicano culture, but which is increasingly rejecting of idealized and romantic stereotypes. While these approaches correspond roughly with the three chronological periods, adherents to each perspective are still to be found today.

Pejorative Depictions of the Mexican American Family

The traditional pejorative view of the Mexican American family can be traced to pathological studies of the Mexican family; works which see *machismo* as the key variable in explaining both the dynamics of Mexican family life and the emergence of Mexican national character (Bermudez, 1955; Gilbert, 1959; Paz, 1961; Ramos, 1962; Diaz-Guerrero, 1975). Based on psychoanalytic assumptions, such studies have assumed the Mexican to be driven by feelings of inadequacy, inferiority, and a rejection of authority. *Machismo* is thus a compensation for powerlessness.

The pathological view of *machismo* and the rigid patriarchal family has been uncritically applied to Mexicans on this side of the border. The father is depicted as the unquestioned authority—the omnipotent, omniscient "lord and master" of the household who is free to come and go as he pleases and to maintain the same lifestyle that he did before marriage.

This empirically unsupported model of Chicano family life, until recently, has been the most prevalent in the social sciences (*cf.* Humphrey, 1944; Jones, 1948; Heller, 1966; and Peñalosa, 1968). According to this view, a man has complete freedom to drink, fight, and carry on extramarital relationships at will. William Madsen (1973:22) has likened the Chicano male to a rooster: "The better man is the one who can drink more, defend himself best, have more sex relations, and have more sons borne by his wife." A man is seen as overly preoccupied with sex and with proving his masculinity and sexual prowess, and "the most convincing way of proving machismo and financial ability is to keep a mistress in a second household" (Madsen, 1973:51).

Not surprisingly, the woman becomes a quiet, saintly, virginal creature who honors and obeys her husband at any cost. According to Madsen (1932:22), the woman is the perfect counterpart to the man: "Where he is strong, she is weak. Where he is aggressive, she is submissive. While he is condescending toward her, she is respectful toward him." So strong is his control that she is expected to accept his marital transgressions and, if she does not, she is likely to be beaten. Moreover, "some wives assert that they are grateful for punishment at the hands of their husbands for such concern with shortcomings indicates profound love" (Madsen, 1973:22).

This patriarchal family system also has been assumed to adversely affect children. Childrearing was presumed to be rigid and authoritarian. The Chicano family was thus the obverse of the middle-class Anglo familial ideal. Where the Anglo family was egalitarian and democratic, the Chicano family was rigid and authoritarian. While the Anglo family encouraged achievement, independence, and a sense of self-worth, the Chicano family engendered passivity and dependence and adversely affected normal personality development. Celia Heller (1966:34–35) has argued that the Chicano family discouraged advancement "by stressing values that hinder mobility—family ties, honor, masculinity, and living in the present." Alvin Rudoff (1971:236–237) has been even more severe in his condemnation of the Chicano family:

> The family constellation is an unstable one as the father is seen as withdrawn and the mother as a self-sacrificing and saintly figure. The Mexican American has little concern for the future, perceives himself as predestined to be poor and subordinate, is still influenced by magic, is gang-minded, distrusts women, sees authority as arbitrary, tends to be passive and dependent, and is alienated from the Anglo culture.

Another commonly assumed effect of the authoritarian and patriarchal structure is family violence. Carroll (1980) has contended that values and norms which are endemic to Chicanos result in a high level of family violence. The democratic Jewish American family, on the other hand, is believed to generate a very low level of violence. Whereas the Chicano family emphasizes severe discipline and violence as a mechanism for conflict resolution, the Jewish American family emphasizes

> the pursuit of knowledge and the use of the mind rather than the body. The value of intellectuality resulting from these values was proposed to lead to the favoring of articulateness, argumentativeness, and bargaining as a way to solve family disputes (Carroll, 1980:80).

Positive Depictions of the Chicano Family

An important outcome of minority movements of the 1960s was that minority scholars began to question social science depictions, which were generally negative or pejorative, and to offer new "insider" (Merton, 1972) perspectives that were not only sensitive and sympathetic to minority cultures but, possibly more valid and consistent with the realities of the minority experience. Given this thrust, it was perhaps inevitable that Chicanos, like blacks, would begin to seriously reevaluate social science perspectives on the Chicano family. Interestingly, while black scholars faced the task of refuting the myth of the "matriarchy" (Staples, 1971), Chicanos had to deal with *machismo* and the issue of male dominance. There emerged, then, a "sympathetic" or "revisionist" view of the Chicano family.

Miguel Montiel (1970, 1972) who not only rejected pathological formulations but suggested that they be replaced with an "appreciative" framework, has been one of the best and most incisive critics of traditional perspectives. Octavio Romano (1973:52) has been similarly critical of social scientists for suggesting that Chicano parents, in effect, "are their children's own worst enemies" and that *la familia* Chicano is "un-American," potentially threatening our "democratic way of life" (1973:50). Alvirez and Bean (1976:277) have responded to the traditional negative view by noting that "only a person who has never experienced the warmth of the Mexican American family would tend to see it primarily from a negative perspective." Another writer to take issue with the traditional view has been Nathan Murillo (1971), who has characterized the Chicano family as a warm and nurturing institution. According to Murillo, family is the most important unit in life and the individual is likely to put the needs of the family above his own. Rather than being rigid and authoritarian, the family is now seen as a stable structure where the individual's place is clearly established and secure. Cooperation among family members is also emphasized. The family "seems to provide more emotional security and sense of belonging to its members" (Murillo, 1971:99). One's status within the family is determined by age and sex. While the father is the ultimate authority, other adults are also respected and honored as "being old and wise" (Goodman and Berman, 1971:111).

Whereas *machismo* was previously synonymous with power, control, and violence, it is now equated with honor, respect, and dignity. "An important part of [the father's] concept of machismo . . . is that [of] using his authority within the family in a just and fair manner" (Murillo, 1971:103). To misuse one's authority is to risk losing respect within the family and in the community.

Another Look at the Patriarchy: The Myth of Machismo

Although there appear to be both positive and negative perspectives of the Chicano family, a closer examination suggests a conversion of the two perspectives (Mirandé 1977:751). Both agree, for example, that male dominance is a persistent feature of the Chicano family, but one sees it as benevolent and the other as malevolent. Interestingly, the position is one held by both supporters and detractors of *la familia,* largely without the benefit of empirical support. When research findings have not supported traditional assumptions, there has been a tendency to resist them, especially by detractors of the Chicano family. "Findings which show that the Chicano family is more egalitarian than was previously assumed have been downplayed or explained away as resulting from increasing acculturation and assimilation" (Mirandé, 1979:475).

A study of California migrant farm families by Hawkes and Taylor (1975) hypothesized that male dominance would prevail. They found instead, that the dominant pattern of decision making and action making among these migrant families was egalitarian. Their response to this unexpected finding was to turn to other factors such as acculturation, urbanization, and the decreasing dependence of women on their husbands in the United States. Only after such attempts proved unsuccessful did the authors begin to question the assumption of male dominance as a prevailing feature of Mexican and Chicano culture (Hawkes and Taylor, 1975:811).

Hawkes and Taylor's findings are significant not so much for what they tell us about migrant farm families but for suggesting a pattern which may not be anomalous or unique to the population studied but characteristic of Chicano families in general. Virtually every systematic study of conjugal roles in the Chicano family has found egalitarianism to be the predominant pattern across socioeconomic groups, educational levels, urban-rural residence, and region of the country. The Mexican-American Study Project, a pioneering effort and one of the most extensive and widely acclaimed studies of the Chicano people, found that Chicanos in Los Angeles and San Antonio did not fall into the traditional patriarchal pattern. Respondent families, especially younger ones and those with higher incomes, were much less patriarchal than previously assumed. There was egalitarianism with respect to the performance of traditional sex-typed tasks, although traditional male tasks appeared to be breaking down more than traditional female tasks, suggesting that Chicanos are increasingly assuming male roles. They found, nonetheless, that sex, age, and income differences were not significant and concluded that "the most striking finding relates not to internal variations in the departure from traditional sex specializations, but rather to the conspicuous presence of a basically *egalitarian* division of household tasks" (Grebler *et al.*, 1970:362–363).

A more recent study of 100 married couples in Fresno, California, also uncovered a basically egalitarian pattern of decision making (Ybarra, 1977). While Ybarra found that conjugal role relations ranged from a patriarchal pattern to a completely egalitarian one, the most prevalent pattern was one in which the husband and wife shared in decisions (Ybarra, 1977:2):

> A large number of Chicano husbands helped their wives with household chores and child care. Also, the Chicanos interviewed were not as obsessed with the idea of machismo as has been suggested in the literature. The overwhelming majority of Chicano husbands preferred to participate in social and recreational activities with their wives and children. Overall, the data indicated that the majority of Chicano wives played an important and/or equal part in most facets of conjugal role relationships.

Factors such as level of acculturation, income, or education were not significantly related to the type of role relationships prevalent in the family. In fact, the only factor that significantly affected the role relationships exhibited was female employment outside the home, with families with working wives demonstrating a more egalitarian pattern relative to decision making, sharing of household tasks, and the caring of children. While couples who are already more egalitarian may be more predisposed to have a working wife, the mere fact of the wife's employment outside the home appears to require adjustments in marital roles and a shift toward a more egalitarian pattern. Yet, Chicanos can work and acquire more power in the family without assimilating or rejecting their ethnicity (Baca Zinn, 1980).

A study of self-report perceptions of spousal dominance among Kansas City Chicanos and blacks similarly failed to support the traditional view of *machismo* in the Chicano family. Cromwell and Cromwell (1978), in studying spousal dominance in decision making and conflict resolution, found that the most common pattern among Chicanos was egalitarianism, rather than male dominance.

After undertaking an extensive review of literature on power and control in the domestic sphere, Maxine Baca Zinn (1975, 1976) has gone a step beyond studies which suggest an egalitarian pattern by proposing that the Chicano family is, in fact, mother-centered. While the family may present a facade of patriarchy because cultural values dictate that the male should be honored and respected as titular head of the household, the day-to-day functioning of the family revolves around *la mujer*. The male has primary responsibility and power outside of the household, but the domestic sphere is the woman's domain (Baca Zinn, 1976). Other studies have suggested that the woman's influence is especially strong relative to children. Mothers not only perform many domestic tasks, but they have primary responsibility for the caring of children and for setting limits on their behavior (Tuck, 1946; Heller, 1966; Rubel, 1966; Goodman and Beman, 1971; Sotomayor, 1972). Ultimately, "as the *madrecita,* entitled to respect and homage, she may actually dominate, in all matters that affect her children" (Tuck, 1946:123).

The questioning of the rigid and authoritarian nature of the Mexican and Chicano family has extended beyond conjugal roles to relations between parents and children. Recent research suggests that parent-child relations may be warm and nurturing rather than cold and rigid. An important assumption that has been challenged is that fathers are necessarily more aloof and authoritarian than mothers. An observational study of Mexican family roles found fathers to be playful and companionable with children (Burrows, 1980). Rubel (1966:66) similarly concluded that "without exception, direct observations note the warmth and affection exhibited by fathers with their young sons and daughters, children under ten years of age." Goodman and Beman (1971:12) were also impressed with the strength and warmth of affection demonstrated in the Chicano family, noting that "the strength of intrafamily affection declared by Barrio children is conspicuous by contrast with responses of the Negro and Anglo children we interviewed." Finally, Bartz and Levine (1978:709) reported that it was black, rather than Chicano parents who were "typified as expecting early autonomy, not allowing wasted time, being both highly supportive and controlling, valuing strictness and encouraging egalitarian family roles." Black fathers were also most controlling. Significantly, of the three groups, Chicano parents were found to be most supportive of increasing permissiveness in parent-child relations (Bartz and Levine, 1978:715).

The Chicano Family: Social and Demographic Characteristics

There are a number of structural and demographic features which distinguish the Chicano family from the dominant American form. One distinctive feature is its high fertility relative not only to white but to black families (Alvirez and Bean,

1976:280–281). Not surprisingly, the Chicano population is a youthful one with a median age of about 21, compared to a median of 30 years for the rest of the population (U.S. Bureau of the Census, 1978:2). Whereas Chicano families average approximately four persons per family, other families average three (1978:11). The vast majority of Chicano children under 18 years of age (81 percent) live with both parents in intact families, 16 percent live with the mother, and only 1 percent live with the father (U.S. Bureau of the Census, 1978:46). Chicano families are about as likely to be maintained by a woman (16 percent) as are other Hispanic or Anglo families, but far less likely to be maintained by a woman than are Puerto Rican families (37 percent). The income of Chicano families is substantially lower than for other families. The median income for Chicano families in 1978 was $12,000, compared to $17,000 for families in the population as a whole (U.S. Department of Commerce, 1978). Twenty-two percent of all Mexican-origin families are below the poverty level, whereas only 9 percent of families not of Spanish origin are classified as poor (U.S. Bureau of the Census, 1978:15).

The marital status of Chicanos does not differ significantly from the general population, with approximately 60 percent of the population in each group classified as married, but Chicanos have a higher proportion of single and a lower proportion of widowed or divorced persons (U.S. Bureau of the Census, 1978:3). Thus, while Chicanos are about as likely to be married as other groups, they are less likely to be divorced. The divorce rate shows greater stability for Chicanos, especially Chicano men (Alvirez and Bean, 1976; Eberstein and Frisbie, 1976).

Since intermarriage has been presumed to be an important index of assimilation, there has been much interest in the outmarriage rates of Chicanos. The conclusions of earlier studies that intermarriage rates of Chicanos suggested a "breakdown of ethnic solidarity in an increasingly open system" (Grebler *et al.*, 1970:471) have been called into question by more recent research. While the overall trend during the present century has been toward intermarriage in the Southwest (Bean and Bradshaw, 1970), the trend appears to have stabilized and, perhaps, reversed in recent years. Murguia and Frisbie (1977:387) concluded after examining recent trends in intermarriage that:

> If the level of Spanish-surname intermarriage is conceived as the most conclusive, objective indicator of the degree of assimilation . . . , it seems probable that the Mexican American population will continue to represent a distinct sociocultural entity for some time to come.

Asian American Families

This minority group has largely been neglected in the family literature. Theory on their family life is nonexistent and empirical studies are sparse and clustered in a few areas. This is due, in part, to their small numbers and geographical concentration. There are approximately 1.5 million individuals of Chinese, Japanese, Korean, Filipino, Vietnamese, Cambodian, Thai, and East Indian ancestries living in the United States (Yamauchi, 1979). In total they constitute less than 1 percent of the American population and represent fewer than 10 percent of our minority groups. Most of them are concentrated in Hawaii and the western part of the United States. In addition, they tend to be underrepresented among social scientists and there are few insiders to develop theory and carry out research on their family lifestyles. Another possible reason is that, as a group, they are not perceived as a "problem" in American society or as very different in their family lifestyles. In the past, Asian men were stereotyped as wily and devious, the women as exotic and mysterious. That image essentially has changed to one of a hardworking, conforming, cohesive family group which is a carrier of a traditional culture similar to that of middle-class Anglo families (Sue and Kitano, 1973). Certainly, they fit better the family ideal of middle-class Americans than do the other minorities. Based on the positive indices of success and family stability, they not only are equal to white Americans, but often fare better in terms of educational achievement, median family income, and marital stability (U.S. Department of Health, Education, and Welfare, 1980).

The new stereotype of Asians as model minorities can be deleterious because it masks the problems they face. While they obviously have different characteristics than other minorities, the variations are not evenly spread across generations in their culture. Asian Americans can be separated chronologically into three groups: pre-1924 immigrants, American-born, and recent immigrants. Many of the pre-1924 immigrants, for instance, were males who came to this country alone and were unable to establish families because of immigration laws that prohibited Asian migration to this country for a long period of time (Lyman, 1968). That group, and the more recent immigrants, have not shared equally in the successes of American-born Asians. Even the American-born Asians are subject to tensions in their family life that remain unexplored by family researchers. Many Asian families contain at least two full-time workers, more than the average American family, and must use their income to support an extended family that is larger than most middle-class nuclear families (Wong, 1976).

Acculturation and assimilation seem to be key concepts in understanding Asian family life. This is particularly true of the younger, American-born group, which has adapted more strongly to American values and traditions (Kuroda et al., 1978). In comparison to the other minorities, Asians have more conservative sexual values, a lower fertility rate, fewer out-of-wedlock births, and more conservative attitudes toward the role of women (Monahan, 1977; Braun and Chao, 1978; Leonetti, 1978). The adoption of American values, however, has proved to be a mixed blessing for young Asian Americans. It has created a schism in the Asian community based on generational differences in language, customs, and values. It makes it difficult to maintain generational continuity and ethnic cohesiveness. Nowhere is this more evident than in high rates of out-marriages among younger Japanese and Chinese Americans (Weiss, 1970; Kikumura and Kitano, 1973). A majority of third generation Japanese Americans marry non-Japanese mates. The majority of out-marriages have involved Japanese women, although the rate for Japanese males in increasing. While many factors account for this high rate of intermarriage, a primary reason is the more acculturated Asian woman's dissatisfaction with the more traditional Japanese male's limited attitude toward women (Kikumura and Kitano, 1973; Braun and Chao, 1978).

Another index of acculturation is child-rearing practices. Studies generally have shown a congruity between third-generation Japanese socialization techniques and American styles of childrearing. However, differences based on some residue of Japanese culture remain. Caudill and Frost (1973) found that young Japanese mothers do more vocal lulling, more breast and bottle feeding, more carrying and more playing with the baby than do American mothers. Connor (1974) also discovered that the legacy of Japanese culture can still be found in third generation Japanese Americans. When compared with whites of the same age and education, the Japanese Americans were significantly different; they were less aggressive, had a greater need for succor and order, and a markedly lesser need for companionship. Johnson (1977) also reported that the Japanese American kinship system operates on a more obligatory basis than the optional basis found in the American kinship system. Her research revealed an increase in kinship contact and sociability among third generation Japanese American families, despite their social mobility and high degree of assimilation.

In sum, culture seems to be the key element in Asian family life. Their traditional culture stressed the importance of the family unit at the expense of the individual, and socialization processes in the family created patterns of self-control which facilitated the achievement of societal goals. These cultural values were very consonant with traditional American values and made them adaptable to the American family system. Class membership does not seem as important since many of the Asian immigrants brought with them values associated with the middle class: i.e., an emphasis on education and a capitalist orientation (Kitano, 1969). However, there are indications that many of these middle-class values are declining among the general American population. With their high degree of acculturation, younger Asian Americans face a clash of generations and a lack of ethnic cohesiveness that may entail a high cost.

Native American Families

While all our minority groups have certain commonalities, Native Americans have several problems which are unique to their particular group. The other minorities have a homeland that theoretically provides a symbolic identity with some other nation. Native Americans have no ties to any other geographical entity. As a group, they are more widely dispersed across North America and are more likely to reside in rural and isolated areas. Furthermore, they are more unalterably opposed to assimilation and integration into mainstream society and culture than any other minority group (Price, 1976). Even within the Native American group, there is a vast amount of diversity. They speak more than 252 languages and are organized into 280 different tribal groupings (Wax, 1971).

Given the existence of these esoteric traits, they cannot be viewed as a monolithic group whose family lifestyles can be easily studied.

In reviewing the family literature on Native Americans, we are hampered by several factors. There is no such institution as a Native American family. There are only tribes, and family structure and values will differ from tribe to tribe. Despite the attempt to impose Western family models on them, various family forms still exist among the different tribal groupings (Unger, 1977). These forms range from polygamy to monogamy, matrilineality to patrilineality (McAdoo, 1978). Most of the literature that is extant can be found in social work and mental health journals. These articles primarily focus upon Native American families as cultural deviants constituting a problem for the larger society. Another body of literature consists of anthropological studies, which again raise the insider-outsider issue. Unlike other minority groups, research done on Native Americans is almost exclusively monopolized by white Americans. Since anthropologists have been outsiders in Native American culture, the few existing Native American social scientists have been critical of outsider perspectives on Native American family life (Redhorse *et al.,* 1978). Oftentimes the outsiders could neither speak the language, nor even locate the living quarters of many Native Americans. In the words of Dorothy Miller (1975:7), a Native-American, "most of us look upon 'surveys' and 'research' as being tools of our suppression and withhold data from white investigators."

In a general sense, Native Americans most closely approximate black American families. Both groups are characterized by a high fertility rate, out-of-wedlock births, a strong role for women, female-headed households, and high rates of unemployment (Witt, 1974; Unger, 1977; U.S. Department of Health, Education, and Welfare, 1980). For many Native Americans, the extended family is the basic unit for carrying out family functions. This is often true despite the absence of extended kin in the same household. Children are actually raised by relatives residing in different, noncontiguous households. The existence of multiple households sharing family functions is quite common. Redhorse (1979) discovered one community where 92 percent of the elderly population resided in independent households, but maintained close functional contact with their children, grandchildren, and great grandchildren. They fulfilled traditional family roles on a daily basis. Fictive kin are also incorporated into the extended family system. An individual, for example, may become a namesake for a child through formal ritual and subsequently assume family obligations and responsibilities for childrearing and role modeling (Momaday, 1976).

In the move from tribal reservations to the urban frontiers, Native Americans often become more isolated and must confront certain vicissitudes of city life without their traditional support system. Certainly, the proportion of Native Americans living off reservations has rapidly increased. In 1930, only 10 percent lived in urban areas. By 1970 that number had grown to 45 percent (U.S. Bureau of the Census, 1974). In their study of 120 urban Native American families, Miller (1975) and her Native American researchers discovered that: (1) one third were female-headed; (2) 27 percent were receiving public welfare; (3) they had an average of three children; and (4) only one third had an adequate income. They found that traditional childrearing techniques were still used by most of the parents. Native American children continued to be trained for independence at significantly earlier ages than either white or black urban children. Their findings support a bicultural model which holds that families who are at home in both the Native American and white world have a greater ability to survive and adapt to the city than do families who only are comfortable in one culture or who feel alienated from both worlds.

The status of Native American families remains in a state of transition. High unemployment and a desire for a better life have propelled many from the reservations into the urban centers. Once in the cities, they encounter a clash of cultures between Native American ways and norms of city life. Moreover, they cannot rely on the extended family system which serves as an anchor of Native American culture and life on the reservations. Hence, there is a constant tension as they seek equilibrium in an alien and hostile environment. In a follow-up study of the urban Native American families, Miller (1980) found that 40 percent had returned to the reservation. Some returned because of dislike for the city, others went back because they could not cope with its demands. Some, however, made a successful bicultural adaptation and returned to their community with leadership and technical skills and an appreciation and understanding of both worlds.

Summary

Our decade review of research and theory on minority families illustrates the fact that there has been an increase in both the quantity and quality of the family literature. Some problems remain. Research continues to be clustered in specific areas while other areas are neglected. In the case of Asian and Native American families, basic studies need to be conducted. Future research needs to focus on the minority family unit as an autonomous system with its own norms, rather than comparing it to or constrasting it with the majority culture using white, middle-class standards. Only by this means will the insider-outsider dichotomy dissipate as a salient issue. Furthermore, both qualitative and quantitative approaches are necessary in the study of minority families. Since these groups remain outside the mainstream of society, the nuances of their cultures cannot be thoroughly understood through the sole use of one-dimensional empirical research. At the same time, we need the solid grounding of quantitative data. Different populations need to be sampled in order to ascertain class and cultural variation within and between minority groups. There is little we can say about class differences among minority families, since few studies have used class controls or accounted for its effect. Finally, while there is no validity to the idea that the family system of a given minority is pathological, there also is little credibility to a philosophical school that assumes that all aspects of minority family life are strong and healthy and that no weaknesses of any kind exist. What we need is theory and research that can give us a balanced account of both strengths and weaknesses of minority families. That remains our task for the next decade.

References

Allen, W.
1978 "Black family research in the United States: A review, assessment and extension." Journal of Comparative Family Studies 9 (Summer): 167–189.

Alvirez, D., and F. Bean
1976 "The Mexican family." Pp. 271–292 in Charles H. Mindel and R. Habenstein (Eds.), Ethnic Families in America. New York: Elsevier.

Aschenbrenner, J.
1975 Lifelines: Black families in Chicago. New York: Holt, Rinehart, and Winston.

Baca Zinn, M.
1975 "Political familism: Toward sex role equality in Chicano families." Aztlan: Chicano Journal of the Social Sciences and the Arts 6 (Winter): 13–26.
1976 "Chicanas: Power and control in the domestic sphere." De Colores 2 (Fall): 19–31.
1980 "Employment and education of Mexican-American women: The interplay of modernity and ethnicity in eight families." Harvard Educational Review 50 (February): 47–62.

Bartz, K., and E. Levine
1978 "Childrearing by black parents: A description and comparison to Anglo and Chicano parents." Journal of Marriage and the Family 40 (November): 709–719.

Bean, F., and B. Bradshaw
1970 "Intermarriage between persons of Spanish and non-Spanish surname: Changes from the mid-nineteenth to the mid-twentieth century." Social Science Quarterly 51 (September): 389–395.

Bermudez, M.
1955 La Vida familar del mexicano. Mexico. D. F.: Antigua Libreria Robredo.

Bianchi, S., and R. Farley
1979 "Racial differences in family living arrangements and economic well-being: An analysis of recent trends." Journal of Marriage and the Family 41 (August): 537–552.

Blassingame, J.
1972 The Slave Community. New York: Oxford University Press.

Braun, J., and H. Chao
1978 "Attitudes toward women: A comparison of Asian-born Chinese and American Caucasians." Psychology of Women Quarterly 2 (Spring): 195–201.

Burrows, P.
1980 "Mexican parental roles: Differences between mother's and father's behavior to children." Paper presented to the annual meeting of the Society for Cross-Cultural Research. Philadelphia (February).

Cade, T.
1970 The Black Woman: An Anthology. New York: Signet Books.

Carroll, J. C.
1980 "A cultural-consistency theory of family violence in Mexican-American and Jewish ethnic groups." Chapter 5 in M. A. Straus and G. T. Hotaling (Eds.), The Social Causes of Husband-Wife Violence. Minneapolis: University of Minnesota Press.

Caudill, W., and L. Frost
1973 "A comparison of maternal care and infant behavior in Japanese-American, American and Japanese families." Unpublished paper, National Institute of Mental Health, Bethesda, Maryland.

Chavis, W., and G. Lyles
1975 "Divorce among educated black women." Journal of the National Medical Association 67 (March): 128–134.

Christensen, H., and L. Johnson
  1978   "Premarital coitus and the southern black: a comparative view." Journal of Marriage and the Family 40 (November): 721–732.
Connor, J.
  1974   "Acculturation and family continuities in three generations of Japanese Americans." Journal of Marriage and the Family 36 (February): 159–168.
Cromwell, V., and R. Cromwell
  1978   "Perceived dominance in decision making and conflict resolution among black and Chicano couples." Journal of Marriage and the Family 40 (November): 749–759.
Dennis, R.
  1976   "Theories of the black family: The weak-family and strong-family schools as competing ideologies." Journal of Afro-American Issues 4 (Summer/Fall): 315–328.
Diaz-Guerrero, R.
  1975   Psychology of the Mexican: Culture and Personality. Austin: University of Texas Press.
Dickinson, G.
  1975   "Dating behavior of black and white adolescents before and after desegregation." Journal of Marriage and the Family 37 (August): 602–608.
Eberstein, I., and W. P. Frisbie
  1976   "Differences in marital stability among Mexican Americans, blacks and Anglos: 1960 and 1970." Social Problems 23 (June): 609–621.
Elkins, S.
  1968   Slavery: A Problem in American Institutional and Intellectual Life. Chicago: University of Chicago Press.
Farley, R.
  1970   Growth of the Black Population. Chicago: Markham.
Fogel, W., and S. Engerman
  1974   Time on the Cross. Boston: Little, Brown and Company.
Frazier, E. F.
  1939   The Negro Family in the United States. Chicago: University of Chicago Press.
Furstenberg, R., Hershberg, T., and J. Modell
  1975   "The origins of the female headed black family: The impact of the urban experience." Journal of Interdisciplinary History 5 (Spring): 211–233.
Genovese, E.
  1974   Roll, Jordan, Roll. New York: Pantheon Press.
Gilbert, G. M.
  1959   "Sex differences in mental health in a Mexican village." The International Journal of Social Psychiatry 3 (Winter): 208–213.
Goodman, M. E., and A. Beman
  1971   "Child's-eye-views of life in an urban barrio." Pp. 109–122 in N. Wagner and M. Haug (Eds.), Chicanos: Social and Psychological Perspectives. St. Louis: C. V. Mosby Company.
Gordon, M.
  1964   Assimilation in American Life. New York: Oxford University Press.
Grebler, L., Moore, J. W., and R. C. Guzman
  1970   The Mexican American People. New York: The Free Press.
Gutman, H.
  1976   The Black Family in Slavery and Freedom: 1750–1925. New York: Pantheon Books.
Halpern, F.
  1973   Survival: Black/White. New York: Pergamon Press.
Hampton, R.
  1979   "Husband's characteristics and marital disruption in black families." Sociological Quarterly (September): 255–266.
Hawkes, G., and M. Taylor
  1975   "Power structure in Mexican and Mexican American farm labor families." Journal of Marriage and the Family 37 (November): 807–811.
Haynes, T., and L. Johnson
  1980   "Changing perspectives on black families in empirical research: Selected journals: 1965–1979." Unpublished manuscript. Washington, D.C., The Urban Institute.

Heer, D.
   1974   "The prevalence of black-white marriage in the United States, 1960 and 1970." Journal of
          Marriage and the Family 35 (February): 246–258.
Heiss, J.
   1975   The Case of the Black Family: A Sociological Inquiry. New York: Columbia University
          Press.
Heller, C.
   1966   Mexican American Youth: Forgotten Youth at the Crossroads. New York: Random House.
Henriques, F.
   1975   Children of Conflict: A Study of Interracial Sex and Marriage. New York: E. P. Hutton.
Hill, R.
   1972   The Strengths of Black Families. New York: Emerson-Hall Publishers.
   1977   Informal Adoption. Washington, D.C.: National Urban League Research Department.
Humphrey, H.
   1944   "The changing structure of the Detroit Mexican family: An index of acculturation."
          American Sociological Review 9 (December): 622–626.
Johnson, C. L.
   1977   "Interdependence, reciprocity and indebtedness: An analysis of Japanese American kinship
          relations." Journal of Marriage and the Family 39 (May): 351–364.
Jones, R. C.
   1948   "Ethnic family patterns: The Mexican family in the United States." American Journal of
          Sociology 53 (May): 450–452.
Kagan, S., and D. Valdez
   in press   "Mexican American family research: A critical review and conceptual framework."
          De Colores.
Kikumura, A., and H. Kitano
   1973   "Interracial marriage: A picture of the Japanese Americans." Journal of Social Issues 29
          (Spring): 67–81.
Kiser, C.
   1970   Demographic Aspects of the Black Community. New York: Milbank Memorial Fund.
Kitano, H.
   1969   Japanese Americans: The Evolution of a Subculture. Englewood Cliffs, New Jersey: Pren-
          tice Hall.
Kuroda, Y., Suzuki, T., and C. Hayashi
   1978   "A cross-national analysis of the Japanese character among Japanese-Americans in Hon-
          olulu." Ethnicity 5 (March): 45–59.
Ladner, J.
   1971   Tomorrow's Tomorrow: The Black Woman. Garden City, New York: Doubleday.
Leonetti, D. L.
   1978   "The biocultural pattern of Japanese-American fertility." Social Biology 25 (Spring):
          38–51.
Lieberman, L.
   1973   "The emerging model of the black family." International Journal of Sociology of the Family
          3 (March): 10–22.
Lyman, S.
   1968   "Marriage and the family among Chinese immigrants to America, 1850–1960." Phylon 29
          (Winter): 321–330.
Madsen, W.
   1973   The Mexican-Americans of South Texas (2nd ed.). New York: Holt, Rinehart, and Winston.
Mannheim, K.
   1936   Ideology and Utopia. New York: Harcourt, Brace, and World.
Martin, E., and J. Martin
   1978   The Black Extended Family. Chicago: University of Chicago Press.
McAdoo, H.
   1978a "Factors related to stability in upwardly mobile black families." Journal of Marriage and
          the Family 40 (November): 762–778.
   1978b "Minority families." Pp. 177–195 in J. Stevens and M. Mathews (Eds.), Mother/Child,
          Father/Child Relationships. Washington, D.C.: National Association of Young Children.

Merton, R. K.
  1972   "Insiders and outsiders: A chapter in the sociology of knowledge." American Journal of
         Sociology 78 (July): 9–48.
Miller, D.
  1975   American Indian Socialization to Urban Life. San Francisco: Institute for Scientific
         Analysis.
  1980   "The Native American family: The urban way." Pp. 441–484 in E. Corfman (Ed.), Families
         Today. Washington, D.C.: U.S. Government Printing Office.
Mirandé, A.
  1977   "The Chicano family: A reanalysis of conflicting views." Journal of Marriage and the
         Family 39 (November): 747–756.
  1979   "Machismo: A reinterpretation of male dominance in the Chicano family." The Family
         Coordinator 28 (October): 473–479
  in press   "Machismo: Rucas, chingasos, y chingaderas." De Colores.
Momaday, N. S.
  1976   The Names. New York: Harper and Row, Publishers.
Monahan, T.
  1977   "Illegitimacy by race and mixture of race." International Journal of Sociology of the Family
  7 (January–June): 45–54.
Montiel, M.
  1970   "The social science myth of the Mexican American family." El Grito: A Journal of
         Contemporary Mexican American Thought 3 (Summer): 56–63.
  1973   "The Chicano family: A review of research." Social Work 18 (March): 22–31.
Moynihan, D. P.
  1965   The Negro Family: The Case for National Action. Washington, D.C.: U.S. Government
         Printing Office.
Murguia, E., and W. P. Frisbie
  1977   "Trends in Mexican-American intermarriage: Recent findings in perspective." Social Sci-
         ence Quarterly 58 (December): 374–389.
Murillo, N.
  1971   "The Mexican American family." Pp. 97–108 in N. Wagner and M. Haug (Eds.), Chicanos:
         Social and Psychological Perspectives. St. Louis: C. V. Mosby Company.
Myrdal, G.
  1944   An American Dilemma. New York: Harper and Row, Publishers.
Noble, J.
  1978   Beautiful, Also, Are the Souls of My Black Sisters: A History of the Black Woman in
         America. Englewood Cliffs, New Jersey: Prentice-Hall.
Nobles, W.
  1978   "Toward an empirical and theoretical framework for defining black families." Journal of
         Marriage and the Family 40 (November): 679–698.
Padilla, A. M., S. Olmedo, and R. Perez
  1978   "Hispanic mental health bibliography." Spanish Speaking Mental Health Research Center,
         University of California, Los Angeles, Monograph No. 6.
Parsons, T., and R. Bales
  1955   Family, Socialization and Interaction Process. Glencoe, Illinois: The Free Press.
Paz, O.
  1961   The Labyrinth of Solitude. New York: Grove.
Peñalosa, F.
  1968   "Mexican family roles." Journal of Marriage and the Family 30 (November): 680–689.
Porter, J.
  1979   Dating Habits of Young Black Americans. Dubuque, Iowa: Kendall Hunt.
Porterfield, E.
  1977   Black and White Mixed Marriages. Chicago: Nelson-Hall.
Price, J.
  1976   "North American Indian families." Pp. 248–270 in C. Mindel and R. Habenstein (Eds.),
         Ethnic Families in America. New York: Elsevier.
Rainwater, L.
  1966   "The crucible of identity: The lower class Negro family." Daedalus 95 (Winter): 258–264.

Ramos, S.
    1962   Profile of Man and Culture in Mexico. Austin: University of Texas Press.
Redhorse, J. G., R. Lewis, M. Feit, and J. Decker
    1978   "Family behavior of urban American Indians." Social Casework 59 (Winter): 67–72. 1979.
            "American Indian elders: Needs and aspirations in institutional and home health care."
            Unpublished manuscript, Arizona State University.
Romano, O. I.
    1973   "The anthropology and sociology of the Mexican Americans: The distortion of Mexican
            American history." Pp. 43–56 in O. Romano (Ed.), Voices: Reading From El Grito.
            Berkeley: Quinto Sol Publications.
Rose, L.
    1980   The Black Woman. Beverly Hills: Sage Publications.
Rubel, A. L.
    1966   Across the Tracks: Mexican-Americans in a Texas City. Austin: University of Texas Press.
Rudoff, A.
    1971   "The incarcerated Mexican-American delinquent." Journal of Criminal Law. Criminology
            and Police Science 62 (June): 224–238.
Scanzoni, J.
    1971   The Black Family in Modern Society. Boston: Allyn and Bacon.
Shimkin, D., E. Shimkin, and D. Frate
    1978   The Extended Family in Black Societies. Chicago: Aldine Publishing Company.
Silverstein, B., and R. Krate
    1975   Children of the Dark Ghetto. New York: Praeger Publishing Company.
Stack, C.
    1974   All Our Kin. New York: Harper and Row, Publishers.
Staples, R.
    1971   "Towards a sociology of the black family: A theoretical and methodological assessment."
            Journal of Marriage and the Family 33 (February): 119–138.
    1973   "The Black Woman in America." Chicago: Nelson-Hall.
    1974   "The black family revisited: A review and a preview." Journal of Social and Behavioral
            Sciences 20 (Spring): 65–78.
    1976a   Introduction to Black Sociology. New York: McGraw-Hill.
    1976   "Race and colonialism: The domestic case in theory and praxis." The Black Scholar 7
            (June): 37–50.
    1978a   "Mental health and black family life." Pp. 73–94 in L. Gary (Ed.), Mental Health: A
            Challenge to the Black Community. Philadelphia: Dorrance.
    1978b   "Race, liberalism–conservatism and premarital sexual permissiveness: A biracial compari-
            son." Journal of Marriage and the Family 40 (November): 78–92.
    in press The World of Black Singles: Changing Patterns of Male/Female Relations. Westport,
            Connecticut: Greenwood.
Stember, C.
    1976   Racial Sexism. New York: Elsevier.
Sotomayor, M.
    1971   "Mexican American interaction with social systems." Social Casework 52 (May): 316–322.
Sue, S., and H. Kitano
    1973   "Asian American stereotypes." Journal of Social Issues 29 (Spring): 83–98.
Tuck, R.
    1946   Not With the Fist. New York: Harcourt, Brace, and World.
U.S. Bureau of the Census
    1974   "A study of selected socio-economic characteristics of ethnic minorities based on the 1970
            Census. Vol. III. American Indians." Washington, D.C.: U.S. Government Printing Office.
    1978   "Persons of Spanish origin in the United States: March, 1977." Series p-20, No. 329.
            Washington, D.C.: U.S. Government Printing Office.
    1979   "The social and economic status of the black population in the United States: An historical
            view, 1790–1978." Series p-28, No. 80. Washington, D.C: U.S. Government Printing
            Office.

U.S. Department of Commerce
    1978   "U.S. Spanish origin population now 12 million census survey shows." August 21, Washington, D.C.: Commerce News.
U.S. Department of Health, Education, and Welfare
    1980   "Health status of minorities and low-income groups." Washington, D.C.: U.S. Government Printing Office.
Unger, S.
    1977   The Destruction of American Families. New York: Association on American Indian Affairs.
Wallace, M.
    1979   Black Macho and the Myth of the Super Woman. New York: Dial Publishing.
Wax, M. L.
    1971   Indian Americans: Unity and Diversity. Englewood Cliffs, New Jersey: Prentice-Hall.
Weiss, M.
    1970   "Selective acculturation and the dating process: The patterning of Chinese-Caucasian interracial dating." Journal of Marriage and the Family 32 (May): 273–278.
Willie, C. V.
    1976   A New Look at Black Families. Bayside, New York: General Hall.
Witt, S. W.
    1974   "Native women today." Civil Rights Digest 6 (Spring): 30–34.
Wong, L.
    1976   "The Chinese experience: From yellow peril to model minority." Journal of Social Issues 9 (Fall): 33–41.
Yamauchi, J. S.
    1979   "Asian American communications: The women's self-concept and cultural accommodations." Paper presented at the conference on the Minority Woman in America. San Francisco (March).
Ybarra, L.
    1977   "Conjugal role relationships in the Chicano family." Unpublished doctoral dissertation. University of California.
    in press   "Marital decision-making and the role of machismo in the Chicano family." De Colores.

Poverty and Family Structure:
The Widening Gap Between Evidence and Public
Policy Issues

William Julius Wilson, with Kathryn Neckerman

In the early and mid-1960s social scientists such as Kenneth B. Clark, Lee Rainwater, and Daniel Patrick Moynihan discussed in clear and forceful terms the relationship between black poverty and family structure and sounded the alarm even then that the problems of family dissolution among poor blacks were approaching catastrophic proportions. These writers emphasized that the rising rates of broken marriages, out-of-wedlock births, female-headed families, and welfare dependency among poor urban blacks were the products not only of race-specific experiences, but also of structural conditions in the larger society, including economic relations. And they underlined the need to address these problems with programs that would attack structural inequality in American society and thereby, in the words of Moynihan, "bring the Negro American to full and equal sharing in the responsibilities and rewards of citizenship."

There is a distinct difference in the way the problems of poverty and family structure were viewed in the major studies of the 1960s and the way they are viewed today, however. Unlike the earlier studies, discussions in the current research of the relationship between black family instability and male joblessness have been overshadowed by discussions that link family instability with the growth of income transfers and in-kind benefits. Because, as we demonstrate [here], the factors associated with the rise of single-parent families—not only among blacks, but among whites as well—are sufficiently complex to preclude overemphasis on any single variable, the recent trend among scholars and policy-makers to neglect the role of male joblessness while emphasizing the role of welfare is especially questionable. But first let us examine the problem of poverty and family structure in its historical context.

Poverty and Family Structure in Historical Perspective

In the early twentieth century the vast majority of both black and white low-income families were intact. Although national information on family structure was not available before the publication of the 1940 census, studies of early manuscript census forms of individual cities and counties make it clear that even among the very poor, a substantial majority of both black and white families were

Reprinted by permission of the publishers from *Fighting Poverty: What Works and What Doesn't*, Sheldon H. Danziger and Daniel H. Weinbert, eds., Cambridge, Mass.: Harvard University Press, Copyright © 1986 by The Board of Regents of the University of Wisconsin System. Footnotes, some text, and all tables and figures, and references to them, have been omitted.

504

two-parent families. Moreover, most of the women heading families in the late nineteenth and early twentieth centuries were widows. Evidence from the 1940 census indicates that divorce and separation were relatively uncommon.

It is particularly useful to consider black families in historical perspective because social scientists have commonly assumed that the recent trends in black family structure that are of concern in this [article] could be traced to the lingering effects of slavery. E. Franklin Frazier's classic statement of this view in *The Negro Family in the United States* informed all subsequent studies of the black family, including the Moynihan report. But recent research has challenged assumptions about the influence of slavery on the character of the black family. Reconstruction of black family patterns from manuscript census forms has shown that the two-parent, nuclear family was the predominant family form in the late nineteenth and early twentieth centuries. Historian Herbert Gutman examined the data on black family structure in the northern urban areas of Buffalo and Brooklyn, New York; in the southern cities of Mobile, Alabama, of Richmond, Virginia, and of Charleston, South Carolina; and in several counties and small towns during this period. He found that between 70 percent and 90 percent of black households were "male-present" and that a majority were nuclear families. Similar findings have been reported for Philadelphia, for rural Virginia, for Boston, and for cities of the Ohio Valley. This research demonstrates that neither slavery, nor economic deprivation, nor the migration to urban areas affected black family structure by the first quarter of the twentieth century.

However, the poverty and degraded conditions in which most blacks lived were not without their consequences for the family. For the most part, the positive association between intact family structure and measures of class, such as property ownership, occupation, or literacy, generally reflected the higher rate of mortality among poor men. Widowhood accounted for about three-quarters of female-headed families among blacks, Germans, Irish, and native white Americans in Philadelphia in 1880. In addition, men sometimes had to live apart from their families as they moved from one place to another in search of work. Given their disproportionate concentration among the poor in America, black families were more strongly affected by these conditions and therefore were more likely than white families to be female headed. For example, in Philadelphia in 1880, 25.3 percent of all black families were female headed, compared to only 13.6 percent of all native white families.

The earliest detailed national census information on family structure is available from the 1940 census. In 1940 female-headed families were more prevalent among blacks than among whites, and among urbanites than among rural residents for both groups. Yet, even in urban areas, 72 percent of black families with children under eighteen were male headed. Moreover, irrespective of race and residence, most women heading families were widows.

The two-parent nuclear family remained the predominant type for both blacks and whites up to World War II. . . . 10 percent of white families and 18 percent of black families were female headed in 1940. The relative stability in gross census figures on female-headed families between 1940 and 1960 obscures the beginnings of current trends in family breakup. More specifically, while widowhood fell significantly during those two decades, marital dissolution was rising. Furthermore, the proportion of out-of-wedlock births was growing. By the 1960s, the proportion of female-headed families had begun to increase significantly among blacks, rising from 22 percent in 1960 to 28 percent in 1970, and then to 42 percent by 1983. This proportion also rose among white families, from 8 percent in 1960 to 12 percent in 1983. The increase in female-headed families with children under eighteen is even more dramatic. By 1983, almost one out of five families with children under eighteen were headed by women, including 14 percent of white families, 24 percent of Spanish-origin families, and 48 percent of black families. To understand the nature of these shifts, it is necessary to disaggregate these statistics and consider factors such as changes in fertility rates, marital status, age structure, and living arrangements.

Changing Family Structure and Demographic Correlates

The unprecedented increases in the proportion of births out of wedlock are a major contributor to the rise of female-headed families in the black community. In 1980, 68 percent of births to black women ages fifteen to twenty-four were outside of marriage, compared to 41 percent in 1955. According to 1981 figures, almost 30 percent of all young single black women have borne a child before the age of twenty. The incidence of out-of-wedlock births has risen to unprecedented levels for young white women as well, although both rates and ratios remain far below those for black women. . . .

These increases in births outside of marriage reflect trends in fertility and marital status, as well as changes in population composition. Age-specific fertility rates for both white and black women have fallen since the peak of the baby boom in the late 1950s. Even fertility rates for teenagers (ages fifteen to nineteen) have fallen overall. What these figures obscure, however, is that the fertility rates of young unmarried women have risen or declined only moderately, while those of married women of these ages have fallen more substantially. . . . In addition, growing proportions of young women are single. For instance, the percentage of never-married women increased dramatically between 1960 and 1980, from 29 percent to 47 percent for whites, and from 30 percent to 69 percent for blacks. Recent data show not only that the incidence of premarital conception has increased, but also that the proportion of those premarital pregnancies legitimated by marriage has decreased. Thus, out-of-wedlock births now comprise a far greater proportion of total births than they did in the past, particularly for black women. . . . The black "illegitimacy ratio" has increased so precipitously in recent years not because the rate of extramarital births has substantially increased, but because the percentage of women married and the rate of marital fertility have both declined significantly.

The decline in the proportion of women who are married and living with their husbands is a function of both a sharp rise in separation and divorce rates and the substantial increase in the percentage of never-married women. The combined impact of these trends has been particularly drastic for black women as the proportion married and living with their husbands fell from 52 percent in 1947 to 34 percent in 1980. . . . [B]lack women have much higher separation and divorce rates than white women, although the differences are exaggerated because of a higher rate of remarriage among white women. Whereas white women are far more likely to be divorced than separated, black women are more likely to be separated than divorced. Indeed, a startling 22 percent of all married black women are separated from their husbands.

Just as important a factor in the declining proportion of black women who are married and living with their husbands is the increase in the percentage of never-married women. Indeed, . . . the proportion of never-married black women increased from 65 percent in 1960 to 82 percent in 1980 for those ages fourteen to twenty-four and from 8 percent to 21 percent for those ages twenty-five to forty-four. On the other hand, while the proportion of black women who are separated or divorced increased from 22 percent in 1960 to 31 percent in 1980 for those ages twenty-five to forty-four, and from 17 percent to 25 percent for those ages forty-five to sixty-four, the fraction divorced or separated actually fell for younger women.

For young women, both black and white, the increase in the percentage of never-married women largely accounts for the decline in the proportion married with husband present. . . . For black women ages twenty-five to forty-four, increases in both the percentage of never-married women and in marital dissolution were important; for white women of the same age-group, marital dissolution is the more important factor. Marriage has not declined among white women ages forty-five to sixty-four; however, among black women in the same age-group, the proportion married with husband present has fallen, due mainly to increases in marital dissolution.

Although trends in fertility and marital status are the most important contributors to the rise of female-headed families, the situation has been exacerbated by recent changes in the age structure, which have temporarily increased the proportion of young women in the population, particularly in the black population. Whereas in 1960, only 36 percent of black women ages fifteen to forty-four were between fifteen and twenty-four years of age, by 1975 that proportion had increased to 46 percent; the comparable increase for white women was from 34 percent in 1960 to 42 percent in 1975. These changes in the age structure increase the proportion of births occurring to young women and, given the higher out-of-wedlock birth ratios among young women, inflate the proportion of all births that occur outside of marriage as well.

Finally, the rise in the proportion of female-headed families reflects an increasing tendency for women to form independent households rather than to live in subfamilies. Until recently, Census Bureau coding procedures caused the number of subfamilies to be significantly underestimated; therefore, an accurate time series is impossible. However, other research suggests that women are becoming more likely to form their own households. For example, Cutright's analysis of components of growth in female-headed families between 1940 and 1970 indicates that 36 percent of the increase in numbers of female family heads between the ages of fifteen and forty-four can be attributed to the higher propensity of such women to form their own households. Bane and Ellwood show that these trends continued during the 1970s. In the period 1969 to 1973, 56 percent of white children and 60 percent of black children born into single-parent families lived in households headed by neither mother nor father (most lived with grandparents). During the years 1974 to 1979, those proportions declined to 24 percent for white children and 37 percent for black children.

Thus, young women comprise a greater proportion of single mothers than ever before. For example, while in 1950, only 26 percent of black female family heads and 12 percent of white female family heads were under the age of thirty-five, in 1983 those proportions had risen to 43 percent for blacks and 29 percent for whites. The number of black children growing up in fatherless families increased by 41 percent between 1970 and 1980, and most of this growth has occurred in families in which the *mother has never been married*. This is not surprising, according to Bane and Ellwood's research: whereas the growth of the number of single white mothers over the last decade is mainly due to the increase in separation and divorce, the growth of the number of single black mothers is "driven by a dramatic decrease in marriage and increase in fertility among never-married women." In 1982 the percentage of black children living with both parents had dipped to 43 percent, only roughly half of the proportion of white children in two-parent homes.

As Bane and Ellwood point out, "Never married mothers are more likely than divorced, separated or widowed mothers to be younger and to be living at home when they have their children." Younger mothers tend to have less education, less work experience, and thus fewer financial resources. Therefore they are more likely initially to form subfamilies, drawing support from parents and relatives. However, it appears that most children of single mothers in subfamilies spend only a small part of their lives in such families. On the basis of an analysis of data from the Panel Study of Income Dynamics (PSID) for the period 1968 to 1979, Bane and Ellwood suggest that by the time children born into subfamilies reach age six, two-thirds will have moved into different living arrangements. Among blacks, two-thirds of the moves are into independent female-headed families, whereas among whites two-thirds are into two-parent families. However, whether the focus is on subfamilies or on independent female-headed families, less than 10 percent of white children and almost half of the black children born into non-two-parent families remain in such families "for their entire childhood." And, as discussed in the next section, these families are increasingly plagued by poverty.

The Poverty Status of Female-Headed Families

. . . The rise of female-headed families has had dire social and economic consequences because these families are far more vulnerable to poverty than are other types of families. Indeed, sex and marital status of the head are the most important determinants of poverty status for families, especially in urban areas. The poverty rate of female-headed families was 36.3 percent in 1982, while the rate for married-couple families was only 7.6 percent. For black and Spanish-origin female-headed families in 1982, poverty rates were 56.2 percent and 55.4 percent, respectively.

Female-headed families comprise a growing proportion of the poverty population. Individuals in female-headed families made up fully a third of the poverty population in 1982. Forty-six percent of all poor families and 71 percent of all poor black families were female headed in 1982. These proportions were higher for metropolitan areas, particularly for central cities, where 60 percent of all poor families and 78 percent of all poor black families were headed by women. The proportion of poor black families headed by women increased steadily from 1959 to 1977, from less than 30 percent to 72 percent, and has remained slightly above 70 percent since then. The total number of poor black female-headed families continued to grow between 1977 and 1982, increasing by 373,000; the proportion of the total number of poor black families did not continue to increase only because of the sharp rise in the number of male-headed families in poverty during this period (from 475,000 to 622,000 in 1982). The proportion of poor white families headed by women also increased from less than 20 percent in 1959 to a high of almost 40 percent in 1977, and then dropping to 35 percent in 1983.

Female-headed families are not only more likely to be in poverty, they are also more likely than male-headed families to be persistently poor. For example, Duncan reports, on the basis of data from the Michigan PSID, that 61 percent of those who were persistently poor over a ten-year period were in female-headed families, a proportion far exceeding the prevalence of female-headed families in the general population.

Causes of the Rise in Female-Headed Families

As the foregoing discussion suggests, to speak of female-headed families and out-of-wedlock births is to emphasize that they have become inextricably tied up with poverty and dependency, often long term. The sharp rise in these two forms of social dislocation is related to the demographic changes in the population that we discussed in the previous section. For example, the drop in the median age of women heading families would lead one to predict a higher rate of poverty among these families, all other things being equal. We only need to consider that young women who have a child out of wedlock, the major contributor to the drop in median age of single mothers, are further disadvantaged by the disruption of their schooling and employment.

However, while a consideration of demographic changes may be important to understand the complex nature and basis of changes in family structure, it is hardly sufficient. Indeed, changes in demographic factors are generally a function of broader economic, political, and social trends. For example, the proportion of out-of-wedlock births has risen among young black women, as a result of a decline in both marriage and marital fertility, coupled with relative stability in out-of-wedlock birth rates (i.e., the number of births per 1,000 unmarried women). This increase in the proportion of extramarital births could be mainly a function of the increasing difficulty of finding a marriage partner with stable employment, or of changes in social values regarding out-of-wedlock births, or of increased economic independence afforded women by the availability of income transfer payments. Broader social and economic forces may also be influencing married women to have fewer children. [Previously] the factors associated with the rise of social dislocations, including female-headed families, in the inner city were examined. In this section we extend that discussion by delineating the role of broader social and economic forces not only on trends in family formation in the inner city, but on national trends in family formation as well. In the process we hope to establish the argument that despite the complex nature of the problem, the weight of existing evidence suggests that the problems of male joblessness could be the single most important factor underlying the rise in unwed mothers among poor black women. Yet, this factor has received scant attention in recent discussions of the decline of intact families among the poor. Let us first examine the contribution of other factors, including social and cultural trends and the growth of income transfers, which in recent years has become perhaps the single most popular explanation of changes in family formation and family structure.

The Role of Changing Social and Cultural Trends

Extramarital fertility among teenagers is of particular significance to the rise of female-headed families. Out-of-wedlock birth rates for teens are generally not falling as they are for older women. Almost 40 percent of all illegitimate births are to women under age twenty. Moreover, adolescent mothers are the most disadvantaged of all female family heads because they are likely to have their schooling interrupted, experience difficulty finding employment, and very rarely receive child support. They are also the most likely to experience future marital instability and disadvantages in the labor market.

Any attempt to explain the social and cultural factors behind the rise of out-of-wedlock teenage fertility must begin with the fact that most teenage pregnancies are reportedly unwanted. Surveys by Zelnik and Kantner have consistently shown that the majority of premarital pregnancies are neither planned nor wanted. In 1979, for instance, 82 percent of premarital pregnancies in fifteen- to nineteen-year-olds (unmarried at the time the pregnancy was resolved) were unwanted.

However, unpublished tabulations from a recent Chicago study of teenage pregnancy indicate that adolescent black mothers reported far fewer pregnancies to be unwanted than did their white counterparts. Moreover, as Dennis Hogan has stated, the Chicago data suggest that "it is not so much that single motherhood is unwanted as it is that it is not sufficiently 'unwanted.' Women of all ages without a strong desire to prevent a birth tend to have limited contraceptive success." This argument would seem especially appropriate to poor inner-city black neighbor-hoods. In this connection, Kenneth Clark has argued that

> In the ghetto, the meaning of the illegitimate child is not ultimate disgrace. There is not the demand for abortion or for surrender of the child that one finds in more privileged communities. In the middle class, the disgrace of illegitimacy is tied to personal and family aspirations. In lower-class families, on the other hand, the girl loses only some of her already limited options by having an illegitimate child; she is not going to make a "better marriage" or improve her economic and social status either way. On the contrary, a child is a symbol of the fact that she is a woman, and she may gain from having something of her own. Nor is the boy who fathers an illegitimate child going to lose, for where is he going? The path to any higher status seems closed to him in any case.

Systematic evidence of expected parenthood prior to first marriage is provided in two studies by Hogan. Drawing upon data collected in a national longitudinal survey of high school students conducted for a National Center for Educational Statistics study (described from here on as the High School and Beyond data), Hogan found that whereas only 1 percent of the white females and 1.4 percent of the white males who were single and childless in 1980 expected to become parents prior to first marriage, 16.5 percent of black females and 21 percent of black males expected parenthood before first marriage. In a follow-up study that focused exclusively on black female adolescents and excluded respondents "who were pregnant or near marriage at the time of the initial interview [1980]," Hogan found that only 8.7 percent expected to become single mothers in 1980, and of these, 19.5 percent actually became unmarried mothers by 1982. On the other hand, of the 91 percent who reported that they *did not* expect to become unmarried mothers, only 7.4 percent gave birth to a child by 1982. Unpublished data from this same study reveal that 20.1 percent of the black girls becoming single mothers by 1982 *expected* to do so in 1980. Thus, although only a small percentage of these adolescent girls expected to become single mothers, those who expressed that view were almost three times as likely to become single mothers as the over-whelming majority who did not.

A number of social structural factors that may influence the development of certain behavior norms may also be directly related to single parenthood. Hogan's research shows that girls from married-couple families and those from households with both mother and grandparent are much less likely to become unwed mothers than those from independent mother-headed households or nonparental homes. The fact that the rate of premarital parenthood of teens who live with both their single mothers and one (usually the grandmother) or more grandparents is as low as that of teens who live in husband-wife families suggests that "the critical effects of one-parent families are not so much attributable to the mother's example of single parenthood as an acceptable status as to the poverty and greater difficulty of parental supervision in one-adult families." Furthermore, Hogan and Kitagawa's analysis of the influences of family background, personal characteristics, and social milieu on the probability of premarital pregnancy among black teenagers in Chicago indicates that those from nonintact families, lower social class, and poor and highly segregated neighborhoods have significantly higher fertility rates. Hogan and Kitagawa estimated that 57 percent of the teenage girls from high-risk social environments (lower class, poor inner-city neighborhood residence, female-headed family, five or more siblings, a sister who is a teenager mother, and loose parental supervision of dating) will become pregnant by age eighteen compared to only 9 percent of the girls from low-risk social backgrounds.

Social structural factors also appear to affect the timing of marriage. Hogan reports that although black teenagers expect to become parents at roughly the same ages as whites, they expect to become married at later ages. Analysis of the High School and Beyond data reveals that when social class is controlled, black adolescents have expected age-specific rates of parenthood that are only 2 percent lower than those of whites, but expected age-specific rates of marriage that are 36 percent lower. While Hogan notes that many whites are delaying marriage and parenthood because of educational or career aspirations, he attributes blacks' expectations of late marriage to the poor "marriage market" black women face. Indeed, available research has demonstrated a direct connection between the early marriage of young people and an encouraging economic situation, advantageous government transfer programs, and a balanced sex ratio. These conditions are not only more likely to obtain for young whites than for young blacks, but as we try to show, they have become increasingly problematic for blacks.

This evidence suggests therefore that attitudes and expectations concerning marriage and parenthood are inextricably linked with social structural factors. Since we do not have systematic longitudinal data on the extent to which such attitudes and aspirations have changed in recent years, we can only assume that some changes have indeed occurred and that they are likely to be responses to broader changes in the society. This is not to ignore the import of normative or cultural explanations, rather it is to underline the well-founded sociological generalization that group variations in behavior, norms, and values often reflect variations in group access to channels of privilege and influence. When this connection is overlooked, explanations of problems such as premarital parenthood or female-headed families may focus on the norms and aspirations of individuals, and thereby fail to address the ultimate sources of the problem, such as changes in the structure of opportunities for the disadvantaged.

It is also important to remember that there are broader social and cultural trends in society that affect in varying degrees the behavior of all racial and class groups. For instance, sexual activity is increasingly prevalent among all teenagers. Growing proportions of adolescents have had sexual experience: according to one survey, the proportion of metropolitan teenage women who reported having premarital intercourse increased from 30 percent in 1971 to 50 percent in 1979. These proportions have risen particularly for white adolescents, thereby narrowing the differentials in the incidence of sexual activity. And they have more than offset the increase in contraceptive use over the past decade, resulting in a net increase in premarital pregnancy. Rising rates of sexual activity among middle-class teens may be associated with various social and cultural trends such as the "sexual revolution," the increased availability of birth control and abortion, and perhaps the growing sophistication of American adolescents, or their adoption of adult social behavior at an increasingly early age. While these trends may also have influenced the sexual behavior of teens from disadvantaged backgrounds, it is difficult to assess their effects independent of the complex array of other factors. Other meager state of knowledge permits us only to say that they probably have some effect, but we do not have even a rough idea as to the degree.

Although our knowledge of the effect of social and cultural trends on the rise of extramarital fertility is scant, we know a little more about the effect of some of these trends on marital dissolution. Multivariate analyses of marital splits suggest that women's labor-force participation and income significantly increase marital dissolution among white women. Labor-force participation rates of white women have nearly doubled from 1940 to 1980 (from 25.6 percent to 49.4 percent), in part due to a decline in marriage and in part to an increase in labor-force participation among married women, particularly those with children. The labor-force participation of black women has also increased, but not as dramatically (from 39.4 percent in 1940 to 53.3 percent in 1980); black women have always worked in greater proportions than white women, a pattern that still holds today for all age-groups except women ages sixteen to twenty-four, an age category with high fertility rates.

Accompanying the increasing labor-force participation of women has been the rise of the feminist movement, which validates work as a source of both independence from men and personal fulfillment, and which has provided practical support not only through legal and political action but also through its role in promoting organizational resources for women in the labor market. Feminism as a social and cultural movement may have directly influenced the marriage decisions of women; it may also have indirectly affected these decisions through its role in women's more active participation in the labor market. In the absence of systematic empirical data, the effect of the feminist movement on the marital dissolution of women, particularly white women, can only be assumed.

It can be confidently asserted, however, that women's increasing employment makes marital breakup financially more viable than in the past. Although marital dissolution means a substantial loss of income, and sometimes severe economic hardship—median income of white female-headed families in 1979 was $11,452, compared to $21,824 for white married-couple families—most white women can maintain their families above poverty with a combination of earnings and income from other sources such as alimony, child support, public-income transfers, personal wealth, and assistance from families. In 1982, 70 percent of white female-headed families were living above the poverty line. In addition, many white single mothers remarry. For most black women facing marital dissolution, the situation is significantly different, not only because they tend to have fewer resources and are far less likely to remarry, but also because the major reasons for their increasing rates of marital disintegration have little to do with changing social and cultural trends.

The Role of Welfare

A popular explanation for the rise of female-headed families and out-of-wedlock births has been the growth of liberal welfare policies, in particular, broadened eligibility for income transfer programs, increases in benefit levels, and the creation of new programs such as Medicaid and food stamps. Charles Murray, for example, argues that relaxed restrictions and increasing benefits of AFDC enticed lower-class women to forego marriage or prolong childlessness in order to qualify for increasingly lucrative benefits. Likewise, Robert Gordon depicts "welfare provisions as a major influence in the decline in two-adult households in American cities."

The effect of welfare on out-of-wedlock births and marital instability became even more of an issue after the costs and caseloads of public assistance programs dramatically increased during the late 1960s and early 1970s. Since that time, a good deal of research has addressed this issue. Because all states have AFDC and food stamp programs, there can be no true test of the effects of welfare on family structure: there is no "control" population that has not been exposed to these welfare programs. However, substantial interstate variations in levels of AFDC benefits and in eligibility rules have provided opportunities for researchers to test the effects of program characteristics. Most studies have examined the level of welfare benefits as one of the determinants of a woman's choice between marriage and single parenthood. Some use aggregate data; others use individual-level data; still others examine the effect of providing cash transfers to intact families under special conditions, such as the Income Maintenance Experiments. But whether the focus is on the relationship between welfare and out-of-wedlock births or that between welfare and marital dissolution, the results have been inconclusive at best.

Many of the studies concerning welfare and out-of-wedlock births have compared illegitimacy rates or ratios across states with varying AFDC benefit levels. Cutright found no association between out-of-wedlock births rates and benefit levels in 1960 or 1970. Using aggregate data, Winegarden's state-level analysis showed no association between measures of fertility and benefit levels, although he did report a small positive association with benefit availability. Fechter and Greenfield and Moore and Caldwell both used state-level cross-sectional data in a multivariate analysis and found no effects of welfare benefit levels on out-of-wedlock births. Finally, Vining showed that for blacks, the illegitimacy ratio in the South was only slightly lower than in nonsouthern states, despite levels of AFDC payments that were less than half those of the rest of the country; for whites, the difference was somewhat larger.

This type of research is vulnerable to the criticism that, in Vining's words, "the overall incidence of illegitimacy could have been rising over time in concert with an overall rise in welfare payments, despite the lack of correlation between cross-state variation in illegitimacy and cross-state variation in welfare levels at any point in time." However, despite frequent references in the literature to rising welfare expenditures, benefit levels have fallen in real terms over the past ten years, while illegitimacy ratios have continued to rise. Both Cutright and Ellwood and Bane examined changes over time in state benefit levels and in illegitimate birth rates and found no association.

Other studies using different approaches and data sets have also yielded inconclusive, largely negative, results. Placek and Hendershot analyzed retrospective interviews of three hundred welfare mothers and found that when the women were on welfare, they were significantly *less* likely to refrain from using contraceptives, *less* likely to desire an additional pregnancy, and *less* likely to become pregnant. Similarly, Presser and Salsberg, using a random sample of New York women who had recently had their first child, reported that women on public assistance desired fewer children than women not on assistance, and were less likely to have planned their first birth. Based on a longitudinal study of low-income New York City women, Polgar and Hiday reported that women having an additional birth over a two-year period were no more likely to be receiving welfare at the start of the period than women who did not get pregnant. Moore and Caldwell reported no relationship between characteristics of AFDC programs and out-of-wedlock pregnancy and childbearing from a microlevel analysis of survey data. Ellwood and Bane examined out-of-wedlock birth rates among women likely and unlikely to qualify for AFDC if they became single mothers, and found no significant effect of welfare benefit levels; a comparison of married and unmarried birth rates in low- and high-benefit states also yielded no effects.

Finally, results from the Income Maintenance Experiments have been inconclusive. Reports from the New Jersey experiments indicate no effect. In the Seattle and Denver experiments, effects of income maintenance payments on fertility varied by race/ethnicity: white recipients had significantly lower fertility, Mexican-Americans had higher fertility, and blacks showed no effect. Because of the relatively short duration of the study, it is not clear if maintenance payments affected completed fertility or simply the timing of births.

The results of studies focusing on the relationship between welfare and family stability have also been inconclusive. Researchers using aggregate data ordinarily look for correlations between rates of female family headship and size of AFDC payments, while controlling for other variables. In some studies, the unit of analysis is the state; in others, most notably Honig and Ross and Sawhill, various metropolitan areas were examined. Analytic models used in most of these studies are similar, but disagreement over specification of the variables and other aspects of the analysis has produced mixed results. Honig found positive effects for AFDC payments on female family headship, although by 1970 the effects had diminished; Minarik and Goldfarb reported insignificant negative effects; Ross and Sawhill found significant positive effects for nonwhites, but not for whites; and Cutright and Madras found that AFDC benefits did not affect marital disruption, but did increase the likelihood that separated or divorced mothers would head their own households.

As Ellwood and Bane observed, despite the sophistication of some of these multivariate analyses of aggregate data, the analyses have "largely ignored the problems introduced by largely unmeasurable differences between states." Introducing a unique and resourceful solution to these problems, they present estimates of welfare effects based on comparisons of marital dissolution and living arrangements among mothers likely and unlikely to be AFDC recipients, and among women who are or are not mothers (and thus eligible for AFDC), in high- and low-benefit states. They also examine changes over time in benefit levels and family structure. The findings based on these three different comparisons are remarkably similar. Ellwood and Bane estimate that in 1975, a $100 increase in AFDC benefits would have resulted in a 10 percent increase in the number of divorced or separated mothers, with a more substantial effect for young women; the same increase in AFDC benefits would have contributed to an estimated 25 percent to 30 percent increase in the formation of independent households, again with much more substantial effects for young mothers.

Studies using individual-level data have yielded mixed results, with some finding modest effects, and some reporting no effect at all of welfare on marital dissolution or family headship. Hoffman and Holmes analyzed Michigan PSID data and reported that low-income families living in states with high AFDC benefits were 6 percent more likely than the average to dissolve their marriages, while similar families in states with low-benefit levels were 6 percent less likely to do so. Ross and Sawhill, in a similar analysis of the same data, found no significant welfare effects, even in a regression performed separately for low-income families. In a recent study, Danziger et al. modeled headship choices using data from 1968 and 1975 *Current Population Surveys* and concluded that a reduction in welfare benefits would result in only a slight decrease in the number of female household heads; the authors also reported that the increase in female-headed families between 1968 and 1975 was greater than the model would have predicted given the changes in the relative economic circumstances of female heads and married women occurring during that period. It seems likely that the decreasing supply of "marriageable men" (examined below) is a constraint on women's marriage decisions that is not accounted for in the model.

Studies of intact families receiving income transfers under the Income Maintenance Experiments show that providing benefits to two-parent families did not tend to reduce marital instability: the split rates for these families were higher, not lower, than those of comparable low-income families, although the results were not consistent across maintenance levels. The Income Maintenance Experiments "increased the proportion of families headed by single females. For blacks and whites, the increase was due to the increase in dissolution; for Chicanos, the increase was due to the decrease in the marital formation rates." Groeneveld, Tuma, and Hannan speculate that nonpecuniary factors such as the stigma, transaction costs, and lack of information associated with the welfare system caused the income maintenance program to have a greater effect on women's sense of economic independence.

To sum up, this research indicates that welfare receipt or benefit levels have no effect on the incidence of out-of-wedlock births. Aid to Families with Dependent Children payments seem to have a substantial effect on living arrangements of single mothers, but only a modest impact on separation and divorce. The extent to which welfare deters marriage or remarriage among single mothers is addressed only indirectly, in studies of the incidence of female-headed households, and here the evidence is inconclusive.

However, if the major impact of AFDC is on the living arrangements of single mothers, it could ultimately have a greater influence on family structure. As we emphasized in our discussion of Hogan's research on the premarital parenthood of adolescents, young women from independent mother-headed households are more likely to become unwed mothers than those from married-couple families and those from female-headed subfamilies living in the homes of their grandparents.

Nonetheless, the findings from Ellwood and Bane's impressive research, and the inconsistent results of other studies on the relationship between welfare and family structure, and welfare and out-of-wedlock births, raise serious questions about the current tendency to blame changes in welfare policies for the decline in the proportion of intact families and legitimate births among the poor. As Ellwood and Bane emphatically proclaim, "Welfare simply does not appear to be the underlying cause of the dramatic changes in family structure of the past few decades." The factor that we have identified as the underlying cause is discussed in the next section.

The Role of Joblessnes

Although the structure of the economy and the composition of the labor force have undergone significant change over the last forty years, labor-force participation patterns of white men have changed little. The labor-force participation rate of white men declined from 82 percent in 1940 to 76 percent in 1980, in part because of a drop in the labor-force activity for men over the age of fifty-five (from 83.9 percent to 72.2 percent for those ages fifty-five to sixty-four). Labor-force participation of white men ages twenty-four and under actually increased over the past decade.

For blacks, the patterns are different. The labor-force participation of black men declined substantially, from 84 percent in 1940 to 67 percent in 1980. Labor-force trends for older black men parallel those of white men of the same ages. But the decline in labor-force participation of young black men and, to a lesser extent, prime-age black men has occurred, while the participation of comparable white men has either increased or remained stable.

Economic trends for black men, especially young black men, have been unfavorable since the end of World War II. While the status of young blacks who are employed has improved with the percentage of white-collar workers among all black male workers, rising from 5 percent in 1940 to 27 percent in 1983, the proportion of black men who are employed has dropped from 80 percent in 1930 to 56 percent in 1983. Unemployment rose sharply for black male teenagers during the 1950s and remained high during the prosperous 1960s; similarly, unemployment rates for black men twenty to twenty-four years of age rose sharply during the mid-1970s and have remained high. In 1979, when the overall unemployment rate had declined to 5.8 percent, the rate for black male teenagers was 34.1 percent. In addition, while blacks have historically had higher labor-force participation levels, by the 1970s labor-force participation of black men had fallen below that of white men for all age-groups, with particularly steep declines for those ages twenty-four and younger. . . .

The adverse effects of unemployment and other economic problems of family stability are well established in the literature. Studies of family life during the Great Depression document the deterioration of marriage and family life following unemployment. More recent research, based on longitudinal data sets such as the PSID and the National Longitudinal Study or on aggregate data, shows consistently that unemployment is related to marital instability and the incidence of female-headed families. Indicators of economic status such as wage rates, income, or occupational status may also be related to marital instability or female headedness, although the evidence is not as consistent. For instance, while Cutright's analysis of 1960 census data indicates that divorce and separation rates are higher among lower-income families, Sawhill et al. find that unemployment, fluctuations in income, and lack of assets are associated with higher separation rates, but that the level of the husband's earnings has an effect only among low-income black families. However, Cohen reports that when the husband's age is controlled, the higher the husband's earnings, the less likely both black and white couples are to divorce.

Nonetheless, the weight of the evidence on the relationship between the employment status of men, and family life and married life suggests that the increasing rate of joblessness among black men merits serious consideration as a major underlying factor in the rise of black single mothers and female-headed households. Moreover, when the factor of joblessness is combined with high black-male mortality and incarceration rates, the proportion of black men in stable economic situations is even lower than that conveyed in the current unemployment and labor-force figures.

The full dimensions of this problem are revealed in [statistics] which show the effect of male joblessness trends, in combination with the effects of male mortality and incarceration rates, [based on] the rates of employed civilian men to women of the same race and age-group. This ratio may be described as a "male marriageable pool index." The number of women is used as the denominator in order to convey the situation of young women in the "marriage market." . . . [M]en sixteen to twenty-four years of age, show similar patterns: a sharp decline in the nonwhite ratios beginning in the 1960, which is even more startling when compared with the rising ratios for white men. . . . [M]en twenty-five to fifty-four years of age show a more gradual decline for black men relative to white men. Clearly, what our "male marriageable pool index" reveals is a long-term decline in the proportion of black men, and particularly young black men, who are in a position to support a family.

As we noted above, the relationship between joblessness and marital instability is well established in the literature. Moreover, available evidence supports the argument that among blacks, increasing male joblessness is related to the rising proportions of families headed by women. By contrast, for whites, trends in male employment and earnings appear to have little to do with the increase in female-headed families. Although lower-income families have higher rates of marital dissolution, trends in the employment status of white men since 1960 cannot explain the overall rise in white separation and divorce rates.

It seems likely that the chief cause of the rise of separation and divorce rates among whites is the increased economic independence of white women as indicated by their increasing employment and improving occupational status. It is not that this growing independence gives white women a financial incentive to separate from or to divorce their husbands; rather, it makes dissolution of a bad marriage a more viable alternative than in the past. That the employment status of white males is not a major factor in white single motherhood or female-headed families can perhaps also be seen in the higher rate of remarriage among white women and the significantly earlier age of first marriage. By contrast, the increasing delay of first marriage and the low rate of remarriage among black women seem to be directly tied to the increasing labor-force problems of men.

Conclusion

In the 1960s scholars readily attributed black family deterioration to the problems of male joblessness. However, in the last ten to fifteen years, in the face of the overwhelming focus on welfare as the major source of black family breakup, concerns about the importance of male joblessness have receded into the background. We argue in this [article] that the available evidence justifies renewed scholarly and public policy attention to the connection between the disintegration of poor families and black male prospects for stable employment.

We find that when statistics on black family structure are disaggregated to reveal changes in fertility rates, marital status, age structure, and residence patterns, it becomes clear, first of all, that the black "illegitimacy ratio" has increased rapidly not so much because of an increase in the incidence of out-of-wedlock births, but mainly because both the rate of marital fertility and the percentage of women married and living with their husbands has declined significantly. And the sharp reduction of the latter is due both to the rise in black divorce and separation and to the increase in the percentage of never-married women. Inextricably connected with these trends are changes in the age structure, which have increased the fraction of all births occurring outside of marriage. The net results has been a 41 percent increase in the number of black children growing up in fatherless families during the 1970s, with most of this increase occurring in families in which the mother has never been married. Furthermore, the substantial racial differences in the timing of first marriage and the rate of remarriage underscore the persistence of black female headedness. And what makes all of these trends especially disturbing is that female-headed families are far more likely than married-couple families to be not only poor, but mired in poverty for long periods of time.

Although changing social and cultural trends have often been invoked to explain some of the dynamic changes in the structure of the family, they appear to have more relevance for shifts in family structure among whites. And contrary to popular opinion, there is little evidence to provide a strong case for welfare as the primary cause of family breakups, female-headed households, and out-of-wedlock births. Welfare does seem to have a modest effect on separation and divorce, especially for white women, but recent evidence suggests that its total effect on the size of the population of female householders is small. As shown in Ellwood and Bane's impressive study, if welfare does have a major influence on female-headed families, it is in the living arrangements of single mothers. We explained why this could ultimately and indirectly lead to an increase in female family headship.

By contrast, the evidence for the influence of male joblessness is much more persuasive. Research has demonstrated, for example, a connection between the early marriage of young people and an encouraging economic situation. In this connection, we have tried to show that black women are more likely to delay marriage and less likely to remarry. We further noted that although black teenagers expect to become parents at about the same ages as whites, they expect to marry at later ages. And we argue that both the black delay in marriage and the lower rate of remarriage, each of which is associated with high percentages of out-of-wedlock births and female-headed households, can be directly tied to the labor-market status of black males. As we have documented, black women, especially young black women, are facing a shrinking pool of "marriageable" (i.e., economically stable) men.

White women are not faced with this problem. Indeed, our "male marriageable pool index" indicates that the number of employed white men per one hundred white women in different age categories has either remained roughly the same or has increased since 1954. We found little reason, therefore, to assume a connnection between the rise in female-headed white families and changes in white male employment. That the pool of "marriageable" white men has not shrunk over the years is reflected, we believe, in the earlier age of first marriage and higher rate of remarriage among white women. For all these reasons, we hypothesize that increases in separation and divorce among whites are due chiefly to the increased economic independence of white women and related social and cultural factors.

Despite the existence of evidence suggesting that the increasing inability of many black men to support a family is the driving force behind the rise of female-headed families, in the last ten to fifteen years welfare has dominated explanations of the increase in female headship. The commonsense assumption that welfare regulations break up families, affirmed by liberals and conservatives alike, buttressed the welfare explanations of trends in family structure. The Subcommittee on Fiscal Policy of the Joint Economic Committee initiated a program of research on the topic in 1971; according to Cutright and Madras, recognition of the increasing monetary value of noncash benefits, in the context of economic theories of marriage, persuaded the subcommittee that welfare was related to the rise of female-headed families despite inconclusive evidence. And despite frequent references to rising social welfare expenditures, the real value of welfare benefits has declined over the past ten years while the number and proportion of female-headed families continue to climb.

Only recently has it been proposed that the rise in female-headed families among blacks is related to declining employment rates among black men. Evidence . . . discussed [here] makes a compelling case for once again placing the problem of black joblessness as a top-priority item in public policy agendas designed to enhance the status of poor black families.

The Family in an Aging Society: A Matrix of Latent Relationships

Matilda White Riley

I am going to talk about families and the revolution in longevity. This revolution has produced configurations in kinship structure and in the internal dynamics of family life at every age that have never existed before.

Over two-thirds of the total improvement in longevity from prehistoric times until the present has taken place in the brief period since 1900 (Preston, 1976). In the United States, life expectancy at birth has risen from less than 50 in 1900 to well over 70 today. Whereas at the start of the century most deaths occurred in infancy and young adulthood, today the vast majority of deaths are postponed to

From *Journal of Family Issues,* Vol. 4, No. 3, September 1983, pp. 439–454. Copyright © 1983 by Sage Publications, Inc. By permission of Sage Publications, Inc.

old age. Indeed we are approaching the "squared" mortality curve, in which relatively few die before the end of the full life span. For the first time in all history, we are living in a society in which most people live to be old.[1]

Though many facts of life extension are familiar, their meanings for the personal lives of family members are elusive. Just how is increasing longevity transforming the kinship structure? Most problematic of all, how is the impact of longevity affecting those sorely needed close relationships that provide emotional support and socialization for family members (see Parsons and Bales, 1955)? To answer such questions, I must agree with other scholars in the conclusion that we need a whole new way of looking at the family, researching it, living in it, and dealing with it in professional practice and public policy.

Indeed, an exciting new family literature is beginning to map and interpret these unparalleled changes; it is beginning to probe beneath the surface for the subjective implications of the protracted and intricate interplay of family relationships. As the kinship structure is transformed, many studies are beginning to ask new questions about how particular relationships and particular social conditions can foster or inhibit emotional support and socialization—that is, the willingness to learn from one another. They are asking how today's family can fill people's pressing need for close human relationships.

From this developing literature, four topics emerge as particularly thought-provoking: (1) the dramatic extension of the kinship structure; (2) the new opportunities this extension brings for close family relationships; (3) the special approaches needed for understanding these complex relationships; and (4) the still unknown family relationships of older people in the future. I shall touch briefly on each of these topics. From time to time I shall also suggest a few general propositions—principles from the sociology of age (see M. W. Riley, 1976; forthcoming) that seem clearly applicable to changing family relationships. Perhaps they will aid our understanding of increasing longevity and the concomitant changes about us. The propositions may guide us in applying our new understanding in research, policy, and practice.

The Changing Configurations of the Kinship Structure

I shall begin with the kinship structure as influenced by longevity. The extent and configurations of this structure have been so altered that we must rethink our traditional view of kinship. As four (even five) generations of many families are now alive at the same time, we can no longer concentrate primary attention on nuclear families of young parents and their children who occasionally visit or provide material assistance to grandparents or other relatives. I have come to think of today's large and complex kinship structure as a matrix of latent relationships—father with son, child with great-grandparent, sister with sister-in-law, ex-husband with ex-wife, and so on—relationships that are latent because they might or might not become close and significant during a lifetime. Thus I am proposing a definition of the kinship structure as a latent web of continually shifting linkages that provide the *potential* for activating and intensifying close family relationships.

The family literature describes two kinds of transformations in this structure that result from increasing longevity: (1) The linkages among family members have been prolonged, and (2) the surviving generations in a family have increased in number and complexity.

Prolongation of Family Relationships

Consider how longevity has prolonged family relationships. For example, in married couples a century ago, one or both partners were likely to have died before the children were reared. Today, though it may seem surprising, couples marrying at the customary ages can anticipate surviving together (apart from divorce) as long as 40 or 50 years on the average (Uhlenberg, 1969, 1980). As Glick and Norton (1977:14) have shown, one out of every five married couples can expect to celebrate their fiftieth wedding anniversary. Because the current intricacy of kinship structures surpasses even the language available to describe it (our step-in-laws might not like to be called "outlaws"), it sometimes helps to do "thought experiments" from one's own life. As marital partners, my husband and I have survived together for over 50 years. What can be said about the form (as distinct from the content) of such a prolonged relationship?

For one thing, we share over half a century of experience. Because we are similar in age, we have shared the experience of aging—biologically, psychologically, and socially—from young adulthood to old age. Because we were born at approximately the same time (and thus belong to the same cohort), we have shared much the same historical experiences—the same fluctuations between economic prosperity and depression, between periods of pacifism and of war, between political liberalism and reactionism, and between low and high rates of fertility. We have also shared our own personal family experiences. We shared the bearing and raising of young children during our first-quarter century together; during our second quarter century we adjusted our couplehood to our added roles as parents-in-law and grandparents. The third quarter-century of our married life, by the laws of probability, should convert us additionally into grandparents-in-law and great-grandparents as well. In sum, prolonged marriages like ours afford extensive common experiences with aging, with historical change, and with changing family relationships.

Such marriages also provide a home—an abiding meeting place for two individuals whose separate lives are engrossed in varied extrafamilial roles. Just as longevity has prolonged the average duration of marriage, it has extended many other roles (such as continuing education, women's years of work outside the home, or retirement). For example, Barbara Torrey (1982) has extimated that people spend at least a quarter of their adult lives in retirement. Married couples, as they move through the role complexes of their individual lives, have many evening or weekend opportunities either to share their respective extrafamilial experiences, to escape from them, or (though certainly not in my own case) to vent their boredom or frustration on one another (see Kelley, 1981).

Thus two features of protracted marriages become apparent. First, these marriages provide increasing opportunity to accumulate shared experiences and meanings and perhaps to build from these a "crescive" relationship, as suggested by Ralph Turner (1970) and Gunhild Hagestad (1981). But second, they also present shifting exigencies and role conflicts that require continual mutual accommodation and reaccommodation. As Richard Lazarus (DeLongis, et al., 1982) has shown, "daily hassles" can be more destructive of well-being than traumatic family events. And Erving Goffman (1959:132) warns that the home can become a "backstage area" in which "it is safe to lapse into an asociable mood of sullen, silent irritability."

Many marriages, not ended by death, are ended by divorce. The very extension of marriage may increase the likelihood of divorce, as Samuel Preston (1976:176-177) has shown. Returning to my personal experience, I was the only one of four sisters who did not divorce and remarry. But as long as their ex-husbands were alive none of my sisters could ever entirely discount the remaining potential linkages between them. These were not only ceremonial or instrumental linkages, but also affective linkages that could be hostile and vindictive, or (as time passes and need arises) could renew concern for one another's well-being. Whatever the nature of the relationship, latent linkages to ex-spouses persist. Thus, a prolonged marriage (even an ex-marriage) provides a continuing potential for a close relationship that can be activated in manifold ways.

The traditional match-making question—"Will this marriage succeed or fail?"—must be replaced and oft-repeated as the couple grows older by a different question: "Regardless of our past, can we—do we want [to]—make the fresh effort to succeed, or shall we fail in this marriage?"

Here I will state as my first proposition: *Family relationships are never fixed:* they change as the self and the significant other family members grow older, and as the changing society influences their respective lives. Clearly, the longer the relationship endures (because of longevity) the greater the opportunity for relational changes.

If, as lives are prolonged, marital relationships extend far behind the original nuclear household, parent-offspring relationships also take on entirely new forms. For example, my daughter and I have survived together so far for 45 years of which only 18 were in the traditional relationship of parent and child. Unlike our shorter-lived forebearers, my daughter and I have been able to share many common experiences although at different stages of our respective lives. She shares a major portion of the historical changes that I have experienced. She also shares my earlier experience of sending a daughter off to college, and will perhaps share my experience of having a daughter marry and raise children. Of course, she and I differ in age. (In Alice Rossi's study of biological age differences, 1980, the consequences for parent-offspring relationships of the reciprocal tensions between a pubescent daughter and her older mother who is looking ahead to the menopausal changes of midlife were explored.)[2] Allthough the relational age between me and my daughter—the 26 years that separate us—remains the same throughout our lives, the implications of this difference change drastically from infancy to my old age.

Number and Stability of Generations

I have dwelt at length on the prolongation of particular relationships to suggest the consequent dramatic changes in the family structure. Longevity has, in addition, increased the stability and the number of generations in a family. A poignant example of this instability (Imhof, n.d.) can be found in an eighteenth century parish where a father could spawn twenty-four offspring of whom only three survived to adulthood—a time in which "it took two babies to make one adult." With increased longevity each generation becomes more stable because more of its members survive. For the young nuclear family in the United States, for example, though the number of children born in each family has been declining over this century, increased longevity has produced a new stability in the family structure. In an important quantitative analysis, Peter Uhlenberg (1980) has shown how the probability of losing a parent or a sibling through death before a child reaches age 15 [has] decreased from .51 in 1900 to .09 in 1976. Compared with children born a century ago, children born today are almost entirely protected against death of close family m .mbers (except for elderly relatives). To be sure, while mortality has been declining, divorce rates have been increasing but less rapidly. Thus, perhaps surprisingly, Uhlenberg demonstrates that disruptions of marriage up through the completion of child rearing have been declining since 1900. In other words, many marriages have been broken by divorce, but overall more have remained intact because of fewer deaths! Thus the young family as well as each of the older generations becomes more stable through survival.

At the same time, the number of older generations has been increasing. Looking up the generational ladder, increasing numbers of a child's four grandparents survive. Among middle-aged couples, whereas back in 1900 more than half had no surviving elderly parents, today half have two or more parents still alive (Uhlenberg, 1980:318). Conversely looking down the generational ladder, each set of elderly parents has adult children with spouses and children of their own. Meanwhile, the increase in divorce and remarriage (four out of five divorced people remarry) compounds the complexity of this elaborate structure, as Andrew Cherlin (1981) has shown. In my own family, for example, each of our two middle-aged children have their own children, and they also have us as two elderly parents; my daughter's husband also has two parents; and my son (who has married twice) has his ex-wife's parents and his current wife's mother, father, and step-mother in addition to us. A complex array!

Of course, as these surviving generations proliferate and overlap, each generation is continually growing older and moving up the generational ladder to replace its predecessor until ultimately the members of the oldest generation die. Because of longevity, every generation—the oldest as well as the youngest—is increasingly stable and more likely to include its full complement of surviving members.

Changing Dynamics of Close Family Relationships

What, then, are the implications of this greatly expanded kinship structure for the dynamics of close family relationships? How does the matrix of latent kinship linkages provide for close ties between particular individual lives, as these lives weave in and out of the intricate and continually shifting kinship network? Under what conditions do some family members provide (or fail to provide) recognition, advice, esteem, love, and tension release for other family members?

The answer, it seems to me, lies in the enlarged kinship structure: It provides many new opportunities for people at different points in their lives to select and activate the relationships they deem most significant. That is, the options for close family bonds have multiplied. Over the century, increased longevity has given flexibility to the kinship structure, relaxing both the temporal and the spatial boundaries of optional relationships.

Temporally, new options have arisen over the course of people's lives because, as we have seen, particular relationships have become more enduring. Particular relationships (even following divorce) are bounded only by the birth and death of members. Now that the experience of losing family members by death is no longer a pervasive aspect of the full life course (and is in fact rare except in old age), people have greater opportunity to plan their family lives. They have time to make mutual adjustments to personal crises or to external threats such as unemployment or the fear of nuclear war. Here we are reminded of my first proposition: Family relationships are never fixed, but are continually in process and subject to change. As family members grow older, they move across time—across history and through their own lives—and they also move upward through the generations in their own families and the age strata of society.[3] As individual family members who each pursue a separate life course, thoughts and feelings for one another are developed; their lives weave together or apart so as to activate, intensify, disregard, or disrupt particular close relationships. Thus the relationship between a mother and daughter can, for example, become close in the daughter's early childhood, her first years of marriage, and again after her children have left home although there may be interim lapses. Or, as current norms permit, couples can try each other out through cohabitation, before deciding whether or not to embark upon marriage.

Just as such new options for close ties have emerged from the prolongation of family relationships, other options have arisen because the number and variety of latent linkages has multiplied across the entire kinship structure. Spatially, close relationships are not bounded by the nuclear households that family members share during their younger lives. Given the intricacy of current kin networks, a wide range of linkages can be activated—between grandchild and grandparent, between distantly related cousins, between the ex-husbands of sisters, or between a child and his or her new step-parent. (Only in Grimm's fairy tales, which reflected the earlier frequency of maternal deaths and successive remarriages, were step-mothers always "wicked.") Aided by modern communication and transportation, affection and interaction can persist even during long periods of separation. On occasion, long-separated relatives or those not closely related may arrange to live together or to join in congregate housing or communes.

Given these options, let me now state a second general proposition: As active agents in directing the course of their own lives, *individuals have a degree of control over their close family relationships*. This control, I submit, has been enhanced because longevity has widened the opportunities for selecting and activating relationships that can provide emotional support and advice when needed.

This part of my discussion suggests a new view of the family. Perhaps we need now to think of a family less as the members of one household with incidental linkages to kin in other households and more as a continuing interplay among intertwined lives within the entire changing kinship structure. The closeness of these intertwined lives and the mutual support they provide depend on many factors (including the predispositions of each individual and the continuing motivation to negotiate and renegotiate their joint lives) but the enlarged kinship structure provides the potential.

New Approaches to Family Research and Practice

Before considering how the oldest family members—those in the added generation—fit into these intertwined lives, let me pause to ask how we can approach these complex and changing family relationships. If the tidy concept of the nuclear family is no longer sufficient, how can we deal in research and in professional practice with the newly emerging concepts? Clearly, special approaches are required for mapping and understanding the centrifugal and centripetal processes of family relationships within the increasing complexity of the kinship matrix. Such approaches must not only take into account my first two propositions (that relationships continually change, and that family members themselves have some control over this change) but must also consider a third proposition: *The lives of family members are interdependent* such that each person's family life continually interacts with the lives of significant relatives. Though long-recognized by students of the family, this proposition takes on fresh significance in the matrix of prolonged relationships.

As case examples, I shall describe two or three studies that illustrate how we can deal with the family as a system of interdependent lives. These studies are also important as they add to our understanding of emotional support and socialization under current family conditions.

In one study of socialization outcomes, Mavis Hetherington et al. (1977) have shown how parental disruption through divorce has a complex impact on the still-intertwined lives of the spouses and on the socialization of their children. Over a two-year period, detailed investigations were made of nursery school boys and girls and their parents, half of whom were divorced and the other half married. Differences were detected: Divorced parents showed comparatively less affection for their children, had less control over them, and elicited more dependent, disobedient, and aggressive child behavior—particularly in mother-son interactions. But relations between the parents also made a difference in these parent-child relationships: If divorced couples kept conflict low and agreed about child rearing, their ineffectiveness in dealing with children could be somewhat offset. This two-year tracing of the three-way interrelationships among spouses and children in disrupted families yields many insights into the interdependence of life course processes.

As family relationships are prolonged, socialization is more frequently recognized as a reciprocal process that potentially extends throughout the lives of parents and children as well as of marital partners. How can socialization operate across generations that belong to differing periods of historical change? One key mechanism, as Marilyn Johnson (1976) has demonstrated, is normative expectations. Parents can influence offspring by expecting behavior that is appropriate to social change, and can in turn be guided by offspring in formulating these expectations. Such subtleties to intergenerational influence are illustrated in a small study which Johnson and I made of high school students in the early 1960s (see Riley, 1982). Just as women's careers were burgeoning, we found that most girls looked forward to combining a career with marriage, whereas most boys did not anticipate marrying wives who worked. How had these young people been socialized to such sharply conflicting norms? We questioned their mothers and fathers to find out. Indeed we learned that, on the whole, parents wanted self-fulfillment for their daughters both in marriage and in work outside the home, while for their sons they wanted wives who would devote themselves fully to home and children. These slight yet provocative findings did presage the future impact of the women's movement on family lives, but I note them here as another instance of research that fits together the differing perspectives of the several interdependent family members.

Analyzing such studies of close relationships impresses one with the problem of studying families from what is often called the "life course" or "lifespan perspective" (see Dannefer, forthcoming). We are indeed concerned with people moving through life. Yet we are concerned not with a single life or a statistical aggregate of lives, but with the dynamic family systems of interdependent lives. An example I often use in teaching comes from the early work of Cottrell and Burgess in predicting success or failure in marriage. Starting with a case study, Cottrell (1933) saw each partner in a marriage as reenacting his or her childhood roles. He showed how the outcome of the marriage depended upon the mesh between these two different sets of early-life experiences—that is, how nearly they would fit together so that each partner met the role expectations of the other. Unfortunately, however, these researchers subsequently departed from this admirable model by questioning large samples of men and women as individuals and then analyzing the data for separate aggregates of men and women rather than for male-female pairs. Each individual was given a score of likely success in marriage, but without considering the success of a marriage between a particular man and a particular woman! Because the interdependent lives were not examined jointly, the central objective of the project was lost.

This difficulty, which I now call "life-course reductionism," still persists. Although many studies purport to study families as systems, they in fact either aggregate individual lives (as Cottrell and Burgess did) or reason erroneously from the lives of single members about the lives of other family members significant to the relationship. The danger of not considering a key family member is highlighted, for example, in Frank Furstenberg's (1981) review of the literature on kinship relations after divorce. Some studies had suggested that divorce disrupts the relations with parents-in-law (that is, with the parents of the ex-spouse) but these studies failed to include the children of the broken marriage. Only after examining the children's generation was it learned that they, by retaining contact with both sets of their grandparents, could help to link divorced spouses to their former in-laws. Supporting this clue from a small study of his own, Furstenberg found that the ties between grandparents and grandchildren did continue to exist in most cases, even though for the divorced parents (the middle generation) the former in-law relationships were largely attenuated or broken. In reconstituted families, then, grandparents can perhaps serve as "kinkeepers."

Among the studies that pursue close relationships across three generations is a national survey of divorce and remarriage now being conducted by Frank Furstenberg, Andrew Cherlin, Nicholas Zill, and James Peterson. In this era of widespread divorce and remarriage, this study is examining the important hypothesis that new intergenerational ties created by remarriage will balance—or more than balance—the losses incurred as a result of divorce. Step-relationships may replace disrupted natural relationships. The intricacy of interdependent lives within our proliferating kinship structure is dramatized by the design of this study. Starting with a sample of children aged 11 to 16 and their parents (who were originally interviewed five years earlier) the research team will now also question these children's grandparents; note that there can be two sets of grandparents where the parents are in intact first marriages or have been divorced, three sets if one parent has remarried after divorce, and four sets (no less than eight grandparents) if both have remarried. Thus, as surviving generations proliferate, their part in the family system will be explored in this study by questioning the many members of the grandparent generation. Surviving generations cannot be fully understood (as many studies of three generations have attempted) by examining a simple chain of single individuals from each of the generations.

These studies, as models for research, reflect the complex family relationships within which people of all ages today can seek or can give affection, encouragement, companionship, or advice.

Older Generations of the Future

About the fourth generation (great-grandparents) that is being contributed by longevity, I want to make three final points.

First, it is too early to tell how an enlarged great-grandparent generation will fit into the kinship structure, or what close family relationships it may form. It is too early because the marked increase in longevity among the old began only in recent decades and are still continuing at a rate far exceeding earlier predictions (Preston, 1976; Manton, 1982; Brody and Brock, n.d.). Will this added generation be regarded as the more familiar generation of grandparents has been regarded—either as a threat to the young adult generation's independence, or as a "social problem" for family and community, requiring care from the mid-generation that is "squeezed" between caring for both young children and aging parents? Or will an added fourth generation mean new coalitions and new forms of personal relationships? And what of five-generation families in which a grandmother can be also a granddaughter (see Hagestad, 1981)? It is still too early to tell what new family norms will develop (see Riley, 1978).

Second, while we do not know how a fourth or even a fifth generation may fit in, we do know that most older family members are not dependent or disabled (some 5 percent of those 65 and over are in nursing homes). For those requiring care or instrumental support, families generally make extraordinary efforts to provide it (see Shanas, 1979). Yet most of the elderly, and especially those who are better educated and more active, are stronger, wiser, more competent, and more independent than is generally supposed. Public stereotypes of old people are far more negative than old people's assessments of themselves (National Council on the Aging, 1981). Healthy members of this generation, like their descendants, must earn their own places in the family and create their own personal ties. They cannot expect obligatory warmth or emotional support.

Third, at the close of their lives, however, old people will need advice and emotional support from kin. This need is not new in the annals of family history. What is new is the fact that terminal illness and death are no longer scattered across all generations but are concentrated in the oldest one. Today two-thirds of all deaths occur after age 65, and 30 percent after age 80 (Brody and Brock, n.d.). And, although most deaths occur outside the home, programs such as the hospice movement are being developed for care of the dying in the home where the family can take part (see J. W. Riley, forthcoming).

In conclusion, I have attempted to trace the impact of the unprecedented increases in longevity on the family and its relationships. In our own time the kinship structure has become more extensive and more complex, the temporal and spatial boundaries of the family have been altered, and the opportunities for close family relationships have proliferated. These relationships are no longer prescribed as strict obligations. They must rather be earned—created and recreated by family members throughout their long lives. Each of us is in continuing need of advice and emotional support from one another, as we contend with personal challenges and troubles, and with the compelling effects of societal changes in the economy, in technology, in culture, and in values. We all must agree with Mary Jo Bane (1976) that the family is here to stay, but in forms that we are beginning to comprehend only now. As members of families and students of the family— whether we are theorists, researchers, counselors, or policy makers—we must begin to realign our thinking and our practice to incorporate the new realities that are being engendered by increasing longevity.

Notes

1. Note that increasing longevity in a society is not necessarily the same as increasing proportions of old people in the population, a proportion influenced in the long-term more by fertility than by mortality. Longevity affects individual lives and family structures, while population composition affects the total society.
2. Gunhild Hagestad (1982) talks even of menopausal grandmothers with pubescent granddaughters.
3. Of course, divisions between generations are only loosely coterminous with age divisions (see the discussion of the difference between "generations" and "cohorts" in the classic piece by Duncan, 1966, and a definitive formulation of this distinction in Kertzer, forthcoming). As Gunhild Hagestad (1981) puts it, "people do not file into generations by cohorts." There are wide ranges in the ages at which particular individuals marry and have children. In addition to the recognized differences by sex, there are important differences by social class. For example, Graham Spanier (Spanier and Glick, 1980) shows how the later marriage age in upper as compared with lower socioeconomic classes postpones many subsequent events in the lives of family members, thus slowing the proliferation in numbers of surviving generations.

References

Bane, M. J.
  1976   Here to Stay: American Families in the 20th Century. New York: Basic Books.
Brody, J. A., and D. B. Brock
  n.d.   "Epidemiologic and statistical characteristics of the United States elderly population." (unpublished)
Cherlin, A. J.
  1981   Marriage, Divorce, Remarriage. Cambridge, MA: Harvard University Press.
Cottrell, L. S., Jr.
  1933   "Roles and marital adjustment." American Sociological Society 27: 107–115.
Dannefer, D.
  forthcoming   "The sociology of the life course." Annual Review of Sociology.
DeLongis, A., J. C. Coyne, G. Dakof, S. Folkman, and R. S. Lazarus
  1982   "Relationship of daily hassles, uplifts, and major life events to health status." Health Psychology 1: 119–136.
Duncan, O. D.
  1966   "Methodological issues in the analysis of social mobility," pp. 51–97 in N. J. Smelser and S. M. Lipsett (eds.), Social Structure and Mobility in Economic Development. Chicago, IL: Aldine.
Furstenberg, F. F., Jr.
  1981   "Remarriage and intergenerational relations," pp. 115–142 in R. W. Fogel et al. (eds.), Aging: Stability and Change in the Family. New York: Academic Press.
Glick, P. C., and A. J. Norton
  1977   "Marrying, divorcing, and living together in the U.S. today." Population Bulletin 32. Washington, D.C. Population Reference Bureau.
Goffman, E.
  1959   The Presentation of Self in Everyday Life. Garden City, NY: Doubleday.

Hagestad, G. O.
   1982   "Older women in intergenerational relations." Presented at the Physical and Mental Health
           of Aged Women Conference, October 21–22, Case Western University, Cleveland, OH.
   1981   "Problems and promises in the social psychology of intergenerational relations," pp. 11–46
           in R. W. Fogel et al. (eds.), Aging: Stability and Change in the Family. New York: Academic
           Press.
Hetherington, E. M., M. Cox, and R. Cox
   1977   "The aftermath of divorce," in J. H. Stevens, Jr. and M. Matthews (eds.), Mother-Child,
           Father-Child Relations, Washington, D.C.: National Association for the Education of Young
           Children.
Imhof, A. E.
   1982   "Life course patterns of women and their husbands—16th to 20th century." Presented at the
           International Conference on Life Course Research on Human Development, September 17,
           Berlin, Germany.
Johnson, M.
   1976   "The role of perceived parental models, expectations and socializing behaviors in the self-
           expectations of adolescents, from the U.S. and West Germany." Dissertation, Rutgers
           University.
Kelley, H. H.
   1981   "Marriage relationships and aging," pp. 275–300 in R. W. Fogel et al. (eds.), Aging:
           Stability and Change in the Family. New York: Academic Press.
Kertzer, D. I.
   forthcoming   "Generations as a sociological problem." Annual Review of Sociology.
Manton, K. G.
   1982   "Changing concepts of morbidity and mortality in the elderly population." Milbank Memo-
           rial Fund Q. 60: 183–244.
National Council on the Aging
   1981   Aging in the Eighties: America in Transition. Washington, D.C.: Author.
Parsons, T., and R. F. Bales
   1955   Family, Socialization and Interaction Process. New York: Free Press.
Preston, S. H.
   1976   Mortality Patterns in National Population: With Special References to Recorded Causes of
           Death. New York: Academic Press.
Riley, J. W., Jr.
   forthcoming   "Dying and the meanings of death: sociological inquiries." Annual Review of
                  Sociology.
Riley, M. W.
   1976   "Age strata in social systems," pp. 189–217 in R. H. Binstock and E. Shanas (eds.),
           Handbook of Aging and the Social Sciences. New York: Van Nostrand Reinhold.
   1978   "Aging, social change, and the power of ideas." Daedalus 107, 4: 39–52.
   1982   "Implications for the middle and later years," pp. 399–405 in P. W. Berman and E. R.
           Ramey (eds.), Women: A Development Perspective NIH Publication No. 82-2298. Washing-
           ton, DC: Dept. of Health and Human Services.
   forthcoming   "Age strata in social systems," in R. H. Binstock and E. Shanas (eds.), The New
                  Handbook of Aging and the Social Sciences.
Rossi, A. S.
   1980   "Aging and parenthood in the middle years," in P. B. Baltes and O. G. Brim, Jr. (eds.), Life-
           Span Development and Behavior 3. New York: Academic Press.
Shanas, E.
   1979   "Social myth as hypothesis: the case of the family relations of old people." The Gerontolo-
           gist 19: 3–9.
Spanier, G. B., and P. C. Glick
   1980   "The life cycle of American families: an expanded analysis." J. of Family History: 97–111.
Torrey, B. B.
   1982   "The lengthening of retirement," pp. 181–196 in M. W. Riley et al. (eds.), Aging from Birth
           to Death, vol. II: Sociotemporal Perspectives, Boulder, CO: Westview.

Turner, R. H.
  1970 Family Interaction. New York: John Wiley.
Uhlenberg, P. R.
  1969 "A study of cohort life cycles: cohorts of native born Massachusetts women. 1830–1920."
       Population Studies 23, 3: 407–420.
  1980 "Death and the family." J. of Family History (Fall): 313–320.

Chapter 11

The Politics of the Family

Motherhood and Morality in America

Kristin Luker

According to interested observers at the time, abortion in America was as frequent in the last century as it is in our own. And the last century, as we have seen, had its own "right-to-life" movement, composed primarily of physicians who pursued the issue in the service of their own professional goals. When abortion reemerged as an issue in the late 1950s, it still remained in large part a restricted debate among interested professionals. But abortion as we now know it has little in common with these earlier rounds of the debate. Instead of the civility and colleagueship that characterized the earlier phases of the debate, the present round of the abortion debate is marked by rancor and intransigence. Instead of the elite male professionals who commanded the issue until recently, ordinary people—and more to the point, ordinary women—have come to predominate in the ranks of those concerned. From a quiet, restricted technical debate among concerned professionals, abortion has become a debate that seems at times capable of tearing the fabric of American life apart. How did this happen? What accounts for the remarkable transformation of the abortion debate?

The history of the debate, as examined in previous chapters in this book, provides some preliminary answers. Technological advances in obstetrics led to a decline in those abortions undertaken strictly to preserve the life of the woman, using the narrowly biological sense of the word *life*. These technological advances, in turn, permitted (and indeed forced) physicians over time to make more and more nuanced decisions about abortion and eventually brought to the fore the underlying philosophical issue that had been obscured by a century of medical control over abortion: is the embryo a person or only a potential per-

From *Abortion and the Politics of Motherhood* by Kristin Luker, pp. 192–215. © 1984 The Regents of the University of California. Reprinted by permission of the University of California Press. Some text has been omitted.

son? . . . [O]nce this question is confronted directly, a unified world view—a set of assumptions about how the world is and ought to be organized—is called into play. . . . [W]orld views are usually the product of values so deeply held and dearly cherished that an assault upon them is a deeply disturbing assault indeed. Thus to summarize the argument of this book up to this point, the abortiion debate has been transformed because it has "gone public" and in so doing has called into question individuals' most sacrosanct beliefs.

But this is only part of the story. This chapter will argue that all the previous rounds of the abortion debate in America were merely echoes of the issue as the nineteenth century defined it: a debate about the medical profession's right to make life-and-death decisions. In contrast, the most recent round of the debate is about something new. By bringing the issue of the moral status of the embryo to the fore, the new round focuses on the relative rights of women and embryos. Consequently, the abortion debate has become a debate about women's contrasting obligations to themselves and others. New technologies and the changing nature of work have opened up possibilities for women outside of the home undreamed of in the nineteenth century; together, these changes give women—for the first time in history—the option of deciding exactly how and when their family roles will fit into the larger context of their lives. In essence, therefore, this round of the abortion debate is so passionate and hard-fought *because it is a referendum on the place and meaning of motherhood.*

Motherhood is at issue because two opposing visions of motherhood are at war. Championed by "feminists" and "housewives," these two different views of motherhood represent in turn two very different kinds of social worlds. The abortion debate has become a debate among women, women with different values in the social world, different experiences of it, and different resources with which to cope with it. How the issue is framed, how people think about it, and, most importantly, where the passions come from are all related to the fact that the battlelines are increasingly drawn (and defended) by women. While on the surface it is the embryo's fate that seems to be at stake, the abortion debate is actually about the meanings of *women's* lives.

To be sure, both the pro-life and the pro-choice movements had earlier phases in which they were dominated by male professionals. Some of these men are still active in the debate, and it is certainly the case that some men continue to join the debate on both sides of the issue. But the data in this study suggest that by 1974 over 80 percent of the activists in both the pro-choice and the pro-life movements in California were women, and a national survey of abortion activists found similar results.

Moreover, in our interviews we routinely asked both male and female activists on both sides of the issue to supply information on several "social background variables," such as where they were born, the extent of their education, their income level, the number of children they had, and their occupations. When male activists on the two sides are compared on these variables, they are virtually indistinguishable from one another. But when female activists are compared, it is dramatically clear that for the women who have come to dominate the ranks of the movement, the abortion debate is a conflict between two different social worlds and the hopes and beliefs those worlds support.

Who Are the Activists?

On almost every social background variable we examined, pro-life and pro-choice women differed dramatically. For example, in terms of income, almost half of all pro-life women (44 percent) in this study reported an income of less than $20,000 a year, but only one-fourth of the pro-choice women reported an income that low, and a considerable portion of those were young women just starting their careers. On the upper end of the income scale, one-third of the pro-choice women reported an income of $50,000 a year or more compared with only one pro-life woman in every seven.

These simple figures on income, however, conceal a very complex social reality, and that social reality is in turn tied to feelings about abortion. The higher incomes of pro-choice women, for example, result from a number of interesting factors. Almost without exception pro-choice women work in the paid labor force, they earn good salaries when they work, and if they are married, they are likely to be married to men who also have good incomes. An astounding 94 percent of all pro-choice women work, and over half of them have incomes in the top 10 percent of all working women in this country. Moreover, one pro-choice woman in ten has an annual *personal* income (as opposed to a family income) of $30,000 or more, thus putting her in the rarified ranks of the top 2 percent of all employed women in America. Pro-life women, by contrast, are far less likely to work: 63 percent of them do not work in the paid labor force, and almost all of those who do are unmarried. Among pro-life married women, for example, only 14 percent report any personal income at all, and for most of them, this is earned not in a formal job but through activities such as selling cosmetics to groups of friends. Not surprisingly, the personal income of pro-life women who work outside the home, whether in a formal job or in one of these less-structured activities, is low. Half of all pro-life women who do work earn less than $5,000 a year, and half earn between $5,000 and $10,000. Only two pro-life women we contacted reported a personal income of more than $20,000. Thus pro-life women are less likely to work in the first place, they earn less money when they do work, and they are more likely to be married to a skilled worker or small businessman who earns only a moderate income.

These differences in income are in turn related to the different educational and occupational choices these women have made along the way. Among pro-choice women, almost four out of ten (37 percent) had undertaken some graduate work beyond the B.A. degree, and 18 percent had an M.D, a law degree, a Ph.D., or a similar postgraduate degree. Pro-life women, by comparison, had far less education: 10 percent of them had only a high school education or less; and another 30 percent never finished college (in contrast with only 8 percent of the pro-choice women). Only 6 percent of all pro-life women had a law degree, a Ph.D., or a medical degree.

These educational differences were in turn related to occupational differences among the women in this study. Because of their higher levels of education, pro-choice women tended to be employed in the major professions, as administrators, owners of small businesses, or executives in large businesses. The pro-life women tended to be housewives or, of the few who worked, to be in the traditional female jobs of teaching, social work, and nursing. (The choice of home life over public life held true for even the 6 percent of pro-life women with an advanced degree; of the married women who had such degrees, at the time of our interviews only one of them had not retired from her profession after marriage.)

These economic and social differences were also tied to choices that women on each side had made about marriage and family life. For example, 23 percent of pro-choice women had never married, compared with only 16 percent of pro-life women; 14 percent of pro-choice women had been divorced, compared with 5 percent of pro-life women. The size of the families these women had was also different. The average pro-choice family had between one and two children and was more likely to have one; pro-life families averaged between two and three children and were more likely to have three. (Among the pro-life women, 23 percent had five or more children; 16 percent had seven or more children.) Pro-life women also tended to marry at a slightly younger age and to have had their first child earlier.

Finally, the women on each side differed dramatically in their religious affiliation and in the role that religion played in their lives. Almost 80 percent of the women active in the pro-life movement at the present time are Catholics. The remainder are Protestants (9 percent), persons who claim no religion (5 percent), and Jews (1 percent). In sharp contrast, 63 percent of pro-choice women say that they have no religion, 22 percent think of themselves as vaguely Protestant, 3 percent are Jewish, and 9 percent have what they call a "personal" religion. We found no one in our sample of pro-choice activists who claimed to be a Catholic at the time of the interviews.

When we asked activists what religion they were raised in as a child, however, a different picture emerged. For example, 20 percent of the pro-choice activists were raised as Catholics, 42 percent were raised as Protestants, and 15 percent were raised in the Jewish faith. In this group that describes itself predominantly without religious affiliation, therefore, only 14 percent say they were not brought up in any formal religious faith. By the same token, although almost 80 percent of present pro-life activists are Catholic, only 58 percent were raised in that religion (15 percent were raised as Protestants and 3 percent as Jews). Thus, almost 20 percent of the pro-life activists in this study are converts to Catholicism, people who have actively chosen to follow a given religious faith, in striking contrast to pro-choice people, who have actively chosen not to follow any.

Perhaps the single most dramatic differences between the two groups, however, is in the role that religion plays in their lives. Almost three-quarters of the pro-choice people interviewed said that formal religion was either unimportant or completely irrelevant to them, and their attitudes are correlated with behavior: only 25 percent of the pro-choice women said they *ever* attend church, and most of these said they do so only occasionally. Among pro-life people, by contrast, 69 percent said religion was important in their lives, and an additional 22 percent said that it was very important. For pro-life women, too, these attitudes are correlated with behavior: half of those pro-life women interviewed said they attend church regularly once a week, and another 13 percent said they do so even more often. Whereas 80 percent of pro-choice people never attend church, only 2 percent of pro-life advocates never do so.

Keeping in mind that the statistical use of averages has inherent difficulties, we ask, who are the "average" pro-choice and pro-life advocates? When the social background data are looked at carefully, two profiles emerge. The average pro-choice activist is a forty-four-year-old married women who grew up in a large metropolitan area and whose father was a college graduate. She was married at age twenty-two, has one or two children, and has had some graduate or professional training beyond the B.A. degree. She is married to a professional man, is herself employed in a regular job, and her family income is more than $50,000 a year. She is not religiously active, feels that religion is not important to her, and attends church very rarely if at all.

The average pro-life woman is also a forty-four-year-old married woman who grew up in a large metropolitan area. She married at age seventeen and has three children or more. Her father was a high school graduate, and she has some college education or may have a B.A. degree. She is not employed in the paid labor force and is married to a small businessman or a lower-level white-collar worker; her family income is $30,000 a year. She is Catholic (and may have converted), and her religion is one of the most important aspects of her life: she attends church at least once a week and occasionally more often.

Interests and Passions

To the social scientist (and perhaps to most of us) these social background characteristics connote lifestyles as well. We intuitively clothe these bare statistics with assumptions about beliefs and values. When we do so, the pro-choice women emerge as educated, affluent, liberal professionals, whose lack of religious affiliation suggests a secular, "modern," or (as pro-life people would have it) "utilitarian" outlook on life. Similarly, the income, education, marital patterns, and religious devotion of pro-life women suggest that they are traditional, hard-working people ("polyester types" to their opponents), who hold conservative views of life. We may be entitled to assume that individuals' social backgrounds act to shape and mold their social attitudes, but it is important to realize that the relationship between social worlds and social values is a very complex one.

Perhaps one example will serve to illustrate the point. A number of pro-life women in this study emphatically rejected an expression that pro-choice women tend to use almost unthinkingly—the expression *unwanted pregnancy*. Pro-life women argued forcefully that a better term would be a *surprise* pregnancy, asserting that although a pregnancy may be momentarily unwanted, the child that results from the pregnancy almost never is. Even such a simple thing—what to call an unanticipated pregnancy—calls into play an individual's values and resources. Keeping in mind our profile of the average pro-life person, it is obvious that a woman who does not work in the paid labor force, who does not have a college degree, whose religion is important to her, and who has already committed herself wholeheartedly to marriage and a large family is well equipped to believe than an unanticipated pregnancy usually becomes a beloved child. Her life is arranged so that for her, this belief is true. This view is consistent not only with her values, which she has held from earliest childhood, but with her social resources as well. It should not be surprising, therefore, that her world view leads her to believe that everyone else can "make room for one more" as easily as she can and that therefore it supports her in her conviction that abortion is cruel, wicked, and self-indulgent.*

It is almost certainly the case that an unplanned pregnancy is never an easy thing for anyone. Keeping in mind the profile of the average pro-choice woman, however, it is evident that a woman who is employed full time, who has an affluent lifestyle that depends in part of her contribution to the family income, and who expects to give a child as good a life as she herself has had with respect to educational, social, and economic advantages will draw on a different reality when she finds herself being skeptical about the ability of the average person to transform unwanted pregnancies into well-loved (and well-cared-for) children.

The relationship between passions and interests is thus more dynamic than it might appear at first. It is true that at one level, pro-choice and pro-life attitudes on abortion are self-serving: activists on each side have different views of the morality of abortion because their chosen lifestyles leave them with different needs for abortion; and both sides have values that provide a moral basis for their abortion needs in particular and their lifestyles in general. But this is only half the story. The values that lead pro-life and pro-choice women into different attitudes

---

*As might be imagined, it is not an easy task to ask people who are anti-abortion activists about their own experiences with a certain kind of unanticipated pregnancy, namely, a premarital pregnancy. Most pro-choice people were quite often open about having had such pregnancies; their pregnancies—and subsequent abortions—were central to their feelings about abortion. Pro-life women, by contrast, were deeply reluctant to discuss the topic. Several of them, after acknowledging premarital pregnancies, said that they did not want people to think that their attitudes on abortion were merely a product of their personal experiences. Thus we have no comparative figures about the extent to which the values represented here are the product of different experiences or just different opinions. We know only that unanticipated pregnancy was common among pro-choice women, and the interviews suggest that it was not uncommon among pro-life women. The difference in experience is, of course, that those in the first group sought abortions and those in the second group, with only a few exceptions, legitimized their pregnancies with a marriage.

toward abortion are the same values that led them at an earlier time to adopt different lifestyles that supported a given view of abortion.

For example, pro-life women have *always* valued family roles very highly and have arranged their lives accordingly. They did not acquire high-level educational and occupational skills, for example, because they married, and they married because their values suggested that this would be the most satisfying life open to them. Similarly, pro-choice women postponed (or avoided) marriage and family roles because they chose to acquire the skills they needed to be successful in the larger world, having concluded that the role of wife and mother was too limited for them. Thus, activists on both sides of the issue are women who have a given set of values about what are the most satisfying and appropriate roles for women, and they have made *life commitments that now limit their ability to change their minds*. Women who have many children and little education, for example, are seriously handicapped in attempting to become doctors or lawyers; women who have reached their late forties with few children or none are limited in their ability to build (or rebuild) a family. For most of these activists, therefore, their position on abortion is the "tip of the iceberg," a shorthand way of supporting and proclaiming not only a complex set of values but a given set of social resources as well.

To put the matter differently, we might say that for pro-life women the traditional division of life into separate male roles and female roles still works, but for pro-choice women it does not. Having made a commitment to the traditional female roles of wife, mother, and homemaker, pro-life women are limited in those kinds of resources—education, class status, recent occupational experiences— they would need to compete in what has traditionally been the male sphere, namely, the paid labor force. The average pro-choice woman, in contrast, is comparatively well endowed with exactly these resources; she is highly educated, she already has a job, and she has recent (and continuous) experience in the job market.

In consequence, anything that supports a traditional division of labor into male and female worlds is, broadly speaking, in the interests of pro-life women because that is where their resources lie. Conversely, such a traditional division of labor, when strictly enforced, is against the interests of pro-choice women because it limits their abilities to use the valuable "male" resources that they have in relative abundance. It is therefore apparent that attitudes toward abortion, even though rooted in childhood experiences, are also intimately related to present-day interests. Women who oppose abortion and seek to make it officially unavailable are declaring, both practically and symbolically, that women's reproductive roles should be given social primacy. Once an embryo is defined as a child and an abortion as the death of a person, almost everything else in a woman's life must "go on hold" during the course of her pregnancy: any attempt to gain "male" resources such as a job, an education, or other skills must be subordinated to her uniquely female responsibility of serving the needs of this newly conceived person. Thus, when personhood is bestowed on the embryo, women's nonreproductive roles are made secondary to their reproductive roles. The act of conception therefore creates a pregnant woman rather than a woman who is pregnant; it creates a woman whose life, in cases where roles or values clash, is defined by the fact that she is—or may become—pregnant.

It is obvious that this view is supportive of women who have already decided that their familial and reproductive roles are the major ones in their lives. By the same token, the costs of defining women's reproductive roles as primary do not seem high to them because they have already chosen to make those roles primary anyway. For example, employers might choose to discriminate against women because they might require maternity leave and thus be unavailable at critical times, but women who have chosen not to work in the paid labor force in the first place can see such discrimination as irrelevant to them.

It is equally obvious that supporting abortion (and believing that the embryo is not a person) is in the vested interests of pro-choice women. Being so well equipped to compete in the male sphere, they perceive any situation that both practically and symbolically affirms the primacy of women's reproductive roles as a real loss to them. Practically, it devalues their social resources. If women are only secondarily in the labor market and must subordinate working to pregnancy, should it occur, then their education, occupation, income and work become potentially temporary and hence discounted. Working becomes, as it traditionally was perceived to be, a pastime or hobby pursued for "pin money" rather than a central part of their lives. Similarly, if the embryo is defined as a person and the ability to become pregnant is the central one for women, a woman must be prepared to sacrifice some of her own interests to the interests of this newly conceived person.

In short, in a world where men and women have traditionally had different roles to play and where male roles have traditionally been the more socially prestigious and financially rewarded, abortion has become a symbolic marker between those who wish to maintain this division of labor and those who wish to challenge it. Thus, on an intimate level, the pro-life movement is women's version of what was true of peasants in the Vendeé, the part of France that remained Royalist during the French Revolution. Charles Tilly has argued that in the Vendeé, traditional relationships between nobles and peasants were still mutually satisfying so that the "brave new world" of the French Revolution represented more loss than gain, and the peasants therefore resisted the changes the Revolution heralded. By the same logic, traditional relationships between men and women are still satisfying, rewarding, and meaningful for pro-life women, and they therefore resist the lure of "liberation." For pro-choice women, however, with their access to male resources, a division of labor into the public world of work and the private world of home and hearth seems to promise only restriction to "second-class" citizenship.

Thus, the sides are fundamentally opposed to each other not only on the issue of abortion but also on what abortion *means*. Women who have many "human capital" resources of the traditionally male variety want to see motherhood recognized as a private, discretionary choice. Women who have few of these resources and limited opportunities in the job market want to see motherhood recognized as the most important thing a woman can do. In order for pro-choice women to achieve their goals, therefore, they *must* argue that motherhood is not a primary, inevitable, or "natural" role for all women; for pro-life women to achieve their goals, they *must* argue that it is. In short, the debate rests on the question of whether women's fertility is to be socially recognized as a resource or as a handicap.

To the extent that women who have chosen the larger public world of work have been successful, both legally and in terms of public opinion and, furthermore, are rapidly becoming the numerical majority, pro-life women are put on the defensive. Several pro-life women offered poignant examples of how the world deals with housewives who do not have an official payroll title. Here is what one of them said:

> I was at a party, about two years ago—it still sticks in my mind, you see, because I'm a housewife and I don't work—and I met this girl from England and we got involved in a deep discussion about the English and the Americans and their philosophies and how one has influenced the other, and at the end of the conversation—she was a working gal herself. I forget what she did—and she says, "Where do you work?" and I said, "I don't." And she looked at me and said, "You don't work?" I said "No." She said, "You're just a housewife . . . and you can still think like that?" She couldn't believe it, and she sort of gave me a funny look and that was the end of the conversation for the evening. And I've met other people who've had similar experiences. [People seem to think that if] you're at home and you're involved with children all day, your intelligence quotient must be down with them on the floor someplace, and [that] you really don't do much thinking or get yourself involved.

Moreover, there are subtle indications that even the pro-life activists we interviewed had internalized their loss of status as housewives. Only a handful of married pro-life activists also worked at regular jobs outside the home; but fully half of those who were now full-time homemakers, some for as long as thirty years, referred to themselves in terms of the work they had given up when they married or had their first child: "I'm a political scientist," "I'm a social worker," "I'm an accountant." It is noteworthy that no one used the past tense as in "I used to be a social worker"; every nonemployed married woman who used her former professional identification used it in the present tense. Since this pattern was not noticed during the interviewing, what the women themselves had in mind must remain speculative. But it does not seem unreasonable to imagine that this identification is an unconscious bow to the fact that "just plain" individuals, and in particular "just plain housewives," lack the status and credibility of professionals. Ironically, by calling on earlier identifications these women may have been expressing a pervasive cultural value that they oppose as a matter of ideology. They seemed to believe that when it comes to making public statements—or at least public statements to an interviewer who has come to ask you about your activities in the abortion debate—*what* you are counts more than *who* you are.

Because of their commitment to their own view of motherhood as a primary social role, pro-life women believe that other women are "casual" about abortions and have them "for convenience." There are no reliable data to confirm whether or not women are "casual" about abortions, but many pro-life people believe this to be the case and relate their activism to their perception of other people's casualness. For example:

> Every time I saw some article [on abortion] I read about it, and I had another friend who had her second abortion in 1977 . . . and both of her abortions were a matter of convenience, it was inconvenient for her to be pregnant at that time. When I talked to her I said, "O.K., you're married now, your husband has a good job, you want to have children eventually, but if you became pregnant now, you'd have an abortion. Why?" "Because it's inconvenient, this is not when I want to have my child." And that bothered me a lot because she is also very intelligent, graduated magna cum laude, and knew nothing about fetal development.

The assertion that women are "casual" about abortion, one could argue, expresses in a short-hand way a set of beliefs about women and their roles. First, the more people value the personhood of the embryo, the more important must be the reasons for taking its life. Some pro-life people, for example, would accept an abortion when continuation of the pregnancy would cause the death of the mother; they believe that when two lives are in direct conflict, the embryo's life can be considered the more expendable. But not all pro-life people agree, and many say they would not accept abortion even to save the mother's life. (Still others say they accept the idea in principle but would not make that choice in their own lives if faced with it.) For people who accept the personhood of the embryo, any reason besides trading a "life for a life" (and sometimes even that) seems trivial, merely a matter of "convenience."

Second, people who accept the personhood of the embryo see the reasons that pro-abortion people give for ending pregnancy as simultaneously downgrading the value of the embryo and upgrading everything else but pregnancy. The argument that women need abortion to "control" their fertility means that they intend to subordinate pregnancy, with its inherent unpredictability, to something else. As the pro-choice activists . . . have told us, that something else is participation in the paid labor force. Abortion permits women to engage in paid work on an equal basis with men. With abortion, they may schedule pregnancy in order to take advantage of the kinds of benefits that come with a paid position in the labor force: a paycheck, a title, a social identity. The pro-life women in this study were often careful to point out that they did not object to "career women." But what they meant by "career women" were women whose *only* responsibilities were in the labor force. Once a woman became a wife and a mother, in their view her primary responsibility was to her home and family.

Third, the pro-life activists we interviewed, the overwhelming majority of whom are full-time homemakers, also felt that women who worked *and* had families could often do so only because women like themselves picked up the slack. Given their place in the social structure, it is not surprising that many of the pro-life women thought that married women who worked outside the home were "selfish"—that they got all the benefits while the homemakers carried the load for them in Boy and Girl Scouts, PTA, and after school, for which their reward was to be treated by the workers as less competent and less interesting persons.*

Abortion therefore strips the veil of sanctity from motherhood. When pregnancy is discretionary—when people are allowed to put anything else they value in front of it—then motherhood has been demoted from a sacred calling to a job.** In effect, the legalization of abortion serves to make men and women more "unisex" by deemphasizing what makes them different—the ability of women to visibly and directly carry the next generation. Thus, pro-choice women are emphatic about their right to compete equally with men without the burden of an unplanned pregnancy, and pro-life women are equally emphatic about their belief that men and women have different roles in life and that pregnancy is a gift instead of a burden.

The pro-life activists we interviewed do not want equality with men in the sense of having exactly the same rights and responsibilities as men do, although they do want equality of status. In fact, to the extent that *all* women have been touched by the women's movement and have become aware of the fact that society often treats women as a class as less capable than men, quite a few said they appreciated the Equal Rights Amendment (ERA), except for its implied stand on abortion. The ERA, in their view, reminded them that women are as valuable *in their own sphere* as men are in theirs. However, to the extent that the ERA was seen as downplaying the differences between men and women, to devalue the female sphere of the home in the face of the male sphere of paid work, others saw it as both demeaning and oppressive to women like themselves. As one of the few married employed pro-life women argued:

> I oppose it [the ERA]. Because I've gotten where I am without it. I don't think I need it. I think a woman should be hired on her merits, not on her sex or race. I don't think we should be hiring on sex or on race. I think we should be taking the competent people that are capable of doing the job. . . . I don't think women should be taking jobs from the breadwinner, you know. I still think that our society should be male . . . the male should be the primary breadwinner. For example, my own husband cannot hope for promotion because he is white and Anglo, you know, I mean white male. He's not going to get a promotion. If he could get the promotion that others of different minorities have gotten over him, I probably wouldn't have to work at all. So from my own point of view, purely selfishly, I think we've got to consider it. On the other hand, if I'm doing the

---

*In fact, pro-life women, especially those recruited after 1972, were *less* likely to be engaged in formal activities such as Scouts, church activities, and PTA than their pro-choice peers. Quite possibly they have in mind more informal kinds of activities, premised on the fact that since they do not work, they are home most of the time.

**The same might be said of all sacred callings—stripped of its layer of the sacred, for example, the job of the clergy is demanding, low status, and underpaid.

same job [as a man], I expect to get the same pay. But I've always gotten it. So I really don't think that's an issue. I see the ERA as causing us more problems than it's going to [solve]. . . . As I see it, we were on a pedestal, why should we go down to being equal? That's my feeling on the subject.

It is stating the obvious to point out that the more limited the educational credentials a woman has, the more limited the job opportunities are for her, and the more limited the job opportunities, the more attractive motherhood is as full-time occupation. In motherhood, one can control the content and pace of one's own work, and the job is *intrinsically meaningful*. Compared with a job clerking in a supermarket (a realistic alternative for women with limited educational credentials) where the work is poorly compensated and often demeaning, motherhood can have compensations that far transcend the monetary ones. As one woman described mothering: "You have this little, rough uncut diamond, and you're the artist shaping and cutting that diamond, and bringing out the lights . . . that's a great challenge."

All the circumstances of her existence will therefore encourage a pro-life woman to highlight the kinds of values and experiences that support childbearing and childrearing and to discount the attraction (such as it is) of paid employment. Her circumstances encourage her to resent the pro-choice view that women's most meaningful and prestigious activities are in the "man's world."

Abortion also has a symbolic dimension that separates the needs and interests of homemakers and workers in the paid labor force. Insofar as abortion allows a woman to get a job, to get training for a job, or to advance in a job, it does more than provide social support for working women over homemakers; it also seems to support the value of economic considerations over moral ones. Many pro-life people interviewed said that although their commitment to traditional family roles meant very real material deprivations to themselves and their families, the more benefits of such a choice more than made up for it.

My girls babysit and the boys garden and have paper routes and things like that. I say that if we had a lot of money that would still be my philosophy, though I don't know because we haven't been in that position. But it's a sacrifice to have a larger family. So when I hear these figures that it takes $65,000 from birth to [raise a child], I think that's ridiculous. That's a new bike every year. That's private colleges. That's a complete new outfit when school opens. Well, we've got seven daughters who wear hand-me downs, and we hope that sometime in their eighteen years at home each one has a new bike somewhere along the line, but otherwise it's hand-me-downs. Those figures are inflated to give those children everything, and I think that's not good for them.

For pro-life people, a world view that puts the economic before the non-economic hopelessly confuses two different kinds of worlds. For them, the private world of family as traditionally experienced is the one place in human society where none of us has a price tag. Home, as Robert Frost pointed out, is where they have to take you in, whatever your social worth. Whether one is a surgeon or a rag picker, the family is, at least ideally, the place where love is unconditional.

Pro-life people and pro-life women in particular have very real reasons to fear such a state of affairs. Not only do they see an achievement-based world as harsh, superficial, and ultimately ruthless; they are relatively less well-equipped to operate in that world. A considerable amount of social science research has suggested, at least in the realm of medical treatment, that there is an increasing tendency to judge people by their official (achieved) worth. Pro-life people have relatively fewer official achievements in part because they have been doing what they see as a moral task, namely, raising children and making a home; and they see themselves as becoming handicapped in a world that discounts not only their social contributions but their personal lives as well.

It is relevant in this context to recall the grounds on which pro-life people argue that the embryo is a baby: that it is genetically human. To insist that the embryo is a baby because it is genetically human is to make a claim that it is both wrong and impossible to make distinctions between humans at all. Protecting the life of the embryo, which is by definition an entity whose social worth is all yet to come, means protecting others who feel that they may be defined as having low social worth; more broadly, it means protecting a legal view of personhood that emphatically rejects social worth criteria.

For the majority of pro-life people we interviewed, the abortions they found most offensive were those of "damaged" embryos. This is because this category so clearly highlights the aforementioned concerns about social worth. To defend a genetically or congenitally damaged embryo from abortion is, in their minds, defending the weakest of the weak, and most pro-life people we interviewed were least prepared to compromise on this category of abortion.

The genetic basis for the embryo's claim to personhood has another, more subtle implication for those on the pro-life side. If genetic humanness equals personhood, then biological facts of life must take precedence over social facts of life. One's destiny is therefore inborn and hence immutable. To give any ground on the embryo's biologically determined babyness, therefore, would by extension call into question the "innate," "natural," and biological basis of women's traditional roles as well.

Pro-choice people, of course, hold a very different view of the matter. For them, social considerations outweigh biological ones: the embryo becomes a baby when it is "viable," that is, capable of achieving a certain degree of social integration with others. This is a world view premised on achievement, but not in the way pro-life people experience the world. Pro-choice people, believing as they do in choice, planning, and human efficacy, believe that biology is simply a minor given to be transcended by human experience. Sex, like race and age, is not an appropriate criterion for sorting people into different rights and responsibilities. Pro-choice people downplay these "natural" ascriptive characteristics, believing that true equality means achievement based on talent, not being restricted to a "women's world," a "black world," or an "old people's world." Such a view, as the profile of pro-choice people has made clear, is entirely consistent with their own lives and achievements.

These differences in social circumstances that separate pro-life from pro-choice women on the core issue of abortion also lead them to have different values on topics that surround abortion, such as sexuality and the use of contraception. With respect to sexuality, for example, the two sides have diametrically opposed values; these values arise from a fundamentally different premise, which is, in turn, tied to the different realities of their social worlds. If pro-choice women have a vested interest in subordinating their reproductive capacities, and pro-life women have a vested interest in highlighting them, we should not be surprised to find that pro-life women believe that the purpose of sex is reproduction whereas pro-choice women believe that its purpose is to promote intimacy and mutual pleasure.

These two views about sex express the same value differences that lead the two sides to have such different views on abortion. If women plan to find their primary role in marriage and the family, then they face a need to create a "moral cartel" when it comes to sex. If sex is freely available outside of marriage, then why should men, as the old saw puts it, buy the cow when the milk is free? If many women are willing to sleep with men outside of marriage, then the regular sexual activity that comes with marriage is much less valuable an incentive to marry. And because pro-life women are traditional women, their primary resource for marriage is the promise of a stable home, with everything it implies: children, regular sex, a "haven in a heartless world."

But pro-life women, like all women, are facing a devaluation of these resources. As American society increasingly becomes a service economy, men can buy the services that a wife traditionally offers. Cooking, cleaning, decorating, and the like can easily be purchased on the open market in a cash transaction. And as sex becomes more open, more casual, and more "amative," it removes one more resource that could previously be obtained only through marriage.

Pro-life women, as we have seen, have both value orientations and social characteristics that make marriage very important. Their alternatives in the public world of work are, on the whole, less attractive. Furthermore, women who stay home full-time and keep house are becoming a financial luxury. Only very wealthy families *or families whose values allow them to place the nontangible benefits of a full-time wife over the tangible benefits of a working wife* can afford to keep one of its earners off the labor market. To pro-life people, the nontangible benefit of having children—and therefore the value of procreative sex—is very important. Thus, a social ethic that promotes more freely available sex undercuts pro-life women two ways: it limits their abilities to get into a marriage in the first place, and it undermines the social value placed on their presence once within a marriage.

For pro-choice women, the situation is reversed. Because they have access to "male" resources such as education and income, they have far less reason to believe that the basic reason for sexuality is to produce children. They plan to have small families anyway, and they and their husbands come from and have married into a social class in which small families are the norm. For a number of overlapping reasons, therefore, pro-choice women value the ability of sex to promote human intimacy more (or at least more frequently) than they value the ability of sex to produce babies. But they hold this view because they can afford to. When they bargain for marriage, they use the same resources that they use in the labor market: upper-class status, an education very similar to a man's, side-by-side participation in the man's world, and, not least, a salary that substantially increases a family's standard of living.

It is true, therefore, that pro-life people are "anti-sex." They value sex, of course, but they value it for its traditional benefits (babies) rather than for the benefits that pro-choice people associate with it (intimacy). Pro-life people really do want to see "less" sexuality—or at least less open and socially unregulated sexuality—because they think it is morally wrong, they think it distorts the meaning of sex, and they feel that it *threatens the basis on which their own marital bargains are built.*

These differences in social background also explain why the majority of pro-life people we interviewed were opposed to "artificial" contraception, and had chosen to use natural family planning (NFP), the modern-day version of the "rhythm method." To be sure, since NFP is a "morally licit" form of fertility control for Catholics, and many pro-life activists are very orthodox Catholics, NFP is attractive on those grounds alone. But as a group, Catholics are increasingly using contraception in patterns very similar to those of their non-Catholic peers. Furthermore, many non-Catholic pro-life activists told us they used NFP. Opposition to contraception, therefore, and its corollary, the use of NFP, needs to be explained as something other than simple obedience to church dogma.

Given their status as traditional women who do not work outside of the home, the choice of NFP as the preferred method of fertility control is a rational one because NFP enhances their power and status as women. The NFP users we talked with almost uniformly stated that men respect women more when they are using NFP and that the marriage relationship becomes more like a honeymoon. Certain social factors in the lives of pro-life women suggest why this may be so. Because NFP requires abstinence during the fertile period, one effect of using it is that *sex becomes a relatively scarce resource.* Rather than something that is simple there—and taken for granted—sex becomes something that disappears from the relationship for regular periods of time. Therefore, NFP creates incentives for husbands to be close and intimate with their wives. The more insecure a woman and the less support she feels from her husband, the more reasonable it is for her to want to lengthen the period of abstinence to be on the safe side.* The increase in

---

*One NFP counselor described a case to me in which a woman found herself unavailable for sex an average of twenty-five days a month in what seemed a deliberate attempt to use sex to control a spouse's behavior. But the interpretation of oneself as fertile (and hence sexually unavailable unless the spouse wishes to risk the arrival of another child) need not be either calculating or conscious. The more insecure a woman is in her marriage the more insecure she may be about interpreting her fertility signs, both because the insecurity in her marriage translates into a more general insecurity and because she may wish to err "on the safe side" if she is worried about the effects of a pregnancy on a shaky relationship.

power and status that NFP affords a woman in a traditional marriage was clearly recognized by the activists who use NFP, as these two quotations suggest:

> The rhythm [method] is the most freeing thing a woman can have, if you want me to tell you the honest-to-God truth. Because if she's married to someone that she loves, and she ought to be, then you know [when she abstains] she's got a romance time, she's got a time when she doesn't have to say she has a headache. He's just got to know, hey, either we're going to have another baby and you're going to pay for it or we're going to read our books tonight. And once in a while we're going to get to read our books, that's the way I look at it. I think it's wonderful, I really do, it might not sound too romantic to people, but it is, this is super romantic.

> You know, if you have filet mignon every day, it becomes kind of disinteresting. But if you have to plan around this, you do some things. You study, and you do other things during the fertile part of the cycle. And the husband and wife find out how much they can do in the line of expressing love for one another in other ways, other than genital. And some people can really express a lot of love and do a lot of touching and be very relaxed. Maybe others would find that they can only do a very little touching because they might be stimulated. And so they would have to find out where their level was. But they can have a beautiful relationship.

NFP also creates an opportunity for both husbands and wives to talk about the wife's fertility so that once again, something that is normally taken for granted can be focused on and valued. Folk wisdom has it that men and women use sexuality in different ways to express their feelings of caring and intimacy: men give love in order to get sex and women give sex in order to get love. If there is some truth to this stereotype (and both popular magazines and that rich source of sociological data, the Dear Abby column, suggest that there is), then it means that men and women often face confusion in their intimate dialogues with one another. Men wonder if their wives really want to have sex with them or are only giving it begrudgingly, out of a sense of "duty." Wives wonder if husbands really love them or merely want them for sexual relief. Natural Family Planning, by making sex periodically unavailable, put some of these fears to rest. Some women said their husbands actually bring them flowers during the period of abstinence. Though husbands were much less forthcoming on this topic; it would seem reasonable that a woman who has been visibly reassured of her husband's caring for her might approach the renewal of sexual activity with the enthusiasm of someone who knows she is cared for as a whole person, to the husband's benefit and pleasure.

Furthermore, a few mutually discreet conversations during our interviews suggest that during abstinence at least some couples find ways of giving each other sexual pleasure that do not involve actual intercourse and hence the risk of pregnancy. Given traditional patterns of female socialization into sexuality and the fact that pro-life women are both traditional and devout women, these periods of mutual caressing may be as satisfying as intercourse for some women and even more satisfying than intercourse for others.*

The different life circumstances and experiences of pro-life and pro-choice people therefore intimately affect the ways they look at the moral and social dilemmas of contraception. The settings of their lives, for example, suggest that the psychological side benefits of NFP, which do so much to support pro-life values during the practice of contraception, are sought in other ways by pro-choice people. Pro-choice people are slightly older when they marry, and the interviews strongly suggest that they have a considerably more varied sexual experience than pro-life people on average; the use of NFP to discover other facets of sexual expression is therefore largely unecessary for them. Moreover, what little we know about sexual practices in the United States (from the Kinsey Report) suggests that given the different average levels of education and religious devoutness in the two groups, such sexual activities as "petting" and oral-genital stimulation may be more frequently encountered among pro-choice people to begin with.**

The life circumstances of the two sides suggest another reason why NFP is popular among pro-life people but not seriously considered by pro-choice people. Pro-choice men and women act on their belief that men and women are equal not only because they have (or should have) equal rights but also because they have substantially similar life experiences. The pro-choice women we met have approximately the same kinds of education as their husbands do, and many of them have the same kinds of jobs—they are lawyers, physicians, college professors, and the like. Even those who do not work in traditionally male occupations have jobs in the paid labor market and thus share common experiences. They and their husbands share many social resources in common: they both have some status outside the home, they both have a paycheck, and they both have a set of peers and friends located in the work world rather than in the family world. In terms of the traditional studies of family power, pro-choice husbands and wives use the same bargaining chips and have roughly equal amounts of them.

*In short, these interviews were describing both "petting" and oral sex. Feminist literature has called to our attention the fact that traditional notions about sexuality are "male-centered"; it is assumed that there will be insertion and that there will be a male ejaculation. Ironically, NFP—the birth control method preferred by the devout, traditional women we interviewed—may come very close to achieving the feminist ideal. Under NFP, the "rules" of "regular" sex are suspended, and each couple must discover for themselves what feels good. For a generation of women who were raised when long periods of "necking" and "petting" occurred before—and often instead of—intercourse, NFP may provide a welcoming change from genitally centered, male-oriented sexual behavior to more diffuse, body-focused "female" forms of sexual expression.

**Kinsey's data suggest that for males the willingness to engage in oral-genital or manual-genital forms of sexual expression is related to education: the more educated an individual, the more likely he is to have "petted" or engaged in oral sex (Alfred Kinsey, *Sexual Behavior in the Human Male*, pp. 337–81, 535–37). For females, the patterns are more complicated. Educational differences among women disappear when age at marriage is taken into account. But as Kinsey notes: "Among the females in the sample, the chief restraint on petting . . . seems to have been the religious tradition against it." The more devout a woman, the less likely she is to have ever petted (Kinsey, *Sexual Behavior in the Human Female*, pp. 247–48).

Pro-choice women, therefore, value (and can afford) an approach to sexuality that, by sidelining reproduction, diminishes the differences between men and women; they can do this *because they have other resources on which to build a marriage.* Since their value is intimacy and since the daily lives of men and women on the pro-choice side are substantially similar, intimacy in the bedroom is merely an extension of the intimacy of their larger world.

Pro-life women and men, by contrast, tend to live in "separate spheres." Because their lives are based on a social and emotional division of labor where each sex has its appropriate work, to accept contraception or abortion would devalue the one secure resource left to these women; the private world of home and hearth. This would be disastrous not only in terms of status but also in terms of meaning; if values about fertility and family are not essential to a marriage, what support does a traditional marriage have in times of stress? To accept highly effective contraception, which actually and symbolically subordinates the role of children in the family to other needs and goals, would be to cut the ground of meaning out from under at least one (and perhaps both) partners' lives. Therefore, contraception, which sidelines the reproductive capacities of men and women, is both useless and threatening to pro-life people.

The Core of the Debate

In summary, women come to be pro-life and pro-choice activists as the end result of lives that center around different definitions of motherhood. They grow up with a belief about the nature of the embryo, so events in their lives lead them to believe that the embryo is a unique person, or a fetus; that people are intimately tied to their biological roles, or that these roles are but a minor part of life; that motherhood is the most important and satisfying role open to a woman, or that motherhood is only one of several roles, a burden when defined as the only role. These beliefs and values are rooted in the concrete circumstances of women's lives—their educations, incomes, occupations, and the different marital and family choices they have made along the way—and they work simultaneously to shape those circumstances in turn. Values about the relative place of reason and faith, about the role of actively planning for life versus learning to accept gracefully life's unknowns, of the relative satisfactions inherent in work and family—all of these factors place activists in a specific relationship to the larger world and give them a specific set of resources with which to confront that world.

The simultaneous and on-going modification of both their lives and their values by each other finds these activists located in a specific place in the social world. They are financially successful, or they are not. They become highly educated, or they do not. They become married and have a large family, or they have a small one. And at each step of the way, both their values and their lives have undergone either ratification or revision.

Pro-choice and pro-life activists live in different worlds, and the scope of their lives, as both adults and children, fortifies them in their belief that their own views on abortion are the more correct, more moral, and more reasonable. When added to this is the fact that should "the other side" win, one group of women will see the very real devaluation of their lives and life resources, it is not surprising that the abortion debate has generated so much heat and so little light.

Bowers v. Hardwick:
Do Homosexuals Have a Right to Privacy?

Justice WHITE delivered the opinion of the Court.

In August 1982, respondent [Hardwick] was charged with violating the Georgia statute criminalizing sodomy by committing that act with another adult male in the bedroom of respondent's home.

. . . This case does not require a judgment on whether laws against sodomy between consenting adults in general, or between homosexuals in particular, are wise or desirable. It raises no question about the right or propriety of state legislative decisions to repeal their laws that criminalize homosexual sodomy, or of state court decisions invalidating those laws on state constitutional grounds. The issue presented is whether the Federal Constitution confers a fundamental right upon homosexuals to engage in sodomy and hence invalidates the laws of the many States that still make such conduct illegal and have done so for a very long time. The case also calls for some judgment about the limits of the Court's role in carrying out its constitutional mandate. . . .

. . . [R]espondent would have us announce, as the Court of Appeals did, a fundamental right to engage in homosexual sodomy. This we are quite unwilling to do. . . .

Proscriptions against [sodomy] have ancient roots. Sodomy was a criminal offense at common law and was forbidden by the laws of the original thirteen States when they ratified the Bill of Rights. In 1868, when the Fourteenth Amendment was ratified, all but 5 of the 37 States in the Union had criminal sodomy laws. In fact, until 1961, all 50 States outlawed sodomy, and today, 24 States and the District of Columbia continue to provide criminal penalties for sodomy performed in private and between consenting adults.

. . . Against this background, to claim that a right to engage in such conduct is "deeply rooted in this Nation's history and tradition" or "implicit in the concept of ordered liberty" is, at best, facetious.

[3] Nor are we inclined to take a more expansive view of our authority to discover new fundamental rights imbedded in the Due Process Clause. The Court

---

From *Bowers v. Hardwick* 106 S.C.t. 2841 (1986). Some text, most footnotes, and most legal citations have been omitted.

is most vulnerable and comes nearest to illegitimacy when it deals with judge-made constitutional law having little or no cognizable roots in the language or design of the Constitution. That this is so was painfully demonstrated by the face-off between the Executive and the Court in the 1930's, which resulted in the repudiation of much of the substantive gloss that the Court had placed on the Due Process Clause of the Fifth and Fourteenth Amendments. There should be, therefore, great resistance to expand the substantive reach of those Clauses, particularly if it requires redefining the category of rights deemed to be fundamental. Otherwise, the Judiciary necessarily takes to itself further authority to govern the country without express constitutional authority. The claimed right pressed on us today falls far short of overcoming this resistance.

Respondent, however, asserts that the result should be different where the homosexual conduct occurs in the privacy of the home. He relies on *Stanley v. Georgia,* 394 U.S. 557 . . . (1969), where the Court held that the First Amendment prevents conviction for possessing and reading obscene material in the privacy of his home: "If the First Amendment means anything, it means that a State has no business telling a man, sitting alone in his house, what books he may read or what films he may watch." . . .

Stanley did protect conduct that would not have been protected outside the home, and it partially prevented the enforcement of state obscenity laws; but the decision was firmly grounded in the First Amendment. The right pressed upon us here has no similar support in the text of the Constitution, and it does not qualify for recognition under the prevailing principles for construing the Fourteenth Amendment. Its limits are also difficult to discern. Plainly enough, otherwise illegal conduct is not always immunized whenever it occurs in the home. Victimless crimes, such as the possession and use of illegal drugs do not escape the law where they are committed at home. *Stanley* itself recognized that its holding offered no protection for the possession in the home of drugs, firearms, or stolen goods. . . . And if respondent's submission is limited to the voluntary sexual conduct between consenting adults, it would be difficult, except by fiat, to limit the claimed right to homosexual conduct while leaving exposed to prosecution adultery, incest, and other sexual crimes even though they are committed in the home. We are unwilling to start down that road.

[4] Even if the conduct at issue here is not a fundamental right, respondent asserts that there must be a rational basis for the law and that there is none in this case other than the presumed belief of a majority of the electorate in Georgia that homosexual sodomy is immoral and unacceptable. This is said to be an inadequate rationale to support the law. The law, however, is constantly based on notions of morality, and if all laws representing essentially moral choices are to be invalidated under the Due Process Clause, the courts will be very busy indeed. Even respondent makes no such claim, but insists that majority sentiments about the morality of homosexuality should be declared inadequate. We do not agree, and are unpersuaded that the sodomy laws of some 25 States should be invalidated on this basis.

Accordingly, the judgment of the Court of Appeals is

Reversed.

Chief Justice BURGER, concurring.

I join the Court's opinion, but I write separately to underscore my view that in constitutional terms there is no such thing as a fundamental right to commit homosexual sodomy.

As the Court notes, . . . the proscriptions against sodomy have very "ancient roots." Decisions of individuals relating to homosexual conduct have been subject to state intervention throughout the history of Western Civilization. Condemnation of those practices is firmly rooted in Judaeo-Christian moral and ethical standards. Homosexual sodomy was a capital crime under Roman law. See Code Theod. 9.7.6; Code Just. 9.9.31. See also D. Bailey, Homosexuality in the Western Christian Tradition 70–81 (1975). During the English Reformation when powers of the ecclesiastical courts were transferred to the King's Courts, the first English statute criminalizing sodomy was passed. 25 Hen. VIII, c. 6. Blackstone described "the infamous crime against nature" as an offense of "deeper malignity" than rape, an heinous act "the very mention of which is a disgrace to human nature," and "a crime not fit to be named." Blackstone's Commentaries *215. The common law of England, including its prohibition of sodomy, became the received law of Georgia and the other Colonies. In 1816 the Georgia Legislature passed the statute at issue here, and that statute has been continuously in force in one form or another since that time. To hold that the act of homosexual sodomy is somehow protected as a fundamental right would be to cast aside millennia of moral teaching.

This is essentially not a question of personal "preferences" but rather of the legislative authority of the State. I find nothing in the Constitution depriving a State of the power to enact the statute challenged here.

Justice BLACKMUN, with whom Justice BRENNAN, Justice MARSHALL, and Justice STEVENS join, dissenting.

This case is no more about "a fundamental right to engage in homosexual sodomy," as the Court purports to declare, . . . than *Stanley v. Georgia* . . . was about a fundamental right to watch obscene movies, or *Katz v. United States* . . . was about a fundamental right to place interstate bets from a telephone booth. Rather, this case is about "the most comprehensive of rights and the right most valued by civilized men," namely, "the right to be let alone." . . .

The statute at issue, Ga.Code Ann. § 16–6–2, denies individuals the right to decide for themselves whether to engage in particular forms of private, consensual sexual activity. The Court concludes that § 16–6–2 is valid essentially because "the laws of . . . many States . . . still make such conduct illegal and have done so for a very long time." . . . But the fact that the moral judgments expressed by statutes like § 16–6–2 may be "natural and familiar . . . ought not to conclude our judgment upon the question whether statutes embodying them conflict with the Constitution of the United States." . . . Like Justice Holmes, I believe that "[i]t is revolting to have no better reason for a rule of law than that so it was laid down in the time of Henry IV. It is still more revolting if the grounds upon which it was laid down have vanished long since, and the rule simply persists from blind imitation of the past." . . . I believe we must analyze respondent's claim in the light of the values that underlie the constitutional right to privacy. If that right means anything, it means that, before Georgia can prosecute its citizens for making choices about the most intimate aspects of their lives, it must do more than assert that the choice they have made is an " 'abominable crime not fit to be named among Christians.' " . . .

I

In its haste to reverse the Court of Appeals and hold that the Constitution does not "confe[r] a fundamental right upon homosexuals to engage in sodomy," . . . the Court relegates the actual statute being challenged to a footnote and ignores the procedural posture of the case before it. A fair reading of this statute and of the complaint clearly reveals that the majority has distorted the question this case presents.

First, the Court's almost obsessive focus on homosexual activity is particularly hard to justify in light of the broad language Georgia has used. Unlike the Court, the Georgia Legislature has not proceeded on the assumption that homosexuals are so different from other citizens that their lives may be controlled in a way that would not be tolerated if it limited the choices of those other citizens. . . . Rather, Georgia has provided that "[a] person commits the offense of sodomy when he performs or submits to any sexual act involving the sex organs of one person and the mouth or anus of another." Ga.Code Ann. § 16–6–2(a). The sex or status of the persons who engage in the act is irrelevant as a matter of state law. In fact, to the extent I can discern a legislative purpose for Georgia's 1968 enactment of § 16–6–2, that purpose seems to have been to broaden the coverage of the law to reach heterosexual as well as homosexual activity.[1] I therefore see no basis for the Court's decision to treat this case as an "as applied" challenge to § 16–6–2, . . . or for Georgia's attempt, both in its brief and at oral argument, to defend § 16–6–2 solely on the grounds that it prohibits homosexual activity. Michael Hardwick's standing may rest in significant part on Georgia's apparent willing-

---

[1] Until 1968, Georgia defined sodomy as "the carnal knowledge and connection against the order of nature, by man with man, or in the same unnatural manner with woman." Ga.Crim.Code § 26–5901 (1933). In *Thompson v. Aldredge,* 187 Ga. 467, 200 S.E. 799 (1939), the Georgia Supreme Court held that § 26–5901 did not prohibit lesbian activity. And in *Riley v. Garrett,* 219 Ga. 345, 133 S.E.2d 367 (1963), the Georgia Supreme Court held that § 26–5901 did not prohibit heterosexual cunnilingus. Georgia passed the act-specific statute currently in force "perhaps in response to the restrictive court decisions such as *Riley,"* Note, The Crimes Against Nature, 16 J.Pub.L. 159, 167, n. 47 (1967).

ness to enforce against homosexuals a law it seems not to have any desire to enforce against heterosexuals. . . . But his claim that § 16–6–2 involves an unconstitutional intrusion into his privacy and his right of intimate association does not depend in any way on his sexual orientation. . . .

II

"Our cases long have recognized that the Constitution embodies a promise that a certain private sphere of individual liberty will be kept largely beyond the reach of government." . . . In construing the right to privacy, the Court has proceeded along two somewhat distinct, albeit complementary, lines. First, it has recognized a privacy interest with reference to certain *decisions* that are properly for the individual to make. . . . Second, it has recognized a privacy interest with reference to certain *places* without regard for the particular activities in which the individuals who occupy them are engaged. . . . The case before us implicates both the decisional and the spatial aspects of the right to privacy.

A

The Court concludes today that none of our prior cases dealing with various decisions that individuals are entitled to make free of governmental interference "bears any resemblance to the claimed constitutional right of homosexuals to engage in acts of sodomy that is asserted in this case." . . . While it is true that these cases may be characterized by their connection to protection of the family . . . the Court's conclusion that they extend no further than this boundary ignores the warning in *Moore v. East Cleveland,* 431 U.S. 494, 501 . . . (plurality opinion), against "clos[ing] our eyes to the basic reasons why certain rights associated with the family have been accorded shelter under the Fourteenth Amendment's Due Process Clause." We protect those rights not because they contribute, in some direct and material way, to the general public welfare, but because they form so central a part of an individual's life. "[T]he concept of privacy embodies the 'moral fact that a person belongs to himself and not others nor to society as a whole.' " . . .

. . . And so we protect the decision whether to marry precisely because marriage "is an association that promotes a way of life, not causes; a harmony in living, not political faiths; a bilateral loyalty, not commercial or social projects." . . . We protect the decision whether to have a child because parenthood alters so dramatically an individual's self-definition, not because of demographic considerations or the Bible's command to be fruitful and multiply. . . . And we protect the family because it contributes so powerfully to the happiness of individuals, not because of a preference for stereotypical households. . . . The Court recognized in *Roberts,* 468 U.S., at 619, . . . that the "ability independently to define one's identity that is central to any concept of liberty" cannot truly be exercised in a vacuum; we all depend on the "emotional enrichment of close ties with others." . . .

Only the most willful blindness could obscure the fact that sexual intimacy is "a sensitive, key relationship of human existence, central to family life, community welfare, and the development of human personality." . . . The fact that individuals define themselves in a significant way through their intimate sexual relationships with others suggests, in a Nation as diverse as ours, that there may be many "right" ways of conducting those relationships, and that much of the richness of a relationship will come from the freedom an individual has to *choose* the form and nature of these intensely personal bonds. . . .

In a variety of circumstances we have recognized that a necessary corollary of giving individuals freedom to choose how to conduct their lives is acceptance of the fact that different individuals will make different choices. For example, in holding that the clearly important state interest in public education should give way to a competing claim by the Amish to the effect that extended formal schooling threatened their way of life, the Court declared: "There can be no assumption that today's majority is 'right' and the Amish and others like them are 'wrong.' A way of life that is odd or even erratic but interferes with no rights or interests of others is not to be condemned because it is different." *Wisconsin v. Yoder,* 406 U.S. 205 . . . (1972). The Court claims that its decision today merely refuses to recognize a fundamental right to engage in homosexual sodomy; what the Court really has refused to recognize is the fundamental interest all individuals have in controlling the nature of their intimate associations with others.

B

The behavior for which Hardwick faces prosecution occurred in his own home, a place to which the Fourth Amendment attaches special significance. The Court's treatment of this aspect of the case is symptomatic of its overall refusal to consider the broad principles that have informed our treatment of privacy in specific cases. Just as the right to privacy is more than the mere aggregation of a number of entitlements to engage in specific behavior, so too, protecting the physical integrity of the home is more than merely a means of protecting specific activities that often take place there. Even when our understanding of the contours of the right to privacy depends on "reference to a 'place,' " . . . "the essence of a Fourth Amendment violation is 'not the breaking of [a person's] doors, and the rummaging of his drawers,' but rather is 'the invasion of his indefeasible right of personal security, personal liberty and private property.' " . . .

The Court's interpretation of the pivotal case of *Stanley v. Georgia,* 394 U.S. 557 . . . (1969), is entirely unconvincing. *Stanley* held that Georgia's undoubted power to punish the public distribution of constitutionally unprotected, obscene material did not permit the State to punish the private possession of such material. According to the majority here, *Stanley* relied entirely on the First Amendment, and thus, it is claimed, sheds no light on cases not involving printed materials. . . . But that is not what *Stanley* said. Rather, the *Stanley* Court anchored its holding in the Fourth Amendment's special protection for the individual in his home:

> " 'The makers of our Constitution undertook to secure conditions favorable to the pursuit of happiness. They recognized the significance of man's spiritual nature, of his feelings and of his intellect. They knew that only a part of the pain, pleasure and satisfactions of life are to be found in material things. They sought to protect Americans in their beliefs, their thoughts, their emotions and their sensations.'
>
> .   .   .   .   .
>
> "These are the rights that appellant is asserting in the case before us. He is asserting the right to read or observe what he pleases—the right to satisfy his intellectual and emotional needs in the privacy of his own home."

. . . "The right of the people to be secure in their . . . houses," expressly guaranteed by the Fourth Amendment, is perhaps the most "textual" of the various constitutional provisions that inform our understanding of the right to privacy, and thus I cannot agree with the Court's statement that "[t]he right pressed upon us here has no . . . support in the text of the Constitution." . . . Indeed, the right of an individual to conduct intimate relationships in the intimacy of his or her own home seems to me to be the heart of the Constitution's protection of privacy.

III

The Court's failure to comprehend the magnitude of the liberty interests at stake in this case leads it to slight the question whether petitioner, on behalf of the State, has justified Georgia's infringement on these interests. I believe that neither of the two general justifications for § 16–6–2 that petitioner has advanced warrants dismissing respondent's challenge for failure to state a claim.

First, petitioner asserts that the acts made criminal by the statute may have serious adverse consequences for "the general public health and welfare," such as spreading communicable diseases or fostering other criminal activity. . . . Inasmuch as this case was dismissed by the District Court on the pleadings, it is not surprising that the record before us is barren of any evidence to support petitioner's claim. In light of the state of the record, I see no justification for the Court's attempt to equate the private, consensual sexual activity at issue here with the "possession in the home of drugs, firearms, or stolen goods," . . . to which *Stanley* refused to extend its protection. . . . None of the behavior so mentioned in *Stanley* can properly be viewed as "[v]ictimless," . . . drugs and weapons are inherently dangerous, . . . and for property to be "stolen," someone must have been wrongfully deprived of it. Nothing in the record before the Court provides any justification for finding the activity forbidden by § 16–6–2 to be physically dangerous, either to the persons engaged in it or to others.[4]

The core of petitioner's defense of § 16–6–2, however, is that respondent and others who engage in the conduct prohibited by § 16–6–2 interfere with Georgia's exercise of the " 'right of the Nation and of the States to maintain a decent society.' " . . . Essentially, petitioner argues, and the Court agrees, that the fact that the acts described in § 16–6–2 "for hundreds of years, if not thousands, have been uniformly condemned as immoral" is a sufficient reason to permit a State to ban them today. . . .

I cannot agree that either the length of time a majority has held its convictions or the passions with which it defends them can withdraw legislation from this Court's scrutiny. . . . As Justice Jackson wrote so eloquently for the Court in *West Virginia Board of Education v. Barnette*, 319 U.S. 624 . . . (1943), "we apply the limitations of the Constitution with no fear that freedom to be intellectually and spiritually diverse or even contrary will disintegrate the social organization. . . . [F]reedom to differ is not limited to things that do not matter much. That would be a mere shadow of freedom. The test of its substance is the right to differ as to things that touch the heart of the existing order." . . . It is precisely because the issue raised by this case touches the heart of what makes individuals what they are that we should be especially sensitive to the rights of those whose choices upset the majority.

The assertion that "traditional Judeo-Christian values proscribe" the conduct involved, Brief for Petitioner 20, cannot provide an adequate justification for § 16–6–2. That certain, but by no means all, religious groups condemn the behavior at issue gives the State no license to impose their judgments on the entire citizenry. The legitimacy of secular legislation depends instead on whether the State can advance some justification for its law beyond its conformity to religious doctrine. . . . Thus, far from buttressing his case, petitioner's invocation of Leviticus, Romans, St. Thomas Aquinas, and sodomy's heretical status during the Middle Ages undermines his suggestion that § 16–6–2 represents a legitimate use

---

[4] Although I do not think it necessary to decide today issues that are not even remotely before us, it does seem to me that a court could find simple, analytically sound distinctions between certain private, consensual sexual conduct, on the one hand, and adultery and incest (the only two vaguely specific "sexual crimes" to which the majority points, . . .), on the other. For example, marriage, in addition to its spiritual aspects, is a civil contract that entitles the contracting parties to a variety of governmentally provided benefits. A State might define the contractual commitment necessary to become eligible for these benefits to include a commitment of fidelity and then punish individuals for breaching that contract. Moreover, a State might conclude that adultery is likely to injure third persons, in particular, spouses and children of persons who engage in extramarital affairs. With respect to incest, a court might well agree with respondent that the nature of familial relationships renders true consent to incestuous activity sufficiently problematical that a blanket prohibition of such activity is warranted. . . . Notably, the Court makes no effort to explain why it has chosen to group private, consensual homosexual activity with adultery and incest rather than with private, consensual heterosexual activity by unmarried persons or, indeed, with oral or anal sex within marriage.

of secular coercive power.[6] A State can no more punish private behavior because of religious tolerance than it can punish such behavior because of racial animus. "The Constitution cannot control such prejudices, but neither can it tolerate them. Private biases may be outside the reach of the law, but the law cannot, directly or indirectly give them effect." . . . No matter how uncomfortable a certain group may make the majority of this Court, we have held that "[m]ere public intolerance or animosity cannot constitutionally justify the deprivation of a person's physical liberty." . . .

Nor can § 16–6–2 be justified as a "morally neutral" exercise of Georgia's power to "protect the public environment." . . . Certainly, some private behavior can affect the fabric of society as a whole. Reasonable people may differ about whether particular sexual acts are moral or immoral, but "we have ample evidence for believing that people will not abandon morality, will not think any better of murder, cruelty and dishonesty, merely because some private sexual practice which they abominate is not punished by the law." H.L.A. Hart, Immorality and Treason, reprinted in The Law as Literature 220, 225 (L. Blom-Cooper ed. 1961). Petitioner and the Court fail to see the difference between laws that protect public sensibilities and those that enforce private morality. Statutes banning public sexual activity are entirely consistent with protecting the individual's liberty interest in decisions concerning sexual relations: the same recognition that those decisions are intensely private which justifies protecting them from governmental interference can justify protecting individuals from unwilling exposure to the sexual activities of others. But the mere fact that intimate behavior may be punished when it takes place in public cannot dictate how States can regulate intimate behavior that occurs in intimate places. See *Paris Adult Theatre I, supra,* at 66, n. 13 ("marital intercourse on a street corner or a theater stage" can be forbidden despite the constitutional protection identified in *Griswold v. Connecticut,* 381 U.S. 479 . . . (1965)).[7]

---

[6] The theological nature of the origin of Anglo-American antisodomy statutes is patent. It was not until 1533 that sodomy was made a secular offense in England. 25 Hen. VIII, cap. 6. Until that time, the offense was, in Sir James Stephen's words, "merely ecclesiastical." 2 J. Stephen, A History of the Criminal Law of England 430 (1883). Pollock and Maitland similarly observed that "[t]he crime against nature. . . . was so closely connected with heresy that the vulgar had but one name for both." 2 F. Pollock & F. Maitland, The History of English Law 554 (1895). The transfer of jurisdiction over prosecutions for sodomy to the secular courts seems primarily due to the alteration of ecclesiastical jurisdiction attendant on England's break with the Roman Catholic Church, rather than to any new understanding of the sovereign's interest in preventing or punishing the behavior involved. Cf. E. Coke, The Third Part of the Institutes of the Laws of England, ch. 10 (4th ed. 1797).

[7] At oral argument a suggestion appeared that, while the Fourth Amendment's special protection of the home might prevent the State from enforcing § 16–6–2 against individuals who engage in consensual sexual activity there, that protection would not make the statute invalid. . . . The suggestion misses the point entirely. If the law is not invalid, then the police *can* invade the home to enforce it, provided, of course, that they obtain a determination of probable cause from a neutral magistrate. One of the reasons for the Court's holding in *Griswold v. Connecticut,* 381 U.S. 479 . . . (1965), was precisely the possibility, and repugnancy, of permitting searches to obtain evidence regarding the use of contraceptives. . . . Permitting the kinds of searches that might be necessary to obtain evidence of the sexual activity banned by § 16–6–2 seems no less intrusive, or repugnant. . . .

The case involves no real interference with the rights of others, for the mere knowledge that other individuals do not adhere to one's value system cannot be a legally cognizable interest, . . . let alone an interest that can justify invading the houses, hearts, and minds of citizens who choose to live their lives differently. . . .

IV

It took but three years for the Court to see the error in its analysis in *Minersville School District v. Gobitis,* 310 U.S. 586 . . . (1940), and to recognize that the threat to national cohesion posed by a refusal to salute the flag was vastly outweighed by the threat to those same values posed by compelling such a salute. . . . I can only hope that here, too, the Court soon will reconsider its analysis and conclude that depriving individuals of the right to choose for themselves how to conduct their intimate relationships poses a far greater threat to the values most deeply rooted in our Nation's history than tolerance of nonconformity could ever do. Because I think the Court today betrays those values, I dissent.

The Family as a Haven in a Heartless World

Christopher Lasch

The family in the form familiar to us took shape in the United States and western Europe in the last half of the eighteenth and the first half of the nineteenth centuries, although its antecedents can be traced back to an earlier period. The chief features of the Western family system can be simply, if somewhat schematically, set forth. Compared with practices in most other societies, marriage takes place at a late age, and large numbers of people remain unmarried. As these demographic facts imply, marriages tend to be arranged by the participants instead of by parents and elders; at best the elders have a veto. Young couples are allowed to court with a minimum of interference from adults, on the understanding that their own self-restraint will take the place of adult supervision—an expectation that is not unreasonable considering that courting couples are typically young adults themselves and that young women in particular have been trained from an early age to accept advances from the other sex without compromising their reputation.

Reprinted by permission of the author and the publisher from *Salmagundi* (Fall 1976), pp. 42–55.

At the same time the habits of self-inhibition acquired during courtship are not easily relinquished in marriage, and the Western marriage system therefore gives rise to much sexual tension and maladjustment, which is more keenly felt than it would be elsewhere because marriage is supposed to be based on intimacy and love. The overthrow of arranged marriage was accomplished in the name of romantic love and a new conception of the family as a refuge from the highly competitive and often brutal world of commerce and industry. Husband and wife, according to this ideology, were to find solace and spiritual renewal in each other's company. Especially the woman was expected to serve, in a well-worn nineteenth-century phrase, as an "angel of consolation."

Her mission of mercy extended of course to her children as well, around whom middle-class family life increasingly centered. A new idea of childhood, as Aries has shown, helped to precipitate the new idea of the family. No longer seen simply as a little adult, the child came to be regarded as a person with distinctive attributes of his own, impressionability, vulnerability, and innocence, that required a warm, protected, and prolonged period of nurture. Whereas formerly children had mixed freely in adult society, parents now sought to segregate them from premature contact with servants and other corrupting influences. Educators and moralists began to stress the child's need for play, for love and understanding, and for the gradual, gentle unfolding of his nature. Child-rearing became more demanding as a result, and emotional ties between parents and children were strengthened at the same time that ties to relatives outside the immediate family were greatly weakened. Here was another source of persistent tension in the middle-class family—the emotional overloading of the parent-child connection.

Still another source of tension was the change in the status of women that the new family system required. The bourgeois family simultaneously degraded and exalted women. On the one hand, it deprived women of many of their traditional employments, as the household ceased to be a center of production and devoted itself to childrearing instead. On the other hand, the new demands of childrearing, at a time when so much attention was being given to the special needs of the child, made it necessary to educate women for their domestic duties. Better education was also required if women were to become suitable companions for their husbands. A thoroughgoing reform and extension of women's education was implicit in the new-style domesticity, as Mary Wollstonecraft, the first modern feminist, was one of the first to appreciate when she insisted that if women were to become "affectionate wives and rational mothers," they would have to be trained in something more than "accomplishments" that were designed to make young ladies attractive to proposition that women should become useful rather than ornamental. In the categories immortalized by Jane Austen, women were called on to give up sensibility in favor of sense. Thus bourgeois domesticity gave rise to its antithesis, feminism. The domestication of woman gave rise to a general unrest, encouraging her to entertain aspirations that marriage and the family could not satisfy. These aspirations were one ingredient in the so-called marriage crisis that began to unfold at the end of the nineteenth century.

To summarize, the bourgeois family system, which had its heyday in the nineteenth century and now seems to be slowly crumbling, was founded on what sociologists have called companionate marriage, on the child-centered household, on the emancipation or quasi-emancipation of women, and on the structural isolation of the nuclear family from the kinship system and from society in general. The family found ideological support and justification in the conception of the family as an emotional refuge in a cold and competitive society. Before turning to the late nineteenth-century crisis of the family, we need to examine a little further the last of these social facts—the concept of the family as a haven in a heartless world. This ideal took for granted a radical separation between work and leisure and between public life and private life. The emergence of the nuclear family as the principal form of family life reflected the high value modern society attached to privacy, and the glorification of privacy in turn reflected the devaluation of work. As production become more complex and efficient, work became increasingly specialized, fragmented, and routine. Accordingly work came to be seen as merely a means to an end—for many, the end of sheer physical survival; for others, of a rich and satisfying personal life. No longer regarded as a satisfying occupation in its own right, work had to be redefined as a way of achieving satisfactions or consolations outside work. Production, in this view, is interesting and important only because it enable us to enjoy the delights of consumption. At a deeper level of mystification, social work—the collective self-realization of mankind through its transformation of nature—appears merely as the satisfaction of private wants.

There is an even deeper sense in which work was degraded when it was mechanized and reduced to a routine. The products of human activity, especially the higher products of that activity such as the social order itself, took on the appearance of something external and alien to mankind. No longer recognizably the product of human invention at all, the man-made world appeared as a collection of objects independent of human intervention and control. Having objectified himself in his work, man no longer recognized it as his own. One of the best examples of this externalization of human creativity is the capitalist economy, which was the collective creation of human ingenuity and toil but was described by the classical economists as a machine that ran according to immutable laws of its own, laws analogous to the laws of nature. These principles, even if they had existed in reality instead of merely in the minds of Adam Smith and Ricardo, were inaccessible to everyday observation, and in the lay mind, therefore, the market economy defied not merely human control but human understanding. It appeared as a complex network of abstractions utterly impenetrable and opaque. John Adams once demonstrated his grasp of modern banking and credit by complaining that "every dollar of a bank bill that is issued beyond the quantity of gold and silver in the vaults represents nothing and is therefore a cheat upon somebody." Jefferson and Jackson, as is well known, held the same opinion. If the governing classes labored under such confusion, we can easily imagine the confusion of the ordinary citizen. He lived in a world of abstractions, where the relations between men, as Marx observed, assumed the fantastic shape of relations between things. Thus labor-power became a commodity, measurable in abstract monetary terms, and was bought and sold on the market like any other commodity.

At bottom, the glorification of private life and the family represented the other side of the bourgeois perception of society as something alien, impersonal, remote, and abstract—a world from which pity and tenderness had been effectively banished. Deprivations experienced in the public world had to be compensated in the realm of privacy. Yet the very conditions that gave rise to the need to view privacy and the family as a refuge from the larger world made it more and more difficult for the family to serve in that capacity.

By the end of the nineteenth century American newspapers and magazines were full of speculation about the crisis of marriage and the family. From the 1890s down to the 1930s, discussion of the decline of the family became increasingly intense. Four developments gave rise to a steadily growing alarm: the rising divorce rate, the falling birth rate among "the better sort of people," the changing position of women, and the so-called revolution in morals.

Between 1870 and 1920 the number of divorces increased fifteen times. By 1923, one out of every seven marriages ended in divorce, and there was no reason to think that the trend toward more and more frequent divorce would reverse itself.

Meanwhile "the diminution of the birth rate among the highest races," as Theodore Roosevelt put it in 1897, gave rise to the fear that the highest races would soon be outnumbered by their inferiors, who reproduced, it was thought, with total disregard for their ability to provide for the rising generation. The middle classes, on the other hand, clearly paid too much attention not only to the future but to their own present comfort. In the opinion of conservatives they had grown soft and selfish, especially middle-class women, who preferred the social whirl to the more serious pleasures of motherhood. Brooks Adams, spokesman for crusty upper-class reaction, described the new woman as the "highest product of a civilization that has rotted before it could ripen." Progressives also worried about the declining birth rate, but they blamed it on the high cost of living and rising standards of comfort, which led young men either to avoid marriage or to postpone it as long as possible. Women were not to blame for "race suicide," according to a leading woman's magazine. The "actual cause" was the "cost of living impelling the masses to pauperdom." The American man, with reason, "is afraid of a large family."

The changing status of women was obvious to the most casual observer. More and more women were going to college, joining clubs and organizations of all kinds, and entering the labor force. What explained all this activity and what did it signify for the future of the family? The feminists had a simple answer, at least to the first of these questions: women were merely "following their work out of the home." Industry had "invaded" the family, stripped it of its productive functions. Work formerly carried on in the household could now be carried out more efficiently in the factory. Even recreation and childrearing were being taken over by outside agencies, the former by the dance-hall and the popular theater, the latter by the school. Women had no choice but to "follow their occupations or starve," emotionally if not literal fact. Confined to the family, women would become parasites, unproductive "consumers upon the state," as a feminist writer put it in 1910.

Faced with an agrument that condemned leisure as a form of parasitism, anti-feminists could have insisted on the positive value of leisure as the precondition of art, learning, and higher forms of thought, arguing that its benefits ought to be extended to the American businessman. But an attack on feminism launched from an essentially aristocratic point of view—an attack that condemned feminism as itself an expression of middle-class moralism and philistinism—hardly recommended itself to those who wished above everything else to preserve the sanctity of the home. American critics of feminism preferred to base their case on the contention that woman's usefulness to society and her own self-fulfilling work lay precisely in her sacred duties as wife and mother. The major premise of feminism—that women should be useful, not ornamental—had to be conceded; even while the conclusions feminists drew from this premise, the conclusions, they would have argued, that followed inevitably, were vigorously repudiated.

For the same reason a total condemnation of the feminist movement had to be avoided. Even the denunciation of "selfishness" was risky. In the mid-nineteenth century, defenders of the home had relied heavily on appeals to woman's duty to sacrifice herself for the good of others; but by 1900 this kind of rhetoric, even when translated into the progressive jargon of "service," had begun to seem decidedly out of date. The view that woman's destiny was to live for others gradually gave way to the view that woman too had a right to self-fulfillment—a right, however, that could best be realized in the home. In a word, the critics of feminism began to argue that motherhood and housewifery were themselves deeply satisfying "careers," which required special training in "homemaking," "domestic science," and "home economics." The invention of such terms expressed an attempt to dignify housework by raising it to the level of a profession. By rationalizing the household and child care, opponents of feminism hoped also to make the family a more effective competitor with the outside agencies that were taking over its functions.

If feminism disturbed the partisans of domesticity with its criticism of the home's inefficiency and its attempt to provide the "restlessness" of modern women with outlets beyond the family, the movement to liberate sexuality from conventional restraints troubled them much more deeply. Feminism at least allied itself with progressivism and with the vision of women's purifying influence over society; indeed the very success with which it identified itself with dominant themes in middle-class culture forced anti-feminists to refrain from attacking it frontally. The "new morality," on the other hand, directly challenged prevailing sexual ethics. It proclaimed the joys of the body, defended divorce and birth control, raised doubts about monogamy, and condemned interference with sexual life on the part of the state or community.

Yet even here the defenders of the family soon learned that unyielding condemnation was by no means the best strategy. In the long run it was no advantage to the family to associate itself with censorship, prudery, and political reaction. Instead of trying to annihilate the new morality, it made more sense to domesticate it—to strip away whatever in the ideology of sexual emancipation was critical of monogamy while celebrating a freer and more enlightened sexuality within marriage. Incidentally this operation provided the housewife with another role to complement her new role of consumer-in-chief—the multifaceted role of sexual partner, companion, playmate, and therapist.

Sex radicals not only called for a revolution in morals, they claimed that such a revolution was already under way. They cited statistical surveys that seemed to show a growing trend toward adultery and premarital sex. Faced with this evidence, the beleaguered champions of marriage executed another strategic retreat. The evidence showed, they argued, that the so-called revolt against marriage was not a revolt against marriage at all, merely an attack on the "sex-monopoly ideal" with which marriage had formerly been rather unnecessarily associated. Since "emphasis on exclusive sex possession" actually had a "destructive effect," it could safely be abandoned. Similarly the "virginity standard"—the requirement that the woman be a virgin at marriage—could be dispensed with. Exclusiveness in sex should be regarded as an ideal to be approximated, not as a standard to be imposed on everyone from without. Each couple should decide for themselves whether they would consider infidelity as evidence of disloyalty.

Another piece of ideological baggage that had to be thrown overboad, according to the emerging body of authoritative opinion on marriage and to spokesmen for arrangements that later came to be known as "open marriage," was the notion that marriage should be free of conflict and tension. Quarrels should be regarded as a normal part of marriage, events that should be taken in stride and even turned to productive purposes. Quarrels might even have a beneficial effect if they were properly "stage-managed" and rounded off with "an artistic consummation."

A fierce attack on romantic love played as important a part in the defense of marriage. Romantic love, it was thought, set impossibly high standards of devotion and loyalty—standards marriage could no longer meet. By undermining "sober-satisfying everyday life," romance wrought as much havoc as prudery, its twin. In the minds of radicals and conservatives alike, romantic love was associated with illusions, dangerous fantasies, and disease—with consumptive heroines, heroes wasting away with feverish desire, and deathbed farewells; with the overwrought, unhealthy music of Wagner, Strauss, and Puccini. Romantic love threatened both psychic and physical stability. The fashionable talk of marriage as an art conveyed a conception of marriage and the family that drew not so much from esthetics as from science and technology—ultimately from the science of healing. When marriage experts said that marriage was the art of personal "interaction," what they really meant was that marriage, like everything else, rested on proper technique—the technique of stage-managing quarrels, the technique of mutual agreement on how much adultery the marriage could tolerate, the technique of what to do in bed and how to do it. The new sex manuals, which began to proliferate in the twenties and thirties, were merely the most obvious examples of a general attempt to rationalize the life of the emotions in the interest of psychic health. That this attempt entailed a vigorous assault on "illusion" and fantasy is highly significant. It implies a concerted attack on the inner life, which was perceived as a threat to stability, equilibrium, and adjustment to reality. Marriage was to be saved at the expense of private life, which it was simultaneously expected to foster. The therapeutic program eroded the distinction between private life and the marketplace, turning all forms of play, even sex, into work. The experts made it clear that "achievement" of orgasm required not only proper technique but effort, determination, and emotional control.

So far I have spoken of the emergence of the nuclear family and its impact on popular thought, with particular attention to the ways in which the popular mind, led by the guardians of public health and morality, struggled with evidences of the family's growing instability. It remains to be seen how the same questions were dealt with at a more exalted level of thought—sociological theory. The social sciences devoted a great deal of attention to the crisis of marriage and the family. In particular the discipline of sociology, having divorced itself from the evolutionary and historical perspectives that had once dominated it, and having defined its field as the study of contemporary institutions and the social relations to which they gave rise, found it necessary to deal in detail with the contemporary family and what was happening to it. Much of what sociology had to say had already been anticipated in popular debate. Indeed it is clear that the sociology of the family in America arose in part as an answer to popular misgivings about the family. The role of sociology was to soothe those apprehensions with the voice of calm scientific detachment. Taking up certain lines of defense that had been suggested by doctors, social workers, psychotherapists, or scholars writing for a popular audience, sociology restated them in far more elaborate and extensive form, at the same time removing them from the polemical context in which they had originated. Claiming to have no stake in the outcome of investigations into the functions of the family, sociology provided the family with an elaborate ideological defense, which soon found its way back into popular thought and helped to bring about an important revival of domesticity and the domestic virtues in the thirties, forties, and fifties.

In effect, sociology revived the nineteenth-century myth of the family as an oasis and restated it in what looked like scientific form. First it dismissed the evidence of the family's decline by translating it into the language of functional analysis; then it showed that loss of certain functions (notably economic and educational functions) had been compensated by the addition of new ones. Ernest W. Burgess, founder of a flourishing school of urban sociology at the University of Chicago, was one of the first to propose, in the early twenties, that what the family had lost in economic, protective, educational, religious, and recreational functions, it had made up in "affectional and cultural" functions. Acording to

Burgess, the family had been "reduced" to an affectional group, "united by the interpersonal relations of its members," but the reduction in its size and scope had strengthened, not weakened, the family by enabling it to concentrate on the interplay of "interacting personalities." As the "institutional" functions of the family declined, the "personality" functions, in the words of W. F. Ogburn, took on greater and greater importance.

The rise of functionalism in social science coincided with, and was made possible by, the repudiation of historical approaches. At one time students of the family (and of other institutions as well) had attempted to arrange various institutional forms of the family in an evolutionary sequence or progression. Theoretical arguments about the family usually boiled down to arguments about historical priority. One group of theorists, following Bachofen, Morgan, and Engels, held that marriage had evolved from promiscuity to monogamy and the family from matriarchal to patriarchal forms. Others, like Westermarck, argued that patriarchal monogamy was the original form of the family. By the 1920s, these disputes had begun to seem inconclusive and heavily ideological, with the adherents of the matriarchal theory predicting the imminent demise of the monogamous family and their opponents seeking to demonstrate its permanence and stability. Sociology now rejected more modest historical theories as well—for example, theories that sought to link the decline of the patriarchal, extended family in Europe to changes in social and economic organization. Instead of attempting to explain the family's history, social science now contented itself with analyzing the way it functioned in various cultures. It was not altogether incidental that this functionalist analysis of the family, worked out first by anthropology in company with psychoanalysis and then applied by sociology to the contemporary family, had reassuring implications for the question of the family's future. The great variety of family forms suggested that while the family varied enormously from one culture to the next, in some form it was always found to be indispensable. The family did not evolve or decline, it merely adapted itself to changing conditions. As industry and the state took over the economic, educational, and protective work of the family, society at the same time became more impersonal and bureaucratic, thereby necessitating the creation of an intimate, protected space in which personal relations could continue to thrive. In the words of the urban sociologist Louis Wirth, "the pecuniary nexus which implies the purchasability of services and things has displaced personal relations as the basis of association"— everywhere, that is, except within the family. Joseph Folsom, a specialist in family sociology, noted in 1934 that modern society gave rise to a "generally increased need for intense affection and romance," while at the same time it "increased the difficulty of satisfying this need." As he put it somewhat quaintly, a "cultural lag" had arisien "between the increasing need for love and the practical arrangements to promote it." Ernest R. Mowrer, another family sociologist, argued along similar lines: "One of the most pronounced and striking phases of modern life is the repression of the emotions"—a tendency from which the family alone is exempt. Accordingly the family becomes "all the more important as the setting for emotional expression." In the rest of life, emotions have no place. "A business man is supposed to be cold, unfeeling, and 'hard-boiled.' Exchange . . . is unemotional and objective." The family, on the other hand, satisfies "the desire for response." Pent-up rage as well as pent-up love find expression in domestic life, and although this rage creates tensions in the family it is also a source of its continuing vitality. Familial tension, Mowrer argued, ought to become the primary concern of sociological study, through which it can be understood and therefore kept under control.

By reviving nineteenth-century conceptions of the family in allegedly scientific form, the sociology of the family accomplished something almost brilliant in its way: it stood the evidence of the family's decline on its head. Sociology invoked loss of functions, the drastic shrinkage of the family, and even the rising divorce rate to prove the stability, not the decline, of the family. Academic scholarship demonstrated that it was precisely the loss of its economic and educational importance that permitted the family to discharge its emotional functions more effectively than ever. The "loss of functions," instead of undermining the family, allowed it to come more fully into its own. There was only one trouble with this line of argument—a major one, however, with ramifying theoretical implications. Having abandoned historical analysis, sociology rested its claims to scientific status on a functional analysis of modern society—an analysis, that is, which purported to show how all the pieces fit together to make up a smoothly function- ing social order. Yet at the same time it saw the family as in conflict with society— a haven of love in a loveless world. Nor could it argue, except by drastically simplifying the problem, that this conflict was itself functional. The view that family life alone provided people with the emotional resources necessary to live and work in modern society remained convincing only so long as the socializing function of the family was ignored. The family might be a haven for adults, but what about the children whom it had to prepare to live in precisely the cold and ugly world from which the family provided a haven? How could children raised under the regime of love learn to "function" in the marketplace? Far from preparing the young for this ordeal, the family, if it operated as sociology insisted it did operate, could only be said to cripple the young, at the same time that it offered a psychological refuge for the cripples, now grown to maladjusted matu- rity, that it had itself produced.

For a time, sociology could deal with these problems by ignoring them—that is, by ignoring the family's role in socializing the child. Some writers went so far as to insist that child-rearing had become incidental to marriage. But the rise of the so-called culture-and-personality school in American anthropology soon made this view untenable. The work of Ruth Benedict, Margaret Mead, and others made it clear that in every culture socialization is the main function of the family. A sociology that confined itself to the analysis of marriage could not stand compari- son with the theoretical achievements of this new anthropology. The sociology of the family had to provide a theory of socialization or collapse into a rather pretentious form of marital counselling. Specifically it had to explain how an institution organized along very different principles from the rest of society could nevertheless train children to become effective members of society.

This was the problem, in effect, to which Talcott Parsons addressed himself in that part of his general theory which dealt with socialization—in Parsonian terminology, with tension-management and pattern-maintenance. Parsons begins by placing the study of the family in a broader social context—already a considerable advance over the work of his predecessors. According to Parsons, the family's famous loss of functions should be seen as part of the more general process of "structural differentiation"—the basic tendency of modern society. As the social division of labor becomes more and more complex, institutions become more specialized in their functions. To take an obvious example, manufacturing is split up into its various components, each of which is assigned to a special unit in the productive system. Specialization of functions increases efficiency, as is well known. Similarly the family performs its emotional services more efficiently once it is relieved of its other functions, which can be more efficiently carried on in institutions expressly designed for those purposes.

Having established a strong link between the development of the family and other social processes, Parsons now has to consider what other sociologists ignored, the family's role in socializing the child. How does the family, an institution in which social roles are assigned by ascription rather than achievement, train the child to enter a society in which roles are achieved rather than ascribed? The isolation of the family from the rest of the kinship system encourages a high degree of dependency between parents and children, yet at the same time the family has to equip the child to break these ties of dependency and to become an independent, self-reliant participant in the larger world. How does it manage to do both of these things at once, to tie children to their parents and yet to lay the ground work for the severance of those ties?

Briefly, Parsons proposed that the emotional security the family gives to the child in his early years is precisely the psychic foundation of the child's later independence. By providing the child with a great deal of closeness and warmth and then by giving him his head, the isolated nuclear family trains a type of personality ideally equipped to cope with the rigors of the modern world. Permissiveness, which many observers mistake for a collapse or abdication of parental responsibility, is actually a new way of training achievement, according to Parsons. It prepares the child to deal with an unpredictable world in which he will constantly face "unstructured situations." In the face of such contingencies he will have little use for hard-and-fast principles of duty and conduct learned from his parents. What he needs is the ability to take care of himself, to make quick decisions, and to adapt quickly to many types of emergencies. In a slower world, parents could indoctrinate their children with moral precepts adaptable to any foreseeable occasion, but modern parents, according to Parsons, can hope only to provide their young with the inner resources they need to survive on their own. This kind of training requires an intense dependency in early childhood followed by what strikes many foreigners as "incredible leeway" later on. But we should not be deceived by this "leeway." What looks like "abdication" is simply realism.

Youth culture, Parsons argues, is a differentiated part of the socialization system, the function of which is to ease the adolescent's transition from particularism to universality, ascription to achievement. Youth culture provides the adolescent with the emotional security of relationships that are "largely ascriptive" yet take him outside his own family. By providing this kind of "emotional support," the subculture of American adolescents fills an important set of needs, complementing the family on one side and the school on the other. Not only does it take young people out of the family but it helps to select and certify them for their adult roles—for example, by reinforcing appropriate ambitions while discouraging ambitions that are beyond the individual's abilities or his family's means to support.

This summary does not do justice to the elegance of the Parsonian theory of the family. We must press on to a further point: that for its elegance, the Parsonian theory has little capacity to explain empirical events, as any theory must. Far from explaining events, it has been overtaken by them. Writing in 1961, on the eve of an unprecedented upheaval of American youth, Parsons thought young people were becoming less hedonistic and more serious and "progressive," but his theory hardly anticipated the emergence of a youth culture that condemned American society in the most sweeping terms, repudiated the desirability of growing up in the usual way, and sometimes appeared to repudiate the desirability of growing up at all. It would be the height of perversity to interpret the youth culture of the sixties and seventies as a culture that sees the transition from childhood to maturity, when the attainment of adult status and responsibilities is seen by the culture as a betrayal of its ideals, by definition a "sell-out," and therefore becomes in the eyes of young people something to be accepted only with deep feelings of guilt. As for the argument that a heightened dependence in childhood is the basis of increased autonomy in adulthood, it does not explain why, in our society, personal autonomy seems more difficult than ever to achieve or sustain. Nor does it explain why so many signs of a massive cultural and psychological regression should appear just at this historical moment when, according to Parsons, the family has emerged from a period of crisis and has "now begun at least to be stabilized."

It is precisely the instability of the family that most emphatically repudiates the Parsonian theory of it. Youth culture itself has made the family a prime target—not just something to "rebel" against but a corrupt and decadent institution to be overthrown. That the new youth culture represents more than adolescent rebellion is suggested by the way its attack on the family reverberates, appealing to a great variety of other groups—feminists, advocates of the rights of homosexuals, cultural and political reformers of all kinds. Hostility to the family has survived the demise of the political radicalism of the sixties and flourished amid the conservatism of the seventies. Even the pillars of society show no great inclination to defend the family, historically regarded as the basis of their whole way of life.

Meanwhile the divorce rate continues to rise, young people avoid or at least postpone marriage, and social life organizes itself around "swinging singles." None of these developments bears out the thesis that "loss of functions" made the family stronger than ever by allowing it to specialize in the work it does best. On the contrary, no other institution seems to work so badly, to judge from the volume of abuse directed against it and the growing wish to experiment with other forms.

Here to Stay: Parents and Children

Mary Jo Bane

Worry about the family is mostly worry about the next generation. Falling birthrates, rising divorce rates, increasing numbers of working mothers, and other indicators of the alleged decline of the family would probably seem much less alarming if adults alone were affected by the making and dissolving of families. People are distressed by these trends not because they signal a decline in the quality and richness of adult lives but because they seem to threaten the next generation. If the trends continue, will there be a next generation? Will it turn out all right? Will it be able to maintain and perhaps even improve the world?

These feelings about the importance of generational continuity lie, I suspect, behind the implicit and explicit comparisons that one generation makes with the generations before it. Modern families and modern methods of child rearing are almost always measured against the families of earlier times. The comparison is usually unfavorable to modern families. In contrast, when modern technology and economic institutions are evaluated against earlier times the judgment is far more often made that things are better. In technology, progress is the standard. In social institutions, continuity is the standard, and when the change occurs, it is seen as decline rather than advance.

Decline and *advance* are not easily defined terms, of course. What some people see as good child rearing, others may see as stifling repression and yet others as rampant permissiveness. But some agreement probably exists on the basic principles of how a society ought to treat its children: Children should receive secure and continuous care; they should be neither abused nor abandoned. Children should be initiated into adult society with neither undue haste nor unduly long enforced dependency—in other words, allowed to be children and permitted to become adults. Probably most important, Americans believe that children should be wanted both by their parents and by society.

Arguments that modern families are failing their children usually cite rising divorce rates and the rising proportion of mothers working as evidence that children are less well cared for by their parents now than in the past, that their environments are less secure and less affectionate. In addition, statistics on falling birthrates are sometimes used as evidence that modern Americans want and value children less than earlier generations. But data on parental care, family size, and the ties between generations can be used to make a different argument: that discontinuities in parental care are no greater than they were in the past; and that changes in fertility rates may lead to an environment that, according to generally agreed on criteria, is more beneficial for children.

Demographic Facts and the Age Structure of Society

Intergenerational relationships are profoundly influenced by the age structure of society, since that structure determines how many generations are alive at any one time and what proportion of the population has living ancestors or decendants. The age structure can also influence whether a society "feels" mature and stable or young and vibrant. Certain activities or patterns may seem characteristic of a society because they are characteristic of the largest age group in the population.

A combination of birth and death rates creates the age structure of a society. These two rates also determine the rate of growth of the population, which can in turn affect the density and structure of living arrangements. Birth and death rates thus define the demographic context within which the relationships between generations must be worked out. As technology provides the basic facts of economic life, demography defines the basic facts of social life.

Today's great-grandparents were born during a period when the population of America was growing at a rapid rate. The European populations from which the American colonists had come had been relatively stable in size, with death rates balancing birthrates over long-term cycles of prosperity followed by epidemics and famines. In the seventeenth-century, death rates began to fall dramatically and steadily, probably because of general improvements in nutrition and the physical environment. Death rates fell at all ages; not only did mature people live longer, but more infants survived to childhood and more children to maturity. And more women lived to have more children. The result was a rapid population growth that has characterized the United States at least since the U.S. Census began in 1790, and probably much earlier.

Falling death rates, however, have been partially balanced by falling birthrates. In the United States, birthrates have been gradually falling for as long as data have been collected. They probably began to fall about 1800 or possibly earlier, and in the last few years they have fallen below replacement level. If they remain at replacement level, the United States will reach a stable population level about the year 2000. In the United States, therefore, the rate of natural population growth

Table 1.   Proportion of American Women Who Are Widows, by Age, 1976

Age group	% Widows
Under 35	1.0%
35–39	1.9
40–44	3.2
45–54	7.2
55–64	19.1
65–74	42.0
75 +	69.7

was probably highest in the early and mid-nineteenth century. Around 1800 the population grew at a rate of almost 3 percent per year. By 1880 it was growing at around 2 percent per year and by 1974, at six-tenths of one percent.

A rapidly growing population is different from a stable population in several ways. One is age structure. Demographers find that the average age of populations that are not growing can range from about twenty-seven years when mortality rates are very high (probably characteristic of pre-industrial Europe) to about thirty-eight years when mortality rates are very low (the United States of the future). In contrast, a rapidly growing population is young. The median age of the population of the United States shown in Table 1 illustrates the point.

As population growth has slowed down, the American population has become gradually older. This aging is perhaps the most important difference between the world of our great-grandparents and our own world, and contributes to many of the changes that have taken place in family and intergenerational relationships.

It may seem strange that a population becomes younger as death rates fall. As people live longer should the population not become older? The reason it does not is that in all the societies that demographers have studied, death rates are highest both late in life and early in life. Declines in death rates are usually most dramatic among infants. More infants survive, contributing more children to the population. More women survive to reproductive age and contribute even more children to the population. Thus lower mortality rates result in a younger average age of the population even though average life expectancy at birth rises.

Imagine, for example, a population in which half the babies died at birth and half lived to be 50. The average life expectancy would be 25 years, and the average age of the population would also be 25 years. Now imagine that infant mortality rates fell, so that everyone lived to be 50. The average life expectancy would then be 50. The average age of the population would still be 25, if the population remained stable in size. But if birthrates remained the same as they were when death rates were high, the population would be bound to grow, since more women would live to reproductive age and there would be more babies and children than older people. Thus mortality rates would have produced a younger rather than an older population.

Another interesting characteristic of a rapidly growing population, related to its age structure, is that working-age adults comprise a relatively small proportion of the population. Working-age adults (age 15–64) made up 58 percent of the rapidly growing population in the United States in 1880. In contrast, 68 percent of the population of the United States in 1940 was made up of working-age adults. The nonworkers in a rapidly growing population are almost all children, since the proportion of old people is extremely low. On the other hand, when death rates are low and the population is stable in size, almost half of the nonworkers are over 65.

A third feature of a rapidly growing population is that it must every year induct a relatively large number of young people into adulthood and into the work force. More must start work than retire. This can put a strain on adult society in general and on the economy in particular. If the economy is not growing as rapidly as the population, the problem of what to do with young people can become acute.

Changes in the rate of population growth produce changes in the age structure of a society that are in turn reflected in the problems the society must cope with, the mechanisms it uses to do so, and the general feel of the society. In a rapidly growing population, children and adolescents must be more visible. A young, childlike society may be a more congenial place for children to live. But it may not. Children may be more precious when they are relatively rare. A more mature society may have more physical and emotional resources to give to the care of children. It may display a greater ease in inducting children—since there are fewer of them—into the adult society.

Teenagers may cause major social problems when they make up a dispropor-tionately large segment of the population. When they are fewer, especially when the number entering the labor force equals the number retiring, they can be integrated much more easily. This interpretation might partially explain cycles of concern over youth. It might also partially explain societal attitudes toward children. Dr. Spock, after all, advocated permissive child-rearing in the first edition of his book in 1947, when children were relatively rare. He changed his mind in 1968, for a variety of reasons no doubt. But whether Spock realized it or not, he may simply have been reacting to what must have seemed a veritable surfeit of children. In the coming decades, children and adolescents will make up a small proportion of the population. Through this simple demographic change, they may become less of a problem and more of a precious resource.

Childlessness and Family Size

Declining birthrates not only change the position of children in society as a whole, but they can also affect the status of children in individual families. Low birthrates that occur because fewer women are having children should probably be interpreted differently from rates that are low because many women are having a smaller number of children. High rates of voluntary childlessness in the society might reflect a cleavage in the society. If people who did not have children were different from those who did—if, for example, they were better educated or concentrated in the professional occupations—the potential for social conflict would be great. Public support for children would certainly be hard to master if only low-status (or only high-status) parents had children. At the same time, the family environments of children would not necessarily change much. If fewer women had children but still had large numbers, most children would continue to be brought up in large families.

If, on the other hand, low birthrates occurred because most people continued to have children but had fewer of them, political divisions between the childless and others would be less likely. But an important change would take place in the family environments of children. More children would be brought up in small families. The consequences would more likely be beneficial to both the children and the society.

Decreasing family size rather than increasing childlessness accounts for most of the declining fertility in the United States. The U.S. Census first gathered data on the total number of children women had had over their reproductive years in 1910. The census data is probably accurate for women born as early as 1846 and as late as 1935, since most women now complete their childbearing before age 35. The fertility of women born after 1935 can be predicted from two sources: from Census Bureau questions that ask women how many children they expect to have, and from projections of fertility rates based on the number of children they have had so far. These combined sources provide fairly accurate descriptions of the fertility history of women born since the middle of the nineteenth century.

Between 90 and 95 percent of women marry at one time or another. The proportion has fluctuated over the years, with a slight increase in recent decades in the proportion of women marrying. The proportion of married women who have no children has also fluctuated over the years—first up, then down. The childless proportion rose from about 8.2 percent of married women born 1846–55 to a high of over 20 percent of the married women born between 1901 and 1910. Childlessness then fell to 7.3 percent among married women born 1931–35.

It is hard to say why childlessness rose during the nineteenth century, but it may have to do with the unhealthful conditions facing women in the factories or the economic difficulties experienced especially by the immigrants. One explanation for the high rates of childlessness among married women born around the turn of the century is the economic depression of the 1930s. When unemployment rates are high, birthrates almost always fall. In the 1930s unemployment reached a new high and birthrates a new low.

The decline in childlessness since the 1930s is equally hard to explain. It may have to do with improvements in general health and with new medical treatments for sterility and infertility. Involuntary childlessness may have virtually disappeared. Predictions about the future are thus predictions about voluntary childlessness, which is now possible through the relative ease of birth control and abortion.

Predictions might be based on the characteristics of women who remained childless in the past. Among women born before 1920 who were surveyed by the

1970 census, those who were childless were more likely to be black, to have been born in the Northeast, to have married at older ages, to have gone to college, to have lived in urban areas, and to have been married to professional or white-collar workers rather than farmers or laborers. In general, the childless were better educated and better off. High rates of childlessness among blacks are the exception and may be explained by health conditions.

These correlates suggest that childlessness should have increased over time as more women became better educated and better off. But that is the opposite of what actually happened. The cross-sectional data also suggest that childlessness should decrease during hard times since fewer people are well-off. But this too is precisely the opposite of the historical fact. The economic and demographic correlates of childlessness are, therefore, not very useful bases for making predictions about what will happen.

Some predictions can be made, however, on the basis of what women say about the number of children they expect to have. In 1975 less than 5 percent of wives who were interviewed about family plans expected to remain childless. This proportion was relatively constant throughout the age groups. The proportion of women who expect to remain childless went up slightly from 1967–1974, but then went down again in 1975. Better-educated women and white women are more likely to expect to remain childless, but the difference is not great.

The most interesting thing about these figures on expected childlessness is that they are so low. If as few women remain childless as say they expect to, the childless proportion among women born between 1940 and 1955 will be the lowest ever recorded. Even if the rate of childlessness for all women were equal to the expected rate for college women, childlessness would still be at its lowest recorded level. Under either condition, however, the country is due for some upswing in births, as those who put off having children begin to have them. One problem with the data is that the Census Bureau interviews only married women about their family plans, not unmarried women who may or may not marry and may or may not expect children in the future. Another is that women who now see themselves as putting off children may later be unable to have them, or decide not to. This problem can be partially corrected by making projections from birthrates by age. One demographic study uses these rates to estimate that 10 percent of women born around 1945 will actually remain childless, rather than the 5 percent who expect to. The Census Bureau made a series of projections from similar data, with similar results. These studies project a slightly higher rate of childlessness than that found among women born during the 1930s, but still lower than that among women born 1901–10. It seems safe to say that the vast majority of American women will continue to have at least one child.

Although there has been no systematic increase over the century in the proportion of women who have no children, there has been a systematic and dramatic decrease in the number of children each mother has. The average married woman in colonial Massachusetts may have had as many as eight children. The average mother born 1846–55 had 5.7 children. The average number of children decreased steadily for sixty years, reaching 2.9 children among women born 1911–15. It then rose for a short period during the postwar baby boom; women born 1931–35 have had an average of 3.4 children per woman with children. It is now once again falling. Yet the proportion of women having no children or having only one child has not increased over the century. The big change has thus been in the proportion of women having very large families, a change which has occurred for all races and education levels. Many fewer women have five or more children; many more women have two or three.

Looking at these numbers from the viewpoint of the children illustrates the change that has taken place over four generations. Statistics about average family size do not accurately reflect the size of the family into which the average child is born. The family of the average child is larger than the average family because more children are born into larger families.

If this sounds like a riddle, imagine ten families distributed as follows:

1-child	4 families
2-child	3 families
3-child	2 families
4-child	1 family

The average family size is $4(1) + 3(2) + 2(3) + 1(4) \div 10 = 2$. But the twenty children are distributed as follows:

1-child families	4 children
2-child families	6 children
3-child families	6 children
4-child families	4 children

The average child is born into a family of $4(1) + 6(2) + 6(3) + 4(4) = 50 \div 20 = 2.5$ children, and has an average of 1.5 brothers and sisters. When large families are included in the calculations the differences between average family size and the average number of brothers and sisters can be very dramatic.

From the point of view of the child, a better indication of family size than average family size is the average number of brothers and sisters that children of different generations have. The great-grandparents of today's children had on the average six brothers and sisters. Their grandparents had five brothers and sisters. Their parents—depression babies—had on the average three brothers and sisters. Today's children may have as few as two. The low birthrates of the depression occurred partly because of high rates of childlessness and only children. There were, however, many large families. In contrast, the low fertility rates of the early 1970s are the product of low rates of childlessness and only children, accompanied by extremely small numbers of large families. Most children in the 1970s are born into two- or three-child families. If these patterns continue, the average child born in the next decade will have only two brothers and sisters.

Small families mean a quite different life for children. Some of the differences are probably detrimental to children, but, on the whole, small families seem to be beneficial. A number of studies suggest that children from small families do better in school and score better on standardized tests than children from large families. Part of the explanation is that small families are usually better off financially. But even when these families are equally well-off, children from large families do not get as much education, as good jobs, or as high earnings as children from small families.

One of the most interesting studies on family size and achievement investigated the reasons for the superior performance of children from small families. The study first looked at the amount of time that parents and other adults spent with children. Middle children in large families received considerably less adult care and attention than children in smaller families or than first and last children in larger families. Parental attention must be shared by more people when the family has more children living at home, a condition that affects middle children in large families more than others.

The study then looked at the effect of family size on achievement. It found that a variable representing the child's share of family time and financial resources had a more important effect on achievement, both educational and occupational, than most other background characteristics.

Children from large families seem to be somewhat slower in physical development than children from small families. Emotional and social differences have not been so clearly documented, although there is some evidence that children from small families are more likely to think well of themselves. On the other hand, cross-cultural studies have shown that children who care for younger children are more nurturing and responsible and less dependent and dominant than others. Because children are more likely to have taken care of younger siblings when they come from larger families, smaller families may produce fewer independent and helpful children. In general, though, the trend toward smaller families among all segments of the population has probably done more to increase and equalize cognitive development and schooling than any other demographic trend.

The data on childlessness and family size, in short, do not suggest a societal abandonment of children. A large increase in childlessness now that involuntary childlessness is almost nonexistent would indicate that a substantial portion of the population wanted no children, but this has not occurred. The vast majority of adults have at least one child. Average family size has decreased, but the decline has taken place mostly in larger families. Family size is converging for the entire population on the two- or three-child ideal. These smaller families seem to be advantageous for children rather than a sign of societal indifference.

Living Arrangements of Children

Another indicator of the place of children in the society is whether parents and children live together. Children who live with their parents are certainly better off than children raised in orphanages. They may or may not be better off than children raised by relatives or foster parents. At any rate, whether or not children live with their parents provides some indication of the strength of ties between parents and children.

Many people assume that the rising divorce rates of the last few decades mean that fewer children now live with their parents. This assumption is not completely accurate. The data suggest that the proportion of children who live with at least one of their parents rather than with relatives, with foster parents, or in institutions has been steadily rising.

The U.S. Census has published information about the living arrangements of people only since 1940. Since then the proportion of children living with at least one of their parents in a separate household has gone steadily up, from about 90 percent in 1940 to almost 95 percent in 1970. The increase seems to have occurred for two reasons. The first reason is that the proportion of children who lost a parent through death and divorce combined fell gradually during the first half of the century and probably fell before that as well. Among children born between 1911 and 1920, about 22 percent lost a parent through death and 5 percent had parents divorce sometime before their eighteenth birthday. Gradually declining death rates meant that fewer children lost parents as the century went on. Smaller families had the same effect, since more children were born to younger parents. The result was that about 20 percent of the children born during the 1940s lost parents through death or divorce. Only for children born around 1960 did rising divorce rates begin to counteract the effects of falling death rates. The proportion of children who experienced a parental disruption fell until then; only recently has disruption increased.

The second reason for the rise in the proportion of children living with at least one parent between 1940 and 1970 is a dramatic increase in the proportion of widowed and divorced women who continued living with their children after their marriage ended. In 1940 only about 44 percent of women with children but without husbands headed their own families. The rest must have sent their children to live with their grandparents or other relatives or to orphanages. By 1970 almost 80 percent of divorced, separated, and widowed women with children headed their own families. Some women, especially the young and unmarried, continue to leave their children with their grandparents. Most, however, now keep the family together. The children may not live with both their parents, but they do live with at least one. In 1975, despite rising divorce rates, only 2.7 percent of children under 14 lived with neither of their parents. The aggregate figures do conceal a racial difference: In the same year, 1975, 7.5 percent of non-white children were living with neither parent, compared with 1.7 percent of white children. But for non-whites as well as whites, the percent living with neither parent has been going down, from 9.8 percent for non-whites in 1968 to the present figure.

Although the proportion of children living with at least one parent has risen, rising divorce rates since 1960 have caused a decrease in the proportion of children under 14 living with both parents. In1960, 88.5 percent of all children under 14 lived with two natural or adoptive parents; by 1974 the number had fallen to 82.1 percent. This trend is likely to continue. Estimates from death and divorce rates indicate that nearly 40 percent of the children born around 1970 will experience a parental death, divorce, or separation and consequently live in a one-parent family at some point during their first eighteen years. The proportion living with neither parent, however, is likely to remain small.

The effects on children of these changes in living arrangements are not well understood. Hardly anyone argues that the divorce or death of parents is good for children, but the extent of the harm done has not been documented. There is some evidence that children from broken homes do not do as well in school as children from unbroken homes. Much of the disadvantage seems to come, however, from the fact that many one-parent homes are also poor. Moreover, children whose parents divorce are no worse off than children whose homes are unbroken but also unhappy. Although the evidence is scanty, it suggests that most children adjust relatively quickly and well to the disruption and that in the case of divorce the disruption may be better than the alternative of living in a tension-filled home.

No studies have looked at the effects on children of various living arrangements after divorce. This is surprising, given the significant change that has taken place over the last thirty years in what normally happens to children. Probably children who stay with their mothers are better off than children with foster parents or relatives, although individual circumstances can vary widely. Staying with the mother may make the event less disruptive and less distressing; only one parent is lost rather than both. The increased tendency of widowed and divorced mothers to keep their children may, therefore, be good for the children.

The effect of the growing tendency of women with children but without husbands to set up separate households rather than live with relatives or friends is less clear. Since single-parent families seem to live on their own whenever they can afford to, they must see advantages to the arrangement. On the other hand, single parents have the almost impossible responsibility of supporting and caring for a family alone. The absence of other adults to relieve the pressure must increase the tension and irritability of single parents (unless, of course, the presence of other adults would increase tension and irritability even more). Children in separate households gain the undivided attention of their mothers and often establish extremely close supportive relationships. But they lose the company of other adults and the exposure to a variety of adult personalities and role models that larger households might provide. Separate households are clearly what most single parents want, but it would be interesting to know exactly what they give up in having them.

Child Care Arrangements

Like data on living arrangements, data on child care arrangements are often cited as evidence of the state of parent-child relationships. People often talk as if children are best off when they are taken care of exclusively by their mothers. The rise in the proportion of mothers who hold paid jobs is, therefore, cited periodically as an indicator of the decline of the family. Most concern, of course, is focused on young children; Americans have long believed that older children should go to school and play on their own, not be continually supervised by mother. But even care arrangements for young children involve more than simply care by the mother. Care arrangements have changed over the century, but it is not clear that families and mothers have become less important. Nor is it clear whether the changes are good or bad.

The most important activity of contemporary children up to the age of 14 is watching television. The average preschooler seems to watch television about thirty-three hours per week, one-third of his waking hours. The average sixth-grade child watches about thirty-one hours. Since television sets only became common during the 1950s, the importance of television has clearly been a development of the last quarter century. It represents a tremendous change in how children of all ages are cared for. Television is by far the most important new child care arrangement in this century.

The next most important activity of children's waking hours is going to school. Children now spend an average of about nineteen hours a week in school. A larger proportion of children of all ages go to school now than ever before. They start school earlier and stay in school longer. The most dramatic change of the last ten years has been in the proportion of very young children enrolled in nursery school and kindergarten. In 1965 about 27 percent of all 3- to 5-year-olds were enrolled in school; by 1973, 41 percent of this age group were in school.

Other important changes have occurred in the length of the school year and in average daily attendance. In 1880 the average pupil attended school about eighty days per year. By the 1960s the typical school year was 180 days and the average pupil attended about 164 days. Both these changes mean that children enrolled in school spend more time there. School, therefore, has steadily gained in importance as a child care arrangement.

Compared with these two dramatic changes in child care arrangements—the growth of television and school—changes caused by mothers working outside the home appear almost trivial. It is true that the proportion of mothers with paid jobs has risen sharply over the last twenty-five years, particularly among mothers of preschool children. In 1950, 12 percent of married women with children under six were in the labor force; by 1974 the proportion had grown to nearly 40 percent. Many of these working mothers arranged their schedules so that they worked only when their children were in school or when fathers were at home to take care of the children. About 70 percent, however, made other child care arrangements. The most common was to have a relative or sitter come to the home and care for the children. Only about 10 percent of the preschool children of working mothers went to day care centers.

How much of a difference these arrangements make in the lives of children depends on what actually happens to them and who actually spends time with them. There is no evidence as to how much time mothers a century ago spent with their children. Undoubtedly, it was less than contemporary nonworking mothers, since mothers of a century ago had more children and probably also had more time-consuming household tasks.

Contemporary nonworking mothers do not spend a great deal of time exclusively with their children. A national study done in 1965 found that the average nonworking mother spent 1.4 hours per day on child care. A study of 1,300 Syracuse families in 1967–68 showed that the average nonworking mother spent sixty-six minutes a day in physical care of *all* family members and forty-eight minutes in other sorts of care on a typical weekday during the school year. The amount of time varied with the age and number of children.

A small 1973 Boston study, by White and Watts, found that of the time they were observed mothers spent about a third interacting with their children (but one expects that mothers being observed by Harvard psychologists might depart somewhat from their normal routines). The children in the study, age 1 to 3, spent most of their time in solitary playing or simply watching what went on around them.

Working mothers spend less time on child care than nonworking mothers, but the differences in the amount of time mothers spend exclusively with their children are surprisingly small. In the Syracuse study, the correlations between the amount of time women spent on physical care of family members and whether or not they are employed were very small, once family size and children's ages were taken into account. When all family members, not just wives, were looked at, the correlations were even smaller. There is some evidence that working mothers especially in the middle class try to make up for their working by setting aside time for exclusive attention to their children. They probably read more to their children and spend more time in planned activities with them than do nonworking mothers.

There is no evidence that having a working mother per se has harmful effects on children. When a mother works because the father is incapacitated, unemployed, or paid poorly, the family may be poor and disorganized and the children may suffer. In these cases, however, the mother's working is a symptom and not a cause of more general family difficulties. In other cases where mothers work, children are inadequately supervised and may get into trouble. Again, though, the problem is general family difficulty. The Gluecks' study of lower-class boys, often cited as evidence that working mothers raise delinquent children, shows no direct link between the mothers' employment and delinquency. It did find that in lower-class homes children of working mothers were less likely to be adequately supervised, and that there was a tie between lack of supervision and delinquency whether the mothers worked or not. In families where the mother's employment is not a symptom of deeper family trouble, children seem not to turn out any differently from other children.

Parents and Teenagers

For the last century or so, Americans have become attuned to the existence and peculiarities of that stage in life between childhood and adulthood that we call adolescence. Adolescence is apparently a creation of relatively recent times; at least its problems have only recently attracted widespread attention. Certainly, as Margaret Mead showed so well, adolescent difficulties do not occur universally. Whatever the distinctive characteristics of the adolescent personality, however, there have been some noticeable changes over the last century in the living and working arrangements of adolescents. The general trend is to tie adolescent boys to parents for an increasing length of time and to begin to liberate adolescent girls.

In mid-nineteenth-century America, it was common practice for young men, and to a lesser extent young women, to leave their parents' house and live for a few years as a lodger or servant in some other older person's house before marrying and setting up independent households. The best information on family structure in the mid-nineteenth century comes from Michael Katz's study of Hamilton, Ontario. Boarders and lodgers were then an important feature of life. In 1851 more than half of the young men aged around 20 were living as boarders in the household of a family other than their own. But industrialization was accompanied by business cycles and increased schooling, which in turn brought striking changes in the lives of young people. By 1861 only a third of Hamilton's young men were living as boarders. More lived at home and went to school. Nearly a third were neither employed nor in school. The nineteenth-century specter of gangs of young men roaming the city streets must have arisen because gangs of young men were indeed roaming the streets.

In the United States also, many young men of the middle and late nineteenth century lived for a time as boarders. Boarding was a different phenomenon, however, in rural and urban areas. In cities young men typically lived with families but worked elsewhere. Rural youth were more often live-in farm help. By 1970, boarding out had virtually disappeared; less than 2 percent of 15- to 19-year-olds were living as boarders or servants. Instead they were living at home and going to school. The rise in school attendance was dramatic. In 1910, about 30 percent of 16- to 19-year-old boys were in school compared to about 73 percent in 1970. The employment situation for teenagers is still, as it was in mid-nineteenth century Hamilton, dreadful. The young men have not been put to work, but they have been induced to stay in school.

Young women, so often forgotten in historical discussions, are working more and going to school more. Typically, young women lived at home performing domestic tasks until they married. In mid-nineteenth-century Hamilton, for example, about 36 percent of the 18- and 19-year-old women were employed and about 5 percent went to school. Another 5 percent were married. The rest must have been living at home, doing domestic chores or doing nothing. During the growth of schooling in the nineteenth century, girls' attendance rates rose even faster than boys'. In 1970 in the United States, young women were still living at home, but they were going to school rather than helping mother. The vast majority (88.6 percent) of the 16- and 17-year-olds and 41.6 percent of the 18- and 19-year-olds were enrolled in school. Most of the rest were working at paid jobs, and some were raising children.

Among both men and women, there seems to have been a slight increase in the last decade in the proportion who live away from their parents during their late teenage years. Even in 1974, however, this group was a minority. Among 18- and 19-year-old men, about 7 percent were married and living with a wife and only about 6 percent were living on their own. Among 18- and 19-year-old women, 21 percent were married and 9 percent were living on their own. Virtually all 14- to 17-year-olds lived with their parents.

In short, there has been no significant emancipation of teenagers from their families. In comparison with nineteenth-century teenagers in urban areas, in fact, contemporary teenage boys are much more dependent on their parents for shelter and support. What they do at home is another matter, but they do live there.

Children in the Family and Society

In summary, demographic materials suggest that the decline of the family's role in caring for children is more myth than fact. None of the statistical data suggests that parental watchfulness over children has decreased over the span of three generations; much suggests that it has increased. The most important difference between today's children and children of their great-grandparents' and grandparents' time is that there are proportionately fewer of them. They make up a smaller proportion of society, and there are fewer of them per family. Like children born during the 1930s, but unlike children born during the 1950s, children of the 1970s face a predominantly adult world. If the rate of population growth continues to stabilize, the society of the next decades will be older and the families smaller than any previously found in America.

Parent-child bonds also persist despite changes in patterns of disruption and living arrangements after disruption. The proportion of children who lose a parent by death has gone steadily down over the generations. The proportion who live with a parent after a death or divorce has gone steadily up. Even in recent years when family disruptions have begun to rise again to high levels, almost no children have gone to relatives, foster homes or institutions.

The trend toward more mothers in the paid labor force has probably not materially affected parent-child bonds. Even though more mothers work outside the home and more children go to school earlier and longer, the quantity and quality of actual mother-child interaction has probably not changed much. In short, the major demographic changes affecting parents and children in the course of the century have not much altered the basic picture of children living with and being cared for by their parents. The patterns of structural change so often cited as evidence of family decline do not seem to be weakening the bonds between parents and children.

Habits of the Heart:
Love and Marriage

Robert N. Bellah, Richard Madsen, William M. Sullivan, Ann Swidler, and Steven M. Tipton

"Finding oneself" is not something one does alone. The quest for personal growth and self-fulfillment is supposed to lead one into relationships with others, and most important among them are love and marriage. But the more love and marriage are seen as sources of rich psychic satisfactions, it would seem, the less firmly they are anchored in an objective pattern of roles and social institutions. Where spontaneous interpersonal intimacy is the ideal, as is increasingly the case, formal role expectations and obligations may be viewed negatively, as likely to inhibit such intimacy. If love and marriage are seen primarily in terms of psychological gratification, they may fail to fulfill their older social function of providing people with stable, committed relationships that tie them into the larger society. . . .

Woman's Sphere

Tocqueville strongly argued the positive social functions of love and marriage. He saw the family, along with religion and democratic political participation, as one of the three spheres that would help to moderate our individualism. The family was central to his concern with "habits of the heart," for it is there that mores are first inculcated. At times he waxes extravagant on the importance of this sphere to the success of American democracy:

> For my part, I have no hesitation in saying that although the American woman never leaves her domestic sphere and is in some respects very dependent within it, nowhere does she enjoy a higher station. . . . if anyone asks me what I think the chief cause of the extraordinary prosperity and growing power of this nation, I should answer that it is due to the superiority of their women.

Tocqueville sees the role of religion in America as in part dependent on its influence on women. Religion, he says, "does direct mores, and by regulating domestic life it helps to regulate the state." The rigor of American mores derives from religion, but not directly through its influence on men. In America,

> religion is often powerless to restrain men in the midst of innumerable temptations which fortune offers. It cannot moderate their eagerness to enrich themselves, which everything contributes to arouse, but it reigns supreme in the souls

of the women, and it is women who shape mores. Certainly of all countries in the world America is the one in which the marriage tie is most respected and where the highest and truest conception of conjugal happiness has been conceived.

Much has changed since Tocqueville's day, and we will be concerning ourselves with the changes in this [article]. Yet the conception of marriage and the family that was being worked out in the late eighteenth and early nineteenth centuries and reached a clear formulation by the 1830s, one that Tocqueville accurately grasped, is in many ways still the dominant American ideal, however subject to criticism and alternative experimentation. This modern American family pattern has been called "patriarchal," but the term is inaccurate and unhelpful here. It is better applied to an earlier phase of family life, one that lasted in America from the settlement to the late eighteenth century (and in rural contexts until much later), in which the family was an economically cooperative whole, where husband, wife, and children worked side by side on the farm or in the shop for the common good of the family. The husband-father in this earlier pattern was indeed a patriarch, responsible for the peace and order of his "family government," deciding on his children's occupations and marriage choices, and controlling the property of his wife, even her wages, if she had any. The new family that was coming into being in the early nineteenth century was not egalitarian to be sure, but it was much more voluntaristic. The power of the father over the children was greatly curtailed, and children by and large made their own choices of occupation and marriage partner. Women were no longer simply subordinate. To a certain degree, they were "separate but equal" in their own sphere—"woman's sphere." This new form of family was closely related to the new commercial and incipiently industrial economy, in which men's occupations took them outside the family into the world of business, the sphere of men. The shift involved a loss of economic functions for affluent women in that they were now confined to the home economy rather than contributing directly to the family business, but it involved a rise in status. With increasing affluence, women were now literate, educated (though mainly in "female academies"), and able to participate in the voluntary associational life of society (though largely within church-affiliated associations). Much of the literature directed to women in the 1830s, frequently written by clergymen, reflected the same attitudes expressed by Tocqueville in exalting "woman's sphere" as one of peace and concord, love and devotion, in contrast to the selfishness and immorality characteristic of "the world." This was the period in which the ideology of the family as a "haven in a heartless world" first came into prominence. It is still a common idea among those to whom we recently talked.

The two "spheres" that were clearly separating in the early nineteenth century are still very much in the minds of contemporary Americans, and the contrast between them is one of the most important ways in which we organize our world. The family, according to David Schneider and Raymond Smith, is a realm of "diffuse, enduring solidarity," as opposed to the anxiety, competitiveness, and achievement-orientation of the occupational realm. The family is a place where one is unconditionally accepted, something almost unknown in the worlds of business and politics. Americans, aware that the family these days is often not as reliable as they might hope, nonetheless define it in terms of this contrast. The family is a place of love and happiness where you can count on the other family members. The family and all familylike relationships receive a strong positive valence relative to the public world.

Given the enormous American emphasis on independence and self-reliance that we described in the previous chapter, the survival of the family, with its strong emphasis on interdependence and acceptance, is striking. In many ways, the family represents a historically older form of life. As opposed to the new time-discipline of the world of business and industry, work in the family has continued to be task-oriented, changing in character in terms of time of day and season, responsive to individual needs and their variations, and intermixing labor and social intercourse. As Nancy Cott puts it, speaking of the early nineteenth century, but in terms that still to some degree apply:

> Despite the changes in its social context adult women's work, for the most part, kept the traditional mode and location which both sexes had earlier shared. Men who had to accept time-discipline and specialized occupations may have begun to observe differences between their own work and that of their wives. Perhaps they focused on the remaining "premodern" aspects of women's household work: it was reassuringly comprehensible, because it responded to immediate needs; it represented not strictly "work" but "life," a way of being.

Morally, too, Cott points out, the family represented an older pattern: "Women's household service alone remained from the tradition of reciprocal service by family members." Thus, while men's work was turning into a career or a job, women's work had the old meaning of a calling, an occupation defined essentially in terms of its contribution to the common good. It was this aspect of unselfishness and concern for others that American clergymen and our French philosopher picked up about the role of women. Contrasting it to the self-aggrandizing individualism of the men, they linked this female familial morality to Christianity and republican virtue. They saw the future of a free society dependent on the nurturing of family mores, passed on to children by mothers and exerted by wives to restrain husbands. That the cost of the moral superiority of women in modern commercial society was their own freedom and participation in the public sphere was already evident in the early nineteenth century. Tocqueville marveled that the independent, self-reliant American girl, so much more able to hold her own in public than her European counterpart, should choose to enter the lifetime commitment of marriage, which would confine her to a limited, if noble, sphere. Probably women did not make the choice as easily as Tocqueville thought—"marriage trauma" was not infrequent and, if severe enough, could lead to women remaining unmarried for life. Yet women did accept much of the ideology of family life and "woman's sphere." Early feminists insisted that public life take on more familial qualities at the same time that they demanded greater public participation and equal rights for women.

At the crux of family life is the relationship between a man and a woman who become husband and wife, father and mother. The love that unites the marriage partners grows into the love between parents and children. It is the characteristic virtue of love that made the family appear as the locus of a morality higher than that of the world. Indeed, the "unselfish love" of a wife and mother for her husband and children was seen as the most visible example of morality itself.

The love between a man and a woman is capable of another set of extended meanings, which has given the family an additional significance in our developing culture. Love implies not only the morality of the family as against the immorality of the business world; love implies feeling as against calculation. As the primary inhabitants of the familial sphere, women were invested with all those characteristics we noted as part of the expressive, rather than the utilitarian, orientation. The nineteenth-century way of characterizing the difference was to identify women with the heart, men with the head. Women acted out of feeling, men out of reason. Nor was the contrast wholly disparaging of women, since the romantic movement exalted feeling above reason as the wellspring of genuine humanity. Women were said to have sensibility, imagination, and gaiety, whereas men were characterized by solidity, judgment, and perseverance.

However strong the contrast between these stereotypes of the sex roles, and the contrast seems to have been greater in the mid-nineteenth century than before or after, men, in one crucial respect, had to participate in what was otherwise "woman's sphere." Love was clearly a matter of the heart, not the head, and love was the essential basis of marriage for both men and women. Even in the seventeenth century, when marriages were largely arranged by parents, the couple was supposed to grow to love one another during the period of espousal and love between husband and wife was, according to Puritan theology, "a duty imposed by God on all married couples." By the nineteenth century, romantic love was the culturally recognized basis for the choice of a marriage partner and in the ideal marriage was to continue for a lifetime. Perhaps it would be too much to speak of expressive *individualism* in connection with nineteenth-century marriage, even though the full set of contrast terms by which we recognize the expressive alternative of utilitarianism was used. But in the twentieth century, marriage has to some extent become separated from the encompassing context of family in that it does not necessarily imply having children in significant sectors of the middle class. Thus marriage becomes a context for expressive individualism, or a "life-style enclave." . . .

To summarize the changes in the American family since the early nineteenth century, the network of kinship has narrowed and the sphere of individual decision has grown. This is truer, even today, among the middle class than among the upper and lower reaches of our population. The nuclear family is not "isolated," as some over-zealous interpreters of that metaphor have implied, but contact with relatives outside the nuclear family depends not only on geographical proximity—not to be taken for granted in our mobile society—but also on personal preference. Even relations between parents and children are matters of individual negotiation once the children have left home.

The sphere of individual decision within the family is growing. For one thing, it is no longer considered disgraceful to remain unmarried. Social pressure to marry is not absent, but it is probably weaker than ever before in American history. Most people still want to marry, but they don't feel they have to. Further, no one has to have children. Having children is a conscious decision, as is the number of children one will have. While most couples want more than one child, large families are, with a few exceptions, a thing of the past. Finally, one can leave a marriage one doesn't like. Divorce as a solution to an unhappy marriage, even a marriage with young children, is far more acceptable today than ever before.

What does all this mean in terms of Tocqueville's claim that marriage and the family are defenses against individualism? The contrast between the family, where love is supposed to rule, and the world, where money rules, is, if anything, sharper today than in Tocqueville's time. And yet individualism is inside the family as well as outside it. Free choice in the family, which was already greater in Tocqueville's day than it had been before, is now characteristic of the decisions of all members of the family except the youngest children. The ideology of "woman's sphere" survives but has suffered severe criticism, particularly when it has been used to restrain women from participation in the occupational world or deny them equal rights in the marital relationship. Men and women both want to preserve "family values," but the justice of a fuller equality between the sexes is also widely recognized. How do all these changes affect the people we interviewed? How do they think about love and marriage in their own lives?

Love and the Self

Americans believe in love as the basis for enduring relationships. A 1970 survey found that 96 percent of all Americans held to the ideal of two people sharing a life and a home together. When the same question was asked in 1980, the same percentage agreed. Yet when a national sample was asked in 1978 whether "most couples getting married today expect to remain married for the rest of their lives," 60 percent said no. Love and commitment, it appears, are desirable, but not easy. For, in addition to believing in love, we Americans believe in the self. Indeed, . . . there are few criteria for action outside the self. The love that must hold us together is rooted in the vicissitudes of our subjectivity. No wonder we don't believe marriage is easy today.

Yet when things go well, love seems so natural it hardly requires explanation. A love relationship is good because it works, because it "feels right," because it is where one feels most at home. Marge and Fred Rowan have been married for twelve years and have two children. They were high school sweethearts. When asked to say how they decided to marry, Fred says "there wasn't a lot of discussion." Marge was always "the kind of girl I wanted to marry" and "some-where along the line" he just assumed "that's where our relationship was headed." There may be reasons, both practical and romantic, for marrying the person one does, but they are almost afterthoughts. What matters is the growing sense that the relationship is natural, right. One does not so much choose as simply accept what already is. Marge, Fred's wife, describes having the sense, before she married, that Fred was the "right person." "It was, like he said, very unspoken, but absolutely that's exactly how we felt. Fred was always 'my guy.' He was just 'mine.' " They were "right on ever since high school," and even when she tried to date someone else in college, "I felt stupid about it because I knew I was in love with Fred. I didn't want to be with anybody else."

Searching for a definition of "real love" becomes pointless if one "feels good" enough about one's relationship. After all, what one is looking for is the "right place" for oneself. As Fred says, "It just felt right, and it was like being caught in the flow. That's just the way it was. It wasn't a matter of deciding, so there could be no uncertainty." A relationship of the kind Fred and Marge describe seems so natural, so spontaneous that it carries a powerful sense of inevitability. For them, their relationship embodies a deep sense of their own identity, and thus a sense that the self has found its right place in the world. Love embodies one's real self. In such a spontaneous, natural relationship, the self can be both grounded and free.

Not every couple finds the easy certainty of love that Fred and Marge convey. But most couples want a similar combination of spontaneity and solidity, freedom and intimacy. Many speak of sharing—thoughts, feelings, tasks, values, or life goals—as the greatest virtue in a relationship. Nan Pfautz, a divorced secretary in her mid-forties, describes how, after being alone for many years, she fell deeply in love. "I think it was the sharing, the real sharing of feelings. I don't think I've ever done that with another man." Nan knew that she loved Bill because "I let all my barriers down. I really was able to be myself with him—very, very comfortable. I could be as gross as I wanted or I could be as funny as I wanted, as silly as I wanted. I didn't worry about, or have to worry—or didn't anyway—about what his reaction was going to be. I was just me. I was free to be me." The natural sharing of one's real self is, then, the essence of love.

But the very sharing that promises to be the fulfillment of love can also threaten the self. The danger is that one will, in sharing too completely with another, "lose oneself." Nan struggled with this problem during her marriage, and afterward still found difficulty achieving the right balance between sharing and being separate. "Before my relationship with Bill, seven, eight years ago now, I seemed to want to hang on to people too much. It was almost as though I devoured them. I wanted them totally to be mine, and I wanted to be totally theirs, with no individuality. Melding . . . I lost all of myself that way and had nothing of *me* left."

How is it that one can "lose" oneself in love, and what are the consequences of that loss? Nan says she lost herself when she lost her "own goals." At first, her marriage was "very good. It was very give and take in those days. It really was. We went skiing the first time together, and I didn't like skiing. From then on, he went skiing on his own, and I did something I wanted to do." Thus not losing yourself has something to do with having a sense of your own interests. What can be lost are a set of independent preferences and the will to pursue them. With the birth of her son, Nan became absorbed in the mother role, and stopped asserting herself. She became "someone to walk on. Very dull and uninteresting, not enthused about anything. Oh, I was terrible. I wouldn't have wanted to be around me at all." The ironic consequence of passively adapting to others' needs is that one becomes less valuable, less interesting, less desirable. Nan's story is particularly interesting because her behavior conformed fairly well to the earlier ideology of "woman's sphere," where unselfish devotion was the ideal of wifely behavior. But giving up one's self, a subtle shift in emphasis from "unselfishness," may, in the contemporary middle class, as in Nan's case, lead to losing precisely the self that was loved—and perhaps losing one's husband.

A younger woman, Melinda Da Silva, married only a few years, has a similar way of describing her difficulties in the first years of her marriage. She acted out the role of the good wife, trying continually to please her husband. "The only way I knew to be was how my mother was a wife. You love your husband and this was the belief that I had, you do all these things for him. This is the way you show him that you love him—to be a good wife, and the fear that if you don't do all these things, you're not a good wife, and maybe you don't love your husband." Trying so hard to be a good wife, Melinda failed to put her *self* into the relationship. In trying so hard so "show Thomas that I loved him," she "was putting aside anything that I thought in trying to figure out what he thought. Everything was just all put aside." What Melinda had "put aside" was her willingness to express her own opinions and act on her own judgment, even about how best to please her husband.

Melinda sought help from a marriage counselor, and came to feel that the problem with her marriage was less her husband than the loss of her self. "That's all I thought about, was what he wanted, thinking that he would love me more if I did what he wanted. I began to realize when Thomas and I went in for counseling I wouldn't voice my opinion, and I was doing things just for him and ignoring things for myself. The very things I was doing to get his approval were causing him to view me less favorably." Thus losing a sense of who one is and what one wants can make one less attractive and less interesting. To be a person worth loving, one must assert one's individuality. Melinda could "give a lot to our marriage" only when she "felt better" about herself. Having an independent self is a necessary precondition to joining fully in a relationship.

Love, then, creates a dilemma for Americans. In some ways, love is the quintessential expression of individuality and freedom. At the same time, if offers intimacy, mutuality, and sharing. In the ideal love relationship, these two aspects of love are perfectly joined—love is both absolutely free and completely shared. Such moments of perfect harmony among free individuals are rare, however. The sharing and commitment in a love relationship can seem, for some, to swallow up the individual, making her (more often than him) lose sight of her own interests, opinions, and desires. Paradoxically, since love is supposed to be a spontaneous choice by free individuals, someone who has "lost" herself cannot really love, or cannot contribute to a real love relationship. Losing a sense of one's self may also lead to being exploited, or even abandoned, by the person one loves.

Freedom and Obligation

Americans are, then, torn between love as an expression of spontaneous inner freedom, a deeply personal, but necessarily somewhat arbitrary, choice, and the image of love as a firmly planted, permanent commitment, embodying obligations that transcend the immediate feelings or wishes of the partners in a love relationship. To trace out the inner logic of these conceptions, let us first contrast two modes of understanding love, each of which emphasizes one side of the dilemma. One approach is a traditional view of love and marriage as founded on obligation, a view we found most strongly held among certain evangelical Christians. The other is what we have called the therapeutic attitude, found among therapists and their clients, but also, at least in the middle-class mainstream, much more widely diffused.

Like the therapeutically inclined, the evangelical Christian worries about how to reconcile the spontaneous, emotional side of love with the obligations love entails. For the Christian, however, the tension is clearly resolved in favor of obligation. Describing how he counsels young singles who come to him with difficulties about relationships, Larry Beckett, a youthful evangelical minister says: "I think most people are selfish, and when they're looking at relationships romantically, they're primarily looking at it for themselves only. And the Scriptures are diametrically opposed to that. They would say, and I would teach, that there is a love that we can have for other people that is generally selfless. We have to learn it. It's actually a matter of the will. I have to decide to go out and love people by action and by will for their own good, not because I enjoy it all the time, but because God commands it. Jesus said, 'Love your enemies.' That's one of His famous sayings. When He said that, He wasn't commanding my emotions or affections, because He can't. But He can command my will and my decision process and my actions, if I allow Him to." Love thus becomes a matter of will and action rather than of feelings. While one cannot coerce one's feelings, one can learn to obey God's commands and to love others in a selfless way. This obedience is not, however, necessarily in conflict with personal freedom. Through training and shaping the will, the Christian can come to want to do what he must do. People can "see their lives as a process of changing," in which they become "less selfish" as they accept "Christ as the standard" and "His ethic as their ethic. And they do that out of a desire to, not out of any compulsion. Their love for God becomes then the motivational source for loving other people," Larry continues. In Christian love, free choice and duty can be combined, but it is obligation that comes first. Then love of God can make one want to do what one is obligated to do.

Just as love is not simply a matter of feeling for Christians, it is also not expressed primarily in internal, emotional form, but in action. "The Scriptures say over and over, if you love in just lip service and not in action, then you're a hypocrite." For the Christian, love means putting another's interests ahead of one's own. The most important examples of love come when conflicts of interest are the most intense.

For the evangelical Christian, a crucial aspect of permanent commitment to marriage involves the relationship of feeling and will. Emotion alone is too unstable a base on which to build a permanent relationship, so Christians must subordinate or tame their feelings so that they follow the mind's guidance. Les Newman, a young businessman married only a few years, is an active member of an evangelical church, and already the father of two children. Describing his marriage, he says, "Before I thought it was all heart, all chemistry. Now I know that chemistry may be a good start, but the only thing that makes it real love that will endure, and the kind of love that is taken into marriages, is that mental decision that you're going to force that chemical reaction to keep going with each other. I think real love is something where there is that chemistry, but there is also that mental decision that there's going to be a conscious effort for two people to do what's best, instead of what's best for one individual." Emotions can be sustained, or even created, by conscious choice. Reliance on that "mental decision," in turn, guarantees a permanence or stability in relationships that would not be possible relying on feelings alone.

Howard Crossland, a scientist from a rural background and an active member of Larry Beckett's evangelical Christian church, poses the problem of reconciling feeling and obligation. Emotional and moral self-control is at the heart of Howard's theory of love. Although he feels that he and his wife, married more than a dozen years, have a good marriage, he says that without his Christian faith, he "probably would have been divorced by now." Only in the Christian faith is it "logical" to say "til death do us part." Otherwise, "if the relationship is giving you trouble, perhaps it is easier to simply dissolve the thing legally, and go your way, than it is to maybe spend five years trying to work out a problem to make a lasting relationship." The difficulty is that in any relationship there will be crises, and Christian faith allows you to "weather the storm until the calm comes back. If you can logically think through and kind of push the emotions to the back, I guess the love is always there. Sometimes it's blotted out."

Although warm, comfortable feelings of love will normally come back if one waits through difficult periods, these emotional reactions do not themselves constitute love. Love is, rather, a willingness to sacrifice oneself for others. "I have a sign hanging in my bedroom: 'Love is when another's needs are greater than your own.' I think maybe that has something to do with it. I bought it for my wife when I went on a trip one time. I felt it was appropriate." With his wife, Howard tries, where possible, to "think of ways to express my love." By this he means to do things he knows she wants, even when they are not his own preferences. These are such small matters as going out occasionally without the children, "even with a limited budget and this inflationary world." "Love" is "saying you come first, even ahead of me, where possible."

In the evangelical Christian view, then, love involves placing duty and obligation above the ebb and flow of feeling, and, in the end, finding freedom in willing sacrifice of one's own interests to others. Additional support for permanence and commitment in this view of marriage comes from an acceptance of social roles. Les Newman, the young businessman quoted earlier, stresses that marriage is a permanent bond, but one based on the fulfillment of social roles. His only expectations of marriage are that "you had that bond with another individual and you spent your lives together." But spending a lifetime together also means that one can count on one's partner. "I guess the big thing is that it's a permanent relationship between two people where they support each other all the way through life, working as a team." Les and his wife have "roles within the marriage." He is "the breadwinner and the father figure" and "the spiritual leader in the family." Susan, his wife, has "the role of the homemaker and taking care of that type of thing." Rather than being artificial, socially imposed constraints that interfere with real intimacy, roles, in this view, naturally hold people together and define their relationship. In language that would be anathema to the therapeutically inclined, the young Christian insists, "It means very much to me that a married couple is in one sense one individual, and whatever affects one, for good or bad, affects both of you. By being two of you, it just makes it that much easier to deal with the world and what's going on, and to carry out the things that you're supposed to do."

Finally, these Christians stress that, at least in modern society, there is no basis for permanent commitment in marriage apart from Christian faith itself. Larry Beckett, the evangelical minister, puts the case most strongly: the only thing that is unchangeable and can be "the foundation" of life is "the spiritual life," because "God doesn't change. Jesus Christ doesn't change." The other values on which people try to build marriage are fragile: "Whether it's career, or family, or romanticism as the center, I believe that those things are innately limited, and they are degenerative. Some time they are going to change, or get boring, or die down. If God is the center and He is unchanging, He's eternal, He is in fact our source and our maker, then by definition of who He is, He is not going to change. So what that does, it gives stability to a family. That is, the family can say, O.K., we're bored with our family life right now, but that in and of itself is not enough reason to say that I don't love you anymore. That's not enough reason to throw in the towel." Faith can tide people over when their ordinary human involvements and their changeable feelings are not enough to sustain a relationship. Les Newman, the young businessman, also insists that a marriage grounded in Christian faith is more meaningful and satisfying than one without it. "There are a lot of people who obviously have very happy marriages and get along quite well. I'd say the biggest difference would be what purpose is there, in the sense, obviously they married each other because they loved each other, but having said that, why do you get married? Why do you live the way you do? A lot of couples that I know aren't Christians are here to have a good time together and enjoy each other's company. But I guess Susan and I, our number one priority is as a pair, as a couple, to work together in the way that we think God wants us to do, and it gives direction to our lives and our relationship that I don't think other people have."

Christian love is, in the view of its practitioners, built of solider stuff than personal happiness or enjoyment. It is, first, a commitment, a form of obedience to God's word. In addition, love rests less on feeling than on decision and action. Real love may even, at times, require emotional self-denial, pushing feelings to the back in order to live up to one's commitments. Most critical in love are a firm decision about where one's obligations lie and a willingness to fulfill these obligations in action, independent of the ups and downs of one's feelings. Of course, these Christians seek some of the same qualities of sharing, communication, and intimacy in marriage that define love for most Americans. But they are determined that these are goods to be sought within a framework of binding commitments, not the reasons for adhering to a commitment. Only by having an obligation to something higher than one's own preferences or one's own fulfillment, they insist, can one achieve a permanent love relationship.

These evangelical Christians seem to be devoted to an older idea of marriage than many others to whom we talked. They are not immune to pressures for the equality of women, but they still accept a version of the traditional distinction between the sphere of men and the sphere of women. They even defend "roles" in marriage that the therapeutically inclined reject. They believe in intimacy and shared feelings in marriage, but they also believe feeling is not enough. Will and intention are also necessary. From their religious point of view, they are aware of the dangers to the family of utilitarian and expressive individualism and are concerned to resist them. Whether the limitations of their grasp on their own tradition hinder the effectiveness of their resistance [is debatable]. But Tocqueville's linkage of religion, family, and mores seems still to some degree to apply to them.

Communicating

Most Americans long for committed, lasting love, but few are willing to accept indissoluble marriage on biblical authority alone. Rather than making a permanent choice, after which feelings of love may come and go, Americans tend to assume that feelings define love, and that permanent commitment can come only from having the proper clarity, honesty, and openness about one's feelings. At the opposite pole from evangelical Christianity, there is something we might call the therapeutic attitude, based on self-knowledge and self-realization. It emerges most fully in the ideology of many practitioners and clients of psychotherapy, but resonates much more broadly in the American middle-class.

This therapeutic attitude . . . begins with the self, rather than with a set of external obligations. The individual must find and assert his or her true self because this self is the only source of genuine relationships to other people.

External obligations, whether they come from religion, parents, or social conventions, can only interfere with the capacity for love and relatedness. Only by knowing and ultimately accepting one's self can one enter into valid relationships with other people.

Asked why she went into therapy, a woman summed up the themes that recur again and again in accounts by therapists and their clients: "I was not able to form close relationships to people, I didn't like myself, I didn't love myself, I didn't love other people." In the therapeutic ideology, such incapacities are in turn related to a failure fully to accept, fully to love, one's self.

As the therapist Margaret Oldham puts it, many of the professionally trained, upper-middle-class young adults who come to her, depressed and lonely, are seeking "that big relationship in the sky—the perfect person." They want "that one person who is going to stop making them feel alone." But this search for a perfect relationship cannot succeed because it comes from a self that is not full and self-sustaining. The desire for relatedness is really a reflection of incompleteness, of one's own dependent needs.

Before one can love others, one must learn to love one's self. A therapist can teach self love by offering unconditional acceptance. As a Rogersian therapist oberves, "There's nobody once you leave your parents who can just say you are O.K. with us no matter what you do." He continues, "I'm willing to be a motherer—to at least with certain parts of a personality, parts of them that they present to me, validate them." Another, more behavioristic therapist concurs, saying he works by "giving them just lots of positive reinforcement in their selves; continually pointing out things that are good about them, feeding them with it over and over again." Thus the initial ingredient in the development of a healthy, autonomous self may be love from the ideal, understanding surrogate parent-lover-friend—the therapist. Unlike that of lovers and friends, however, the purpose of the therapist's love is not to create a lasting relationship of mutual commitment, but to free people of their dependence so that ultimately they can love themselves.

Becoming a more autonomous person means learning self-acceptance. While another's love or approval may help, to be a firmly autonomous individual, one must ultimately become independent of others. To be able to enjoy the full benefits of a love relationship, one must stop needing another's love to feel complete. A California therapist in his forties says, "I think people have to feel somewhat whole, and that includes liking yourself—maybe hating yourself, parts of yourself—but accepting who you are, and feeling that you can make it in this world without a partner. If what a relationship means is that you can be dependent on someone, you can say I need you at times, but I think that unless you feel you also can do without that person, then you cannot say I need you. If you have been saying that I need you as a substitute because you do not think you can make it on your own, you are in trouble."

Therapy can help individuals become autonomous by affirming over and over again that they are worthy of acceptance as they are. But the ultimate purpose of the therapist's acceptance, the "unconditional positive regard" of post-Freudian therapy, is to teach the therapeutic client to be independent of anyone else's standards. Another therapist comments, "Ultimately I think people want to know that they're O.K., and they're looking for somebody to tell them that, but I think what's really needed is to be able to have themselves say that I, Richard, am O.K. personally. What people really need is a self-validation, and once people can admit that they're O.K., even though I have shortcomings, everybody has short-comings, but once they can admit that, all right I've got these, but I'm really O.K., somehow, they get miraculously better." Thus the therapeutic ideal posits an individual who is able to be the source of his own standards, to love himself before he asks for love from others, and to rely on his own judgment without deferring to others. Needing others in order to feel "O.K." about oneself is a fundamental malady that therapy seeks to cure.

Discovering one's feelings allows one to get close to others. A behaviorist therapist describes how he teaches clients gradually to be more spontaneous by giving them positive feedback, telling them "there's a big difference in you now than last time. You seem more at ease; you tell me how you feel; you laugh; you smile." When they relax, he "provides praise for them and teaches them that it's O.K. to share your feelings." This ability to share feelings can then be carried over from therapy to other relationships. He continues: "That's how you get close to somebody, because you relax, you're spontaneous, you act like yourself and you open up to somebody and share those intimacies with somebody that in turn responds similarly." Thus sharing of feelings between similar, authentic, expressive selves—selves who to feel complete do not need others and do not rely on others to define their own standards or desires—becomes the basis for the therapeutic ideal of love.

Therapy not only teaches people to avoid problems in love relationships by overcoming excessive dependence or unrealistic demands on those they love. It also changes the ideal of love itself. When Melinda Da Silva feared she was "losing herself" in the early years of her marriage, she went to a marriage counselor, who taught her to assert what she wanted rather than always deferring to her husband's wishes. She came to feel that only by becoming more independent could she really love, or be loved by, her husband. For Melinda, the ideal of love changed from self-sacrifice to self-assertion. "The better I feel about myself, I feel I have a whole lot that I can contribute to Thomas, so I can value him more as opposed to idolize him. It's easier to love someone you're on a par with. You can be 'in love' with someone you idolize, but you can't 'love' someone you idolize." Thus she cannot really love unless she is enough of an independent person to make her own contribution to the relationship, rather than doing only what "I thought he wanted." Loving someone implies an active, free involvement that is incompatible with the helpless thralldom of being "in love."

This egalitarian love between therapeutically self-actualized persons is also incompatible with self-sacrifice. It must be based on the autonomous needs of two separate individuals—needs that may come into conflict. Melinda says, "Being in love one day can mean, like, being selfish. I mean, doing something just for yourself, which I never thought you can and still love." When asked to give an example, she replies, "I guess like just thinking about myself and sitting and telling Thomas. Not considering what his day was like when he comes home. Just when he comes in, saying I have to talk to him and sit him down and talk to him, which I never would have done before. There are times when I don't even think about his day, but I can still love him." In the therapeutic view, a kind of selfishness is essential to love.

Therapy also redefines the ideal love relationship. Indeed, therapy becomes in some ways the model for a good relationship, so that what truly loving spouses or partners do for each other is much akin to what therapists do for their clients. Melinda, now herself in training to be a counselor, expresses part of this therapeutic ideal of marriage. A "good relationship" requires, "first for both people to be able to be strong and weak together at different times. Our relationship, our marriage, changed as I became stronger. That allowed Thomas to be able to come home and say, 'My job was horrible today,' or 'I was really upset,' or 'I was in a situation where I got anxious again.' That allowed Thomas to be weaker, and for me to be stronger, so it felt a little more balanced." Both partners in a relationship become therapists in a reciprocal exchange, each willing to listen, to understand, to accept the other's weaknesses, and in turn ready to share their own anxieties and fears.

In its pure form, the therapeutic attitude denies all forms of obligation and commitment in relationships, replacing them only with the ideal to full, open, honest communication among self-actualized individuals. Like the classic obligation of client to therapist, the only requirement for the therapeutically liberated lover is to share his feelings fully with his partner. A divorced woman, now a social services administrator, feels uncomfortable with the word *love*: "I got married believing that I was in love, and that I was going to do everything for this person, and I did a lot. I gave up a lot, supported him financially through school, and I began to realize that I was not getting anything in return." The obligations and self-sacrifice promised by the word *love* turned out to be a false promise of security and a dangerous illusion, inducing her to give up protecting her own interests. Now she values relationships that are balanced, in which if she gives a lot, she gets a lot back. Asked what would be the worst thing in a relationship, she says: "If I felt communication was no longer possible, the relationship would be over. If I felt I could not really say what I felt. If I was not caring about how he felt about things, then it would be over. Lack of communication, I think it would be the end." In a world of independent individuals who have no necessary obligations to one another, and whose needs may or may not mesh, the central virtue of love—indeed the virtue that sometimes replaces the ideal of love—is communication.

For therapeutically liberated individuals, obligation of any kind becomes problematic in relationships. A counselor who runs a therapy group of divorced women tries to help them feel more independent. She wants them to enjoy doing things for themselves and one another and to develop confidence in their ability to live alone. Relationships are better when the partners "do not depend just on themselves or each other." When pressed to consider obligation in relationships, she answers, "I guess, if there is anyone who needs to owe anybody anything, it is honesty in letting each other know how they feel about each other, and that if feelings change, to be open and receptive, to accept those changes, knowing that people in relationships are not cement."

The therapeutic attitude liberates individuals by helping them get in touch with their own wants and interests, freed from the artificial constraints of social roles, the guilt-inducing demands of parents and other authorities, and the false promises of illusory ideals such as love. Equally important, the therapeutic attitude redefines the real self. Money, work, and social status are not central to the authentic self, which instead consists of the experience and expression of feelings. For such expressive selves, love means the full exchange of feelings between authentic selves, not enduring commitment resting on binding obligation.

Ideological Confusions

Although we have drawn a sharp contrast between the therapeutic attitude, grounded in a conception of authentic self-knowledge, and an ethic that rests on absolute and objective moral obligations, found in one form among some evangelical Christians, most Americans are, in fact, caught between ideals of obligation and freedom.

The language and some of the assumptions of the therapeutic attitude have penetrated quite deeply, at least into middle-class mainstream culture. Even Les Newman, the young Christian businessman who spoke so fervently about the need to ground marriage in larger religious truth, answers a question about what makes a relationship good by saying, "I'd say a big part of it is just being able to understand, sympathize, and empathize with each other's problems. Just to be able to talk to each other and share each other's problems, sort of counsel each other a little bit. Just helping each other deal with the world." Here the ideal of mutual help and support blends with a more therapeutic image of empathy and psychological understanding as the major goods spouses can offer each other.

Even as the therapeutic attitude spreads, however, it meets, and sometimes blends with, the countervailing aspiration of many Americans to justify enduring relationships and the obligations that would sustain such relationships. For Melinda Da Silva, for example, her enthusiastic embrace of the therapeutic ideal of love is embedded in a larger sense that a marriage should last. The richer, more equal communication she and her husband worked to develop in marriage counseling was a way of sticking with her marriage rather than running away at the first sign of difficulties. "When I married him, I said that he was the person, not that I have to spend forever and ever with, but at least I'm going to make some kind of social commitment, and say I'm going to try to work things out with this person, have a family with him, and be a family with him. If we hadn't been married, I don't know that I would have gone through couseling, marriage counseling, or couple counseling." Here reasons for commitment that go beyond the terms of the therapeutic ethic are provided by the traditional social form of marriage, her sense of being a "family" with her husband, and a pride in sticking by commitments she has made. Therapy taught Melinda to "be selfish" as a way of loving, but it also gave her a way of working through the first hard times in her marriage. Yet she still has difficulty justifying her willingness to work for an enduring marriage. She gives credit to a childhood in which "family was an important value," but she hesitates to say that that value is objectively important, that it could apply to everyone. When asked whether people should stay married to the same person their whole lives she says, "Not everyone . . . I don't know how you could stop people wanting to change. I think that a lot of things that happen in divorce are that these changes occur. You're not 'in love' anymore, and being 'in love' seems so important to everyone. When they get to a point where they're not 'in love,' they don't know what else there is, so the easiest thing is to leave that and find another 'in love.' " The search for one "in love" after another strikes Melinda as unrealistic or immature, but her choice to look for more in marriage comes down fundamentally to a matter of personal preference, based on her own idiosyncratic background. The therapeutic attitude provides her with a way of deepening the bond in her own marriage, even while validating a view of the world in which people change, relationships easily end, and the self is ultimately alone.

Despite its rejection of relationships based on socially grounded obligations, the therapeutic attitude can enrich the language through which people understand their connections to others. Those influenced by the therapeutic attitude often express extreme ambivalence about ideals of obligations and self-sacrifice, particularly when they consider their own parents' marriages. They long for the unquestioning commitment their parents seemed to have, yet they are repelled by what they take to be the lack of communication, the repression of difficulties, and, indeed, the resigned fatalism such commitment seems to imply. These respondents both envy their parents and vow never to be like them.

What sometimes replaces the social obligations of marriage is a sense that relationships can be based not only on individuals maximizing their own interests and being true to their authentic feelings, but on a shared history in which two people are bound together in part by what they have been through together. Describing her sense of how her parents "love each other very much, in their sense of the word," even though they are not "in love," Melinda Da Silva says, "I never understood until the past year, after Thomas and I had gone through counseling and everything. We shared experiences together. It's different than being in love. It's real different—because we have shared things together, time and experiences, all that." For Melinda and others like her, the therapeutic attitude, with its rich description of the selves who love and the authentic feelings such selves can share, can give texture to a sense of shared history, even if it is a history of private struggles over feelings, disconnected from any larger community of memory or meaning.

The therapeutic attitude reinforces the traditional individualism of American culture, including the concept of utilitarian individuals maximizing their own interests, but stresses the concept of expressive individuals maximizing their experience of inner psychic goods. Melinda was able to blend the commitments arising from her upbringing in a large, loving traditional family with the therapeutic stress on self-assertion and communication to become a fuller participant in her own marriage. But even Ted Oster, the success-oriented young lawyer, . . . uses aspects of the expressive individualist culture to go beyond his primarily utilitarian view of the world. It was Ted Oster who referred to life as "a big pinball game" in which in order to "enjoy it" you have to "move and adjust yourself to situations," and "to realize that most things are not absolute." He has left his family's conventional Protestantism behind, and he claims few loyalties to any ideal or standard of conduct beyond his own happiness, but this psychologically oriented pragmatist, married more than ten years, feels that he is married to the "special person" who is right for him. He acknowledges that, rationally speaking, "you see a lot of people successfully married," and "that many coincidences couldn't happen all the time." But the romantic in him insists that even if there is "more than one special person" or "quite a few people with whom you could be equally happy in a different way, you've got to find somebody from that group."

Like Melinda Da Silva, Ted Oster feels that communication and the sharing of feelings are at the heart of a good marriage. And relationships require work. "You can't have something as good as a love relationship without putting a lot of effort into it. It's a wonderful thing, but it's not going to keep going by itself just because it's wonderful. That person is not forever just because you found that special person." Unlike Melinda, however, Ted Oster does not cite his family upbringing or the public commitment of marriage in describing why he wants a lasting relationship. In his utilitarian individualist vocabulary, the fundamental reason is that he has found the best possible partner, the one who will bring him the most happiness. He is unsure whether he has any obligations to his marriage or stays married only because he continues to prefer his wife to the available alternatives. Even when asked explicitly about obligation, he rapidly returns to what works: "I think there is an element, a small element of obligation. But I think mostly it's just, you know, this person is really good. It's worked so well up to now, and it continues to do that because you expect it to, and it does, by and large." It would be "wrong" to break up his marriage only in the sense, first, that he would feel "a sense of failure at making the relationship work, because I know you have to work at it," and, second, because it would be wrong for their children "not to be able to grow up in a family." Yet despite his utilitarian language, Ted Oster deeply values an enduring marriage. When pushed, he is finally able to say why in terms that go beyond both the romantic idea that his wife Debby is "special" and pragmatic concerns about the unpleasantness of divorce. Here he relies heavily on the idea of a shared history. When he is asked why one should not go from one relationship to another if one is tired of one's spouse or finds someone else more exciting, he begins, once again, with a statement of his preferences, but moves rapidly to a discussion of the virtues of sharing: "It [shifting relationships] is just not some-thing that interests me. I have seen us get from a good relationship in terms of sharing with each other and so on to one that's much, much deeper. I mean, we still have our hard times and good times, but it's a deeper, deeper relationship." This "deeper" sharing in turn suggests the value of a shared life, a sense of historical continuity, a community of memory. Ted continues, "You can't develop a deeper relationship over a brief period of time, and also I think it is probably harder to develop with somebody new at this stage in your life. Your having grown through the twenties with someone is good. Having first children and doing all those things, you could never do it again with somebody else." He concludes by moving from the notion that life is more enjoyable when shared with one person to the idea that only a shared history makes life meaningful. "I get satisfaction in growth with Debby in proceeding through all these stages of life together. That's what makes it all really fun. It makes life meaningful and gives me the opportunity to share with somebody, have an anchor, if you will, and understand where I am. That, for me, is a real relationship."

Here the ideal of sharing, derived in part from therapy that produces a "deeper relationship," goes at least part way toward filling the gap in Ted Oster's predomi-nantly utilitarian moral language. At times, he seems to claim only that a lasting marriage is good for him because it is what he personally finds most satisfying, but he also develops a distinctive life-course argument, finally involving a larger sense of the purpose and direction of life, to explain why the value of a lifelong marriage transcends even the virtues of the "special person" he has married. Thus Ted Oster resourcefully finds ways to describe why for him a lasting relationship is, in fact, a good way to live, good not only in the pragmatic sense that it pleases him, but good in the sense that it is virtuous, given the nature of human beings and of a fulfilling life. Yet all these arguments continually threaten to collapse into the claim that for him, because of his own background or the peculiarities of his own psyche, this way of life is simply more enjoyable. His therapeutic ethic provides a partial way of describing why his bond to his wife transcends immediate self-interest. But he has difficulty, without a widely shared language of obligation and commitment, justifying his sense that a lasting relationship is more than a matter of personal preference.

We may now return briefly to Marge and Fred Rowan, the high school sweet-hearts, now married many years, whom we met early in this chapter. They illustrate both the strengths and the confusions that result from the blending of a therapeutic world view with an ethic of commitment or obligation.

Marge and Fred see themselves as a traditional couple for whom marriage and family are the center of life, in Marge's words "home-body as opposed to jet-setter" types, whose love relationship is "just a way of living, just what we are." Unlike many participants in the therapeutic culture, they do not insist on putting self first, and indeed relish a kind of old-fashioned absorption in home and family. Marge says, "I think our relationship has always been the base of just about everything I do. Sometimes I almost feel guilty if I'm out on my own too much."

But the Rowans did go through active induction into the therapeutic culture through Marge's and then Fred's participation in *est* (Erhard Seminars Training). Marge, in particular, had to "find out that one little thing—that I'm O.K.," in order to assert herself more fully in her marriage and in the wider world. She echoes Melinda Da Silva's conviction that affirming herself made her a fuller participant in her own marriage. Both Marge and Fred stress the depth of communication their experience of the *est* program brought to their marriage. Fred describes the new sense of security he felt after he and Marge had worked through major problems in their marriage: "It felt safer to be here. I felt more secure in the relationship. I felt like there was more support here for me as a person."

The Rowans, like the Da Silvas and the Osters, have found a way to integrate a therapeutic understanding of self and relationship (the conviction that one must know that he or she is "O.K." before one can fully enter a relationship with another) with quite traditional views of love and marriage. For the Rowans, self-discovery went hand in hand with renewed commitment to their relationship. Therapeutic language affirmed the "rightness" they had felt about each other since high school. Yet even for this stable, committed couple, therapeutic language with its stress on openness, self-development, and change, undermines a larger language of commitment. Fred stresses the excitement that their involvement in the human potential movement brought to their marriage. "I want our relationship to keep changing. I don't want it to stay exactly the way it is. Even at moments when I am just overcome with how great our relationship is, I don't even want it to stay that way. I want it to be different. I don't want it to be stagnant or boring." Marge and Fred expect their "relationship to go on forever." But they now reject any language in which permanence could be grounded in something larger than the satisfactions provided by the relationship itself. Discussing the possibility that the changes he finds so exciting might be dangerous to their relationship, Fred says, "Intellectually I think I can justify that they might be dangerous, but I feel pretty secure about our relationship, and if one of those changes happens to be something that ends our relationship, then that's probably the way the relationship was headed anyhow. If that happens it's because our relationship didn't have what it takes or took." Marge continues his thought: "Or not that it didn't have what it takes or took, but it's just what the relationship led to."

For the Rowans, as for many others, adoption of the therapeutic language leads to a paradox. They turned to the human potential movement as a way of revitalizing their marriage and working through problems. They became more committed to the marriage by doing what Americans have classically done—each, as an individual, making a fuller, freer choice of the other based on a truer, more authentic sense of self. Both Fred and Marge had to find out that they were "O.K." as individuals precisely so that they could make a genuine commitment to their relationship—because, for them, as for most Americans, the only real social bonds are those based on the free choice of authentic selves.

For the classic utilitarian individualist, the only valid contract is one based on negotiation between individuals acting in their own self-interest. For the expressive individualist, a relationship is created by full sharing of authentic feelings. But both in hard bargaining over a contract and in the spontaneous sharing of therapeutically sophisticated lovers, the principle is in basic ways the same. No binding obligations and no wider social understanding justify a relationship. It exists only as the expression of the choices of the free selves who make it up. And should it no longer meet their needs, it must end.

Love and Individualism

How Americans think about love is central to the ways we define the meaning of our own lives in relations to the wider society. For most of us, the bond to spouse and children is our most fundamental social tie. The habits and modes of thought that govern intimate relationships are thus one of the central places where we may come to understand the cultural legacy with which we face the challenges of contemporary social life. Yet in spite of its great importance, love is also, increasingly, a source of insecurity, confusion, and uncertainty. The problems we have in thinking about love are an embodiment of the difficulty we have thinking about social attachment in general.

A deeply ingrained individualism lies behind much contemporary understanding of love. The idea that people must take responsibility for deciding what they want and findings relationships that will meet their needs is widespread. In this sometimes somber utilitarianism, individuals may want lasting relationships, but such relationships are possible only so long as they meet the needs of the two people involved. All individuals can do is be clear about their own needs and avoid neurotic demands for such unrealizable goods as a lover who will give and ask nothing in return.

Such a utilitarian attitude seems plausible for those in the throes of divorce or for single people trying to negotiate a world of short-term relationships. It is one solution to the difficulties of self-preservation in a world where broader expectations may lead to disappointment or make one vulnerable to exploitation. Then love becomes no more than an exchange, with no binding rules except the obligation of full and open communication. A relationship should give each partner what he or she needs while it lasts, and if the relationship ends, at least both partners will have received a reasonable return on their investment.

While utilitarian individualism plays a part in the therapeutic attitude, the full significance of the therapeutic view of the world lies in its expressive individualism, an expanded view of the nature and possibilities of the self. Love then becomes the mutual exploration of infinitely rich, complex, and exciting selves. Many of our respondents stress that their own relationships are much better than their parents' marriages were. They insist on greater intimacy, sharing of feelings, and willingness to "work through" problems than their parents found possible.

It is true that the evangelical Christians we interviewed and others who maintain continuity with a religious tradition—liberal Protestant, Catholic, and Jewish traditions as well—find relationships deepened by being part of a wider set of purposes and meanings the partners share. Les Newman and Howard Crossland say that their marriages are strong because they share commitment to the religious beliefs of their respective churches with their wives.

Accepting religious authority as a way of resolving the uncertainties and dilemmas of personal life was relatively unusual among those to whom we talked, as was the extreme version of the therapeutic attitude that puts self-realization ahead of attachment to others. But in the middle-class members of America's mainstream, we found therapeutic language very prevalent, even among those who also retain attachment to other modes of thinking about and experiencing the world. Therapeutic understandings fit many aspects of traditional American individualism, particularly the assumption that social bonds can be firm only if they rest on the free, self-interested choices of individuals. Thus even Americans who do not share the quest for self-actualization find the idea of loving in spite of, not because of, social constraints very appealing.

On the whole, even the most secure, happily married of our respondents had difficulty when they sought a language in which to articulate their reasons for commitments that went beyond the self. These confusions were particularly clear when they discussed problems of sacrifice and obligation. While they wanted to maintain enduring relationships, they resisted the notion that such relationships might involve obligations that went beyond the wishes of the partners. Instead, they insisted on the "obligation" to communicate one's wishes and feelings honestly and to attempt to deal with problems in the relationship. They had few ideas of the substantive obligations partners in a relationship might develop. Ted Oster began to hint at some of these when he discussed how having lived your life with someone, having a shared history, bound you to her in ways that went beyond the feelings of the moment. He seemed to reach for the idea that the interests, and indeed the selves of the partners, are no longer fully separable in a long-lasting relationship, but his utilitarian individualist language kept pulling him back. In the end, he oscillated between the idea that it might in some larger sense be wrong to leave his marriage and the simple idea that he and Debby would stay together because they were well suited to each other.

Similarly, while the evangelical Christians welcomed the idea of sacrifice as an expression of Christian love, many others were uncomfortable with the idea. It was not that they were unwilling to make compromises or sacrifices for their spouses, but they were troubled by the ideal of self-denial the term "sacrifice" implied. If you really wanted to do something for the person you loved, they said, it would not be a sacrifice. Since the only measure of the good is what is good for the self, something that is really a burden to the self cannot be part of love. Rather, if one is in touch with one's true feelings, one will do something for one's beloved only if one really wants to, and then, by definition, it cannot be a sacrifice. Without a wider set of cultural traditions, then, it was hard for people to find a way to say why genuine attachment to others might require the risk of hurt, loss, or sacrifice. They clung to an optimistic view in which love might require hard work, but could never create real costs to the self. They tended instead to believe that therapeutic work on the self could turn what some might regard as sacrifices into freely chosen benefits. What proved most elusive to our respondents, and what remains most poignantly difficult in the wider American culture, are ways of understanding the world that could overcome the sharp distinction between self and other.

Marriage and Mores

We have seen that marriage and the family continue to be important for Americans—in some ways, more important than ever. We have seen that the satisfactions of marriage and family life have been increasing, though as institutions they are more fragile and difficult to maintain than ever. We would argue that the family is not so much "fading," as some have said, as changing.

Marriage and the family, while still desirable, are now in several ways optional. The authors of *The Inner American* report as the most dramatic of their findings the change between 1957 and 1976 in "increased tolerance of people who reject marriage as a way of life." Whereas the majority of Americans believed it was "sick," "neurotic," or "immoral" to remain unmarried thirty years ago, by the late seventies only a third disapproved and 15 percent thought it was preferable, while a majority felt it was up to the individual. That getting married, having children, and staying married are now matters of choice, rather than things taken for granted, creates a new atmosphere for marriage and a new meaning for family life. In this more tolerant atmosphere, alternate forms of committed relationship long denied any legitimacy, such as those between persons of the same sex, are becoming widely accepted. To the extent that this new atmosphere creates more sensitive, more open, more intense, more loving relationships, as it seems to have done, it is an achievement of which Americans can justly be proud. To the extent that the new atmosphere renders those same relationships fragile and vulnerable, it threatens to undermine those very achievements.

All of this means that marriage and the family may be found wanting when it comes to providing "diffuse, enduring solidarity" and "unconditional acceptance." From Tocqueville's point of view, the family today is probably less able to tie individuals securely into a sustaining social order than it was in his day, though our family in many ways simply displays a further stage of the tendency he observed for "natural feeling" to increase as deference and formality declined.

It is also more difficult today for the wife and mother to be the moral exemplar that Tocqueville so admired in American women. All studies agree that women are less satisfied with family life than men. Women have entered the work force in increasing numbers, so that now the majority of married women and mothers work. This they do partly to express their feelings of self-worth and desire for public involvement, partly because today many families would not survive without two incomes, and partly because they are not at all sure their marriages will last. The day of the husband as permanent meal-ticket is over, a fact most women recognize, however they feel about "women's liberation." Yet women's work is largely low-status work and the differential between men's pay and women's pay is large, though women are increasingly breaking into formerly male occupations. On top of demeaning work and low pay, working wives and mothers come home to families where the men still expect them to do the preponderance of housework and child care. There have been considerable changes in expectation in this area but not much change in actual behavior. When women are more disgruntled with marriage than men, there is good reason. If women do more than their share of caring for others, it may not be because they enjoy it, but because custom and power within the family make them have to. We should not rule out the possibility that women have developed sex-specific moral sensitivities that have much to contribute to society. Carol Gilligan and Sara Ruddick, among others, argue as much. But women today have begun to question whether altruism should be their exclusive domain.

One resolution would be to see that the obligations traditionally associated with "woman's sphere" are human obligations that men and women should share. There is anxiety, not without foundation, among some of the opponents of feminism, that the equality of women could result in complete loss of the human qualities long associated with "woman's sphere." The present ideology of American individualism has difficulty, as we have seen, justifying why men and women should be giving to one another at all. Traditionally, women have thought more in terms of relationships than in terms of isolated individuals. Now we are all supposed to be conscious primarily of our assertive selves. To reappropriate a language in which we could all, men and women, see that dependence and independence are deeply related, and that we can be independent persons without denying that we need one another, is a task that has only begun.

What would probably perplex and disturb Tocqueville most today is the fact that the family is no longer an integral part of a larger moral ecology tying the individual to community, church, and nation. The family is the core of the private sphere, whose aim is not to link individuals to the public world but to avoid it as far as possible. In our commercial culture, consumerism, with its temptations, and television, with its examples, augment that tendency. Americans are seldom as selfish as the therapeutic culture urges them to be. But often the limit of their serious altruism is the family circle. Thus the tendency of our individualism to dispose "each citizen to isolate himself from the mass of his fellows and withdraw into the circle of family and friends," that so worried Tocqueville, indeed seems to be coming true. "Taking care of one's own" is an admirable motive. But when it combines with suspicion of, and withdrawal from, the public world, it is one of the conditions of the despotism Tocqueville feared.

The History of Love:
Theories and Debates

Francesca M. Cancian

The debate on the family focuses on how far we have moved from role to self and on whether the change is good or bad. Underlying the debate are different theoretical ideas about the causes of family change, and the nature of a good society. Scholars generally agree on the directions of change: the split between the feminine home and the masculine workplace in the nineteenth century, and the shift towards self-development in the twentieth century. But is the family being undermined by the trend to androgyny and self-development? Do we need traditional roles in order to maintain committed relationships? On these questions there is considerable disagreement.

Observers such as Christopher Lasch and Robert Bellah* believe that contemporary blueprints of love are destroying enduring relationships and real self-development. Mutual commitment and a shared moral code are necessary, they argue, to sustain an intimate relationship and develop coherent selves. But the human potential movement encourages people to reject these commitments, and to manage their private lives according to the selfish individualism of the marketplace. For other critics, the women's movement and the trend to androgyny are the main danger, because they threaten us with a society where women as well as men care mostly about their individual success.

In contrast to this pessimistic outlook, I am optimistic about the shift from role to self. I argue that the Interdependence blueprint is a workable guide to intimacy and personal growth, a blueprint that has many advantages over the major alternative—Companionship marriage and feminized love.

Causes of Change

Critics of the trend to self-development typically imply that the family is on the verge of collapse. They underestimate the persistence of traditional family and gender roles because they ignore the stability of two social factors that maintain these roles: the division of labor, and relations of dependency between women and men.

The new division of labor accompanying capitalism or industrialism was the most important cause of modern family and gender roles, according to both functionalist theorists like Talcott Parsons, and Marxists like Eli Zaretsky. This

---

*[See selections by these authors in Chapter 11 of this volume.]

From *Love in America: Gender and Self-Development* by Francesca M. Cancian, pp. 49–65. Copyright © 1987 by Cambridge University Press. Reprinted with permission. Footnotes and cross-references to within the original have been omitted.

609

division of labor differentiated the public and private sphere by: (1) separating economic production from the household, and (2) organizing the economy around impersonal, competitive relations and the family around personal, loving relations. It also polarized gender roles by: (3) specializing activities, so wives were responsible for family relations and husbands were responsible for earning money, and (4) basing gender identity on these specialized activities, so that femininity focused on love and masculinity on work. This division of labor was the foundation of the Family Duty and Companionship blueprints. It polarized gender roles, feminized love, and led Americans to look to the family and private life as their haven in a heartless world.

The separation of public and private spheres has not changed appreciably since the nineteenth century. Gender roles have changed, with a dramatic increase in wives working and a shift towards more androgynous conceptions of masculinity and femininity. But most Americans continue to expect the husband to be the main breadwinner; women continue to do most of the childrearing, and the stereotypes of the loving woman and the competent man persist.

Continuity in the division of labor has produced considerable continuity in family and gender roles. . . . The problems of oppressive roles are still with us—isolated men obsessed with work and submissive women obsessed with intimacy. The weakening of family ties is not our only problem.

Obviously family life and images of love have shifted a great deal towards emphasizing self-fulfillment and more flexible roles, but the critics of self-development exaggerate the degree of change. As long as the division of labor remains stable, something like the Companionship family will persist as one important blueprint for close relationships.

Relations of economic and emotional dependency between women and men, which are related to the division of labor, have also persisted, maintaining the roles of dominant, independent husbands and submissive, dependent wives. Mutual dependency is the root of power relations, as sociological exchange theory makes clear. Power, in this perspective, comes from owning or controlling a valued resource and supplying it to someone who needs it. Thus the balance of power between a man and a woman depends on the balance of resources that the other overtly needs; covert or repressed needs do not affect power. The resource may be love, money, or assistance—anything a person believes he needs from another and cannot get from an alternative source, although money is especially important in our culture. Most researchers seem to agree on the link between dependency and power, but except for feminists and Marxists, they often neglect to use it in interpreting family relationships.

The division of labor established in the nineteenth century increased the power of husbands over wives by making women more economically dependent on men. As more wives earned money, this dependency lessened, but it will persist as long as women's wages continue to be substantially lower than men's wages. Women also became more emotionally dependent on men, as intimate relations with men became the focus of their daily lives. Beliefs about gender that emphasized women's need for heterosexual love and minimized men's need for love further amplified the imbalance in dependency and power between the sexes. The imbalance is lessening, as men place more value on their close relationships and women focus more on friends and work, but according to recent surveys, love is still more important to women than to men. As long as the imbalance in material and emotional dependency persists, so will many aspects of traditional family and gender roles.

Evaluating the Trend from Role to Self: Classic Issues

However far we have traveled on the road to androgynous love, is this change mostly beneficial or harmful for our private lives? The answer is partly an empirical issue, and hinges on which blueprint of love is dominant—Independence or Interdependence. But classic theoretical issues are also involved. First, there is the issue of constraint versus freedom: do people need stronger social values and roles to provide security and structure, or do they need more freedom and power to direct their own lives and develop their potential? Gender is the second issue: is it more natural and socially useful if women focus on love and men on work, or if they are both androgynous? These have been central questions in social theory since the nineteenth century. The answers proposed by classic theorists—especially Emile Durkheim and Karl Marx—provide a framework for evaluating the trend from role to self and for understanding the current debate about the family.

The Need for Constraint

Durkheim and Marx offer opposing views on whether constraint or freedom is the basic problem of modern society. Steven Lukes observed that "Durkheim saw human nature as essentially in need of limits and discipline," while Marx assumed that the full realization of human powers requires

> a world in which man is free to apply himself to whatever activity he chooses and where his activities and his way of seeing himself and other men are not dictated by a system within which he and they play specific roles . . . Social constraint is for Marx a denial and for Durkheim a condition of human freedom and self-realization.

Durkheim argued that people need rules to limit their desires and define a meaningful way of life that binds them together in a secure moral community. They need to believe in values and obligations that they experience as external and constraining and that are enforced by the authority of the group. Shared beliefs and values not only can restrain disruptive emotions and promote mutual commitment and support; they are also essential for developing a separate, coherent self capable of meaningful choices. Our actions have meaning only in the context of a world view or belief system, and commitment to a world view depends on being part of a group that supports our beliefs. Being with the group intensifies our personal vitality, our sense that we are real and worthwhile because our way of life is good and makes sense. Without this social integration, we become excessively self-centered and despairing, and may even turn to suicide. Thus, committed relationships and self-development require restrictive rules and a potentially repressive moral community. Anomie, or the collapse of traditional values and community ties, is the root of our troubles. From Durkheim's perspective, the change from strong family roles to tolerance of diversity is a change for the worse.

There is an anti-democratic, pro-authority bias in Durkheim's position. He exaggerates the dangers of pluralism and uncertainty, and minimizes the dangers of a uniform moral code—the intolerance, sexism, and justification of inequality that typify periods of moral consensus like the fifties. But he is probably correct in pointing to the need for some constraining beliefs in order to achieve a secure relationship and a meaningful sense of self. Security seems to encourage self-development. The positive psychological effects of economic security are shown by studies of unemployment and economic depressions; and security in close relationships also seems to be important—the confidence that one's partner will not leave and will be supportive and behave in expected ways. A world view that structures and justifies one's self and one's relationships is also likely to encourage self-development, as Durkheim argued. Enduring relationships and self-development thus depend on constraining beliefs and expectations that are shared with others. These "others," however, can be limited to one's partner and a network of friends and acquaintances. Beliefs that are part of a unified national culture, such as marital roles, usually are overly restrictive and are part of an oppressive hierarchy of power. Contrary to Durkheim, I am arguing that values and rules do not need to be experienced as external and as embodied in superior authorities. They can be developed and changed by the participants themselves, as the cases I describe later illustrate. Such a decentralized and democratized culture can provide the benefits of shared beliefs with a minimum of restriction and domination.

Contemporary critics of self-development who praise moral codes, following Durkheim, also tend to glorify the traditional rural community, following decline-of-community theorists. Decline-of-community theorists celebrate rural village life in which family ties were strong and people knew each other and were united by bonds of cooperation and shared religion. They see these warm communities as having been destroyed by modernization, especially the development of an impersonal market place, urbanization, mobility, and the decay of traditional beliefs. The modern concern with freedom, self-development, and individualism is for them a sign of the decay of community. If we want secure attachments, they argue, we will have to return to the more restricted way of life of the past; love and self-development cannot be integrated.

The father of the decline-of-community perspective is Ferdinand Tönnies. He distinguished between warm, familial "community" relationships (*Gemeinschaft*), and cold, efficient "society" relationships (*Gesellschaft*). According to Tönnies, the nuclear family is the prototype of *Gemeinschaft* and combines emotional bonds and instrumental exchange. Relations are based on blood and kinship and are strengthened by living together for a long time, helping each other, and sharing possessions and experiences. Less intense forms of *Gemeinschaft* relations are extended kinship, neighborhood, and friendship. In all these relations, people do not treat each other as means to an end; the relationship is an end in itself. *Gesellschaft* relations are also based on exchanging goods and services, but relations are "transitory and superficial," limited to the specific things to be exchanged. Each individual "is by himself and isolated," relating to others as a means to increase his private goods.

Tönnies's emphasis on material interdependence in all relationships is useful. He does not restsrict love to women and the private sphere—*Gemeinschaft* includes the relationships between fathers and children and among friends, neighbors, and co-workers. But his major theme, counter to my position, is that warm human relationships are incompatible with self-development. For Tönnies, as for Bellah and other contemporary critics, modern individualism rests on independence and isolation, not interdependence.

The decline-of-community position implies that we have become a society of iolated individuals without strong family bonds or other dependable human ties, but this exaggerates the degree of change and romanticizes the past. There is strong demographic evidence that the past was not much warmer or more secure than the present. The proportion of marriages broken by death *and* divorce did not rise significantly in the twentieth century because the rise in divorce was offset by a decline in mortality until around 1970. Geographical mobility was very high in the working class in the nineteenth century, and also has not increased greatly for the average American in the past hundred years. Although there probably was more contact and interdependence among extended kin in the past, for centuries most people in Europe and North America have lived in nuclear households.

Durkheimian and decline-of-comnmunity theorists also ignore the rich social life that is possible in modern society. Many studies have documented the vitality of friendship networks, specialized subcultures, voluntary associations, and urban neighborhoods. The decline of community ties, for most Americans, has not been very large, and the decreasing authority of the national culture has been partly offset by the increasing authority of subcultures.

For Durkheim and Tönnies, the underlying problem of modern life is that we are cut off from family and community ties and confused by a jumble of conflicting beliefs and life styles. What we lack is security, connection, and constraining beliefs that define our goals and limit our desires.

The Need for Freedom

For Marx, in contrast, our major problem stems from the exploitation and domination of the many by the few. What people need is more freedom to develop their potential, more power in controlling their society and determining how they will live.

Marx argues that individuals must be free or self-directed at work in order to develop their potential. The economy and the state must be organized in such a way that people collectively control what they produce and determine how it will be distributed. But—to greatly simplify his theory—modern society creates alienation, not freedom, because of private property and the class structure. Some people control economic production and take more than their share of the goods, while others are forced to work for the ruling groups in order to support themselves and their families. The rigid division of labor also blocks self-development by denying people the variety, creativity, and conscious choice they need to develop their potential. The solution, for Marxists, is to abolish private property and create a society of free individuals who collectively control the economy and are unfettered by repressive roles.

But Marx is not clear on what will bind people together and ensure stable attachments in this ideal society. He sees social laws and rules as repressive and ignores their positive contribution. Thus, Marxists tend to fall back on a "natural love" argument: if people were not corrupted and oppressed by class differences and ideology, their natural loving tendencies would create a harmonious society in which everyone could find both love and freedom.

Two Marxist ideas are especially useful in interpreting the trend from role to self. Firstly, Marx emphasizes the value of being free to develop one's full potential. Secondly, he identifies social conditions that promote self-development: democratizing economic and political relations so that people would be more powerful or self-directed, and changing the division of labor so that people would engage in a broader variety of activities.

However, most Marxists are pessimistic about the recent trend to self-development because it has not been accompanied by change in property and the control of economic production. Real self-development, in their view, cannot be restricted to the private sphere and the expression of feelings.

The pessimism of most Marxists is exaggerated, in my view. They typically discount gradual reform and see all developments in capitalist society as destructive and oppressive. This unrelieved negativism is contradicted by evidence that the quality of life has improved substantially for the average American in the past fifty years; for example, economic security, education, and leisure time have increased and mental and physical health have improved. Capitalism does block self-development in many ways, as the Marxists charge: inequality deprives poorer Americans of economic security, lowers their self-esteem, and severely restricts their freedom; and most Americans remain relatively powerless in the public sphere. None the less, there have been significant reforms and improvements, including, I argue, the change from Companionship marriage to Interdependent relationships.

In sum, emphasizing the need for constraint leads to a negative evaluation of the trend to self-development. Emphasizing the need for freedom leads to a positive evaluation unless, like many Marxists, one assumes that positive trends in capitalist America are very unlikely.

Split Gender Roles versus Androgyny

The desirability of polarized gender roles is the second theoretical issue shaping people's evaluation of the trend from role to self. A closely related issue is the impact of separating the public and private spheres. Those who value androgyny and the integration of public and private life will be more likely to welcome the trend from role to self. Those who believe that women's place is in the home, and that women are naturally more loving than men, will disapprove of the trend to self-development, and will support the separation of public and private life.

Some scholars argue that biological sex differences make it preferable to follow traditional family and gender roles. However, historical and cross-cultural variation in gender shows that the American split between the expressive wife and the instrumental husband is not built into the human organism. . . . Others use theories about the functional requirements of society to justify polarized gender roles, and a sharp division between the private and public spheres.

According to Talcott Parsons, the most influential functionalist in recent decades, the split between the feminine, expressive family and the masculine, instrumental workplace is a social arrangement that fulfills the needs of individuals and of society. The modern family and the economy specialize in different functions and need to emphasize different kinds of social relations. Family relations need to be emotionally expressive, accepting, and concerned with the whole person in order to carry out the functions of raising children and maintaining the personality of adults. Relations at work need to emphasize rationality, performance, and impersonal standards to fulfill the function of efficient production. The division of labor between family and economy is necessarily linked to polarized gender roles. Because women bear children, they focus on the expressive home while men's lives focus on the instrumental workplace. These gender roles are beneficial and will persist, according to Parsons, although he also describes the strains in the feminine role.

Other theorists legitimate polarized gender roles by using gender-linked conceptions of self-development and love. They emphasize the masculine aspects of self-development—being instrumental, independent, and rational—and portray the ideal adult as an independent person with a successful career, unrestricted by obligations to care for others. Directions of development where women are likely to excel such as attachment to others, are ignored. This view implies that some people—presumably women—must forego self-development and specialize in caring for others, since a society without care and nurturance is difficult to imagine. Polarized gender roles are also supported by feminine conceptions of love that emphasize verbal self-disclosure and expressing tender feelings. Such conceptions ignore masculine styles of love like providing protection and practical help, and imply that only women really know how to love.

On the other hand, the benefits of androgyny are also a persistent theme in social theory and research. Most feminists have advocated moving towards androgyny, and integrating public and private life. Marxists too have criticized traditional gender roles as a form of oppression, and have forecast a more androgynous future in which women and men would be loving, productive, and creative. For Marxists, given their focus on power and material exchange, it is obvious that the marriage of an instrumental man who controls the money and property and an expressive woman who controls "love" will result in the woman being powerless and exploited.

The benefits of androgyny are also supported by research, although the findings are not conclusive. Illness and early death are more likely to occur among men who are preoccupied with work and women who are preoccupied with relationships, as I will discuss later, and children seem to develop better if both parents are emotionally expressive and there is no sharp differentiation between an expressive mother and an instrumental father. Androgynous individuals tend to be more flexible and have higher self-esteem, according to psychological studies, but some researchers find the highest levels of adjustment among individuals who rate high on masculinity. Finally, marriages in which partners want a high degree of companionship are happier if both husband and wife can be expressive. In general, androgynous individuals seem to have better close relationships.

Criticism of the trend from role to self is rooted in two ideas about what is good for individuals and society. Firstly, people need constraining rules and strong community ties. Secondly, love and work are accomplished better if women specialize in love and men specialize in work. Since there is good reason to doubt both propositions, much criticism of self-development and androgyny rests on shaky foundations. A positive evaluation of self-development is rooted in the opposing ideas that people need to be free of domination and oppressive roles, and that the split between masculine and feminine, public and private, is destructive.

The Current Debate: In Praise of Constraint and Authority

The growing interest in self-development has been condemned by most contemporary scholars, who follow Durkheim and the decine-of-community theorists. *The Triumph of the Therapeutic,* written by Philip Rieff in the sixties, presented the major issues. Culture, according to Rieff, is based on faith and on obedience to the authorities that embody moral demands. By submitting to cultural controls, we are saved from chaos and emptiness, and gain a commitment to larger "communal purposes in which alone the self can be realized and satisfied." The emerging therapeutic world view is an anti-culture, substituting individual feelings and well-being for faith in collective morality. Therapy undermines faith and authority by teaching a tolerant, skeptical attitude towards all moral codes. It advocates "limiting the power of the super-ego and therewith, of culture."

In *Habits of the Heart,* Robert Bellah *et al.* make a similar critique of the "therapeutic ethic," although they are more cautious and balanced than Rieff. "The meaning of one's life for most Americans," they assert, "is to become one's own person," a process that is largely negative, and involves "breaking free from family, community, and inherited ideas." In the pursuit of freedom "we have jettisoned too much," and need to revitalize our biblical and republican moral traditions.

As our culture becomes increasingly voluntaristic, individual preferences and experience have become our only moral guide, Bellah observes, and we lack "any objectifiable criteria of right and wrong." Instead of real communities that integrate private and public life, and bring together a variety of people, modern Americans belong to "lifestyle enclaves" of their choice—a network of similar people that focus on some segment of private life. Instead of a language for talking about relationships that justifies commitments to others, people are adopting a therapeutic language that "denies all forms of obligations and commitment in relationships, replacing them only with the ideal of full, open, honest communication among self-actualized individuals . . ."

Without the guidance of a moral code, Bellah argues, our search for self-development and intimacy will fail. A coherent self requires a shared vision that links individual lives to the wider society. Enduring close relationships depend on moral traditions that legitimate mutual commitments and obligations. The search for self-fulfillment undermines commitment because it legitimates only self-interest and the expression and sharing of feelings. When these individual needs are no longer met, the relationship must end.

This evaluation of the trend from role to self has a strong negative bias and elitist, anti-democratic implications, even though that is not the authors' intention. Bellah *et al.* underestimate the costs of moral communities—how they justify exploitation and inequality, and oppress women and other "deviants." They point to these problems in passing, but their main argument is that Americans suffer from an "individualism grown cancerous" and need less freedom and more commitment to a shared moral code. Their criticism of "lifestyle enclaves" is also elitist, implying that cultural standards cannot be diverse and decentralized. Research findings, however, suggest that subcultures and networks of similar people can successfully anchor a person's identity and provide guidelines for action. Finally, they underestimate the positive features of the popular search for self-development. They miss the importance of interdependence and mutual support in contemporary relationships, both in people's behavior and in the language they use in talking about relationships. And they misrepresent therapy as a cool relationship that teaches people to be distanced and manipulative. Thus, the couples who turn to therapy to improve their relationships are victims of "ideological confusion," in their view. In fact, the warm relationship that is gradually established in successful intensive therapy often does teach people to be more intimate, as I will show later.

A more legitimate criticism by Bellah *et al.* is that the average American is more narrowly focused on his or her private life than in the past, producing an increasing separation of the self from the public sphere. However, others conclude that the plethora of self-help groups, local activists, and single-issue groups indicate a rising level of community involvement.

One would expect contemporary Marxists to be less elitist and more sympathetic to self-improvement than the Durkheimians, but most of them are not. A prime example is Christopher Lasch, who rejects Marx's stress on the freedom to develop one's potential, emphasizing instead the usefulness of social constraint, and using some of the same arguments as Rieff and Bellah. Lasch mourns the decay of traditional authority and moral commitments and implies that life was better in the fifties, when clear family and gender roles ordered our lives. The elements of Marxism that Lasch retains are a concern with political and economic factors, a criticism of all developments in capitalist society, and occasional references to the need for a socialist revolution.

For Lasch, the growing concern with intimacy and self-development is a symptom of the destruction of family bonds and all human relationships by capitalism. Preoccupation with the self is part of the ideology of independence and competition fostered by capitalism. We are becoming a society of isolated individuals, increasingly oppressed by the ruling class, corporate managers, experts, and the government. Even when individuals manage to obtain what they want, they are not free, because their wants have been manipulated by the mass media and the cultural apparatus of our consumer society.

Real self-development requires becoming aware of the conflicts within oneself and within society and working for social change, argue Lasch and other Marxist social critics. But self-development has been co-opted by the establishment. People now remain unaware of their internal conflicts, accept the status quo, and seek instant self-development by paying for a weekend workshop on personal growth. Similarly, real intimacy requires long-term interdependence and commitments, and an expressive, non-market orientation. But capitalist culture lures people to seek intimacy through acquiring the right cars, clothes, and social skills and attracting someone who will immediately make them feel good. The new therapies contribute to the breakdown of personal relations by instructing people to avoid investing themselves in relationships. Private life has become as stressful as work, and "the family—the last refuge of love and decency," which "has been slowly coming apart for more than a hundred years," is decaying.

Part of the decay of the nuclear family, Lasch argues, is that parents, especially fathers, have lost their power. Psychologists, social workers, and other experts have invaded the family, destroying the confidence of parents and making them confused and anxious, so they offer their children neither an intense emotional relationship nor clear standards for behavior. Their children develop an ethic of immediate gratification instead of internalizing a coherent set of values that would lead them to sacrifice for others, and help them achieve real self-development and intimacy.

Many of Lasch's criticisms of contemporary culture are partly valid—they reveal the weaknesses of the Independence blueprint and the need for commitment to other people and to moral standards. But his analysis displays the usual problems of a Durkheimian, decline-of-community approach: he exaggerates the collapse of social ties, romanticizes the past, and underestimates the costs of patriarchal authority. The elitist tendencies of *Habits of the Heart* are magnified in Lasch's work, and he discounts the popular search for intimacy and self-development as a futile, self-defeating enterprise. However, most people are not as deluded and victimized by the system as Lasch asserts, according to numerous studies of contemporary Americans. Most seekers for self-development seem to be following the Interdependence blueprint, and they are making small but substantial steps to a better private life.

The Current Debate: Possibilities of Freedom

Marxist scholars who are positive about the trend to self-development have more respect for the desires and opinions of "common" people. They retain Marx's idea that the goal of progressive change is to give individuals freedom to develop their potential, and observe an expansion of this freedom for the average American in recent decades.

Eli Zaretsky, one of the few Marxist social critics who is positive about the human potential movement, shares some of my optimism about the trend from role to self. He sees the development of personal life and the concern with self-fulfillment as a product of capitalism that has contradictory effects on individual freedom. In nineteenth-century America, "proletarianization split off the outer world of alienated labor from an inner world of personal feeling," Zaretsky argues, in a historical analysis. . . . This development of a separate sphere of personal life, together with the shortening of the work week, created new needs for intimate relationships and self-gratification among the masses of people, needs that were strengthened by advertising.

The growing interest in self-development reflects an expansion of freedom and power, a "profound democratization" of "the ethic of personal fulfillment," compared to previous eras when personal fulfillment was restricted to the elite. But there are also new sources of alienation and powerlessness. The needs for intimacy generated by capitalism tend to be all-engulfing and mystifying, Zaretsky argues, because they are experienced as completely subjective—split off from the outside world of community, work, and politics. People experience their love life as mysterious—one day they fall in love and then for some inexplicable reason love fades and they are alone again. In a socialist society, he believes, people would better understand the material and social bases of love, and their personal needs would be fulfilled in the workplace and the community as well as at home.

Other observers are more positive about recent trends. The most enthusiastic, who are popular writers, embrace even the worst features of the trend from role to self—the overemphasis on independence and the alienation from public life. A more balanced optimistic view is presented by Peter Clecak. The quest for self-fulfillment, he argues, has produced a "democratization of personhood" and a greater involvement in the public sphere for most Americans, although it also has had negative consequences such as encouraging selfishness. This quest includes the human potential movement, the political activists of the sixties, contemporary feminists, and the Christian revival. They are united by "their accent on personal experience; their wish for a community of affective, touching selves; and their comparatively light regard for authority, doctrine, and received institutions." These movements have successfully challenged the political and cultural domination of the male W.A.S.P. elite, Clecak concludes, creating a more decentralized, pluralistic society that provides greater self-fulfillment for the average American.

Where Bellah and Lasch see misguided individualists or deluded victims of capitalism, seeking self-fulfillment and intimacy, but achieving empty isolation, Clecak sees successful creators of new social forms that provide more love and self-development. Studies of contemporary Americans tend to support Clecak's more optimistic assessment.

The Current Debate: Split Gender Roles vs. Androgyny

The nature of gender is the second dimension underlying current debates on the trend from role to self. One would expect feminists to support the quest for self-development, because it is linked to androgyny, and anti-feminists on the radical right to oppose it. But there is more opposition in both groups than support.

For the radical right, the Parsonian ideal of an instrumental husband and an expressive wife is the natural and right kind of family. For example, Marabel Morgan's national best seller, *The Total Woman,* proclaims that "God ordained man to be the head of the family, its president," while his wife is ordained to be "the executive vice-president," charged with maintaining an affectionate, sexually exciting marriage, raising the children, and imparting religion.

Love and marriage are a woman's life, says Morgan, in language reminiscent of the Victorian celebration of woman's special sphere: "It is only when a woman surrenders her life to her husband, reveres and worships him, and is willing to serve him, that she becomes really beautiful to him. She becomes a priceless jewel, the glory of femininity, his queen." A wife has absolute power in the sphere of domestic affection. It is possible for almost any wife "to have her husband absolutely adore her in just a few weeks' time." But to be a powerful queen at home, a woman must sacrifice any claims to independent achievement outside the home. "Only after you have met your spiritual needs, the needs of your husband and your children, should you think of your profession or the public." The same message comes from Phyllis Schlafly, the organizer of a powerful anti-E.R.A. (Equal Rights Amendment) organization, who is scornfully quoted in a feminist pamphlet as asserting that "self-fulfillment is not compatible with a happy marriage, with family life or with motherhood . . . Motherhood has to be self-sacrificing: this is what marriage and motherhood is all about."

But the radical right also tries to incorporate some contemporary themes into its call for a return to the past. Thus on the first page of her book, Marabel Morgan confides that when she was first married, she and her husband "had marvelous communication, so things looked very promising." But they gradually stopped talking and had a "communication breakdown." Then she developed her Total Woman program and applied it to her marriage "with stunning results." Her husband Charlie "began to talk to me in his old way. At times he could hardly get his words out fast enough . . . He began to share his dreams and activities eyeball to eyeball again . . . With communication reopened, romance was not far behind." Thus the main reward that Morgan promised her many women readers was the modern goal of intimate communication with their husbands.

The radical right ignores the disadvantages of polarized gender roles, and the contradiction between expecting intimacy in marriage and advising spouses to be unequal in power and dissimilar in their activities and attitudes. They present an idealized image of the happy traditional family that conveys a sexist and conservative political message: the world will be a happy place again if women just go back home and put the family in order—economic and political problems are not the issue.

The strength of the radical right position is that it voices many people's concerns about their families and their own emotional security and offers a clear solution— revitalize the Companionship family—even though the solution is unrealistic given the high rates of divorce and female employment. The radical right acknowledges the superior power and financial resources of men and the demands of childrearing, and implicitly or explicitly advises women to make the most of their dependent position.

Feminists, as one would expect, oppose the radical right on all these issues and reject the Companionship family roles that subjugate women. Modern feminists like Betty Friedan welcome the trend from role to self and envision a new form of the family where women and men share equally in childrearing and providing money. But most feminist scholars seem to reject the possibility of androgynous marriage in our time. Given the persistent inequality in men's and women's power, income, and childrearing responsibilities, they argue, heterosexual relationships will oppress women and should be avoided.

Marxist or socialist feminists attack the trend towards self-development as another pernicious outgrowth of capitalism, just as Lasch does, although they do not share Lasch's nostalgia for the past. Thus Barbara Ehrenreich and Dierdre English charge that the ideas of the human potential movement lead to a "ruthless self-centeredness" and an extension of the capitalist market mentality into close relationships.

> The primary assumption is that each person in a relationship has a set of emotional, sexual, or other 'needs' which he or she wants met. If they are no longer being satisfied by a friend or sexual partner, then that bond may be broken just as reasonably as a buyer would take his business away from a seller if he found a better price. The *needs* have an inherent legitimacy—the *people* are replaceable.

As individual needs become all-important, women are abandoning their traditional nurturant roles, and are adopting the instrumental attitudes of men. And men, encouraged by the human potential movement and attacks on the traditional male role, are choosing a life of self-centered consumerism and personal growth instead of providing for their wives and children, Ehrenreich argues in a more recent book.

The split gender roles of the past "denied women any future other than service to the family," according to Ehrenreich and English, but "the new psychology seemed to deny human bonds altogether—for women or for men." They conclude on a pessimistic note. "The alternative to the suffocation of domesticity turns out to be the old rational nightmare: a world dominated by the Market, socially atomized, bereft of 'human' values." Like Lasch, Ehrenreich and English focus on the Independence blueprint and on the evils of capitalism, and can see nothing positive in the trend from role to self.

The hostility of most feminist and Marxist scholars towards the new images of love is surprising, since they advocate androgyny and self-development as general goals. One explanation may be their negativism—their skepticism about all developments in a capitalist or sexist society. Another factor may be the difficulty of breaking away from gender-linked conceptions of love and self. Love traditionally means something women do in traditional families, even for feminists and Marxists. Thus the only way to protect enduring love is to forfeit women's rights to develop themselves, something that Lasch seems willing to recommend, but feminists reject, leaving them no positive alternative. Self-development means a ruthless pursuit of individual needs—an extension of the ideology of the self-made man—not developing new capacities within an interdependent, mutually supportive relationship. Thus, scholars with socialist sympathies often reject the trend to self-development.

There are some signs that Marxists and feminists are becoming more positive about the human potential movement, perhaps because it is becoming clearer that interdependence and mutual support is part of self-development for many Americans. For example, Barbara Ehrenreich, in a recent book, praises the human potential movement for freeing men and women from oppressive roles, and for increasing "the possibility of honest communication between the sexes . . ." Feminists and Marxist scholars should nourish and guide the progressive aspects of the human potential movement, in addition to criticizing its faults, given their assumptions about human nature and a good society. Hopefully, more of them will follow the example of people like Eli Zaretsky, and provide this intellectual leadership.

In sum, classic issues of social theory shape our understanding of the history of love and the family. If we attend to the social foundations of heterosexual love—the division of labor and the balance of dependence—we conclude that gender inequality and traditional family forms will persist for some time. We are not on the verge of becoming a society of equal and isolated individuals pursuing our selfish interests. Companionship marriage and the roles of expressive wife and instrumental husband will be part of American society for many dcades, but only as one acceptable life style among others, not as the only right way to love.

Our evaluation of changes in the family depends on our ideas about freedom and gender, and about the possibilty of gradual progress in American society. These basic questions about human nature and society can be clarified by evidence, but probably not resolved. Those who emphasize the fundamental differences between the sexes and the need for authority and a constraining moral code, will condemn the trend to self-development and androgyny, and will support a revitalization of traditional family and gender roles. Those who emphasize the similarity between men and women and need for greater freedom to develop one's self, are more likely to see the benefits of current trends and the costs of feminized love.